ACCOUNTING
FOR NON-ACCOUNTING STUDENTS

Eighth Edition

John R. Dyson

**Financial Times
Prentice Hall**
is an imprint of

PEARSON

Harlow, England • London • New York • Boston • San Francisco • Toronto • Sydney • Singapore • Hong Kong
Tokyo • Seoul • Taipei • New Delhi • Cape Town • Madrid • Mexico City • Amsterdam • Munich • Paris • Milan

Pearson Education Limited

Edinburgh Gate
Harlow
Essex CM20 2JE
England

and Associated Companies throughout the world

Visit us on the World Wide Web at:
www.pearsoned.co.uk

First edition published in Great Britain under the Pitman Publishing imprint in 1987
Second edition 1991
Third edition 1994
Fourth edition published under the Financial Times Pitman Publishing imprint in 1997
Fifth edition 2001
Sixth edition 2004
Seventh edition 2007
Eighth edition 2010

ISBN: 978-0-273-72297-7

British Library Cataloguing-in-Publication Data
A catalogue record for this book is available from the British Library

Library of Congress Cataloging-in-Publication Data
Dyson, J. R. (John R.)
    Accounting for non-accounting students / John R. Dyson. -- 8th ed.
        p. cm.
    ISBN 978-0-273-72297-7 (pbk.)
    1. Accounting. I. Title.
    HF5636.D97 2010
    657--dc22
                                                    2010005340

10 9 8 7 6 5
14 13 12

Typeset in 10.5/13pt Minion by 30
Printed and bound by Rotolito Lombarda, Italy

Brief contents

Contents

Supporting resources

Visit www.pearsoned.co.uk/dyson to find valuable online resources:

Companion Website for students
- Multiple choice questions to help test your learning
- Extra question material
- Links to relevant sites on the web
- Glossary explaining key terms mentioned in the book

For instructors
- Complete, downloadable Lecturer's Guide
- PowerPoint slides that can be downloaded and used for presentations
- Answers to extra question material in the Companion Website
- Extra case studies and guidelines on using them with students

Also: The Companion Website provides the following features:
- Search tool to help locate specific items of content
- E-mail results and profile tools to send results of quizzes to instructors
- Online help and support to assist with website usage and troubleshooting

For more information please contact your local Pearson Education sales representative or visit www.pearsoned.co.uk/dyson

Preface

Why study accounting?

This book provides a solid introduction to accounting for those students who are required to study it as part of a non-accounting course. It is also of benefit to those managers in business, government or industry whose work involves them in dealing with accounting information.

Non-accountants are often puzzled why they are required to take a course in accounting, and even more so when they have to take a demanding examination at the end of it. The fact is that these days, no matter what your job, you need to have some knowledge of accounting matters. The main reason for this is that for different specialists to talk to each other they have to speak in a language that everyone understands. In business (in its widest sense) that language is money and that happens to be the accountants' language. The use of a common language enables all the various activities that take place within a business to be translated into monetary terms and for all reports to be prepared on the same basis. So if you need to know what is going on in other departments (as you almost certainly will) you will find it much easier if you speak the language of accounting.

The book's purpose

The problem with many accounting textbooks is that they are written primarily for accounting students. As a result they go way beyond what a non-accountant needs. This book is different. The subject is not covered superficially but it avoids going into the technical detail that is of relevance only to accountants. Nevertheless, by the time you get to the end of the book you will have gained a perfectly adequate knowledge and understanding of accounting that will enable you to talk to accountants with great confidence and which will help you to do your job much more effectively.

Some guidance for lecturers

The book is divided into four parts. Part 1 introduces students to the world of accounting, Part 2 deals with financial accounting, Part 3 with financial reporting and Part 4 with management accounting.

As you will probably be aware, many further and higher education institutions now operate a modular structure for the delivery of their courses. This book is particularly useful if your own institution does the same. Some accounting syllabi for non-accounting students combine both financial accounting and management accounting in one module while others split them between separate modules. The book is designed so that it can easily be adapted irrespective of whether you combine them or split them.

It is highly unlikely, of course, that the contents of the book will match precisely the syllabus requirements of your own course. There are bound to be topics to which you give more or less emphasis and there will be others that are not covered at all in the book. Nevertheless, the book has now been widely used throughout the UK and in many overseas countries for over 25 years. From the feedback that has been received the contents appear to continue to meet the main requirements of most introductory accounting courses for non-accounting students.

There is one topic, however, that splits opinion right down the middle: double-entry book-keeping. Some lecturers are absolutely convinced that non-accounting students need to have a grounding in this topic if they are to understand where the information comes from, what problems there are with it and how it can be used. Other lecturers are adamant that it is totally unnecessary for non-accounting students.

As opinion is so evenly divided on this subject we have decided to retain double-entry book-keeping in the main part of the book. If you do not include the topic in your syllabus it can be easily left out by skipping the whole of Chapter 3 (Recording data) and possibly parts of Chapter 4 (Sole trader accounts). You could then pick up the thread of the book in Chapter 5 (Company accounts) provided you are sure that your students know something about a trial balance, a profit and loss account, and a balance sheet.

In this edition we have taken the opportunity to revise and update the seventh edition. Two structural changes have been made to this edition:

1 The old Chapter 9 (Information disclosure) has been merged with the old Chapter 2 (Accounting rules) to become a new, largely rewritten Chapter 2 (Accounting rules and regulations).
2 The old Chapters 4 and 5 (Sole trader accounts and Last minute adjustments) have been combined to form a single chapter (the new Chapter 4 with the same title as the old one).

By their nature substantial additions and revisions have had to be made to two other chapters: the old Chapter 13 (Contemporary issues), and the old Chapter 22 (Emerging issues). It has not been too difficult to select contemporary financial issues for the new Chapter 11 because the various accounting bodies have a clearly established development programme.

It has proved much more difficult to select emerging management accounting issues for the new Chapter 20. Management accounting is not as fast moving as financial accounting and, as yet, there is no such body as a 'management accounting standards board' driving the discipline forward. The main source comes from accountants pursuing academic research in universities but as yet there is no consensus on what changes are needed. When preparing this chapter, therefore, we examined the syllabi of several accounting bodies and also took note of various suggestions made by reviewers. These two sources enabled us to select some likely emerging management issues over the next few years.

A new feature has been introduced into this edition: news clips. News clips are brief extracts or summaries of recent newspaper articles that are of relevance to the particular chapters in which they are placed. They are intended to demonstrate that the accounting matters discussed in the various chapters are not theoretical but that they are of practical importance and relevance in the real world.

The news stories introduced into an earlier edition at the beginning of each chapter have been replaced with more recent ones. As before, broad questions on each of these stories may then be found towards the end of the chapter. Students are strongly encouraged to have a go at answering these questions even though some of the issues covered may sometimes appear to be somewhat beyond non-accountants. However, it would be surprising if this were to be the case since most of them were first published in newspapers intended for a general audience.

As publicly traded companies in the European Union (EU) are now required to prepare their financial statements in accordance with International Accounting Standards (IASs) various amendments have had to be made throughout the text. This has caused a problem for a book aimed at non-accountants as financial statements have become more and more difficult to understand. However, strenuous attempts have been made to keep the text as simple and as relevant as possible.

An additional complexity is that non-listed companies in the UK can adopt UK accounting standards while listed companies must adopt international ones. A similar problem may arise in other EU countries if non-listed companies are allowed to adopt their own accounting standards.

This problem was particularly acute when preparing the cash flow chapter. So what we have done is to show how a simple cash flow statement may be prepared using both UK standards and IASs. As far as published accounts are concerned we have limited our discussion to IAS-prepared statements as these are of relevance to *all* EU-based students as well as to students based in other non-EU countries.

Some guidance for college and university students

If you are using this book as part of a formal course, your lecturer should have provided you with a work scheme. The work scheme will outline just how much of the book you are expected to cover each week. In addition to the work done in your lecture you will probably have to read each chapter at least twice.

As you work through a chapter you will come across a number of 'activities'. Most of them require you to do something or to find something out. The idea of these activities is to encourage you to stop your reading of the text at various points and to think about what you have just read.

There are few right and wrong answers in accounting so we want you to gain some experience in deciding for yourself what you would do if you were faced with the type of issues covered in the activities.

You are also recommended to attempt as many of the questions that follow each chapter as you can. The more questions that you do, the more confident you will be that you really do understand the subject matter. However, avoid looking at the answers (there are some at the back of the book) until you are absolutely certain that you do not know how to do the question. If the answer is not at the back of the book, ask your lecturer to download it for you from the *Lecturer's Guide*.

Some guidance for students studying on their own

If you are studying accounting without having the opportunity of having face-to-face tuition, we suggest that you adopt the following study plan.

1 Organize your private study so that you have covered every topic in your syllabus at least two weeks before your examination. A proven method is to divide the number of weeks (or perhaps days!) you have available by the number of topics. This gives you the *average* time that you should spend on each topic. Allow for some topics requiring more time than others but don't rush though a topic just because you are behind your timetable. Instead, try to put in a few extra hours that week.

2 Read each chapter slowly. Be careful to do each activity and to work through each example. Don't worry if you do not understand each point immediately. Read on to the end of the chapter.

3 Read the chapter again, this time making sure that you understand each point. If necessary, go back and re-read and repeat until you do understand the point.

4 Attempt as many questions at the end of each chapter as you can, but do not look at the answers until you have completed the question or you are certain that you cannot do it. The questions are generally graded so the more difficult ones come towards the end. If you can do them all without too much difficulty then you can move on to the next chapter with great confidence. However, before you do it is not a bad idea to re-read the chapter again.

More guidance for all students

At this early stage of your accounting career we want to emphasize that accounting involves much more than being good at doing simple arithmetic (contrary to popular opinion it is not highly mathematical). The solution to many accounting problems often calls for a considerable amount of personal judgement and this means that there is bound to be an element of subjectivity in whatever you decide to do.

The simplified examples used in this book illustrate some complicated issues and problems in the real world that are not easily solved. You should, therefore, treat the suggested answers with caution and use them as an opportunity to question the methodology adopted. This will mean that when you are presented with some accounting information in your job, you will automatically subject it (rightly) to a great deal of questioning. That is as it should be because, as you will shortly discover, if you were an accountant and you happened to be asked '*What do 2 + 2 make?*' you might well reply by asking another question: '*What do you want it to make?*'

Puzzled? Intrigued? Then read on – and good luck with your studies.

An explanation

In order to avoid tedious repetition and tortuous circumlocution, the masculine pronoun has generally been adopted throughout this book. No offence is intended to anyone, most of all to our female readers, and we hope that none will be taken.

Guided tour

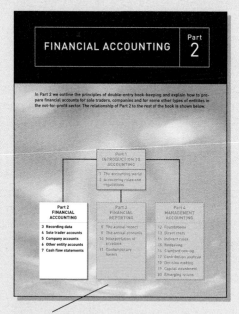

Part openers contain a diagram to help you find your way around the book.

Chapter openers feature a topical news article relating chapter content to the real world, and there are shorter **News clips** throughout.

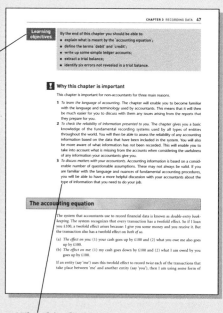

Learning objectives are provided in each chapter.

Why this chapter is important explores the applications and benefits of chapter content for the non-accountant.

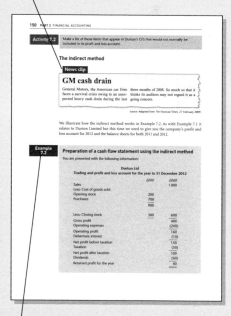

Examples are spread throughout the chapter.

Activities test student understanding at regular intervals throughout the chapter.

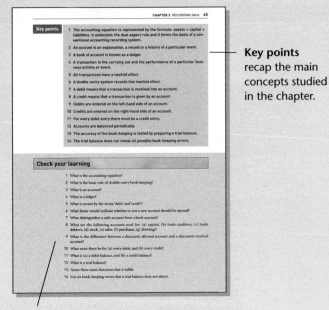

Key points recap the main concepts studied in the chapter.

Questions you should ask are questions business managers might ask to assist in the decision-making process.

Check your learning tests absorption of chapter content and offers a useful revision aid.

News story quizzes provide thought-provoking questions relating to topical news articles.

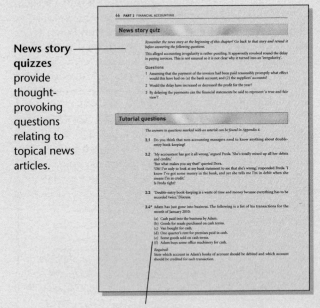

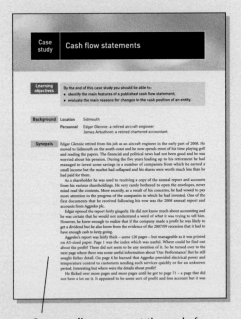

Tutorial questions offer ideas for assignments or class discussion.

Case studies appear at the end of parts.

Visit the Companion Website at www.pearsoned.co.uk/dyson to find further practice questions, study material and links to relevant sites on the World Wide Web. See page xi for full contents.

Acknowledgements

We are grateful to the following for permission to reproduce copyright material:

Figures

Figure 20.2 adapted from Using the balanced scorecard as a strategic management system, *Harvard Business Review*, January/February (Kaplan, R.S. and Norton, D.P. 1996), with permission from Harvard Business School Publishing; Figure 20.3 after A framework for functional coordination, *Atlanta Economic Review*, 23(6), 8-11 (Fox, H. 1973), with permission from the Federal Reserve Bank of Atlanta.

Text and other materials

J. Smart & Co. (Contractors) PLC for data and materials extracted from the J. Smart & Co. (Contractors) PLC and Subsidiary Companies Annual Report and Accounts 2008; Aggreko plc for data and materials extracted from the Aggreko plc Annual Report and Accounts 2008; A.G. Barr plc for data and materials extracted from the A.G. Barr plc Annual Report and Accounts 2008 – 2009; Cairn Energy plc for data and materials extracted from the Cairn Energy plc Annual Report and Accounts 2008; Devro plc for data and materials extracted from the Devro plc Annual Report and Accounts 2008; Robert Wiseman Dairies plc for data and materials extracted from the Robert Wiseman Dairies plc Annual Reports and Accounts/Financial Statements for 2005, 2006, 2007, 2008 and 2009; Article on page 2 from Management Today, 27 October 2008, Email bulletin, www.managementtoday.co.uk/newsalerts/article/857179, reproduced from MT magazine with the permission of the copyright owner, Haymarket Business Publications Limited.; Article on page 22 from Article by Paul Grant, 17 June 2009, www.accountancyage.com/2244250; Extract on page 35 from IASB, with permission from International Accounting Standards Board; Article on page 46 from 15 September 2008, www.accountancyage.com/2226049; Article on page 126 from *Financial Management* (2009 (May)), CIMA; Article on page 145 by Judith Tydd, 9 October 2008, www.accountancyage.com/2227851; Article on page 178 by Kevin Reed, 24 October 2008, www.accountancyage.com/2229007; Article on page 195 from FT.com, 2 March 2009, with permission from Philip Whitchelo, Interim M&A Partners Ltd, London, E1; Article on page 213 by David Jetuah, 7 May 2009, www.accountancyage.com/2241782; Article on page 249 from Accounting board could lose power to set rules, *The Observer*, 7 June 2009 (Mathiason, N.), Copyright Guardian News & Media Ltd 2009; Article on page 270 by David Jetuah, 30 April 2009, www.accountancyage.com; Article on page 300 from *Aviation Week* (*online 09/01/2009*) (Meeham, M.), with permission from McGraw-Hill Education; Article on page 347 from AccountingWEB US blogs, 2 April 2009, AccountingWEB.com; Article on page 445 from Accountants given green reporting guidance, *Accountancy Age 12/02/2009* (Singh, R.), all Accountancy Age materials with permission from Incisive Media Ltd.

The Financial Times

Article on page 73 from FT.com, 3 March 2009; Article on page 103 from FT.com, Joe Leahy, 8 January 2009; Article on page 284 from FT.com, Daniel Schäfer, 26 April 2009; Article on page 371 from FT.com, Andrew Parker, 30 July 2009; Article on page 396 from FT.com, Andrew Taylor, 8 January 2009; Article on page 419 from FT.com, Stephen Pritchard, 13 May 2009; all at www.ft.com.

In some instances we have been unable to trace the owners of copyright material, and we would appreciate any information that would enable us to do so.

Abbreviations

AAT	Association of Accounting Technicians
ABB	Activity-based budgeting
ABC	Activity-based costing
ABCM	Activity-based cost management
ABM	Activity-based management
AC	Average cost
ACCA	Association of Chartered Certified Accountants
AMT	Advanced manufacturing technology
ARR	Accounting rate of return
ASB	Accounting Standards Board
ASC	Accounting Standards Committee
ASSC	Accounting Standards Steering Committee
BB	Beyond budgeting/Better budgeting
BBC	British Broadcasting Corporation
CA	Chartered Accountant/Companies Act
CE	Capital employed/expenditure
CFS	Cash flow statement
CI	Capital investment
CIMA	Chartered Institute of Management Accountants
CIPFA	Chartered Institute of Public Finance and Accountancy
Cr	Credit
DCF	Discounted cash flow
Dr	Debit
EA	Environmental accounting
ED	Exposure draft
EMA	Environmental management accounting
EPS	Earnings per share
EU	European Union
FA	Financial accounting
FASB	Financial Accounting Standards Board
FIFO	First in, first out
FRC	Financial Reporting Council
FRP	Financial Reporting Panel
FRS	Financial Reporting Standard
FSA	Financial Services Authority
FTSE	Financial Times and London Stock Exchange
GAAP	Generally accepted accounting principles
GBV	Gross book value
HCA	Historic cost accounting
HP	Hire purchase
IAS	International Accounting Standard
IASB	International Accounting Standards Board

IASC	International Accounting Standards Committee
IASCF	International Accounting Standards Committee Foundation
ICAEW	Institute of Chartered Accountants in England and Wales
ICAI	Institute of Chartered Accountants in Ireland
ICAS	Institute of Chartered Accountants of Scotland
IFAC	International Federation of Accountants
IFRS	International Financial Reporting Standard
IRR	Internal rate of return
JIT	Just-in-time
KPI	Key performance indicator
LCC	Life cycle costing
LIFO	Last-in, first-out
LLP	Limited liability partnership
LSE	London Stock Exchange
LTD	Limited
MA	Management accounting
MV	Market value
NBV	Net book value
NCF	Net cash flow
NPV	Net present value
PBIT	Profit before interest and tax
P/E	Price/earnings ratio
PFI	Private finance initiative
PI	Performance indicator
PLC	Public limited company
PLCC	Product/project life cycle costing
R&D	Research and development
RI	Residual income
ROCE	Return on capital employed
SBU	Strategic business unit
SC	Standard cost/costing
SI	Statutory Instrument
SMA	Strategic management accounting
SME	Small and medium-sized enterprise
SSAP	Statement of Standard Accounting Practice
TB	Trial balance
TOC	Theory of constraints
TQM	Total quality management
UK	United Kingdom
VA	Value added
VCA	Value chain analysis
WACC	Weighted average cost of capital
ZBB	Zero base budgeting

INTRODUCTION TO ACCOUNTING

Part 1

This book is divided into four main parts, as shown below. Part 1 contains two chapters. In Chapter 1 we provide some background about accounting, the accountancy profession, and the organizations that accountants work for. In Chapter 2 we outline the rules and regulations that accountants are expected to follow when preparing accounting statements.

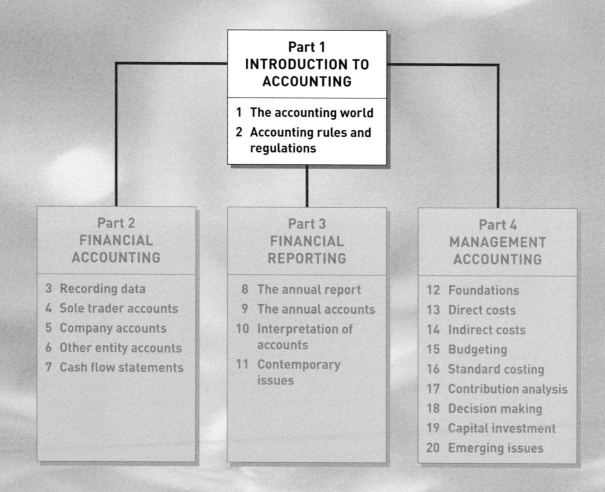

Part 1
INTRODUCTION TO ACCOUNTING

1 The accounting world
2 Accounting rules and regulations

Part 2
FINANCIAL ACCOUNTING

3 Recording data
4 Sole trader accounts
5 Company accounts
6 Other entity accounts
7 Cash flow statements

Part 3
FINANCIAL REPORTING

8 The annual report
9 The annual accounts
10 Interpretation of accounts
11 Contemporary issues

Part 4
MANAGEMENT ACCOUNTING

12 Foundations
13 Direct costs
14 Indirect costs
15 Budgeting
16 Standard costing
17 Contribution analysis
18 Decision making
19 Capital investment
20 Emerging issues

As others see us . . .

But we are cool, insist accountants

It's one of the most enduring stereo-types in the business world: ever since the days of Monty Python's Lion Tamer sketch, accountancy has become a byword for dull, straight-laced stuffi-ness. But now the grey men are fighting back: an indignant survey reports that accountants are actually a lot more dynamic, tech-savvy and generally 'down with the kids' than everyone makes them out to be. And if you don't believe them, they've got the spreadsheets to prove it...

The report, from tax and account-ancy information provider CCH, 'exposes the gulf' between people's perception of accountants and the real-ity – or at least, the reality according to accountants. Take technology, just 28% of the public surveyed thought account-ancy was a dynamic profession embracing new technologies, whereas 53% of accountants think their profes-sion is the height of tech-saviness. Indeed, so achingly hip are accountants that a staggering 74% can use an iPod – miles more than the public's guess of just 59%!

What's more, accountants are also 'down' with social networking sites: 58% are apparently regular users (com-pared to the public perception of 44%). CCH reckons accountants are 50% more likely to have a Facebook profile than the average punter – 60% of those under 35 have a page, compared to the national average of 23%. Even if we ignore the inevitable socio-economic bias in that statistic, we're not totally sure whether this proves that they're cool, or the direct opposite (although it does go a long way towards explaining the existence of a 12,000-strong Facebook group called 'Accountants are Sexy').

According to CCH, this marvellous embrace of new technologies is proof positive of a new, dynamic younger generation of accountants, who are 'breathing new life into the profession'. And as such, their enduring reputation for terminal tediousness is wholly undeserved. 'Even in these hyper PC times, it seems that accountants are still unfairly viewed as being behind the times,' laments CCH executive director Martin Casimir.

On the other hand, we can't help feeling that life could be a lot worse for these poor accountants – after all, they could be bankers, in the Monty Python sketch, accountant Michael Palin ini-tially jumps at the idea of working his way up to lion taming via banking: 'That's a man's life, isn't it?' he exclaims, 'Travel, excitement, adven-ture, thrills, decisions affecting people's lives...' Prophetic words – and it explains exactly why bankers are cur-rently a hell of a lot more unpopular than accountants have ever been...

Management Today, 27 October 2008.

Source: Reproduced from *MT* magazine with the permission of the copyright owner, Haymarket Business Publications Limited.

Questions relating to this news story can be found on page 20 ➡

About this chapter

This chapter sets the scene for the rest of the book.

The chapter begins with an explanation of why it is important for you as a non-accountant to study accounting. It then gives a brief explanation of the nature and purpose of accounting and of its historical development. This is followed by an outline of the main branches of accounting and a description of the accountancy profession. The last main section of the chapter gives a brief overview of the economic structure of the United Kingdom (UK).

Learning objectives

By the end of this chapter you should be able to:

- summarize the nature and purpose of accounting;
- outline its history;
- explain why you need to know something about it;
- identify the main branches;
- list the principal UK accountancy bodies;
- describe the most important types of public and private entities in the UK.

! Why accounting is important

News clip

Financial meltdown

According to the Deputy President of the Association of Chartered Certified Accountants the failure to tackle financial illiteracy could be as devastating as global warming. She urges financial professionals to help with financial education in schools 'to put something back'. How is not clear but perhaps this book is a step in that direction.

Source: Adapted from *Accountancy Magazine*, January 2007, p. 10.

You've probably got hold of this book because you're a student. You may be doing a certificate, diploma or degree course in perhaps business, engineering, languages, law, management or one of the sciences. And then you find to your horror that you have to do some accounting. Why?

OK, we'll try to explain. You probably have a vague idea that accounting has something to do with balance sheets and profits and tax and, er, *stuff* but you are certainly not sure what that has to do with the subject you're studying. And you resent it.

Right. Now accounting is basically about collecting information and letting people who need it have it, like shareholders and managers. Perhaps just like you hope to be. 'So what?' you might well ask. 'If I need it or want it I'll just ask the accountants to get it for me.' That's fine, but if you were a manager would you really be quite happy to accept *all* that the accountants gave you? Would you know what it meant, how reliable it was and what you were supposed to do with it? We suspect that if you really think about the repercussions of *not* questioning what your accountants gave you, you would be (to say the least) a little unhappy. Maybe even a bit worried, especially if you were legally responsible for it all.

The point we are making is that accountants provide a service for other people. Most accountants are probably highly qualified, experienced and good at their job, but as accountants they should not take the *decisions*. That is the manager's job – it could be your job and you will know much more about your business than any accountant. Rest assured that there is no doubt that you will be able to make even *better* decisions (a) if you have some knowledge and some understanding of the nature of accounting information; and (b) what it can and what it cannot do in helping you plan and control your business.

So in a sentence – if you know something about accounting you will become a *better* manager. By the end of this book you will be well on the way to becoming one.

This first chapter sets the scene for what follows. It is important because it provides you with the necessary background information to enable you to become a better manager.

Nature and purpose

We begin our accounting studies by giving a brief explanation of what accounting is and what it *does*. We will then tell you something of what it *doesn't* do. For our purposes we will use the following definition of accounting:

> **Accounting is a service provided for those who need information about an entity's financial performance, its assets and its liabilities.**

This definition contains a number of features that require some explanation.

- *Service*. Accounting is of assistance to other people – if nobody wanted the service there would be no such thing as accounting.
- *Information*. The information traditionally collected by accountants is restricted to what can be quantified and translated into monetary terms.
- *Entity*. An entity is a jargon term used by accountants to describe any type of organization, e.g. a person running his (or her) own business or a company.
- *Financial performance*. The financial performance is usually judged by matching incomes received with expenditure incurred over a period of time (usually one year).
- *Assets*. In accounting an asset is regarded as being something that will result in a future economic benefit as a result of a past event. For example, the purchase of plant and machinery will provide a benefit over very many years and thereby help the entity generate income in those years.
- *Liabilities*. A liability in accounting is defined as an obligation arising from a past event. For example, you may have bought some furniture but you don't have to start paying for it until next year. So for the time being, what you owe is a debt or an obligation, i.e. a liability.

The above summary shows that accounting information is somewhat restricted:

- It relates to only one entity.
- It has to be quantifiable.
- It must be capable of being converted into monetary terms.
- It relates to an arbitrary period of time.

- A distinction is made between economic benefits that relate to past, current and future periods.

Non-accountants are often surprised when they realize that accounting information is restricted in such ways. This gives rise to what is sometimes called the *expectations gap*, i.e. when users expect accounting to do more than it can.

The expectations gap often causes considerable misunderstanding between accountants and the public, especially when an 'accounting scandal' erupts from time to time. Such scandals are often the result of genuine accounting problems but the public tend to think that they can all be put down to fraud. This was especially so in the early 2000s when there was a great many accounting scandals. The best known one in recent times involved an American company called Enron. Its problems were caused mainly by fraud but some questionable accounting practices probably made it easier to perpetrate the fraud.

We now move on to give you a review of the historical development of accounting. We do so in the next section.

Activity 1.1	Look up the definition of accounting in three different dictionaries. Copy the definitions into your notebook. Then frame your own definition based on the information that you have extracted from your dictionaries.

Historical development

The word *account* in everyday language is often used as a substitute for an *explanation* or a *report* of certain actions or events. If you are an employee, for example, you may have to explain to your employer just how you have been spending your time, or if you are a manager you may have to report to the owner on how the business is doing. In order to explain or to report, you will, of course, have to remember what you were doing or what happened. As it is not always easy to remember, you may need to keep some written record. In effect, such records can be said to provide the basis of a rudimentary accounting system.

In a primitive sense, man has always been involved in some form of accounting. It may have gone no further than a farmer measuring his worth simply by counting the number of cows or sheep that he owned. However, the growth of a monetary system enabled a more sophisticated method to be developed. It then became possible to calculate the increase or decrease in individual wealth over a period of time, and to assess whether a farmer with perhaps ten cows and fifty sheep was wealthier than one who had sixty pigs. Figure 1.1 illustrates just how difficult it would be to assess the wealth of a farmer in a non-monetary system.

Even with the growth of a monetary system, it took a very long time for formal documentary systems to become commonplace, although it is possible to trace the origins of modern book-keeping back to at least the twelfth century. We know that from about that time, traders began to adopt a system of recording information called *double-entry book-keeping*. By the end of the fifteenth century, double-entry book-keeping was widely used in Venice and the surrounding areas (the first-known book on the subject was published in 1494 by an Italian mathematician called Pacioli). Modern book-keeping systems are still based on principles established in the fifteenth century, although they have had to be adapted to suit modern conditions.

His possessions	A year ago	Now	Change
Cows	••••••••••	••••••••••••••••	+5
Hens [• = 10]	••••••••••	•••••••	–30
Pigs	••••••	••••	–2
Sheep [• = 10]	•••••	•••••••	+20
Land [• = 1 acre]	••••	••••	no change
Cottage	•	•	no change
Carts	•••	•	–2
Ploughs	•	••	+1

Figure 1.1 Accounting for a farmer's wealth

There are two main reasons why a recording system devised in medieval times has lasted for so long:

- It provides an accurate record of what has happened to a business over a given period of time.
- Information extracted from the system can help the owner or the manager to operate the business much more effectively.

In essence, the system provides the answers to three basic questions that both owners and managers want to know. They are as follows.

- What profit has the business made?
- How much does the business owe?
- How much is owed to it?

These three questions are illustrated in pictorial form in Figure 1.2.

The medieval system dealt largely with simple agricultural and trading entities. In the eighteenth century, however, the UK underwent an *Industrial Revolution*. Economic activity gradually moved away from growing things to making or manufacturing them. In the early days of the Industrial Revolution managers had to depend upon the type of information supplied to the owners. The owners' need was for *financial* purposes, i.e. to calculate how much profit they had made and how much they owed and what was owed to them. Financial information was prepared infrequently (perhaps only once a year) and then not in any great detail. Managers needed information largely for *costing* purposes, so they could work out the cost of making individual products. The information required needed to be in much more detail and prepared much more frequently.

As a result of the different information needs of owners and managers, separate accounting systems were developed. However, as much of the basic data were common to both systems they were gradually brought together. It would be rare now to find any entity that had a separate financial accounting system and a separate costing system.

Another change in more recent years is that it is possible to identify more than two user groups. Besides owners and managers, information may also now be required by other users such as creditors, employees, the government and investors.

While accounting gradually evolved into two main branches in the late nineteenth century (financial accounting and cost accounting), there were additional developments in the twentieth century. We examine the structure of accounting as it is today in the next section.

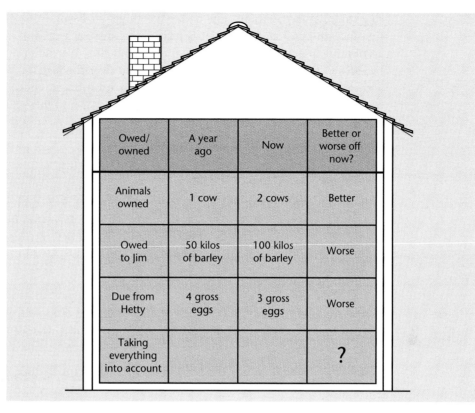

Figure 1.2 An owner's vital questions

Complete the following sentences:

(a) The word _____ in everyday language means an explanation or a report.
(b) Traders in the fifteenth century began to adopt a system of _____ to record information.
(c) The owners of a business want to know how much _____ a business has made.
(d) An _____ is a term used to describe any type of organization.
(e) In the eighteenth century the United Kingdom underwent an _____ _____.

Branches

Among the top 100

A new survey shows that more than half the chief executives of companies in the FTSE 100 share index have a strong financial background in accounting, banking or finance. It appears that a strong background in such sectors is the best way to 'fast track' to the top jobs in UK business.

Source: Adapted from Robert Half International, 26 March 2009.

The work that accountants now undertake ranges far beyond that of simply preparing financial and cost statements. It is possible to identify at least six main branches of accounting and a number of important sub-branches. We will deal with each of them broadly in the order that they have developed over the last 100 years, i.e. financial accounting, management accounting, auditing, taxation, financial management, and bankruptcy and liquidation. You will see from Figure 1.3 how they all fit together.

Financial accounting

Until about the middle of the nineteenth century the nature, purpose and development of accounting described in the last two sections was mainly about the type of accounting that we would now describe as *financial* accounting. We do not, therefore, need to add much more to our outline except to give you a more formal definition of financial accounting. We will adopt that used by the Chartered Institute of Management Accountants (CIMA). It is as follows:

> *Classification and recording of the monetary transactions of an entity in accordance with established concepts, principles, accounting standards and legal requirements and their presentation, by means of income statements, balance sheets and cash flow statements, during and at the end of an accounting period. (CIMA, Official Terminology, 2005)*

'Concepts, principles, accounting standards and legal requirements' are the rules and regulations that govern accounting. We shall be dealing with them in Chapter 2. 'Income statements, balance sheets and cash flow statements' are dealt with in Part 2 of this book. But in brief, an income statement is a summary of what profit or loss you might have made over a period of time. A balance sheets is a summary of what you own and what you are owed at the end of that time, and a cash flow statement is a summary of what cash you have received and what cash you have paid in that particular period. Income statements (or profit and loss accounts), balance sheets and cash flow statements are known collectively as the *financial statements*.

A distinction is sometimes made between *financial accounting* and *financial reporting*. We do so in this book mainly for practical reasons in order to break the information down into manageable parts. *Financial accounting* may be regarded as being the accounting process that ends with the preparation of the financial statements. *Financial reporting* is the process of analysing, communicating and supplementing the information included in the financial statements to those users who either need it or want it.

Book-keeping

An important sub-branch of financial accounting is *book-keeping*. Indeed, book-keeping may be regarded as the foundation on which the entire discipline of accounting is built. It is a mechanical task involving the collection of basic financial data. The data are entered in special records known as *books of account* and they are then extracted in the form of a *trial balance*. The trial balance enables the financial statements to be prepared. The CIMA definition of book-keeping is:

> *Recording of monetary transactions, appropriately classified, in the financial records of an entity. (CIMA, Official Terminology, 2005)*

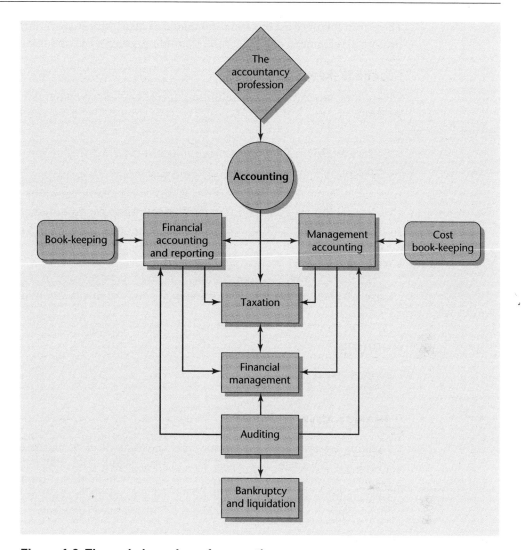

Figure 1.3 The main branches of accounting

Management accounting

Management accounting has grown out of nineteenth century financial accounting. The CIMA definition is:

> *The application of the principles of accounting and financial management to create, protect, preserve and increase value for the stakeholders of for-profit and not-for-profit enterprises in the public and private sectors. (CIMA, Official Terminology, 2005)*

This definition is accompanied by a statement explaining that:

> *Management accounting is an integral part of management. It requires the identification, generation, presentation, interpretation and use of relevant information to:*

There then follows a list of various functions of management accounting. The list includes strategy development, planning, control, funding, governance, and information supply.

Cost book-keeping

CIMA does not give a specific definition of cost book-keeping but it does define the verb 'to cost':

> *To ascertain the cost of a specified thing or activity. (CIMA, Official Terminology, 2005)*

So by combining this definition of 'cost' with the definition of 'book-keeping' given earlier, we can arrive at a suitable working definition of cost book-keeping:

> *The recording of monetary transactions, appropriately classified, in the financial records of an entity in order to ascertain the cost of a specified thing or activity.*

Auditing

News clip

Help somebody

Auditors are apparently easy scapegoats when there is a financial scandal. This is put down to what stakeholders expect and what auditors are actually paid to do. Steps taken in recent years to make the position clear do not appear have been successful. The author of this article appears to think that it may not be possible to do much about people who make 'ill-informed comments'.

Source: Adapted from *Accountancy Age*, 13 November 2008, p. 3.

CIMA defines an audit as being:

> *Systematic examination of the activities and status of an entity, based primarily on investigation and analysis of its systems, controls and records. (CIMA, Official Terminology, 2005)*

So auditing is the process of carrying out that investigation.

Not all entities have their accounts audited but it is a legal requirement for some entities, e.g. large limited liability companies.

Auditors are usually trained accountants who specialize in checking whether the accounts are credible, i.e. whether they can be believed. There are two main types of auditor.

1 *External auditors.* External auditors are entirely independent. They come from outside the entity, they are not employees of it and they do not answer to its managers. When they have finished their work they present their findings to the owners. They do not report to any of its managers.

External auditors formally report to the owners on whether the financial accounts represent what is called 'a true and fair view' of the entity's affairs. They may do some detailed checking of its records in order to be able to come to such a view but normally they would be selective. If they are then satisfied they will be able to report their findings to the owners. The public often believe that the job of an auditor is to discover whether any fraud has taken place. This is not so. This misconceived perception forms part of the expectations gap discussed earlier in the chapter.

2   *Internal auditors.* Some entities employ internal auditors. Internal auditors are appointed by the managers of the entity; they are employees of the entity and they answer to its management. Internal auditors perform routine tasks and undertake some detailed checking of the entity's accounting procedures. Their task may also go beyond the financial accounts e.g. they may examine the planning and control procedures and conduct 'value-for-money' tests.

External auditors and internal auditors usually work together very closely. Nevertheless, they do have separate roles and responsibilities. External auditors have always to remember that internal auditors are employees of the entity and they may be subject to the same pressures as other employees such as job security, pay and promotion prospects. But even external auditors are not completely independent. In the case of a public company, for example, the directors *recommend* the appointment of the company's auditors to the shareholders. As the shareholders usually accept whom the directors suggest, the directors are in a strong position if they want to dismiss the auditors. The auditors can then appeal directly to the shareholders but the shareholders usually back the directors.

Taxation

Taxation is a highly complex and technical branch of accounting. Those accountants who are involved in tax work are responsible for calculating the amount of tax payable both by business entities and by individuals. It is not necessary for anybody or any entity to pay more tax than is required by the law. It is, therefore, perfectly legitimate to search out all legal means of minimizing the amount of tax that might be demanded by the government. This is known as *tax avoidance.* The non-declaration of sources of income on which tax might be payable is known as *tax evasion.* Tax evasion is a very serious offence and it could lead to a long prison sentence. The borderline between tax avoidance and tax evasion is a narrow one and tax accountants have to steer a fine line between what is lawful and what is not.

Financial management

Financial management is a relatively new branch of accounting that has grown rapidly over the last 30 years. Financial managers are responsible for setting financial objectives, making plans based on those objectives, obtaining the finance needed to achieve the plans and generally safeguarding all the financial resources of the entity. They are much more likely to be involved in the general management of an entity than are other types of accountant. Their responsibilities involve them in drawing on a much wider range of disciplines (such as economies and mathematics) than is traditional in other branches of accounting and they use more non-financial and more qualitative data.

Bankruptcy and liquidation

One other highly specialist branch of accounting that you may sometimes read about is that connected with *insolvency*, i.e. bankruptcies and liquidation. This branch of accounting is extremely specialized. It has a long history but it is not one that most accountants will have had either anything to do with or indeed know much about.

Bankruptcy is a formal legal procedure. The term is applied to individuals when their financial affairs are so serious that they have to be given some form of legal protection from their creditors. The term *liquidation* is usually applied to a company when it gets into serious financial difficulties and its affairs have to be 'wound up', i.e. arrangements made for it to go out of existence in an orderly fashion.

Companies do not necessarily go immediately into liquidation if they get into financial difficulties. An attempt will usually be made either to rescue them or to protect certain types of creditors. In these situations, accountants sometimes act as *administrators*. Their appointment freezes creditors' rights. This prevents the company from being put into liquidation during a period when the administrators are attempting to manage the company. By contrast, *receivers* may be appointed on behalf of loan creditors. The creditors' loans may be secured on certain property. The receivers will try to obtain the income from that property or they may attempt to sell it.

We hope that you never come into contact with insolvency practitioners and so we will move on swiftly to have a look at another topic, namely the structure of the accountancy profession.

Activity 1.3	State whether each of the following statements is true or false:

(a)	An auditor's job is to find out whether a fraud has taken place.	*True/false*
(b)	Management accounts are required by law.	*True/false*
(c)	Tax avoidance is lawful.	*True/false*
(d)	A balance sheet is a list of assets and liabilities.	*True/false*
(e)	Companies have to go into liquidation if they get into financial difficulties.	*True/false*

The accountancy profession

News clip

Not up to standard

The President of the Association of Chartered Certified Accountants believes that there are a number of people out there who call themselves accountants even though they are not professionally qualified. They are perfectly entitled to do so but he argues that an awful lot of them do not measure up to the sort of standards that clients would reasonably expect from an 'accountant'.

Source: Adapted from *Accountancy Age*, 31 July 2007.

There are six major accountancy bodies operating in the United Kingdom. They are:

- Institute of Chartered Accountants in England and Wales (ICAEW)
- Institute of Chartered Accountants in Ireland (ICAI)
- Institute of Chartered Accountants of Scotland (ICAS)
- Association of Chartered Certified Accountants (ACCA)
- Chartered Institute of Management Accountants (CIMA)
- Chartered Institute of Public Finance and Accountancy (CIPFA)

The Irish Institute (ICAI) is included in the UK list because it has a strong influence in Northern Ireland.

Although all six major professional accountancy bodies now have a Royal Charter, it is still customary to refer only to members of ICAEW, ICAI, and ICAS as *chartered accountants* (CAs). Such chartered accountants have usually had to undergo a period of training in a practising office, i.e. one that offers accounting services directly to the public. This distinguishes them from members of the other three bodies because their auditing experience enables them to become approved (in the legal sense) auditors. Much practice work is involved, not just in auditing but also in tax. After qualifying, many CAs go to work in commerce or industry. ACCA members may also obtain their training in practice but relevant experience elsewhere counts towards their qualification (apart from in auditing). CIMA members usually train and work in industry, while CIPFA members specialize almost exclusively in central and local government.

Apart from the six major bodies, there are a number of important (although far less well-known) smaller accountancy associations and societies, e.g. the Association of Certified Public Accountants, the Institute of Cost and Executive Accountants and the Institute of Financial Accountants. Such bodies offer some form of accountancy qualification but they have not yet managed to achieve the status or the prestige of the six major bodies. They are usually referred to as *secondary bodies*.

There is also another very important accountancy body, the Association of Accounting Technicians (AAT). The association was formed in 1980 as a professional organization especially for those accountants who *assist* qualified accountants in preparing accounting information. In order to become an accounting technician, it is necessary to take (or be exempt from) the association's examinations. The AAT's examinations are less technical and perhaps more practical than those of the six major bodies but they are not easy.

The overall organization of the accountancy profession is shown in Figure 1.4.

Activity 1.4	Which is the odd one out among the following professional accountancy bodies? Give your reasons.

(a) AAT
(b) CIMA
(c) CIPFA
(d) ICAEW

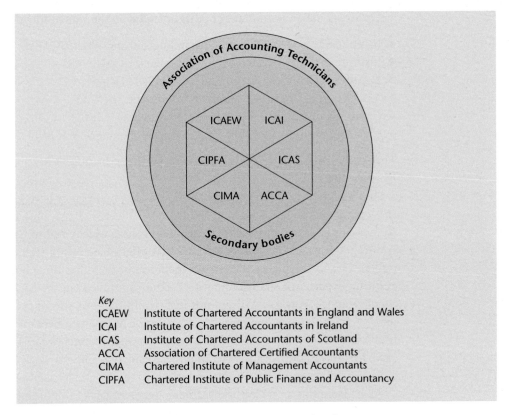

Key

ICAEW	Institute of Chartered Accountants in England and Wales
ICAI	Institute of Chartered Accountants in Ireland
ICAS	Institute of Chartered Accountants of Scotland
ACCA	Association of Chartered Certified Accountants
CIMA	Chartered Institute of Management Accountants
CIPFA	Chartered Institute of Public Finance and Accountancy

Figure 1.4 Organization of the UK accountancy profession

Public and private entities

The main aim of this section is to introduce you to the two main types of entities with which we shall be primarily concerned in this book – *sole traders* and *companies*. Before we can do this we need to explain a little bit about the economic structure of the United Kingdom.

In order to simplify our analysis, we will classify the UK economy into two broad groupings – the *profit-making sector* and the *not-for-profit sector*. Within each of these sectors it is then possible to distinguish a number of different types of entities (see Figure 1.5). We begin by examining the profit-making sector.

The profit-making sector

The profit-making sector is extremely diverse, but it is possible to recognize three major subdivisions. These are the manufacturing sector, the trading sector and the service sector.

The *manufacturing sector* is involved in purchasing raw materials and component parts, converting (or incorporating) them into finished goods and then selling them to customers. Examples of manufacturing enterprises include the chemicals, glass, iron and steel, and textile industries.

The *trading sector* purchases finished goods and then sells them to their customers without any further major conversion work normally being done on them. Trading

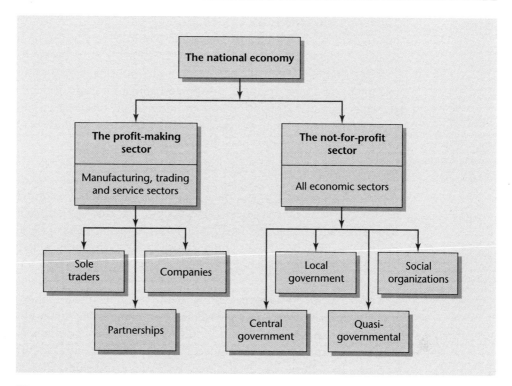

Figure 1.5 Public and private entities

enterprises are found in the retailing and wholesaling sectors. The sector includes entities such as builders' merchants, shops and supermarkets.

The *service sector* provides advice or assistance to customers or clients, e.g. hairdressing, legal and travel services. Unlike the manufacturing and trading sectors, the service sector does not usually deal in physical or tangible goods. There are some exceptions: the hotel and restaurant trade, for example, is normally classed as part of the service sector even though it provides major tangible services such as accommodation, food and drink.

The accounting systems required of manufacturing, trading and service sector entities are all slightly different, although they are based on similar principles and procedures. Manufacturing entity accounts are the most complex, trading entity accounts are fairly straightforward, while service entity accounts are usually quite simple.

Until about 30 years ago the manufacturing sector was of major significance in the UK. It is now much less important and the service sector has largely taken its place.

The products or the services offered by the manufacturing, trading or service sectors may be different but the way that they are organized is still very similar. Within each sector you will find three main types of entities: *sole traders*, *partnerships* and *companies*. The basic distinction between them reflects their ownership, how they are financed and what the law requires of them.

Sole traders

The term 'sole trader' is rather misleading for two reasons:

- 'sole' does not necessarily mean that only one person is involved in the entity;
- manufacturing and service entities may also be organized as sole traders.

The term really reflects the *ownership* of the entity; the main requirement is that only one individual should own it. The owner would normally also be the main source of finance and he would be expected to play a reasonably active part in its management.

Sole trader entities usually operate on a very informal basis and some private matters relating to the owner are often indistinguishable from those of the business. Sole trader accounts are fairly straightforward and there is no specific legislation that covers the accounting arrangements. We shall be using sole trader accounts in Chapters 3 and 4 in order to demonstrate some basic accounting techniques.

Partnerships

A partnership entity is very similar to a sole trader entity except that there must be at least *two owners* of the business. Partnerships often grow out of a sole trader entity, perhaps because more money needs to be put into the business or because the sole trader needs some help. But it is also quite common for a new business to begin as a partnership, e.g. when some friends get together to start a home-decorating service or to form a car-repair business.

The partners should agree among themselves how much money they will each put into the business, what jobs they will do, how many hours they will work, and how the profits and losses will be shared. In the absence of any agreement (whether formal or informal), partnerships in the United Kingdom are covered by the Partnership Act 1890.

Since 2001 there has been a new type of partnership called a *Limited Liability Partnership* (LLP). An LLP has a separate legal personality from that of its owners (like a company) and so it protects the partners from personal bankruptcy.

Partnership accounts are very similar to those of sole traders and we shall not be dealing with them in this book.

Companies

A company is another different type of business organization. There are many different forms of companies but basically a company is an entity that has a separate existence from that of its owners. We are going to be primarily concerned with *limited liability companies*. The term 'limited liability' means that the owners of such companies are required to finance the business only up to an agreed amount. Once they have contributed that amount they cannot be called on to contribute any more, even if the company gets into financial difficulties.

Activity 1.5	Insert in the following table one advantage and one disadvantage of operating a business as (a) a sole trader, (b) a partnership, and (c) a limited liability company.

Type of entity	Advantage	Disadvantage
(a) Sole trader		
(b) Partnership		
(c) Limited liability company		

As there is a risk that limited liability companies may not be able to pay what they owe, Parliament has had to give some legal protection to those parties who may become involved with them. The details are contained within the Companies Act 2006. We will be dealing with company accounts in some detail in Chapters 5 to 9.

The not-for-profit sector

By 'not-for-profit' we mean those entities whose primary purpose is to provide a service to the public rather than to make a profit. We will consider this sector under four main headings: central government, local government, quasi-governmental bodies and social organizations.

Within the three governmental groups, there is a wide variety of different types of entity. Governmental accounting is extremely specialized and it would require a book of its own to deal with it. We shall not be covering it in any depth.

Central government

Central government is responsible for services such as macro-economic policy, education, defence, foreign affairs, health and social security. These responsibilities are directly controlled by Cabinet ministers who answer to Parliament at Westminster for their actions. In 1999, some of these central government responsibilities were 'devolved', i.e. they became the direct responsibility of elected bodies in Northern Ireland, Scotland and Wales.

Local government

Devolution is not new in the UK. For well over a century central government has also devolved many of its responsibilities to local authorities, i.e. smaller units of authority that have some geographical and community coherence. Councillors are elected by the local community. They have responsibility for those services that central government has delegated or devolved, e.g. the local administration of education, housing, the police and social services.

Quasi-governmental bodies

Central government also operates indirectly through quasi-governmental bodies such as colleges and universities and the British Broadcasting Corporation (BBC). Such bodies are nominally independent of central government, even though their main funds normlally come from central government and their senior managers may be appointed by government ministers.

Activity 1.6 Into which category may the following functions/services best be placed? Tick the appropriate column.

Function/service	Central government	Local government	Quasi-governmental	Social organization
1 Broadcasting				
2 Famine relief				
3 Postal deliveries				
4 Social services				
5 Work and pensions				

Social organizations

This category covers a wide range of cultural, educational, recreational and social bodies. Some are formally constituted and professionally managed, such as national and international charities, while others are local organizations run by volunteers on a part-time basis, e.g. bridge and rugby clubs.

! Questions you should ask

This is an introductory chapter so at this stage there are not many technical questions that you might want to ask. Your questions are more likely to be about the accountants themselves and the organization of the accounting function. The following is a sample of the types of general question that as a non-accountant you might like to put to your own entity's accountants.

- How many accountants do we employ?
- How many are members of each of the six main professional accounting bodies?
- How is the accounting function organized?
- What can the accountants do to help me do a better job?
- What information do the accountants want from me?
- When is it wanted?
- What is it to be used for?
- What do I get back in return?
- What am I supposed to do with it?
- In future how can managers and accountants become a better team?

Conclusion

The main aim of this chapter has been to introduce non-accountants to the world of accounting. The chapter has stressed that the main purpose of accounting is to provide financial information to those parties that need it.

Information must be useful if it is to have any purpose but as a non-accountant you may feel reluctant to question any accounting information that lands on your desk. You may also not understand why the accountant is always asking you irrelevant questions and so you respond with any old nonsense. You then perhaps feel a bit guilty and a little frustrated; you would like to know more but you dare not ask. We hope that by the time you have worked your way through this book, you will have the confidence to ask and, furthermore, that you will understand the answer. Good luck!

Now that the world of accounting has been outlined, we can turn to more detailed subject matter. The first task is to learn the basic rules and regulations governing accounting. These are covered in the next chapter.

Key points

1 To account for something means to give an explanation or to report on it.

2 Owners of an entity want to know (a) how well it is doing, (b) what it owes, and (c) how much is owed to it.

3 Accounting is important for non-accountants because (a) they must make sure their own entity complies with any legal requirements, and (b) an accounting system can provide them with information that will help them do a better job.

4 There are seven main user groups: investors, lenders, suppliers and other trade creditors, employees, customers, governments and their agencies, and the public.

5 The six main branches of accounting are auditing, financial accounting and reporting, financial management, management accounting, taxation, and bankruptcy and liquidation.

6 Sub-branches of accounting include book-keeping (a function of financial accounting) and cost book-keeping (a function of management accounting).

7 There are six major professional accountancy bodies in the UK: the Institute of Chartered Accountants in England and Wales, the Institute of Chartered Accountants in Ireland, the Institute of Chartered Accountants of Scotland, the Association of Chartered Certified Accountants, the Chartered Institute of Management Accountants and the Chartered Institute of Public Finance and Accountancy.

8 The Association of Accounting Technicians is an important secondary accountancy body. Its members primarily provide technical assistance to professionally qualified accountants although they themselves are often in senior positions.

9 There are two economic sectors within the UK economy: the profit-making sector and the not-for-profit sector. Within each sector business operations can be classified into manufacturing, trading or service entities. Individual entities may then be organized as sole traders, partnerships or companies.

10 The not-for-profit sector includes central government and local government operations, quasi-governmental bodies and social organizations. Governmental operations are extremely complex and the accounting requirements are highly specialized. Social organizations are also diverse. They include various associations, charities, clubs, societies and sundry voluntary organizations. Their accounting requirements are similar to those in the profit-making sector.

Check your learning

The answers to these questions can be found within the text.

1 What is accounting?

2 What is meant by an 'entity'?

3 Give three reasons why accounting is an important subject for non-accountants to study.

4 What is meant by the word 'account'?

5 What name is given to the system that accountants use to record information?

6 What are the three basic questions that the owner of a business might ask?

7 What economic event happened in the UK during the eighteenth century?

8 What happened to the ownership and management of businesses during the nineteenth century?

9 Why did managers in nineteenth century industrial entities require more detailed information?

10 List three user groups of accounting information.

11 What are the six main branches of accounting?

12 Of which main branch of accounting does cost accounting form a part?

13 What is the difference between 'book-keeping' and 'cost book-keeping'?

14 Explain the difference between 'bankruptcy' and 'liquidation'.

15 List the six major UK professional accountancy bodies.

16 What function does the *Association of Accounting Technicians* fill?

17 Name three types of entity that fall within the profit-making sector of the UK.

18 What is meant by 'limited liability'?

19 What role do local authorities play in the not-for-profit sector?

20 Name one quasi-governmental body.

News story quiz

Remember the news story at the beginning of this chapter? Go back to that story and re-read it before answering the following questions.

In a sense this is an old story: our perceptions of ourselves are quite different from what other people think of us. It is often quite a shock to find that out. In this case the story is specifically about accountants, and it is no surprise to find that there is quite a big perception gap.

Questions

1 Have you seen the *Monty Python* 'Lion Tamer' sketch?

2 What is your perception of an accountant?

3 Where does your perception of an accountant come from?

4 Do you think that the accountancy profession is a dynamic one?

5 What immediately springs to mind when/if you think of the accountancy profession?

Tutorial questions

The answers to questions marked with an asterisk can be found in Appendix 4.

1.1 'Accountants stifle managerial initiative and enterprise.' Discuss.

1.2 Do you think that auditors should be responsible for detecting fraud?

1.3 The following statement was made by a student: 'I cannot understand why accountants have such a high status and why they have so much influence.' How would you respond to such assertions?

1.4* Why should a non-accountant study accounting?

1.5* Describe two main purposes of accounting.

1.6* What statutory obligations require a public limited company to prepare management accounts?

1.7 State briefly the main reasons why a company may employ a team of accountants.

1.8* What statutory obligations require limited liability companies to prepare financial accounts?

1.9 Why does a limited liability company have to engage a firm of external auditors?

1.10 Assume that you are a personnel officer in a manufacturing company, and that one of your employees is a young engineering manager called Joseph Sykes. Joseph has been chosen to attend the local university's business school to study for a diploma in management. Joseph is reluctant to attend the course because he will have to study accounting. As an engineer he thinks that it will be a waste of time for him to study such a subject.

Required:
Draft an internal memorandum addressed to Joseph explaining why it would be of benefit to him to study accounting.

1.11 Clare Wong spends a lot of her time working for a large local charity. The charity has grown enormously in recent years and the trustees have been advised to overhaul their accounting procedures. This would involve its workers (most of whom are voluntary) in more book-keeping and there is a great deal of resistance to this move. The staff have said that they are there to help the needy and not to get involved in book-keeping.

Required:
As the financial consultant to the charity, prepare some notes that you could use in speaking to the voluntary workers in order to try to persuade them to accept the new proposals.

Further practice questions, study material and links to relevant sites on the World Wide Web can be found on the website that accompanies this book. The site can be found at **www.pearsoned.co.uk/dyson**

Accounting rules and regulations

A principled approach

FSA should avoid 'lengthy rule book' says ICAEW

Paul Grant

The Financial Services Authority needs to avoid drawing up a 'lengthy rule book' in response to the financial crisis and instead adopt a principles-based approach in its reform of banking regulation.

In its submitted response to the Turner Review, the ICAEW said the City regulator should instead address operational fallings as well as weaknesses in system design and regulatory policy. It should also strive to avoid losing the positive aspects of the work it had previously undertaken from the pressure to change.

'The arguments that the FSA should move towards a more principles-based approach remain valid not least in that such an approach deals better with changing financial markets than a lengthy rule book,' said PwC partner and chair of the ICAEW Financial Service Faculty's Risk and Regulation Committee, John Tattersall.

Iain Coke, head of Financial Services Faculty, added: 'Communication, cooperation and coordination between the tripartite authorities can, and should, be improved. It is vital, however the system is structured, that it is made to work effectively at both policy and operational levels. Part of the solution here is for there to be closer dialogue between the FSA and the audit profession on systematic risks.'

Accountancy Age, 17 June 2009.

Source: Reproduced with permission from Incisive Media Ltd.

Questions relating to this news story can be found on page 41 ➡

About this chapter

In this chapter we outline the conventional accounting rules that are commonly adopted in practice and the legislation that governs accounting. We then examine the role of the UK's Accounting Standards Board along with the International Accounting Standards Board in the preparation of financial statements. The chapter closes with a review of the attempts made to develop a framework of accounting based on generally accepted principles.

Learning objectives

By the end of this chapter you should be able to:

- identify fourteen conventional accounting rules;
- summarize the UK legal requirements covering financial reporting;
- outline the role of the Accounting Standards Board in that process;
- examine the legal authority the International Accounting Standards Board has in UK financial reporting.

! Why this chapter is important

This chapter is important for non-accountants for the following reasons.

1 It underpins almost the entire contents of this book. So if you are to understand what accountants do and why they do it, you must be familiar with the rules and regulations that they adopt.

2 You need to have some familiarity with the legal requirements governing accounting in the UK.

3 Similarly it is necessary to have some knowledge of the quasi-legal role that the Accounting Standards Board and the International Accounting Standards Board play in UK financial reporting.

4 You must have a grasp of the attempts made to base accounting practice on generally accepted accounting principles (GAAP).

The need for rules

Most games have an agreed set of rules. Rules define the game and they provide a structure that every player is expected to follow. If you are a footballer, for example, you are expected to follow the rules that apply to football. Without them football (as we know it) would just become a totally uncoordinated and chaotic kick-about.

Unlike football or any other game, no one actually sat down and devised a set of accounting rules. What happened was that over a long period of time entities (mainly sole traders) gradually adopted similar procedures for recording their transactions and assessing how the business had performed at a regular and fixed interval. In other words, such procedures eventually became generally accepted and they became the rules that virtually everyone adopted. The development of accounting rules over the centuries to where we are today is shown in Figure 2.1.

There was nothing indisputable about such rules, of course, in the sense that if you drop an apple it falls to the ground. The accounting rules that evolved were man-made and you could argue against them. You were also free to choose whether to adopt them or follow your own rules. If you did, of course, you might cause a great deal of confusion (just as you would in football if you adopted your own rules) but that would be up to you.

Many accountants these days do not like to describe conventional accounting procedures as 'rules' because that gives the impression that they are prescriptive. So you will come across a bewildering number of different terms such as assumptions, axioms,

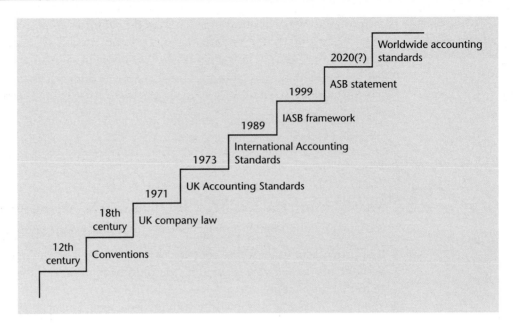

Figure 2.1 The development of accounting rules

concepts, objectives, policies, postulates, principles and procedures. It is quite easy to have an argument about each of these descriptions. For example, if you are told that 'this procedure is a *principle* of accounting' it sounds as though there is a moral code underpinning how that procedure should be dealt with, like being told that 'murder is wrong' and 'hanging is the answer'. Whereas in accounting all we are really saying is that 'this is the way that we usually do it', i.e. it is a convention.

We do not believe that it is necessary to get bogged down in such arguments so, in this book, for convenience and to avoid repetition we will generally refer to conventional accounting practices as 'accounting rules'. But why do we need some rules? Surely there is nothing more to accounting than the equivalent of adding 2 and 2 together and making sure that the answer is 4? Well, not quite.

In order to explain why, we need to re-examine what we mean by 'accounting'. In Chapter 1 we gave you the following definition:

> *Accounting is a service provided for those who need information about an entity's financial performance, its assets and it liabilities.*

Now even with perhaps such a broad definition it is possible to spot fairly quickly some of the difficulties involved in carrying out that brief. Some of the questions we might ask are as follows.

1 Why is the type of information? Qualitative, quantitative or both?
2 Who wants it? Owners? Workers? Customers? Are their wants the same?
3 What is meant by an entity? Where do you draw the line?
4 How do you report the information that you are going to provide? On the basis of numbers, e.g. six cows and a hundred sheep? Or do you use a common measure such as translating everything into monetary values?
5 Do you report on a regular basis? And over what period? Every week or every five years?

It is in response to such questions that over the centuries common procedures have evolved. Unfortunately, they are no longer necessarily suitable for a fast-moving highly technological age. The questions may remain the same but we need to come up with different answers. The search is on.

However, before we set off on that journey we need to review the answers that used to be acceptable. We do so in the next section.

Activity 2.1

Consult the most comprehensive dictionary you can find in your college/university library. Write down the meaning of the following words. They may have several meanings so extract the one that relates more to fact or truth.

(1) assumptions; (2) axioms; (3) concepts; (4) conventions; (5) postulates; (6) principles; and (7) procedures.

Consider carefully the definitions that you have extracted. Do they all have a similar meaning?

Conventional accounting rules

Dozens of conventional rules have been adopted over the centuries but it is possible to identify fairly clearly the most common ones. We have selected fourteen for our purposes. For convenience we have grouped them into three categories: boundary rules, measurement rules and ethical rules (see Figure 2.2). We start with what we call 'boundary' rules, i.e. where we draw the line at what should be reported.

Boundary rules

There are four important boundary rules: entity, periodicity, going concern and quantitative.

Entity

It is customary to keep strictly separate the affairs of a business from the private affairs of its owners. In practice, it is not always easy to distinguish precisely between what is 'business' and what is 'private', especially in the cases of sole trader and partnership entities. The close interrelationship between what are effectively two separate entities is shown in Figure 2.3.

Periodicity

The main accounting period is usually considered to be twelve months. This is an arbitrary period of time especially in the case of entities that have an unlimited life. In the western agrarian world it does reflect the four seasons of the year although this is now of little relevance to manufacturing and service entities. Indeed, in the fashion industry, for example, a much shorter accounting period might by more appropriate since fashions and tastes change quite quickly. A year is, however, a practical period of time because most people can relate to what happened last year, whereas it is much more difficult over (say) a five-year period.

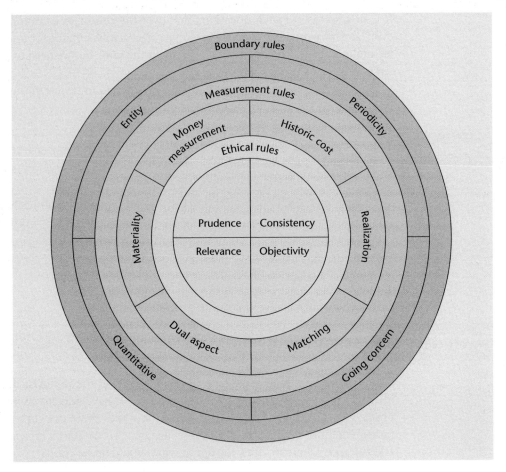

Figure 2.2 The basic accounting rules

| **Activity 2.2** | List three advantages and disadvantages of preparing financial accounts only once a year. |

Advantages	Disadvantages
1	1
2	2
3	3

Going concern

Irrespective of the chosen accounting period it is usual to assume that an entity will continue in business for the foreseeable future. If this is not the case then different accounting procedures would be adopted. But how is it possible to determine with any certainty whether an entity is a 'going concern' especially when business is bad such as in a recession?

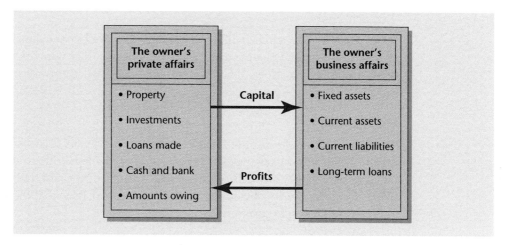

Figure 2.3 The entity rule: separation of business and private affairs

News clip

Liverpool FC concern

Liverpool FC's parent company may not be able to continue trading as a going concern. KPMG auditors warned that it needs to refinance its £350m debt. The parent company, Kop Football Holding, suffered a £42.6m loss last year with interest payments accounting for £36.5m of that loss. The Club itself had a turnover of £159.1m and a net profit of £10.2m.

Source: Adapted from www.accountancyage.com, 5 June 2009.

Quantitative

Accounting information is usually restricted to that which can be easily quantified. Value considerations, such as how long the business has been in existence or the length of service of the staff are usually ignored. And yet surely these factors are worth something to a long-established entity compared with a newly created business?

Measurement rules

Measurement rules determine how data should be recorded. There are six important ones. They are: money measurement, historic cost, realization, matching, dual aspect and materiality. First, the money measurement rule.

Money measurement

Such information that can be easily quantified is given a monetary value. But the value of money changes over a period of time. During inflationary periods its value goes down, i.e. the same quantity of money buys fewer goods and services than the year before. Deflationary periods can also occur but they are quite rare and they are usually quite short. In inflationary and deflationary circumstances it is misleading to compare one year's results with that of another without allowing for the effect of the value of money either going up or going down.

Historic cost

Assets (such as cars) and liabilities (such as amounts owed to a creditor) are usually valued at their historic cost, i.e. at the price paid for them when they were originally purchased or sold. However, apart from the impact of inflation or deflation, assets and liabilities may change their value owing to such factors as wear and tear and obsolescence.

Realization

When goods are sold or purchased or sold on credit terms it is customary practice to treat them as being exchanged at the point when the legal title to the goods is transferred, i.e. when they are realized. In modern manufacturing and trading conditions that point is not necessarily obvious and it remains a major issue that the accountancy profession is still trying to sort out.

Activity 2.3	A contracting company divides each of its sales into five stages: (1) on order; (2) on despatch; (3) on installation; (4) on commissioning; and (5) on completion of a 12-month warranty period.
	Assume that an order for Contract A for £100,000 was signed on 1 January 2011. The contract is expected to be completed on 31 December 2013 and the warranty period will end on 31 December 2014. In which year would you consider that the £100,000 has been 'realized'?

Matching

The matching rule is illustrated in Figure 2.4.

This rule is closely related to the realization rule. Accounts are not usually prepared on the basis of cash received and cash paid during (say) a 12-month period because there is often a delay between the receipt and the payment of cash depending on the credit period given. This means that a comparison based on cash received/cash paid may

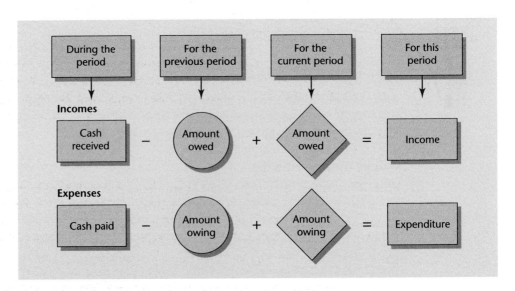

Figure 2.4 The matching rule

be misleading when one year is compared with another. When preparing the accounts at the end of a year, therefore, it is necessary to allow for what was *owed to* the entity and *owing* by it at both the beginning and the end of the year, i.e. opening and closing debtors and creditors. This procedure often involves making an estimate of the amounts due to be received and sometimes the amounts due to be paid. Any estimate, of course, can be wrong because it is likely that some debts will not be settled. If this proves to be the case then the accounts for that year will be incorrect.

Dual aspect

Any transaction involves someone giving something and someone else receiving it. So the basic rule is: *record **every** transaction twice* even if it is an internal transaction. As a result a recording system known as *double-entry book-keeping* evolved. This system has many practical advantages and most entities (apart from perhaps very small ones) now adopt it.

Materiality

The adoption of many of the conventional accounting procedures can result in a tremendous amount of work, e.g. in estimating the amount of bad debts. However, if the eventual results of that extra work are likely to be immaterial or insignificant, i.e. they do not have any meaningful effect on the overall results, then there does not appear to be much point in sticking strictly to the 'rules'. It would not be customary, for example, to estimate the value of small amounts of stationery at the year end and include them in 'stocks' or 'inventories'. But what does 'small' mean in this context? Stationery worth £200 may be material to a one-woman business but mean nothing to a multinational company. So materiality is a matter of context; it requires judgement and different people will come to a difference conclusion.

Ethical rules

Ethical rules relate to the moral code or principles expected to be adopted in the preparation of accounts. There are four main ethical rules. They are: prudence, consistency, objectivity and relevance.

Prudence

This is perhaps a rule which has helped to preserve the cautious, careful and pernickety perception of the typical old-fashioned accountant. The rule states that if there is some doubt over the treatment of a particular transaction, then income should be underestimated and expenditure overestimated. By following this rule the overall profit is likely to be lower and so there is less danger of it being paid out to the owners and hence not being recoverable.

Consistency

The same accounting policies and rules should be followed in successive accounting periods unless there is a fundamental change in circumstances that makes such a change justifiable. It is not usually acceptable, for example, to adopt a different accounting method simply because the profit for a particular accounting period is low.

Objectivity

This rule requires you to avoid personal bias and prejudice when selecting and applying the accounting rules. This is not always easy, of course, but an important part of your college or university education is to train you to argue both sides of a case irrespective of just how you feel. This training helps you to deal with problems objectively without letting your own personal feelings overwhelm a particular decision.

Relevance

Financial statements should not include matters that prevent users from gaining what they need to know. The overall picture may be obscured if too much information or too much detail is given. So, in short, the information provided must be *relevant*. In the jargon of the accountancy profession this means that financial statements should give a true and fair view of the financial affairs of the entity.

You are going to come across all the rules that we have discussed in this section in one form or another throughout the rest of the book but we now need to examine which professional and statutory requirements cover accounting. We turn to this topic in the next section.

Activity 2.4	Review the 14 conventional rules we have outlined in this section. Then on the table below score each one according to whether you think that in practice it is easy to apply. Use the following scale: (1) very easy; (2) easy; (3) neither easy nor difficult; (4) difficult; and (5) very difficult.

Boundary rules	Score	Measurement rules	Score	Ethical rules
Entity		Money measurement		Prudence
Periodicity		Historic cost		Consistency
Going concern		Realization		Objectivity
Quantitative		Matching		Relevance
		Dual aspect		
		Materiality		

Sources of authority

The application of the rules summarized in the previous section in an increasingly sophisticated banking, commercial, industrial, political, technological and social society began to cause problems for accountants and the users of financial statements as the twentieth century progressed. A number of fire-fighting solutions were then put forward in all attempt to deal with the numerous problems that began to erupt. During the 1960s it became obvious that the system had begun to break down and that something needed to be done.

What did happen was that the UK accountancy profession began to develop what are called *accounting standards*. It was not long before *international accounting standards* also began to be developed. Such standards now play a very important part in the UK regulatory framework. We shall be examining them in detail in later sections of this chapter.

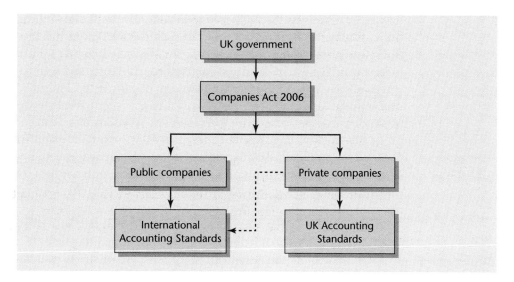

Figure 2.5 Sources of authority

Parliament also played its part in an attempt to come up with some solutions to the financial reporting problem. It takes time to get legislation through Parliament but even so it managed to pass seven Companies Acts in 22 years (between 1967 and 1989). It then took another 17 years before another Companies Act was passed in 2006 (a massive one as it turned out). We will have a look at it a little later in the chapter.

There is also another source of authority: the London Stock Exchange (LSE). The LSE is regulated by the Financial Services Agency (FSA). The FSA is an independent non-governmental body set up by the Financial Service and Market Act 2000. It is responsible for the UK financial services industry and its powers are wide-ranging. They include rule-making, investigatory powers and enforcement powers.

The LSE plays a very important part in financial reporting but much of it is irrelevant for our purposes. This means that there are three main sources of authority governing accounting regulation in the UK that we need to examine: (1) the Companies Act 2006; (2) UK Accounting Standards; and (3) International Accounting Standards (IASs). These three sources are examined in some detail in the following sections. The relationship between these sources is shown in Figure 2.5.

Activity 2.5	Do you think that by law shareholders should have complete freedom of information, i.e. the right to be given all the information that they want about a company in which they hold shares? What practical problems might arise if this were the case?

Companies Act 2006

There are no specific legal or statutory requirements dealing with sole trader and partnership accounts in the Companies Act or elsewhere. This means that the owners and managers of such entities may keep what accounting records that suit them (if any) and prepare periodic accounts when and in what form they wish. However, if they are registered for Value Added Tax they will need to keep adequate records that satisfy the somewhat severe requirements of Her Majesty's Revenue and Customs. Similarly, as the owners of a business they will need to include any profit due to them on their own personal income tax return. As a result of such considerations most entities have to keep some basic accounting records and to compile a rudimentary profit and loss account once a year. The precise form and content of such records and accounts is up to them.

As we mentioned in Chapter 1, a new form of partnership, limited liability partnerships, was introduced in 2001. The 2006 Companies Act also covers some aspects of this type of entity but as we are not covering LLPs in this book we do not need to go into the details.

In this book we are mainly concerned with the limited liability company type of entity. The legislation dealing with the formation, management, operation (including the accounting requirements) and reporting of such entities is now contained in the new Act of 2006 although it only became fully operable in October 2009. The Act is extremely detailed and complex. It is the largest Act ever passed by Parliament. No doubt you will be relieved to know that for your purposes (at least at this stage of your career) most of it is way beyond this book. And that includes the accounting bits!

Right, so what *do* you need to know for now? We will try to give you the answer to this question as plainly and as simply as we can. The following is an extremely brief summary of what you need to know.

1 The Act deals with the entire operation and management of companies so it encompasses much more than simply 'the accounts'. The 'Accounts and Records' are covered in Part 15. This part forms a relatively small section of the entire Act and much of it is based on earlier legislation.

2 It classifies companies into 'small', 'medium' and 'large'. This classification is based on a requirement to satisfy two out of three criteria: turnover, balance sheet totals and number of employees. The respective quantitative amounts are given in the Act but they are subject to amendment from time to time by Statutory Instrument (SI), which we come back to later.

3 A company has a duty to keep what are referred to as 'adequate accounting records'. This means that (a) the company's transactions can be shown and explained; (b) the financial position of the company can be disclosed at any time; (c) its accounts comply with either the Act or with European Union (EU) requirements.

4 A company must keep a daily record of money received and paid and a record of its assets and liabilities.

5 Companies dealing in stocks (apart from retail traders) have to keep a record of their purchases and sales during a financial year, details of their suppliers and customers, and their year end stocks.

6 The Act makes a distinction between (a) publicly traded companies and (b) non-publicly traded companies. A publicly traded company is basically a company that is permitted to offer its shares to the public on a regulated market, i.e. a Stock Exchange. In the United Kingdom you should be able to recognize such companies fairly easily because they have to put PLC, plc or public limited company after their name. Similarly, non-publicly traded companies must put LTD, ltd or limited after their name.

7 PLCs in member states of the EU must use what are called *International Accounting Standards* (IASs) when preparing *consolidated* accounts, i.e. when all the accounts forming part of a family of closely connected companies are combined. The accounts are then known as the *group* accounts. This requirement applies to every one of the 27 member countries of the EU.

8 In preparing their accounts non-publicly traded companies in the UK have a choice. They can use either (a) the accounting requirements of the Companies Act 2006 plus UK Accounting Standards; or (b) just IASs.

The 'Annual Accounts' section of the Act (in Part 15) is much broader in scope than was the case in earlier Companies Acts, the precise detail being left to the Secretary of State to determine. The form, content and terminology of accounts, for example, are not set out in the legislation (as they were in the 1985 and 1989 Companies Acts). This does not mean that companies are free to decide these things for themselves. Instead the details are decided by the Secretary of State and he (it's usually a 'he') issues his instructions in the form of an SI This is known as *secondary legislation.*

SIs enable the Secretary of State to make changes to *primary* legislation without needing to put another Bill before Parliament. Such a procedure is perfectly legitimate because Parliamentary time is short and the government's legislative programme is usually very full. The SI procedure enables changes to be made to non-controversial matters contained in legislation when circumstances change, e.g. the definition of 'small', 'medium' and 'large' companies. Turnover and balance sheet totals (in sterling) can get out of date very quickly, so it makes sense if they are kept up to date on a regular basis without having to introduce even more legislation.

An SI dealing with the form and content of accounts was issued about 18 months after the Companies Act 2006 received the Royal Assent. As it turned out the requirements were almost identical to those detailed in the 1985 and 1989 Companies Acts. This is a good example of the Act, despite its size, not having a major impact on conventional accounting practices – at least for those companies that did not have to switch to IASs.

We now turn to examine the second main source of accounting authority: UK Accounting Standards'. We do so below.

Activity 2.6	How confusing do you think it is in the UK to have two options in preparing a company's financial statements: (1) UK company law + UK Accounting Standards; and (2) IASs? Mark your score on the following scale: 1 = totally confusing; 5 = no confusion.

Totally confusing   no confusion

| 1 | 2 | 3 | 4 | 5 |

UK Accounting Standards

It would be helpful if we first define what is meant by an 'accounting standard'. The Companies Act 2006 gives us a definition although it is not a particularly clear one. According to the Act, accounting standards are:

> ...statements of standard accounting practice issued by such body as may be prescribed by regulations. (CA 2006, S464(1))

In less legalistic language this means that: statements of standard accounting practice (SSAPs) are authorative pronouncements that explain how to deal with specific accounting problems such as the valuation of closing stocks or the treatment of research expenditure. The regulations referred to above usually come in the form of SIs. In the UK there is currently one such prescribed body called the Accounting Standards Board (ASB). Many other countries have a similar body. A brief history of the ASB now follows.

News clip

John Varley

John Varley, the Chief Executive Officer of Barclays Bank, has called for global con-sistency of accounting standards if another financial crisis is to be avoided in future.

Source: Adapted from www.accountancyage.com/articles, 23 April 2009.

During the 1960s a number of contentious company mergers and takeovers took place. These events received a great deal of publicity and they both annoyed and puzzled the general public in equal measure. What was particularly puzzling to the public was that at the beginning of the week one set of accountants could decide that a company had made a profit and then by the end of that week another set of accountants would decide that it had actually made a loss. 'How was it possible,' many people asked, 'for different accountants to arrive at such conflicting results when they both used the same informa-tion?' It then began to dawn on the public that there was much more to accounting than simply adding up a lot of figures. And when reality struck home there was outrage. The figures could be fiddled: accountants were not saints after all!

The Institute of Chartered Accountants in England and Wales (ICAEW) was the first professional body to act. In 1970 it founded what was initially called the Accounting Standards Steering Committee (ASSC). It was renamed as the Accounting Standards Committee (ASC) in 1976 but in 1990 it was replaced by the Accounting Standards Board (ASB). By 1996 all the other five major professional accountancy bodies had become ASB members. Throughout this entire period the basic role of the ASSC/ASC/ASB remained unchanged, i.e. to develop definitive standards for financial reporting.

The ASB's main aim is to establish and to improve standards of financial accounting and reporting for the benefit of users, preparers and auditors of financial information. It aims to do so by achieving a number of objectives. In summary they are as follows:

1 To develop accounting principles.
2 To provide a framework to resolve accounting issues.
3 To issue accounting standards.
4 To amend existing accounting standards.
5 To address promptly any urgent accounting issues.
6 To work with other accounting standard setting bodies and institutions.

The ASB operates under the umbrella of the *Financial Reporting Council* (FRC). The FRC is a private limited company. Its main objectives are (i) to provide support for the ASB and the Financial Reporting Panel; and (ii) to encourage good financial reporting. Its funds come from a number of sources such as the accounting profession, the banking and insurance companies, the London Stock Exchange and the government.

Most of the ASB's funds come from the FRC. This arrangement might suggest that the FRC has ultimate control over the formulation and issue of accounting standards. This is not the case. The ASB has complete autonomy over them.

ASB standards are called *Financial Reporting Standards* (FRSs). By the spring of 2010, 30 FRSs had been issued. In addition, 12 ASB standards, known as *Statements of Standard Accounting Practice* (or SSAPs) were still mandatory although they will eventu-ally be phased out. The accounting problems covered in FRSs include acquisitions and mergers (FRS 6), goodwill and intangible assets (FRS 10), and life assurance (FRS 27).

SSAPs that have not yet been withdrawn cover topics such as stocks and long-term contracts (SSAP 9) and accounting for pension costs (SSAP 24). The SSAPs still in existence give you some indication that they deal with issues that are either less controversial or more difficult to deal with.

We now turn to have a look at the third main source of accounting regulation in the UK: International Accounting Standards.

Activity 2.7	From what you know so far about the ASB what are your views?

1   Do you think that there is a need for such a body? [Yes] [No]
2   If yes, (a) it should it be (i) state owned [ ] or (ii) privately owned [ ]? and (b) should it lay down (i) detailed rules [ ] or (ii) give just general guidance [ ]? (tick your responses).
3   If no, why not? Give your reasons.

International Accounting Standards

News clip

ACCA backs International Accounting Standards

Accountancy Age has reported that the Association of Chartered Certified Accountants has called on world leaders at a forthcoming G20 summit to throw their weight behind international financial reporting standards. The Association regards it 'a major failing that IFRS are not already the global accounting language for all financial professionals'.

Source: Adapted from www.accountancyage.com/articles, 10 March 2009.

International Accounting Standards are issued by what is now called the International Accounting Standards Board (IASB). The IASB was originally created in 1973 as the International Accounting Standards Committee (IASC) but it changed its name in 2001. The main aim of the IASC was to make financial statements much more comparable on an international basis. It was hoped to achieve this aim by issuing International Accounting Standards (IASs).

The IASB's aim is similar. It is as follows:

> *Our mission is to develop, in the public interest, a single set of high quality, understandable and international financial reporting standards (IFRSs) for general purpose financial statements.*

The IASB operates through a body called the International Accounting Standards Committee Foundation (IASCF). The IASCF is an independent, private, not-for-profit sector organization governed by 22 trustees from a number of different countries and professional backgrounds. It is funded by a voluntary system of donors from international accounting firms, business associations and organizations and central banks. The IASC Foundation appoints the IASB's board of 14 members who are recruited from many wide-ranging backgrounds. It also finances, governs and oversees the IASB.

The IASB works closely with national standard setting bodies (such as the ASB in the UK) to ensure that accounting standards throughout the world are as comparable as possible. The number of countries either permitting or requiring the use of its standards continued to grow to 120 by the beginning of 2010. The big breakthrough came in 2002 when the EU decided that as from 2005 publicly traded companies should adopt its standards. The next big hurdle facing the IASB is to encourage the USA to adopt its standards. Discussions have been taking place for some years. The indications are that the USA is 'mindful' to do so (using diplomatic language) but up to date the discussions have not been successful. We return to this point later in the chapter.

The IASB's standards are called *International Financial Reporting Standards* (IFRSs). Between 2001 and the spring of 2010, eight IFRSs had been issued and were still effective. This may not seem very many but the work programme had been deliberately slowed down between 2005 and 2009 to allow more time for new IFRSs to be implemented. The topics that they deal with include such matters as insurance contracts (IFRS 4) and operating segments (IFRS 8). The slow-down meant that 29 of the original *International Accounting Standards* (IASs) were still in use in the spring of 2010. The problems that they deal with range from the presentation of financial statements (IAS 1) to one coping with agriculture activity (IAS 41). Many of these accounting standards are highly technical and are certainly way beyond what you need to know until you become a very senior manager.

Now that we have given you some idea of the importance and status of both the ASB and the IASB in accounting regulation we are in a position to examine what these two bodies have done to improve their performance. We do so in the next section.

Activity 2.8	Log on to the IASB website. Insert the current date:

Answer the following questions:

1 How many countries have now adopted IFRSs?
2 How many IFRSs have now been issued.
3 How many IASs are still in use?

An accounting framework

News clip

A principled approach to standards

In a recently issued policy paper on the international accounting standard setting process, the International Federation of Accountants has argued that the key to successful standard setting is the identification of 'the underlying principles'.

Source: Adapted from *Financial Management*, February 2009, p. 7.

Until 2005 IASs and IFRSs were not a significant feature of UK financial reporting and SSAPs and FRSs took priority in the preparation of financial statements. The ASB certainly did not ignore the work of the IASB and the two bodies had a close working relationship but the ASB had a legal and professional status in the UK which the IASB did not have. That all changed in 2005 once the EU decided to adopt International Accounting Standards. As a member of the EU the UK was bound to accept the decision.

There were two basic differences between UK Accounting Standards and International Accounting Standards:

1 They did not always deal with the same accounting problems. This was perhaps because what was a contentious issue in the UK was not necessarily so in the rest of the world (and vice versa).

2 If the ASB and the IASB did issue an accounting standard dealing with the same problem, the IASB's solution tended to be more generalized (possibly because it had to be acceptable in so many different and disparate countries). This was an advantage for the UK because it meant that compliance with a UK standard almost automatically meant compliance with the equivalent IAS one.

The ASB and the IASB did have one thing in common when framing their respective accounting standards: they were largely fire-fighting exercises dealing with what happened to be a problem at that particular time. This meant that there was often little consistency in the way that the various issues were tackled. It eventually became apparent that accounting standards should be built on a basic framework or foundation. This would then enable solutions to different problems to be based on the same basic principles or rules. As a result, accounting standards would have a common theme running through them.

Academic accountants had argued for years that there was a need for such a framework. They referred to it as a *conceptual* framework which no doubt frightened the more practically trained accountants to death. Nevertheless, both the ASB and the IASB and similar standard setting bodies in many other countries were working on such a project. The IASB was the first to publish its ideas in a document called *Framework for the Preparation and Presentation of Financial Statements* (note that it did not include the word 'concept' in its title). The ideas in it relied very heavily on work done on the same subject in the USA as well as in Australia and Canada. We shall refer to it as the *Framework* from now on.

The ASB took a great deal longer to produce its own framework. It was not until 1999 that it published what it called *Statement of principles for financial reporting*. It is very similar to the Framework. As it is, in effect, a more up-to-date version of it, we will use the Statement to summarize what we need for this chapter. The relevant points are as follows.

1 The *objective* of financial statements is: to provide information about the reporting entity's financial performance and financial position that is useful to a wide range of users for assessing the stewardship of the entity's management and for making economic decisions.

2 The *users* of financial statements are: (i) investors; (ii) lenders; (iii) suppliers and other trade creditors; (iv) employees; (v) customers; (vi) governments and their agencies; and (vii) the public. These users are depicted in Figure 2.6.

3 The *reporting entity* is a cohesive economic unit, its boundary being determined by what it can control both directly and indirectly.

4 The *qualitative characteristics* of financial information are summarized below. Note how they relate very closely to the four ethical accounting rules we discussed earlier in the chapter, i.e. prudence, consistency, objectivity and relevance.

(a) *Relevance.* Financial statements should meet the needs of users and be *timely*, i.e. not to be so out of date that they have become irrelevant for decision making purposes. This characteristic, in effect, presupposes the incorporation of the *materiality* concept because information that is not helpful for decision making is irrelevant.

(b) *Reliability.* Users should be able to rely on the information contained within the financial statements. It should be free from material error, represent faithfully what it is supposed to represent, be free from bias (i.e. it should be **neutral**), and be compatible with the substance of transactions and not simply just because it is lawful. It should also be complete provided that it is material, and a *prudent* approach should be adopted when it is unclear how a particular transaction should be accounted for. So materiality, prudence and also objectivity are all inherent in this characteristic.

(c) *Comparability.* Financial statements containing the results for comparative periods should be prepared on a consistent basis. In other words, they should be prepared on the same basis each year. Comparability is almost the same concept as our consistency rule.

(d) *Understandability.* Financial statements should be capable of being understood by those users who have some knowledge of accounting, business activities and economic affairs and who are willing to study the financial statements diligently. The financial statements themselves should not, however, to be so simple that the information becomes meaningless.

5 The *elements* of financial information are the 'building blocks' used in the construction of the financial statements. They include what assets and liabilities the entity owns, what interest the owners have in the entity, what contributions and distributions the owners have made, and what has been paid out to them.

6 The Statement recognises that assets and liabilities need to be *measured* so that they can be included in the financial statements. They can be included at either their historical cost or at their current value. Historical cost is the more usual. Current cost is a method that relates to the loss an entity would suffer if the entity was deprived of an asset. So it is sometimes called 'deprival value' or 'loss to the business'. We shall not be dealing with current value accounting in this book.

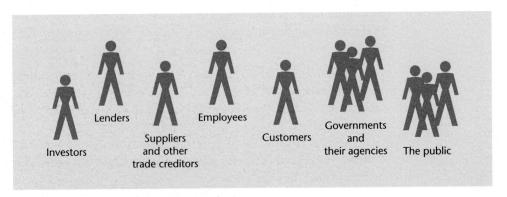

Figure 2.6 The main users of financial statements

Source: Statement of Principles for Financial Reporting, ASB 1999.

7 Financial statements should be presented clearly, effectively, simply and straightforwardly. When you reach Chapters 8 and 9 of this book you may begin to question whether the authors of the Companies Act 2006 and the compilers of accounting standards were aware of this requirement.

You might also think that despite the fuss that we have made in this chapter about the need to develop a workable framework, the outcome so far has not been very impressive. Both the Framework and the Statement are quite vague in their requirements and perhaps they lack a more prescriptive approach.

You would be right but if the profession went down that road we would be moving to what is called a *rules-based* approach to accounting. The main problems with this approach are that (i) it is difficult to formulate rules that accommodate every eventuality and (ii) ways will always be found of getting round whatever rules are formulated. So a culture develops and creates a climate whereby the attitude becomes '*if it's not in the rules you can do what you like*'. As we indicated earlier in the chapter, the USA has adopted a *rules-based* approach while EU countries all use a *principles-based* approach. This approach allows for individual circumstances to be taken into account but it can result in apparent inconsistencies in the accounts of different entities. This fundamental difference between the EU's and the USA's methods of accounting is the main reason why the USA has been reluctant to adopt IASs but political considerations have, no doubt, also played a part.

Activity 2.9	UK Accounting Standards are based on generally accepted *principles*. Some other countries prefer a *rules-based system*. Which approach do you favour?

1 (a) principles   [ ]   (b) rules-based   [ ]   (tick which).
2 Give three reasons for your choice.

❗ Questions you should ask

This is an important chapter. It not only prepares you for what follows in the rest of the book but it outlines a number of accounting issues that will face you when you become a manager in the real world. We suggest that among the long list of questions that you might well ask are the following.

● Are we subject to the Companies Act 2006?

● Do we adopt International Accounting Standards or UK (or own country's) standards?

● What accounting rules do we follow in the preparation of our financial statements?

● Are we without doubt a going concern?

● How do we determine what is an immaterial item?

● To what extent does neutrality override the need to be prudent?

Conclusion

In this chapter we have identified 14 conventional accounting rules and introduced you to the accounting provisions of Companies Act 2006 along with the additional semi-statutory requirements specified by the Accounting Standards Board and the International Accounting Standards Board.

The chapter enables you to grasp the fundamentals of what accountants do, why they do it and what the law requires them to do. In subsequent chapters we will show you how to prepare financial statements based on what is required. By knowing why and how they are prepared you will find that they will be of much greater benefit to you in making and taking the types of decision that your job requires.

Key points

1 In preparing financial statements, accountants use a number of conventional accounting rules (sometimes called principles); these rules have evolved over many centuries.

2 Such rules may be classified into boundary rules (entity, periodicity, going concern and quantitative); measurement rules (money measurement, historic cost, realization, matching, dual aspect and materiality); and ethical rules (prudence, consistency, objectivity and relevance).

3 The main source of legislation affecting accounting matters in the UK is the Companies Act 2006; the Act is primarily concerned with companies and limited liability partnerships.

4 The Act delegates much of the detail involving the preparation and reporting of financial statements to the International Accounting Standards Board (for publicly quoted group companies) and the UK Accounting Standards Board (for other companies).

5 The IASB issues International Financial Reporting Standards (IFRSs) and the ASB Financial Reporting Standards (FRSs) to help companies deal with contentious and difficult accounting matters. Other countries have their own accounting standards boards but many of them also use IASs.

6 Financial statements in the UK have always been prepared on a custom and practice basis but both the IASB and the ASB have issued a framework outlining the principles that entities are expected to follow in preparing such statements. Both frameworks are similar and they incorporate in one form or another all the 14 rules detailed in the first part of this chapter.

Check your learning

1 In an accounting context name three other terms that are similar in meaning to 'rules'.

2 Identify three categories of accounting rules.

3 What accounting rule is used to describe a defined period of time?

4 What is a going concern?

5 What is matching?

6 What does dual aspect mean?

7 When is a transaction not material?

8 What criteria are used to determine whether items are relevant?

9 Name three important sources of authority governing accounting matters affecting UK companies?

10 What do the following initials stand for: (a) CA; (b) SI; (c) ASB; (d) IASB; (e) SSAP; (f) IAS; (g) FRS; (h) IFRS?

11 What is an accounting standard?

12 What is a conceptual framework?

13 What is the objective of financial statements?

14 List seven user groups of accounting information.

15 What is a reporting entity?

16 List the qualitative characteristics of financial information.

News story quiz

Remember the news story at the beginning of the chapter? Go back to that story and reread it before answering the following questions.

This article relates back to the financial crisis that in 2007 struck the banking system in Britain and in many other countries. However, the points raised in the article are also relevant today as well as for other economic sectors.

Questions

1 What is the difference between a rule book and a principles approach to accounting matters?

2 Why does a principles approach necessarily deal better with changing financial markets and by implication with financial statements?

3 Closer dialogue is seen to be partly the answer for dealing with problems of systematic risk in auditing, but what else might be needed?

Tutorial questions

The answers to questions marked with an asterisk can be found in Appendix 4.

2.1 Do you think that when a set of financial accounts is being prepared, neutrality should override prudence?

2.2 'The law should lay down precise formats, contents and methods for the preparation of limited liability company accounts.' Discuss.

2.3 The Accounting Standards Board bases its Financial Reporting Standards on what is sometimes called a 'conceptual framework'. How far do you think that this approach is likely to be successful?

In questions 2.4, 2.5 and 2.6 you are required to state which accounting rule the accountant would most probably adopt in dealing with the various problems.

2.4* (a) Electricity consumed in Period 1 and paid for in Period 2.
(b) Equipment originally purchased for £20,000 which would now cost £30,000.
(c) The company's good industrial relations record.
(d) A five-year construction contract.
(e) A customer with a poor credit record might go bankrupt owing the company £5000.
(f) The company's vehicles, which would only have a small scrap value if the company goes into liquidation.

2.5* (a) A demand by the company's chairman to include every detailed transaction in the presentation of the annual accounts.
(b) A sole-trader business which has paid the proprietor's income tax based on the business profits for the year.
(c) A proposed change in the methods of valuing stock.
(d) The valuation of a litre of petrol in one vehicle at the end of accounting Period 1.
(e) A vehicle which could be sold for more than its purchase price.
(f) Goods which were sold to a customer in Period 1 but for which the cash was only received in Period 2.

2.6* (a) The proprietor who has supplied the business capital out of his own private bank account.
(b) The sales manager who is always very optimistic about the creditworthiness of prospective customers.
(c) The managing director who does not want annual accounts prepared as the company operates a continuous 24-hour-a-day, 365-days-a-year process.
(d) At the end of Period 1, it is difficult to be certain whether the company will have to pay legal fees of £1000 or £3000.
(e) The proprietor who argues that the accountant has got a motor vehicle entered twice in the books of account.
(f) Some goods were purchased and entered into stock at the end of Period 1, but they were not paid for until Period 2.

2.7 The following is a list of problems which an accountant may well meet in practice.

(a) The transfer fee of a footballer.

(b) Goods are sold in one period but the cash for them is received in a later period.

(c) The proprietor's personal dwelling house has been used as security for a loan which the bank has granted to the company.

(d) What profit to take in the third year of a five-year construction contract.

(e) Small stocks of stationery held at the accounting year end.

(f) Expenditure incurred in working on the improvement of a new drug.

Required:

(1) Which accounting rule would the accountant most probably adopt in dealing with each of the above problems?

(2) State the reasons for your choice.

2.8 *FRS 18* (accounting policies) states that profits shall be treated as realized and included in the profit and loss account only when the cash due 'can be assessed with reasonable certainty' (para. 28).

How far do you think that this requirement removes any difficulty in determining in which accounting period a sale has taken place?

2.9 The adoption of the realization and matching rules in preparing financial accounts requires a great deal of subjective judgement.

Required:

Write an essay examining whether it would be fairer, easier and more meaningful to prepare financial accounts on a cash received/cash paid basis.

Further practice questions, study material and links to relevant sites on the World Wide Web can be found on the website that accompanies this book. The site can be found at www.pearsoned.co.uk/dyson

FINANCIAL ACCOUNTING

Part 2

In Part 2 we outline the principles of double-entry book-keeping and explain how to prepare financial accounts for sole traders, companies and for some other types of entitites in the not-for-profit sector. The relationship of Part 2 to the rest of the book is shown below.

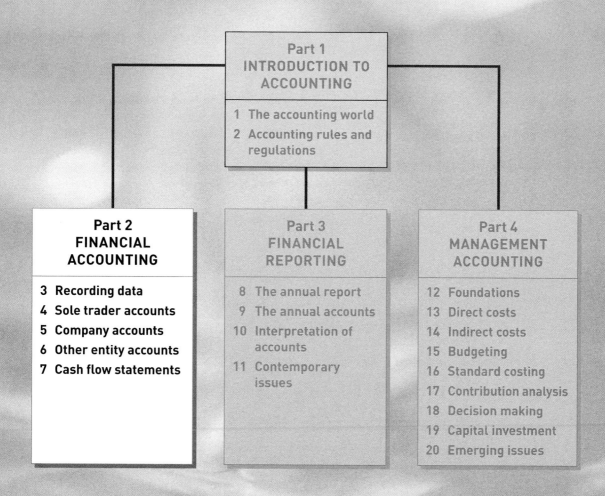

Part 1
INTRODUCTION TO ACCOUNTING

1 The accounting world
2 Accounting rules and regulations

Part 2
FINANCIAL ACCOUNTING

3 Recording data
4 Sole trader accounts
5 Company accounts
6 Other entity accounts
7 Cash flow statements

Part 3
FINANCIAL REPORTING

8 The annual report
9 The annual accounts
10 Interpretation of accounts
11 Contemporary issues

Part 4
MANAGEMENT ACCOUNTING

12 Foundations
13 Direct costs
14 Indirect costs
15 Budgeting
16 Standard costing
17 Contribution analysis
18 Decision making
19 Capital investment
20 Emerging issues

A book-keeping error?

KPMG forewarned XL board of accounting woes

KPMG resigned as auditor of XL, forewarning its board it had ignored 'potential accounting irregularities'

KPMG resigned in 2006 as auditor of the collapsed travel company XL Leisure, after forewarning its board it had ignored 'potential accounting irregularities' and was replaced by BDO Stoy Hayward.

The *Sunday Times* reports KMPG said in a strongly worded resignation letter the company had 'not satisfactorily addressed the concerns we had raised about other arrangements and potential accounting irregularities in the financial statements'.

KPMG resigned after staff at XL held up the payment of invoices to airline catering company Alpha Airports. The delay inflated XL's figures leading up to the listing of its then parent company Avion on the Icelandic stock exchange.

The discovery triggered the departures of Alpha's chairman, chief executive and finance director, as well as the departure of Steve Tomlinson, XL chief operating officer, and Paul Robinson, chief financial officer.

Source: *Accountancy Age*, 15 September 2008.

Source: Reproduced with permission from Incisive Media Ltd.

Questions relating to this news story can be found on page 66 ➡

About this chapter

In the last chapter we outlined some fundamental accounting rules. We indicated that some 'rules' are merely conventions, i.e. they have become generally accepted over a long period of time by custom and practice. You may recall that one convention that we dealt with in Chapter 2 is called the *dual aspect rule*. There is no iron law either of man or of nature that requires this rule to be adopted. It is merely a highly practical and useful one that has been shown to work over many centuries.

The dual aspect rule is a logical method of recording accounting data that enables (a) an accurate record to be kept of an entity's activities on a regular basis; and (b) an entity to assess its performance over and at the end of a defined period of time.

We cover the practical application of the dual aspect rule in this chapter.

Learning objectives	By the end of this chapter you should be able to:

By the end of this chapter you should be able to:

- explain what is meant by the 'accounting equation';
- define the terms 'debit' and 'credit';
- write up some simple ledger accounts;
- extract a trial balance;
- identify six errors not revealed in a trial balance.

! Why this chapter is important

This chapter is important for non-accountants for three main reasons.

1 *To learn the language of accounting.* The chapter will enable you to become familiar with the language and terminology used by accountants. This means that it will then be much easier for you to discuss with them any issues arising from the reports that they prepare for you.

2 *To check the reliability of information presented to you.* The chapter gives you a basic knowledge of the fundamental recording systems used by all types of entities throughout the world. You will then be able to assess the reliability of any accounting information based on the data that have been included in the system. You will also be more aware of what information has *not* been recorded. This will enable you to take into account what is missing from the accounts when considering the usefulness of any information your accountants give you.

3 *To discuss matters with your accountants.* Accounting information is based on a considerable number of questionable assumptions. These may not always be valid. If you are familiar with the language and nuances of fundamental accounting procedures, you will be able to have a more helpful discussion with your accountants about the type of information that you need to do your job.

The accounting equation

The system that accountants use to record financial data is known as *double-entry book-keeping.* The system recognizes that every transaction has a twofold effect. So if I loan you £100, a twofold effect arises because: I give you some money and you receive it. But the transaction also has a twofold effect on *both of us.*

(a) *The effect on you:* (1) your cash goes up by £100 and (2) what you owe me also goes up by £100.

(b) *The effect on me:* (1) my cash goes down by £100 and (2) what I am owed by you goes up by £100.

If an entity (say 'me') uses this twofold effect to record *twice* each of the transactions that take place between 'me' and another entity (say 'you'), then I am using some form of double-entry book-keeping. The most commonly used system has evolved over at least the last six hundred years and it is now used on a worldwide basis. Before we describe how it works, however, we must first make sure that you are clear about three important accounting terms. They are as follows:

- *Assets*: These are possessions or resources *owned* by an entity. They include physical or tangible possessions such as property, plant, machinery, stock, and cash and bank balances. They also include intangible assets, i.e. non-physical possessions such as copyright and patent rights, as well as debts owed to the entity such as trade and other debtors.
- *Capital*: This is the term used to describe the amount that the owners have invested in an entity. In effect, 'capital' is the amount owed by the entity to its owners.
- *Liabilities*: These are the opposite of assets. They are the amounts owed *by* an entity to outside parties. They include loans, bank overdrafts, creditors, i.e. amounts owing to parties for the supply of goods and services to the entity that still have to be paid for.

There is a close relationship between assets, capital and liabilities. It is frequently presented in the form of what is called the 'accounting equation' (also see Figure 3.1):

$$\text{Assets} = \text{capital} + \text{liabilities}$$

The equation tells us in clear and simple terms that what the entity owns (or possesses) was obtained using a combination of contributions from the entity's owners and borrowings from other people.

$$A = C + L$$

Figure 3.1 The accounting equation

We will illustrate the use of the accounting equation with a simple example. Let us assume that you have decided to go into business. You do so by transferring £2000 in cash from your own private bank account. The entity rule means that we are not interested in your private affairs, so we only want to keep track of how the business deals with your £2000.

The business now has £2000 invested in it. This is its capital but it also has £2000 in cash. The cash is an asset. So the £2000 asset equals the £2000 of capital. Or in equation form:

Assets			Capital	
Cash	£2000	=	Capital	£2000

The equation captures the twofold effect of the transaction: the assets of the business have been increased by the capital contributed by the owner.

Now suppose that you then decide to transfer £1500 of the cash to a business bank account. The effect on the equation is:

Assets				Capital		
		£				£
Bank		1500	=	Capital		2000
Cash		500				
		2000				2000

As you can see, there has simply been a change on the *assets* side of the equation.

Suppose now that you borrow £500 in cash from one of your friends to help finance the business. The assets will be increased by an inflow of £500 in cash, but £500 will be owed to your friend. The £500 owed is a liability and your friend has become a creditor of the business. The business has total assets of £2500 (£1500 at the bank and £1000 in cash). Its capital is £2000 and it has a liability of £500. The equation then reads:

Assets			Capital			Liabilities	
	£			£			£
Bank	1500	=	Capital	2000	+	Creditor	500
Cash (500 + 500)	1000						
	2500			2000			500

If £800 of goods were then purchased in cash for subsequent resale to the entity's customers, the equation would read:

Assets			Capital			Liabilities	
	£			£			£
Stocks	800		Capital	2000		Creditor	500
Bank	1500	=			+		
Cash (1000 – 800)	200			2000			500
	2500						

Again there has been a change on the assets side of the equation when £800 of the cash (an asset) was used to purchase £800 of goods for resale (i.e. stocks), another asset.

The equation is now becoming somewhat complicated but it does enable us to see the effect that *any* transaction has on the entity. The vital point to remember about the accounting equation is:

> If an adjustment is made to one side of the equation, you *must* make an identical adjustment *either* to the other side of the equation *or* to the same side.

This maxim reflects the basic rule of double-entry book-keeping:

> **Every transaction must be recorded twice.**

We will explain how the recording is done in the next section.

Activity 3.1

What are the missing words in the following statements?

(a) The accounting equation is represented by _____ = _____ + _____ .
(b) Every transaction must be recorded _____ .

News clip

An expensive mistake

The book-keeping of the US mortgage lenders Freddie Mac and Fannie May has 'long been questioned' according to a report in *Accountancy Age*. It appears that several years ago they both had been forced 'to restate billions in earnings after federal regulators [had] discovered accounting irregularities at both companies'.

Source: Adapted from www.accountancyage.com, 30 September 2008.

Double-entry book-keeping

We are going to explain how a *handwritten* double-entry book-keeping system works, even though these days most systems are computerized. We do so because both systems use the same accounting principles and the principles are much easier to follow in a simple handwritten system.

Just as the accounting equation reflects the twofold effect of every transaction, so does a double-entry book-keeping system. This means that each transaction must be recorded twice. A change to the accounting system is called an *entry* and so we talk about making entries in the accounts (remember that an *account* is simply a history or a record of a particular type of transaction). Accounts used to be kept in various bound books referred to as ledgers and all the *ledgers* used in a particular accounting system are known collectively as the *books of account*.

The effect of entering a particular transaction once in one ledger account and again in another ledger account causes the balance on each of the two accounts either to go up or to go down (like the accounting equation). So a transaction can either *increase* or *decrease* the total amount held in an account. In other words, an account either *receives* (i.e. accepts) an additional amount or it *gives* (i.e. releases) it. This receiving and giving effect has given rise to two terms from Latin that are commonly used in accounting:

> *debit: meaning to receive, or value received;*
> *credit: meaning to give, or value given.*

Accountants judge the twofold effect of all transactions on particular accounts from a receiving and giving point of view and each transaction is recorded on that basis. So when a transaction takes place, it is necessary to ask the following two questions:

● Which account should *receive* this transaction, i.e. which account should be debited?
● Which account has *given* this amount, i.e. which account should be credited?

Accounts have been designed to keep the debit entries separate from the credit entries. This helps to emphasize the opposite, albeit equal, effect that each transaction has within the recording system. In a handwritten system the separation is achieved by recording the debit entries on the left-hand side of the page, and the credit entries on the right-

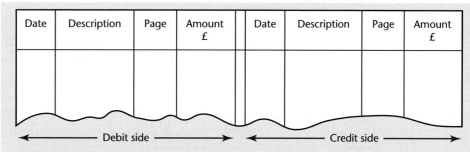

Date	Description	Page	Amount £	Date	Description	Page	Amount £

←———— Debit side ————→   ←———— Credit side ————→

Notes
1 The columnar headings would normally be omitted.
2 The description of each entry is usually limited to the *title* of the corresponding account in which the equal entry and opposite entry may be found.
3 The page column is used to refer to the page number of the corresponding account.
4 This example of a ledger account may nowadays only be found in a fairly basic handwritten book-keeping system. The debit and credit columns in a computerized account would normally be side-by-side.

Figure 3.2 Example of a ledger account

hand side. Each account is normally kept on a separate page in a ledger (i.e. a book of account). A traditional handwritten ledger account is illustrated in Figure 3.2.

In the next section we will show you how particular transactions are recorded in ledger accounts.

Activity 3.2

In one sentence describe what is meant by each of the following terms:

(a) An account is _____ .
(b) A ledger is _____ .
(c) Debit means _____ .
(d) Credit means _____ .

Working with accounts

There are four specific purposes behind this section:

1 to outline what type of transactions are included in an account;
2 to show how they are entered in an account;
3 to explain what is meant by a debit balance and a credit balance;
4 to demonstrate what happens at the end of an accounting period.

We should stress that we are not trying to turn you into a book-keeper. We just think that you need to know something about how accounting information is recorded and summarized before it is presented to you as a manager. If you have that knowledge then we believe that information will be much more useful to you in deciding what to do with it.

Choice of accounts

There is no specified or statutory list of accounts that *must* be used. Much will depend on the size and nature of the entity and whether it is in the private or public sector. Sometimes it is not clear, even to accountants, what account to use so they then adopt the maxim *if in doubt, open another account.* It really does not matter how many accounts are used – they can always be dropped if some of them become superfluous.

Some of the more common types of accounts that you may come across in your career are summarized below. Figure 3.3 also shows you how they are all so closely interlinked.

Capital

The *Capital Account* records what the owner has contributed (or given) to the entity out of private resources in order to start the business and keep it going. In other words, it shows what the business owes the owner.

Cash at bank

The *Bank Account* records what money the entity keeps at the bank. It shows what has been put in (e.g. cash and cheques) and what has been taken out (e.g. cheque and direct debit payments).

Cash in hand

The *Cash Account* works on similar lines to the Bank Account, except that it records the physical cash received (such as notes, coins and cheques) before they are paid into the bank. The cash received may be used to purchase goods and services or it may be paid straight into the bank. From a control point of view, it is best not to pay for purchases directly out of cash receipts but to draw an amount out of the bank specifically for sundry cash purchases. Any large amount should always be paid through the bank account.

Creditors

Creditor Accounts record what the entity owes its suppliers for goods or services purchased or supplied on credit (see also *trade creditors*).

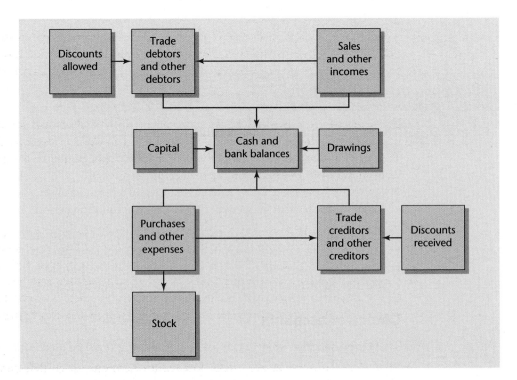

Figure 3.3 Interlinking of accounts

Debtors

Debtor Accounts record what is owed to the entity by its customers for goods or services sold to them on credit (see also *trade debtors*).

Discounts allowed

Discounts allowed are cash discounts granted to the entity's customers for the prompt settlement of any debts due to the entity. The amount of cash received from debtors who claim a cash discount will then be less than the total amount for which they have been invoiced.

Discounts received

Discounts received relate to cash discounts given by the entity's suppliers for the prompt payment of any amounts due to them. So the amount paid to the entity's creditors will be less than the invoiced amount.

Drawings

The term *drawings* has a special meaning in accounting. The *Drawings Account* is used to record what cash (or goods) the owner has withdrawn from the business for his personal use.

Petty cash

The *Petty Cash Account* is similar to both the Bank Account and the Cash Account. It is usually limited to the recording of minor cash transactions, such as bus fares or tea and coffee for the office. The cash used to finance this account will normally be transferred from the Bank Account.

Sales

The *Sales Account* records the value of goods sold to customers during a particular accounting period. The account includes both cash and credit sales. It does not include receipts from (say) the sale of a motor car originally purchased for use within the business.

Stock

Stock includes goods which have not been sold at the end of an accounting period. In accounting terminology, this would be referred to as *closing stock*. The closing stock at the end of one period becomes the *opening stock* at the beginning of the next period. The term *inventory* is now beginning to replace the term *stock*.

Purchases

The term *purchases* has a restricted meaning in accounting. It relates to those goods that are bought primarily with the intention of selling them (normally at a profit). The purchase of some motor cars, for example, would not usually be recorded in the *Purchases Account* unless they have been bought with the intention of selling them to customers. Goods not intended for resale are usually recorded in separate accounts. Some purchases may also require further work to be done on them before they are eventually sold.

Trade creditors

Trade Creditor Accounts are similar to Creditor Accounts except that they relate specifically to trading items, i.e. purchases.

Trade debtors

Trade Debtor Accounts are similar to Debtor Accounts except that they also relate specifically to trading items, i.e. sales.

Trade discounts

Trade discounts are a form of special discount. They may be given for placing a large order, for example, or for being a loyal customer. Trade discounts are deducted from the normal purchase or selling price. They are not recorded in the books of account and they will not appear on any invoice.

Once the book-keeper has chosen the accounts in which to record all the transactions for a particular accounting period, it is then necessary to decide which account should be debited and which account should be credited. We examine this problem in the next subsection.

Activity 3.3

Which two ledger accounts would you use in recording each of the following transactions?

(a) cash sales
(b) rent paid by cheque
(c) wages paid in cash
(d) a supplier of goods paid by cheque
(e) goods sold on credit to Ford.

Entering transactions in accounts

When entering a transaction in an account always make sure that you:

> **Debit the account which receives**

and

> **Credit the account which gives.**

Example 3.1 illustrates the use of this rule. It contains some common ledger account entries.

Example 3.1

Examples of some common ledger account entries

Entry 1
The proprietor contributes some cash to the business.

Debit: Cash Account   *Credit*: Capital Account

Reason: The Cash Account receives some cash given to the business by the owner. His Capital Account is the giving account and the Cash Account is the receiving account.

Entry 2
Some cash in the till is paid into the business bank account.

Debit: Bank Account   *Credit*: Cash Account

Reason: The Cash Account is the giving account because it is releasing some cash to the Bank Account.

Entry 3

A van is purchased for use in the business; it is paid for by cheque.

Debit: Van Account   *Credit*: Bank Account

Reason: The Bank Account is giving some money in order to pay for a van, so the Bank Account must be credited as it is the giving account.

Entry 4

Some goods are purchased for cash.

Debit: Purchases Account   *Credit*: Cash Account

Reason: The Cash Account is giving up an amount of cash in order to pay for some purchases. The Cash Account is the giving account, so it must be credited.

Entry 5

Some goods are purchased on credit terms from Fred.

Debit: Purchases Account   *Credit*: Fred's Account

Reason: Fred is supplying the goods on credit terms to the business. As he is the giver, his account must be credited.

Entry 6

Some goods are sold for cash.

Debit: Cash Account   *Credit:* Sales Account

Reason: The Cash Account receives the cash from the sale of goods and the Sales Account is credited because it is the giving or supplying account.

Entry 7

Some goods are sold on credit terms to Sarah.

Debit: Sarah's Account   *Credit:* Sales Account

Reason: Sarah's Account is debited because she is receiving the goods, and the Sales Account is credited because it is supplying (or giving) them.

Activity 3.4

Is there anything wrong with the following abbreviated bank account?

Debit		£000	Credit		£000
10.3.12	Wages paid	1000	6.6.12	Interest received	500

It is not always easy to think of the receiving and of the giving effect of each transaction. You will find that it is very easy to get them mixed up and to then reverse the entries. If we look at Entries 6 and 7 in Example 3.1, for example, it is difficult to understand why the Sales Account should be credited. Why is the Sales Account the giving account? Surely it is *receiving* an amount and not giving anything? In one sense it is receiving something, but then that applies to any entry in any account. So in the case of the sales account, regard it as a *supplying* account because it gives (or releases) something to another account.

If you find this concept difficult to understand, think of the effect on the opposite account. A cash sale, for example, results in cash being increased. The cash account must, therefore, be the *receiving* account and it must be debited. Somebody (say Jones) must have given the cash, but a cash sale is credited straight to the sales account as the *supplying* account. If the sales had been sold to Jones on credit, his account would have been debited (because his account is the *receiving* account) and credited to sales (again because it is the *supplying* account).

Activity 3.5

State which account should be debited and which account should be credited in respect of each of the following transactions:

(a) cash paid to a supplier
(b) office rent paid by cheque
(c) cash sales
(d) dividend received by cheque.

A ledger account example

This section illustrates the procedure adopted in entering various transactions in ledger accounts. It brings together the basic material covered in the earlier part of this chapter. It also demonstrates the use of various accounts as well as the debiting and crediting effect of different types of transactions.

Example 3.2

Joe Simple: a sole trader

The following information relates to Joe Simple, who started a new business on 1 January 2012:

1	1.1.12	Joe started the business with £5000 in cash.
2	3.1.12	He paid £3000 of the cash into a business bank account.
3	5.1.12	Joe bought a van for £2000 paying by cheque.
4	7.1.12	He bought some goods, paying £1000 in cash.
5	9.1.12	Joe sold some of the goods, receiving £1500 in cash.

Required:

Enter the above transactions in Joe's ledger accounts.

Answer to Example 3.2

Joe Simple's books of account

Cash Account

		£			£
1.1.12	Capital (1)	5 000	3.1.12	Bank (2)	3 000
9.1.12	Sales (5)	1 500	7.1.12	Purchases (4)	1 000

Capital Account

		£			£
			1.1.12	Cash (1)	5 000

Bank Account

		£			£
3.1.12	Cash (2)	3 000	5.1.12	Van (3)	2 000

Van Account

	£		£
5.1.12 Bank (3)	2 000		

Purchases Account

	£		£
7.1.12 Cash (4)	1 000		

Sales Account

	£		£
		9.1.12 Cash (5)	1 500

Tutorial notes

1 The numbers in brackets after each entry refer to the example notes; they have been inserted for tutorial guidance only.

2 The narration relates to that account in which the equal and opposite entry may be found.

After entering all the transactions for a particular period in appropriate ledger accounts, the next stage in the exercise is to calculate the balance on each account at the end of an accounting period. We show you how to do this in the next section.

Balancing the accounts

News clip

Past problem

The American Italian Pasta Company has paid out $1m to settle allegations that it engaged in fraudulent accounting includ-ing capitalising period costs, the recording of false receivables, and the failure to write-off obsolete or missing parts.

Source: Adapted from www.accountancyage.com, 16 September 2008.

During a particular accounting period, some accounts (such as the bank and cash accounts) will include a great many debit and credit entries. Some accounts may be made up of mainly debit entries (e.g. the purchases account) or largely credit entries (e.g. the sales account). It would be somewhat inconvenient to allow the entries (whether mainly debits, credits or a mixture of both) to build up without occasionally striking a balance. Furthermore, the owner will almost certainly want to know not just what is in each account, but also its overall or *net* balance (i.e. the total of all the debit entries less the total of all the credit entries). So in order to meet these requirements it will be necessary to calculate the balance on each account on a regular basis.

Balancing an account requires the book-keeper to add up all the respective debit and credit entries, take one total away from the other, and arrive at the net balance.

Accounts may be balanced fairly frequently, e.g. once a week or once a month, but some entities may only do so when they prepare their annual accounts. In order to keep a tight control on the management of the business, it is advisable to balance the accounts at reasonably short intervals. The frequency will depend on the nature and the size of the entity but once a month is probably sufficient for most entities.

The balancing of the accounts is part of the double-entry procedure and the method is quite formal. In Example 3.3 below we show how to balance an account with a *debit* balance (i.e. when the total debit entries exceed the total credit entries).

Example 3.3	**Balancing an account with a debit balance**

Cash Account

		£			£
1.1.12	Sales (1)	2 000	10.1.12	Jones (1)	3 000
15.1.12	Rent received (1)	1 000	25.1.12	Davies (1)	5 000
20.1.12	Smith (1)	4 000			
31.1.12	Sales (1)	8 000	31.1.12	Balance c/d (2)	7 000
	(3)	15 000		(3)	15 000
1.2.12	Balance b/d (4)	7 000			

Note: The number shown after each narration relates to the tutorial notes below.

Tutorial notes

1 The total debit entries equal £15,000 (2000 + 1000 + 4000 + 8000). The total credit entries equal £8000 (3000 + 5000). The net balance on this account, therefore, at 31 January 2012 is a *debit balance* of £7000 (15,000 − 8000). Until both the debit entries and the credit entries have been totalled, of course, it will not usually be apparent whether the balance is a debit one or a credit one. However, it should be noted that there can never be a credit balance in a cash account, because it is impossible to pay out more cash than has been received.

2 The debit balance of £7000 is inserted on the *credit* side of the account at the time that the account is balanced (in this case, at 31 January 2012). This then enables the total of the credit column to be balanced so that it agrees with the total of the debit column. The abbreviation 'c/d' means carried down. In this example the debit balance is carried down in the account in order to start the new period on 1 February 2012.

3 The £15,000 shown as a total in both the debit and the credit columns demonstrates that the columns balance (they do so, of course, because £7000 has been inserted in the credit column to make them balance). The totals are double-underlined in order to signify that they are a final total.

4 The balancing figure of £7000 is brought down ('b/d') in the account to start the new period on 1 February 2012. The double entry has been completed because £7000 has been debited below the line (i.e. below the £15,000 debit total), and the £7000 balancing figure credited above the line (i.e. above the £15,000 credit total).

Example 3.3 demonstrates how an account with a debit entry is balanced. In Example 3.4 we illustrate a similar procedure, but this time the account has a *credit* balance.

Example 3.4	**Balancing an account with a credit balance**

Scott's Account

		£			£
31.1.12	Bank (1)	20 000	15.1.12	Purchases (1)	10 000
31.1.12	Balance c/d (2)	5 000	20.1.12	Purchases (1)	15 000
	(3)	25 000		(3)	25 000
			1.2.12	Balance b/d (4)	5 000

Note: The number shown after each narration relates to the tutorial notes below.

Tutorial notes to Example 3.4

1 Apart from the balance, there is only one debit entry in Scott's account: the bank entry of £20,000. The total credit entries amount to £25,000 (10,000 + 15,000). Scott has a *credit balance*, therefore, in his account as at 31 January 2012 of £5000 (10,000 + 15,000 – 20,000). With many more entries in the account it would not always be possible to tell immediately whether the balance was a debit one or a credit one.

2 The credit balance of £5000 at 31 January 2012 is inserted on the *debit* side of the account in order to enable the account to be balanced. The balance is then carried down (c/d) to the next period.

3 The £25,000 shown as the total for both the debit and the credit columns shows that the account balances. This has been made possible because of the insertion of the £5,000 balancing figure on the debit side of the account.

4 The balancing figure of £5000 is brought down (b/d) in the account in order to start the account in the new period beginning on 1 February 2012. The double-entry has been completed because the debit entry of £5000 above the £25,000 line on the debit side equals the credit entry below the £25,000 line on the credit side.

Activity 3.6	Write down in you notebook what is meant by (a) an account having a debit balance (b) an account having a credit balance.

The next stage after balancing each account is to check that the double-entry procedure has been completed throughout the entire book-keeping system. This is done by compiling what is known as a *trial balance*.

The trial balance

A trial balance (TB) is a working paper compiled at the end of a specific accounting period. It does not form part of the double-entry procedure. It has three main purposes: (1) to check that all of the transactions for a particular period have been entered correctly in the ledger system; (2) to confirm that the balance on each account is correct; and (3) to assist in the preparation of the profit and loss account and the balance sheet.

A sales glitch

The formal global audit firm Arthur Andersen has been fined £75,000 and ordered to pay £100,000 in costs for 'failing to spot that sales had been booked into the wrong accounting period'. For some reason not explained it appears that the firm was 'reluctant to contact customers to verify sales' (a normal audit procedure).

Source: Adapted from www.accountancyage.com, 29 January 2009.

The trial balance lists each debit and each credit balance in columns side by side. The total of each column is then added up. If the two totals agree we can be reasonably confident that the double-entry procedures have been carried out correctly. There are, however, some errors that do not show up. We will explain what they are later in the chapter.

We show how to prepare a trial balance below in Example 3.5.

Example 3.5	**Edward – compilation of a trial balance**

Edward started a new business on 1 January 2012. The following transactions took place during his first month in business.

2012
  1.1   Edward commenced business with £10,000 in cash.
  3.1   He paid £8000 of the cash into a business bank account.
  6.1   He bought a van on credit from Perkin's garage for £3000.
  9.1   Edward rented shop premises for £1000 per quarter; he paid for the first quarter immediately by cheque.
 12.1   He bought goods on credit from Roy Limited for £4000.
 15.1   He paid shop expenses amounting to £1500 by cheque.
 18.1   Edward sold goods on credit to Scott and Company for £3000.
 21.1   He settled Perkin's account by cheque.
 24.1   Edward received a cheque from Scott and Company for £2000; this cheque was paid immediately into the bank.
 27.1   Edward sent a cheque to Roy Limited for £500.
 31.1   Goods costing £3000 were purchased from Roy Limited on credit.
 31.1   Cash sales for the month amounted to £2000.

Required:
(a) Enter the above transactions in appropriate ledger accounts, balance off each account as at 31 January 2012, and bring down the balances as at that date.
(b) Extract a trial balance as at 31 January 2012.

Answer to Example 3.5(a)

Cash Account

		£			£
1.1.12	Capital (1)	10 000	3.1.12	Bank (2)	8 000
31.1.12	Sales (12)	2 000	31.1.12	Balance c/d	4 000
		12 000			12 000
1.2.12	Balance b/d	4 000			

Capital Account

		£			£
			1.1.12	Cash (1)	10 000

Bank Account

		£			£
3.1.12	Cash (2)	8 000	9.1.12	Rent payable (4)	1 000
24.1.12	Scott and		15.1.12	Shop expenses (6)	1 500
	Company (9)	2 000	21.1.12	Perkin's garage (8)	3 000
			27.1.12	Roy Limited (10)	500
			31.1.12	Balance c/d	4 000
		10 000			10 000
1.2.12	Balance b/d	4 000			

Van Account

		£			£
6.1.12	Perkin's Garage (3)	3 000			

Perkin's Garage Account

		£			£
21.1.12	Bank (8)	3 000	6.1.12	Van (3)	3 000

Rent Payable Account

		£			£
9.1.12	Bank (4)	1 000			

Purchases Account

		£			£
12.1.12	Roy Limited (5)	4 000			
31.1.12	Roy Limited (11)	3 000	31.1.12	Balance c/d	7 000
		7 000			7 000
1.2.12	Balance b/d	7 000			

Roy Limited Account

		£			£
27.1.12	Bank (10)	500	12.1.12	Purchases (5)	4 000
31.1.12	Balance c/d	6 500	31.1.12	Purchases (11)	3 000
		7 000			7 000
			1.2.12	Balance b/d	6 500

Shop Expenses Account

		£			£
15.1.12	Bank (6)	1 500			

Sales Account

		£			£
			18.1.12	Scott & Company (7)	3 000
31.1.12	Balance c/d	5 000	31.1.12	Cash (12)	2 000
		5 000			5 000
			1.2.12	Balance b/d	5 000

Scott and Company Account

		£			£
18.1.12	Sales (7)	3 000	24.1.12	Bank (9)	2 000
			31.1.12	Balance c/d	1 000
		3 000			3 000
1.2.12	Balance b/d	1 000			

Tutorial notes

1 The number shown after each narration has been inserted for tutorial guidance only in order to illustrate the insertion of each entry in the appropriate account.

2 There is no need to balance an account and carry down the balance when there is only a single entry in one account (see Edward's Capital Account).

3 Note that some accounts may not have a balance (e.g., *Perkin's Garage Account*).

Answer to Example 3.5(b)

Trial Balance at 31 January 2012

	Dr	Cr
	£	£
Cash	4 000	
Capital		10 000
Bank	4 000	
Van	3 000	
Rent payable	1 000	
Purchases	7 000	
Roy Limited		6 500
Shop expenses	1 500	
Sales		5 000
Scott and Company	1 000	
	21 500	21 500

Tutorial notes

1 The total debit balance agrees with the total credit balance and so the trial balance balances thus confirming that the transactions appear to have been entered in the books of account correctly.

2 The total amount of £21,500 shown in both the debit and credit columns of the trial balance does not have any significance except to prove that the trial balance balances.

Trial balance errors

A trial balance confirms that the books of account balance arithmetically. This means that the following procedures have all been carried out correctly:

● for every debit entry there appears to be a credit entry – a cardinal rule in double-entry book-keeping;
● the value for each debit and credit entry has been entered in appropriate accounts;
● the balance on each account has been calculated, extracted and entered correctly in the trial balance;
● the debit and credit columns in the trial balance are the same.

As we indicated earlier, there are, however, some errors that are not disclosed by the trial balance. They are as follows.

- *Omission*: a transaction could have been completely omitted from the books of account.
- *Complete reversal of entry*: a transaction could have been entered in (say) Account A as a debit and in Account B as a credit, when it should have been entered as a credit in Account A and as a debit in Account B.
- *Principle*: a transaction may have been entered in the wrong *type* of account, e.g. the purchase of a new delivery van may have been debited to the purchases account instead of to the delivery vans account.
- *Commission*: a transaction may have been entered in the correct type of account but in the wrong *personal* account, e.g. in Bill's account instead of in Ben's account.
- *Compensating*: an error may have been made in (say) adding the debit side of one account and an identical error made in adding the credit side of another account; the two errors would then cancel each other out.
- *Original entry*: a transaction may have been entered incorrectly in both accounts, e.g. as £291 instead of as £921.

Such errors may only be discovered if some transactions are double-checked later on in the period. They may also become apparent when the financial statements are prepared and the results are compared with previous periods. Similarly, some errors may also come to light if they affect creditor and debtor balances and suppliers and customers begin to complain about unpaid or incorrect invoices. Notwithstanding these possible errors the compilation of a trial balance is still useful because:

- the arithmetical accuracy of the entries made in the books of account can be confirmed;
- the balance owed or owing on each account can easily be extracted;
- the preparation of the financial statements is simplified.

Activity 3.7	State whether each of the following errors would be discovered as a result of preparing a trial balance.

State whether each of the following errors would be discovered as a result of preparing a trial balance.

(a) £342 has been entered in both ledger accounts instead of £432.   *Yes/no*
(b) The debit column in Prim's account has been overstated by £50.   *Yes/no*
(c) £910 has been put in Anne's account instead of Agnes's.   *Yes/no*

> **! Questions you should ask**
>
> As a non-accountant it is highly unlikely that you will become involved in the detailed recording, extraction and summary of basic accounting information. Your particular responsibility as a senior manager will be to ensure that:
>
> - adequate accounting records are kept;
> - they are accurate;
> - an appropriate profit and loss account and a balance sheet (as required by any legislation) can be prepared from such records.
>
> As a minimum you should ensure that the accounting records are capable of dealing with all cash received and paid by the entity and that they contain details of all its assets and liabilities.

In order to satisfy yourself about these requirements you should ask the following questions.

● Do we use a double-entry book-keeping system?

● If not, why not?

● Is it a manual or a computerized one?

● Does the system include a cash book in which all cash and bank transactions are entered?

● Is the balance shown in the cash book checked regularly against the balance disclosed in the bank's statements of account?

● Is a separate account kept for each identifiable group of fixed assets, current assets and current liabilities?

● What is included in such groups?

● Is a balance calculated regularly for each of the accounts?

● How often is a trial balance prepared?

● What steps are taken to ensure that errors not disclosed in a trial balance are minimized?

● What is the system for the separation of duties affecting the recording of the accounting information and the preparation of the trial balance?

● Does a senior manager (not involved with the accounting function) receive a copy of the trial balance?

Conclusion

This book is specifically aimed at non-accountants. In this chapter we have deliberately avoided going into too much detail about double-entry book-keeping. In your managerial role you will almost certainly be supplied with information that has been extracted from a ledger system. In order to assess its real benefit to you, we believe that it is most important that you should know something about where it has come from, what it means, and what reliability can be placed on it.

The chapter has, therefore, covered the following features of a double-entry book-keeping system:

● the accounting equation;
● the type of accounts generally used in practice;
● the meaning of the terms 'debit' and 'credit';
● the definition of the terms 'debtor' and 'creditor';
● the method of entering transactions in ledger accounts;
● the balancing of ledger accounts;
● the compilation of a trial balance.

Key points	

1 The accounting equation is represented by the formula: assets = capital + liabilities. It underpins the dual aspect rule and it forms the basis of a conventional accounting recording system.

2 An account is an explanation, a record or a history of a particular event.

3 A book of account is known as a ledger.

4 A transaction is the carrying out and the performance of a particular business activity or event.

5 All transactions have a twofold effect.

6 A double-entry system records that twofold effect.

7 A debit means that a transaction is received into an account.

8 A credit means that a transaction is given by an account.

9 Debits are entered on the left-hand side of an account.

10 Credits are entered on the right-hand side of an account.

11 For every debit entry there must be a credit entry.

12 Accounts are balanced periodically.

13 The accuracy of the book-keeping is tested by preparing a trial balance.

14 The trial balance does not reveal all possible book-keeping errors.

Check your learning

1 What is the accounting equation?

2 What is the basic rule of double-entry book-keeping?

3 What is an account?

4 What is a ledger?

5 What is meant by the terms 'debit' and 'credit'?

6 What factor would indicate whether or not a new account should be opened?

7 What distinguishes a cash account from a bank account?

8 What are the following accounts used for: (a) capital, (b) trade creditors, (c) trade debtors, (d) stock, (e) sales, (f) purchases, (g) drawings?

9 What is the difference between a discounts allowed account and a discounts received account?

10 What must there be for (a) every debit, and (b) every credit?

11 What is (a) a debit balance, and (b) a credit balance?

12 What is a trial balance?

13 Name three main functions that it fulfils.

14 List six book-keeping errors that a trial balance does not detect.

News story quiz

Remember the news story at the beginning of this chapter? Go back to that story and reread it before answering the following questions.

This alleged accounting irregularity is rather puzzling. It apparently revolved round the delay in paying invoices. This is not unusual so it is not clear why it turned into an 'irregularity'.

Questions

1 Assuming that the payment of the invoices had been paid reasonably promptly what effect would this have had on (a) the bank account; and (2) the suppliers' accounts?

2 Would the delay have increased or decreased the profit for the year?

3 By delaying the payments can the financial statements be said to represent 'a true and fair view'?

Tutorial questions

The answers to questions marked with an asterisk can be found in Appendix 4.

3.1 Do you think that non-accounting managers need to know anything about double-entry book-keeping?

3.2 'My accountant has got it all wrong,' argued Freda. 'She's totally mixed up all her debits and credits.'
'But what makes you say that?' queried Dora.
'Oh! I've only to look at my bank statement to see that she's wrong,' responded Freda. 'I know I've got some money in the bank, and yet she tells me I'm in debit when she means I'm in credit.'
Is Freda right?

3.3 'Double-entry book-keeping is a waste of time and money because everything has to be recorded twice.' Discuss.

3.4* Adam has just gone into business. The following is a list of his transactions for the month of January 2010:

(a) Cash paid into the business by Adam.
(b) Goods for resale purchased on cash terms.
(c) Van bought for cash.
(d) One quarter's rent for premises paid in cash.
(e) Some goods sold on cash terms.
(f) Adam buys some office machinery for cash.

Required:
State which account in Adam's books of account should be debited and which account should be credited for each transaction.

3.5* The following is a list of Brown's transactions for February 2011:

(a) Transfer of cash to a bank account.
(b) Cash received from sale of goods.
(c) Purchase of goods paid for by cheque.
(d) Office expenses paid in cash.
(e) Cheques received from customers from sale of goods on cash terms.
(f) A motor car for use in the business paid for by cheque.

Required:
State which account in Brown's books of account should be debited and which account should be credited for each transaction.

3.6 Corby is in business as a retail distributor. The following is a list of his transactions for March 2012:

1 Goods purchased from Smith on credit.
2 Corby introduces further capital in cash into the business.
3 Goods sold for cash.
4 Goods purchased for cash.
5 Cash transferred to the bank.
6 Machinery purchased, paid for in cash.

Required:
State which account in Corby's books of account should be debited and which account should be credited for each transaction.

3.7 Davies buys and sells goods on cash and credit terms. The following is a list of her transactions for April 2010:

1 Capital introduced by Davies paid into the bank.
2 Goods purchased on credit terms from Swallow.
3 Goods sold to Hill for cash.
4 Cash paid for purchase of goods.
5 Dale buys goods from Davies on credit.
6 Motoring expenses paid by cheque.

Required:
State which account in Davies' books of account should be debited and which account should be credited for each transaction.

3.8 The following transactions relate to Gordon's business for the month of July 2011:

1 Bought goods on credit from Watson.
2 Sold some goods for cash.
3 Sold some goods on credit to Moon.
4 Sent a cheque for half the amount owing to Watson.
5 Watson grants Gordon a cash discount.
6 Moon settles most of his account in cash.
7 Gordon allows Moon a cash discount that covers the small amount owed by Moon.
8 Gordon purchases some goods for cash.

Required:
State which account in Gordon's books of accounts should be debited and which account should be credited for each transaction.

3.9 Harry started a new business on 1 January 2012. The following transactions cover his first three months in business:

1 Harry contributed an amount in cash to start the business.
2 He transferred some of the cash to a business bank account.
3 He paid an amount in advance by cheque for rental of business premises.
4 Bought goods on credit from Paul.
5 Purchased a van paying by cheque.
6 Sold some goods for cash to James.
7 Bought goods on credit from Nancy.
8 Paid motoring expenses in cash.
9 Returned some goods to Nancy.
10 Sold goods on credit to Mavis.
11 Harry withdrew some cash for personal use.
12 Bought goods from David paying in cash.
13 Mavis returns some goods.
14 Sent a cheque to Nancy.
15 Cash received from Mavis.
16 Harry receives a cash discount from Nancy.
17 Harry allows Mavis a cash discount.
18 Cheque withdrawn at the bank in order to open a petty cash account.

Required:
State which account in Harry's books of account should be debited and which account should be credited for each transaction.

3.10* The following is a list of transactions which relate to Ivan for the first month that he is in business:

1.9.10	Started the business with £10,000 in cash.
2.9.10	Paid £8000 into a business bank account.
3.9.10	Purchased £1000 of goods in cash.
10.9.10	Bought goods costing £6000 on credit from Roy.
12.9.10	Cash sales of £3000.
15.9.10	Goods sold on credit terms to Norman for £4000.
20.9.10	Ivan settles Roy's account by cheque.
30.9.10	Cheque for £2000 received from Norman.

Required:
Enter the above transactions in Ivan's ledger accounts.

3.11* Jones has been in business since 1 October 2011. The following is a list of her transactions for October 2011:

1.10.11	Capital of £20,000 paid into a business bank account.
2.10.11	Van purchased on credit from Lang for £5000.
6.10.11	Goods purchased on credit from Green for £15,000.
10.10.11	Cheque drawn on the bank for £1000 in order to open a petty cash account.
14.10.11	Goods sold on credit for £6000 to Haddock.
18.10.11	Cash sales of £5000.
20.10.11	Cash purchases of £3000.
22.10.11	Miscellaneous expenses of £500 paid out of petty cash.
25.10.11	Lang's account settled by cheque.
28.10.11	Green allows Jones a cash discount of £500.
29.10.11	Green is sent a cheque for £10,000.

| 30.10.11 | Haddock is allowed a cash discount of £600. |
| 31.10.11 | Haddock settles his account in cash. |

Required:
Enter the above transactions in Jones's ledger accounts.

3.12 The transactions listed below relate to Ken's business for the month of November 2012:

1.11.12	Started the business with £150,000 in cash.
2.11.12	Transferred £14,000 of the cash to a business bank account.
3.11.12	Paid rent of £1000 by cheque.
4.11.12	Bought goods on credit from the following suppliers:

	Ace	£5000
	Mace	£6000
	Pace	£7000

| 10.11.12 | Sold goods on credit to the following customers: |

	Main	£2000
	Pain	£3000
	Vain	£4000

15.11.12	Returned goods costing £1000 to Pace.
22.11.12	Pain returned goods sold to him for £2000.
25.11.12	Additional goods purchased from the following suppliers:

	Ace	£3000
	Mace	£4000
	Pace	£5000

26.11.12	Office expenses of £2000 paid by cheque.
27.11.12	Cash sales for the month amounted to £5000.
28.11.12	Purchases paid for in cash during the month amounted to £4000.
29.11.12	Cheques sent to the following suppliers:

	Ace	£4000
	Mace	£5000
	Pace	£6000

| 30.11.12 | Cheques received from the following customers: |

	Main	£1000
	Pain	£2000
	Vain	£3000

| 30.11.12 | The following cash discounts were claimed by Ken: |

	Ace	£200
	Mace	£250
	Pace	£300

| 30.11.12 | The following cash discounts were allowed by Ken: |

	Main	£100
	Pain	£200
	Vain	£400

| 30.11.12 | Cash transfer to the bank of £1000. |

Required:
Enter the above transactions in Ken's ledger accounts.

3.13* The following transactions relate to Pat's business for the month of December 2010:

| 1.12.10 | Started the business with £10,000 in cash. |
| 2.12.10 | Bought goods on credit from the following suppliers: |

| | Grass | £6000 |
| | Seed | £7000 |

10.12.10	Sold goods on credit to the following customers:
	Fog £3000
	Mist £4000
12.12.10	Returned goods to the following suppliers:
	Grass £1000
	Seed £2000
15.12.10	Bought additional goods on credit from Grass for £3000 and from Seed for £4000.
20.12.10	Sold more goods on credit to Fog for £2000 and to Mist for £3000.
24.12.10	Paid office expenses of £5000 in cash.
29.12.10	Received £4000 in cash from Fog and £6000 in cash from Mist.
31.12.10	Pat paid Grass and Seed £6000 and £8000, respectively, in cash.

Required:

(a) Enter the above transactions in Pat's ledger accounts.

(b) Balance off the accounts as at 31 December 2010.

(c) Bring down the balances as at 1 January 2011.

(d) Compile a trial balance as at 31 December 2010.

3.14* Vale has been in business for some years. The following balances were brought forward in his books of account as at 1 January 2011:

	£ Dr	£ Cr
Bank	5000	
Capital		20000
Cash	1000	
Dodd		2000
Fish	6000	
Furniture	10000	
	22000	22000

During the year to 31 December 2011 the following transactions took place:

1 Goods bought from Dodd on credit for £30,000.
2 Cash sales of £20,000.
3 Cash purchases of £15,000.
4 Goods sold to Fish on credit for £50,000.
5 Cheques sent to Dodd totalling £29,000.
6 Cheques received from Fish totalling £45,000.
7 Cash received from Fish amounting to £7000.
8 Office expenses paid in cash totalling £9000.
9 Purchase of delivery van costing £12,000 paid by cheque.
10 Cash transfers to bank totalling £3000.

Required:

(a) Compile Vale's ledger accounts for the year 31 December 2011, balance off the accounts and bring down the balances as at 1 January 2012.

(b) Extract a trial balance as at 31 December 2011.

3.15 Brian started in business on 1 January 2012. The following is a list of his transactions for his first month of trading:

1.1.12	Opened a business bank account with £25,000 obtained from private resources.
2.1.12	Paid one month's rent of £2000 by cheque.
3.1.12	Bought goods costing £5000 on credit from Linda.
4.1.12	Purchased motor car from Savoy Motors for £4000 on credit.
5.1.12	Purchased goods costing £3000 on credit from Sydney.
10.1.12	Cash sales of £6000.
15.1.12	More goods costing £10 000 purchased from Linda on credit.
20.1.12	Sold goods on credit to Ann for £8000.
22.1.12	Returned £2000 of goods to Linda.
23.1.12	Paid £6000 in cash into the bank.
24.1.12	Ann returned £1000 of goods.
25.1.12	Withdrew £500 in cash from the bank to open a petty cash account.
26.1.12	Cheque received from Ann for £5500; Ann also claimed a cash discount of £500.
28.1.12	Office expenses of £250 paid out of petty cash.
29.1.12	Sent a cheque to Savoy Motors for £4000.
30.1.12	Cheques sent to Linda and Sydney for £8000 and £2000, respectively. Cash discounts were also claimed from Linda and Sydney of £700 and £100, respectively.
31.1.12	Paid by cheque another month's rent of £2000.
31.1.12	Brian introduced £5000 additional capital into the business by cheque.

Required:

(a) Enter the above transactions in Brian's ledger accounts for January 2012, balance off the accounts and bring down the balances as at 1 February 2012.

(b) Compile a trial balance as at 31 January 2012.

3.16 An accounts clerk has compiled Trent's trial balance as at 31 March 2010 as follows:

	Dr	Cr
	£	£
Bank (overdrawn)	2 000	
Capital	50 000	
Discounts allowed		5 000
Discounts received	3 000	
Dividends received	2 000	
Drawings		23 000
Investments		14 000
Land and buildings	60 000	
Office expenses	18 000	
Purchases	75 000	
Sales		250 000
Suspense (unexplained balance)		6 000
Rates		7 000
Vans	20 000	
Van expenses		5 000
Wages and salaries	80 000	
	310 000	310 000

Required:

Compile Trent's corrected trial balance as at 31 March 2010.

3.17 Donald's transactions for the month of March 2012 are as follows:

	£
Cash receipts	
Capital contributed	6 000
Sales to customers	3 000
Cash payments	
Goods for sale	4 000
Stationery	500
Postage	300
Travelling	600
Wages	2 900
Transfers to bank	500
Bank receipts	£
Receipts from trade debtors:	
Smelt	3 000
Tait	9 000
Ure	5 000
Bank payments	£
Payments to trade creditors:	
Craig	2 800
Dobie	5 000
Elgin	6 400
Rent and rates	3 200
Electricity	200
Telephone	100
Salaries	2 000
Miscellaneous expenses	600
Other transactions	
Goods purchased from:	
Craig	3 500
Dobie	7 500
Elgin	7 500
Goods returned to Dobie	400
Goods sold to:	
Smelt	4 000
Tait	10 000
Ure	8 000
Goods returned by Ure	900
Discounts allowed:	
Smelt	200
Tait	500
Ure	400
Discounts received:	
Craig	50
Dobie	100
Elgin	200

Required:

(a) Enter the above transactions in appropriate ledger accounts.

(b) Balance each account as at 31 March 2012.

(c) Extract a trial balance as at that date.

Further practice questions, study material and links to relevant sites on the World Wide Web can be found on the website that accompanies this book. The site can be found at **www.pearsoned.co.uk/dyson**

Another tale of woe

Cattles suspends executives and issues new alert

By Jane Croft and Maggie Urry

Shares in Cattles plummeted 40 per cent on Tuesday after the subprime lender suspended three senior executives in Welcome Financial Services, its main operating company, and warned 2008 profits were likely to be 'substantially lower' than market expectations.

Cattles had previously warned profits would be 'substantially lower' just 11 days ago and said it expected it would be required to enter into talks with its banks and bondholders, which raised concerns among analysts that it might breach its lending covenants. Cattles shares, which peaked at more than 400p in early 2007, yesterday fell 2.1p to close at 3.1p.

The lender has asked Deloitte to review its bad debt impairment provisions and said it believed that there had been a breakdown in internal controls that had resulted in its impairment policies having being applied incorrectly.

Analysts raised concerns that Cattles, which has delayed its 2008 results, could breach its banking covenants, which would trigger all £2.6bn of its group debt to fall due.

Analysts had predicted Cattles would report profits of £170m in 2008 before its previous two profit warnings, but banking covenants would be breached if interest cover slipped below 1.75 times.

James Hamilton, analyst at Numia, said he believed interest cover would fall below that level if bad debt impairments were 15–16 per cent above his forecast.

'Cattles dramatically expanded its loan book at the top of the economic cycle and used accounting policies that would allow the group to have loans 240 days in arrears before any impairment was taken to the profit and loss,' he said.

Cattles is due to refinance a £500m debt facility with a syndicate of 22 banks led by Royal Bank of Scotland later this summer, plus a further £135m facility that falls due to Royal Bank of Scotland in December. It has stopped lending to new customers.

It is feared that some of the banks may not roll over their loans and Cattles is conserving cash so it can repay some or all of that debt if necessary.

www.ft.com, 3 March 2009.

Source: Reproduced with permission from *The Financial Times*.

Questions relating to this news story can be found on page 93 ➡

About this chapter

The last chapter finished by showing you how to prepare a trial balance. The trial balance has two main purposes: (i) to confirm that all transactions have been entered correctly in the double-entry system; and (ii) to provide the information necessary to prepare an entity's basic financial statements. Such statements usually include a trading account, a profit and loss account, and a balance sheet.

In this chapter we show you how to prepare such statements for a trading entity. A trading entity is a fairly simple organization so it enables us to demonstrate the basic procedures without too many complications. The knowledge and experience that you gain from working your way through this chapter will then give you the foundation necessary for studying more complex organizations.

<table>
<tr><td>

Learning objectives

</td><td>

By the end of this chapter you should be able to:

- prepare a simple set of financial statements for a trading entity;
- make adjustments in sets of financial statements for stock, depreciation, accruals and prepayments, and bad and doubtful debts;
- list the main defects of historical cost accounting;
- explain why accounting profit is not the same as an increase in cash.

</td></tr>
</table>

! Why this chapter is important

This chapter is important for non-accountants for the following reasons.

1 *To distinguish between capital and revenue items.* This is often a matter of judgement and it is not one that is always easy to make. You should not leave the decision entirely to your accountants because it has a major impact on the profit that your entity makes. Make sure that you get involved in the decision!

2 *To be aware that subjective judgements are involved.* Subjective judgements are involved in preparing annual (or periodic) accounts. The main adjustments are for stock, depreciation, accruals and prepayments, and bad and doubtful debts. The decisions that are taken can have significant effect on how much profit you make. So once again, don't leave it to your accountants to decide what to do.

3 *To understand that cash is not the same as profit.* It is vital that you understand the difference between *cash* and *profit.* If you don't your entity is likely to go bankrupt. Just because you have made a profit doesn't necessarily mean that you've got the same amount of money in the bank. All sorts of adjustments are made to the cash position before accountants arrive at what is called 'profit'. Profit is *not*, repeat **NOT**, therefore, simply the difference between cash received less cash paid.

Preparing basic financial statements

News clip

A profitable change

A change in accounting rules has meant that Deutsche Bank has made a profit instead of a loss. The bank was able to reclassify €25bn as 'loans' instead of 'assets'. Price movements on loans do not have to be charged to the profit and loss account.

Source: Adapted from www.accountancyage.com/articles, 31 October 2008.

In this section we are going to explain how to prepare a basic set of financial statements. Such a set is usually made up of a trading account a profit and loss account, and a balance sheet. You can see how they relate to each other in Figure 4.1. If an entity is not trading in goods but in services (say), a trading account will not, of course, be necessary.

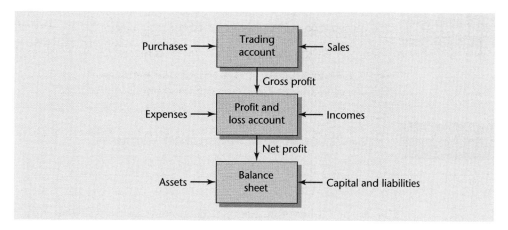

Figure 4.1 A trading entity's basic accounts

In order to keep our explanation simple we are going to assume for the time being that once the trial balance has been prepared no further adjustments are required. Then later on in the chapter we deal with a number of adjustments that usually have to be made at the period end (it's usually a year). In practice the trial balance would normally be prepared before any adjustments are allowed for. They would then be entered in the books of accounts once everything has been agreed for that year.

We suggest that you adopt the following approach if you become involved in the year end procedures.

1 Double-check that your trial balance (TB) balances.
2 Go through the TB line by line, inserting against each balance 'C' (for a capital item) and 'R' (for a revenue item). Capital expenditure is expenditure that is likely to provide a benefit to the entity for more than one accounting period. Revenue expenditure is expenditure that is likely to provide a benefit for just one period. Capital income (a term not normally used) includes the finance provided by the owners and long-term loans. Revenue income includes income from sales, dividends and rents. It is not always easy to make a distinction between capital and revenue items and some difficult decisions may have to be taken.
3 Insert the 'R' balances either in the trading account or in the profit and loss account. The recommended layout (or format) is shown in Example 4.1.
4 Transfer the 'C' balances to the balance sheet. See Example 4.1 for the format.
5 Calculate the gross profit (or loss) in the trading account, i.e. by deducting the cost of purchases from the trading income. Balance the account. Transfer the balance (i.e. the gross profit) to the profit and loss account.
6 Calculate the net profit (or net loss) by deducting the expenses from the gross profit plus any non-trading income. The balance is the net profit for the year (it could be a net loss). Balance the account. Transfer the balance to the balance sheet.
7 Separate all the capital income balances (including the net profit for the year) from all the capital expenditure items and classify them as shown in Example 4.1. Balance the balance sheet.

Activity 4.1		
	(a) Accounting profit = cash received less cash paid	*True/false*
	(b) Capital expenditure is normally the difference between cash received and cash paid.	*True/false*
	(c) Capital expenditure only provides a short-term benefit.	*True/false*

Example 4.1	

Preparation of basic financial statements

The following trial balance has been extracted from Bush's books of account as at 30 June 2012.

Name of account		Dr £	Cr £
Bank (1)	(C)	5 000	
Capital (at 1 July 2011) (2)	(C)		11 000
Cash (3)	(C)	1 000	
Drawings (4)	(C)	8 000	
Motor vehicle at cost (5)	(C)	6 000	
Motor vehicle expenses (6)	(R)	2 000	
Office expenses (7)	(R)	3 000	
Purchases (8)	(R)	30 000	
Trade creditors (9)	(C)		4 000
Trade debtors (10)	(C)	10 000	
Sales (11)	(R)		50 000
		65 000	65 000

Notes:
There were no opening or closing stocks.
R = Revenue items; C = Capital balances.

Required:
Prepare Bush's trading and profit and loss account for the year to 30 June 2012 and a balance sheet as at that date.

Answer to Example 4.1	

Bush
Trading and profit and loss account for the year to
30 June 2012

	£	£
Sales (11)		50 000
Less: cost of goods sold:		
Purchases (8)		30 000
Gross profit		20 000
Less: expenses		
Motor vehicle expenses (6)	2 000	
Office expenses (7)	3 000	5 000
Net profit for the year		15 000

Bush
Balance sheet at 30 June 2012

	£	£
Fixed assets		
Motor vehicles at cost (5)		6 000
Current assets		
Trade debtors (10)	10 000	
Bank (1)	5 000	
Cash (3)	1 000	
	16 000	
Current liabilities		
Trade creditors (9)	4 000	12 000
		18 000
Capital		
Balance at 1 July 2011 (2)		11 000
Add: Net profit for the year*	15 000	
Less: Drawings (4)	8 000	7 000
		18 000

* Obtained from the profit and loss account.
The bracketed number after each narration refers to the account number of each balance extracted from the trial balance.

Tutorial notes

1 Both the trading account and the profit and loss account cover a period of time. In this example it is for the year *to* (or, alternatively, *ending*) 30 June 2012. The balance sheet is prepared at a particular moment in time. It depicts the balances as they were at a specific date. In this example they are shown as at 30 June 2012.

2 The trading account, the profit and loss account, and the balance sheet are presented in what is called the *vertical* format, i.e. on a line-by-line basis starting at the top of the page and working downwards. This is in contrast to the *horizontal* format. This format lists expenditure balances in the trading and profit and loss account and liability balances in the balance sheet on the left-hand side of the page, while income and asset balances are shown on the right-hand side. The horizontal format is now out-of-date and is rarely used. Using the vertical format, the *gross profit* of £20,000 is not only the last line in the trading account but also the first line of the profit and loss account.

3 Both the trading account and the profit and loss accounts are accounts in their own right and they form part of the double-entry system. The balance sheet is merely a list of balances left in the accounting system after the profit and loss account has been prepared. The last line of the profit and loss account shows a net profit of £15,000. This balance remains within the accounting system and so it will be carried forward to the next accounting period. It must, therefore, be included in the balance sheet, otherwise the balance sheet would not balance. You will find the £15,000 towards the bottom of the balance sheet.

4 The balance sheet is divided into two main sections. The first section shows that Bush owned *net assets* worth £18,000 at 30 June 2012. It is split between *fixed assets* of £6000, i.e. those assets that are intended for long-term use in the business, and current assets, i.e. those assets that are constantly being turned over and replaced such as stock, debtors and cash. However, *current liabilities* of £4000 have been deducted from the current assets of £16,000 to show that there was £12,000 of *net current assets*. Current liabilities are amounts owing to various parties that will be due for payment within the next 12 months.

**Answer to
Example 4.1
*continued***

5 The second section shows how the £18,000 of net assets has been financed, i.e. where the money has come from. There were two sources: £11,000 contributed by the owner as capital; and profit left in the business of £7000 – the £15,000 profit made for the year less £8000 taken out (in the form of cash or goods) by Bush during the year, presumably in anticipation that the entity would make a profit. Note that it is not customary to include proprietor's drawings in the profit and loss account.

6 In a more detailed example the expense section in the profit and loss account, and the fixed assets, current assets, current liabilities and capital section in the balance sheet would include many more balances. The profit and loss account balances would be grouped in sections, e.g. administration expenses, distribution costs, selling expenses. In the balance sheet, both fixed asset and current asset balances would be shown in the order of the least liquid (or realizable) assets balances being placed first, e.g. property before machinery, stocks before debtors. Similarly, current liabilities would be listed in the order of those that are going to be paid *last* being placed *first*, e.g. short-term loans would come before creditors. If there are a number of capital balances they too would be placed on 'a last should be first' basis, i.e. capital would come before retained profits.

Activity 4.2	In what order should the following balances be shown in a balance sheet? (a) furniture and fittings; land; plant and machinery; property. (b) cash; bank; insurance paid in advance; other debtors; trade debtors; stocks. (c) bank overdraft; electricity owing; other creditors; trade creditors.

Year end adjustments

We can now move on to deal with a number of year end adjustments. These are events that are normally only made at the end of the year when the financial statements are being prepared. We are going to deal with four of them. They involve allowing for opening and closing stock, writing off some capital expenditure, dealing with outstanding debtors and creditors, and making an allowance for likely bad and doubtful debts (see Figure 4.2).

We begin with stock.

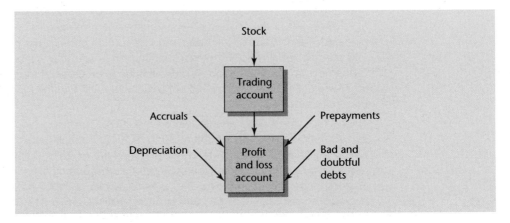

Figure 4.2 Main adjustments

Stock

It is most unlikely that all the purchases that have been made during the year will have been sold by the end of it and so there will almost certainly be some goods still left in the stores. In accounting terminology, purchases still on hand at the period end are referred to as *stock* (the Americans use the term *inventory*).

When calculating the gross profit for the year, therefore, it is necessary to make some allowance for *closing* stock, since we want to match the sales revenue earned for the period with the cost of goods sold and not the cost of all of those goods actually purchased during the year. This means that we have to check the quantity of stock we have on hand at the end of the year and then put some value on it. In practice, this is an extremely difficult exercise. We shall be returning to it in a little more detail in Chapter 13. But we have another problem in dealing with stock. Closing stock at the end of one period becomes the opening stock at the beginning of the next period so we have to allow for *opening* stock as well. This means that the cost of goods sold is made up of three elements: opening stock, purchases and closing stock. Expressed as a formula:

Cost of goods sold = (opening stock + purchases) – closing stock

By making an adjustment for opening and closing stock, the trading account should now appear as in Example 4.2.

Example 4.2

Example of a trading account with stock adjustments

	£	£
Sales		4 000
Less: Cost of goods sold		
Opening stock	1 000	
Purchases	2 000	
	3 000	
Less: Closing stock	1 500	1 500
Gross profit		2 500

Activity 4.3

Assume that Company A has a sales revenue of £10 000 for the year. The opening stock had a value of £2000 and during year the company made purchases of £6000. What would be the gross profit if the closing stock was valued at:

(a) £1500
(b) £2000
(c) £2500?

We now move on to the second of our year end adjustments: depreciation.

Depreciation

Expenditure that covers more than one accounting period is known as *capital expenditure*. Capital expenditure is not normally included in either the trading account or the profit and loss account but it would be misleading to exclude it altogether from the calculation of profit.

Expenditure on fixed assets (such as plant and machinery, motor vehicles and furniture) is necessary in order to help provide a general service to the business. The benefit received from the purchase of fixed assets must (by definition) extend beyond at least one accounting period. So the cost of the benefit provided by fixed assets ought to be charged to those accounting periods that benefit from such expenditure. The problem is in determining what charge to make. In accounting terminology, such a charge is known as *depreciation*.

There is also another reason why fixed assets should be depreciated. By *not* charging each accounting period with some of the cost of fixed assets, the level of profit will be correspondingly higher and the owner would then be able to withdraw more profit from the business. If this happens, insufficient cash may be left in the business and the owner may then find it difficult to buy new fixed assets.

It is not easy to measure the benefit provided to each accounting period by some groups of fixed assets and most depreciation methods tend to be somewhat simplistic. The method most commonly adopted is known as *straight-line depreciation*. This method charges an equal amount of depreciation to each accounting period that benefits from the purchase of a fixed asset. The annual depreciation charge is calculated as follows:

$$\frac{\text{original cost of the asset} - \text{estimated residual value}}{\text{estimated life of the asset}}$$

Another method that you might come across (although it is far less common than straight-line depreciation) is *reducing balance*. A percentage depreciation rate is applied to the original cost of the asset **after** deducting any depreciation charged in previous periods. Example 4.3 shows how it works.

The reducing balance method of calculating depreciation results in a much higher charge in the early life of the asset than does straight depreciation. So it is much more suitable for fixed assets such as vehicles because they tend to depreciate very quickly in the first two or three years.

You can see that in order to calculate the annual depreciation charge using either the straight-line method or the reducing balance method it is necessary to work out (a) how long the asset is likely to last; (b) what it can be sold for, and (c) its useful life.

It is customary to include fixed assets at their historic (i.e. original) cost in the balance sheet but some fixed assets (such as property) may be revalued at regular intervals. If this is the case, the depreciation charge will be based on the revalued amount and not on the historic cost. It should also be noted that even if the asset is depreciated on the basis of its revalued amount there is still no guarantee that it can be replaced at that amount. A combination of inflation and obsolescence may mean that the eventual replacement cost is far in excess of either the historic cost or the revalued amount. It follows that when the fixed asset eventually comes to be replaced, the entity may not have sufficient cash available to replace it.

Example 4.3	**Reducing balance method of depreciating fixed assets**

A fixed asset costs £1000. Assume that the depreciation rate to be applied is 50%. The depreciation rate per year would then be as follows.

Year		£
1. 01.01	Original cost	1000
31.12.01	Depreciation charge for the year (50%)	500
	Reduced balance	500
31.12.02	Depreciation charge for the year (50%)	250
	Reduced balance	250
31.12.03	Depreciation charge for the year (50%)	125
	Reduced balance	125

Tutorial notes

1 Depreciation would be charged each year until eventually the original cost of the asset is written off completely.

2 We have used a depreciation rate of 50% in this example in order to make it easier to follow. In practice the depreciation rate would be calculated by using the formula:

$$r = 1 - \sqrt[n]{\frac{R}{C}}$$

where r = the depreciation rate to be applied; n = the estimated life of the asset; R = the residual (scrap) value; and C = its historic cost.

Activity 4.4	The cost of a company's plant was £50,000. It was estimated that the plant would have a life of 20 years and that it could then be sold for £5000.

Using the straight-line method of depreciation, how much depreciation would you charge to the profit and loss account in Year 1?

The depreciation charge for the year is charged to the profit and loss account as an expense. The balance sheet would include the following details for each group of fixed assets:

1 the historic cost (or revalued amount), i.e. the gross book value (GBV);
2 the accumulated depreciation;
3 the net book value (NBV).

In other words, line 1 minus line 2 = line 3.

These balance sheet requirements are illustrated in Example 4.4.

<table>
<tr><td>**Example 4.4**</td><td colspan="4">**Balance sheet disclosure of fixed assets**</td></tr>
</table>

Fixed assets	Cost	Depreciation	Net book value
	£	£	£
Buildings	100 000	30 000	70 000
Equipment	40 000	25 000	15 000
Furniture	10 000	7 000	3 000
	150 000	62 000	88 000
Current assets			
Stocks		10 000	
Debtors		8 000	
Cash		2 000	
			20 000
			108 000

Activity 4.5

What depreciation policy would you recommend? (a) straight-line for all assets; (b) reducing balance for all assets; (c) reducing balance for certain types of fixed assets and straight-line for all other assets; (d) other methods (state what).

Your answer:
Why?

Accruals and prepayments

The third of our last minute adjustments relates to accruals and prepayments.

News clip

Accrual mistake

Ex-executives of the USA company Krispy Kreme Doughnuts have settled a claim that the company allegedly under-accrued or reversed previously accrued incentive com-pensation expenses with the intention of apparently inflating the company's earn-ings. The personnel involved agreed to give up money allegedly made illegally.

Source: Adapted from www.cfo.com/article, 6 March 2009.

We will deal with each of these adjustments separately.

Accruals

An accrual is an amount owing for a service provided during a particular accounting period but still unpaid for at the end of it. For example, the entity may have paid the last quarter's electricity bill one week before the year end. In its accounts for that year, therefore, it needs to allow for (or *accrue*) the amount that it will owe for the electricity consumed during the last week of the year. The amount due will normally be settled in cash a few days after the year end.

The accrual will be based on an estimate of the likely cost of one week's supply of electricity, or as a proportion of the amount payable (if it has already received the invoice).

The accrual will be included in the amount charged to the profit and loss account for the period as part of the cost of the service provided. The formula is:

(amounts paid during the year + closing accruals) – opening accruals

The closing accruals will be shown on the balance sheet as part of the current liabilities.

Activity 4.6	You owed £500 to the telephone company at 31 December 2010. During the year to 31 December 2011 you paid the company £4000. At 31 December 2011 you owed the company £1000.
	What amount for telephone charges would you debit to the profit and loss account for the year to 31 December 2011?

Prepayments

A prepayment is an amount paid in cash during an accounting period for a service that will be provided in a subsequent period. For example, assume a company's year end is 31 December. It buys a van halfway through 2011 and licences it for 12 months, so half of the fee paid will relate to 2011 and half to 2012. It is necessary, therefore, to adjust 2011's accounts so that only half of the fee is charged in that year. The other half will eventually be charged to 2012's accounts.

Prepayments made during the year will be deducted from the amount charged to the profit and loss account. The formula is:

(amount paid during the year + opening prepayments) – closing prepayments

The closing prepayments will be shown in the balance sheet as part of the current assets.

Activity 4.7	Jill had paid £3000 in advance for insurance at 31 December 2010. During the year to 31 December 2011 she paid the insurance company £10,000. At 31 December 2011 she estimated that she had paid £2000 for insurance cover that related to the following year.
	What amount for insurance charges should Jill debit to her profit and loss account for the year to 31 December 2011?

Bad and doubtful debts

News clip

Exemplar España

The Bank of Spain's policy of forcing banks to provide for bad loans suggests that Spain can now be considered to be at 'the cutting edge of accounting innovation'. Its regulators were determined that its banks would not get involved in cookie-jar accounting 'where executives excessively pad out provisions in good times and then quietly let the excess flow out in the tough times to disguise poor performance'.

Source: Adapted from www.ft.com/cms/s, 9 March 2009.

The fourth main adjustment made in finalizing the annual accounts involves making adjustments for bad debts, and provisions for bad and doubtful debts.

The realization rule allows us to claim profit for any goods that have been sold, even if the cash for them is not received until a later accounting period. This means that we are taking a risk in claiming the profit on those goods in the earlier period, even if the legal title has been passed to the customer. If the goods are not eventually paid for, we will have overestimated the profit for that earlier period. Fortunately, there is a technique whereby we can build in an allowance for any possible *bad debts,* as they are called. This is quite a tricky operation and so we will need to explain it in two stages: first, how to account for bad debts; and, second, how to allow for the possibility that some debts may be *doubtful.*

Bad debts

Once it is clear that a debt is bad (i.e. it is highly unlikely it will ever be paid), then it must be written off to the profit and loss account immediately as an expense. This means that we have to charge it to the current year's profit and loss account even though it may relate to an earlier period. This is because it is usually impractical to change accounts once they have been finalized because the owner may have already taken his profit out of the business in cash. On the balance sheet we then show trade debtors *after* deducting any bad debts that have been written off.

Activity 4.8

Gibson's trade debtors at 31 December 2010 amount to £75,000. One of the trade debtors has owed Gibson £5000 since 2004. Gibson thinks that the debtor now lives abroad in exile.

Should Gibson write off the £5000 as a bad debt to the profit and loss account for the year to 31 December 2010? If so, which account should be debited and which account should be credited? And what amount for trade debtors should be shown in Gibson's balance sheet at 31 December 2010?

Provisions for bad and doubtful debts

The profit in future accounting periods would be severely distorted if the entity suffered a whole series of bad debts. So it seems prudent to allow for the possibility that some debts may become bad. We can do this by setting up a *provision* for bad and doubtful debts (a provision is simply an amount set aside for something that is highly likely to happen), and debiting an annual charge to a special account. In order to calculate the charge, it is necessary to estimate the likely level of bad debts. The estimate will normally be based on the experience that the entity has had in dealing with specific bad debts. In simple book-keeping exercises, the provision is usually expressed as a percentage of the outstanding trade debtors.

The procedure is illustrated in Example 4.5.

Example 4.5	**Accounting for bad and doubtful debts**

You are presented with the following information for the year to 31 March 2011:

	£
Trade debtors at 1 April 2010	20 000
Trade debtors at 31 March 2011 (including £3000 of specific bad debts)	33 000
Provision for bad and doubtful debts at 1 April 2010	1 000

Note: A provision for bad and doubtful debts is maintained equivalent to 5 per cent of the trade debtors as at the end of the year.

Required:
(a) Calculate the increase required in the bad and doubtful debts provision account for the year to 31 March 2011.
(b) Show how both the trade debtors and the provision for bad and doubtful debts account would be featured in the balance sheet at 31 March 2011.

Answer to Example 4.5(a)

	£
Trade debtors as at 31 March 2011	33 000
Less: Specific bad debts to be written off to the profit and loss account for the year to 31 March 2011	3 000
	30 000
Provision required: 5% thereof	1 500
Less: Provision at 1 April 2010	1 000
Increase in the bad and doubtful debts provision account*	500

* This amount will be charged to the profit and loss account for the year to 31 March 2011

Tutorial notes   The balance on the provision for bad and doubtful debts account will be higher at 31 March 2011 than it was at 1 April 2010. This is because the level of trade debtors is higher at the end of 2011 than it was at the end of 2010. The required increase in the provision of £500 will be *debited* to the profit and loss account. If it had been possible to reduce the provision (because of a lower level of trade debtors at the end of 2011 compared with 2010) the decrease would have been *credited* to the profit and loss account.

**Answer to
Example 4.5(b)
continued**

Balance sheet extract at 31 March 2011

	£	£
Current assets		
Trade debtors	30 000	
Less: Provision for bad and doubtful debts	1 500	
		28 500

As a non-accountant it is important for you to grasp just two essential points about the treatment of bad debts and doubtful debts.

- A debt should never be written off until it is absolutely certain that it is bad, because once it is written off, it is highly likely that no further attempt will ever be made to recover it.
- It is prudent to allow for the possibility of some doubtful debts. Nevertheless, it is perhaps rather a questionable decision to reduce profit by an arbitrary amount, e.g. by guessing whether it should be 3 per cent or 5 per cent of outstanding debtors. Obviously, the level that you choose can have a big effect on the profit for the period in question.

Activity 4.9

Watson keeps a provision for bad and doubtful debts account. It is maintained at a level of 3% of his total outstanding trade debtors as at the end of the year. The balance on the provision account at 1 January 2011 was £9000. His trade debtors at 31 December 2011 amounted to £250,000.

What balance on his provision for bad and doubtful debts does he need to carry forward as at 31 December 2011? What amount does he need to write off to the profit and loss account for that year? And will it increase or decrease his profit?

A comprehensive example

In this section, we bring together the material covered in this chapter in a comprehensive example.

Accounting defects

In previous sections of the book, we have emphasized that the calculation of accounting profit calls for a great deal of subjective judgement. Accounting involves much more than merely being very good at mastering some complicated arithmetical examples. So we think that it would be helpful (indeed essential) if we summarized the major defects inherent in the traditional method of calculating accounting profit. (*Continues on page 89*).

Example 4.6	**Example of basic accounting procedures**

Wayne has been in business for many years. His accountant has extracted the following trial balance from his books of account as at 31 March 2011:

	£	£
Bank	1 200	
Capital		33 000
Cash	300	
Drawings	6 000	
Insurance	2 000	
Office expenses	15 000	
Office furniture at cost	5 000	
Office furniture: accumulated depreciation at 1 April 2010		2 000
Provision for bad and doubtful debts at 1 April 2010		500
Purchases	55 000	
Salaries	25 000	
Sales		100 000
Stock at 1 April 2010	10 000	
Trade creditors		4 000
Trade debtors	20 000	
	139 500	139 500

Notes: The following additional information is to be taken into account.

1 Stock at 31 March 2011 was valued at £15,000.
2 The insurance included £500 worth of cover which related to the year to 31 March 2012.
3 Depreciation is charged on office furniture at 10 per cent per annum of its original cost (it is assumed not to have any residual value).
4 A bad debt of £1000 included in the trade debtors balance of £20,000 is to be written off.
5 The provision for bad and doubtful debts is to be maintained at a level of 5 per cent of outstanding trade debtors as at 31 March 2011, i.e. after excluding the bad debt referred to in note 4 above.
6 At 31 March 2011, there was an amount owing for salaries of £1000.

Required:
(a) Prepare Wayne's trading and profit and loss account for the year to 31 March 2011.
(b) Prepare a balance sheet as at that date.

Answer to Example 4.6	(a)

Wayne
Trading and profit and loss account for the year to 31 March 2011

	£	£	(Source of entry)
Sales		100 000	(TB)
Less: Cost of goods sold:			
Opening stock	10 000		(TB)
Purchases	55 000		(TB)
	65 000		
Less: Closing stock	15 000		(QN 1)
		50 000	

Answer to Example 4.6 continued

	£	£	£	(Source of entry)
Gross profit			50 000	
Less: Expenses:				
Insurance (2000 – 500)		1 500		(Wkg 1)
Office expenses		15 000		(TB)
Depreciation: office furniture (10% × 5000)		500		(Wkg 2)
Bad debt		1 000		(QN 4)
Increase in provision for bad and doubtful debts		450		(Wkg 3)
Salaries (25 000 + 1000)		26 000		(Wkg 4)
			44 450	
Net profit for the year			5 550	

(b)
Wayne
Balance sheet at 31 March 2011

Fixed assets	Cost £	Accumulated depreciation £	Net book value £	(Source of entry)
Office furniture c/f	5 000	2 500	2 500	(TB and Wkg 5)
b/f	5 000	2 500	2 500	
Current assets				
Stock		15 000		(QN 1)
Trade debtors				
(20 000 – 1000)	19 000			(Wkg 3)
Less: Provision for bad and doubtful debts	950	18 050		(Wkg 3)
Prepayment		500		(QN 2)
Cash at bank		1 200		(TB)
Cash in hand		300		(TB)
		35 050		
Less: Current liabilities				
Trade creditors	4 000			(TB)
Accrual	1 000			(QN 6)
		5 000	30 050	
			32 550	
Financed by:				
Capital				
Balance at 1 April 2010			33 000	(TB)
Add: Net profit for the year		5 550		(P&L a/c)
Less: Drawings		6 000	(450)	
			32 550	

Key:
TB = from trial balance;
QN = extracted straight from the question and related notes;
Wkg = workings (see below);
P&L a/c = balance obtained from the profit and loss account.

Workings

	£
1 Insurance:	
As per the trial balance	2 000
Less: Prepayment (QN 2)	500
Charge to the profit and loss account	1 500
2 Depreciation:	
Office furniture at cost	5 000
Depreciation: 10% of the original cost	500
3 Increase in provision for bad and doubtful debts:	
Trade debtors at 31 March 2011	20 000
Less: Bad debt (QN 4)	1 000
	19 000
Provision required: 5% thereof	950
Less: Provision at 1 April 2010	500
Increase in provision: charge to profit and loss	450
4 Salaries:	
As per the question	25 000
Add: Accrual (QN 6)	1 000
	26 000
5 Accumulated depreciation:	
Balance at 1 April 2010 (as per TB)	2 000
Add: Depreciation for the year (Wkg 2)	500
Accumulated depreciation at 31 March 2011	2 500

As a non-accountant, it is most important that you appreciate one vital fact: the method that we have outlined for calculating the profit for a period results in an *estimate* of what the accountant thinks the profit should be. You must not place too much reliance on the *absolute* level of accounting profit. It can only be as accurate and as reliable as the assumptions upon which it is based. If you accept the assumptions, then you can be fairly confident that the profit figure is reliable. You will then not go too far wrong in using the information for decision-making purposes. But you must know what the assumptions are and you must support them. So we recommend that you *always question accounting information before accepting it.*

The main reasons why you should not place too much reliance on the *actual* level of accounting profit (especially if you are unsure about the assumptions upon which it is based) are summarized below.

- Goods are treated as being sold when the legal title to them changes hands and not when the customer has paid for them. In some cases, the cash for some sales may never be received.
- Goods are regarded as having been purchased when the legal title to them is transferred to the purchaser, although there are occasions when they may not be received, e.g. if a supplier goes into receivership.
- Goods that have not been sold at the period end have to be quantified and valued. Counting stock can be a complex operation and valuing it involves a considerable amount of subjective judgement.

- There is no clear distinction between capital and revenue transactions.
- Estimates have to be made to allow for accruals and prepayments.
- The cost of fixed assets is apportioned between different accounting periods using methods that are fairly simplistic and highly questionable.
- Arbitrary reductions in profit are made to allow for bad and doubtful debts.
- Historic cost accounting makes no allowance for inflation. So the value of £100 (say) at 1 January 2011 is not the same as £100 at 31 December 2011. As a result profit tends to be overstated largely because of low closing stock values and low depreciation charges.

The defects of historic cost accounting as listed are serious but no one as yet has been able to suggest a better method of accounting. For the time being, therefore, all we can do is to take comfort in the old adage that 'it is better to be vaguely right than precisely wrong'.

We would like to emphasize one point before we leave this chapter. Many students are mystified when they begin their study of accounting why 'profit' is not the same as an increase in cash. Now that you have worked your way through this chapter you should be clear why this is not the case. So remember that:

> **Accounting profit is not the same as an increase in cash.**

Why? Most of the reasons are contained within the above list of accounting defects. We have also demonstrated the distinction pictorially in Figure 4.3. Basically, some cash items are excluded from the profit and loss account (e.g. capital expenditure) while some non-cash items are included in it such as a provision for bad and doubtful debts. You can perhaps compile your own list of reasons by having a go at answering Activity 4.10.

Activity 4.10	List as many examples as you can of (a) cash transactions that are not normally included in a trading or profit and loss account; and (b) non-cash items that are usually included in such financial statements.

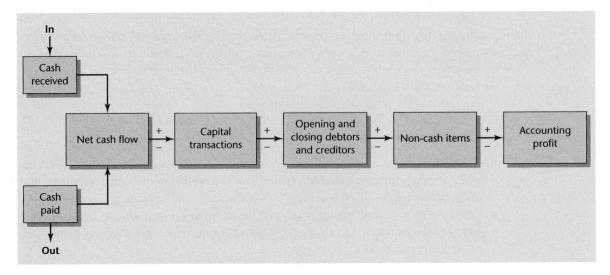

Figure 4.3 Cash vs accounting profit

> ## ! Questions you should ask
>
> It is important that as a non-accountant you should grasp the significance of this chapter. The decisions that your accountants will have taken in making a series of year end adjustments to the financial accounts (particularly for stocks, depreciation, accruals and prepayment, and bad and doubtful debts) will have a considerable effect on the amount of profit that the entity reports for the year.
>
> We suggest that you ask the following questions.
>
> - What criteria have been used for distinguishing between capital and revenue items?
> - Which items included in the financial statements may or may not be capital (or revenue)?
> - What is the definition that you have used to determine revenue?
> - Was a physical stock check done at the year end?
> - What method was used to value the closing stock?
> - What depreciation method has been used?
> - Has historic cost been used to depreciate the fixed assets?
> - If not, how has the cost of fixed assets been determined?
> - How has the expected life of the assets been assessed?
> - How do such lives compare with those used by our competitors?
> - How have any residual values for the fixed assets been estimated?
> - How have estimated values been determined for any accruals and prepayments?
> - Have any bad debts been written off?
> - How can we be certain that they are indeed bad?
> - What basis is used to determine an appropriate level of provision for bad and doubtful debts?

Conclusion

We began this chapter by showing you how to prepare a basic set of financial statements working from a trial balance and where there were no year end adjustments. We then went on to deal with four important adjustments that an entity usually has to make at the year end once the trial balance has been balanced. These four adjustments relate to opening and closing stocks, an allowance for depreciation on capital assets, adjusting for accruals and prepayments, and making allowances for bad and doubtful debts.

These four types of adjustment lead to many inherent deficiencies in the way that accounting profit is conventionally calculated. In concluding the chapter we summarized such deficiencies while at the same time reminding you that an increase in profit does not necessarily lead to an increase in cash.

Key points

1 A trial balance provides the basic data for the preparation of the financial accounts.

2 The basic financial statements of a trading entity normally include a trading account, a profit and loss account, and a balance sheet.

3 Revenue balances are transferred to either the trading account or the profit and loss account, and capital balances to the balance sheet.

4 The trading account and the profit and loss account form part of the double-entry system. The balance sheet is merely a listing of the balances that remain in the ledger system once the trading and profit and loss accounts have been prepared.

5 The basic financial accounts are nowadays normally presented in a vertical format.

6 Following the completion of the trial balance, some year end adjustments have usually to be made to the financial statements. The main adjustments are stock, depreciation, accruals and prepayments, and bad and doubtful debts.

7 Accounting profit is merely an estimate. The method used to calculate it is highly questionable and it is subject to very many criticisms. Undue reliance should not be placed on the actual level of profit shown in the accounts. The assumptions upon which profit is based should be carefully examined and it should be viewed merely as a guide to decision making.

8 Accounting profit is not the same as an increase in cash.

Check your learning

The answers to these questions can be found within the text.

1 Name two important functions of a trial balance.

2 What are the three financial statements that make up a set of basic accounts?

3 What are the two broad groups into which all transactions may be classified?

4 Name the two stages involved in preparing the basic accounts.

5 What term is given to the difference between sales revenue and the cost of goods sold?

6 What term is given to the difference between the total of all revenue incomes and the total of all revenue expenditures?

7 What two formats may be used for the presentation of financial statements?

8 Which format is the one now commonly used?

9 What is meant by 'stock'?

10 What is the American term for stock?

11 What is meant by 'opening stock' and 'closing stock'?

12 What three items make up the closing stock?

13 To which account are opening and closing stock transferred?

14 Is opening stock shown on the balance sheet at the end of an accounting period?

15 Is closing stock shown on the balance sheet at the end of an accounting period?

16 What is depreciation?

17 Name two methods of depreciating fixed assets.

18 How are each of those methods calculated?

19 What is meant by the terms 'gross book value' and 'net book value'?

20 What amount for depreciation is shown on the balance sheet?

21 What is (a) an accrual, and (b) a prepayment?

22 Where are they normally disclosed in the profit and loss account?

23 Where are they to be found in the balance sheet?

24 What is (a) a bad debt, and (b) a doubtful debt?

25 What is a provision for bad and doubtful debts?

26 On what might the provision be based?

27 List eight reasons why the calculation of accounting profit is an arbitrary exercise.

News story quiz

Remember the news story at the beginning of this chapter? Go back to that story and reread it before answering the following questions.

Yet again another alleged 'accounting irregularity' involving an inadequate provision for bad debts.

Questions

1 How could 'a breakdown in internal controls' affect a decision to set aside a specific provision for bad debts?

2 Why might the company break its banking covenants if all the £2.6bn group debt fell due?

3 What is meant by the explanation 'before any impairment was taken to the profit and loss account'?

4 Do you think that 240 days is an exceptionally long period of time for loans to be in arrears?

Tutorial questions

The answers to questions marked with an asterisk can be found in Appendix 4.

4.1 Explain why an increase in cash during a particular accounting period does not necessarily mean that an entity has made a profit.

4.2 'The differentiation between so-called capital and revenue expenditure is quite arbitrary and unnecessary.' Discuss.

4.3 How far does a balance sheet tell users how much an entity is worth?

4.4 'Depreciation methods and rates should be prescribed by law.' Discuss.

4.5 Explain why it is quite easy to manipulate the level of gross profit when preparing a trading account.

4.6 How far is it possible for an entity to build up hidden amounts of profit (known as *secret reserves*) by making some adjustments in the profit and loss account for bad and doubtful debts?

4.7* The following trial balance has been extracted from Ethel's books of accounts as at 31 January 2010:

	Dr £	Cr £
Capital		10 000
Cash	3 000	
Creditors		3 000
Debtors	6 000	
Office expenses	11 000	
Premises	8 000	
Purchases	20 000	
Sales		35 000
	48 000	48 000

Required:
Prepare Ethel's trading and profit and loss account for the year to 31 January 2010 and a balance sheet as at that date.

4.8* Marion has been in business for some years. The following trial balance has been extracted from her books of account as at 28 February 2011:

	Dr £000	Cr £000
Bank	4	
Buildings	50	
Capital		50
Cash	2	
Creditors		24
Debtors	30	
Drawings	55	
Heat and light	10	
Miscellaneous expenses	25	
Purchases	200	
Sales		400
Wages and salaries	98	
	474	474

Required:
Prepare Marion's trading and profit and loss account for the year to 28 February 2011 and a balance sheet as at that date.

4.9 The following trial balance has been extracted from Jody's books of account as at 30 April 2012:

	Dr £000	Cr £000
Capital (as at 1 May 2011)		30
Cash	1	
Electricity	2	
Maintenance	4	
Miscellaneous expenses	7	
Purchases	40	
Rent and rates	6	
Sales		85
Vehicle (at cost)	30	
Wages	25	
	115	115

Required:

Prepare Jody's trading and profit and loss account for the year to 30 April 2012 and a balance sheet as at that date.

4.10 The following trial balance has been extracted from the books of Garswood as at 31 March 2010:

	Dr £	Cr £
Advertising	2 300	
Bank	300	
Capital		55 700
Cash	100	
Discounts allowed	100	
Discounts received		600
Drawings	17 000	
Electricity	1 300	
Investments	4 000	
Investment income received		400
Office equipment	10 000	
Other creditors		800
Other debtors	1 500	
Machinery	20 000	
Purchases	21 400	
Purchases returns		1 400
Sales		63 000
Sales returns	3 000	
Stationery	900	
Trade creditors		5 200
Trade debtors	6 500	
Wages	38 700	
	127 100	127 100

Required:

Prepare Garswood's trading and profit and loss account for the year to 31 March 2010 and a balance sheet as at that date.

4.11 Pete has extracted the following trial balance from his books of account as at 31 May 2011:

	Dr £000	Cr £000
Bank		15
Building society account	100	
Capital (as at 1 June 2010)		200
Cash	2	
Heat, light and fuel	18	
Insurances	10	
Interest received		1
Land and property (at cost)	200	
Long-term loan		50
Long-term loan interest paid	8	
Motor vehicles (at cost)	90	
Motor vehicle expenses	12	
Plant and equipment (at cost)	100	
Property maintenance	7	
Purchases	300	
Repairs to machinery	4	
Rent and rates	65	
Sales		900
Wages and salaries	250	
	1166	1166

Required:
Prepare Pete's trading and profit and loss account for the year to 31 May 2011 and a balance sheet as at that date.

4.12* The following information has been extracted from Lathom's books of account for the year to 30 April 2010:

	£
Purchases	45 000
Sales	60 000
Stock (at 1 May 2009)	3 000
Stock (at 30 April 2010)	4 000

Required:
(a) Prepare Lathom's trading account for the year to 30 April 2010.
(b) State where the stock at 30 April 2010 would be shown on the balance sheet as at that date.

4.13 Rufford presents you with the following information for the year to 31 March 2011:

	£
Purchases	48 000
Purchases returns	3 000
Sales	82 000
Sales returns	4 000
Stock at 1 April 2010	4 000

He is not sure how to value the stock as at 31 March 2011. Three methods have been suggested. They all result in different closing stock values, namely:

	£
Method 1	8 000
Method 2	16 000
Method 3	4 000

Required:

(a) Calculate the effect on gross profit for the year to 31 March 2011 by using each of the three methods of stock valuation.

(b) State the effect on gross profit for the year to 31 March 2012 if Method 1 is used instead of Method 2.

4.14*Standish has been trading for some years. The following trial balance has been extracted from his books of account as at 31 May 2012:

	Dr	Cr
	£	£
Capital		22 400
Cash	1 200	
Creditors		4 300
Debtors	6 000	
Drawings	5 500	
Furniture and fittings	8 000	
Heating and lighting	1 500	
Miscellaneous expenses	6 700	
Purchases	52 000	
Sales		79 000
Stock (at 1 June 2011)	7 000	
Wages and salaries	17 800	
	105 700	105 700

Note: Stock at 31 May 2012: £12 000.

Required:

Prepare Standish's trading and profit and loss account for the year to 31 May 2012 and a balance sheet as at that date.

4.15 Witton commenced business on 1 July 2009. The following trial balance was extracted from his books of account as at 30 June 2010:

	Dr	Cr
	£	£
Capital		3 000
Cash	500	
Drawings	4 000	
Creditors		1 500
Debtors	3 000	
Motor car at cost	5 000	
Office expenses	8 000	
Purchases	14 000	
Sales		30 000
	34 500	34 500

Additional information:

1 Stock at 30 June 2010: £2000.
2 The motor car is to be depreciated at a rate of 20 per cent per annum on cost; it was purchased on 1 July 2009.

Required:
Prepare Witton's trading and profit and loss account for the year to 30 June 2010 and a balance sheet as at that date.

4.16 The following is an extract from Barrow's balance sheet at 31 August 2011:

Fixed assets	Cost	Accumulated depreciation	Net book value
	£	£	£
Land	200 000	–	200 000
Buildings	150 000	60 000	90 000
Plant	55 000	37 500	17 500
Vehicles	45 000	28 800	16 200
Furniture	20 000	12 600	7 400
	470 000	138 900	331 100

Barrow's depreciation policy is as follows:

1 A full year's depreciation is charged in the year of acquisition, but none in the year of disposal.
2 No depreciation is charged on land.
3 Buildings are depreciated at an annual rate of 2 per cent on cost.
4 Plant is depreciated at an annual rate of 5 per cent on cost after allowing for an estimated residual value of £5000.
5 Vehicles are depreciated on a reduced balance basis at an annual rate of 40 per cent on the reduced balance, i.e. on the net book value as at the end of the previous year.
6 Furniture is depreciated on a straight-line basis at an annual rate of 10 per cent on cost after allowing for an estimated residual value of £2000.

Additional information:

1 During the year to 31 August 2012 new furniture was purchased for the office. It cost £3000 and it is to be depreciated on the same basis as the old furniture. Its estimated residual value is £300.
2 There were no additions to, or disposals of, any other fixed assets during the year to 31 August 2012.

Required:
(a) Calculate the depreciation charge for each of the fixed asset groupings for the year to 31 August 2012.
(b) Show how the fixed assets would appear in Barrow's balance sheet as at 31 August 2012.

4.17*Pine started business on 1 October 2011. The following is his trial balance at 30 September 2012:

	£	£
Capital		6 000
Cash	400	
Creditors		5 900
Debtors	5 000	
Furniture at cost	8 000	
General expenses	14 000	
Insurance	2 000	
Purchases	21 000	
Sales		40 000
Telephone	1 500	
	51 900	51 900

The following information was obtained after the trial balance had been prepared:

1 Stock at 30 September 2012: £3000.
2 Furniture is to be depreciated at a rate of 15 per cent on cost.
3 At 30 September 2012, Pine owed £500 for telephone expenses, and insurance had been prepaid by £200.

Required:
Prepare Pine's trading and profit and loss account for the year to 30 September 2012 and a balance sheet as at that date.

4.18 Dale has been in business for some years. The following is his trial balance at 31 October 2010:

	Dr	*Cr*
	£	£
Bank	700	
Capital		85 000
Depreciation (at 1 November 2009):		
Office equipment		14 000
Vehicles		4 000
Drawings	12 300	
Heating and lighting	3 000	
Office expenses	27 000	
Office equipment, at cost	35 000	
Rates	12 000	
Purchases	240 000	
Sales		350 000
Stock (at 1 November 2009)	20 000	
Trade creditors		21 000
Trade debtors	61 000	
Vehicles at cost	16 000	
Wages and salaries	47 000	
	474 000	474 000

Additional information (not taken into account when compiling the above trial balance):
1 Stock at 31 October 2010: £26 000.
2 Amount owing for electricity at 31 October 2010: £1500.
3 At 31 October 2010, £2000 had been paid in advance for rates.
4 Depreciation is to be charged on the office equipment for the year to 31 October 2010 at a rate of 20 per cent on cost, and on the vehicles at a rate of 25 per cent on cost.

Required:
Prepare Dale's trading and profit and loss account for the year to 31 October 2010 and a balance sheet as at that date.

4.19 The following information relates to Astley for the year to 30 November 2011:

Item	Cash paid during the year to 30 November 2011	As at 1 December 2010 Accruals/ Prepayments		As at 30 November 2011 Accruals/ Prepayments	
	£	£	£	£	£
Electricity	26 400	5 200	–	8 300	–
Gas	40 100	–	–	–	4 900
Insurance	25 000	–	12 000	–	14 000
Rates	16 000	–	4 000	6 000	–
Telephone	3 000	1 500	–	–	200
Wages	66 800	1 800	–	–	–

Required:
(a) Calculate the charge to the profit and loss account for the year to 30 November 2011 for each of the above items.
(b) Demonstrate what amounts for accruals and prepayments would be shown in the balance sheet as at 30 November 2011.

4.20 Duxbury started in business on 1 January 2012. The following is his trial balance as at 31 December 2012:

	Dr	Cr
	£	£
Capital		40 000
Cash	300	
Delivery van, at cost	20 000	
Drawings	10 600	
Office expenses	12 100	
Purchases	65 000	
Sales		95 000
Trade creditors		5 000
Trade debtors	32 000	
	140 000	140 000

Additional information:
1 Stock at 31 December 2012 was valued at £10 000.
2 At 31 December 2010 an amount of £400 was outstanding for telephone expenses, and the business rates had been prepaid by £500.
3 The delivery van is to be depreciated at a rate of 20 per cent per annum on cost.
4 Duxbury decides to set aside a provision for bad and doubtful debts equal to 5 per cent of trade debtors as at the end of the year.

Required:

Prepare Duxbury's trading and profit and loss account for the year to 31 December 2012 and a balance sheet as at that date.

4.21 Beech is a retailer. Most of his sales are made on credit terms. The following information relates to the first four years that he has been in business:

	2010	2011	2012	2013
Trade debtors as at 31 January:	£60 000	£55 000	£65 000	£70 000

The trade is one that experiences a high level of bad debts. Accordingly, Beech decides to set aside a provision for bad and doubtful debts equivalent to 10 per cent of trade debtors as at the end of the year.

Required:

(a) Show how the provision for bad and doubtful debts would be disclosed in the respective balance sheets as at 31 January 2010, 2011, 2012 and 2013.

(b) Calculate the increase/decrease in provision for bad and doubtful debts transferred to the respective profit and loss accounts for each of the four years.

4.22 The following is Ash's trial balance as at 31 March 2011:

	Dr £	Cr £
Bank		4 000
Capital		20 500
Depreciation (at 1 April 2010): furniture		3 600
Drawings	10 000	
Electricity	2 000	
Furniture, at cost	9 000	
Insurance	1 500	
Miscellaneous expenses	65 800	
Provision for bad and doubtful debts (at 1 April 2010)		1 200
Purchases	80 000	
Sales		150 000
Stock (at 1 April 2010)	10 000	
Trade creditors		20 000
Trade debtors	21 000	
	199 300	199 300

Additional information:

1 Stock at 31 March 2011: £15 000.

2 At 31 March 2011 there was a specific bad debt of £6000. This was to be written off.

3 Furniture is to be depreciated at a rate of 10 per cent per annum on cost.

4 At 31 March 2011 Ash owes the electricity board £600, and £100 had been paid in advance for insurance.

5 The provision for bad and doubtful debts is to be set at 10 per cent of trade debtors as at the end of the year.

Required:

Prepare Ash's trading and profit and loss account for the year to 31 March 2011 and a balance sheet as at that date.

4.23 Lime's business has had liquidity problems for some months. The following trial balance was extracted from his books of account as at 30 September 2012:

	Dr £	Cr £
Bank		15 200
Capital		19 300
Cash from sale of office equipment		500
Depreciation (at 1 October 2011):		
office equipment		22 000
Drawings	16 000	
Insurance	1 800	
Loan (long-term from Cedar)		50 000
Loan interest	7 500	
Miscellaneous expenses	57 700	
Office equipment, at cost	44 000	
Provision for bad and doubtful debts		
(at 1 October 2011)		2 000
Purchases	320 000	
Rates	10 000	
Sales		372 000
Stock (at 1 October 2011)	36 000	
Trade creditors		105 000
Trade debtors	93 000	
	586 000	586 000

Additional information:
1 Stock at 30 September 2012: £68 000.
2 At 30 September 2012, accrual for rates of £2000 and insurance prepaid of £200.
3 Depreciation on office equipment is charged at a rate of 25 per cent on cost. During the year, office equipment costing £4000 had been sold for £500. Accumulated depreciation on this equipment amounted to £3000. Lime's depreciation policy is to charge a full year's depreciation in the year of acquisition and none in the year of disposal.
4 Specific bad debts of £13 000 are to be written off.
5 The provision for bad and doubtful debts is to be made equal to 10 per cent of outstanding trade debtors as at 30 September 2012.

Required:
Prepare Lime's trading, and profit and loss account for the year to 30 September 2012, and a balance sheet as at that date.

Further practice questions, study material and links to relevant sites on the World Wide Web can be found on the website that accompanies this book. The site can be found at www.pearsoned.co.uk/dyson

Company accounts

Riding a tiger

Indian outsourcing group chief admits to $1bn accounting fraud

By Joe Leahy

The head of one of India's biggest outsourcing groups has confessed to fixing the company's books in a $1bn ($662m) fraud.

B. Ramalinga Raju, chairman and chief executive of Satyam Computer Services, resigned yesterday after admitting that he had manipulated the accounts for 'several' years to show hugely inflated profits and fictitious assets.

The scandal will raise questions about how outsourcing groups are regulated and audited. Satyam was audited by PwC and was the first Indian company to list on three international stock exchanges – Mumbai, New York and Amsterdam – yet the fraud went unnoticed for years.

In a letter to the Satyam board, Mr Raju confessed and said he would resign and 'subject myself to the laws of the land'. He said that the cover up started as an attempt to disguise a poor quarterly performance by inflating group profit and got out of hand.

'It was like riding a tiger, not knowing when to get off without being eaten,' Mr Raju wrote.

The Securities and Exchange Board of India, the regulator, said it was launching an inquiry and would 'check whether the audit was done properly'.

Mr Raju said the accounts in the quarter ended last September included a cash pile of Rs53.61bn (£728m), of which 94 per cent was 'fictitious'. Among other irregularities, the operating margin was inflated to 24 per cent of revenue against an actual figure of 3 per cent, Mr Raju said.

www.ft.com, 8 January 2009.

Source: Reproduced with permission from *The Financial Times*.

Questions relating to this news story can be found on page 119 ⬛▶

About this chapter

In the previous chapter we have shown you how to prepare a set of basic financial statements for a sole trader entity. The management and organization of such entities are not normally very complex, so we have been able to cover the overall procedures without becoming *too* bogged down in the detail (although this may rather surprise you).

Many non-accountants using this book are, however, likely to work for a *company*. There are many different types of companies but the most common ones are private limited liability companies and public limited liability companies (as we explained in Chapter 2). By law, all companies have to prepare a set of annual accounts and supply a copy to their shareholders. They also have to file a copy with the Registrar of Companies, i.e. send it to the Registrar. This means that the accounts are then open to inspection by the public. The amount of detail disclosed or published in company accounts (i.e. included) depends upon their type and size.

We shall be dealing with the disclosure requirements of companies in Chapters 8 and 9. In this chapter we explain how to prepare a company's financial accounts for the *internal* management. There are no legal requirements covering the presentation and contents of financial accounts for such a purpose, so a company can do more or less as it wants. Nevertheless, in order to cut down on the amount of work involved, most companies probably produce internal accounts that are similar to the ones required for external purposes, except that they are likely to be much more detailed.

> ### Learning objectives
>
> By the end of this chapter you should be able to:
> - explain what is meant by limited liability;
> - distinguish between private and public companies;
> - describe how companies are organized;
> - prepare a basic set of financial statements for a company.

❗ Why this chapter is important

This chapter is important for a non-accountant because it shows how the material covered in earlier chapters can be adapted for use in preparing company accounts. As many non-accountants work for a company (while others will have contact with one) this chapter will help them to do a better job if they know something about the origin, structure and operation of companies. They will be even better placed if they can then use the available accounting information to assess the past and future performance of their own company and compare it with its competitors. In order to be able to do so, it is necessary to know where the accounting information comes from, what it includes, how it has been summarized and any deficiencies that it may have. This can be best achieved by being able to prepare a simple set of financial statements for a company. This chapter provides non-accountants with that opportunity.

We start our study of company accounts with an explanation of what is meant by 'limited liability'.

Limited liability

There is a great personal risk in operating a business as a sole trader or as a partnership. If the business runs short of funds, the owners may be called upon to settle the business's debts out of their own private resources. This type of risk can have a damaging effect on the development of new businesses. So there is a need for a different type of entity that will neither make the owners bankrupt nor inhibit new developments. This need became apparent in the nineteenth century following the Industrial Revolution when enormous amounts of capital were required to finance new and rapidly expanding industries such as the railways and shipbuilding.

These sorts of ventures were undertaken at great personal risk. By agreeing to become involved in them many investors faced bankruptcy if the ventures were unsuccessful (as they often were). It became apparent that the development of industry would be hindered unless some means could be devised of restricting the personal liability of prospective investors.

So the concept of *limited liability* was born although it was not entirely an innovation of the nineteenth century. It eventually received legal recognition in 1855 when the Limited Liability Act was passed. The Act only remained in force for a few months before it was repealed and incorporated into the Joint Stock Companies Act 1856. By distinguishing between the private and public affairs of business proprietors, the 1855 Act effectively created a new form of legal entity. Since the 1850s Parliament has passed a number of other Companies Acts, all of which have continued to give legal recognition to the concept of limited liability.

The important point about a limited liability company is that no matter what financial difficulties it may get into, its members cannot be required to contribute more than an agreed amount of capital, so there is no risk of its members being forced into bankruptcy.

The concept of limited liability is often very difficult for business owners to understand, especially if they have formed one out of what was originally a sole trader or a partnership entity (this point is illustrated in Figure 5.1). Unlike such entities, companies are bound by some fairly severe legal operating restrictions. The legal restrictions can be somewhat burdensome but they are necessary for the protection of all those parties who might have dealings with the company (such as creditors and employees). This is because if a limited liability company runs short of funds the creditors and employees might not get paid. It is only fair, therefore, to warn all those people who might have dealings with it that they run a risk in doing business with it. So companies have to be more open about their affairs than do sole traders and partnerships.

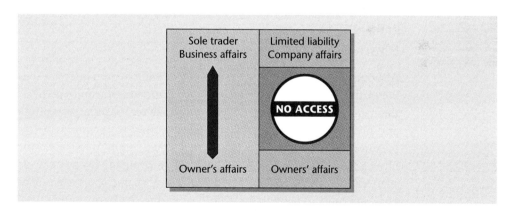

Figure 5.1 Access: sole trader vs limited liability company

Structure and operation

In this section we examine the structure and operation of limited liability companies. In order to make it easier to follow we have broken down our examination into a number of subsections. A summary of the section is also presented in diagrammatic format in Figure 5.2.

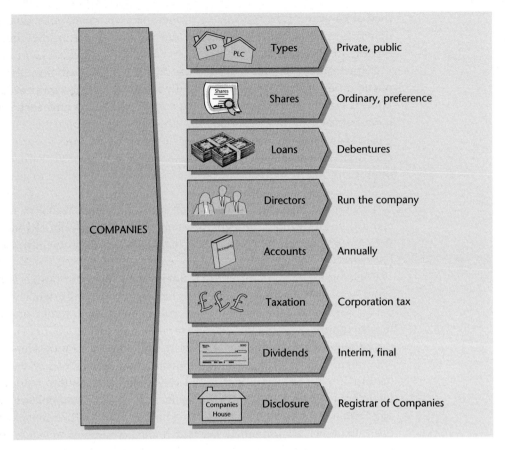

Figure 5.2 Structure and operation of companies

Share capital

Although the law recognizes that limited liability companies are separate beings with a life of their own, i.e. separate from those individuals who collectively own and manage them, it also accepts that someone has to take responsibility for promoting the company and giving it life. Only one person is required to form a private company and that person (or persons if there is more than one) agrees to make a capital contribution by buying a number of shares. The capital of a company is known as its *share capital*. The share capital will be made up of a number of shares of a certain denomination, such as 10p, 50p or £1. Members may hold only one share, or many hundreds or thousands depending upon the total share capital of the company, the denomination of the shares and the amount that they wish to contribute.

The maximum amount of capital that the company envisages ever raising has to be stated. This is known as its *authorized share capital*, although this does not necessarily mean that it will issue shares up to that amount. In practice, it will probably only issue sufficient capital to meet its immediate and foreseeable requirements. The amount of share capital that it has actually issued is known as the *issued share capital*. Sometimes, when shares are issued, prospective shareholders are only required to pay for them in instalments. Once all the issued share capital has been paid for, it is described as being *fully paid*.

There are two main types of shares: *ordinary shares* and *preference shares*. Ordinary shares do not usually entitle the shareholder to any specific level of dividend. Preference shareholders are normally entitled to a fixed level of dividend and they have priority over the ordinary shareholders if the company is liquidated. Sometimes the preference shares are classed as *cumulative*; this means that if the company cannot pay its preference dividend in one year, the amount due accrues until such time as the company has the profits to pay all of the accumulated dividends.

We show the share capital structure of companies in Figure 5.3.

Types of companies

A prospective shareholder may invest in either a public company or a private company. A *public company* must have an authorized share capital of at least £50 000, and it becomes a public company merely by stating that it is a public company. In fact, most public limited companies in the United Kingdom have their shares listed on the London Stock Exchange and so they are often referred to as *listed* (or quoted) companies. As a warning to those parties who might have dealings with them, public companies have to include the term 'public limited liability company' after their name (or its abbreviation 'plc').

Any company that does not make its shares available to the public is regarded as being a *private company*. Like public companies, private companies must also have a stated amount of authorized share capital although no minimum amount is prescribed. Otherwise, their share capital requirements are very similar to public companies.

Private companies also have to warn the public that their liability is limited. They must do so by describing themselves as 'limited liability companies' and attaching the term 'limited' after their name (or the abbreviation 'ltd').

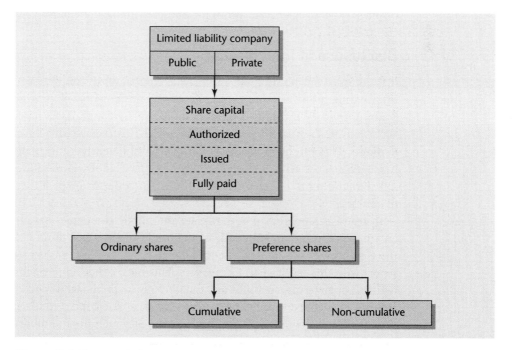

Figure 5.3 Types of shares

Activity 5.1	Limited liability companies have to disclose some information about their operations as well as putting 'limited' ('ltd') or public limited company ('plc') after their name in order to warn the public that their liability is limited.
	Do you think that such safeguards are adequate? What more can be done? How far do you think that it is fair for individuals to set up businesses under the protection of limited liability? The business may then go into liquidation and the creditors will be left without any means of getting their money back from the owners of the company. Is this acceptable if the concept of limited liability encourages new businesses to be formed?

Loans

Besides obtaining the necessary capital from their shareholders, companies often borrow money in the form of *debentures*. A company may invite the public to loan it some money for a certain period of time (the period can be unspecified) at a certain rate of interest. A debenture loan may be secured on specific assets of the company, on its assets generally or it might not be secured at all. If the loan is secured and the company cannot repay it on its due repayment date, the debenture holders may sell the secured assets and use the amount to settle what is owing to them.

Debentures, like shares, may be bought and sold freely on the Stock Exchange. The nearer the redemption date for the repayment for the debentures, the closer the market price will be to their nominal value, i.e. their face, or stated paper value. If they are to be redeemed at a premium, i.e. in excess of their nominal value, the market price may exceed the nominal value.

Debenture holders are not shareholders of the company and they do not have voting rights. From the company's point of view, one further advantage of raising capital in the form of debenture loans is that for taxation purposes the interest can be charged as a business expense against the profit for the year (unlike dividends).

Disclosure of information

It is necessary for both public and private companies to supply a minimum amount of information to their members. The detailed requirements will be examined in Chapters 8 and 9. You might find it surprising to learn that shareholders have neither a right of access to the company's premises nor a right to receive any information that they demand. This might not seem fair but it would clearly be difficult for a company's managers to cope with thousands of shareholders, all of whom suddenly turned up one day demanding to be let into the building in order to inspect the company's books of account.

Instead, shareholders in both private and public companies have to be supplied with an annual report containing at least the minimum amount of information required by the Companies Act 2006. The company also has to file (as it is called) a copy of the report with the Registrar of Companies. This means that on payment of a small fee the report is open to inspection by any member of the public who wants to consult it. Some companies (defined as small or medium-sized) are permitted to file an abbreviated version of their annual report with the registrar, although the full report must still be sent to their shareholders.

The disclosure requirements are shown in summary form in Figure 5.4.

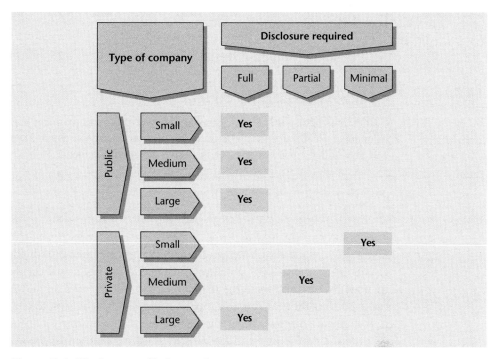

Figure 5.4 Disclosure of information

Accounts

Company accounts are very similar to those of sole traders. They do, however, tend to be more detailed and some modifications have to be made in order to comply with various legal requirements.

Directors

A limited liability company must always be regarded as a separate entity, i.e. separate from those shareholders who own it collectively and separate from anyone who works for it. This means that all those who are employed by it are its employees, no matter how senior they are. Nevertheless, someone has to take responsibility for the management of the company and so the shareholders usually delegate that responsibility to *directors.*

Directors are the most senior level of management. They are responsible for the day-to-day running of the company and they answer to the shareholders. Any remuneration paid to them as directors is charged as an expense of the business. They may also be shareholders but any dividends that they receive are regarded as being a private matter. They should not be confused with any payments that they receive as directors.

The distinction between employees and shareholder–employees is important even if the sole member of a private company works full time in the business. The same requirement applies to public companies except that they must have at least two members. As we have emphasized throughout the chapter, in law the company is regarded as being a separate entity. Even if there are just two shareholders who both work full-time for the company, the company is still treated as distinct from that of the two individuals who happen to own it. They may take decisions that appear to affect no one else except themselves but because they operate the company under the protection of limited liability they have certain obligations as well as rights. As a result they are not as free to run the company as they would be if it were (say) a partnership.

Dividends

News clip

Dividend pay-out

Between 2000 and 2006 Sanyo, the Japanese electronics group, admitted that it had added up its figures incorrectly. This meant that its losses over this period were greater than had been reported and that it had paid out 28 billion yen too much in dividends.

Source: Adapted from *The Guardian*, 27 December 2007, p. 38.

Profits are usually distributed to shareholders in the form of a dividend. A dividend is calculated on the basis of so many pence per share. The actual dividend will be recommended by the directors to the shareholders. It will be based on the amount of net profit earned during the year and how much profit the directors want to retain in the business.

A dividend may have been paid during the year as an *interim dividend*, i.e. a payment on account. At the year end the directors may recommend a *final* dividend. The final dividend has to be approved by the shareholders at a general meeting.

Taxation

Taxation is another feature which clearly distinguishes a limited liability company from that of a sole trader entity. Sole traders do not have tax levied on them as entities. Instead, tax is levied on the amount of profit the owner has made during the year. The tax payable is a private matter and in accordance with the entity rule, it lies outside the boundary of the entity. Any tax that appears to have been paid by the entity on the owner's behalf is treated as part of the owner's drawings, i.e. an amount paid as part of the share of the profits.

Activity 5.2

Assume that you would like to start a small business of your own. You have heard that a limited liability company will not make you bankrupt if it is unsuccessful. So you decide to form a company.

List three advantages and three disadvantages in the table below of running your business as a limited liability company.

Advantages	Disadvantages
(1)	(1)
(2)	(2)
(3)	(3)

Companies are treated quite differently. They are taxed in their own right like individuals. They have their own form of taxation known as *corporation tax*. Corporation tax was introduced in 1965 and all companies are eligible to pay it. It is based on the company's accounting profit for a particular financial year. The accounting profit has to be adjusted, however, because some items are treated differently for tax purposes, e.g. the depreciation of fixed assets. Any corporation tax due at the year end is treated as a current liability.

Now that we have outlined the basic structure and operation of limited liability companies we can begin to examine company accounts in some detail. We start with the profit and loss account.

The profit and loss account

News clip

Concealed costs

A £16.5m fraud was uncovered at the Scottish mineral water division of Greencore, the Irish good group. It appears that the internal auditors found that 'significant costs' had been concealed.

Source: Adapted from www.accountancyage.com/2223234.

As we suggested earlier, the preparation of a company's trading and profit and loss account is basically no different from that of sole trader entities. Almost an identical format or structure may be adopted and it is only after the net profit stage that some differences become apparent. Company accounts usually include a *profit and loss appropriation account*. Such an account is usually placed below the profit and loss account although no clear dividing line may be drawn between them. An example of a company's profit and loss appropriation account is shown in Example 5.1.

Example 5.1

A company's profit and loss appropriation account

	£000
Net profit for the year before taxation	1 000
Taxation	(300)
Net profit for the year after taxation	700
Dividends	(500)
Retained profit for the year	200

You can see from Example 5.1, that the company's net profit for the year is appropriated (or used) in three ways:

- to pay tax;
- to pay dividends;
- for retention within the business.

Activity 5.3

Complete the following equations.

(a) _____ – taxation = net profit for the year after taxation.

(b) Net profit for the year after taxation – _____ = retained profit for the year.

The balance sheet

Going, going ...

ITN's accounts show a £39.9 million pension deficit, an increase of £17.7 million over the previous year. The deficit was likely to be 'significantly higher' in the following year. It is possible that the broadcasting giant would be unable to continue trading as there is 'uncertainty over future funding requirements'.

Source: Adapted from www.accountancyage.com/articles, 29 May 2009.

The structure of a limited liability company's balance sheet is also very similar to that of a sole trader. The main difference arises because of the company's capital structure although there are some other features that are not usually found in non-company balance sheets.

The main features of a company's balance sheet are shown in Example 5.2. It includes a number of tutorial notes which will help you as you work through the example.

Example 5.2

A company's balance sheet

Exhibitor Ltd
Balance sheet at 31 March 2011

	£000	£000	£000
Fixed assets			600
Investments (1)			100
Current assets		6 000	
Less: Current liabilities			
Trade creditors	2 950		
Accruals	50		
Corporation tax (2)	300		
Proposed dividend (3)	500	3 800	2 200
			2 900

	Authorized	Issued and fully paid
Financed by:		
Capital and reserves (4):		
	£000	£000
Ordinary shares of £1 each (5)	2 000	1 500
Preference shares of £0.50 each (5)	500	500
	2 500	2 000
Capital reserves (6)		200
Revenue reserves (7)		600
Shareholders' funds (8)		2 800
Loans (9)		100
		2 900

Note: The number shown after each narration refers to the tutorial notes below.

Tutorial notes to Example 5.2

1 *Investments.* This item usually represents long-term investments in the shares of other companies. Short-term investments (such as money invested in bank deposit accounts) would be included in current assets. The shares may be either in public or private limited liability companies. The market price of the investments should be stated. A directors' valuation should be obtained if this is not available.

2 *Corporation tax.* This represents the outstanding tax due on the company's profits for the year.

3 *Proposed dividend.* This will probably be due for payment very shortly after the year end, and so it will usually be shown as a current liability.

4 *Capital and reserves.* Details of the authorized, issued and fully paid-up share capital should be shown.

5 *Ordinary shares and preference shares.* Details about the different types of shares that the company has issued should be disclosed.

6 *Capital reserves.* This section may include several different reserve accounts of a capital nature, i.e. amounts that are not available for distribution to the shareholders as dividend. It might include, for example, a share premium account (an extra amount paid by shareholders in excess of the nominal value of the shares). The premium does not rank for dividend but prospective shareholders are sometimes willing to pay it if they think that the shares are particularly attractive. Another example of a capital reserve is that of an asset that has been revalued. The difference between the original cost and the revalued amount will be credited to a *revaluation* reserve account.

7 *Revenue reserves.* Revenue reserve accounts are amounts that are available for distribution to the shareholders. Any profits retained in the business and not paid out to shareholders may be included under this heading. Retained profits are normally shown separately under the heading 'profit and loss account'.

8 *Shareholders' funds.* The total amount available to shareholders at the balance sheet date is equal to the share capital originally subscribed plus all the capital and revenue reserve account balances.

9 *Loans.* The loans section of the balance sheet will include all the long-term loans obtained by the company, i.e. those loans that do not have to be repaid for at least twelve months, such as debentures and long-term bank loans.

Activity 5.4	State in which section of the balance sheet you are likely to find the following items.

(a) Amount owing for corporation tax.
(b) Debenture stock.
(c) Plant and machinery.
(d) Preference shares.
(e) Trade debtors.

A comprehensive example

Example 5.3 brings together the material covered in this chapter.

Example 5.3	**Preparation of a company's accounts**

The following information has been extracted from the books of Handy Ltd as at 31 March 2011:

	Dr £	Cr £
Bank	2 000	
Capital: 100 000 issued and fully paid ordinary shares of £1 each		100 000
50 000 issued and fully paid 8% preference shares of £1 each		50 000
Debenture loan stock (10%: repayable 2025)		30 000
Debenture loan stock interest	3 000	
Dividends received		700
Dividends paid: Ordinary interim	5 000	
Preference	4 000	
Freehold land at cost	200 000	
Investments (listed: market value at 31 March 2011 was £11 000)	10 000	
Office expenses	47 000	
Motor van at cost	15 000	
Motor van: accumulated depreciation (at 1 April 2010)		6 000
Motor van expenses	2 700	
Purchases	220 000	
Retained profits (at 1 April 2010)		9 000
Sales		300 000
Share premium account		10 000
Stocks at cost (at 1 April 2010)	20 000	
Trade creditors		50 000
Trade debtors	27 000	
	555 700	555 700

Additional information:
1 The stocks at 31 March 2011 were valued at their historical cost of £40,000.
2 Depreciation is to be charged on the motor van at a rate of 20 per cent per annum on cost. No depreciation is to be charged on the freehold land.

3 The corporation tax for the year has been estimated to be £10,000.

4 The directors propose a final ordinary dividend of 10p per share.

5 The authorized share capital of the company is as follows:

    (a) 150,000 ordinary shares of £1 each; and

    (b) 75,000 preference shares of £1 each.

Required:

(a) Prepare Handy Ltd's trading and profit and loss account for the year to 31 March 2011.

(b) Prepare a balance sheet as at that date.

Answer to Example 5.3(a)

Handy Ltd
Trading and profit and loss account for the year to 31 March 2011

	£	£	£
Sales			300 000
Less: Cost of goods sold:			
Opening stocks		20 000	
Purchases		220 000	
		240 000	
Less: Closing stocks		40 000	200 000
Gross profit			100 000
Add: Incomes:			
Dividends received			700
Less: Expenditure:			100 700
Debenture loan stock interest		3 000	
Motor van depreciation (1)	3 000		
Motor van expenses	2 700	5 700	
Office expenses		47 000	
			55 700
Net profit for the year before taxation			45 000
Less: Corporation tax (2)			10 000
Net profit for the year after taxation			35 000
Less: Dividends (3):			
Preference dividend paid (8%)		4 000	
Interim ordinary paid (5p per share)		5 000	
Proposed final ordinary dividend			
(10p per share)		10 000	19 000
Retained profit for the year			16 000
Retained profits brought forward			9 000
Retained profits carried forward (4)			25 000

Answer to Example 5.3(b)

Handy Ltd Balance sheet at 31 March 2011

	£	£	£
Fixed assets	Cost	Accumulated depreciation	
Freehold land (5)	200 000	–	200 000
Motor van (6)	15 000	9 000	6 000
	215 000	9 000	206 000
c/f			206 000

Answer to Example 5.3(a) *continued*

	£	£	£
	b/f		206 000
Investments			
At cost (market value at 31 March 2011: £11 000) (7)			10 000
Current assets			
Stocks at cost		40 000	
Trade debtors		27 000	
Bank		2 000	
		69 000	
Less: Current liabilities			
Trade creditors	50 000		
Corporation tax (8)	10 000		
Proposed ordinary dividend (9)	10 000	70 000	
Net current assets			(1 000)
			215 000

	Authorized	Issued and fully paid
Financed by:		
Capital and reserves		
Ordinary shares of £1 each (10)	150 000	100 000
Preference shares of £1 each (10)	75 000	50 000
	225 000	150 000
Share premium account (11)		10 000
Retained profits (12)		25 000
Shareholders' funds (13)		185 000
Loans (14)		
10% debenture stock (repayable 2025)		30 000
		215 000

Note: The number shown after each narration refers to the following tutorial notes.

Tutorial notes

1 Depreciation has been charged on the motor van at a rate of 20 per cent per annum on cost (as instructed in question note 2).

2 Question note 3 requires £10,000 to be charged as corporation tax. Corporation tax is applied to the taxable profit and not to the accounting profit. The taxable profit has not been given in the question.

3 A proposed ordinary dividend of 10p has been included as instructed in question note 4.

4 The total retained profit of £25,000 is carried forward to the balance sheet (see tutorial note 12 below).

5 Question note 2 states that no depreciation is to be charged on the freehold land.

6 The accumulated depreciation for the motor van of £9000 is the total of the accumulated depreciation brought forward at 1 April 2010 of £6000, plus the £3000 written off to the profit and loss account for the current year (see tutorial note 1 above).

7 Note that the market value of the investments has been disclosed on the face of the balance sheet.

**Answer to
Example 5.3(b)**
continued

8 The corporation tax charged against profit (question note 3) will be due for payment in 2012. The amount due is treated as a current liability (this requirement is different for public companies).

9 The proposed ordinary dividend will be due for payment shortly after the year end and so it is also a current liability. The interim dividend and the preference dividend have already been paid so they are not current liabilities.

10 Details of the authorized, issued and fully paid share capital should be disclosed.

11 The share premium is a capital account: it cannot be used for the payment of dividends. It will normally remain unchanged in successive balance sheets although there are a few highly restricted purposes for which it may be used.

12 The retained profits become part of a revenue account balance that could be used for the payment of dividends. The total retained profits of £25,000 is the amount brought in to the balance sheet from the profit and loss account.

13 The total amount of shareholders' funds should always be shown.

14 The loans are long-term loans. Loans are not part of shareholders' funds and so they need to be shown separately in the balance sheet.

❗ Questions you should ask

Many of the questions that we have suggested in previous chapters that non-accountants should ask are of relevance in this chapter. For example, the various accounting rules adopted by the accountants in preparing the company's profit and loss and balance sheet, especially those with a significant impact on revenue, stock valuation, depreciation and provisions for bad and doubtful debts.

The following questions relate particularly to this chapter.

- Can our accounting records disclose with reasonable accuracy (as the 2006 Companies Act requires) our financial position at any time?
- Do the accounting records contain entries for all money received and spent?
- Do they also contain a record of all assets and all liabilities?
- Do the accounting records include a statement of the stock held at the financial year end?
- Are there details of stocktaking from which the statement of stock has been compiled?
- Is a record kept of all goods sold and purchased as well as all the buyers and sellers so that they can all be identified?
- Have both the profit and loss account and the balance sheet been prepared in accordance both with the requirements of the Companies Act 2006 and with recommended practice?
- Do the accounts genuinely represent a 'time and fair' view of the company's affairs?

Conclusion

This chapter has briefly examined the structure and content of limited liability company accounts using a number of simple examples. Although a great deal of information can be obtained from studying the annual accounts of a company, it is difficult to extract the most relevant and significant features. Some further guidance is needed, therefore, in how to make the best use of the financial accounting information presented to you. This will be provided in Chapters 7 to 10, but first we need to examine some other types of account. We do so in the next chapter.

Key points

1 The financial statements of a company are similar in format (i.e. structure) to those of sole traders.

2 The profits of a company are taxed separately (like an individual). The tax is based on the accounting profit for the year. Any tax due at the year end will be shown in the balance sheet as a current liability.

3 The net profit after tax may be paid to shareholders in the form of a dividend although some profit will normally be retained in the business. Proposed dividends should be shown in the balance sheet as a creditor. This requirement is, however, different for public companies. See Chapter 9.

Check your learning

The answers to these questions can be found within the text.

1 What is meant by 'limited liability'?

2 When was it first incorporated into company law?

3 Why was it found necessary to do so?

4 Distinguish between the authorized, issued and fully paid share capital of a company.

5 Name two main types of shares.

6 What is the basic difference between them?

7 What are the two main types of limited liability companies?

8 What is a debenture loan?

9 What is meant by 'disclosure of information'?

10 Why do companies have to let the Registrar of Companies have certain types of information?

11 What is a director?

12 What is a dividend?

13 Name two types of dividend.

14 What name is given to the tax that a company pays on its profits?

15 Name three ways in which a company's profits are appropriated.

16 List three types of assets.

17 Name three items that may be included under the heading of 'current liabilities'.

18 Distinguish between a capital reserve and a revenue reserve.

19 What is a share premium account?

20 What is meant by 'shareholders' funds'?

21 What is the difference between a short-term loan and a long-term loan?

News story quiz

Remember the news story at the beginning of this chapter? Go back to that story and reread it before answering the following questions.

This is yet another report of a fraud – this time in India. You will recall that it is not the duty of the external auditors to discover any fraud that might have taken place. Their responsibility is to report that the accounts represent 'a true and fair view' (at least in the UK). Based on what you have learned so far about accounting and book-keeping, suggest some plausible answers to the following questions.

Questions

1 How could one man on his own fix the company's books on such a grand scale?

2 How do you think it was possible to inflate the group's profit by a margin of 24 per cent?

3 How is it possible for 94 per cent of cash (£685m out of £728m) to be 'fictitious'?

Tutorial questions

The answers to question marked with an asterisk may be found in Appendix 4.

5.1 'The concept of limited liability is an out-of-date nineteenth-century concept.' Discuss.

5.2 Appleton used to operate her business as a sole trader entity. She has recently converted it into a limited liability company. Appleton owns 80 per cent of the ordinary (voting) shares, the remaining 20 per cent being held by various relatives and friends. Explain to Appleton why it is now inaccurate for her to describe the company as 'her' business.

5.3 How far do you think that the information presented in a limited liability company's profit and loss account and balance sheet is useful to the owners of a small business?

5.4* The following balances have been extracted from the books of Margo Ltd for the year to 31 January 2010:

	Dr	Cr
	£000	£000
Cash at bank and in hand	5	
Plant and equipment:		
At cost	70	
Accumulated depreciation (at 31.1.10)		25
Profit and loss account (at 1.2.09)		15
Profit for the financial year (to 31.1.10)		10
Share capital (issued and fully paid)		50
Stocks (at 31.1.10)	17	
Trade creditors		12
Trade debtors	20	
	112	112

Additional information:
1 Corporation tax owing at 31 January 2010 is estimated to be £3000.
2 Margo Ltd's authorized share capital is £75,000 of £1 ordinary shares.
3 A dividend of 10p per share is proposed.

Required:
Prepare Margo Ltd's profit and loss account for the year to 31 January 2010 and a balance sheet as at that date.

5.5* Harry Ltd was formed in 2003. The following balances as at 28 February 2011 have been extracted from the books of account after the trading account has been compiled:

	Dr	Cr
	£000	£000
Administration expenses	65	
Cash at bank and in hand	10	
Distribution costs	15	
Dividend paid (on preference shares)	6	
Furniture and equipment:		
At cost	60	
Accumulated depreciation at 1.3.10		36
Gross profit for the year		150
Ordinary share capital (shares of £1 each)		100
Preference shares (cumulative 15% of £1 shares)		40
Profit and loss account (at 1.3.10)		50
Share premium account		20
Stocks (at 28.2.11)	130	
Trade creditors		25
Trade debtors	135	
	421	421

Additional information:
1 Corporation tax owing at 28 February 2011 is estimated to be £24,000.
2 Furniture and equipment is depreciated at an annual rate of 10 per cent of cost and it is all charged against administrative expenses.

3 A dividend of 20p per ordinary share is proposed.
4 All the authorized share capital has been issued and is fully paid.

Required:
Prepare Harry Ltd's profit and loss account for the year to 28 February 2011 and a balance sheet as at that date.

5.6* The following balances have been extracted from the books of Jim Ltd as at 31 March 2011:

	Dr £000	Cr £000
Advertising	3	
Bank	11	
Creditors		12
Debtors	118	
Furniture and fittings:		
At cost	20	
Accumulated depreciation (at 1.4.10)		9
Directors' fees	6	
Profit and loss account (at 1.4.10)		8
Purchases	124	
Rent and rates	10	
Sales		270
Share capital (issued and fully paid)		70
Stock (at 1.4.10)	16	
Telephone and stationery	5	
Travelling expenses	2	
Vehicles:		
At cost	40	
Accumulated depreciation (at 1.4.10)		10
Wages and salaries	24	
	379	379

Additional information:
1 Stock at 31 March 2011 was valued at £14,000.
2 Furniture and fittings, and the vehicles are depreciated at a rate of 15 per cent and 25 per cent, respectively, on cost.
3 Corporation tax owing at 31 March 2011 is estimated to be £25,000.
4 A dividend of 40p per share is proposed.
5 The company's authorized share capital is £100,000 of £1 ordinary shares.

Required:
(a) Prepare Jim Ltd's trading and profit and loss account for the year to 31 March 2011 and a balance sheet as at that date.
(b) Why would the business not necessarily be worth its balance sheet value as at 31 March 2011?

5.7 The following trial balance has been extracted from Carol Ltd as at 30 April 2012:

	Dr £000	Cr £000
Advertising	2	
Bank overdraft		20
Bank interest paid	4	
Creditors		80
Debtors	143	
Directors' remuneration	30	
Freehold land and buildings:		
At cost	800	
Accumulated depreciation at 1.5.11		102
General expenses	15	
Investments at cost	30	
Investment income		5
Motor vehicles:		
At cost	36	
Accumulated depreciation (at 1.5.11)		18
Preference dividend paid	15	
Preference shares (cumulative 10% shares of £1 each)		150
Profit and loss account (at 1.5.11)		100
Purchases	480	
Repairs and renewals	4	
Sales		900
Share capital (authorized, issued and fully paid ordinary shares of £1 each)		500
Share premium account		25
Stock (at 1.5.11)	120	
Wages and salaries	221	
	1900	1900

Additional information:
1 Stock at 30 April 2012 was valued at £140,000.
2 Depreciation for the year of £28,000 is to be provided on buildings and £9000 for motor vehicles.
3 A provision of £6000 is required for the auditors' remuneration.
4 £2000 had been paid in advance for renewals.
5 Corporation tax owing at 30 April 2012 is estimated to be £60,000.
6 The directors propose an ordinary dividend of 10p per share.
7 The market value of the investments at 30 April 2012 was £35,000.

Required:
Prepare Carol Ltd's trading and profit and loss account for the year to 30 April 2012 and a balance sheet as at that date.

5.8 Nelson Ltd was incorporated in 2003 with an authorized share capital of 500,000 £1 ordinary shares, and 200,000 5 per cent cumulative preference shares of £1 each. The following trial balance was extracted as at 31 May 2011:

	Dr £000	Cr £000
Administrative expenses	257	
Auditor's fees	10	
Cash at bank and in hand	5	
Creditors		85
Debentures (12%)		100
Debenture interest paid	6	
Debtors	225	
Directors' remuneration	60	
Dividends paid:		
Ordinary interim	20	
Preference	5	
Furniture, fittings and equipment:		
At cost	200	
Accumulated depreciation at 1.6.10		48
Investments at cost (market value at 31.5.11:		
£340 000)	335	
Investment income		22
Ordinary share capital (issued and fully paid)		400
Preference share capital		200
Profit and loss account (at 1.6.10)		17
Purchases	400	
Sales		800
Share premium account		50
Stock at 1.6.10	155	
Wages and salaries	44	
	1 722	1 722

Additional information:
1 Stock at 31 May 2011 was valued at £195,000.
2 Administrative expenses owing at 31 May 2011 amounted to £13,000.
3 Depreciation is to be charged on the furniture and fittings at a rate of $12\frac{1}{2}$ per cent on cost.
4 Salaries paid in advance amounted to £4000.
5 Corporation tax owing at 31 May 2011 is estimated to be £8000.
6 Provision is to be made for a final ordinary dividend of 1.25p per share.

Required:
Prepare Nelson Ltd's trading and profit and loss account for the year to 31 May 2011 and a balance sheet as at that date.

5.9 The following trial balance has been extracted from the books of Keith Ltd as at 30 June 2011:

	Dr £000	Cr £000
Advertising	30	
Bank	7	
Creditors		69
Debentures (10%)		70
Debtors (all trade)	300	
Directors' remuneration	55	
Electricity	28	
Insurance	17	
Investments (quoted)	28	
Investment income		4
Machinery:		
At cost	420	
Accumulated depreciation at 1.7.10		152
Office expenses	49	
Ordinary share capital (issued and fully paid)		200
Preference shares		50
Preference share dividend	4	
Profit and loss account (at 1.7.10)		132
Provision for bad and doubtful debts		8
Purchases	1 240	
Rent and rates	75	
Sales		2 100
Stock (at 1.7.10)	134	
Vehicles:		
At cost	80	
Accumulated depreciation (at 1.7.10)		40
Wages and salaries	358	
	2 825	2 825

Additional information:
1 Stock at 30 June 2011 valued at cost amounted to £155,000.
2 Depreciation is to be provided on machinery and vehicles at a rate of 20 per cent and 25 per cent respectively on cost.
3 Provision is to be made for auditors' remuneration of £12,000.
4 Insurance paid in advance at 30 June 2011 amounted to £3000.
5 The provision for bad and doubtful debts is to be made equal to 5 per cent of outstanding trade debtors as at 30 June 2011.
6 Corporation tax owing at 30 June 2011 is estimated to be £60,000.
7 An ordinary dividend of 10p per share is proposed.
8 The investments had a market value of £30,000 at 30 June 2011.
9 The company has an authorized share capital of 600,000 ordinary shares of £0.50 each and of 50,000 8 per cent cumulative preference shares of £1 each.

Required:

(a) Prepare Keith Ltd's trading and profit and loss account for the year to 30 June 2011 and a balance sheet as at that date.

(b) Explain why shareholders of Keith Ltd would not necessarily have been able to sell the business for its balance sheet value as at 30 June 2011.

Further practice questions, study material and links to relevant sites on the World Wide Web can be found on the website that accompanies this book. The site can be found at **www.pearsoned.co.uk/dyson**

Other entity accounts

Getting better . . .

Unqualified sign-off for EU accounts

The National Audit Office has issued a report summarising the results of the European Court of Auditors' examination of the European Union's accounts for 2007 and progress on initiatives by the European Commission and member states. For the first time the court gave a positive statement of assurance, without qualification, on the reliability of the accounts in effect, confirming that they provide a true and fair view. But for the 14th successive year it did not provide a positive statement of assurance on whether the underlying transactions conformed to the applicable laws and regulations.

The most troublesome area is cohesion policy funds, which are designed to reduce disparities in the level of development between regions of the EU – for example, by supporting infrastructure projects. The court estimates that at least 11 per cent of expenditure on cohesion schemes should not have been reimbursed by the commission in 2007. This reflects weakness in controls at member state level as well as the difficulty of implementing such complex programmes. But the commission has increased the rate at which it recovers incorrect payments for cohesion schemes from member states: from €287m in 2007 to €843m to September 2008.

'Recent initiatives have started to improve the financial management of EU funds, but a positive statement of assurance on the legality and regularity of expenditure has yet to be achieved' said Tim Burr, head of the National Audit Office. 'The implementation of cohesion policy remains the chief source of error. The commission will soon start work with member states on the design of future programmes.'

Source: *Financial Management*, May 2009.

Source: Reproduced with permission from CIMA.

Questions relating to this news story can be found on page 142 ➡

About this chapter

In previous chapters we have shown you how to compile a set of financial statements and explained what they tell you by using examples from private sector sole trader businesses and limited liability companies. However, we would be presenting an unbalanced and unhelpful view of accounting if we did not also refer to the many other types of private and public entities.

In a book of this nature we cannot possibly deal with every conceivable type of entity that you may come across but fortunately we do not need to. In broad terms the accounting requirements are usually similar to those of sole traders and companies and all that is possibly required is some technical specialist advice, e.g. if the entity is an investment bank or an insurance company. The main difference is more in the way that their financial statements are presented rather than in their accounting methods.

By the time that you get to the end of this book you will find that you will have gained sufficient knowledge and confidence to be able to find your way around almost any type of financial statement no matter whether it is in the private or the public sector and irrespective of its organization, size and type.

This chapter is yet another step towards achieving that goal.

Learning objectives

By the end of this chapter you should be able to:

- **prepare a simple manufacturing account;**
- **describe the type of financial statements required by service sector entities;**
- **compare and contrast financial statements in the profit-making sector with those in the not-for-profit sector;**
- **state why accounting procedures in the public sector may be different from those in the private sector.**

! Why this chapter is important

This chapter is important for non-accountants because it will give you a more balanced and a more well-rounded appreciation of accounting and the presentation of accounting information in different types of entities.

Most accounting textbooks concentrate on looking at accounting practices in the private profit-making sector, especially those relating to manufacturing and trading entities. However, the service sector now forms a significant element in the private sector, so it would be misleading to ignore the accounting procedures in that sector. Similarly, in the not-for-profit sector there are many types of entities (such as charities and voluntary bodies) that play an important part in the life of many people. The Government too has a major impact on economic life and so we must also have a brief look at its method of accounting.

The relatively few other types of entity that we cover in this chapter will give you an indication of how basic accounting practices are used (with some modification) in other kinds of entity. You will also find that if you are involved in such entities you can adapt your accounting knowledge to suit the requirements of different entity. Many non-accountants, for example, will be members of various social and sporting clubs so the accounting knowledge that you have gained by working your way through this book will enable you to assess the financial position and future prospects of such entities with relative ease. Indeed, you may already have come across misleading statements prepared by club treasurers, such as calling a summary of cash received and cash paid a 'balance sheet'! Mistakes like this may not be very serious but they will certainly confuse the club members and give them a false impression of the club's assets and liabilities.

It is to be hoped that after reading this book in general, and this chapter in particular, you will not make such mistakes – or other, much more serious ones.

Manufacturing accounts

An organization that purchases or obtains raw materials and converts them to a finished goods state is known as a *manufacturing* entity. The finished goods are then sold to customers. Manufacturing entities are normally to be found in the private sector and they may operate as sole traders, partnerships or companies.

Unlike the examples we have used in previous chapters, manufacturing entities are not likely to use a *purchases* account. This is because they normally buy raw materials and then process them before they are sold as *finished goods*. So before the trading account can be compiled it is necessary to calculate the cost of converting the raw materials into finished goods. The conversion cost is called the *manufacturing cost* and it is the equivalent of a trading entity's purchases.

In order to calculate an entity's manufacturing cost, we need to prepare a *manufacturing account*. A manufacturing account forms part of the double-entry system and it is included in the periodic financial statements. It normally contains only manufacturing *costs* since it is rare to have any manufacturing *incomes*.

Manufacturing costs are debited to the manufacturing account. They are usually classified into *direct* and *indirect* costs. Direct costs are those costs that can be easily and economically identified with a particular segment (economically means at the least possible cost). A segment may be a department, a section, a product or a unit. Indirect costs are those costs that cannot be easily and economically identified with a particular segment. Indirect costs are sometimes referred to as 'overhead' or 'overheads'.

The format of the manufacturing account is straightforward. Normally, it contains two main sections itemizing the direct and the indirect costs. Each section is then analysed into what are called the *elements of cost*. The elements of cost include materials, labour and other expenses.

Example 6.1 illustrates the format of a typical manufacturing account. A detailed explanation of its contents follows.

Construction of the account

In this section, we are going to explain how to construct a manufacturing account. We use Example 6.2 to do so.

Example 6.1	**Format of a basic manufacturing account**		
		£000	*£000*
	Direct costs (1)		
	Direct materials (2)	20	
	Direct labour (3)	70	
	Other direct expenses (4)	5	
	Prime cost (5)		95
	Manufacturing overhead (6)		
	Indirect material cost (7)	3	
	Indirect labour cost (7)	7	
	Other indirect expenses (7)	10	
	Total manufacturing overhead incurred (8)		20
	Total manufacturing costs incurred (9)		115
	Work-in-progress (10)		
	Opening work-in-progress	10	
	Closing work-in-progress	(15)	(5)
	Manufacturing cost of goods produced (11)		110
	Manufacturing profit (12)		11
	Market value of goods produced transferred to the trading account (13)		121

Notes:

(a) The number shown after each item refers to the tutorial notes. The values have been inserted purely for illustrative purposes.

(b) The term 'factory' or 'work' is sometimes substituted for the term manufacturing.

Tutorial notes to Example 6.1

1 *Direct costs.* The exhibit relates to a *company's* manufacturing account. It is assumed that the direct costs listed for materials, labour and other expenses relate to those expenses that have been easy to identify with the specific products manufactured by the company.

2 *Direct materials.* The charge for direct materials will be calculated as follows:

direct material cost = (opening stock of raw materials + purchases of raw materials) – closing stock of raw materials

The total of direct material cost is sometimes referred to as *materials consumed*. Direct materials will include all the raw material costs and component parts that have been easy to identify with particular products.

3 *Direct labour.* This will include all those employment costs that have been easy to identify with particular products.

4 *Other direct expenses.* Besides direct materials and direct labour costs, there are sometimes other direct expenses that are easy to identify with particular products, e.g. the cost of hiring a specific machine. Such expenses are relatively rare.

5 *Prime cost.* The total of direct material costs, direct labour costs and other direct expenses is known as prime cost.

6 *Manufacturing overhead.* Overhead refers to the total of all indirect costs and so any manufacturing costs that are not easy to identify with specific products will be classified separately under this heading.

Tutorial notes to Example 7.1 continued

7 *Indirect material cost, indirect labour cost and other indirect expenses.* Manufacturing overhead will probably be shown separately under these three headings.

8 *Total manufacturing overhead incurred.* This item represents the total of indirect material cost, indirect labour cost and other indirect expenses.

9 *Total manufacturing costs incurred.* The total of prime cost and total manufacturing overhead incurred equals the total manufacturing costs incurred.

10 *Work-in-progress.* This represents the estimated cost of incomplete work that is not yet ready to be transferred to finished stock. There will usually be some opening and closing work-in-progress.

11 *Manufacturing cost of goods produced.* This equals the total manufacturing costs incurred plus (or minus) the difference between the opening and closing work-in-progress.

12 *Manufacturing profit.* The manufacturing cost of goods produced may be transferred straight to the finished goods stock account. The finished goods stock account is the equivalent of the purchases account in a trading organization. Sometimes a manufacturing profit is added to the manufacturing cost of goods produced before it is transferred to the trading account. The main purpose of this adjustment is to enable management to compare more fairly the company's total manufacturing cost (inclusive of profit) with outside prices (since such prices will also normally include some profit). The profit added to the manufacturing cost of goods produced may simply be an appropriate percentage or it may represent the level of profit that the industry generally expects to earn. Any profit element added to the manufacturing cost (irrespective of how it is calculated) is an internal bookkeeping arrangement, because the profit has not been earned or *realized* outside the business. It is what accountants call a 'book entry'.

13 *Market value of goods produced.* As explained in note 12 above, the market value of goods produced is the amount that will be transferred (i.e. debited) to the trading account.

Activity 6.1

Do you think that the structure of a manufacturing account makes it easy to follow? Check that you clear about the meaning of each individual item. What does the information tell you about the cost of manufacturing during the period in question?

Example 6.2

Constructing a manufacturing account

The following balances, *inter alia*, have been extracted from the Wren Manufacturing Company as at 31 March 2011:

	Dr
	£
Carriage inwards (on raw materials)	6 000
Direct expenses	3 000
Direct wages	25 000
Factory administration	6 000
Factory heat and light	500
Factory power	1 500
Factory rent and rates	2 000
Factory supervisory costs	5 000
Purchase of raw materials	56 000
Raw materials stock (at 1 April 2010)	4 000
Work-in-progress (at 1 April 2010)	5 000

Additional information:
1   The stock of raw materials at 31 March 2011 was valued at £6000.
2   The work-in-progress at 31 March 2011 was valued at £8000.
3   A profit loading of 50 per cent is added to the total cost of manufacture.

Required:
Prepare Wren's manufacturing account for the year to 31 March 2011.

Answer to Example 6.2

Wren Manufacturing Company
Manufacturing account for the year to 31 March 2011

	£	£	£
Direct materials			
Raw material stock at 1 April 2010		4000	
Purchases	56000		
Carriage inwards (1)	6000	62000	
		66000	
Less: Raw material stock at 31 March 2011		6000	
Cost of materials consumed			60000
Direct wages			25000
Direct expenses			3000
Prime cost			88000
Other manufacturing costs (2)			
Administration		6000	
Heat and light		500	
Power		1500	
Rent and rates		2000	
Supervisory		5000	
Total manufacturing overhead expenses		15000	
			103000
Work-in-progress			
Add: Work-in-progress at 1 April 2010		5000	
Less: Work-in-progress at 31 March 2011		(8000)	(3000)
Manufacturing cost of goods produced			100000
Manufacturing profit (50%) (3)			50000
Market value of goods produced (4)			150000

Tutorial notes

1   Carriage inwards (i.e. the cost of transporting goods to the factory) is normally regarded as being part of the cost of purchases.

2   Other manufacturing costs include production overhead expenses. In practice there would be a considerable number of other manufacturing costs.

3   A profit loading of 50 per cent has been added to the manufacturing cost (see question note 3). The manufacturing profit is a debit entry in the manufacturing account. The corresponding credit entry will eventually be made in the profit and loss account.

4   The market value of goods produced will be transferred to the finished goods stock account.

Links with the other accounts

Example 6.2 deals with the manufacturing account in isolation. However, once the manufacturing account has been prepared it will then be linked with the trading account and the profit and loss account by transferring either the *manufacturing cost* of the goods produced or the *market value* of the goods produced to the trading account. The manufacturing cost or the market value of the goods produced is, therefore, the equivalent of 'purchases' in the trading account of a non-manufacturing entity. Apart from this minor amendment, the preparation of a trading account for a manufacturing entity is exactly the same as that for a trading entity. This relationship is shown in outline in Figure 6.1.

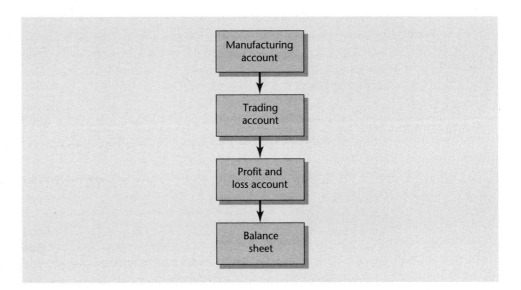

Figure 6.1 The relationship between the main accounts

Service entity accounts

The profit-making sector is made up of a great many other types of entity beside those that may be classified as manufacturing or trading. For convenience we will describe them as *service entities*. Unlike manufacturing or trading entities, service entities do not normally deal in physical or tangible goods. Instead they offer advice and provide assistance to their customers, clients, patients or passengers. In recent years the manufacturing sector in the United Kingdom has declined and the service sector has become much more important.

The service sector is extremely diverse, but there are a number of recognizable categories. Some of the main ones are as follows.

- *Hotels and catering.* Such entities are generally regarded as being part of the service sector although the service they offer includes a physical or tangible element, e.g. the supply of food and drink.
- *Leisure and recreational activities.* Services included in this category include cinema, concerts and theatre productions, leisure and sports centres, and travel agencies.

● *Personal.* Examples of personal services include beauticians, hairdressing and manicuring.
● *Professional.* The more common professional services include accounting, legal and medical (including chiropody and optical).
● *Transportation.* Transportation services include the movement of goods and passengers by air, land and sea.

<table>
<tr><td>**Activity 6.2**</td><td>Think of the main street in your own town or city. List six different types of service entitity.</td></tr>
</table>

It will be apparent from the above summary that there is an extremely wide variety of different types of service entities. This means that the accounts of different entities will also be somewhat different, e.g. the accounts of a beautician will not be identical to those of a railway company. Nevertheless, there are some basic features that are common to all service sector entities and that distinguish them from manufacturing and trading entities. These may be summarized as follows:

1 *No manufacturing and trading accounts.* These accounts are irrelevant in service entities because they do not normally manufacture products or trade in tangible goods.
2 *No gross profit.* As service entities do not prepare trading accounts the calculation of gross profit is irrelevant.
3 *Primacy of the profit and loss account.* Details of the income and expenditure for a particular accounting period are shown almost entirely in the profit and loss account.
4 *Format.* The format of a service-sector profit and loss account is very similar to that of a trading entity. However, sometimes specific groups of expenditure are deducted from specific groups of income, the net amount then being highlighted in the profit and loss account. For example, suppose an entity sells food for £1000 and its cost was £600. The £1000 income *could* be shown in the income section of the profit and loss account with the £600 being shown separately as an expenditure item. But as there is a close relationship between the income and the expenditure, it is helpful to users if it is grouped as in Example 6.3.

<table>
<tr><td>**Example
6.3**</td><td colspan="3">**Extract from the profit and loss account**</td></tr>
<tr><td></td><td></td><td>£</td><td>£</td></tr>
<tr><td></td><td>Income from sale of food</td><td>1 000</td><td></td></tr>
<tr><td></td><td>*Less*: cost of provision</td><td>600</td><td>400</td></tr>
</table>

5 *Segmentation.* Similar categories of income or expenditure are usually grouped together in the same part of the profit and loss account with the subtotal of each category being shown separately.

We illustrate the presentation of a set of financial statements for a service entity in Example 6.4. As you will see, the presentation of the profit and loss account and the balance sheet is very similar to the examples used in previous chapters.

<table>
<tr><td>Example
6.4</td><td colspan="3">

A service entity account

</td></tr>
</table>

Mei Loon: Educational training consultant

Profit and loss account for the year to 31 March 2012

	£	£
INCOME (1)		
Article fees	5 000	
Author's licensing and collecting payments	2 000	
Consultation fees	90 000	
Lecture fees	30 000	
Public lending right payment	1 000	
Royalties	20 000	148 000
EXPENDITURE (2)		
Computing	5 000	
Depreciation : equipment (3)	2 000	
: furniture (3)	500	
Heat and light	1 000	
Insurances	600	
Photocopying	200	
Postage	100	
Rates	1 500	
Secretarial	30 000	
Stationery (4)	700	
Subscriptions	400	
Travelling	6 000	48 000
Net profit for the year (5)		100 000

Balance sheet at 31 March 2012

	£	£
FIXED ASSETS (6)		
Office equipment	10 000	
Less: accumulated depreciation	4 000	6 000
Office furniture	5 000	
Less: accumulated depreciation	1 500	3 500
		9 500
CURRENT ASSETS		
Stock of stationery (7)	200	
Debtors (8)	15 000	
Prepayments (9)	3 000	
Cash at bank and in hand	52 300	
	70 500	
CURRENT LIABILITIES		
Creditors (10)	2 000	
Accruals (11)	1 000	
	3 000	67 500
		77 000

	£	£
CAPITAL		
At 1 April 2011 (12)		17 000
Net profit for the year (13)	100 000	
Less: drawings (14)	40 000	60 000
Balance at 31 March 2012		77 000

Tutorial notes to Example 6.4

1 All six of the listed income items will have been compiled on an accruals and pre-payments basis, i.e. the cash received during the period will have been adjusted for any opening and closing debtors.

2 Apart from depreciation the expenditure items will have been adjusted for any opening or closing accruals and prepayments.

3 Mei Loon appears to be depreciating her office furniture by 10 per cent per annum on cost [(£500 ÷ £5000) × 100%], and her office equipment by 20 per cent per annum on cost [(£2000 ÷ £10,000) × 100%].

4 The stationery costs for the year have been reduced by the stock at 31 March 2012 (see note 7).

5 The net profit for the year has been added to Mei Loon's capital at 1 April 2011 (see note 12).

6 The fixed assets are shown at their gross book value less the accumulated depreciation. The difference is known as 'net book value'.

7 Mei Loon has valued the stock of stationery that she held at 31 March 2012 at £200.

8 The debtors entry probably represents what is owed to Mei Loon for various fees as at 31 March 2012.

9 The prepayments represent what she has paid in advance at the end of the year for various services, such as insurances or heat and light, from which she would expect to benefit in the year to 31 March 2013.

10 The creditors represent what she owes at the end of the year for various goods and services supplied during the year.

11 The accruals are similar to the creditors, but they probably relate to services such as insurances or heat and light (see note 9).

12 Mei Loon's opening capital balance is shown as £17,000. This would be composed of her original capital contribution plus previous years' profits that she had not drawn out of the business.

13 The net profit for the year is the balance on the profit and loss account.

14 Mei Loon has drawn £40,000 out of the business during the year for her own private use. Some of the £40,000 probably relates to previous years' profits that she has drawn out during the current year, along with various amounts drawn out in advance of this year's profits.

Activity 6.3

Referring to Example 6.4, examine Mei Loon's profit and loss account and balance sheet. What does the information tell you? How well has her consultancy done during the year to 31 March 2012? Is she likely to go bankrupt in the near future?

Not-for-profit entity accounts

News clip

Accounting for charities

In a recent review the Charity Commission has argued that accounting and reporting requirements are important tools for charities. The Commission believes that such requirements help them balance their books, plan for the future, and account for their income and spending. The report also highlighted a lack of proper controls which made existing problems harder to sort out.

Source: Adapted from www.accountancyage.com/articles/print/2225722, 10 September 2008.

As the term suggests, not-for-profit entities are in business solely to provide some sort of service without necessarily needing to or wanting to make a profit. Examples include charities such as 'Save the Children', bridge clubs, music societies and sports organizations. It is possible that such bodies might be engaged in some sort of trading (or even manufacturing) but the profit motivation would not be their main consideration.

If not-for-profit entities have some manufacturing or trading activities, they will prepare manufacturing and trading accounts. The balance on the manufacturing account would be transferred to the trading account and the balance on the trading account (i.e. the gross profit) to an *income and expenditure account*. An income and expenditure account is almost identical to a profit and loss account except that the title is different and the balance on the account is described as the *excess of income over expenditure* (or expenditure over income) instead of *profit* (or *loss*).

An example of an income and expenditure account and a balance sheet for a social club is shown in Example 6.5. The preparation of such accounts is very similar to that for trading entities.

Example 6.5

A social club's accounts

Balli Social Club
Income and expenditure account for the year to 31 March 2011

	£	£
INCOME (1)		
Bar sales (2)	60 000	
Less: purchases	40 000	20 000
Building society interest		200
Dances (2)	1 600	
Less expenses	900	700
Food sales (2)	8 000	
Less: purchases	4 500	3 500
Members' subscriptions		36 200
c/f		60 600

	b/f		60 600
EXPENDITURE (3)			
Accountants' fees	250		
Depreciation: furniture and fittings	3 900		
Insurances	600		
Electricity	1 400		
Office expenses	22 000		
Rates	2 000		
Salaries and wages	14 000		
Telephone	3 100		
Travelling expenses	13 000	60 250	
Excess of income over expenditure for the year (4)		350	

Balance sheet at 31 March 2011

	£	£	£
	Cost	Accumulated	
FIXED ASSETS (5)		depreciation	
Club premises	18 000	–	18 000
Furniture and equipment	39 000	17 900	21 100
	57 000	17 900	39 100
CURRENT ASSETS (5)			
Stocks	1 500		
Prepayments	200		
Members' subscriptions (in arrears)	7 000		
Building society account	2 700		
Cash	5 500	16 900	
CURRENT LIABILITIES (5)			
Trade creditors	2 000		
Members' subscriptions (paid in advance)	800		
Accruals	1 250	4 050	12 850
			51 950
ACCUMULATED FUND (6)			
Balance at 1 April 2010 (7)			51 600
Excess of income over expenditure for the year (8)			350
Balance at 31 March 2011 (9)			51 950

Tutorial notes to Example 6.5

1 The income items will have been calculated on an accruals and prepayments basis.

2 Details relating to the bar, dances and food sales (and other similar activities) may require separate disclosure. If so, individual accounts would be prepared for these activities, the balance on such accounts then being transferred to the income and expenditure account.

3 Expenditure items would be calculated on an accruals and prepayments basis.

4 The balance on the account (the excess of income over expenditure for the year) is transferred to the Accumulated Fund account (see note 6).

5 Fixed assets, current assets and current liabilities are calculated and presented in exactly the same way that they are for profit-making entities.

Tutorial notes to
Example 6.5
continued

6 The Accumulated Fund is the equivalent of the capital element in the accounting equation. The total amount of £51,950 represents what the members have invested in the club as at 31 March 2011, and what could have been paid back to them (in theory) if the club had been closed down at that date. In practice, of course, the various items on the balance sheet would not necessarily have been disposed of at their balance sheet values.

7 This was the balance in the Accumulated Fund at the beginning of the club's financial year.

8 This balance has been transferred from the income and expenditure account.

9 This is the balance in the Accumulated Fund as at the end of the club's financial year.

Activity 6.4

Referring to Example 6.5, how satisfactory do you think the Balli Social Club's financial performance has been during the year to 31 March 2011?

Government accounts

News clip

Whitehall needs accountants

It has been reported that there are only a small number of civil servants working in Whitehall who have an adequate financial qualification. Edward Leigh, Chairman of the House of Commons Public Accounts Committee, is quoted as saying, 'You would think that no department would contemplate implementing a policy without first estimating what it is going to cost. But only 20 per cent of departments based policy decisions on a thorough assessment of their financial implications.'

Source: Adapted from www.accountancyage.com/articles/print/2225631, 10 September 2009.

Another important set of entity accounts relate to the government sector of the economy. Such accounts may generally be regarded as part of the not-for-profit service sector. There are three broad categories: central government accounts, local government accounts, and quasi-governmental accounts.

Central government accounts incorporate the results of major departments such as defence, the environment, social security and trade and industry. Until a few years ago they were prepared on a cash basis, i.e. cash received for the year was matched with cash paid during that year but then the government switched to what it calls *resource accounting*. This is just another term for accounts prepared on an accruals and prepayments basis.

Resource accounting was introduced because government services needed to become more efficient, i.e. to offer a better service to the public for every pound spent. Cash accounting resulted in a lack of control of operations and projects. If a project was costing more than had been budgeted for it, for example, payments to suppliers would be delayed because this made the cash position look better.

Resource accounting has required government departments to adopt a different approach to the way that they manage their affairs. It involves setting objectives, laying down long-term and short-term plans, the tight management of funds and resources, and statutory reporting similar to that required in the private sector.

Resource accounting involves producing sets of accounts that include operating cost statements. These are similar to profit and loss accounts and balance sheets. It is claimed that they have the following advantages:

- costs are charged to departments when they are incurred and not when they are paid for;
- distortions are removed between when goods and services are received, when they are paid and when they are consumed;
- departmental budgets are more realistic;
- it is much more difficult to disguise the overall cost of departmental activities;
- there is greater control over the safeguarding of fixed and current assets, e.g. stocks, and the monitoring of current liabilities such as creditors.

These are substantial claims. Bearing in mind the difficulties that the commercial world has in dealing with 'accruals and prepayment' accounting, it is doubtful whether resource accounting is operating quite as smoothly as the government had expected.

Activity 6.5	Consider the benefits listed above that the switch to resource accounting was supposed to bring to government activities. How far do you think that they are being met? Is the absence of the profit motive in the not-for-profit sector a major difficulty?

An important part of the government sector is *local government*. Local government accounts include income and expenditure details relating to major services such as education, housing, police and social services. The annual budget (running from 1 April to 31 March) determines the amount of cash that the local authority needs to raise from its council tax payers in order to finance its projected expenditure for the forthcoming year. This is a highly political consideration and councillors are usually more concerned about the impact that a forthcoming budget may have on the electorate than about expenditure that has already been incurred.

News clip

Outsourcing local government

According to *The Economist* one way that local councils could cut their costs is 'to do less by getting others to do more'. This policy requires councils to contract private sector and not-for-profit organizations to manage facilities and provide necessary services for them. If this policy is done right, it is argued, the facilities and the local budget are improved although it is admitted that if it is done wrong, 'services vanish'.

Source: Adapted from *The Economist*, 11 April 2009, p. 30.

Another part of the government sector includes *quasi-government* bodies. They include those entities that are owned by the government but operated at arm's length (i.e. indirectly) through specially appointed authorities and councils. Examples include the British Broadcasting Corporation (BBC), secondary and tertiary education colleges, the Royal Mail and universities. Such entities are often heavily dependent on the Government for providing a great deal of their operational income.

London Olympics in a hole

Apparently the finances of the London Olympics are in a hole because it has been discovered that the Directorate failed to make a provision for between £60m and £100m to cover a compensation claim for local businesses forced to relocate from the Olympic site.

Source: Adapted from www.accountancyage.com/articles/print/2244697, 27 June 2009.

Overall, government accounting generally is a highly specialist activity, although the basics are similar to the procedures used in the private sector. As it is so specialized, we will not consider it any further in this book.

! Questions you should ask

This chapter covers a number of different types of entity so the following questions may not be relevant in all instances.

- How do you distinguish between 'direct costs' and 'indirect costs'?
- Why bother with manufacturing profit?
- How has the amount added for manufacturing profit been calculated?
- Are there any problems in deciding what income to take to the income and expenditure account?
- How have the depreciation rates for the fixed assets been arrived at?
- Should we allow for any bad debts or any doubtful ones? [A very important question in the case of social clubs.]
- What method has been used to estimate them?
- How have any accruals and prepayments been taken into account?

Conclusion

We began this chapter by describing the nature and purpose of manufacturing accounts and demonstrating how they may be compiled. We then moved the focus away from manufacturing and trading accounts toward other types of accounts used in the service sector and the non-for-profit sector.

You will have noticed that there is a great deal of similarity between manufacturing and trading accounts and the accounts of service sector entities. Manufacturing, trading and service sector entities all usually adopt an accruals and prepayments basis for preparing their financial statements and they are presented in the form of a profit and loss account (or equivalent) and a balance sheet.

The main difference is in the detail. Non-manufacturing and trading entities have few (if any) raw material stocks, work-in-progress or finished goods, and product costing is largely irrelevant. There are also a few differences in the way that information is presented in the profit and loss account (or the income and expenditure account) and the balance sheet. So if you can work your way through a manufacturing entity's accounts, you should not have too much difficulty with non-manufacturing, non-trading and service sector accounts. Government accounts are, however, a different matter!

Key points

1 Entities that convert raw materials and component parts into finished goods may need to prepare a manufacturing account.

2 A manufacturing account is part of the double-entry system. Normally it will be prepared annually along with the other main financial accounts. It usually comes before the trading account.

3 The main elements of a manufacturing account include direct materials, direct labour, direct expenses and various indirect manufacturing costs.

4 A direct cost is a cost that can be easily and economically identified with a particular department, section, product, process or unit. An indirect cost is a cost that cannot be so easily and economically identified.

5 The type of manufacturing account described in this chapter would not be required if an entity had a management accounting system.

6 Service sector entities do not normally deal in physical or tangible goods or services. So they do not need to prepare a manufacturing or a trading account, their basic accounts consisting of a profit and loss account and a balance sheet. The preparation of such financial statements is similar to that required for compiling manufacturing and trading entity accounts.

7 The accounts of not-for-profit entities are very similar to those of service entities, except that the profit and loss account is referred to as an income and expenditure account.

8 Government accounts are highly specialized although their basic structure is now similar to that adopted in the private sector.

Check your learning

The answers to these questions can be found within the text.

1 What is a manufacturing account?

2 What is (a) a direct cost, (b) an indirect cost?

3 What is meant by the term 'prime cost'?

4 How does an allowance for profit in the manufacturing account affect the cash position of the entity?

5 To which account is the 'market value of goods produced' transferred?

6 What is meant by the 'service sector'?

7 List five different groups of service sector entities.

8 Name four different types of businesses operating in the service sector.

9 What is meant by a 'not-for-profit' entity?

10 What terms are applied to its main financial statement?

11 Can a not-for-profit entity make profits?

12 What is the balance called that is transferred to the accumulated fund at the end of a financial period?

13 What is meant by an 'accumulated fund'?

14 What term does the government use to describe its method of accounting?

15 Name two types of local government activities.

16 Name two quasi-governmental entities.

News story quiz

Remember the news story at the beginning of this chapter? Go back to that story and reread it before answering the following question.

This article reflects a worrying state of affairs in the management of the European Union. You would expect that an organization as big and as important as the EU could manage its finances effectively and efficiently. Unfortunately this has not been the case although this article indicates that recently there has been some improvement. The issues raised in this article are highly complex but we suggest that you have a go at answering the following questions by using a combination of your accounting knowledge and a certain amount of common sense.

Questions

1 How do you think a supposedly sophisticated organization could present accounts over a number of years that are not 'reliable', i.e. they do not represent a true and fair view?

2 What would the consequences be if a *company* presented accounts that were unreliable?

3 What steps would you suggest could be taken to ensure that there is greater control in releasing funds to cover expenditure on infrastructure projects?

Tutorial questions

The answers to questions marked with an asterisk can be found in Appendix 4.

6.1 A direct cost has been defined as 'a cost that that can be easily and economically identified with a particular department, section product or unit'. Critically examine this definition from a non-accounting manager's perspective.

6.2 Although a manufacturing account may contain a great deal of information, how far do you think that it helps managers who are in charge of production cost centres?

6.3 It has been asserted that the main objective of a profit-making entity is to make a profit, while that of not-for-profit entity is to provide a service. Discuss this assertion in the context of the accounting requirements of different types of entities.

6.4* The following information relates to Megg for the year to 31 January 2010:

	£000
Stocks at 1 February 2009:	
Raw material	10
Work-in-progress	17
Direct wages	65
Factory: Administration	27
Heat and light	9
Indirect wages	13
Purchases of raw materials	34
Stocks at 31 January 2010:	
Raw material	12
Work-in-progress	14

Required:
Prepare Megg's manufacturing account for the year to 31 January 2010.

6.5* The following balances have been extracted from the books of account of Moor for the year to 28 February 2011:

	£
Direct wages	50 000
Factory indirect wages	27 700
Purchases of raw materials	127 500
Stocks at 1 March 2010:	
Raw material	13 000
Work-in-progress	8 400
Stocks at 28 February 2011:	
Raw material	15 500
Work-in-progress	6 300

Required:
Prepare Moor's manufacturing account for the year to 28 February 2011.

6.6 The following balances have been extracted from the books of Stuart for the year to 31 March 2012:

	£000
Administration: Factory	230
Direct wages	330
Purchases of raw materials	1 123
Stocks at 1 April 2011:	
Raw material	38
Work-in-progress	29
Additional information:	
Stocks at 31 March 2012:	
Raw material	44
Work-in-progress	42

Required:
Prepare Stuart's manufacturing account for the year to 31 March 2012.

6.7 The following balances have been extracted from the books of the David and Peter Manufacturing Company as at 30 April 2011:

	£000
Direct wages	70
Factory equipment: at cost	360
General factory expenses	13
Heat and light (factory $\frac{3}{4}$; general $\frac{1}{4}$)	52
Purchases of raw materials	100
Stocks at 1 May 2010:	
Raw material	12
Work-in-progress	18
Rent and rates (factory $\frac{2}{3}$; general $\frac{1}{3}$)	42

Additional information:

1 Stocks at 30 April 2011:   £000

   Raw material   14

   Work-in-progress   16

2 The factory equipment is to be depreciated at a rate of 15 per cent per annum on cost.

Required:
Prepare the David and Peter Manufacturing Company's manufacturing account for the year to 30 April 2011.

Further practice questions, study material and links to relevant sites on the World Wide Web can be found on the website that accompanies this book. The site can be found at www.pearsoned.co.uk/dyson

Cash flow statements

Crunch highlights cash flow

Judith Tydd

Economic instability is forcing a growing number of corporations to look at the way in which cash flow management is applied.

Bill Dodwell, tax partner at Deloitte, said the consensus among businesses prior to the collapse of global markets was to relegate cash flow management behind more compliance related areas.

'People haven't previously focused on it nearly as much as what they are now,' he said.

VAT systems are of particular significance to companies as this has a direct impact on cash flow from sales produced and, according to Dodwell, resulting VAT numbers have the potential to be 'huge'.

'Companies haven't bothered to look at whether their system is proper. It's about ensuring you're paying the right amount of tax at the right time,' he said.

Richard Mannion, national tax director at Smith & Williamson, said any well-run businesses should be aware of its cash flow management system. 'It's critical for people to be doing cash flow very carefully. It has come as a shock for business plans put in place last year which hadn't factored in the downturn in the market,' he said.

Source: Accountancy Age, 9 October 2008.

Source: Reproduced with permission from Incisive Media Ltd.

Questions relating to this news story can be found on page 163 ➡

About this chapter

This chapter deals with *cash flow statements* (CFS). A CFS is a financial statement listing all the cash receipts and all the cash payments for a certain period of time. It is now considered to be one of the main financial statements along with the profit and loss account and the balance sheet. Its importance was clearly recognized in 1991 when cash flow became the very first *Financial Reporting Standard* (FRS 1). The subject is also covered by an IASB requirement (IAS 7).

By the end of this chapter you should be able to:

- explain what is meant by a cash flow statement;
- describe its purpose;
- prepare a simple cash flow statement;
- outline the main structure of a cash flow statement in accordance with FRS 1 and IAS 7;
- identify the main causes of a change in cash flow during an accounting period.

! Why this chapter is important

This chapter is exceptionally important for non-accountants, especially those who are hoping to become senior managers in any entity no matter what its type or size. No entity can survive unless it takes in more cash than it is paying out and that applies both in the short term and in the long term. So all managers have to make sure that there is enough cash available (or they can borrow enough) to meet their debts. If they cannot then their business will go bankrupt.

It follows that managers must monitor their cash position constantly. One way of doing this is for their accountants to give them a cash flow statement on a frequent and regular basis.

As a manager, a CFS will not mean much to you if you do not know where the information has come from, what it means and what you should do with it. This chapter gives you the knowledge to make full use of all that it will tell you.

Nature and purpose

News clip

More about the Olympics

The British Olympic Association has had to have a £2m advance as it faced a cash crisis resulting from £1m spent on consultants and pay-offs for ex-staff. The move was necessary to give it time to renegotiate its overdraft. The BOA made a £1.5m pre-tax loss in 2008.

Source: Adapted from *The Guardian*, 18 June 2009, p. 10.

A cash flow statement (CFS) is a summary of all the cash that an entity has received for a period of account and all the cash payments that it has made during the same period. The net balance is then usually added (or deducted) to the opening balance to arrive at the closing balance. An example of a simple CFS is shown in Figure 7.1.

A CFS is now considered to be one of the main financial statements along with the profit and loss account and the balance sheet. It has become so because it provides vital information about an entity's cash position that is not disclosed in either the profit and loss account or the balance sheet, i.e. how it got to its current cash position.

Belton Limited
Cash flow statement for the year to 31 March 2012

	2011 £000	2012 £000
Receipts		
Trade debtors	1,410	1,990
Debenture interest	–	400
	1,410	2,390
Payments		
Trade creditors	720	1,400
Expenses	430	560
Development costs	20	250
Fixed assets	95	455
Debenture stock	100	–
Tax paid	20	70
Dividends paid	30	60
	1,415	2,795
Net payments	(5)	(405)
Opening cash	10	5
Closing cash	5	(400)

Figure 7.1 Example of a cash flow statement

After working your way through this book so far, you might find this argument some-what contradictory. You would have a point. In previous chapters we have emphasized just how important it is to show where the entity's *profit* has come from and now we are arguing for *cash*.

The truth is that both cash and profit are important: cash because an entity will not last overnight if it has not got the money to pay what it owes and profit because it will not survive in the long-run if it does not make a profit.

So, in summary: remember that (1) cash received less cash paid is not the same as profit; (2) an entity needs enough cash to keep going; and (3) it has to make a profit in the long-run. So users of accounts need information about an entity's cash position **and** its profitability.

In the next section we explain how to prepare a CFS so that when you come across one you will know where the information has come from, what it means and what you should do about it.

Activity 7.1

Go through Figure 7.1 identifying the main item that explains why a favourable cash balance of £5000 has turned into an unfavourable one of £400,000.

Preparation

There are two recognized ways of preparing a CFS: the *direct method* and the *indirect method*. The direct method is basically a summary of all the entries made in the cash book. In theory it is an easy and simple way of preparing a CFS. In practice it can involve a lot of extra work because all the accounting entries need to be converted back on to a cash basis. So most entities opt for the indirect method. This method simply extracts and adapts where necessary the data included in the profit and loss account and the balance sheet. As a result this method shows a clear link and a close relationship between the CFS and the financial statements, as can be seen in Figure 7.2.

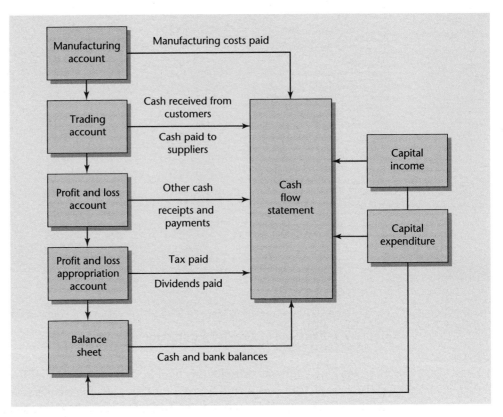

Figure 7.2 The interrelationship between the main financial statements

During your career you might well come across both the direct and the indirect methods so we will show you both methods using the same example. First the direct method.

The direct method

<table>
<tr><td>**Example 7.1**</td><td>

Preparation of a cash flow statement

You are presented with the following information:

Durton Ltd
Cash book summary for the year to 31 December 2012

Receipts	£000	Payments	£000
Balance b/f	25	Trade creditors	680
Trade debitors	970	Operating expenses	135
10% debenture stock	100	Debenture interest	10
		Taxation	40
		Dividends	30
		Fixed assets	150
		Balance c/f	45
	1 095		1 095

Required:
Prepare Durton's cash flow statement for the year to 31 December 2012 using the direct method.
</td></tr>
</table>

Answer to Example 7.1

Durton Ltd
Cash flow statement for the year to 31 December 2012 using the direct method

	Tutorial notes	£000
Cash receipts		
Sale of goods	1	970
Issue of 10% debenture stock	2	100
		1 070
Cash payments		
Purchases of goods	3	680
Operating expenses		135
Debenture interest paid	4	10
Tax paid	5	40
Dividends paid	6	30
Fixed assets purchased	7	150
		1 045
Increase in cash during the year	8	25
Cash at 1 January 2012		20
Cash at 31 December 2012		45

Tutorial notes

1 This amount has been received in cash from trade debtors during the year.

2 The cash received from the sale of the debenture stock will not be shown in the profit and loss account.

3 This amount is what has been paid to trade creditors during the year.

4 The debenture stock has apparently been issued on 1 January 2012 because £10 000 is the total amount of interest for a full year.

5 An amount paid during the year but we do not know to which year or years it relates.

6 The dividends may or may not be related to 2012 or they could be a final dividend declared in 2011 and paid in 2012.

7 The cost of fixed assets, of course, would not be included in the profit and loss account.

8 The increase in cash during the year is probably a mixture of cash received and paid during 2012 some of which relates to 2011 and some to 2013.

As you worked your way through Example 7.1 you probably found it fairly easy because you were given a highly summarized version of the cash book and this provided most of the information you needed. It would have been a little more difficult to prepare if you had had to extract what you wanted from a poorly kept handwritten cash book (still found these days even with the benefits of computerization). But even if the CFS is fairly easy to prepare the information provided appears to be independent of the other two main financial statements: the profit and loss account and the balance sheet. This means that they tend to be viewed in isolation. It can also be confusing for those users of financial statements who are not clear about the difference between 'cash' and 'profit'. The indirect method gets over these problems even if it is perhaps a little more difficult to understand. So now to the indirect method.

Activity 7.2	Make a list of those items that appear in Durton's CFS that would not normally be included in its profit and loss account.

The indirect method

News clip

GM cash drain

General Motors, the American car firm faces a survival crisis owing to an unexpected heavy cash drain during the last three months of 2008. So much so that it thinks its auditors may not regard it as a going concern.

Source: Adapted from *The Financial Times*, 27 February 2009.

We illustrate how the indirect method works in Example 7.2. As with Example 7.1 it relates to Durton Limited but this time we need to give you the company's profit and loss account for 2012 and the balance sheets for both 2011 and 2012.

Example 7.2	**Preparation of a cash flow statement using the indirect method**

You are presented with the following information:

Durton Ltd
Trading and profit and loss account for the year to 31 December 2012

	£000	£000
Sales		1 000
Less: Cost of goods sold:		
Opening stock	200	
Purchases	700	
	900	
Less: Closing stock	300	600
Gross profit		400
Operating expenses		(240)
Operating profit		160
Debenture interest		(10)
Net profit before taxation		150
Taxation		(50)
Net profit after taxation		100
Dividends		(60)
Retained profit for the year		40

Durton Ltd
Balance sheet at 31 December 2012

	2011		2012	
	£000	£000	£000	£000
Fixed assets at cost	900		1 050	
Less: Accumulated depreciation	150	750	255	795
Current assets				
Stocks	200		300	
Trade debtors	120		150	
Cash	20		45	
	340		495	
Less: Current liabilities				
Trade creditors	70		90	
Taxation	40		50	
Proposed dividend	30		60	
	140	200	200	295
		950		1 090
Capital and reserves				
Ordinary shares of £1 each		750		750
Profit and loss account		200		240
		950		990
Loans				
Debenture stock (10%: issued 1 January 2012)		–		100
		950		1 090

Required:
Prepare a cash flow statement for the year to 31 December 2012 using the indirect method.

Answer to Example 7.2

Durton Ltd
Cash flow statement for the year to 31 December 2012

	Tutorial notes	£000
Cash receipts		
Sale of goods	1	970
Issue of debenture stock	2	100
		1 070
Cash payments		
Purchases of goods	3	680
Operating expenses	4	135
Debenture interest paid	5	10
Taxation	6	40
Dividends	7	30
Purchases of fixed assets	8	150
		1 045
Increase in cash during the year 2012		25
Cash at 1 January 2012		20
Cash at 31 December 2012		45

Answer to Example 7.2 continued

1   Sale of goods = (opening debtors + sales) – closing debtors: $(1\,000 + 120) - 150 = 970$.

2   Issue of debenture stock: $100 - 0 = 100$.

3   Purchases of goods: $700 + 70 - 90 = 680$.

4   Operating expenses – depreciation: $240 - 105* = 135$ [*accumulated depreciation balances: $255 - 150$].

5   Debenture interest: $10\% \times 100 = 10$.

6   Taxation: 40. Only last year's has been paid as the taxation in the profit and loss account is the same amount shown in the balance sheet.

7   Dividends: 30. Only last year's has been paid as the dividends in the profit and loss account is the same balance as shown in the balance sheet.

8   Purchase of fixed assets: $1\,050 - 900 = 150$.

We can now begin to work out what Durton's CFS is telling us. The balance sheet shows that at 31 December 2011 the company had a cash balance of £20,000. By 31 December 2012, the cash balance was £45,000, an increase of £25,000. The retained profit for the year of £40,000 was more than the £25,000 increase in cash during the year. We do not, of course, need to prepare a CFS to find out such information but we do need some help in determining why there is a difference. A CFS provides us with the evidence. Most of the cash received for the year came from sales and much of it was spent on buying goods, but if you look at the CFS a little more closely, however, you will also see that £100,000 was raised by issuing some debenture stock and that £150,000 was incurred on purchasing some fixed assets. These items do not appear in the profit and loss account. There is probably a connection between them: the debentures might have been issued to finance the purchase of the fixed assets. Certainly, without the debentures the cash position at the end of the year would have been very different, e.g. an overdrawn amount of £55,000 (45,000 – 100,000) instead of a favourable balance of £45,000. Similarly, if the taxation balance of £50,000 and the proposed dividend of £60,000 at 31 December 2012 had had to be paid early in 2013, the cash position would have been extremely vulnerable. Durton Ltd would then have to depend on its trade debtors (£150,000 at 31 December 2012) settling their debts before it could pay its trade creditors of £90,000.

Durton's CFS is a simplified example of a company's cash flow statement. Nevertheless, it does enable the major cash items to be highlighted and to bring them to the attention of the managers and to the owners of the company. Although it is to be hoped that the cash position of Durton was being closely monitored during the year, an annual CFS enables the year's results to be put into context.

Activity 7.3

Durton Limited retained profits of £40,000 for the year to 31 December 2012 and yet its cash balance only increased from £20,000 at the beginning of the year to £45,000 at the end of it. The managing director (a salesperson) thinks that someone has defrauded the company of £15,000. Let him have a note (via email) explaining to him why this is not so.

The layout that we have used in preparing the solution to Example 7.2 does not demonstrate very clearly the close relationship between the profit and loss account, the balance sheet and the CFS. The various changes that have been made are also somewhat difficult to trace. If it is possible, a CFS should be presented in such a way that its close relationship with the profit and loss account and the balance sheet is much more apparent.

Both the ASB and the ISAB have issued an accounting standard covering CFSs: FRS 1 and IAS 7 respectively. They are not identical: slightly different accounting policies are used to prepare them, some terminology is different and the formats (e.g. the headings) are not the same. Overseas students (especially those from EU countries) are likely to use the IASB's version. However, UK students will probably come across both FRS 1 and IAS 7 so we will deal with each of them. First FRS 1.

FRS 1 presentation

FRS 1 was first issued in 1991 and revised in 1996. It is quite a complicated standard but we will make matters easier for you by dealing only with a CFS for single entities. We are only going to cover the indirect method as this is the method that you are much more likely to come across. Our discussion will be in two parts: (1) an example of a CFS as required by FRS 1; and (2) an explanation of some of its main features.

We will use Durton Limited's accounts as our example because by now you should be familiar with the details.

Example 7.3

Preparation of a cash flow statement in accordance with FRS 1 using the individual method

Using the data from Durton Limited, Example 7.2 on pages 150–151, prepare a cash flow statement in accordance with FRS 1 using the indirect method.

Durton Ltd
Cash flow statement for the year to 31 December 2012

	Tutorial notes	£000
Net cash inflow from operating activities	1	155
Returns on investments and servicing of finance		
Interest paid	7	(10)
Taxation	8	(40)
Capital expenditure		
Payments to acquire tangible fixed assets	9	(150)
Equity dividends paid	10	(30)
		(75)
Management of liquid resources and financing		
Issue of debenture stock	11	100
Increase in cash	12	25

Note 1   Reconciliation of operating profit to net cash inflow from operating activities

	Tutorial notes	£000
Operating profit	2	160
Depreciation	3	105
(Increase) in stocks	4	(100)
(Increase) in trade debtors	5	(30)
Increase in trade creditors	6	20
Net cash inflow from operating activities	1	155

➡

*Example 7.3
continued*

Note 2 Reconciliation of net cash flow to movement in debt

	Tutorial notes	£000
Increase in cash during the period	12	25
Cash from issuing debentures	13	(100)
Change in net debt	14	(75)
Net funds at 1 January 2012	15	20
Net debt at 31 December 2012	16	55

Note 3 Analysis of change in net debt

	At 1.1.12	Cash flows	At 31.12.12
	£000	£000	£000
Cash	20 (15)	25 (12)	45 (17)
Debt due after one year	– (15)	(100) (13)	(100)(13)
Total	20 (15)	(75) (14)	(55)(16)

*Tutorial notes to
Example 7.3*

1 The calculation of the net cash inflow from operating activities totalling £155,000 is shown in **Note 1** to the CFS. This note is required although it is not a formal part of the CFS 1.

2 The operating profit of £160,000 has been obtained from the profit and loss account.

3 The depreciation charge has been obtained from the balance sheet. It is the difference between the accumulated depreciation of £255,000 as at 31 December 2012 and £150,000 as at 31 December 2011.

4 The increase in stocks has been obtained from the two balance sheets. It is the movement between the two balances of £300,000 and £200,000. Note that an increase in stocks is the equivalent of a *reduction* in cash because more cash will have been paid out.

5 The increase in trade debtors of £30,000 represents the movement between the opening and closing trade debtors as obtained from the two balance sheets. An increase in trade debtors represents a *reduction* in cash because less cash has been received by the entity.

6 The increase in trade creditors of £20,000 is again obtained from the balance sheets. The £20,000 represents an *increase* in cash because less cash has been paid out of the business.

7 The interest paid of £10,000 has been obtained from the profit and loss account.

8 The taxation amount of £40,000 is the balance shown on the previous year's balance sheet. As £50,000 was charged to this year's profit and loss account for taxation and this amount features on this year's balance sheet, only £40 000 must have been paid during the year.

9 The capital expenditure amount of £150,000 is the difference between the two balance sheet amounts for fixed assets, of £1,050,000 and £900,000 respectively. No further details are given.

10 The equity dividends of £30,000 represent the dividends paid out to ordinary shareholders during the year (there are no other groups of shareholders in this example). The amount has been obtained from the 2011 balance sheet.

The 2012 balance sheet shows an amount of £60,000, which is the same amount as disclosed in the profit and loss account. This means that only last year's dividend has been paid during the current year. Sometimes, there would also be other payments during the year.

11 The debenture stock balance has been obtained from the 2012 balance sheet. There was no such balance at the end of 2011, and so all the debenture must have been issued during 2012, as indeed is stated in the example.

12 After making all the above adjustments to the financial accounts, the net increase in cash during 2012 is found to be £25,000.

13 See note 11 above.

14 Without the issue of the debentures, there would have been a £75,000 net outflow of cash during the year.

15 The company only had cash at 1 January 2012; it did not have any debt.

16 The entity's net debt at 31 December 2012 was £55,000, i.e. the debenture stock of £100,000 less the cash in hand of £45,000.

17 This was the cash balance at 31 December 2012, as shown in the balance sheet at that date.

Main features

We hope that you have been able to work your way carefully through Example 7.3 line by line and note by note without too much difficulty. We think that you will agree that it is not particularly easy to follow even if you are familiar with the data. We will now try to pull out some of the main features and difficulties in order to enable you to compile simple CFSs for yourself. If you can do that then you should be able to cope with more complex presentations that you may come across in your job.

Layout

FRS 1 requires eight main headings, as summarized in Table 7.1 below. Example 7.3 only uses six headings because in this example there are no data for one heading (acquisitions and disposals) and two headings may be combined (management of liquid resources and financing) as long as they are shown separately elsewhere.

Cash

You might think that there is no need to define what is meant by 'cash'. After all, everyone knows it is just notes and coins that you have in your pocket, tucked under the mattress or perhaps kept at the bank. FRS 1's definition is a little wider than this. It is as follows:

Cash = cash in hand + deposits – overdrafts

The definition of cash is not a problem: coins and bank notes and cash at the bank that give you instant access. Similarly you almost certainly know all about overdrafts! The definition of deposits is, however, a little trickier. According to FRS 1 deposits are regarded as the same as 'cash' when they are with a 'qualifying institution' (i.e. an entity that accepts deposits or other repayable funds and grants credits for its own account) and that are repayable on demand within at least 24 hours. Both cash and deposits may be in foreign currencies.

Table 7.1 Structure of a cash flow statement according to FRS 1

Heading[a]	Contents[b]
1 Net cash inflow from operating activities	Operating or trading activities[c]
2 Returns on investments and servicing of finance	Investment income. Interest payments on loans. Dividends paid to preference shareholders
3 Taxation	Tax paid on profits
4 Capital expenditure and financial investment[d]	Purchases and sales of fixed assets. Loans to other entities received and paid
5 Acquisitions and disposals	Sales and purchases of other entities or of investments in them
6 Equity dividends paid	Dividends paid to ordinary shareholders
7 Management of liquid resources[e]	Purchases and sales of current asset investments
8 Financing[e]	Receipts and payments relating to share issues and redemptions, debentures, loans and other long-term borrowings

Notes:
(a) Headings may be omitted if no cash transaction has taken place either in the current period or in the previous period. They must be in the order listed. A subtotal should be included for each heading.
(b) The contents reflect only the *cash* flow for each transaction. Cash includes cash in hand, deposits repayable on demand, and overdrafts. *Cash flow* is an increase or decrease in cash during the period.
(c) FRS 1 requires a reconciliation to be made between the operating profit and the net cash flows from operating activities.
(d) The heading 'capital expenditure' may be used if there are no cash flows relating to financial investment (such as loans).
(e) Headings 7 and 8 may be combined under one heading provided that each of their respective cash flows are shown separately and that separate subtotals are given for each heading.

This definition of cash is important because, as you will see later, IAS 7's definition is not the same.

Notes

FRS 1 requires three main significant notes to accompany the CFS: one reconciling the operating profit to operating cash flow; one reconciling net cash flow to the movement in debt; and one analysing the change in net debt. These are all tricky notes to compile and they require some thought. So be warned!

1 Note reconciling operating profit to operating cash flows

This reconciliation basically converts the traditional profit and loss account items prepared on an accruals and payments basis back to a cash basis. We do this by adding to or deducting any increase or decrease in opening and closing debtors, prepayments, creditors and accruals. So, for example, if closing trade debtors are greater than the opening trade debtors we *deduct* the increase from the operating profit. We do this because, other things being equal (*ceteris paribus*), less cash has been received during the year. If the closing trade debtors are less than opening ones we *add* the decrease to the operating profit. Again we do this because, *ceteris paribus,* more cash has been received during the year.

This notion of adding or deducting the movement between the opening and closing current asset and current liability balances is sometimes quite difficult to grasp and so to work out. In order to make it much easier for you we have summarized the procedure in Table 7.2 below.

Table 7.2 The effect of working capital movements on cash flow

Item	Movement (closing balance less opening balance)	Effect on cash
Stocks	Increase	Down (more cash has been spent on stocks). Insert the movement in brackets
	Decrease	Up (less cash has been spent on stocks)
Trade debtors, other debtors and prepayments	Increase	Down (less cash has been received). Insert the movement in brackets
	Decrease	Up (more cash has been received)
Trade creditors, other creditors and accruals (excluding taxation payable and proposed dividends)	Increase	Up (less cash has been spent)
	Decrease	Down (more cash has been paid). Insert the movement in brackets

Activity 7.4

State whether each of the following statements is true or false.

(a) Operating activities reflect total cash inflows.   *True/false*

(b) Depreciation decreases the cash position.   *True/false*

(c) Tax paid decreases the tax position.   *True/false*

(d) A proposed dividend increases the cash position.   *True/false*

(e) A decrease in debtors increases the cash position.   *True/false*

(f) An increase in creditors decreases the cash position.   *True/false*

2 Note reconciling net cash flow to movement in net debt

The second note required by FRS 1 involves preparing a schedule reconciling the difference between the net debt at the beginning of the period and net debt at the end of it. Net debt is basically the difference between long-term loans and any cash and bank balances (net *funds* if the cash and bank balances are greater than the net debt). This note helps users of financial statements to assess the liquidity position of the company and to determine its solvency.

Such a note is usually quite a simple one to prepare. It has three main elements:

● the change in the cash for the period;
● the movement in debt during the period;
● the net debt at the end of the period.

The note is usually shown immediately after the CFS itself.

3 Note analysing changes in net debt

The third note involves analysing the changes that have taken place in the net debt position during the period. Net debt is split between cash and debt. These two elements are then analysed into:

● the balances at the beginning of the period;
● changes that happened during the period;
● the balances at the end of the period.

This note usually follows Note 2.

We now leave FRS 1 and in the next section we explain how to prepare and present a CFS in accordance with IAS 7.

IAS 7 FORMAT

News clip

BA Cuts

In order to save cash and reduce losses British Airways is reducing capacity and cutting jobs. This move involves reducing capital expenditure and deferring deliveries of new aircraft.

Source: Adapted from *The Financial Times*, 4/5 July 2009, p. 12.

In this section we examine a CFS prepared according to IAS 7. We will follow a similar procedure to the one we adopted in the last section, i.e. a CFS example and an outline of its main features. And again we are going to limit our discussion to the indirect method.

Example 7.4

Preparation of a cash flow statement in accordance with IAS 7 using the individual method

Using the data from Durton Limited, Example 7.2 on pages 150–151, prepare a cash flow statement in accordance with IAS 7 using the indirect method.

Durton Ltd
Statement of cash flows as at 31 December 2012

	Tutorial notes	2012 £000	£000
Cash flows from operating activities			
Profit before taxation	1	160	
Adjustments for:			
Depreciation	2	105	
		265	
Increase in trade and other receivables	3	(30)	
Increase in inventories	4	(100)	
Increase in trade payables	5	20	
Cash generated from operation		155	
Interest paid	6	(10)	
Income tax paid	7	(40)	
Net cash from operating activities			105
Cash flows from investing activities			
Purchase of property, plant and equipment	8	(150)	
Net cash used in investing activities			(150)
c/f			(45)

	Tutorial notes	2012	
		£000	£000
b/f			(45)
Cash flow from financing activities			
Proceeds from long-term borrowings	9	100	
Dividends paid	10	(30)	
Net cash used in financing activities			70
Net increase in cash and cash equivalents	11		25
Cash and cash equivalents at 1 January 2012			20
Cash and cash equivalents at 31 December 2012			45

Tutorial notes to Example 7.4

1 Net profit before taxation + debenture interest: 150 + 10 = 160.

2 Depreciation: 255 − 150 = 105.

3 Increase in trade and other receivables: 150 − 120 = 30.

4 Increase in inventories: 300 − 200 = 100.

5 Increase in trade payables: 90 − 70 = 20.

6 Interest paid: 10 (10% × 100).

7 Income tax paid: 40 + 50 − 50 = 40.

8 Purchase of property, plant and equipment: 1 050 − 900 = 150.

9 Proceeds from long-term borrowings: 100 − 0 = 100.

10 Dividends paid: 30 + 60 − 60 = 30.

11 Net increase in cash and cash equivalents: 45 − 20 = 25.

Note:

We have used exactly the same data from Durton Limited to prepare a CFS under both FRS 1 and IAS 7. In practice this would not normally be possible without some amendments since the ASB and the IASB have slightly different accounting policies. The example is fictitious, however, and our purpose in this chapter is only illustrative.

Main features

Both the ASB and the IASB accept that entities should produce a CFS. There are differences, between them, such as layout, terminology and detail. These differences are, however, relatively minor.

Layout

You will see from Example 7.4 that a CFS prepared under IAS 7 only has three main headings (compared with FRS 1's eight): *operating activities, investing activities* and *financing activities*. The standard allows a great deal of discretion about what to include under each heading.

Operating activities include those incomes and expenses that you would normally find in the profit and loss account suitably adjusted for debtors, creditors, accruals and prepayments plus depreciation. The adjustments that you need to make are identical to the ones we outlined for you in the previous section (see Table 7.2). Investing activities may include the purchases and sales of long-term assets and investments while financing activities include cash from the sale and purchase of the company's own shares, debentures and loans. In practice, when dealing with the affairs of a large company, it is not always easy to decide between investing and financing activities.

Cash and cash equivalents

IAS 7's definition of cash is a little wider than that of FRS 1 as it includes *cash equivalents*. Cash equivalents are:

> **Short-term, highly liquid investments that are readily convertible to known amounts of cash and which are subject to insignificant risk of changes in value.**

A maturity date of up to three months is usually taken as a guide to what is meant by 'short-term, highly liquid investments'.

Notes

An IAS 7 prepared CFS does not require specific notes about the movement in net debt and an analysis of the changes in net debt.

News clip

The biggest headaches

A recent survey shows that credit and cash flow management are the biggest headaches affecting finance leaders. The survey shows that 75% of Chief Financial Officers are most concerned about credit and 51% of them about cash flow management.

Source: Adapted from *accountancymagazine*, November 2008, p. 37.

The differences between an ASB prepared CFS and one prepared under IASB requirements are not particularly significant and its precise format does not really matter. What does matter is that as a manager (a) you receive some sort of CFS; (b) that you know what it is; and (c); and you know what action to take when you receive it. It could help to save your job and your company!

Activity 7.5
Compare and contrast Durton Limited's CFSs given in this chapter (Example 7.3 and Example 7.4, pages 153–154 and 158–159) prepared under FRS requirements and the other prepared under IASB requirements. List what you like and what you dislike about each format and then come to a conclusion about which format you prefer.

Questions you should ask

It is unlikely that as a non-accountant you will have to prepare cash flow statements. Your accountants will do that for you and present you with them from time to time.

We will assume that after studying this chapter you know where the information comes from and what it means. So what questions should you ask? We suggest that the following may be appropriate.

- Why has there been an increase or a decrease in cash during the period?
- What are the main items that have caused it?
- Did we anticipate them happening?
- What caused them?
- What did we do about any likely problems?
- Are we going to be short of cash in the immediate period?
- Will the bank support an extension of our overdraft?
- Can we borrow some funds from elsewhere?
- Might we need to borrow some on a long-term basis?
- How will that affect our future cash position?
- And what impact will it have on our profitability?

Conclusion

A cash flow statement for management contains some extremely useful information because it gives a lot more detail about the movement in the cash position. This is vital as it is possible for an entity to be profitable without necessarily having the cash resources to keep it going. Strict control over cash resources is absolutely essential, and a cash flow statement can help in this respect especially one prepared using the indirect method as it links directly with the profit and loss account and the balance sheet.

Key points

1 Entities may have a long-term profitable future but in the short term they may be short of cash. This may curb their activities and in extreme cases they may be forced out of business.

2 To avoid this happening owners and managers should be supplied with information about the cash movement and resources of the entity, i.e. about its liquidity. This can be done by preparing a cash flow statement.

3 A cash flow statement can be prepared using any format. Listed companies in the EU must use IAS 7 in preparing their *group* financial statements as they are required to adopt IASB requirements. Non-listed companies in the UK may use either IAS 7 or the ASB's FRS 1. Non-listed companies in other EU countries may have a similar arrangement.

Key points continued

4 Both IAS 7 and FRS 1 permit the use of either the direct method or the indirect method. The direct method is basically a list of the receipts and payments extracted from the cash book. The indirect method takes the respective balances from the profit and loss account and the balance sheet and converts them back from an accruals and payments basis to a cash basis. This method is to be preferred because it establishes an obvious and clear link between the CFS and the other two financial statements.

Check your learning

The answers to these questions can be found within the text.

1 List five reasons why the accounting profit for a period will not necessarily result in an improvement in an entity's cash position.

2 Identify two balance sheet items that may change an entity's cash position.

3 How does depreciation affect the cash balance?

4 What two methods may be used for preparing a CFS?

5 What Financial Reporting Standard covers the preparation of CFSs?

6 How many headings does the standard suggest for a CFS?

7 What are they?

8 Does an *increase* in (a) stocks, (b) debtors, and (c) creditors increase or decrease the cash position?

9 Does a *decrease* in (a) stocks, (b) debtors, and (c) creditors increase or decrease the cash position?

10 What is (a) net debt, (b) net funds?

11 What International Accounting Standard covers the preparation of a CFS?

12 How many headings does this standard require?

13 What are they?

14 What UK entities may adopt IAS 7?

15 What type of EU entity must adopt IAS 7?

16 List the assumptions and estimates that have to be made when compiling a CFS.

17 How reliable is a CFS?

18 What action would you expect a manager to take on receiving a CFS based on (a) historical data, (b) forecasted data?

News story quiz

Remember the news story at the beginning of this question? Go back to that story and reread it before answering the following questions.

The credit crunch that began to have a major impact on the UK economy in 2007 resulted in much more attention being given to cash flow. This article is one of many reports about what companies have had to do since that time.

Questions

1 Why is VAT an important element of cash flow management?

2 Why is it particularly significant during a recession?

3 What factors may cause inefficient cash management during periods of boom?

Tutorial questions

The answers to questions marked with an asterisk can be found in Appendix 4. Questions 7.4 to 7.9 may be answered by following the requirements of either FRS 1 or IAS 7.

7.1 'Proprietors are more interested in cash than profit.' Discuss.

7.2 Unlike traditional financial accounting, cash flow accounting does not require the accountant to make a series of arbitrary assumptions, apportionments and estimates. How far, therefore, do you think that there is a case for abandoning traditional financial accounting?

7.3 Does a cash flow statement serve any useful purpose?

7.4* You are presented with the following information:

Dennis Limited
Balance sheet at 31 January 2010

		31 January 2009		31 January 2010	
		£000	£000	£000	£000
Fixed assets					
Land at cost			600		700
Current assets					
Stock		100		120	
Debtors		200		250	
Cash		6		10	
	c/f	306	600	380	700

		31 January 2009		31 January 2010	
		£000	£000	£000	£000
	b/f	306	600	380	700
Less: Current liabilities					
Creditors		180	126	220	160
			726		860
Capital and reserves					
Ordinary share capital			700		800
Profit and loss account			26		60
			726		860

Required:
(a) Prepare Dennis Limited's cash flow statement for the year ended 31 January 2010.
(b) Outline what it tells the managers of Dennis Limited.

7.5* The following balance sheets have been prepared for Frank Limited:

Balance sheets at:	28.2.11		28.2.12	
	£000	£000	£000	£000
Fixed assets				
Plant and machinery at cost		300		300
Less: Depreciation		80		100
		220		200
Investments at cost		–		100
Current assets				
Stocks	160		190	
Debtors	220		110	
Bank	–		10	
	380		310	
Less: Current liabilities				
Creditors	200		160	
Bank overdraft	20		–	
	220	160	160	150
		380		450
Capital and reserves				
Ordinary share capital		300		300
Share premium account		50		50
Profit and loss account		30		40
		380		390
Shareholders' funds				
Loans				
Debentures		–		60
		380		450

Additional information:
There were no purchases or sales of plant and machinery during the year.

Required:
(a) Prepare Frank Limited's cash flow statement for the year ended 28 February 2012.
(b) What does it tell the managers of Frank Limited?

7.6   You are presented with the following information:

Starter
Profit and loss account for the year to 31 March 2012

	£	£
Sales		10 000
Purchases	5 000	
Less: Closing stock	1 000	4 000
Gross profit		6 000
Less: Depreciation		2 000
Net profit for the year		4 000

Balance sheet at 31 March 2012

	£	£
Van		10 000
Less: Depreciation		2 000
		8 000
Stock	1 000	
Trade debtors	5 000	
Bank	12 500	
	18 500	
Less: Trade creditors	2 500	16 000
		24 000
Capital		20 000
Add: Net profit for the year		4 000
		24 000

Note: Starter commenced business on 1 April 2011.

Required:
(a) Compile Starter's cash flow statement for the year ended 31 March 2012.
(b) What does it tell the owners of Starter?

7.7   The following is a summary of Gregory Limited's accounts for the year ended 30 April 2010.

Profit and loss account for the year ended 30 April 2010

	£000
Net profit before tax	75
Taxation	25
	50
Dividend (proposed)	40
Retained profit for the year	10

Balance sheet at 30 April 2010

	30.4.09		30.4.10	
	£000	£000	£000	£000
Fixed assets				
Plant at cost		400		550
Less: Depreciation		100		180
c/f		300		370

	30.4.09		30.4.10	
	£000	£000	£000	£000
b/f		300		370
Current assets				
Stocks	50		90	
Debtors	70		50	
Bank	10		2	
	130		142	
Less: Current liabilities				
Creditors	45		55	
Taxation	18		25	
Proposed dividend	35		40	
	98	32	120	22
		332		392
Capital and reserves				
Ordinary share capital		200		200
Profit and loss account		132		142
		332		342
Loans		–		50
		332		392

Additional information:
There were no sales of fixed assets during the year ended 30 April 2010.

Required:
(a) Prepare Gregory Limited's cash flow statement for the year ended 30 April 2010.
(b) Outline what it tells the managers of Gregory Limited.

7.8 The following summarized accounts have been prepared for Pill Limited:

Profit and loss account for the year ended 31 May 2011

	2010	2011
	£000	£000
Sales	2400	3000
Less: Cost of goods sold	1600	2000
Gross profit	800	1000
Less: Expenses:		
Administrative expenses	310	320
Depreciation: vehicles	55	60
furniture	35	40
	400	420
Net profit	400	580
Taxation	120	150
	280	430
Dividends	200	250
Retained profits for the year	80	180

Balance sheet at 31 May 2011

	31.5.10		31.5.11	
	£000	£000	£000	£000
Fixed assets				
Vehicles at cost	600		800	
Less: Depreciation	200	400	260	540
Furniture	200		250	
Less: Depreciation	100	100	140	110
		500		650
Current assets				
Stocks	400		540	
Debtors	180		200	
Cash	320		120	
	900		860	
Less: Current liabilities				
Creditors	270		300	
Corporation tax	170		220	
Proposed dividends	150		100	
	590	310	620	240
		810		890
Capital and reserves				
Ordinary share capital		500		550
Profit and loss account		120		300
Shareholders' funds		620		850
Loans				
Debentures (10%)		190		40
		810		890

Additional information:
1 There were no sales of fixed assets during the year ended 31 May 2011.
2 The debentures were paid back at the beginning of the year.

Required:
(a) Compile Pill Limited's cash flow statement for the year ended 31 May 2011.
(b) What does it tell the managers of Pill Limited?

7.9 The following information relates to Brian Limited for the year ended 30 June 2012:

Profit and loss account for the year to 30 June 2012

	£000	£000
Gross profit		230
Administrative expenses	76	
Loss on sale of vehicle	3	
Increase in provision for doubtful debts	1	
Depreciation on vehicles	35	115
Net profit		115
Taxation		65
		50
Dividends		25
Retained profit for the year		25

Balance sheet at 30 June 2012

	2011		2012	
	£000	£000	£000	£000
Fixed assets				
Vehicle at cost		150		200
Less: Depreciation		75		100
		75		100
Current assets				
Stocks		60		50
Trade debtors	80		100	
Less: Provision for bad and				
doubtful debts	4	76	5	95
Cash		6		8
		142		153
Current liabilities				
Trade creditors	(60)		(53)	
Taxation	(52)		(65)	
Proposed dividend	(20)	(132)	(25)	(143)
		85		110
Capital and reserves				
Ordinary share capital		75		75
Profit and loss account		10		35
		85		110

Additional information:

1 The company purchased some new vehicles during 2012 for £75,000.
2 During 2012 the company also sold a vehicle for £12,000 in cash. The vehicle had originally cost £25,000, and £10,000 had been set aside for depreciation.

Required:

(a) Prepare a cash flow statement for Brian Limited for the year ended 30 June 2012.
(b) Outline what it tells the managers of Brian Limited.

Further practice questions, study material and links to relevant sites on the World Wide Web can be found on the website that accompanies this book. The site can be found at www.pearsoned.co.uk/dyson

Preparation of financial statements

By the end of this case study you should be able to:

- identify the accounting rules adopted in preparing a set of accounts;
- evaluate the format and presentation of such accounts;
- suggest a more meaningful way of presenting them.

Background **Location**   Bleasedale

Personnel   Alan Marshall: a member of the Calder Rambling Club
Wendy Hargreaves: Treasurer, Calder Rambling Club

Synopsis   Alan Marshall has recently joined the Calder Rambling Club based in Bleasedale. A few
months after joining he attended the annual general meeting.

Among the items on the agenda was the treasurer's report. Alan did not know a great
deal about accounting and so he was somewhat mystified by the 'accounts' presented by
the treasurer, Wendy Hargreaves. He took the opportunity to ask her a few questions but
he did not understand the explanations. A copy of the accounts as presented at the meeting is shown in the appendix to this case study. They were described as a 'balance sheet'
and all the information was presented on one page.

After the meeting Alan learnt that Wendy had been in post for 25 years and the
accounts had always been presented in that way. As long as the club had some money in
the bank nobody else seemed concerned about them.

When he got home, Alan decided to write to Wendy asking for clarification about certain items contained in the 'balance sheet'. She was very helpful and she provided him with
more information. He was still not satisfied that the accounts presented a clear picture of
the club's financial position for the year 2010/11. He also suspected that this was probably
true for the preceding year as well. Alan's questions and Wendy's answers are shown below.

A: *What is 'Mr Smith's bequest'?*
W: A legacy left by ex-chairman Arthur Smith to the club some years ago.

A: *On the left-hand side, what does the item 'Cheques not through bank' mean?*
W: Cheques that had not gone through the bank at the end of the year.

A: *On the right-hand side what do the 'Deposits' mean?*
W: The New Year deposit relates to a booking made at a youth hostel for the forthcoming New Year. The Slide Show deposit is a payment to the hotel for the room
booking for the slide show in December.

A: *On the right-hand side, what does the item 'Through bank' mean?*
W: Cheques that had not gone through the bank at the beginning of the year.

A: *Were any amounts paid in 2009/10 for 2010/11?*

W: Yes – a deposit of £88 paid to the rugby club for the Christmas party held in December 2010.

A: *Did we receive any money in 2009/10 that related to 2010/11?*

W: Yes – subscriptions of £50 in total from five members.

Required:

(a) Identify those accounting rules that the treasurer appears to have adopted in preparing the Calder Rambling Club's accounts and explain what each of them means.

(b) Giving your reasons, indicate what other accounting rules might be appropriate for the treasurer to adopt.

(c) Prepare the club's accounts in a format that you believe would more clearly present its financial performance and position during and at the end of the year.

Appendix

Calder Rambling Club
Balance sheet of accounts for year 2010/11

	£		£
Bank balance at 13.9.10	4365	Affiliation fees	20
Subscriptions	1920	Rights of Way membership	150
Donations	5	Mountain Hut membership	30
Profits from:		Youth Hostel membership	6
Bus cancellation fees	406	Youth Hostel donation	100
Private buses	144	National Trust donation	50
Christmas party	173		
Cheese and wine	17	**Expenses:**	
		Printing and stationery	330
Mr Smith's bequest	96	Leaders' expenses	16
Bank interest (2010/11)	83	Recce expenses	1072
Subscriptions (2011/12)	30	Postage/telephones	6
		Secretary	131
		Treasurer	36
		Sundry items:	
		Hire of halls	285
		Insurance	88
		General	42
		Deposits:	
		New Year 2011/12	128
		Slide show 16.12.11	50
		Losses:	
		High tea	5
		Lecture	17
		Through bank	297
Cheques not through bank	841	**Balance in bank 23.8.11**	5221
TOTAL	**£8080**	TOTAL	**£8080**

Learning objectives

By the end of this case study you should be able to:

- outline the meaning of various conventional accounting policies used in preparing financial statements;
- explain the effect each policy has on the profit or loss for a particular period.

Background

Location	Aberdeen
Personnel	Clare Marshall: Potential investor
	Kate Moorfield: Chartered Accountant

Synopsis

After leaving Birmingham University, Clare Marshall took up a marketing job in an Aberdeen oil firm. During her first five years with the company she earned a good salary and she was paid some highly satisfactory bonuses. She had managed to put a deposit down and take out a mortgage on a flat in Aberdeen, furnish it, buy a car and still have plenty of money for taking advantage of Aberdeen's amenities. She had also fallen in love with Scotland, and with a postgraduate student at Aberdeen University. So she was pretty certain that she would not be moving away from Scotland.

She had realized, however, that she might not always be earning a lot of money so she decided that she must start investing what little spare cash she had. She decided that as her future probably lay in Scotland she might as well invest in the country. Clare had taken a basic course in accounting when she was at university and her job gave her some knowledge of business life around the world, but she did not know very much about suitable companies in which to invest. So she decided to collect a number of Scottish companies' annual reports and accounts. They were delivered to her flat in dribs and drabs but eventually she was able to go through them all in detail.

It was hard going. Some of the reports were long and technical (especially and rather ironically, the oil company ones). However, one of the reports was from an Edinburgh-based construction company called J. Smart & Co. (Contractors) plc. Its 2008 report was only 50 pages long, so she started to go through it without feeling too daunted. But she found even this report hard going and she wished fervently that she had listened more carefully to her accounting lecturer when she was at university.

She got frustrated and bored, and so she decided to ring Kate Moorfield, one of the many new friends that she had made in Aberdeen. After they had discussed their respective boyfriends, Clare mentioned what she had been trying to do. Kate had recently passed her chartered accountancy examinations and she offered to go round to help Clare.

Kate was in her element. She took Clare through Smart's report pretty smartly, stressing what she said were two very important points:

- the preparation of accounting statements requires a great deal of individual judgement;
- apart from their relative brevity the format and content of Smart's accounts were no different from most other public companies.

Clare was reassured about the second point but concerned about accounts apparently needing a lot of 'individual judgement'.

'OK,' said Kate, 'let's look at Note 1 on pages 24 to 29. Rather interestingly they've called them accounting policies and *estimation* techniques. That makes my point. Apart from a few things that relate more to a construction company, they are pretty well what you will find in most reports.' Clare was beginning to feel a little less concerned.

Kate continued, 'If we go through a few of the policies, I can explain why some individual judgement is required and what impact the policies may have on the company's results.' 'How do you mean?' queried Clare. 'Are they flexible?' 'Oh yes,' replied Kate with the enthusiasm expected of a newly qualified chartered accountant. 'What do you mean exactly?' queried Clare rather anxiously. 'Now don't look so concerned,' said Kate, 'It's simply that depending on what accounting policies are adopted and what assumptions are made, it is possible to arrive at almost any figure for profit that you want. That is the case in the preparation of *any* accounting statement.'

Kate may have been overstating the point and Clare's face once more began to register alarm, so Kate began to explain the company's accounting policies while Clare listened very carefully. But it wasn't long before they decided to go out for a coffee and it was several weeks later before Clare bought some shares in ... well, we'd better not say.

Required:

Some of Smart's accounting policies are outlined in the appendix to this case study.
(a) Explain what each of the accounting policies means.
(b) Demonstrate how the application of each these policies can affect the level of accounting profit (or loss) for a particular period.

Appendix

J. Smart & Co. (Contractors) plc
Accounting policies and estimation techniques

Basis of preparation
The accounts have been prepared under the historical cost convention.

The accounting policies set out below have been consistently applied to all periods presented in these accounts.

The preparation of financial statements requires management to make estimates and assumptions concerning the future that may affect the application of accounting policies and the reported amounts of assets and liabilities and income and expenses. Management believes that the estimates and assumptions used in the preparation of these accounts are reasonable. However, actual outcomes may differ from those anticipated.

Revenue
Revenue, which is stated net of value added tax, represents the invoiced value of goods sold, except in the case of long-term contracts where revenue represents the sales value of work done in the year.

Profits on long-term contracts are calculated in accordance with International Financial Reporting Standards and do not relate directly to revenue. Profit on current contracts is only taken at a stage near enough to completion for that profit to be reasonably certain after making provision for contingencies, whilst provision is made for all losses incurred to the accounting date together with any further losses that are foreseen in bringing contracts to completion.

The value of construction work transferred to investment properties is excluded from revenue.

Revenue from investment properties comprises rental income, service charges and other recoveries, and is disclosed as other operating income in the Consolidated financial statements.

Rental income from investment property leased out under an operating lease is recognized in the Income Statement on a straight-line basis over the term of the lease.

Surrender premiums from tenants vacating the property are deferred and released to revenue over the original lease term. When the unit is re-let all deferred amounts are released to revenue at that point.

Inventories and work in progress

Inventories are valued at the lower of cost and net realizable value.

Land held for development is included at the lower of cost and net realizable value.

Work in progress other than long-term contract work in progress is valued at the lower of cost and net realizable value.

Cost includes materials on a first-in, first-out basis and direct labour plus attributable overheads based on normal operating activity, where applicable. Net realizable value is the estimated selling price less anticipated disposal costs.

Long-term contracts

Amounts recoverable on contracts which are included in debtors are stated at cost as defined above, plus attributable profit to the extent that this is reasonably certain after making provision for maintenance costs, less any losses incurred or foreseen in bringing contracts to completion, and less amounts received as progress payments.

For any contracts where receipts exceed the book value of work done, the excess is included in trade and other payables as payments on account.

Depreciation

Depreciation is provided on all items of property, plant and equipment, other than investment properties including those under construction and freehold land, at rates calculated to write off the cost of each asset over its expected useful life, as follows:

Freehold building	over 40 to 66 years
Plant, machinery and vehicles	15% to $33\frac{1}{3}$% reducing balance or straight line as appropriate.

Cash flow statements

Learning objectives

By the end of this case study you should be able to:

- identify the main features of a published cash flow statement;
- evaluate the main reasons for changes in the cash position of an entity.

Background **Location**   Sidmouth

Personnel Edgar Glennie: a retired aircraft engineer
James Arbuthnot: a retired chartered accountant

Synopsis   Edgar Glennie retired from his job as an aircraft engineer in the early part of 2008. He moved to Sidmouth on the south coast and he now spends most of his time playing golf and reading the papers. The financial and political news had not been good and he was worried about his pension. During the five years leading up to his retirement he had managed to invest some savings in a number of companies from which he earned a small income but the market had collapsed and his shares were worth much less than he had paid for them.

As a shareholder he was used to receiving a copy of the annual report and accounts from his various shareholdings. He very rarely bothered to open the envelopes, never mind read the contents. More recently, as a result of his concerns, he had vowed to pay more attention to the progress of the companies in which he had invested. One of the first documents that he received following his vow was the 2008 annual report and accounts from Aggreko plc.

Edgar opened the report fairly gingerly. He did not know much about accounting and he was certain that he would not understand a word of what it was trying to tell him. However, he knew enough to realize that if the company made a profit he was likely to get a dividend but he also knew from the evidence of the 2007/09 recession that it had to have enough cash to keep going.

Aggreko's report was fairly thick – some 120 pages – but manageable as it was printed on A5-sized paper. Page 1 was the index which was useful. Where could he find out about the profit? There did not seem to be any mention of it. So he turned over to the next page where there was some useful information about 'Our Performance'. But he still sought futher detail. On page 4 he learned that Aggreko provided electrical power and temperature control to customers needing such services quickly or for an unknown period. Interesting but where were the details about profit?

He flicked over more pages and more pages until he got to page 71 – a page that did not have a lot on it. It appeared to be some sort of profit and loss account but it was called a Group Income Statement. Ha! But it did give him the profit for the year: nearly £123 million compared with about £81 million for 2007. Good, now what about the dividend? There was no mention of it on that page.

He turned over to page 72: the Group Balance Sheet. This was a much longer statement but he did find an amount called 'cash and cash equivalents' (whatever they were) of £15.3 million compared with the previous year of £9.8 million. He wondered where all the profit had gone. Glancing at the opposite page he noticed that there was another statement called a 'Group Cash Flow Statement' but it showed 'cash and cash equivalents' of £10.3 million at the end of 2008 and £9.6 million at the end of 2007.

Realising that his own knowledge of accounting was too limited for him to sort it all out he decided to have a word with James Arbuthnot, a golfing friend of his. James had been a partner in a small firm of Chartered Accountants in Sidmouth until he had retired some years ago.

When Edgar telephoned James and told him what he had discovered James said that of course he would be glad to help him. Some days later they got together in the golf club bar and James began to take him through Aggreko's report and accounts. He began where Edgar had left off – at the Group Cash Flow Statement ...

Required:

(a) The Aggreko' Group Cash Flow Statement for 2008 is shown in the appendix. Assume that you were James. Explain how a profit for the year after tax of £122.7 million only resulted in an increase in cash and cash equivalents of £10.3 million and why there appears to be a difference between the cash and cash equivalent balances on the group balance sheet and the group cash flow statement.

Appendix

Aggreko plc
Group cash flow statement for the year ended 31 December 2008

	2008 £million	2007 £million
Cash flow from operating activities		
Cash generated from operations	276.1	230.2
Tax paid	(39.6)	(21.4)
Net cash generated from operating activities	236.5	208.8
Cash flows from investing activities		
Acquisitions (net of cash acquired)	(15.9)	(0.4)
Purchase of property, plant and equipment (PPE)	(265.2)	(180.6)
Proceeds from sale of PPE	9.0	8.1
Net cash used in investing activities	(272.1)	(172.9)
Cash flows from financing activities		
Net proceeds from sale of ordinary shares	1.3	1.8
Increase in long-term loans	185.7	66.0
Repayment of long-term loans	(107.1)	(62.6)
Net movement in short-term loans	4.9	(7.1)
Interest received	0.5	1.5
Interest paid	(14.6)	(12.8)
Dividends paid to shareholders	(23.7)	(19.2)
c/f	47.0	32.4

		2008 £million	2007 £million
	b/f	47.0	32.4
Purchase of Treasury shares		(13.2)	(4.2)
Sale of own shares by Employee Benefit Trust		0.9	–
Net cash from/(used in) financing activities		34.7	(36.6)
Net decrease in cash and cash equivalents		(0.9)	(0.7)
Cash and cash equivalents at beginning of year		9.6	10.0
Exchange gain on cash and cash equivalents		1.6	0.3
Cash and cash equivalents at end of year		10.3	9.6

Notes

(1) Cash flow from operating activities

	2008 £ million	2007 £ million
Profit for year	122.7	80.7
Adjustments for:		
Tax	67.3	43.5
Depreciation	115.9	92.8
Amortization of intangibles	1.9	1.6
Finance income	(0.5)	(1.5)
Finance cost	15.3	13.2
Profit on sale of PPE (see below)	(4.2)	(3.0)
Share-based payments	7.8	4.6
Changes in working capital (excluding the effects of exchange differences on consolidation):		
Increase in inventories	(20.4)	(18.6)
Increase in trade and other receivables	(51.7)	(13.4)
Increase in trade and other payables	23.8	34.7
Net movements in provisions for liabilities and charges	(1.8)	(4.2)
Net retirement benefit cost	–	(0.2)
Cash generated from operations	276.1	230.2

In the cash flow statement, proceeds from sale of PPE comprise:

	2008 £ million	2007 £ million
Net book amount	4.8	5.1
Profit on sale of PPE	4.2	3.0
Proceeds from sale of PPE	9.0	8.1

(2) Cash and cash equivalents

	2008 £million	2007 £million
Cash at bank and in hand	14.8	9.1
Short-term bank deposits	0.5	0.7
	15.3	0.7
Cash and cash equivalents *	15.3	0.7
Bank overdrafts +	(5.0)	(0.2)
	10.3	9.6

* as per the Group Balance Sheet
+ the bank overdrafts are included in the Group Balance Sheet under **Borrowings**

FINANCIAL REPORTING

In Part 3 we deal with the subject of *financial reporting*. The distinction between financial accounting (as covered in Part 2) and financial reporting is blurred. Indeed, at one time no such distinction would be made. However, financial accounting is now regarded as a rather mechanical and technical process that ends with the preparation of the profit and loss account, balance sheet and a cash flow statement. Financial reporting is more concerned with how accounting data can best be communicated to users of financial statements in accordance with legal and professional requirements.

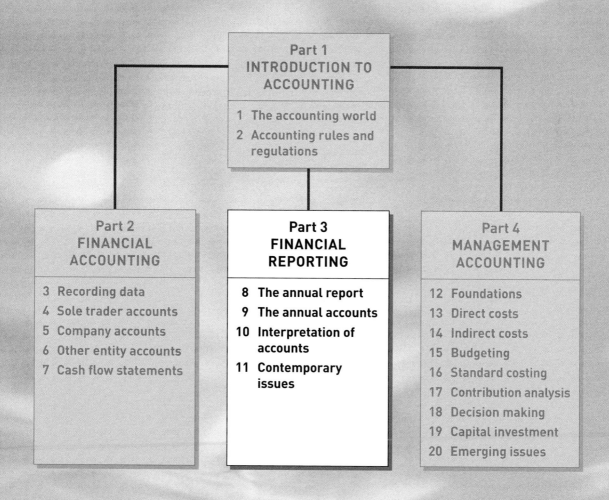

Part 1
INTRODUCTION TO ACCOUNTING

1 The accounting world
2 Accounting rules and regulations

Part 2
FINANCIAL ACCOUNTING

3 Recording data
4 Sole trader accounts
5 Company accounts
6 Other entity accounts
7 Cash flow statements

Part 3
FINANCIAL REPORTING

8 The annual report
9 The annual accounts
10 Interpretation of accounts
11 Contemporary issues

Part 4
MANAGEMENT ACCOUNTING

12 Foundations
13 Direct costs
14 Indirect costs
15 Budgeting
16 Standard costing
17 Contribution analysis
18 Decision making
19 Capital investment
20 Emerging issues

The annual report

Does more mean less?

Narrative reporting taking over annual reports

Kevin Reed

Narrative reporting is taking up a greater proportion of annual reports, according to **Deloitte's research**.

While the size of annual reports grew by just 2% on 2007 to an average 96 pages, narrative reporting makes up 54% of the reports, which is a 3% increase on the previous year.

Annual reports are 35% longer than they were in 2005.

'The main message from this year's survey is the realisation of how much the narrative reporting requirements have grown like topsy over the years,' said Deloitte audit partner Isobel Sharp.

'New requirements have been bolted on and new extensions will be added in 2008/9. The result is that the narrative sections of annual reports can have similarities with the famous Ronnie Corbett monologues, namely lots of diversions.

'Unfortunately new rules governing narrative reporting mean that this is unlikely to change in the future.'

A new requirement for a directors' responsibility statement, introduced by the Financial Services Authority and emanating from the EU Transparency Obligations Directive, was met only by 54% of relevant companies.

Accountancy Age, 24 October 2008.

Source: Reproduced with permission from Incisive Media Ltd.

Questions relating to this news story can be found on page 194 ➡

About this chapter

The Companies Act 2006 requires companies to prepare accounts for each financial year. They are then obliged to send a copy of the accounts to every shareholder and every debenture holder of the company. The Act also requires them to report on other aspects of their operations along with a number of legislative and professional requirements. The additional information is usually provided in report form. The reports and the accounts and are then combined to form one document.

A copy of the report and accounts must also to be filed with the Registrar of Companies, i.e. sent to him; he then makes it available for public inspection. This process is what accountants mean when they talk about 'disclosure of information' or 'published accounts'.

Annual reports and accounts can be quite lengthy. Those for a relatively small plc, for example, can easily stretch to 50 pages while those for a large international plc may go well beyond 100 pages. So for shareholders and debenture holders there is an awful lot to read. In addition, much of the content is complex, highly technical and full of jargon. It is very difficult to believe that most annual report and accounts mean very much to the average shareholder and there is, in fact, some strong empirical evidence to suggest that very few are actually read.

In this book we have provided you with the necessary background information and knowledge that should enable you make sense of a company's annual report and accounts. But even so you probably need some additional help in order to see how the material we have covered so far in this book relates to the published information. We provide that help in two chapters as the subject is too big to cover in one chapter. In this chapter we deal with 'reports' and in the next chapter the 'accounts'.

In both chapters we will be primarily concerned with the published reports and accounts of public limited liability companies and we will be making frequent references to examples extracted from such a source.

Learning objectives	By the end of this chapter you should be able to: • list the types of reports found in a company's annual report and accounts; • separate such reports from the accounts section; • identify the introductory material; • outline the contents of a chairman's report; • explain what is meant by corporate governance; • specify the nature of a business review; • identify the main sections of a directors' report; • summarize the contents of a directors' remuneration report.

❗ Why this chapter is important

This chapter is important for non-accountants because at some time or other in whatever career you pursue you are going to come across company annual reports and accounts. Most entities of any size prepare such a document but by law companies are required to do so. As a result, published reports and accounts tend to act as a model for other types of entities irrespective of their nature and size.

It is highly likely that in your job you will be involved to a lesser or greater degree in the preparation of *the* annual report and accounts. And as you become more senior you will have greater and greater responsibility to ensure that your company complies with legal and professional requirements. Furthermore, given that the company has to produce such a document, you will want to make sure that as far as possible it is readable and understandable. That means you will need to have a good eye for presentation and an ability to spot what reads well and what does not. This chapter will help you to develop your knowledge and skill in what is required.

There is perhaps another reason why this chapter is important. In your private life you will probably want to become a shareholder in a company. One document at least that you will need to study before making an investment is its annual report and accounts; thereafter you will use it to monitor its progress. The chances are that once trained in the mysteries of annual reports and accounts you will find them helpful when making your own personal investment decisions.

Activity 8.1	Obtain the annual report and accounts of three UK public limited liability companies.

Guidance: If some of your friends or relatives have shares in a company they should automatically receive a copy of its annual report and accounts. See if they will let you have it. Otherwise write to the Company Secretary of each company. Most companies will let you have a set without any questions being asked. You may also be able to download some reports from the Internet. Choose commercial or industrial companies. Avoid banking and insurance companies as they have different reporting requirements.

Note: It is important that you do as requested above otherwise you will find it more difficult to work your way through both this chapter and the next one.

Overview

News clip

Longer and longer

A report by Deloitte shows that annual reports have nearly doubled in size over ten years. In 1996 the average length was 45 pages. By 2006 the average length was 89 pages and by 2007, 96 pages (*refer back to the news story on page 178*).

Source: Adapted from *Accountancy Age*, 6 December 2007, p. 1.

You will find that with most annual reports and accounts it is relatively easy to separate the 'reports' from the 'accounts' no matter where they appear in the overall document or what they are called. The reports will usually come before the accounts and they will probably be put into various groupings although there is no statutory requirement to do so. The number of categories adopted can range from only two or three categories to as many as ten.

We will opt for a fairly broad approach in our discussion. As can be seen from Figure 8.1, we have decided to group the report section into the three main categories: (1) introductory material; (2) corporate reporting; and (3) shareholder information.

We start our discussion with the introductory material section. You are likely to find it in the first few pages of any annual report and accounts.

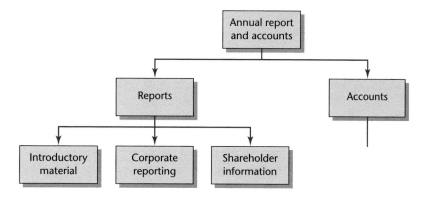

Figure 8.1 Annual reports: structure

Introductory material

There are no statutory or professional requirements that specifically cover the introductory section although what is reported must not conflict with other reports. The section is usually confined to the first few pages of the document (including sometimes the use of the inside page of the front cover). The information provided will probably tell you something about the company: what it does, where it has done it and how it was done, i.e. its history, location and a summary of its financial results.

The information that is likely to be disclosed may be broken down into four broad categories, as shown in Figure 8.2. They are: (1) highlights, i.e. specific matters to which the company particularly wants to draw attention; (2) a financial summary of the results for the year; (3) some promotional material; and (4) the chairman's statement.

We will discuss each of these categories in turn starting with the 'highlights'.

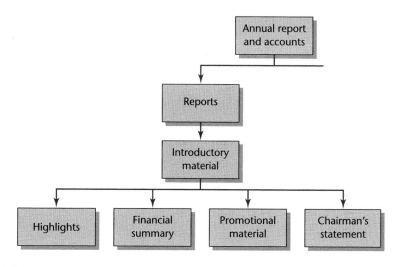

Figure 8.2 Annual reports: introductory material

Highlights

An overview of the company and its performance is useful for those readers who have neither the time nor the inclination to go beyond the introductory material. Such material will probably be outlined in no more than one or two pages but sometimes it may be very brief. Sig plc, for example, in its 2008 Annual Report and Accounts adopts an A4-size page and then uses the inside page of the front cover to report in large white letters on a red background that:

> *SIG plc is a leading European supplier of insulaton, exteriors, interiors and specialist construction products.*

A four-line sentence (in much smaller white letters) outlining the company's strategy then follows. This in turn is followed by a summary of its three core principles (in much larger letters) and a two-and-a-half-line sentence explaining what these principles enable the Group to do. The contents of the Report and Accounts are then listed in small type at the bottom of the page.

The introductory section of the report includes on page 1 a summary of the Group's performance, on page 2 a list of its activities, on page 3 a review of the year, and on pages 4 and 5 we find the Chairman's statement. So in Sig's case the highlights section is just six pages long (including the inside cover).

By contrast Aggreko's 2008 Annual Report and Accounts uses A5-size pages. The front inside cover is covered in tiny print; it is too small to read and the user is perhaps not meant to do so (as it is probably presentational). Page 1 (and 3) lists the contents. Page 2 summarises 'Our performance'. Pages 4 to 13 then give the reader some information about the company using such headings (in large orange type) as 'What We Do', 'Where We Do It', 'Our Fleet', 'Our Business Models', and 'The Market' (the latter taking up five pages). Pages 14 to 16 are given over to the Chairman's statement. All of this information is included in what is titled the 'Directors' Report' which altogether takes up 52 of the entire 120 page document.

Financial summary

Most companies usually give a brief financial summary of the group's performance for the year. This usually takes up no more than one page. Often it is a combination of numbers and graphs. Devro's 2008 report is a good example. On page 1 under the heading 'Financial Highlights' four small bar charts are given showing data for four years: earnings per share, group revenue, operating profit, and operating profit margin. Underneath is a small table of the 2007 and 2008 results which we have reproduced in Figure 8.3. The information is so compact that there has even been room to include on the same page a list of the contents of the entire document.

Some of the information shown in Figure 8.3 will not mean much to you just yet so you can appreciate just how difficult it must be for those readers who have not had *any* training in accounting.

Promotional material

Many companies take the opportunity of promoting the company's products in their annual report and accounts. This makes sound business sense. Shareholders are also consumers and if there are thousands of them the company might as well encourage them to buy its products.

DEVRO plc	FINANCIAL HIGHLIGHTS	
	2008	2007*
Dividends per share	**4.45p**	4.45p
Operating profit before exceptional items	**£20.6m**	£17.7m
– margin	**11.2%**	11.3%
Exceptional items	**£(3.5)m**	£0.7m
Profit before tax	**£15.3m**	£16.2m
Cash generated from operations	**£31.3m**	£23.4m
Capital expenditure	**£12.7**	£11.1m
Net debt	**£24.0m**	£27.3m
Gearing	**21.5%**	28.7%

* on a continuing operations basis

Figure 8.3 Introductory material: example of a financial summary

Source: Devro plc, *Annual Report and Accounts*, 2008.

A good example of how this can be done is A.G. Barr plc, the soft drinks manufacturer best known as the makers of *Irn Bru*. Its 2009 report and accounts is particularly striking. The 87-page report is bound in a double-page-thick front and back piece thereby giving it an extra eight pages in a vivid multi-colour display of its range of products. Barr then goes even further than most companies. The last page of the document and the two inside pages of its double back cover is given over to a remarkable display of 25 reproductions of its products in what can only be described as the 'beer mat' format. By contrast J. Smart & Co (Contractors) PLC, a much smaller company than Barr, has a very slim and sober presentation. Its 2008 report and accounts does not have any introductory material of any kind, still less any promotional material! But then construction companies are not into the mass consumer market.

Activity 8.2

Consult your copies of the three sets of annual reports and accounts that you obtained when completing Activity 8.1. Read through the introductory material. Write down the content of each company's material in just a few words in three adjacent columns. Then compare your results for the three companies. On a scale of 1 to 5 (5 being the highest) rate how informative you find each company's introductory material section.

Chairman's statement

Most company chairmen like to include a report or statement of their own in the annual report. There are no statutory, ASB/IASB or Stock Exchange requirements for chairmen to publish a report so the format and content will vary from company to company. A relatively brief chairman's report is shown in Figure 8.4.

You will probably find the chairman's statement in the first few pages of the annual report. You can expect it to be anything from one to four pages in length. It will be largely narrative in style although there will almost certainly be some quantitative information. Research evidence suggests that chairmen's statements are the most widely read section of an annual report, perhaps because they are mainly narrative.

Chairmen tend to adopt an upbeat approach about the recent performance of the company and they are usually extremely optimistic about the future. You must, therefore, read their reports with some degree of scepticism and you should check their comments against the detailed results contained elsewhere within the overall annual report and accounts. Nevertheless, chairmen have to be careful that they do not become too optimistic. Their remarks can have a significant impact on the company's share price and they might have to answer to the Stock Exchange authorities if they publish misleading statements.

J. Smart & Co. (Contractors) PLC

CHAIRMAN'S REVIEW

ACCOUNTS

Group profits for the year before tax, including an unrealised deficit in revalued property, as required by the International Financial Reporting Standards, were less than last year turning out at £5,849,000. This compares with the figure for last year of £8,144,000 which includes an unrealised gain in revalued property. If the impact of revalued property on the figures is disregarded then a truer reflection of Group Performance emerges in the form of an underlying profit before tax of £8,504,000 (including £3,890,000 profit from property sales) for the year under review which would compare with a figure for the previous year of £6,200,000 (including £2,129,000 profit from property sales).

The Board is recommending a Final dividend of 10.50p nett making a total for the year of 13.50p nett which compares with 13.15p nett for the previous year. After waivers by members holding approximately 51% of the shares, the Dividends will cost the Company £664,000.

Profit adjusted for pension scheme deficit, dividends paid and fair value reserve when added to opening shareholders' funds brings the total equity of the Group to £97,314,000.

TRADING ACTIVITIES

Group turnover increased by 27%, own work capitalised decreased by 53% and other operating income increased by 4%. Total Group profits decreased by 28%. Underlying Group profits excluding an unrealised deficit in revalued property increased by 37%.

Turnover in contracting increased but a small loss was sustained. Private housing sales declined again. Sales in precast concrete manufacture increased slightly and a small profit was made.

The mixed commercial and residential development in McDonald Road, Edinburgh continues apace. We have completed the residential Joint Venture with Kiltane Developments Ltd (formerly Keane Develpments Ltd) at Duff Street, Edinburgh. Over 50% of the flats have been sold.

FUTURE PROSPECTS

Rental income is expected to increase.

We have almost completed the second and final phase of our Joint Venture with Walker Group at Prestonfield Park, Edinburgh, comprising five Industrial Units, four of which are let or pre-let and one of which is partly let.

We have commenced a second speculative office block at Glenbervie Business Park, Larbert and a medium sized speculative industrial unit which is capable of sub-division into four smaller units at Bilston Glen, near Edinburgh.

The amount of contract work in hand is more than at this time last year. The majority of this work has been obtained on a negotiated and/or design and construct basis and the balance by traditional competitive tender, however, costs have been rising significantly. Private house sales have stalled.

These are uncertain times which make forecasting difficult. However, disregarding the impact on the Income Statement of including unrealised gains/deficits in revalued property, I anticipate that the underlying profit for the current year will be less than last year.

J. M. SMART
Chairman

18th November 2008

Figure 8.4 A chairman's statement
Source: J. Smart & Co. (Contractors) PLC, *Annual Report and Accounts*, 2008.

The contents of a typical chairman's statement could include the following items:

- *Results.* A summary of the company's results for the year covering turnover, pre- and post-tax profits, earnings per share and cash flow.
- *Dividend.* Details about any interim dividend paid for the year and any proposed final dividend.
- *Prospects.* A summary of how the chairman sees the general economic and political outlook and the future prospects for the company.

- *Employees.* A comment about the company's employees including any notable successes, concluding with the Board's thanks to all employees for their efforts.
- *Directors.* A similar note may be included about the Board of Directors including tributes to retiring directors.

We now turn to what we have called the 'corporate reporting' section of a company's annual report and accounts.

Activity 8.3	Referring to your three sets of annual reports and accounts, find the chairman's statement and in each set go through them very carefully. Are there any items not included in the summary shown above?
	List the main contents of each chairman's statement.

Corporate reporting

Some companies call this section of the annual report and accounts 'the directors' report' but this can be a little confusing as the Companies Act uses the same term to refer to a much narrower type of report. We have, therefore, called this section 'corporate reporting' and classified it into three broad categories (as can be seen in Figure 8.5): (1) corporate governance; (2) the statutory directors' report; and (3) the directors' remuneration report.

Corporate governance

Strictly speaking the Companies Act 2006 requires much of the material disclosed in this section to be included in a statutory directors' report although it is permitted to present it elsewhere within the overall report and accounts. Many companies do just that and we will do the same because it simplifies our discussion.

As far back as 1991 the accounting profession, the Financial Reporting Council and the London Stock Exchange set up a committee (known as the Cadbury Committee) to examine what has become to be known as 'corporate governance'. The term refers to the way that companies and other entities are controlled and managed. The Committee

Figure 8.5 Annual reports: corporate reporting

reported in 1992 and since that time there have been a number of other influential committees that have worked on the practice and development of 'corporate governance'.

While shareholders own companies, they appoint directors to run the companies for them. So it seems reasonable that the shareholders want to be assured that the directors know what they are doing, how they are going about it, and how successful they have been. Nonetheless, Parliament has largely left the business and financial communities to deal with the matter and there has not been any detailed legislation. The specific requirements are laid down by the London Stock Exchange for all listed companies in a document called the *The Combined Code.*

The Code *is* extremely detailed. It deals with both companies and institutional shareholders. In this chapter we are particularly interested in what the company and the directors have to disclose in their annual report and accounts. The details are included in Schedule C of the Code: *Disclosure of corporate governance arrangements.* There are two and a half pages listing the disclosure requirements so no doubt you will appreciate why this helps to increase the size (and weight) of annual reports and accounts. In summary, the main disclosure requirements are as follows.

- Application of the Code's principles.
- Compliance or not with all the Code's principles and if not, which, for how long and why.
- Details of the Board's operations including the names of the chairman, deputy chairman, chief executive, senior independent director, independent non-executive directors and the names and members of the nomination, audit and remuneration committee members.
- The Chairman's commitments along with any changes.
- Evaluation of the Board's performance, its committees and the directors.
- Ways the Board keeps in contact with shareholder opinion.
- Description of the work of the nomination committee (i.e. to the Board) and the (directors') remuneration committee.
- Directors' duties in the preparation of the accounts and the auditors' reporting responsibilities.
- Statement by the directors that the company is a going concern (this is particularly important at a time of recession).
- A review of internal control procedures.
- Reasons why there is no internal audit function (if that is so), duties and responsibilities of the audit committee, the appointment or otherwise of the external auditor and details of the external auditor's non-audit services.

There are also various clauses covering the disclosure of some additional information on the company's website about the nomination, remuneration and audit committees, the appointment of non-executive directors and the use of remuneration consultants. Similarly, additional information about the election of directors and the appointment of the external auditor has to be given in papers sent to shareholders.

Even in summary the above list of disclosure requirements is formidable. In order to give you some ideas of what is required Figure 8.6 shows the main headings used in two annual reports and accounts: those of Cairn Energy plc and Devro plc.

Activity 8.4
Once again turn to your three sets of annual reports and accounts. Check whether there is a specific corporate governance statement. Read each one. Then copy the headings into adjacent columns, listing as far as possible similar items on the same line opposite each other.

Cairn Energy plc 2008	Devro plc 2008
Opening paragraph (not titled)	1 Statement
The board	2 Board composition 8 Directors' training and development
Performance evaluation	9 Board performance evaluation
Independence of non-executive directors	
Hamish Grossart	9 Board performance evaluation
Board committees	3 Board and committee proceedings
1 Audit committee report	5 Report from audit committee 6 Auditor independence
2 Remuneration committee report	4 Directors' remuneration
3 Nomination committee report	10 Report from the nomination committee
Succession planning	
Organisational planning	
Directors' attendance at board and board committee meetings	
Relations with shareholders	7 Relationship with shareholders
Annual general meeting	
Directors' responsibility statement	
Going concern	13 Going concern
Internal control	12 Internal control
1 Strategic direction	
2 Operating management	
3 Risk management	
4 Assurance	11 Financial reporting
Compliance with the Combined Code	14 Compliance with the Code

Note: Devro presented its corporate governance statement in numbered paragraphs (as above). These have been placed as closely as possible to Cairn's paragraph headings.

Figure 8.6 Corporate governance statements: two examples

Sources: Cairn Energy plc, *Annual Report and Accounts*, 2008; Devro plc, *Annual Report and Accounts*, 2008.

Directors' report

The Companies Act 2006 requires company directors to prepare a report for each financial year. You will usually find it towards the end of the corporate governance section. The report is likely to be a very long one and to make up a high proportion of the overall annual report and accounts. No set format is required but it will probably be presented as a series of paragraphs under appropriate headings. The content of each paragraph will be mainly narrative but it is likely that some statistical information will also be included.

The information required to be disclosed by the Act is specified in three sections. The details are summarized below.

General contents

The general disclosure requirements are fairly minimal. However, the Secretary of State has the authority to put forward other requirements by way of 'regulations' so it is possible that over time this section will grow as new issues arise. The current requirements are as follows.

- The names of those persons who have been directors during the year.
- The principal activities of the company in the course of the year.
- The amount recommended by the directors to be paid by way of dividend.

Business review

The business review is likely to take up most of the directors' report. Its purpose is to provide information to members of the company in order to help them assess how successful the directors have been in performing their duty in promoting the success of the company. Among the mandatory items to be included in the business review are the following.

- A fair review of the company's business.
- A description of risks and uncertainties facing it.
- A balanced and comprehensive analysis of its development and performance of the company's business during the year.
- A similar analysis of the company's business position at the end of the year.
- The main trends and factors likely to affect its future development, performance and position.
- The disclosure of information relating to the company's policies, the impact and effectiveness of such matters as the environment, the company's employees, and social and community issues.
- Information about persons who have essential contractual or other arrangements with the company.
- An analysis of the company's business incorporating key financial, environmental, employee and performance indicators.
- A reference to, and some additional explanations of, amounts included in the annual accounts.
- The steps taken to make sure that the auditors get all the information that they need in order to prepare their report.

Auditors

The 2006 Companies Act has six subsections dealing with matters that relate to the auditors. The following matters are of particular relevance.

- The directors' report must contain a statement that the directors are aware that all relevant information has been given to the auditors, i.e. all the information that they need in order to be able to complete their report.
- The directors have taken steps to be aware of all relevant information that the auditors might need and that the auditors in turn are aware of that information.

The statutory and listing disclosure information required in a directors' report is quite formidable. This part of the annual report and accounts can take up many pages. This is not the case with Cairn Energy plc's 2008 annual report and accounts. It is only four pages long but even so there is a lot of technical detail to absorb, as can be seen from the main headings reproduced in Figure 8.7.

Opening paragraph (not titled)
Results and dividend
Principal activities and business review (there is a detailed separate business review)
Change of control
Directors
Share capital
Voting rights
Restrictions on voting
Variation of rights
Transfer of shares
Major interests in share capital
Charitable and political donations
Creditor payment policy and practice
Financial instruments
Election/re-election of directors
Powers of the directors
Articles of association
Disclosure of information to auditors
Reappointment of auditors
AGM 2009

Figure 8.7 Directors' report: main headings for Cairn Energy plc 2008

Source: Cairn Energy plc, *Annual Report and Accounts*, 2008.

Activity 8.5

Search through each of your three sets of annual reports and accounts. Find the section called 'Business Review' (or some such title). List the headings used in the review. Does it include all the requirements that we have listed in the above section? What is missing? If some items are missing try to find them elsewhere in the respective report and accounts.

Directors' remuneration report

The Companies Act 2006 requires that the directors of a quoted company must prepare a directors' remuneration report for each financial year. The Act does not explain the purpose of such a report so we can only go off its title.

It seems reasonable to assume that the purpose of a directors' remuneration report is to let shareholders know what the company is paying the directors to act on the shareholders' behalf. In practice the directors determine their own pay although it has to be approved by the shareholders. They very rarely object or get anywhere if they try to do so. The total amount paid to the directors may be very large indeed. It will usually be made up of a complex package of fees, salaries, bonuses, pension contributions and share options.

The Act itself does not go into much detail about what should be disclosed but the Secretary of State has the power to do so by 'regulation'. The current disclosure requirements are similar to those that have been required for many years. We outline some of the main requirements below.

Information not subject to audit

- Names of directors and others involved in the consideration of the directors' remuneration.
- Statement of the company's policy on directors' remuneration.
- A performance graph plotting total shareholder return against a broad equity market index.
- Details of the directors' service contracts.

Information subject to audit

- Amount of each director's emoluments and compensation.
- Each director's share option arrangements.
- Long-term incentive schemes for directors.
- Pensions.
- Excess retirement benefits of directors and past directors.
- Compensation for past directors.
- Sums paid to third parties for a director's services.

The above requirements can lead to a very lengthy directors' remuneration report. For example, Robert Wiseman Dairies' report is 10 pages long and Cairn Energy just over 12 pages. Directors' remuneration reports are presented mainly in a narrative style in paragraphs under relevant headings. There can, however, be some quantitative and statistical data and (as required) at least one performance graph.

We do not have the space here to reproduce an actual directors' remuneration report but what we have done in Figure 8.8 is to extract the main headings used in Devro's directors' remuneration report. Its report is a relatively short one: it is only four pages long!

Activity 8.6	Once more turn to your three sets of annual reports and accounts. Find the directors' remuneration report. Read through each one. List all the main headings in each report in three adjacent columns. Try to put similar headings opposite each other. Is there a regular pattern? Or are there some items that are specific to one company? Note the differences.

Shareholder information

Following on from the directors' remuneration report you will then almost certainly come across the 'accounts'. We will come back to this section in the next chapter. After the accounts you may then find some miscellaneous information that is of particular relevance to the shareholders. If it is not at the back of the report then it may be included in the introductory section. The shareholder information is likely to include the following information.

Opening paragraph (not a heading)
Composition of the non-executive directors' remuneration committee
Policy on non-executive directors' remuneration
Composition of the executive directors' remuneration committee ('the committee')
Compliance
Company policy on contracts of service
Performance graph total shareholder return
Shareholding qualification
External directorships
Auditable information
Company pensions policy regarding executive directors
Directors' detailed emoluments
The Devro 2003 performance share plan
Directors' interests

Figure 8.8 Directors' renumeration report: main headings for Devro plc 2008

Source: Devro plc, *Annual Report and Accounts*, 2008.

Administrative matters

This may include notice of the annual general meeting, when the dividend may be paid, details about online shareholder services and share dealing, the names and addresses of the company officers and advisers, a financial calendar, and a list of the principal companies of the group.

Financial summary

A summary of the financial results over the last five years (possibly ten) may be included in this part of the annual report and accounts. It will probably give some quantitative and statistical data and some graphs depicting the main results covering such items as the revenue earned, profits, capital expenditure and number of employees. Such a summary is sometimes included in the accounts section of the overall annual report and accounts.

Glossary of terms

Some companies provide a list of the financial and technical terms used in their annual report and accounts.

Activity 8.7

List the shareholder information included in each of your three sets of annual reports and accounts. In most companies this information will be at the back but some of it may be at the front. Are there any items not included in the text above? If so, add them to the list outlined in the text.

> **!** **Questions you should ask**
>
> In previous chapters we have stressed that the accounting information presented to you will have been prepared by your accountants and that you are unlikely to be involved in the detailed preparation. This chapter is different. The matters with which we have been dealing will be the responsibility of a large team of non-accountants with the assistance of the accountants. So what do you need to ask if you are involved in preparing your company's annual report? We suggest the following.
>
> - What information is legally and professionally required and where should it be shown?
> - What corporate governance information and other matters are we duty bound to disclose and where is the best place to put it?
> - Are we sure that any statements made are in line with the financial data presented in the annual accounts?
> - Do we have some evidence to justify any predictions we make about our future prospects?
> - Are we presenting too much information to our shareholders and if so, can we cut it back?
> - Is the design, format and general content of the material likely to encourage users to read it?
> - Do the various reports contain any jargon and if so, can we either cut it out or reduce it?
> - Are the publicity pages likely to annoy our shareholders?

Conclusion

A company usually publishes an annual report and accounts. It then supplies a copy to each shareholder and files one with the Registrar of Companies for public inspection. In this chapter we have examined the annual *report* section of an annual report and accounts. The next chapter examines the annual *accounts* section.

In order to make our study of an annual report a little easier, we have suggested that it can be broken down into three main sections. The first few pages usually contain some introductory material about the company such as its objectives and a summary of the financial year. In consumer-orientated companies there may also be many pages advertising the company's products. A chairman's report may be considered to be part of this section. You will probably find it towards the end of the introductory material. It will normally be narrative in style and upbeat in tone. The Chairman usually summarizes the financial performance for the year and reviews the prospects for the following year.

Following the introductory section most annual reports and accounts contain what we have called a 'corporate reporting' section although other terms are used. This section may be broken down into a number of categories. We have identified three: the corporate governance of the company, the directors' report and the directors' remuneration report. Much of the information disclosed in this section is now mandatory as part of the London Stock Exchange listing requirements but some of it is also a statutory requirement.

Thereafter there will almost certainly be a detailed section dealing with the 'accounts' (discussed in the next chapter) and following the accounts a brief section outlining some administrative matters that are of particular relevance for the shareholders. Such matters include company names and addresses, details of the AGM, a financial summary, and sometimes a glossary.

Key points	

1 A company's annual report and accounts contains a great many reports and statements, some of which are voluntary and some of which are mandatory. In this chapter we have dealt with annual reports.

2 It is possible to identify three main sections of an annual report, although the detailed content and structure varies from company to company. The length of such reports also varies depending partly on the size of the company and partly on its type, e.g. whether it is a manufacturing or a service-based company.

3 The introductory section contains some details about the company, a summary of its financial results for the year, the chairman's statement details about the governance of the company and possibly some publicity material.

4 The specific reports that follow include a directors' report and a directors' remuneration report.

5 The annual accounts will normally then be presented followed by the last few pages of the overall document containing some miscellaneous information largely for the benefit of the shareholders.

Check your learning

The answers to these questions can be found within the text.

1 List three items that may be included in the introductory section of a company's annual report.

2 What mandatory requirement covers the contents of a chairman's statement?

3 List three items that will normally be included in a chairman's statement.

4 Identify three main sections under which the 'report of the directors' may be classified.

5 What is meant by corporate governance?

6 What is *The Combined Code*?

7 Name six of its provisions.

8 What three items should be included in the general contents section of a directors' report?

9 What is a business review?

10 Identify six items that it should include.

11 What information about the auditors should directors include in their report?

12 What is a directors' remuneration report?

13 Name six matters that should be included in it.

14 Identify three items that may be included in 'shareholder information'.

News story quiz

Remember the news story at the beginning of this chapter? Go back to that story and reread it before answering the following questions.

Research over many years has indicated that most users of annual reports and accounts have difficulty in coping with quantitative information. They are much happier when the information is presented in a narrative style. For this reason it is not surprising that the chairman's report is thought to be more widely read than most of the other reports.

Questions

1 Is it possible for financial statements to be presented in such a way that non-trained users will be able to understand them?

2 To what extent do you think that narrative reporting makes financial statements more understandable?

3 Does more information lead to less understanding?

Tutorial questions

8.1 'A limited liability company's annual report should be made easier to understand for the average shareholder.' Discuss.

8.2 Examine the argument that annual reports are a costly irrelevance because hardly anyone refers to them.

8.3 Should companies be banned from including non-financial data in their annual reports?

Further practice questions, study material and links to relevant sites on the World Wide Web can be found on the website that accompanies this book. The site can be found at www.pearsoned.co.uk/dyson

Say what you think ...

Accounting sleights of hand replaced by puffery

Philip Whitchelo

In 1992, Terry Smith published the first edition of his best selling exposé *Accounting for Growth*, of the methods by which some UK companies in the 1980s and 1990s had used (apparently legitimate) accounting techniques to turn losses into profits, expenditure into assets and debt into somebody else's liability.

Funnily enough, many of the companies that used such techniques (such as Tiphook, Queens Moat and Trafalgar House) had the nasty habit of blowing up as soon as the recession of the early 1990s took hold.

The most egregious examples of accounting trickery have since been outlawed by the Accounting Standards Board through the development of more robust accounting standards, recommended practices and other strictures, such that the investor of the late 2000s could be forgiven for thinking that published company annual reports were in some way a useful guide to a company's business and to the likely risks (and rewards) that an investor in the equity of such companies could expect.

Nothing could be further from the truth.

A review of the published annual report and accounts of the banks that have imploded and showered us all with their toxic debris shows that the accounting sleights of hand of the 1980s have been replaced by a thick, glossy catalogue of useless puffery, where mindless box ticking compliance and endless committees stupefy the reader with page after page of irrelevant disclosure and really important information such as the CO_2 output of bank branches, and per employee, and details of the water saving toilet-flushing system installed in head office.

Of the impending maelstrom, not a whisper.

The proper purpose of a company report and accounts – an honest description of a company's business model a realistic assessment of the risks and rewards to which the business is subject and a true picture of the balance sheet – has become almost totally obliterated

It is time for regulators, auditors and companies to put a halt to this farce and to return the annual report to its rightful place as a source of meaningful information for investors.

www.ft.com, 2 March 2009.

Source: Reproduced with permission from Philip Whitchelo, Interim M&A Partners Ltd, London.

Questions relating to this news story can be found on page 211 ➡

About this chapter

This chapter is a continuation of Chapter 8. In that chapter we dealt with the various reports that you will find in a listed company's annual report and accounts. In this chapter we are going to look at what may be found in its annual *accounts*, such as a profit and loss account and a balance sheet. Figure 9.1 gives you an overview of what we will be covering in this chapter.

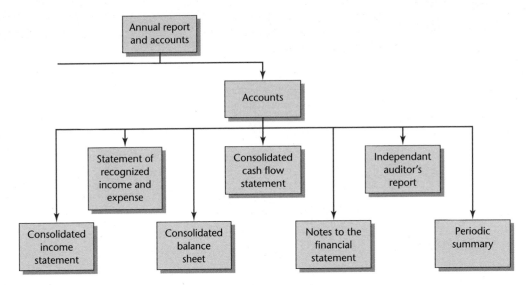

Figure 9.1 Annual accounts: structure

Learning objectives

By the end of this chapter you should be able to:

- list the main seven reports and statements that are included in a public limited company's published annual accounts;
- outline what each of these reports and statements contain;
- locate additional information in the notes to the accounts;
- extract meaningful and useful information about the company's performance from the accounts;
- evaluate the significance of the auditor's report;
- review the company's financial performance over the longer term.

❗ Why this chapter is important

The various *reports* included in a company's published annual report and accounts are important for non-accountants because they provide a great deal of background information about the company and its operations. Much of this information is now mandatory either by statute or by professional requirements.

Apart from the periodic summary most of the accounts section is mandatory. The information that it contains is considered vital because it tells shareholders and other users what profit the company has made, what its cash flow is like, what assets it owns and what liabilities it has incurred. Such information can provide the basis for a rigorous analysis of the company's performance in order to help assess its future prospects.

In the next chapter we shall explain how you can go about undertaking such an analysis. Accountants refer to it as 'interpreting the accountants', or as the man in the street might say, 'reading between the lines of the balance sheet'. This chapter provides you with the basic information that will enable you to interpret a set of accounts.

Activity 9.1	Turn to the three sets of the annual report and accounts that you used in the previous chapter. Find out what accounts are included in each of them and then list their titles in three adjacent columns.

Setting the scene

News clip

No better off?

A recent study suggests that IFRS prepared financial statements are not
necessarily easier to compare than they
were under locally determined generally

accepted accounting principles. However,
the study showed that profits were higher
under IFRS but balance sheets worse off.

Source: Adapted from www.accountancyage.com/articles/2229902.

This section is divided into two parts. In the first part we give you a brief reminder of some of the material we covered in Chapter 2, while in the second part we explain what is meant by group accounts.

International financial reporting standards

Unlike most of the previous chapters in this book, in this one we are dealing with the *published* accounts of a limited liability company. And if the accounts have been pub-lished then that probably means that the company is *listed*, i.e. it is a public limited liability company and you can buy its shares on the Stock Exchange. We will also assume that it is incorporated in the United Kingdom but most of the points that we cover in this chapter are relevant even if the company is incorporated in one of the other 26 member countries of the European Union.

It is important that we make the above assumptions clear, particularly about the EU. In the UK the accounting requirements are included in the Companies Act 2006. As we mentioned in Chapter 2, the Act requires group listed companies to prepare accounts under IAS requirements. In this respect the Act simply incorporates EU law into British law. Other EU countries have had to do the same thing. This means that *all* group listed companies throughout the EU have had to adopt IAS requirements. So perhaps apart from the language and the currency you should find that group listed company accounts throughout the EU look similar in both content and presentation.

The main requirements affecting the presentation of published accounts under the IASB programme may be found in *IAS 1* (*Presentation of Financial Information*), *IAS 7* (*Cash Flow Statements*), *IAS 27* (*Consolidated and Separate Financial Statements*), and *IAS 28* (*Accounting for Investments in Associates*). All IASs will eventually be replaced by IFRSs but the old IASs remain valid until that happens.

There are two other matters that will also be new to you when you come across a set of published accounts although these have not come about as a result of adopting the international accounting standards. They are:

- corresponding figures for the preceding year will be included side by side with the current year;
- most published accounts will be for a *group* of companies.

We deal with group accounts in a little more detail below.

Group accounts

We referred to 'groups' in Chapter 2. A group of companies is like a family. One company (say Company A) may buy shares in another company (say Company B). When Company A owns more than 50 per cent of the voting shares in Company B, B becomes a *subsidiary* of A. If A were to own more than 20 per cent but less than 50 per cent of the voting shares in B, B would be known as an *associated company* of A. In effect, B is considered to be the offspring of A. Of course B might have children of its own, say Company C and Company D. So C and D become part of the family, i.e. part of the A group of companies. An example of a group structure is shown in Figure 9.2.

The main significance of these relationships is that you can expect the published accounts to be those of the *group*, i.e. in effect, as though it were one entity so that any intergroup activities (such as sales between group companies or transfers of funds) are ignored. This involves adding together all the accounts of the group companies, or *consolidating* them. Using IASB terminology you can, therefore, expect a published set of accounts to include a *consolidated* income statement, a *consolidated* statement of recognized income and expense (or changes in equity), a *consolidated* balance sheet and a *consolidated* cash flow statement. Note that instead of using the term 'consolidated' some companies substitute 'group'. Such statements are now considered in turn in the following sections.

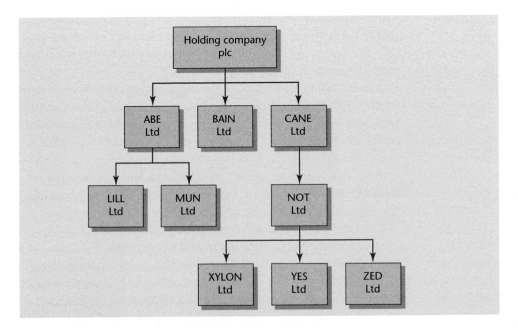

Figure 9.2 Example of a group company structure

Consolidated income statement

News clip

Scots invade England

A.G. Barr, the Scottish soft drink manu-facturer, reported better results than expected. Sales were boosted by a free glass promotion and increased penetration of the English market.

Source: Adapted from *The Guardian*, 4 September 2008, p. 28.

We show a consolidated income statement prepared under IASB requirements in Example 9.1.

Example 9.1

A consolidated income statement

A.G. Barr plc
Consolidated income statement for the year to 31 January 2009

	Tutorial notes	£000
Revenue	1	169698
Cost of sale	2	84962
Gross profit	3	84736
Net operating expenses	4	61552
Operating profit	5	23184
Operating profit before exceptional items	6	23054
Exceptional item (credit)	6	(130)
Operating profit	7	23184
Finance income	8	1062
Finance costs	9	(1037)
Profit before tax	10	23209
Tax on profit	11	6134
Profit attributable to equity shareholders	12	17075
Earnings per share		
Basic earnings per share	13	89.12p
Diluted earnings per share	13	88.16p
Dividends		
Dividends per share paid	14	39.60p
Dividend paid (£000)	15	7604
Dividend per share proposed	16	30.40p
Dividend proposed (£000)	17	5916

A.G. Barr plc, *Annual Report and Accounts*, January 2009.

Note:
References to the formal notes and the notes themselves have not been reproduced in the above example.

Tutorial notes to Example 9.1 continued

1 *Revenue.* The net invoiced sales value exclusive of value added tax of goods and services supplied to external customers during the year.

2 *Cost of sales.* No details were disclosed except that the amount does not include distribution costs and administration expenses (see Tutorial Note 4 below). As there are no other operating expenses we can assume that it includes only raw material and production costs.

3 *Gross profit.* Gross profit is normally defined as the difference between sales revenue and purchase costs (after allowing for opening and closing stock). In published accounts production costs are also usually included.

4 *Net operating expenses.* Distribution costs and administrative expenses reduced by a provision for £130,000 no longer required.

5 *Operating profit.* This is the profit that the company has earned during the year on its normal manufacturing and selling activities.

6 *Operating profit before exceptional items.* The operating profit as above less the exceptional item of £130,000. The provision of £130,000 is no longer needed so it is written back to the income statement. Exceptional items are costs and income that are not expected to recur in the normal course of business.

7 *Operating profit.* As above.

8 *Finance income.* Interest receivable.

9 *Finance costs.* Interest payable.

10 *Profit before tax.* The profit made on the company's activities during the year before taking into account any taxation due on it.

11 *Tax on profit.* The tax amount will be mainly corporation tax payable on the profits for the year adjusted for amounts relating to other years.

12 *Profit attributable to equity holders.* This is the overall profit for the year after allowing for tax. In theory it could all be paid out to the shareholders.

13 *Earnings per share.* The basic earnings per share are the profit for the year attributable to equity holders divided by the weighted average number of ordinary shares in issue during the year. The diluted earnings per share are calculated similarly to the basic earnings per share except that an allowance is made for some shares that *might* be issued if the right to take them up is exercised.

14 *Dividend per share.* What shareholders received in dividend during 2008/09 for each share that they held. It includes dividends relating to the previous year plus an interim dividend for 2008/09 both paid out during the current year.

15 *Dividend paid.* This is the total cost of the dividends paid out during 2008/09.

16 *Dividend per share proposed.* The dividend per share held that the directors recommend should be paid, i.e. the 'final' dividend for the year. If approved by the shareholders it will be paid out during 2009/10.

17 *Dividend proposed.* This is the total cost of the proposed final dividend.

Barr has presented its consolidated income statement by aggregating its expenses according to *function*, i.e. by itemizing the cost of sales, distribution costs and administrative expenses. This is known as the *operational* format and most companies adopt it. An alternative format is to aggregate expenses according to their *nature* by itemizing changes in inventories of finished goods and work in progress, raw materials and consumables, depreciation and amortization expenses, and other operating expenses. This is known as the *type of expenditure* format. The chances are that you will not come across this format very often. There is no difference in presentation between the two formats after the operating profit line.

Activity 9.2	Refer to your three sets of annual accounts and turn to the page that includes the consolidated income statement. Read down through the statement on a line-by-line basis. If you do not understand a particular item look it up in the 'notes to the accounts'. Compare your three statements with Example 9.1 and list any significant differences between them.

Statement of recognized income and expense

Besides an income statement IAS require another primary statement called the *Statement of Changes in Equity*. However, an alternative version is permitted: the Statement of *Total Recognized Gains and Losses*. This version is the one that we have chosen to adopt in this chapter as it is the one you are most likely to come across in the UK. Both types of statement serve a similar purpose.

The objective of the statement is to disclose *all* gains and losses of the company during the financial year and not just those that have been included in the income statement. Gains or losses on the revaluation of property, for example, are not normally taken to the income statement until they have been realized, i.e. when the property has been sold. So until they are, any gains or losses should be included in this particular statement. Other examples include currency translation differences on foreign currency net investments, unrealized gains or losses on trade investments, and adjustments that relate to the previous year.

The statement should be presented immediately following the income statement. Example 9.2 shows Cairn Energy's statement of recognized income and expense for 2008.

Example 9.2	**A statement of recognized income and expense**

Cairn Energy plc
Statement of recognized income and expense for the year ended 31 December 2008

	Tutorial notes	Group 2008 $m
Income and expense recognized directly in equity		
(Deficit)/surplus on valuation of financial assets	1	(14.0)
Currency translation differences	2	(150.6)
Total (expense)/income recognized directly in equity		(164.6)
Profit/(loss) for the year	3	366.7
Total recognized income and expense for the period		202.1
Attributable to:		
Equity holders of the parent	4	236.5
Minority interests	5	(34.4)
		202.1

Cairn Energy plc, *Annual Report and Accounts*, 2008.

Note:
Reference to the formal notes, the notes themselves, the company's results and the 2007 results have not been reproduced.

Tutorial notes to
Example 9.2
continued

1 Investments.

2 Unrealized foreign exchange gains less losses.

3 The profit for the year brought in from the income statement.

4 The group majority shareholders' share of the realized and unrealized income for the year after allowing for the minority shareholders' share.

5 The remaining shareholders' share of the realized and unrealized income for the year.

Activity 9.3

Look up the statement of recognized income and expense in each of your three accounts. List all the various items (there should not be many) in each statement in adjacent columns.

Consolidated balance sheet

Most published balance sheets are now presented in the vertical format (like the other financial statements), i.e. the items are listed on a line-by-line basis from the top of the page to the bottom. It is also customary to group the items into various categories, such as fixed assets and current assets. This is the approach adopted by the IASB.

There is no prescribed format but current assets should be separated from non-current assets and liabilities. Otherwise you can expect variations in the way that companies present the information that *must* be disclosed on the face of the balance sheet. Generally, however, you will probably find that most companies start with the non-current assets, followed by the current assets to arrive at *total assets*. This will then be followed in sequence by three sections listing the capital and reserves, the non-current liabilities and the current liabilities. The total will be described as the *total equity and liabilities*. This balance should, of course, be the same as the total assets.

News clip

Swings and roundabouts

The IASB is proposing that certain types of investment held by banks and insurance companies should be shown on the balance sheet at their market value. This is likely to mean that the balance sheet will be much more meaningful. However, the profit for the year will be become more erratic because any changes in the market value from year to year will be written off to it.

Source: Adapted from *The Financial Times*, 15 July 2009.

Example 9.3 is a reasonably simple presentation of a group balance sheet although we have not included the previous year's balance sheet or the formal notes relating to the current one.

Example 9.3	**An example of a published balance sheet**

J. Smart & Co (Contractors) PLC and Subsidiary Companies
Consolidated Balance Sheet as at 31 July 2008

	Tutorial notes	2008 £000
Non-current assets		
Property, plant and equipment	1	4 331
Investment properties	2	68 148
Investments in joint ventures	3	2 067
Financial assets	4	1 533
Trade and other receivables	5	3 176
Deferred tax assets	6	936
		80 191
Current assets		
Inventories	7	8 184
Trade and other receivables	5	3 833
Cash at bank and in hand		18 390
		30 407
Total assets		110 598
Non-current liabilities		
Retirement benefit obligations	8	1 089
Deferred tax liabilities	6	5 944
		7 033
Current liabilities		
Trade and other payables	9	5 518
Current tax liabilities		733
		6 251
Net assets		13 284
Total equity		97 314
Equity		
Called up share capital	10	1 088
Fair value reserve	11	(127)
Retained earnings	12	96 433
Total equity		97 314

J. Smart & Co (Contractor) PLC, *Annual Report and Accounts*, 2008.

Tutorial notes to Example 9.3

1 Shown at cost or valuation after allowing for additions, disposals and depreciation.

2 Properties earning rental income. Shown at cost or valuation after allowing for additions, disposals, and gains and deficits on valuation.

3 Joint ventures are contractual activities taken with other parties subject to the control of them all. So these are investments in companies where there is such an arrangement.

4 Listed investments.

5 Non-current assets are loans to joint venture companies. Current assets include: trade debtors, other receivables, prepayments, and amounts recoverable on contracts.

6 Deferred taxation: tax due to or from the tax authorities beyond the financial year.

Tutorial notes to
Example 9.3
continued

7 Long-term contracts balances, land, raw materials, consumables and finished goods.

8 Liabilities under the company's pension scheme.

9 Trade creditors, other creditors and loans from joint venture companies.

10 Ordinary shares of 10p each.

11 Fair value: amounts at which assets could be exchanged or liabilities settled; so this is an amount set aside for that purpose.

12 Profit retained within the business for future investment.

Activity 9.4

Referring to your set of three published accounts, work your way down each of the three consolidated balance sheets. If you do not understand what any of the items mean, consult the 'notes to the accounts'. Then compare Smart's main section headings to those in each of your three balance sheets. Note any differences in the description of the headings and the order in which they are presented. Assuming that there are some differences between them, which format do you think is the easiest to follow?

Consolidated cash flow statement

We dealt with cash flow statements (CFSs) in Chapter 7. Towards the end of that chapter we used a simple example to explain the difference between an ASB prepared CFS and an IASB one. The requirements are spelt out in the ASB's FRS 1 and the IASB's IAS 7. The main differences between them are as follows:

- *Exemptions*: IAS 7 does not permit any exemptions.
- *Definition of cash*: FRS 1 uses a narrow definition of cash whereas IAS 7 includes 'cash equivalents'.
- *Presentation*: FRS 1 requires eight main headings: operating activities, returns on investments and servicing of finance, taxation, capital expenditure and financial investment, acquisitions and disposals, equity dividends paid, management of liquid resources, and financing. IAS 7 uses three main headings: operating, investing and financing.
- *Disclosures*: FRS 1 requires some disclosures to be made about 'net debt'; IAS 7 does not make this a formal requirement.

With these differences in mind we can now look at a group CFS prepared under IASB requirements. We do so in Example 9.4.

In Example 9.4 we haven't reproduced either the 2007 comparative figures or the notes (there were three including one converting the profit for the year into 'cash generated from operations'). Aggreko did also include a reconciliation of net cash flow to the movement in net debt. The company used A5-sized paper for its annual report and accounts but even with the net debt reconciliation its CFS took up less than one page. It looks, therefore, highly presentable and straightforward. Whether the contents actually mean much to the average reader is a different matter.

Activity 9.5

Turn to the cash flow statements in each of your three accounts. Examine the terminology, the presentations and layout of each CFS along with Aggreko's. Are there any substantial differences between the four CFSs? If there are, make a note of them. Then extract the two or three most significant items in each CFS that have resulted in an increase or a decrease in cash and cash equivalents during the year.

Example 9.4	**Example of a published cash flow statement for a plc**

Aggreko plc
Group cash flow statement for the year ended 31 December 2008

	2008 £m
Cash flows from operating activities	
Cash generated from operations	276.1
Tax paid	(39.6)
Net cash generated from operating activities	236.5
Cash flows from investing activities	
Acquisitions (net of cash acquired)	(15.9)
Purchases of property, plant and equipment (PPE)	(265.2)
Proceeds from sale of PPE	9.0
Net cash used in investing activities	(272.1)
Cash flows from operating activities	
Net proceeds from issue of ordinary shares	1.3
Increase in long-term loans	185.7
Repayment of long-term loans	(107.1)
Net movement in short-term loans	4.9
Interest received	0.5
Interest paid	(14.6)
Dividends paid to shareholders	(23.7)
Purchase of treasury shares	(13.2)
Sale of own shares by Employee Benefit Trust	0.9
Net cash from/(used in) financing activities	34.7
Net decrease in cash and cash equivalents	
Cash and cash equivalents at beginning of year	(0.9)
Exchange gain on cash and cash equivalents	1.6
Cash and cash equivalents at end of year	10.3

Aggrego plc, *Annual report and accountants*, 2008.

Notes to the financial statements

The income statement, the statement of recognized income and expense and the balance sheet are usually supported by a great deal of additional notes. These notes serve two main purposes:

- they avoid too much detail being shown on the face of the financial statements;
- they make it easier to provide some supplementary information.

IASB requirements specify what information *must* be disclosed on the face of the financial statements. This means that the notes can stretch to many pages. Aggreko's 2008 notes to the accounts, for example, are 33 pages long (on A5 paper). Cairn Energy, one of the top 100 companies in the UK, has 51 pages of notes (on A4 paper). This is an awful lot of information to plough through and you have to be a dedicated shareholder to do so. The ASB, in its 1999 *Statement of Principles for Financial Reporting*, expected financial information to be understandable, but only if users had:

> *a reasonable knowledge of business and economic activities and accounting and a willingness to study with reasonable diligence the information provided.*

After studying the information in some financial statements (no doubt reasonably diligently) you could perhaps be forgiven if you felt that the ASB was being just a little bit too optimistic in its expectations.

Independent auditor's report

News clip

Concern over Southampton FC

Southampton Football Club's parent company has failed to publish its results and its shares have been suspended. Apparently the auditors have not signed the accounts as there are doubts that the company is able to operate as a 'going concern'.

Source: Adapted from www.accountancyage.com/articles/print/2239558.

In some companies you will find the independent (i.e. external) auditor's report before the financial statements, while others include it after the 'notes to the accounts'.

The independent auditor is required to do the audit and then to report to the shareholders in accordance with relevant legal and regulatory requirements. Most reports will be short – probably no longer than one page – and unless some highly unusual events have taken place, most auditors' reports will be very similar. Aggreko's independent auditors' report (note the plural) is reproduced in Figure 9.3. Read through it very carefully. The following features are of particular interest.

1 The independent auditors have audited not only the financial statements but also parts of the director's remuneration report (as required).
2 There is quite a long statement explaining the respective responsibilities of the directors and of the auditors. Note what they are.
3 The audit has been conducted on the basis of international auditing standards (UK and Ireland).
4 The auditors explain what was involved in doing the audit (basis of audit opinion).
5 The auditors confirm that the group financial statements give a 'true and fair' view for the period in question.
6 This opinion is in accordance with IFRS requirements and the provision of the 1985 Companies Act (in later years this will become the 2006 Companies Act) and IAS regulations.

Independent Auditors' Report to the Members of Aggreko plc

We have audited the Group financial statements of Aggreko plc for the year ended 31 December 2008 which comprise the Group Income Statement, the Group Statement of Recognised Income and Expense, the Group Balance Sheet, the Group Cash Flow Statement and the related notes. These group financial statements have been prepared under the accounting policies set out therein.

We have reported separately on the parent company financial statements of Aggreko plc for the year ended 31 December 2008 and on the information in the Directors' Remunation Report that is described as having been audited.

Respective responsibilities of directors and auditors

The directors' responsibilities for preparing the Annual Report and the group financial statements in accordance with applicable law and International Financial Reporting Standards (IFRSs) as adopted by the European Union are set out in the Statement of Directors' Responsibilities.

Our responsibility is to audit the group financial statement in accordance with relevant legal and regulatory requirements and International Standards on Auditing (UK and Ireland). This report, including the opinion, has been prepared for and only for the company's members as a body in accordance with Section 235 of the Companies Act 1985 and for no other purpose. We do not, in giving this opinion, accept or assume responsibility for any other purpose or to any other person to whom this report is shown or into whose hands it may come save where expressly agreed by our prior consent in writing.

We report to you our opinion as to whether the group financial statements give a true and fair view and whether the group financial statements have been properly prepared in accordance with the Companies Act 1985 and Article 4 of the IAS Regulation. We also report to you whether, in our opinion, the Directors' Report is consistent with the group financial statements.

In addition we report to you if, in our opinion, we have not received all the information and explanations we require for our audit, or if information specified by law regarding directors' remuneration and other transactions is not disclosed.

We review whether the Corporate Governance Statement reflects the company's compliance with the nine provisions of the Combined Code (2006) specified for our review by the Listing Rules of the Financial Services Authority, and we report if it does not. We are not required to consider whether the board's statements on internal control cover all risks and controls, or form an opinion on the effectiveness of the group's corporate governance procedures or its risk and control procedures.

We read other information contained in the Annual Report and consider whether it is consistent with the audited group financial statements. The other information comprises only the Directors' Report, the Chairman's Statement and the Corporate Governance Statement. We consider the implications for our report if we become aware of any apparent misstatements or material inconsistencies with the group financial statements. Our responsibilities do not extend to any other information.

Basis of audit opinion

We conducted our audit in accordance with International Standards on Auditing (UK and Ireland) issued by the Auditing Practices Board. An audit includes examination, on a test basis, of evidence relevant to the amounts and disclosures in the group financial statements. It also includes an assessment of the significant estimates and judgements made by the directors in the preparation of the group financial statements, and of whether the accounting policies are appropriate to the group's circumstances, consistently applied and adequately disclosed.

We planned and performed our audit so as to obtain all the information and explanations which we considered necessary in order to provide us with sufficient evidence to give reasonable assurance that the group financial statements are free from material misstatement, whether caused by fraud or other irregularity or error. In forming our opinion we also evaluated the overall adequacy of the presentation of information in the group financial statements.

Figure 9.3 An example of an independent auditors' report *(continues overleaf)*

Opinion

In our opinion

- the group financial statements give a true and fair view, in accordance with IFRSs as adopted by the European Union, of the state of the group's affairs as at 31st December 2008 and of its profit and cash flows for the year then ended; and
- the group financial statements have been properly prepared in accordance with the Companies Act 1985 and Article 4 of the IAS Regulation; and
- the information given in the Directors' Report is consistent with the Group financial statements.

PricewaterhouseCoopers LLP

PricewaterhouseCoopers LLP
Chartered Accountants and Registered Auditors, Glasgow
5 March 2009

Figure 9.3 (*continued*) **An example of an independent auditors' report**

Source: Aggreko plc, *Annual Report and Accounts*, 2008.

Activity 9.6
Find the auditor's report in each of your three accounts. Read through them. Does the auditor state that the accounts represent a 'true and fair' view or are there any qualifications or reservations about something in the financial statements? If there are any qualifications (probably introduced by the phrase 'except for …'), list them.

Periodic summary

Many companies include a periodic summary as part of their accounts. The usual period covered is five years but sometimes it may be ten. The summary will usually be found after the 'notes to the accounts'.

As there are no IASB requirements to produce such a summary companies are free to choose how it should be presented and what to put in it. Even so the independent auditor is required to report 'on other information contained in the Annual Report' to ensure that 'it is consistent with the audited Group financial statements' (see Figure 9.3). So companies are not entirely free to publish just what suits them.

We suggest that in most periodic summaries you will find some details about the sales revenue, gross profit, profit before tax, and dividends paid. You might also find some items extracted from the balance sheet such as fixed assets, some non-current liabilities, and the retained earnings.

Although periodic statements are limited in scope they can help users to assess the company's performance over a much longer period than the two years that are legally required (the current year's result and the previous one). This is a significant point because conventional financial statements prepared on an annual basis may not suit some companies whose activities are much more long-term. As a result the preparation of financial statements on such a short-term basis may be highly misleading. Periodic summaries may help, therefore, to give a much fairer picture of the company's affairs although there does not appear to be any current plans to make them mandatory.

A typical periodic summary is shown in Example 9.5.

Example 9.5	**Example of a periodic summary**

Devro plc

Financial summary for the year ended 31 December 2008

	2008 £million	2007 £million	2006 £million	2005 £million	2004 £million
Revenue	183.1	156.3	152.8	152.5	148.9
Operating profit before exceptional items	20.6	17.7	19.7	21.6	21.9
Exceptional items	(3.5)	0.6	(1.0)	6.3	–
Operating profit	17.1	18.3	18.7	27.9	21.9
Profit before tax	15.3	16.2	16.9	25.8	18.0
Profit after tax	12.4	12.0	12.4	18.7	12.9
Net assets	111.3	95.1	73.2	61.4	53.3
Earnings per share:					
– Basic	7.6p	7.4p	7.7p	11.5p	8.0p
– Diluted	7.6p	7.4p	7.6p	11.4p	7.9p
– Before exceptional items	8.2p	6.4p	8.1p	8.7p	8.0p
Dividends per share	4.45p	4.45p	4.45p	4.4p	4.0p
Net assets per share	68.3p	58.4p	44.9p	37.9p	33.0p

Source: Devro plc, *Annual report and accounts*, 2008.

Note:

Two brief explanatory notes have not been reproduced in the above example.

! Questions you should ask

It is probably only at a very senior level that you would be in a position to ask questions about your company's draft annual report and accounts prepared for publication, but if you get the opportunity the following ones might be pertinent.

● Are we absolutely confident that we have complied with the minimum statutory and mandatory accounting statements?

● Can we reduce the number of pages without missing out any essential information?

● Would it be possible to use different formats so that users not trained in accounting can follow them more easily?

● Can any item be left out to make it easier for users to understand?

● Could we avoid professional jargon and substitute terms that the layperson would understand?

Conclusion

In this chapter we have examined the accounts section of a number of listed companies' annual report and accounts. We have suggested that it is possible to group the various types of financial statements into seven major categories:

- income statement
- statement of recognized income and expense
- balance sheet
- cash flow statement
- notes to the accounts
- auditor's report
- periodic summary.

All these statements, except the periodic summary, are mandatory for UK and other EU group listed companies. This now means that they have to be prepared in accordance with IASB requirements. When they are combined with the 'reports' (discussed in the last chapter) they can form quite a formidable document especially for a very large international group of companies. Overall the annual report and accounts is supposed to provide sufficient information for shareholders to be satisfied that their company is being managed effectively and efficiently. However, it may be that the sheer amount of information does not enable shareholders to be entirely reassured. There can be such a thing as 'information overload'!

Key points

1 An annual report and accounts contains a great many statements but those relating to the accounts (often referred to as the 'financial statements') may take up to about half of the entire contents.

2 The accounts section will include an income statement, a statement of recognized income and expense, a balance sheet (two if the accounts deal with a group of companies), a cash flow statement, notes to the accounts, an auditor's report and a periodic summary.

3 As a part of the EU all UK group listed companies are required to adopt IASB standards in the preparation of their financial statements.

4 *IAS 1* specifies the format of the income statement and the balance sheet, the contents and the sectional heading. *IAS 7* covers the cash flow statement.

5 A minimum amount of information is usually shown on the face of the various statements with the remaining mandatory information being shown in notes to the accounts.

Check your learning

The answers to these questions can be found within the text.

1 What is meant by 'disclosure'?

2 What is a group of companies?

3 What are consolidated accounts?

4 Which main international accounting standard covers the presentation of accounts?

5 What is meant by the 'operational' and 'type of expenditure' formats for the presentation of the income statement?

6 Is is permissable for a company to include any proposed dividends in its income statement?

7 Name two items that you might find in a statement of recognized income and expense.

8 What is meant by the terms 'current' and 'non-current' in a company's balance sheet?

9 Give an example of a non-current liability.

10 What international accounting standard covers the preparation of a listed company's cash flow statement?

11 How many main headings are there in a listed company's cash flow statement?

12 Why are 'notes to the accounts' used?

13 What opinion does an independent auditor usually express about a company's financial statements?

14 What mandatory requirements cover the publication of a periodic summary statement?

News story quiz

Remember the news story at the beginning of this chapter? Go back to that story and reread it before answering the following questions.

You will gather that the writer of this letter published in the *Financial Times* is fairly critical of published company reports and accounts.

Questions

1 Do you think that current reports and accounts are a 'thick, glossy catalogue of useless puffery'?

2 Is the reader of published accounts supplied with 'page after page of irrelevant disclosure' at the exclusion of more important matters?

3 How far do you agree with the writer's view of the purpose of company reports and accounts?

Tutorial questions

9.1 What items do you think could be taken out of a listed company's published income statement and its balance sheet without affecting the usefulness of such statements?

9.2 Describe what is meant by a 'qualified audit report' illustrating your answer with appropriate examples.

9.3 Suggest ten items that should be disclosed in a listed company's periodic summary statement.

Further practice questions, study material and links to relevant sites on the World Wide Web can be found on the website that accompanies this book. The site can be found at www.pearsoned.co.uk/dyson

Interpretation of accounts

Two years too old

'Insolvencies are not our fault,' says Euler chief

David Jetuah

The CEO of Britain's biggest credit insurer has dismissed accusations that companies have been driven into administration by the withdrawal of cover from suppliers, and warned that businesses can no longer rely on statutory accounts for their credit ratings.

Fabrice Desnos, CEO of Euler Hermes UK, said: 'it's got nothing to do with us. If anything, it proves how difficult it is to analyse credit risk based on statutory accounts, because some statements in the public domain are not as strong as they first look.

'Historical accounts are getting too old to be meaningful. In a time of crisis, you can't rely on performance figures on a period two years in the past.'

Desnos's remarks follow claims that companies would be forced out of business because insurers were beginning to withdraw trade credit insurance if management accounts were not made available instead of statutory accounts lodged with Companies House.

Desnos said he was not unsympathetic to the plight of companies in the current climate, and the most timely set of figures could only help companies secure cover,

'Not disclosing information to the credit insurer means you don't think your suppliers need to know up to date information about the company.'

He added: 'Companies have to realise that when they are sharing this information with the credit insurer they are sharing it confidentially.'

Source: Accountancy Age, 7 May 2009.

Source: Reproduced with permission from Incisive Media Ltd.

Questions relating to this news story can be found on page 241 ➡

About this chapter

In this chapter we cover what accountants call the 'interpretation of accounts'. In essence, all that this means is that you dig behind the figures shown in the financial statements in order to make more sense of them and to put them into context. You will often see, for example, a newspaper screaming in large headlines that Company X has made a profit of (say) £50 million. In absolute terms £50 million is certainly a lot of money but what does it mean? Is it a lot compared with what it took to make it? Is it a lot compared with other similar companies? How does it compare with previous years? And is it up to expectations?

These questions cannot always be answered directly from the financial statements themselves. The figures may have to be reworked and then compared with other similar data. So interpreting accounts is a type of detective work: you look for the evidence, you analyse it and then you give your verdict.

This chapter explains how you do the detective work. There are various ways of going about it but we will be concentrating on *ratio analysis*. This is one of the most common methods used in interpreting accounts and we shall be spending a lot of time on it.

Learning objectives	By the end of this chapter you should be able to: ● define what is meant by the 'interpretation of accounts'; ● outline why it is needed; ● summarize the procedure involved in interpreting a set of accounts; ● explain the usefulness and importance of ratio analysis; ● calculate 15 main accounting ratios; ● explore the relationship between those ratios.

! Why this chapter is important

For non-accountants this chapter is one of the most important in the book. In your professional life you could rely entirely on your accountants to present you with any financial information that *they* think you might find useful. In time and with some experience you might understand most of it. The danger is that you might take the figures at their face value, just as you might when you read an eye-catching newspaper headline.

You could be misled by such headlines and then take what might turn out to be a most unwise decision, e.g. buying or selling shares or perhaps even making a takeover bid for a company! For example, an alleged £15 billion profit might be a record but how can we be certain that it is significant? The short answer is that we can't unless we relate it to something else, such as what sum of money it took to earn that profit or what profit other similar companies have made.

Accountants refer to the explanation process as the *interpretation of accounts*. After working your way through the chapter you too will be able to interpret a set of accounts so that when you read a story in the newspaper or you come across some financial statements you can make much more sense of the information and you can put it into context, i.e. compare it with something meaningful. This is sometimes referred to as 'reading between the lines of the balance sheet'. We hope that by the end of the chapter you too can read between these lines, and for that matter between the lines of all the other financial statements as well. Such a skill is vital if you are to become a *really* effective manager.

Nature and purpose

News clip

Distortion fear

The recession has increased pressure to distort earnings figures. According to a survey of 1000 internal auditors from 25 countries, 86% of them believe that there is now a greater risk of 'inappropriate earnings management and other misconduct'.

Source: Adapted from www.accountancyage.com/news, 9 July 2009.

In this section we explain what accountants mean when they talk about interpreting a set of accounts, why such an exercise is necessary and who might have need of it.

Definition

The verb 'to interpret' has several different meanings. Perhaps the most common is 'to convert' or 'to translate' the spoken word of one language into another, but it also has other meanings such as 'to construe', 'to define' or 'to explain'. We will use the latter meaning. Our definition of what we mean by the *interpretation of accounts* may then be expressed as follows:

> *A detailed explanation of the financial performance of an entity incorporating data and other quantitative and qualitative information extracted from both internal and external sources.*

Limited information

By this stage of your accounting studies you will no doubt have realized that the amount of information contained in a set of accounts prepared for *internal* purposes is considerable. Even published accounts can be quite detailed. The 2008 annual report and accounts of Cairn Energy plc, for example, an oil and gas exploration and production company, covers 136 pages. You would think that accounts of this length would provide you with all the information that you would ever want to know about the company but unfortunately this is not necessarily the case. There are three main reasons why this may not be so.

● *Structural.* Financial accounts are prepared on the basis of a series of accounting rules. Even financial accounts prepared for internal purposes contain a restricted amount of information and this is especially the case with published accounts. Only information that can be translated easily into quantitative financial terms is usually included, and also some highly arbitrary assessments have to be made about the treatment of certain matters such as stock valuation, depreciation and bad debts. Furthermore financial accounts are also usually prepared on a historical basis so they may be out-of-date by the time that they become available, the details may relate at best to one or two accounting periods and probably no allowance will have been made for inflation.

- *Absolute.* The monetary figures are presented almost solely in absolute terms. For example, Cairn's revenue for 2008 was $299.3 million and its profit before tax was $440.9 million. So how, you might ask, can the profit be higher than the sales revenue? Exactly. This is a good example of why we need to dig behind the figures; it's why we need to *interpret* them.
- *Contextual.* Even if you could grasp the size and significance of what sales of $300 million and profits of $440 million meant, in isolation they do not tell us very much. In order to make them more meaningful they need to be put in context perhaps by comparing them with previous years' results or with companies in the same industry.

Users

Company law concentrates almost exclusively on shareholders but as we explained in Chapter 2, there are many other user groups. We reproduce the seven main user groups listed in that chapter in Table 10.1. Beside each group we have posed a question that a user in each particular group may well ask.

The questions in Table 10.1 cannot always be answered directly from the financial statements. For example, investors asking the question 'What's the dividend like?' will find that the annual report and accounts gives them the dividend per share for the current and the previous year in *absolute* amounts. Somewhere within the annual report and accounts the percentage increase may be given but that still does not really answer the question. Investors will probably want to know how their dividend relates to what they have invested in the company (what accountants call the 'yield'). As most investors probably paid different amounts for their shares it would be impossible to show each individual shareholder's yield in the annual account, so investors have to calculate it for themselves.

Table 10.1 Users of financial accounts and their questions

User group	Questions asked
Customers	How do its prices compare with its competitors?
Employees	Has it enough money to pay my wages?
Governments and their agencies	Can the company pay its taxes?
Investors	What's the dividend like?
Lenders	Will I get my interest paid?
Public	Is the company likely to stay in business?
Suppliers and other creditors	Will we get paid what we are owed?

Activity 10.1

Taking the seven user groups listed in Table 10.1, what other questions do you think that each user group would ask? List each user group and all the questions that you think each would ask. Then insert:

(a) where the basic information could be found in the annual report and accounts to answer each question; and

(b) what additional information would be required to answer each question fully.

Procedure

In this section we outline the basic procedure involved in interpreting a set of accounts. The scale and nature of your investigation will clearly depend on its purpose so we can only point you in the right direction. For example, if you were working for a large international company proposing to take over a foreign company, you would need a vast amount of information and it might take months before you had completed your investigation. By contrast, if you were a private individual proposing to invest £1000 in Tesco plc, you might just spend part of Saturday morning reading what the city editor of your favourite newspaper had to say about the company (although we would recommend you to do much more than that).

In essence an exercise involving the interpretation of accounts involves four main stages:

- collecting the information;
- analysing it;
- interpreting it;
- reporting the findings.

Collecting the information

This stage involves you first conducting a fairly general review of the international economic, financial, political and social climate and a more specific one of the *country* in which the entity operates. In broad terms, you are looking to see whether it is politically and socially stable with excellent prospects for sound and continuing economic growth. Then you should look at the particular *industry* in which it operates. Ask yourself the following questions.

- Is the government supportive of the industry?
- Is there an expanding market for its products?
- Is there sufficient land and space available for development?
- Is there a reliable infrastructure, e.g. utility supplies and a transport network?
- Are there grants and loans available for developing enterprises?
- Is there an available and trained labour force near by?

Once you have got all this macro and micro information you will need to obtain as much information about the *entity* as you can get. This will involve finding out about its history, structure, management, operations, products, markets, labour record and financial performance. These days you should be able to obtain much of this information from the Internet but don't forget about old-fashioned sources such as the company's interim and annual reports and accounts, press releases, trade circulars and analysts' reviews.

By the end of this early stage of your investigation you will probably already have a 'feel' or a strong impression about the entity but your work is not yet over. Indeed, there is still a great deal more work to do.

Analysing the information

Analysing the information involves putting together all the information you have collected and making sense of it. In this book as we are primarily concerned with the accounting aspects of business so we will concentrate on how you can begin to make sense of the *financial* information that you have collected.

The main source of such information will normally be the entity's annual report and accounts. In order to make our explanation easier to follow we will assume that we are dealing primarily with public limited liability companies (although you will find that much of what we have to say is relevant when dealing with other types of entities).

There are four main techniques that you can use in interpreting a set of financial statements: horizontal analysis, trend analysis, vertical analysis and ratio analysis. Figure 10.1 depicts a diagrammatic representation of these different types of analyses. A brief description of each one is outlined below.

1 *Horizontal analysis.* This technique involves making a line-by-line comparison of the company's accounts for each accounting period chosen for the investigation. You may

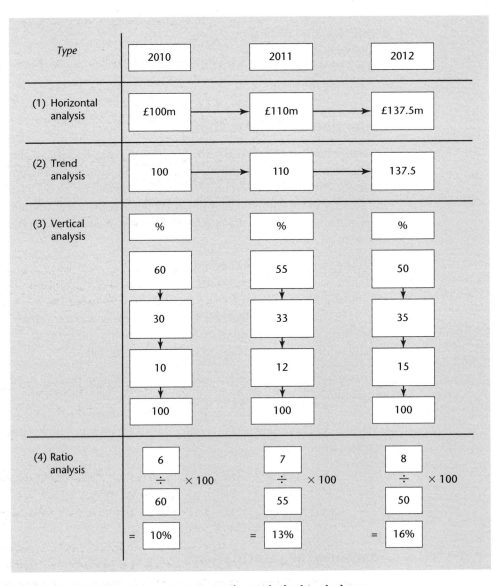

Figure 10.1 Interpreting accounts: main analytical techniques

have noted, for example, that the sales for the year 2010 were £100m, £110m in 2011 and £137.5m in 2012 and so on. This type of comparison across a row of figures is something that we do naturally but such a casual observation is not very effective when we are faced with a great many detailed figures. In order to grasp what they mean, at the very least we would need to calculate the changes from one year to the next. Even then their significance might still be hard to take in. So we would probably have to calculate the *percentage* increases year-by-year (10% for 2011 and 25% in 2012 in the above example) and this could involve an awful lot of work with a pen, paper and a calculator, or preferably a spreadsheet.

2   *Trend analysis.* This is similar to horizontal analysis except that all the figures in the first set of accounts in a series are given a base line of 100 and the subsequent sets of accounts are converted to that base line. So if the sales for 2010 were £50m, £70 for 2011 and £85m for 2012, the sales of £50m for 2010 would be given a base line of 100; the 2011 sales would then become 140 (70 × 100/50) and the 2012 sales 170 (85 × 100/50). This method enables us to grasp much more easily the changes in the absolute costs and values shown in the financial statements. For example, if we told you that the sales were £202,956,000 for 2011 and £210,161,000 in 2012 it is not too difficult to calculate that they have gone up by about £7m but the figures are still too big for most of us to absorb. The changes that have taken place would be much easier to take in if they are all related to a base line of 100. In this example, the sales for 2011 would then be given a value of 100, with 103 (210 161 × 100/202 956) for 2012, an increase of about 3% (it's actually 3.6%). The figures then begin to mean something because by converting in this way they relate more to our experience of money terms and values in our everyday life.

3   *Vertical analysis.* This technique requires the figures in each financial statement (usually restricted to the profit and loss account and the balance sheet) to be expressed as a percentage of the total amount. For example, assume that a company's trade debtors were £10m in 2011 and the balance sheet total was £50m; in 2012 the trade debtors were £12m and the balance sheet total was £46m. Trade debtors would then be shown as representing 20% of the balance sheet total (10 × 100/50) in 2011 and 26% in 2012 (12 × 100/46). This would be considered quite a large increase so the reasons for it would need to be investigated. The modern practice of using lots of sectionalized accounts and subtotals means that it is not always easy to decide what *is* the total of a particular financial statement. If you come across this difficulty we suggest that you use the sales revenue figure for the total of the profit and loss account and the total of net assets (or shareholders' funds, it should be the same figure!) for the total of the balance sheet.

4   *Ratio analysis.* A ratio is simply the division of one arithmetical amount by another arithmetical amount expressed as a percentage or as a factor. Ratio analysis is a most useful means of comparing one figure with another because it expresses the relationship between lots of amounts easily and simply. If the cost of sales for 2011 was £12m, for example, and the sales revenue was £20m, we would express the relationship as 60% (12 × 100/20) sales or 0.6 to 1 (12/20). Ratio analysis is such an important technique in the interpretation of accounts that we will be dealing with it in some detail a little later in the chapter.

Activity 10.2	State whether the following assertions are true or false:	
	(a) Ratio analysis is only one form of analysis that can be used in interpreting accounts.	*True/false*
	(b) Ratio analysis aims to put the financial results of an entity into perspective.	*True/false*
	(c) Ratio analysis helps to establish whether or not an entity is a going concern.	*True/false*

Interpreting the information

This is the third stage in a broad interpretative exercise. By this stage of your investigation you would have collected a great deal of information about the company you are investigating and you would have put that information into context by subjecting it to a whole battery of analyses. Now you have to use all the information that you have before you to interpret or to *explain* what has happened. Some of the questions you might ask yourself include the following.

- What does it tell me about the company's performance?
- Has the company done well compared with other financial periods?
- How does it compare with other companies in the same sector of the economy?
- Are the world economic, political and social circumstances favourable to trade generally?
- What are they like for this company's industry?
- What are the prospects for the region in which this company does its business?

Asking and answering such questions might seem a formidable task but like anything else, the more practice you get, the easier it becomes. In any case, by this time your initial research and your various analyses will have given you a strong indication about the company's progress and its future prospects. You will have realized that there are a number of obvious strengths and weaknesses and a variety of positive and negative factors and trends.

When you have come to a conclusion based on the evidence and the analysis that you have framed, you have one further task: report it to whoever asked you to do the study in the first place.

Reporting the findings

In most interpretive exercises of the type described in this chapter you will probably have to write a written report. Many people are fearful of having to commit themselves to paper and they find this part of the exercise very difficult. However, having to write something down helps you to think more clearly and logically. It may also throw up gaps in your argument, so regard this part of the exercise as more of an opportunity than a threat.

The format of your report will depend on its purpose but basically it should be broken down into three main sections. Your first section should be an *introduction* in which you outline the nature and purpose of your report including a brief outline of its structure. The second part should contain your *discussion* section in which you present your evidence and your assessment of what the evidence means. In the third *concluding* section summarize briefly the entire study, list your conclusions and state your recommendations.

In the next section we consider in much more detail one of the analytical techniques mentioned earlier in the chapter: *ratio analysis.*

Ratio analysis

We are now going to spend the rest of the chapter dealing with ratio analysis in some detail. Before we begin you should note the following points.

● There are literally hundreds of ratios that we could produce but most accountants have just a few favourites.
● Always check the definition of a particular ratio you come across because while the name may be familiar to you, the definition could be different from the one that you use.
● There is no standard system for grouping ratios into representative categories.
● Strictly limit the number of ratios you adopt. If you use 20 different types of ratio, for example, and you are covering a five-year period, you have 100 ratios to calculate *and* to incorporate in your analysis. That's a lot to handle!

In this book we are going to limit the number of accounting ratios that we cover to just 15. In order to simplify our discussion, we will also group them into four broad categories (although there is some overlap between them):

● liquidity ratios;
● profitability ratios;
● efficiency ratios;
● investment ratios.

A diagrammatic representation of this classification and the names of the ratios included in each grouping are shown in Figure 10.2.

We start our detailed study with what we call *liquidity* ratios.

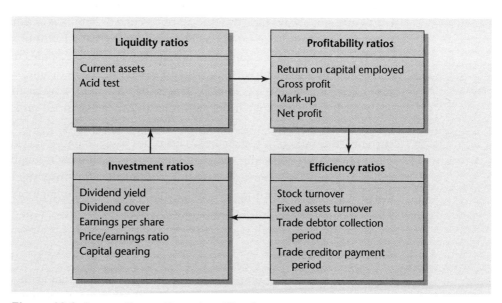

Figure 10.2 Accounting ratios: classification

Liquidity ratios

News clip

Insolvencies soar

Liquidations went up by 56% in the first quarter of 2009 compared with the same period in 2008. The recession is blamed as backers of companies do not want to throw more good money after bad. As a result companies are experiencing some severe liquidity problems.

Source: Adapted from www.accountancyage.com/articles/print/2241538, 1 May 2009.

Liquidity ratios measure the extent to which assets can be turned into cash quickly. In other words, they try to assess how much cash the entity has available in the short term (this usually means within the next twelve months). For example, it is easy to extract the total amount of trade debtors and trade creditors from the balance sheet, but are they too high? We cannot really tell until we put them into context. We can do this by calculating two liquidity ratios known as the *current assets ratio* and the *acid test ratio*.

Current assets ratio

The *current assets ratio* is calculated as follows:

$$\frac{\text{current assets}}{\text{current liabilities}}$$

It is usually expressed as a factor, e.g. 3 to 1, or 3 : 1 although you will sometimes see it expressed as a percentage (300% in our example, i.e. $\frac{3}{1} \times 100$).

The term 'current' means receivable or payable within the next twelve months. The entity may not always have to settle all of its current liabilities within the next week or even the next month. Be careful before you assume that a factor of (say) 1 : 2 suggests that the company will be going into immediate liquidation. Some creditors, such as tax and dividends, may not have to be paid for several weeks. In the meantime, the company may receive regular receipts of cash from its debtors and it may be able to balance these against what it has to pay to its creditors. In other instances, some entities (such as supermarkets) may have a lot of cash trade, and it is possible that they then may have a current assets ratio of less than 2 : 1. This is not likely to be a problem for them because they are probably collecting sufficient amounts of cash daily through the checkouts. In some cases, however, a current assets ratio of less than 2 : 1 may signify a serious financial position, especially if the current assets consist of a very high proportion of stocks. This leads us on to the second liquidity ratio, the *acid test ratio*.

Acid test ratio

It may not be easy to dispose of stocks in the short term as they cannot always be quickly turned into cash. In any case, the entity would then be depriving itself of those very assets that enable it to make a trading profit. It seems sensible, therefore, to see what would happen to the current ratio if stocks were not included in the definition of current assets. This ratio is called the acid test (or quick) ratio. It is calculated as follows:

$$\frac{\text{current assets} - \text{stocks}}{\text{current liabilities}}$$

Like the current ratio, the acid test ratio is usually expressed as a factor (or occasionally as a percentage). It is probably a better measure of an entity's immediate liquidity position than the current assets ratio because it may be difficult to dispose of the stocks in the short term. Do not assume, however, that if current assets less stocks are less than current liabilities, the entity's cash position is vulnerable. As we explained above, some of the current liabilities may not be due for payment for some months. Some textbooks suggest that the acid test ratio must be at least 1 : 1, but again there is no evidence to support this assertion so use it only as a guide.

Activity 10.3	Fill in the blanks in the following equations.

(a) $\dfrac{\text{Current assets}}{\text{Current liabilities}} = \dfrac{£65\,500}{\underline{\hspace{2cm}}} = 1.60$

(b) $\dfrac{\text{Current assets} - \underline{\hspace{3cm}}}{\text{Current liabilities}}$

Profitability ratios

News clip

Spotting trouble

A number of UK firms are running summer schools in order to help junior auditors spot companies facing financial difficulties. They will be trained to look for unrealistic cash flow forecasts and other forecasts as well as covenant and financing arrangements that might cause problems.

Source: Adapted from www.accountancyage.com/2223899, 14 August 2008.

Users of accounts will want to know how much profit a business has made, and then to compare it with previous periods or with other entities. The absolute level of accounting profit will not be of much help, because it needs to be related to the size of the entity and how much capital it has invested in it. There are four main profitability ratios. We examine each of them below.

Return on capital employed ratio

The best way of assessing profitability is to calculate a ratio known as the *return on capital employed* (ROCE) ratio. It can be expressed quite simply as

$$\frac{\text{profit}}{\text{capital}} \times 100$$

This ratio is usually expressed as a percentage and it is one of the most important. Even so, there is no common agreement about how it should be calculated. The problem is that both 'profit' and 'capital' can be defined in several different ways. As a result, a variety of ROCE ratios can be produced merely by changing the definitions of either profit or capital. For our purposes you need to be aware of only four definitions of ROCE. They are as follows.

(1)
$$\frac{\text{net profit before taxation}}{\text{shareholders' funds}} \times 100$$

This definition measures the pre-tax profit against what the shareholders have invested in the entity. Use it if you want to know how profitable the entity has been as a whole.

(2)
$$\frac{\text{net profit after taxation}}{\text{shareholders' funds}} \times 100$$

This definition is similar to the previous one except that it measures post-tax profit against the shareholders' investment in the company. Taxation is normally regarded as an *appropriation* of profit and not as an expense. The tax payable will be based on the profit for the year and a company has no option other than to pay it. The distinction between tax as an appropriation and tax as a profit is blurred, and some accountants prefer to use this definition as a measure of overall profitability. However, bear in mind that the taxation charge in the accounts can be subject to various accounting adjustments so you would have to be careful using this definition in comparing one company with another company.

(3)
$$\frac{\text{net profit after taxation and preference dividends}}{\text{shareholders' funds} - \text{preference dividends}} \times 100$$

This definition should be used if you want to assess how profitable the company has been from an *ordinary* shareholder's point of view. It measures how much profit could be distributed to ordinary shareholders as a proportion of what they have invested in the business.

(4)
$$\frac{\text{profit before taxation and interest}}{\text{shareholders' funds} + \text{long-terms loans}} \times 100$$

This definition measures what profit has been earned in relation to what has been used to *finance* the entity in total. Interest is a cost of borrowing money so it is added back to the profit made. Similarly long-term loans are added to the shareholders' funds because that gives us the *total* financial investment in the entity. Use this definition if you want to know how profitable the entity has been in relation to what it has taken to finance it.

The above definitions use the closing shareholders' funds but sometimes a simple average, is adoped, e.g. (opening + closing shareholders funds) ÷ 2.

Activity 10.4	There are many other ways of calculating ROCE other than the four listed above. Divide a page into two broad columns. In the left-hand column list all the various levels of profit that you would find in a published profit and loss account (e.g. operating profit). In the right-hand column list all the various levels or types of capital shown in a published balance sheet (e.g. total assets). Then try to relate each definition of profit to a compatible definition of capital.
	Remember that what you are trying to do is to find how much profit (however defined) has been earned for the particular level or type of capital invested. So the numerator (profit) has got to be compatible with the denominator (the capital employed).

Gross profit ratio

The *gross profit ratio* enables us to judge how successful the entity has been at trading. It is calculated as follows:

$$\frac{\text{gross profit}}{\text{sales}} \times 100$$

The gross profit ratio measures how much profit the entity has earned in relation to the amount of sales that it has made. The definition of gross profit does not usually cause any problems. Most entities adopt the definition we have used in this book, namely sales less the cost of goods sold [the cost of sales being (opening stock + purchase) – closing stock] and so meaningful comparisons can usually be made between different entities. However, if you are using published accounts, sales may be described as 'turnover' and the cost of sales may well include production costs (which are not usually disclosed). Be wary, therefore, if you are using publishing accounts to make comparisons between different companies.

Mark-up ratio

The gross profit ratio complements another main trading ratio, which we will refer to, for convenience, as the *mark-up ratio*. This is calculated as follows:

$$\frac{\text{gross profit}}{\text{cost of goods sold}} \times 100$$

Mark-up ratios measure the amount of profit added to the cost of goods sold. The cost of goods sold plus profit equals the sales revenue. The mark-up may be reduced to stimulate extra sales activity, but this will have the effect of reducing the gross profit. However, if extra goods are sold there may be a greater volume of sales and this will help to compensate for the reduction in the mark-up on each unit.

Net profit ratio

Owners sometimes like to compare their net profit with the sales revenue. This can be expressed in the form of the *net profit ratio*. It is calculated as follows:

$$\frac{\text{net profit before taxation}}{\text{sales}} \times 100$$

It is difficult to compare the net profit ratio for different entities fairly. Individual operating and financing arrangements vary so much that entities are bound to have different levels of expenditure no matter how efficient one entity is compared with another. So it may only be realistic to use the net profit ratio in making *internal* comparisons. Over a period of time a pattern may emerge and it might then be possible to establish a trend. If you use the net profit ratio to make intercompany comparisons, make sure you allow for different circumstances.

In published accounts you might also want to substitute 'operating profit' or 'profit on ordinary activities before tax' for net profit.

Efficiency ratios

News clip

Late payment problems

Three in five businesses are being affected by late payments according to a survey done by Tenon Recovery. Its national head said that cash flow is fundamental to business survival and late payments are part of it. He argued that businesses must adopt a responsible attitude to avoid the domino effect of businesses collapsing. They should also have clear payment terms, credit control procedures, chase slow-paying customers and make their own payments on time.

Source: Adapted from www.accountancyage.com/articles/print2240410, 15 April 2009.

Traditional accounting statements do not tell us how *efficiently* an entity has been managed, i.e. how well its resources have been looked after. Accounting profit may, to some extent, be used as a measure of efficiency. However, as we have explained in earlier chapters, it is subject to a great many arbitrary adjustments and in this context it can be misleading. What we need to do is to make comparisons between different periods and with other similar companies.

There are very many different types of ratios that we can use to measure the efficiency of a company, but in this book we will cover only the more common ones.

Stock turnover ratio

The stock turnover ratio may be calculated as follows:

$$\frac{\text{cost of goods sold}}{\text{closing stock}}$$

The stock turnover ratio is normally expressed as a number (e.g. 5 or 10 times) and not as a percentage.

Instead of using the cost of goods sold, sometimes it is necessary to substitute sales revenue. This should be avoided if at all possible as the sales revenue will include a profit loading. As this may be subject to change, the stock turnover will become distorted so making it difficult to make meaningful comparisons.

As far as the closing stock is concerned some accountants prefer to use an average, often a simple average, i.e. opening stock + closing stock/2, especially if trade is seasonal or the year end falls during a quiet period.

The greater the turnover of stock, the more efficient the entity would appear to be in purchasing and selling goods. A stock turnover of 2 times, for example, would suggest that the entity has about six months of sales in stock. In most circumstances this would appear to be a high relative volume, whereas a stock turnover of (say) 12 times would mean that the entity had only a month's normal sales in stock.

Fixed assets turnover ratio

Another important area to examine, from the point of view of efficiency, relates to fixed assets. Fixed assets (such as plant and machinery) enable the business to function more efficiently, and so a high level of fixed assets ought to generate more sales. We can check this by calculating a ratio known as the fixed asset turnover ratio. This may be done as follows:

$$\frac{\text{sales}}{\text{fixed assets at net book value}}$$

The more times that the fixed assets are covered by the sales revenue, the greater the recovery of the investment in fixed assets. The fixed assets turnover ratio may also be expressed as a percentage.

This ratio is really only useful if it is compared with previous periods or with other companies. In isolation it does not mean very much. For example, is a turnover of 5 good and one of 4 poor? All we can suggest is that if the trend is upwards, then the investment in fixed assets is beginning to pay off, at least in terms of increased sales. Note also that the ratio can be strongly affected by the company's depreciation policies. There is a strong argument, therefore, for taking the *gross* book value of the fixed assets and not the *net* book value.

| Activity 10.5 | A company has a turnover of £4,000,000 for the year to 31 December 2012. At that date the gross book value of its fixed assets was £22,000 and the net book value £12,000. When measuring the efficiency with which its uses its fixed assets, is it more meaningful to use the gross book value in relation to turnover or the net book value? Give your reasons. |

Gross book value ☐   Net book value ☐

Reason: _____

Trade debtor collection period ratio

Investing in fixed assets is all very well but there is not much point in generating extra sales if the customers do not pay for them. Customers might be encouraged to buy more by a combination of lower selling prices and generous credit terms. If the debtors are slow at paying, the entity might find that it has run into cash flow problems. So it is important for it to watch the trade debtor position very carefully. We can check how successful it has been by calculating the *trade debtor collection period*. The ratio may be calculated as follows:

$$\frac{\text{closing trade debtors}}{\text{credit sales}} \times 365$$

The average trade debtors term is sometimes used instead of the closing trade debtors, i.e $\frac{1}{2}$ (opening trade debtors + closing trade debtors).

It is important to relate trade debtors to *credit* sales if at all possible and so cash sales should be excluded from the calculation. The method shown above for calculating the ratio would relate the closing trade debtors to *x* days' sales, but it would be possible to substitute weeks or months for days. It is not customary to express the ratio as a percentage.

An acceptable debtor collection period cannot be suggested as much depends on the type of trade in which the entity is engaged. Some entities expect settlement within 28 days of delivery of the goods or on immediate receipt of the invoice. Other entities might expect settlement within 28 days following the end of the month in which the goods were delivered. On average this adds another 14 days (half a month) to the overall period of 28 days. If this is the case, a company would appear to be highly efficient in collecting its debts if the average debtor collection period was about 42 days. The United Kingdom experience is that the *median* debtor collection period is about 50 days.

Like most of the other ratios, it is important to establish a trend. If the trend is upwards, then it might suggest that the company's credit control procedures have begun to weaken.

Activity 10.6	A company's sales for 2012 were £4452 million and its trade debtors for that year were £394 million. Assuming that all the sales were made on credit terms, do you think that its debtor collection was efficient?
	Yes ☐ No ☐
	Reason: _____

Trade creditor payment period

A similar ratio can be calculated for the trade creditor payment period. The formula is as follows:

$$\frac{\text{closing trade creditors}}{\text{total credit purchases}} \times 365$$

Average trade creditors may be substituted for the closing trade creditors like the trade debtor collection period ratio and this may be a simple average (opening trade debtors +

closing trade debtors/2) or a more complex one. The trade creditors should be related to credit purchases (although this information will often not be available), and weeks or months may be substituted for the number of days. Again, like the trade debtor collection period, it is not usual to express this ratio as a percentage.

In published accounts you might have to calculate the purchases figure for yourself. The accounts should disclose the opening and closing stock figures and the cost of sales. By substituting them in the equation [(opening stock + purchases) – closing stock = cost of sales] you can calculate the purchases. Other expenses may have been included in the cost of sales but unless these have been disclosed you will just have to accept the cost of sales figure shown in the accounts.

An upward trend in the average level of trade creditors would suggest that the entity is having some difficulty in finding the cash to pay its creditors. Indeed, it might be a sign that it is running into financial difficulties.

Investment ratios

News clip

Football clubs face financial meltdown

According to *The Observer* British football clubs face financial meltdown as a result of excessive debt and massive wages paid to players. The paper reports that there will be some insolvencies since in the summer clubs do not earn much income while they have the same overhead expenditure. Those clubs that are highly geared both financially and operationally face particular difficulties as season ticket sales, sponsorship earnings and corporate box deals all begin to drop.

Source: Adapted from *The Observer*, 5 April 2009, p. 6 Business.

The various ratios examined in the previous sections are probably of interest to all users of accounts, such as creditors, employees and managers, as well as to shareholders. There are some other ratios that are primarily (although not exclusively) of interest to prospective investors. These are known as *investment ratios*.

Dividend yield

The first investment ratio that you might find useful is the *dividend yield*. It usually applies to ordinary shareholders and it may be calculated as follows:

$$\frac{\text{dividend per share}}{\text{market price per share}} \times 100$$

The dividend yield measures the rate of return that an investor gets by comparing the cost of his shares with the dividend receivable (or paid). For example, if an investor buys 100 £1 ordinary shares at a market rate of 200p per share, and the dividend was 10p per share, the yield would be 5 per cent (10/200 × 100). While he may have invested £200 (100 × £2 per share), as far as the company is concerned he will be registered as holding 100 shares at a nominal value of £1 each (100 shares × £1). He would be entitled to a dividend of £10 (10p × 100 shares) but from his point of view he will only be getting a return of 5 per cent, i.e. £10 for his £200 invested.

Dividend cover

Another useful investment ratio is called *dividend cover*. It is calculated as follows:

$$\frac{\text{net profit} - \text{taxation} - \text{preference dividend}}{\text{ordinary dividends}}$$

This ratio shows the number of times that the ordinary dividend could be paid out of current earnings. The dividend is usually described as being *x* times covered by the earnings. So if the dividend is covered twice, the company would be paying out half of its earnings as an ordinary dividend.

Earnings per share

Another important investment ratio is that known as *earnings per share* (EPS). This ratio enables us to put the profit into context and to avoid looking at it in simple absolute terms. It is usually looked at from the ordinary shareholder's point of view. The following formula is used to calculate what is called the *basic* earnings per share:

$$\frac{\text{net profit} - \text{preference shares}}{\text{number of ordinary shares}}$$

In published accounts you will sometimes see other definitions of the EPS. The calculations involved in obtaining them are often highly complex. We recommend you to stick to the above definition, i.e. basically, net profit less preference dividends divided by the number of ordinary shares.

EPS enables a fair comparison to be made between one year's earnings and another by relating the earnings to something tangible, i.e. the number of shares in issue.

Price to earnings ratio

Another common investment ratio is the *price to earnings ratio* (P/E). It is calculated as follows:

$$\frac{\text{market price per share}}{\text{earnings per share}}$$

The P/E ratio enables a comparison to be made between the earnings per share (as defined above) and the market price. It tells us that the market price is *x* times the earnings. It means that it would take *x* years before we recovered the market price paid for the shares out of the earnings (assuming that they remained at that level and that they were all distributed). So the P/E ratio is a multiple of earnings. A high or low ratio can only be judged in relation to other companies in the same sector of the market.

A high P/E ratio means that the market thinks that the company's future is a good one. The shares are in demand, so the price of the shares will be high. Of course it would take you a long time to get your 'earnings' back (even if the company paid them all out as dividends) but the expectation is that the company will be able to increase its earnings and that sometime in the future it will be able to pay out a higher dividend. As a result the shares are a good buy from that point of view.

Activity 10.7	At 5 October 2009 Dawson's P/E ratio was 88.2 while Experian's was 2.4. Both are grouped in the 'support services' sector of the economy. What do these P/E ratios tell you about the market's perception of these two companies?

Capital gearing ratio

The last ratio that we are going to consider is the *capital gearing ratio*. As we saw in Chapter 5, companies are financed out of a mixture of share capital, retained profits and loans. Loans may be long-term (such as debentures) or short-term (such as credit given by trade creditors). In addition, the company may have set aside all sorts of provisions (e.g. for taxation) which it expects to meet sometime in the future. These may also be regarded as a type of loan. From an ordinary shareholder's point of view, even preference share capital can be classed as a loan because the preference shareholders may have priority over ordinary shareholders both in respect of dividends and upon liquidation. So if a company finances itself from a high level of loans, there is obviously a higher risk in investing in it. This arises for two main reasons:

- the higher the loans, the more interest the company will have to pay; that may affect the company's ability to pay an ordinary dividend;
- if the company cannot find the cash to repay its loans then the ordinary shareholders may not get any money back if the company goes into liquidation.

There are many different ways of calculating capital gearing but we prefer the following formula.

$$\frac{\text{preference shares} + \text{long-term loans}}{\text{shareholders' funds} + \text{long-term loans}} \times 100$$

A company that has financed itself out of a high proportion of loans (e.g. in the form of a combination of preference shares and long-term loans) is known as a highly-geared company. Conversely, a company with a low level of loans is regarded as being low-geared. Note that 'high' and 'low' in this context are relative terms. A highly-geared company is potentially a higher risk investment as it has to earn sufficient profit to cover the interest payments and the preference dividend before it can pay out any ordinary dividend. This should not be a problem when profits are rising but if they are falling then they may not be sufficient to cover even the preference dividend.

We have now reviewed 15 common accounting ratios. There are many others that could have been included. However, the 15 selected are enough for you to be able to interpret a set of accounts. Many of the ratios are not particularly helpful if they are used in isolation but as part of a detailed analysis they can be invaluable.

| Activity 10.8 | Company A has a capital gearing of 10%, Company B 40%, and Company C 60%. What effect will such gearing ratios have on each company's reported profits when they are (a) rising steeply; (b) or falling sharply? |

Company	Effect on profits	
	Rising	*Falling*
A		
B		
C		

For your convenience a summary of the 15 ratios is included in an appendix at the end of this chapter (see pages 247–248). We will now show how they can be used to interpret the accounts of a small company.

An illustrative example

In this section we bring together much of the material that we have covered so far in this chapter in the form of a practical example. The example is meant to provide you with a framework for interpreting accounts. We have tried to make it as simple as possible and to reduce the arithmetic involved.

When you are faced with having to interpret a set of accounts in your work or in your private life you will probably be faced with a huge amount of additional information. And yet some information that you will probably need will be missing. For example, published accounts almost certainly only give you the 'cost of sales' and not the 'cost of goods sold' as defined in this book. This means that you will not be able to calculate the gross profit using the conventional formula. Besides some missing information much of what is available will be highly complex and technical and you will have to sort it out for yourself using the notes attached to the accounts.

All of this may seem that you will face an almost impossible task. This is not so. With the guidance specifically provided in this chapter and more generally throughout the rest of the book, you should soon be able to interpret a set of accounts. Here goes.

Example 10.1	**Interpreting company accounts**

You are presented with the following information relating to Gill Limited.

Gill Limited
Profit and loss account for the year to 31 March 2012

	2011	2012
	£000	£000
Sales	160	200
Cost of goods sold	(96)	(114)
Gross profit	64	86
Operating expenses	(30)	(34)
Debenture interest	(5)	(5)
Net profit before tax	29	47
Tax	(9)	(12)
Net profit after tax	20	35
Dividends paid		
Preference shares	(2)	(2)
Ordinary shares	(8)	(10)
	(10)	(12)
Retained profit	10	23

Balance sheet at 31 March 2012

	2011	2012
	£000	£000
Fixed assets (at net book value)	300	320
Current assets		
Stocks	15	20
Trade debtors	40	50
Cash and bank	3	1
	58	71
Current liabilities		
Trade creditors	(25)	(35)
Net current liabilities	33	36
	333	356
Capital and reserves		
Share capital (£1 ordinary shares)	200	200
Preference shares (£1 shares; 8%)	25	25
Retained earnings	58	81
	283	306
Long-term liabilities		
Debentures (10%)	50	50
	333	356

➡

Example 10.1
continued

Additional information:

1   All sales and all purchases are on credit terms.
2   The opening stock at 1 April 2010 was £20,000.
3   There were no accruals or prepayments at the end of either 2011 or 2012.
4   Assume that both the tax and the dividends had been paid before the end of the year.
5   The market price of the ordinary shares at the end of both years was estimated to be 126p and 297p respectively.

Required:

(a) Calculate appropriate liquidity, profitability, efficiency and investment ratios for both 2011 and 2012.

(b) Comment briefly on the company's financial performance for the year to 31 March 2012.

Answer to Example 10.1

(a) Significant accounting ratios

Gill Limited

	2011	*2012*

Liquidity ratios

Current assets:

$$\frac{\text{Current assets}}{\text{Current liabilities}}$$

	$\dfrac{58}{25}$	$\dfrac{71}{35}$
	$= 2.3$	$= 2.0$

Acid test:

$$\frac{\text{Current assets} - \text{stock}}{\text{Current liabilities}}$$

	$\dfrac{58 - 15}{25}$	$\dfrac{71 - 20}{35}$
	$= 1.7$	$= 1.5$

Profitability ratios

Return on capital employed:

$$\frac{\text{Net profit before tax}}{\text{Shareholders' funds}} \times 100$$

	$\dfrac{29}{283} \times 100$	$\dfrac{47}{306} \times 100$
	$= 10.2\%$	$= 15.4\%$

$$\frac{\text{Net profit after tax}}{\text{Shareholders' funds}} \times 100$$

	$\dfrac{20}{283} \times 100$	$\dfrac{35}{306} \times 100$
	$= 7.1\%$	$= 11.4\%$

$$\frac{\text{Profit after tax and preference dividend}}{\text{Shareholders' funds} - \text{preference shares}} \times 100$$

	$\dfrac{18}{283 - 25} \times 100$	$\dfrac{33}{306 - 25} \times 100$
	$= 7.0\%$	$= 11.7\%$

$$\frac{\text{Profit before tax and interest}}{\text{Shareholders' funds} + \text{long-term loans}} \times 100$$

	$\dfrac{29 + 5}{333} \times 100$	$\dfrac{47 + 5}{356} \times 100$
	$= 10.2\%$	$= 14.6\%$

Gross profit ratio:

$$\frac{\text{Gross profit}}{\text{Sales}} \times 100$$

$$\frac{64}{160} \times 100 = 40\%$$

$$\frac{86}{200} \times 100 = 43\%$$

Mark-up ratio:

$$\frac{\text{Gross profit}}{\text{Cost of goods sold}} \times 100$$

$$\frac{64}{96} \times 100 = 66.7\%$$

$$\frac{86}{114} \times 100 = 75.4\%$$

Net profit ratio:

$$\frac{\text{Net profit before tax}}{\text{Sales}} \times 100$$

$$\frac{29}{160} \times 100 = 18.1\%$$

$$\frac{47}{200} \times 100 = 23.5\%$$

Efficiency ratios

Stock turnover:

$$\frac{\text{Cost of goods sold}}{\text{Stock}}$$

$$\frac{96}{15} = 6.4 \text{ times}$$

$$\frac{114}{20} = 5.7 \text{ times}$$

Fixed assets turnover:

$$\frac{\text{Sales}}{\text{Fixed assets (NBV)}}$$

$$\frac{160}{300} = 0.5 \text{ times}$$

$$\frac{200}{320} = 0.6 \text{ times}$$

Trade debtor collection period:

$$\frac{\text{Trade debtors}}{\text{Credit sales}} \times 365$$

$$\frac{40}{160} \times 365 = 92 \text{ days}$$

$$\frac{50}{200} \times 365 = 92 \text{ days}$$

Trade creditor payment period:

$$\frac{\text{Trade creditors}}{\text{Purchases}} \times 365$$

$$\frac{25}{91} \times 365 = 101 \text{ days}$$

$$\frac{35}{119} \times 365 = 108 \text{ days}$$

Purchases:

Opening stock +	20	15
Purchases*	91	119
	111	134
– Closing stock =	15	20
Cost of goods sold	96	114

* by deduction

Investment ratios

Dividend yield:

$$\frac{\text{Dividend per share}}{\text{Market price per share}} \times 100$$

$$\frac{4^*}{126} \times 100 = 3.2\%$$

$$\frac{5^*}{297} \times 100 = 1.7\%$$

Dividend per share:

$$\frac{\text{Dividends}}{\text{Issued share capital}}$$

$$\frac{8}{200} \times 100 = 4p$$

$$\frac{10}{200} \times 100 = 5p$$

Answer to Example 10.1 continued

Dividend cover:

Net profit after tax and preference dividend		
Ordinary dividends	$\dfrac{20-2}{8}$	$\dfrac{35-2}{10}$
	= 2.25 times	= 3.3 times

Earnings per share:

Net profit after tax and preference dividend		
Number of shares	$\dfrac{20-2}{200}$	$\dfrac{35-2}{200}$
	= 9p	= 16.5p

Price/earnings:

Market price per share		
Earnings per share	$\dfrac{126}{9}$	$\dfrac{297}{16.5}$
	= 14	= 18

Capital gearing:

$$\frac{\text{Preference shares} + \text{long-term loans}}{\text{Shareholders' funds} + \text{long-term loans}} \times 100$$

$\dfrac{25+50}{333} \times 100$	$\dfrac{25+50}{356} \times 100$
= 22.5%	= 21.1%

(b) Comments on the company's financial performance for the year to 31 March 2012

In answering Part (b) of the question we will confine our comments to just a few brief points.

Liquidity

Cash flow

The company had a small cash balance at the end of each year (£3000 and £1000 respectively). We have not been provided with a cash flow statement but it is possible to prepare a simple one for 2012.

Cash flow statement for the year to 31 March 2012

	£000
Net profit before debenture interest and taxation (47 + 5)	52
Increase in stock	(5)
Increase in trade debtors	(10)
Increase in trade creditors	10
Increase in fixed assets	(20)
Interest paid	(5)
Tax paid	(12)
Dividends paid	(12)
Decrease in cash during the year	(2)
Cash at 1.4.11	3
Cash at 31.3.12	1

● Increases in stock and trade debtor balances of £15,000 were offset by a smaller increase in trade creditors of £10,000. An increase in fixed assets and tax paid was largely responsible for a decrease in the cash position at the end of 2012.

● Both the current assets and the acid test ratios were well within the generally accepted ranges.

Profitability

● All measures of profit show a healthy return on capital employed in both years with an increase in 2012.

● We do not, however, know how the ROCE ratios compare with other companies. The increases may have been partly due to a significant increase in mark-up on sales. If this is so, this would suggest that the company is selling in an elastic market and that it has been able to increase its selling prices without any great difficulty resulting in an increase in sales of 25% (from £160,000 to £200,000).

● The gross profit ratio showed a reasonable increase in 2012.

● Similarly the net profit ratio shows a healthy increase indicating that operational expenses are under control despite the company being busier.

Efficiency

● The stock turnover ratio has fallen from 6.4 times to 5.7 times. In other words the stock is not being used in production quite as quickly in 2012 as it was in 2011. This needs to be investigated. It may well be that the company has purchased more stock than was needed to meet the 25% increase in sales.

● The fixed assets turnover is very low in both years although it did increase slightly in 2012. Indeed it would appear that the company is not recovering in sales what it has invested in fixed assets. Perhaps this is because there is a long time-lag between the installation of plant and machinery and the expected upturn in sales. Again this is something that needs further investigation.

● The trade debtor position is very high (92 days in each year). This may be the industrial sector norm but it still needs investigation. The company could run into cash flow problems if its customers are slow to pay. This ratio may be related to the even higher trade creditor payment period (101 days and 108 days respectively). If the company is not receiving cash from its debtors it will not have the cash to pay its creditors. There is, therefore, a danger that it could possibly be going to run into a severe cash flow problem.

Investment

● This is a private company so it is difficult to read too much into the investment ratios. The dividend yield has fallen by nearly half but the dividend cover shows a healthy increase.

● The increase in the earnings per share is much more than healthy: it increased by over 83% in 2012.

● The market appears to view the prospects for the company favourably as the price/earnings ratio increased from 14 to 18.

● At just over 20% the capital gearing is sufficiently low to satisfy the ordinary shareholders that if future profits increase their dividends are likely to grow without any problems arising. Similarly if profits fall, the payments to both debenture holders and preference shareholders will not swallow up a huge proportion of whatever profits are made, leaving the ordinary dividend fairly safe.

Conclusion

● There are a few caveats: (1) we don't have any information about the overall environment in which the company operates; (2) we are provided with only limited internal data; (3) we only have the accounts for a two-year period; and (4) we don't know how this company compares with other private companies in the same industry.

● The company appears to be profitable, generally efficient and not a huge investments risk. There is a peculiar relationship between the fixed assets and the sales and

**Answer to
Example 10.1**
continued

the underlying cash flow position is weak because the company is not chasing up its debtors fast enough. As a result it is not able to pay its creditors very quickly. This means that if they begin to demand quicker payment the company could find itself facing great financial difficulties. If it cannot obtain the necessary credit then there may even be questions about whether it is able to continue as a going concern and it might then have to go into liquidation.

! Questions you should ask

As far as this chapter is concerned, there are two situations in which you might find yourself: either with a set of financial accounts that will have been interpreted for you or some that you might have to interpret for yourself. Irrespective of which situation you find yourself in, you might find it useful to ask (or ask yourself) the following questions.

● How reliable is the basic accounting information underpinning this information in front of me?

● Have consistent accounting policies been adopted throughout the period covered?

● If not, has each year's results been adjusted on to the same accounting basis?

● Were there any unusual items in any year that may have distorted a comparative analysis?

● Was the rate of inflation significant in any year covered by the report?

● If so, should the basic accounting data be adjusted to allow for it?

● What are the three or four most significant changes in these accounts during the period they cover?

● Are there any apparent causal links between them, such as greater efficiency resulting in a higher level of profitability or higher profits causing cash flow problems?

● What are the most important factors that this report tells me about the company's progress during the period in question and its prospects for the future?

Conclusion

This chapter has explained how you can examine the financial performance of a company (or other entity) over a certain period of time. If a detailed examination is required it may be necessary to examine the general business environment and economic sector in which it operates. Much information will also be collected about the company itself. One of the main sources of information will be its annual report and accounts.

While a great deal of information may be found in the annual reports and accounts that information has to be put into context as the absolute numbers disclosed are often large, do not mean much in isolation, and are often difficult to understand. This means that the accounts need to be analysed. There are four main types of analysis:

● horizontal analysis, involving a line-by-line inspection across the various time periods;
● trend analysis, in which all the data are indexed to a base of 100;
● vertical analysis, where each period's data is expressed as a percentage of a total;
● ratio analysis, which requires a comparison to be made of one item with another item expressing the relationship as either a percentage or a factor.

All of these four types of analyses rely primarily on the accounting data. Such data are subject to a number of reservations, such as the accounting policies and the methods used in preparing the accounts. These reservations must be allowed for when interpreting a set of accounts, especially when a comparison is made with other companies since accounting policies and methods are often different.

Ratio analysis is the most important of the four types of analyses. There are literally hundreds of ratios that could be calculated, plus some highly specialist ones that relate to particular industries. In this chapter we have selected just 15 common but important ratios and grouped them under four headings:

- liquidity ratios, which help to decide whether an entity has enough cash to continue as a going concern;
- profitability ratios, which measure the profit an entity has made;
- efficiency ratios, which ratios show how well the entity has used its resources;
- investment ratios, which help to consider the investment potential of an entity.

Irrespective of the category into which they fall, ratios should only be regarded as a signpost: in themselves they do not actually *interpret* the accounts for you. They are merely an arithmetical device that points you in the right direction and help you to assess what *has* happened and to predict what *might* happen. They provide you with the evidence, but you have to use that evidence to come to a verdict.

Key points

1 The interpretation of accounts involves examining financial accounts in some detail so as to be able to explain what has happened and to predict what is likely to happen.

2 The examination can be undertaken by using a number of techniques, such as horizontal analysis, trend analysis, vertical analysis and ratio analysis.

3 Ratio analysis is a common method of interpreting accounts. It involves comparing one item in the accounts with another closely related item. Ratios are normally expressed in the form of a percentage or a factor. There are literally hundreds of recognized accounting ratios (excluding those that relate to specific industries) but we have restricted our study to just 15.

4 Not all of the ratios covered in this chapter will be relevant for non-manufacturing, non-trading or not-for-profit entities. It is necessary to be selective in your choice of ratios.

5 When one item is related to another item in the form of a ratio, it is important to make sure that there is a close and logical correlation between the two items.

6 In the case of some ratios, different definitions can be adopted. This applies particularly to ROCE and capital gearing. In other cases annual averages are used instead of year end balances. This applies especially to ratios relating to stocks, debtors and creditors.

7 Assessing trends and calculating ratios is not the same as interpreting a set of financial accounts. Interpretation involves using a wide range of information sources as well as the incorporation of various types of analyses into a cohesive appraisal of an entity's past performance and its future prospects.

Check your learning

The answers to these questions can be found within the text.

1 What is meant by the term 'interpretation of accounts'?

2 Give three reasons why the absolute data shown in financial accounts may need to be interpreted.

3 List the users of accounts and suggest one piece of information that each user group may require from a set of financial accounts.

4 What is the difference between (a) horizontal analysis, (b) trend analysis?

5 What is vertical analysis?

6 What is (a) a ratio, (b) ratio analysis?

7 What four main categories may be used for classifying accounting ratios?

8 What does 'ROCE' mean and how may it be calculated?

9 What is the difference between the gross profit ratio and the mark-up ratio?

10 Why might it be misleading to compare the net profit ratio of one entity with that of another entity?

11 Why is liquidity important and what two ratios may be used for assessing it?

12 How would you assess whether stock turnover and fixed asset turnover ratios were good or bad?

13 What is meant by the 'trade debtor collection period'. Is a 60-day period worrying?

14 What is meant by the 'trade creditor payment period'. Is a 100-day period worrying?

15 Which two investment ratios take market prices into account?

16 Explain why there may be a difference between the dividend payable and its yield.

17 What is meant by 'EPS' and where might you find it in a set of published accounts?

18 What is the P/E ratio, and what is its importance?

19 What is capital gearing and how might it be calculated?

20 What is a possible link between the following ratios: (a) profitability and efficiency; (b) profitability and liquidity; (c) profitability and investment, and (d) efficiency and liquidity?

21 Outline the main steps you would take if you were asked to appraise the financial performance of a company using its annual report and accounts.

News story quiz

Remember the news story at the beginning of this chapter? Go back to that story and reread it before answering the following questions.

This is an interesting news story suggesting that historical accounts are too old to be meaningful when times are difficult and that management accounts would be much more useful. We shall be moving on shortly to examine management accounting in some detail but for the moment you might need to refer back to Chapter 1 to give you a brief reintroduction to its nature and purpose.

Questions

1 What performance measures might indicate that 'some statements in the public domain are not as strong as they first look'?

2 Why might historical accounts relating to two years in the past be 'too old to be meaningful'?

3 Why do you think that Fabrice Desnos believes that 'management accounts' would be any better than financial accounts in assessing performance?

Tutorial questions

The answers to questions marked with an asterisk may be found in Appendix 4.

10.1 'Accounting ratios are only as good as the data on which they are based.' Discuss.

10.2 How far do you accept the argument that the return on capital employed ratio can give a misleading impression of an entity's profitability?

10.3 Is ratio analysis useful in understanding how an entity has performed?

10.4* The following information has been extracted from the books of account of Betty for the year to 31 January 2011:

Trading and profit and loss account for the year to 31 January 2011

	£000	£000
Sales (all credit)		100
Less: Cost of goods sold:		
Opening stock	15	
Purchases	65	
	80	
Less: Closing stock	10	70
Gross profit		30
Administrative expenses		16
Net profit		14

Balance sheet at 31 January 2011

	£000	£000
Fixed assets (net book value)		29
Current assets		
Stock	10	
Trade debtors	12	
Cash	3	
Less: Current liabilities	25	
Trade creditors	6	19
		48
Financed by:		
Capital at 1 February 2010		40
Add: Net profit	14	
Less: Drawings	6	8
		48

Required:

Calculate the following accounting ratios:

(a) gross profit
(b) net profit
(c) return on capital employed
(d) current ratio
(e) acid test
(f) stock turnover
(g) debtor collection period.

10.5* You are presented with the following summarized accounts:

James Ltd
Profit and loss account for the year to 28 February 2012

	£000
Sales (all credit)	1 200
Cost of sales	600
Gross profit	600
Administrative expenses	(500)
Debenture interest payable	(10)
Profit on ordinary activities	90
Taxation	(30)
	60
Dividends	(40)
Retained profit for the year	20

James Ltd
Balance sheet at 28 February 2012

	£000	£000	£000
Fixed assets (net book value)			685
Current assets			
Stock		75	
Trade debtors		200	
		275	
Less: Current liabilities			
Trade creditors	160		
Bank overdraft	10		
Taxation	30		
Proposed dividend	40	240	35
			720
Capital and reserves			
Ordinary share capital			600
Profit and loss account			20
Shareholders' funds			620
Loans:			
10% debentures			100
			720

Required:

Calculate the following accounting ratios

(a) return on capital employed

(b) gross profit

(c) mark-up

(d) net profit

(e) acid test

(f) fixed assets turnover

(g) debtor collection period

(h) capital gearing.

10.6 You are presented with the following information relating to three companies:

Profit and loss accounts for the year to 31 March 2009

	Mark Limited £000	Luke Limited £000	John Limited £000
Profit before tax	64	22	55

Balance sheet (extracts) at 31 March 2009

	Mark Limited £000	Luke Limited £000	John Limited £000
Capital and reserves			
Ordinary share capital of £1 each	100	177	60
Cumulative 15% preference shares of £1 each	–	20	10
Share premium account	–	70	20
Profit and loss account	150	60	200
Shareholders' funds	250	327	290
Loans			
10% debentures	–	–	100
	250	327	390

Required:

Calculate the following accounting ratios:

(a)   return on capital employed

(b)   capital gearing.

10.7   The following information relates to Helena Limited:

Trading account year to 30 April

	2008 £000	2009 £000	2010 £000	2011 £000	2012 £000
Sales (all credit)	130	150	190	210	320
Less: Cost of goods sold:					
Opening stock	20	30	30	35	40
Purchases (all in credit terms)	110	110	135	145	305
	130	140	165	180	345
Less: Closing stock	30	30	35	40	100
	100	110	130	140	245
Gross profit	30	40	60	70	75
Trade debtors at 30 April	45	40	70	100	150
Trade creditors at 30 April	20	25	25	30	60

Required:

Calculate the following accounting ratios for each of the five years from 30 April 2008 to 2012 inclusive:

(a)   gross profit

(b)   mark-up

(c)   stock turnover

(d)   trade debtor collection period

(e)   trade creditor payment period.

10.8 You are presented with the following information relating to Hedge public limited company for the year to 31 May 2011:

1 The company has an issued and fully paid share capital of £500,000 ordinary shares of £1 each. There are no preference shares.
2 The market price of the shares at 31 May 2011 was £3.50.
3 The net profit after taxation for the year to 31 May 2011 was £70,000.
4 The directors are proposing a dividend of 7p per share for the year to 31 May 2011.

Required:
Calculate the following accounting ratios:
(a) dividend yield
(b) dividend cover
(c) earnings per share
(d) price/earnings ratio.

10.9 The following information relates to Style Limited for the two years to 30 June 2011 and 2012 respectively:

Trading and profit and loss accounts for the years

	2011		2012	
	£000	*£000*	*£000*	*£000*
Sales (all credit)		1 500		1 900
Less: Cost of goods sold:				
Opening stock	80		100	
Purchases (all on credit terms)	995		1 400	
	1 075		1 500	
Less: Closing stock	100	975	200	1 300
Gross profit		525		600
Less: Expenses		420		495
Net profit		105		105

Balance sheet at 30 June

	2011		2012	
	£000	*£000*	*£000*	*£000*
Fixed assets (net book value)		685		420
Current assets				
Stock	100		200	
Trade debtors	375		800	
Bank	25		–	
	500		1 000	
Less: *Current liabilities*				
Bank overdraft	–		10	
Trade creditors	80		200	
	80	420	210	790
		1 105		1 210
Capital and reserves				
Ordinary share capital		900		900
Profit and loss account		205		310
Shareholders' funds		1 105		1 210

Required:

(a) Calculate the following accounting ratios for the two years 2011 and 2012 respectively:

    1 gross profit

    2 mark-up

    3 net profit

    4 return on capital employed

    5 stock turnover

    6 current ratio

    7 acid test

    8 trade debtor collection period

    9 trade creditor payment period.

(b) Comment on the company's performance for the year to 30 June 2012.

Further practice questions, study material and links to relevant sites on the World Wide Web can be found on the website that accompanies this book. The site can be found at www.pearsoned.co.uk/dyson

Appendix: Summary of the main ratios

Liquidity ratios

$$\text{Current assets ratio} = \frac{\text{current assets}}{\text{current liabilities}}$$

$$\text{Acid test ratio} = \frac{\text{current assets} - \text{stocks}}{\text{current liabilities}}$$

Profitability ratios

$$\text{ROCE} = \frac{\text{net profit before taxation}}{\text{shareholders' funds}} \times 100$$

$$\text{ROCE} = \frac{\text{net profit after taxation}}{\text{shareholders' funds}} \times 100$$

$$\text{ROCE} = \frac{\text{net profit after taxation and preference dividends}}{\text{shareholders' funds} - \text{preference shares}} \times 100$$

$$\text{ROCE} = \frac{\text{profit before taxation and interest}}{\text{shareholders' funds} + \text{long-term loans}} \times 100$$

$$\text{Gross profit ratio} = \frac{\text{gross profit}}{\text{sales}} \times 100$$

$$\text{Mark-up ratio} = \frac{\text{gross profit}}{\text{cost of goods sold}} \times 100$$

$$\text{Net profit ratio} = \frac{\text{net profit before taxation}}{\text{sales}} \times 100$$

Efficiency ratios

$$\text{Stock turnover} = \frac{\text{cost of goods sold}}{\text{stock}}$$

$$\text{Fixed assets turnover} = \frac{\text{sales}}{\text{fixed assets at net book value}}$$

$$\text{Trade debtor collection period} = \frac{\text{trade debtors}}{\text{credit sales}} \times 365 \text{ days}$$

$$\text{Trade creditor payment period} = \frac{\text{trade creditors}}{\text{total credit purchases}} \times 365 \text{ days}$$

Investment ratios

$$\text{Dividend yield} = \frac{\text{dividend per share}}{\text{market price per share}} \times 100$$

$$\text{Dividend cover} = \frac{\text{net profit} - \text{taxation} - \text{preference dividend}}{\text{paid and proposed ordinary dividends}}$$

$$\text{Earnings per share} = \frac{\text{net profit}}{\text{number of ordinary shares}}$$

$$\text{Price/earnings ratio} = \frac{\text{market price per share}}{\text{earnings per share}}$$

$$\text{Capital gearing} = \frac{\text{preference shares} + \text{long-term loans}}{\text{shareholders' funds} + \text{long-term loans}} \times 100$$

Contemporary issues

A ticking clock

Accounting board could lose power to set rules

Nick Mathiason

SIR DAVID Tweedie, chairman of the International Accounting Standards Board (IASB), is to be grilled on Tuesday by European finance ministers and senior EU commissioners.

The development comes as speculation mounts that the IASB will be reformed as a result of the financial crisis. It could even lose powers to set international accounting standards.

A senior source close to the European Commission said 'There's a lot of anxiety in many countries and they wonder if the IASB is the right body for future rule setting. The clock is ticking.'

A growing body of opinion is unhappy with the IASB. It approved accounting principles that allowed financial institutions to book profits from unrealised assets.

The principle, enshrined in a rule called IAS 39, arguably allowed banks to fuel a speculative frenzy using financial instruments, and exacerbated institutions' deterioration as values plunged.

There are also concerns among European power brokers, particularly within France and Germany, that the IASB is an 'interconnected old boy's network'. A third of its board had worked for KPMG or firms that KPMG later acquired.

A senior City fund manager said: 'There's a recognition on the part of fund managers that were brought in during the good times. And there's a lot of resistance from technical accounting specialists who believe they have the true view of life.'

A spokesman for the IASB said: 'We're planning to provide a response of the IASB to the financial crisis, including an update to replace IAS 39.'

The Observer, 7 June 2009.

Source: Copyright Guardian News & Media Ltd 2009.

Questions relating to this news story can be found on page 262 ➡

About this chapter

In this chapter we look ahead over the next five to ten years to see what changes may take place in financial accounting and reporting. As this is a book for non-accountants we will not speculate about those possible developments that would be of particular concern to professional accountants. Instead we have identified five issues that are of relevance to all managers irrespective of their discipline (see Figure 11.1). They are: (1) the pronouncements of the International Accounting Standards Board; (2) the work of the Accounting Standards Board; (3) the development of a conceptual framework in accounting; (4) the treatment of revenue in financial statements; and (5) the role of the auditors.

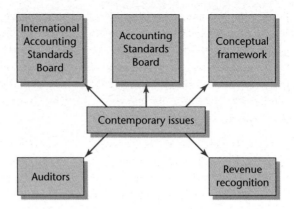

Figure 11.1 Contemporary issues: chapter contents

Learning objectives

By the end of this chapter you should be able to:

● identify the major changes that are likely to take place in financial reporting practice between 2010 and 2015;

● assess the importance of the Accounting Standards Board and the International Accounting Standards Board in financial reporting during that period;

● summarize the changes that may be made to the conceptual framework currently underpinning accounting practice;

● explain why the treatment of revenue is a major problem in financial reporting;

● outline the role auditors have in approving the financial statements of companies.

! Why this chapter is important

Accounting is a dynamic discipline. It has to be in order to cope with a rapidly changing world. New problems and new issues arise and some way has to be found of dealing with them as quickly as possible. There may then be a need to report them to interested parties and, if so, how and what form should the report take?

Accountants are expected to take a lead on the reporting issues. This is their expertise but non-accountants should also be heavily involved because the impact of many issues is far too wide-ranging to be left to just one group of specialists. For example, a decision to write-off goodwill to the profit and loss account instead of leaving it on the balance sheet can have a significant effect on a company's reported profit, the dividend it pays and on its share price.

It is as a result of such consequences that non-accountants need to know what new accounting and reporting issues are currently under discussion in the business, economic, financial and political worlds and what proposals are being suggested to deal with them. Space does not allow us to deal with all of them in this book but we can give you an indication of some of the changes that are likely to take place in the next five years. We have chosen five of the major ones but you are encouraged to read the business and financial press regularly to keep up with emerging issues in financial reporting.

In summary, then, we suggest that this chapter is particularly important for non-accountants for the following reasons.

- To be briefed about the general business environment in which accounting operates both nationally and internationally.
- To be informed about some contemporary issues in financial accounting and reporting.
- To advise your senior manager of any changes that may affect your own sphere of responsibility.
- To take an active part in any debate on the effect of any proposed financial reporting changes on your own entity.

Overview

We cannot be absolutely certain what changes will take place in financial accounting and reporting over the next few years. Some changes that appear highly likely at the moment may be abandoned altogether, while others may be radically amended or delayed well into the long term. We can, however, be reasonably confident that:

- There will be no new UK Companies Act before 2020.
- The International Accounting Standards Board will have become the preeminent worldwide body responsible for setting accounting standards.
- The UK's Accounting Standards Board will have lost much of its influence.
- Most entities in the UK will have decided to adopt IASB standards.
- Company annual reports and accounts will have become much longer and even more difficult to understand than they are now.

We hope that we are wrong on the last point. There are signs that the problem is recognized (see the News clip below) but we are certainly not confident that much will or can be done about it.

News clip

Towards easy reading

'The Financial Reporting Council (FRC), the UK's independent regulator responsible for promoting confidence in corporate reporting and governance, has published a discussion paper arising from its project on reducing complexity in financial reporting.'

Source: Adapted from Press Release (FRC PN 269), Financial Reporting Council, 4 June 2009.

We now move on to the first of our five topics: what the IASB is likely to require during the next five years.

IASB projects

Rules danger

'... there is a danger of standards becoming rules based because of the addition of more and more guidance for detailed situations, rather than sticking with broad principles.'

Source: Andy Simmonds, www.accountancyage.com/articles/print/2222281, 23 July 2008.

In this section we are going to summarize the main projects that the IASB was working on in the summer of 2009. This will give you a good idea of the changes that are likely to take place in financial reporting practice over the following five years. In the UK and the other EU countries its requirements will, of course, only be mandatory for publicly listed group companies. Nonetheless, they will inevitably have an influence on other types of entity.

The Board had divided its projects into five main groups: (i) financial crisis-related projects; (ii) new standards; (iii) amendments to existing standards; (iv) work on a conceptual framework; and (v) research and other related projects.

Financial crisis projects

This group includes six projects that will eventually lead to new IASs. They deal with matters that may be described as 'advanced' financial reporting and they are, therefore, beyond this book. All of them should have become standards by the end of 2010 but as new standards usually only become effective some 6 to 18 months after publication they will not be operable until perhaps 2012.

New standards

The new standards group is divided into two sections:

(a) *Proposals out for public comment.* There are three such proposals: revenue recognition, leases, and income tax. We will be returning to 'revenue recognition' later in the chapter. Both the proposed standard on leases and the one on income tax will have become standards by the end of 2011.

(b) *Developments currently being advanced.* This group includes nine projects. They range from 'emissions trading schemes' to 'post-employment benefits' (including pensions). However, one project, 'financial statement presentation', is of interest to us in this book but it is not scheduled to be published until 2011 (to be effective perhaps as late as June 2012) so we can put it to one side for the time being. One other proposal in this group relates to small and medium-sized enterprises (SMEs).

Amendments to existing standards

This group includes nine projects: one relating to annual improvements 2008–2010 and another for annual improvements 2009–2012. The seven other projects relate specifically to a number of standards such as earnings per share (IAS 33) and liabilities (IAS 37). All seven of them are fairly technical. They should be completed and published in their amended form by the end of 2011.

Conceptual framework

We are going to deal with this project as a separate section later in the chapter.

Research and other projects

There is only one such project: extractive activities. Apparently it is being prepared for the IASB by the national standard setters of Australia, Canada, Norway and South Africa. However, 'common control transactions' was added to the agenda in December 2007 and work will begin on it when staff become available. Similarly work on government grants had been deferred but this time until progress has been made on the revenue recognition, related parties, and emissions projects. Presumably their requirements will have a strong influence on what is recommended for the treatment of government grants.

You will appreciate that some of the estimated publication dates indicated by the IASB for its various projects may well be put back. We can certainly expect some projects to be delayed as sudden urgent issues arise, unforeseen difficulties occur in dealing with some issues, and some may even be abandoned as a result of political difficulties in some countries. Nonetheless we hope that the above summary gives you some idea of the depth and breadth of issues that the IASB is facing over the next five to ten years.

We now turn to have a look at what the Accounting Standards Board in the UK expects to be doing over the same period.

Activity 11.1	Log on to the IASB's website. Find the link relating to current projects. Identify those projects that do not appear in the above summary.

ASB projects

News clip

Accounting crossroads

'UK GAAP is indeed at a crossroads, and it appears that the ASB will have to stay at that crossroads for some time – perhaps two years or so – before deciding which road to follow.'

Source: Peter Holgate, *Accountancy*, January 2007, pp. 84–5.

Like the IASB the ASB has an active work programme. In the summer of 2009 its main activities fell into three categories: (i) convergence projects; (ii) other projects; and (iii) current proposals.

Convergence projects are those that involve examining some of the ASB's existing standards and bringing them into line with similar IASB standards. The ASB had five such projects in the summer of 2009: (1) business combinations; (2) inventories; (3) property, plant and equipment costs; (4) disposal of non-current assets and presentation of discontinued operations; and (5) accounting standard setting in a changing environment: the role of the Accounting Standards Board. The first four projects are somewhat technical and we do not need to consider them any further. The fifth project is about the future role of the ASB and this one is of considerable interest to us because it will have a major impact on both accountants and non-accountants. We return to this topic shortly.

The ASB has 14 *other projects* under consideration. Like the convergence projects, most are of a highly technical nature, e.g. intangible assets, 'financial instruments, and insurance. There are, however, two projects that are of particular interest to us: one looking at a conceptual framework and the other examining revenue recognition. We are going to deal with both these projects in separate sections later in the chapter.

The third grouping, *current proposals*, relates to documents that are in issue and are out for comment. At the time of writing there were ten such projects. Two projects went back as far as 2002 but they were almost at the accounting standards stage. The most recent project was a discussion paper on heritage assets; it was issued in January 2006.

We can see from the above work programme that the change to IASB requirements for listed companies in the EU has had a major impact on the role and influence of the UK Accounting Standards Board. It no longer is quite the premier standard setting body in the UK that it used to be and its influence is likely to diminish further as the IASB's dominance in world accounting increases.

The ASB has set out how it sees its future role in a series of pronouncements. It believes that it lies in contributing to the development of high quality global accounting standards by working closely with the IASB and other standard setting bodies. Its specific activities now fall under five main heads:

1 Contributing directly to the development of the IASB.
2 Influencing EU accounting standards policy.
3 Achieving convergence of UK standards with IFRS.
4 Improving 'other aspects' of UK standards.
5 Improving communication between companies and investors.

The above summary is extracted from the ASB's website. It appears that once UK standards have become compatible with ISAB standards the ASB will become, in effect, a sub-branch of the IASB albeit with special responsibility for acting on behalf of the UK. This might only be likely, however, if IASB requirements become mandatory for both private and public companies. They are not at present. They only apply to listed group companies. So it would appear that for the time being the ASB still has a major role to play in developing and issuing accounting standards for entities that do not fall into this category.

We now turn to an issue we introduced in Chapter 2 and one which the IASB is considering: the search for a *conceptual framework*.

Activity 11.2	**Opportunity knocks** Log on to the ASB's website. Check through the list of projects. What are the new projects?

A conceptual framework

The ASB is working with the US Financial Accounting Standards Board (FASB) on a joint project to '*develop an improved common conceptual framework that provides a sound foundation for developing future accounting standards*'. The two Boards believe that such a framework is *essential* (their word) to fulfil the Boards' goal of developing standards that are *principles based*. In addition, such standards should be 'internally consistent, and

News clip

IASB

'The IASB could use the financial tur-
moil as an opportunity to establish
definitely its long-delayed conceptual
framework for financial reporting. The
fair value crisis has shown the need for
clarification of the purpose of accounts so
that expectations of stakeholders are
appropriately set and a clear framework
established for the improvement and
application of standards.'

Source: ACCA, The G-20 Summit, April 2009, p. 2.

internationally converged'; they should also lead to 'financial reporting that provides the information capital providers need to make decisions in their capacity as capital providers'.

Just to remind you of some points we made in Chapter 2. In simple terms a conceptual framework is merely a list of rules that accountants use in preparing financial statements. Such a framework is necessary because otherwise different accountants would use different accounting rules in preparing financial statements. This would clearly confuse and mislead users and so they would have difficulty in making sense of the information that they were given. So what the IASB and the FASB are both trying to do is to agree a set of rules that all accountants in all countries could and should adopt.

The current IASB/FASB project was started in 2004. The work was divided into eight phases (A to H) and our comments relate to the position in the late summer of June 2009. Only Phases A to D had by then been reported as being currently active, so clearly the project has a long way to go. We will review the progress on Phases A to D but not in any detail as we cannot be certain that what may already have been decided will necessarily be included in the final draft.

Phase A deals will the objective and qualitative characteristics of financial reporting. Its aims are to consider in respect of financial reporting: (1) the objectives; (2) the qualitative characteristics; and (3) the trade-offs among qualitative characteristics and how they relate to materiality and cost–benefit relationships.

So far the Boards have tentatively agreed that:

1 The term 'faithful representation' should replace the characteristic of reliability.
2 Relevance and faithful representation are regarded as fundamental characteristics.
3 The concepts of neutrality, completeness and freedom from error cannot be 'absolutes', i.e. completely unlimited or unrestricted.
4 Verifiability, comparability, timeliness and understandability are enhancing characteristics.
5 Materiality and cost are constraints on financial reporting.

There is nothing particularly remarkable about decisions 1, 2 and 4: they are largely confirmations of existing practice. Decision 3 is a little hard to understand: the Board uses the term 'absolutes'; in other words, no one can ever be absolutely neutral, there will always be an element of bias, and it is impossible to guarantee that there will never be any errors. Finally, Decision 5 is just a recognition of reality.

Phase B covers 'elements' and 'recognition'. Its objectives are (1) to revise and clarify the definition of an asset and a liability; (2) resolve differences and definitions about other elements; and (3) revise and eliminate differences and provide a basis for resolving derecognition and unit of account issues. So this phase is largely about definitions. Of particular interest to us is the proposed definition of an asset and a liability:

Asset. A present economic resource to which the entity has a right or other access that others do not have. All these terms were then defined.

Liability. A present economic obligation for which the entity is the obligor. These terms were again defined.

Phase C provides guidance for selecting measurement bases in financial reporting so that they satisfy the objectives and qualitative characteristics of financial reporting. Work continues on the phase and no specific decisions had been taken. The Boards had simply agreed, in effect, to continue their work in this area.

Phase D. The objective of this phase is to determine what constitutes a reporting entity for the purposes of financial reporting. This phase is still largely at the discussion stage.

The overall impression given by the joint IASB/FASB project on the formulation of an agreed conceptual framework is that we are not going to get anything that is particularly new or earth shattering. It is more likely to be confirmation of the type of conceptual framework that had already been adopted in many countries during the previous 20 years. Its real significance would be that the USA was clearly willing to work with other countries and that it no longer insisted on its own conceptual framework being accepted by the international community.

We now move on to consider another contentious issue in financial reporting: revenue recognition.

Activity 11.3	Log on to the FASB's website. What is the current status of the FASB/IASB's joint conceptual framework project?

Revenue recognition

News clip

Revenue and commission

Andy Halford, the Chief Financial Officer of Vodaphone has called for clarity in the way that accounting rules relate to statutory reporting because there is an increasing risk that financial and non-financial staff interpret them differently. This is alleged to cause problems for his staff when they calculate their commission on sales because of different ways of recognising revenue.

Source: Adapted from Andy Halford, Vodaphone CFO, *Accountancy Age*, 7 May 2009, p. 15.

Revenue may be defined as:

> *The gross inflow of economic benefits during the period arising in the course of the ordinary operating activities of an entity when those inflows result in increases in equity, other than increases relating to contributions from equity participants. (IAS 18, para. 7)*

IAS 18 then goes into considerable detail as to when revenue should be recognized. Apart from the rather stiff language its intentions appear to be reasonably clear, so what is the problem? The main problem arises from having to apply general pronouncements to specific circumstances. As a result a considerable number of gaps and loopholes begin to appear and preparers of financial statements are left to decide for themselves just how they should be filled.

The problem is so fundamental that the IASB has joined together with the FASB with the intention of publishing an accounting standard that would satisfy both bodies and their members. The project began in 2002 but an agreed standard is not expected until at least 2011. The driving force behind the project is a realization that *revenue* is a crucial element in financial statements because it helps users to assess a company's performance and its prospects. However, the experience of most countries is that the definition and recognition of revenue is quite unsatisfactory and as a result users are being fed highly unreliable information. It follows that something has to be done to correct a most unsatisfactory situation.

Revenue is usually the largest single item in financial statements and the two Boards suggest that there are a number of practical and conceptual reasons why a standard is necessary. In summary they are as follows.

- Revenue recognition problems are the main cause of errors and fraud in financial statements.
- Insufficient information is shown in them about the individual items making up the total revenue figure.
- Revenue accounting policies are too general to be useful.
- There is little guidance for emerging industries and for service entities.
- There is little comparability among different entities and industries.
- Revenue recognition in the USA is not based on a conceptual framework, there is no comprehensive standard, and there are over 200 pronouncements about the treatment of revenue.

It follows from the above list of problems that the main objective of the project is to deal with them by developing a coherent conceptual framework for revenue recognition. Such a framework would:

1 Eliminate inconsistencies in existing conceptual guidance and in existing standards.
2 Provide conceptual guidance.
3 Fill those voids where there is no revenue recognition guidance.
4 Establish a single comprehensive standard on revenue recognition.

The above outline of the IASB/FASB's revenue recognition project is taken from various publications and updates issued by the FASB on behalf of both bodies. If you want to read more about the project and you want an update, you will find the FASB's website very helpful (log on to: www.fasb/org/project/revenue-recognition).

In December 2008 the Boards published a discussion paper for comment on its preliminary views on revenue recognition 'in contracts with customers'. A single recognition 'model' was suggested for application across a range of industries and geographical regions. Revenue would be recognized when it satisfied 'the performance obligations in the contract', i.e. when it fulfilled a promise to provide a good or service to the customer. This pronouncement does not seem particularly different from existing practice but the Boards believe that by applying and clarifying the principle it will improve the comparability and understandability of revenue for users of financial statements.

The discussion paper was open for discussion until June 2009. Following a review by the Boards and, no doubt, some modification, it was then hoped that an Exposure Draft would be issued, possible in early 2010. The standard was still scheduled to be issued in 2011. It could then take another 6 to 18 months before it becomes operative. It is, therefore, going to take a very long time before the various revenue recognition problems we identified earlier are sorted out. That is, of course, assuming that the new standard fulfils all its objectives.

Activity 11.4	A building has now been under construction for three years. It is expected to be completed in two years' time. The agreed contract price is £1,000,000. The costs to date are £400,000 and it is expected that another £200,000 will be spent on the building before it is completed. What amount of revenue would you recognize in each year?

Year 1   Year 2   Year 3   Year 4   Year 5

Auditors

News clip

Auditors' powers

As a result of poor trading, Bay Trading Company has collapsed into administration. The auditors of the parent company, Alexon, said they were likely to issue an 'emphasis of matter' paragraph when they publish the company's audit report. This gives a signal that the company may have difficulty in continuing as a going concern.

Source: Adapted from *The Financial Times*, 23 April 2009, p. 56.

Auditors are usually qualified accountants who specialize in checking financial statements and who are employed by a firm of chartered or certified accountants. Most firms of accountants are very small and they don't have either the staff or the experience to audit large public companies. Indeed, in the UK there are probably only about four or five firms of accountants capable of doing a very large audit for an international group of companies.

There is no evidence to suggest that auditors in the UK colluded in the type of scandals that took place in the early 2000s although they were undoubtedly placed in a very difficult position. This was partly due to their role in company auditing and partly because they had little guidance on what accounting practices the new industries such as electronics and information technology should adopt.

The law states that shareholders appoint the auditors of the company. In practice they cannot do so because it is impossible for them all to get together and vote on the merits of the various firms. So it is usually left to the directors to select a firm and put the name forward to the shareholders at a general meeting for their formal approval. As it is rare for the shareholders to vote against the directors' recommendation, the auditors are well aware that if they fall out with the directors they are likely to lose the audit. Auditors are not, therefore, as independent as is sometimes believed.

The auditors' independence may also be compromised because of a number of other factors:

- They may become heavily dependent on the fee earned for a particular audit.
- The staff generally, and the partner in charge particularly, may become too friendly with the directors.
- It is common for staff to leave an audit firm and take up a full-time position with the client company.
- Audit firms often do lucrative non-audit work for the company, such as management consultancy and tax advice.

All these factors are of very real concern because they could compromise the audit firm's independence. So if a company engages in dubious financial practices then the auditors may be accused of not doing anything about it because they are in the directors' pockets.

This may be so in some cases but a more likely cause is the *expectations gap* that we referred to in Chapter 1, i.e. the public think that the auditors are there to do one job, whereas in reality they are there to do an entirely different one. Their job is primarily to confirm that the accounts represent a true and fair view and not to discover if there has been any fraud.

So what about the questionable accounting practices that some companies might be tempted to adopt and which would then receive a lot of media coverage along the lines of '**another accounting scandal!**'? It might not always be obvious, of course, that some practices *are* questionable. As we have argued throughout this book, accounting is not a form of simple arithmetic where 2 + 2 always = 4. There are often difficult decisions to take and the directors may then have to convince the auditors that what they want to do is fairer and more reasonable than what the auditors want to do. It may only be well after the year end that what seemed fair and reasonable at the time does not seem so two or three years later.

Referring back to Activity 11.4, what was your decision? Recognizing revenue in the construction industry is not easy. As in this case, projects often take longer than one year. So should you wait until a project is finished before you recognize any revenue? That would be a highly prudent approach. Should you instead recognize some revenue in each year of the contract? That would normally be regarded as being highly imprudent. Or might you recognize some revenue when the project is nearing completion? That is the conventional accounting approach. But then, of course, you have to decide in which year you begin and how much to take in each subsequent year. A further complication is that you would also have to charge some of the costs in each year that you recognized some revenue. The conventional approach is to take some profit based on the contract price less the costs to date and an estimate of the costs to completion. The balance (i.e. the estimated profit) would then probably be adjusted by an arbitrary factor, e.g. two-thirds. All of these decisions are likely to go horribly wrong and the contract may eventually result in a considerable loss.

There are no absolutely right or wrong ways of dealing with such situations. Ultimately it is largely a matter of experience and judgement of what to do: the directors may take an optimistic view while the auditors may take a much more pessimistic one. The latter approach was certainly the one that auditors appeared to be taking during the recession which hit the UK in 2007. It became obvious just how many auditors were concerned about whether a particular company was a 'going concern' and whether the financial statements needed to be 'qualified'.

This brings us back to the conflict between two accounting concepts: neutrality and prudence. Accountants are trained to be cautious about financial matters, i.e. prudent. If you did not need to be extremely cautious then you have still got the money in the bank but if you were too optimistic, the profit will have long since been paid out to shareholders. The deep recession in the first part of the twenty-first century was probably caused by caution being thrown out of the window and as a result the UK (among many other countries) is still paying for it. All that those accountants trained in the old school can do is to shake their heads and mutter, *'It wasn't like that when I was young: we were trained not to take risks'*:

Activity 11.5	
(a) Should an independent body appoint company auditors?	yes/no
(b) Should auditors be allowed to do other work for their clients in addition to auditing?	yes/no
(c) Should auditors be allowed to take up full-time employment with a former client?	yes/no
(d) Should auditors be allowed to do an audit for only a limited period?	yes/no

---

❗ Questions you should ask

Allowing for changes that *may* have taken place since the book was published, you might like to pose the following questions.

- Have we had to change our treatment of any accounting matters as a result of new IFRSs/FRSs?
- Has the ASB published anything during this last year that affects us?
- Are there any new accounting concepts that we have incorporated into our financial statements this year?
- What definition of revenue do we adopt?
- What methods do we use to recognize the amount of revenue we take to the profit and loss account?
- Have our auditors raised any concern about our financial statements?

Conclusion

This chapter has looked ahead to some of issues that may affect financial accounting and reporting practices over the next five to ten years.

We have reviewed the current work of both the IASB and the ASB as it was in the summer of 2009 and highlighted those projects that are likely to result in changes to financial reporting over the next few years. We have also considered in a little more detail two projects that are being undertaken by the IASB: the development of a new conceptual framework, and the introduction of a completely new standard covering revenue recognition.

Finally, we examined the role external auditors play in financial reporting and the conflict that arises between their responsibilities to shareholders and the dilemma they face in not antagonizing the directors.

Key points

1 Both the IASB and the ASB have an active development programme which should result in new standards coming on stream within the next five years. Most of their projects are highly technical and they are not of immediate relevance to non-accountants.

2 The IASB is working jointly with the FASB on a new conceptual framework, i.e. a statement of accounting principles.

3 Of particular interest is another joint programme the IASB has with the FASB: an accounting standard on revenue recognition.

4 Auditors act on behalf of shareholders but they cannot afford to fall out with a company's directors. They also face difficult decisions about supporting the directors in the treatment of certain contentious accounting matters. In more recent times it has been difficult to determine whether or not a company is actually a going concern.

Check your learning

The answers to these questions can be found within the text.

1 What do the initials ASB, IASB and FASB represent?

2 When do IASB standards normally become effective?

3 What do the initials EPS mean?

4 Why has work on government grants been deferred?

5 What is convergence?

6 With who or what is the ASB converging?

7 What five specific activities has the ASB set itself?

8 What is a conceptual framework?

9 Who has become the IASB's partner?

10 What is another term for faithful representation?

11 Why are neutrality, completeness and freedom from error not absolutes?

12 Give an example of a fundamental characteristic.

13 Give two examples of enhancing characteristics.

14 What are two constraints on financial reporting?

15 What is revenue?

16 What is meant by recognition?

17 Give three reasons why an accounting standard on revenue recognition is needed.

18 What is an auditor?

19 What is an external auditor's basic job?

20 Give three reasons why an external auditor's independence may be compromised.

21 Why might an auditor disagree with the accounting treatment a client may have adopted?

News story quiz

Remember the news story at the beginning of this chapter? Go back to that story and reread it before answering the following questions.

Questions

1 How would it be possible for the IASB to lose its powers?

2 What could replace the IASB if the European Union abandoned IASB's requirements for its member countries?

3 What would be the implications for international financial reporting if the IASB was disbanded?

Tutorial questions

11.1 Examine the prospects of one set of accounting standards being applicable on a worldwide basis.

11.2 Assess the likely future of the UK's Accounting Standards Board?

11.3 Outline the accounting principles that you think should be included in a conceptual framework.

11.4 Explain why revenue recognition is a major problem in financial reporting.

11.5 Discuss the relationship between a company's external auditor and its directors.

> Further practice questions, study material and links to relevant sites on the World Wide Web can be found on the website that accompanies this book. The site can be found at www.pearsoned.co.uk/dyson

The communication of financial information

After preparing this case study you should be able to:

- identify significant features in a company's profit and loss account, balance sheet and cash flow statement;
- describe the financial performance of a company using the above statements;
- prepare a chairman's report based on the information extracted from the financial statements and from other sources.

Background

Location   Moodiesburn, Scotland

Company   Devro plc

Synopsis

Devro plc is a Scottish-based company with its headquarters at Moodiesburn near Glasgow. It is one of the world's leading producers of manufactured casings ('skins') for the food industry. It supplies a wide range of products along with technical support to manufacturers of sausage, salami, hams and other cooked meats. The company concentrates on producing edible collagen products. Collagen is a common form of animal protein. In recent years such products have been replacing gut casings in all of the company's markets.

Besides its operations in Scotland, Devro has production plants in Australia, the Czech Republic and the USA. It also services markets from appropriately located offices around the world and through agents and distributors.

The appendix to this case study includes some information about Devro's activities for the year ended 31 December 2008.

Required:

Based on the above information and that contained in the appendix, draft a chairman's statement covering the year to 31 December 2008.

Appendix

Board changes

Retirements: Pat Barrett, Chairman at the next AGM. John Neilson, Finance Director since 1993, on 1 May 2008. Successor: Peter Williams. Board now has five directors: three executive (two appointed since 2006) and two non-executive directors (again both appointed since 2006).

Dividend

	2008	2007
	£000	£000
Final paid of 3.025 pence per share (2007: 3.025 pence)	4927	4926
Interim paid of 1.425 pence per share (2007: 1.425 pence)	2321	2321
Unclaimed dividends from previous years	(5)	(2)
	7243	7245

The directors proposed a final dividend in respect of the financial year ended 31 December 2008 of 3.025 pence per share, which it was estimated would absorb £4,927,000 of shareholders' funds. It was planned to be paid on 15 May 2009 to shareholders who were on the register at close of business on 17 April 2009.

Financial

	2008	2007
Before exceptional items:	£000	£000
Revenue	183125	156252
Operating profit	20595	17692
Profit before tax	18818	15567
Profit after tax	3286	10323
Basic earnings per share	8.2p	6.0p
Exceptional items*:		
Operating profit	(3478)	651
Taxation	2641	1044
Basic earnings per share	(0.6p)	1.0p
Cash and cash equivalents at 31 December	4243	9495

* Mostly due to reorganization of manufacturing activities in the Czech Republic (£3.7 million) less profit on sale of Moodiesburn land (£238,000).

Operational

Sales to external customers	2008	2007
Business segmental revenue:	£000	£000
Collagen casings	144695	125104
Distributed products	21523	18080
Other products	16907	13068
	183125	156252
Geographical segmental revenue:		
Europe	107289	92515
Americas	33627	28778
Asia/Pacific	42209	34959
	183125	156252

Prices were raised by 3.2% on average during 2008. Raw material costs were broadly similar to those in 2007.

Outlook

It was thought likely that the banking crisis in the UK would be a major headache during 2009 and beyond and that credit would also be very tight. The UK's national debt was considered huge and that it would take many years before it could be brought down to a sustainable level. Taxes would probably have to rise and government capital and revenue expenditure would be cut fairly severely.

The outlook for Devro was much healthier. Increased investment in capital expenditure would help (up from £10,469,000 in 2007 to £12,949,000 in 2008). Most of its income was earned overseas and like the UK other countries were also in economic difficulties.

Note: For further information about Devro plc log on to its website (www.devro.plc.uk).

Interpretation of accounts

**Learning
objectives**

After preparing this case study you should be able to:

- evaluate a set of financial statements for a public limited company;
- identify the main changes in the company's financial position over a period of time;
- summarize the information contained within such statements.

Background

Location	Scotland
Company	Robert Wiseman Dairies PLC

Synopsis

Robert Wiseman Dairies is a public limited company. Its head office is in East Kilbride near Glasgow. The group's revenue and profits arise wholly from the processing and distribution of liquid milk and associated products. It operates entirely within the UK with seven major processing dairies at Aberdeen, East Kilbride, Glasgow, Manchester, Droitwich Spa, Okehampton and Bridgwater. The average number of persons employed by the group during the year to 4 April 2009 was 4508 (3888 on production and distribution, and 620 on administration).

The company was originally a small family business. In recent years it has expanded rapidly. It has done this partly by natural growth and partly through acquiring other companies. It became a public company in 1994.

The appendix to this case study shows some data extracted from the Group's annual report and accounts for 2005, 2006, 2007, 2008 and 2009.

Required:

Analyse the company's financial performance for the five years 2005 to 2009 inclusive.

Appendix

Robert Wiseman Dairies plc
Five-year financial statement summary

For the year ended	2005	2006	2007	2008	2009
	£000	£000	£000	£000	£000
Income statement					
Revenue	489 168	568 564	605 289	721 983	847 702
Cost of sales	(373 400)	(429 883)	(448 594)	(551 829)	(667 309)
Gross profit	115 768	138 681	156 695	170 154	180 393
Profit from operations	25 077	27 495	35 659	31 645	35 147
Profit before tax	25 221	26 726	34 592	29 184	30 767
Profit for the year	21 551	18 450	24 156	19 320	6 581
Balance sheet					
Property, plant and equipment	146 228	150 119	176 309	216 455	221 881
Inventories	6 826	7 037	7 079	8 887	10 581
Trade receivables	32 237	39 876	41 958	53 310	57 130
Current assets	49 851	56 328	59 432	71 607	80 995
Trade payables	(38 321)	(44 803)	(52 155)	(63 140)	(69 906)
Current liabilities	(67 889)	(76 170)	(81 798)	(101 861)	(107 173)
Total equity	114 069	119 258	139 796	139 509	134 521
Cash flow statement					
Operating activities	31 424	36 010	44 109	52 937	57 964
Investing activities	(18 953)	(23 871)	(41 679)	(62 731)	(30 983)
Financing activities	(20 585)	(15 724)	(3 737)	10 563	(21 978)
Net increase/(decrease) in cash and cash equivalents	(8 114)	(3 585)	(1 307)	859	5 003
Cash and cash equivalents at start of year	16 431	8 317	4 732	3 425	4 284
Cash and cash equivalents at end of year	8 317	4 732	3 425	4 284	9 287
Statistics					
Basic earnings per share (p)	28.38	25.35	33.38	26.76	9.19
Dividends per share (p)	8.00	9.00	12.00	14.00	15.00
Market price per share (p)	270	312	459	458	324

Notes:

(1) According to the notes to the financial statements (p. F29), the current year's tax (2009) was significantly affected by a change in legislation phasing out an industrial building allowance. The deferred tax impact on the Group was over £17 million. There was no immediate cash impact, i.e. it was a 'book' entry. This change was not expected to occur again.

(2) Additional information may be obtained by logging on to Wiseman's website (www.wiseman-diaries.co.uk).

MANAGEMENT ACCOUNTING

Part 4

Part 4 deals with management accounting. Chapter 12 provides a foundation for a study of the subject. Chapters 13 and 14 deal with some basic costing accounting matters, Chapters 15 and 16 with planning and control procedures, and Chapters 17, 18 and 19 with some decision-making issues. Finally, Chapter 20 reviews some emerging issues in management accounting.

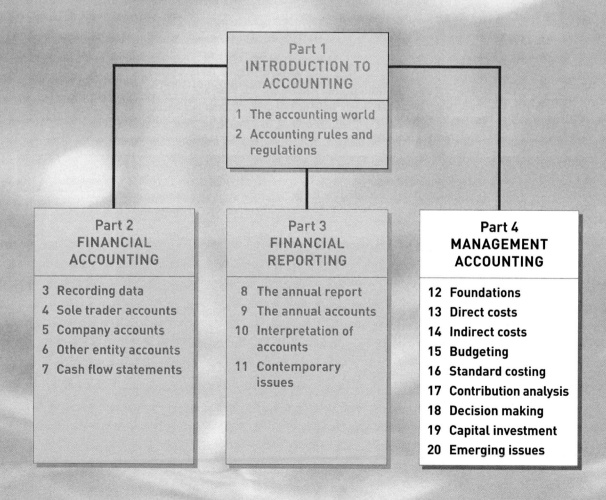

Part 1
INTRODUCTION TO ACCOUNTING

1 The accounting world
2 Accounting rules and regulations

Part 2
FINANCIAL ACCOUNTING

3 Recording data
4 Sole trader accounts
5 Company accounts
6 Other entity accounts
7 Cash flow statements

Part 3
FINANCIAL REPORTING

8 The annual report
9 The annual accounts
10 Interpretation of accounts
11 Contemporary issues

Part 4
MANAGEMENT ACCOUNTING

12 Foundations
13 Direct costs
14 Indirect costs
15 Budgeting
16 Standard costing
17 Contribution analysis
18 Decision making
19 Capital investment
20 Emerging issues

Wanted: management accounts!

Whitehall backs demands for 'sensitive accounts'

David Jetuah

The government's efforts to provide more trade credit insurance will reinforce the controversial demands of insurers to be supplied with highly sensitive management accounts instead of relying on statutory filings at Companies House.

Alistair Darling announced in the Budget a £5bn war chest to aid businesses that had seen their trade credit cover withdrawn or cut.

Last week *Accountancy Age* revealed the world's biggest insurer Euler Hermes had withdrawn cover from suppliers to frozen food company McCain because it had refused to provide management accounts when asked.

But the chancellor's announcement means companies can now expect the government to bolster demands for accounts that would otherwise not be made available and would normally only be used for internal purposes.

'Whatever accounts the industry uses to get their impression of a company, that's what we'll be using,' said a DBERR spokeswoman.

After the collapse of Bay Trading last week, one credit referencing agency boss said government backing credit insurers on management accounts could be the prelude to more collapses.

'If insurers pull cover because they don't get management accounts this could lead to investors in a jittery market saying "what do they know that we don't", and taking action,' said Martin Williams of Graydon.

Matthew Fell, the CBI's director of company affairs, said companies were getting 'more and more onerous information requests including management accounts'.

Accountancy Age, 30 April 2009.

Source: Reproduced with permission from Incisive Media Ltd.

Questions relating to this news story can be found on page 282 ➡

About this chapter

In Parts 1 to 3 of this book we have concentrated on financial accounting and financial reporting. In Part 4 we turn to management accounting – one of the most important branches of accounting. In this chapter we outline the nature and purpose of management accounting, trace its historical development, describe its main functions and examine the impact it has on the behaviour of those coming into contact with it.

The chapter provides you with a foundation for the subject. It then makes it easier for you to deal with the eight other chapters that cover management accounting in some depth.

Learning objectives

By the end of this chapter, you should be able to:

- describe the nature and purpose of management accounting;
- trace its historical development;
- outline the six main functions of management accounting;
- assess its impact on human behaviour.

! Why this chapter is important

The previous chapters in this book covered mainly financial accounting and financial reporting. It is logical to start a study of accounting in this way because financial accounting practices have strongly influenced the development of much else in accounting. This is especially true of management accounting. Nevertheless, until you become a senior manager it is unlikely that you will be involved to any great extent in the financial accounting and reporting requirements of an entity. This is not the case with management accounting. Even as a junior manager you are likely to have to provide information for management accounting purposes and to receive reports of your departmental or sectional performance.

At the very least, therefore, it is helpful to know what that information is for and what the various reports mean, especially when you are asked to act on them. It also suggests that all employees in an entity should know something about management accounting if they want to be really good at their jobs.

It follows that this chapter is important because it provides the background for a detailed study of management accounting that is covered in the remaining chapters.

Nature and purpose

News clip

Call for disclosure

Small and medium-sized enterprises (SMEs) are being encouraged to disclose their management accounts if they want to end the 'curse' of being scored badly by the credit rating agencies. The report indicates that statutory reports are considered useless for this purpose because they may be two years out of date before they are filed.

Source: Adapted from www.accountancyage.com/business, 9 July 2009.

You will recall from Chapter 1 that accounting is a specialized service function involving the collection, recording, storage and summary of *data* (primarily of a financial nature), and the communication of *information* to interested parties. It has six main branches, the two most prominent being financial accounting and management accounting. *Financial accounting* deals mainly with information normally required by parties that are *external* to an entity, e.g. shareholders or government departments. *Management accounting* has a similar role, except that the information supplied is normally for parties *within* an entity, e.g. management.

In Chapter 1 we also gave you CIMA's definition of management accounting. For convenience, we will repeat it here.

> *Management accounting is the application of the principles of accounting and financial management to create, protect, preserve and increase value for the stakeholders of for-profit and not-for-profit enterprises in the public and private sectors. (CIMA, Official Terminology, 2005)*

This is a fairly wide definition of management accounting. Its *primary* purpose is to supply accounting information for use *within* an entity but that information may also be of interest to external parties such as banks, credit rating agencies and the government. Clearly, therefore, in that respect at least it is very similar to financial accounting. However, we can distinguish many differences between financial accounting and management accounting. We summarize them for you below; they are also depicted in Figure 12.1.

- *Non-mandatory*: there are no statutory or mandatory professional requirements covering management accounting.
- *Data*: more quantitative data are normally incorporated into a management accounting system.
- *Qualitative data*: management accounting information increasingly includes a great deal of qualitative data.
- *Non-monetary*: data that cannot be translated into monetary terms is incorporated into management accounting reports.
- *Forecasted and planned*: data of both a historic and a forecasted or planned nature is of considerable importance and relevance in management accounting.
- *Users*: management accounting is primarily concerned with providing information for use *within* an entity.

It follows from the above that unlike financial accountants management accountants have considerably more freedom in providing the type of information that meets the specific requirements of interested parties. The main party will normally be the entity's managers.

Companies				
Management accounting	Main user	Financial accounting		
Management		Shareholders		
None	Regulations	Statutory	Professional	
Non-monetary : Quantitative : Qualitative	Data	Financial		
Historical : Forecasted : Planned : Budgeted				

Figure 12.1 Management accounting vs financial accounting: main differences

Activity 12.1	The above section has provided you with some idea of what management accountants do. But *how* could they help you do a better job? Jot down what help you think that they could give you.

Historical review

Until the eighteenth century Britain was primarily an agrarian society and there were comparatively few recognizable industrial entities. Furthermore, most entities (of whatever type) were relatively small and they were financed and managed by individuals or their families. As a result, it was unnecessary to have formal documentary systems for planning, control and reporting purposes because the entities were small enough for the owners to assess these considerations for themselves on a day-to-day basis.

During the eighteenth century, Britain became the first country in the world to undergo an industrial revolution. In just a short period of time it changed from a predominantly agricultural society to an industrial one and by the late nineteenth century it had become a major industrial power in the world. There were two specific consequences of this development. Firstly, the new industrial enterprises needed large amounts of capital. This could not be provided by just a few individuals. Capital had to be sought from 'investors' whose interest in the enterprise was largely financial. Such investments were extremely risky and there was the strong possibility of personal bankruptcy. So Parliament intervened and introduced the concept of *limited liability* into company law. Secondly, the new enterprises needed specialist staff to operate and manage them. Such staff had often to be recruited from outside the immediate family circle.

These two consequences resulted in the ownership of the enterprise often being divorced from its management. A number of Companies Acts passed in the nineteenth and twentieth centuries gave shareholders in limited liability companies the right to receive a minimum amount of information annually, and that auditors should be appointed to report to them about the company's performance.

The complexity, scale and size of the new industrial enterprises meant that it was difficult for professional managers to exercise control on the basis of personal knowledge and casual observation. It became necessary to supply them with information that was written down. At first this revolved round the statutory annual accounts, but it soon became clear that such accounts were produced too late, too infrequently and in too little detail for effective day-to-day managerial control. As a consequence, during the period from 1850 to about 1900, a more detailed recording and reporting system gradually evolved. We now refer to this as a *cost accounting system*. Its main purposes were to provide sufficient information for the valuation of closing stock, work-in-progress and finished goods, and for calculating the costs of individual products. In the early days it was common for financial accounting systems and cost accounting systems to run side-by-side but they eventually merged when it became clear that they used much of the same basic data. The development of management accounting is shown in Figure 12.2. Notice how the pace of development quickens after the eighteenth century.

The really major developments in management accounting occurred in the United States at the beginning of the twentieth century. By 1925 most of the practices and techniques used today were established. Indeed, between 1925 and 1980 few new developments in management accounting took place. The position has changed somewhat during the

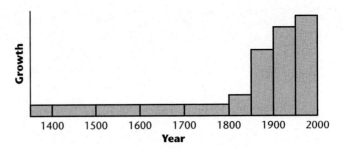

Figure 12.2 Management accounting: development

last 30 years or so, and many new ideas have now been put forward. Some of them have been incorporated into practice, albeit mainly by large companies.

The new management accounting techniques were rapidly developed and practised fairly widely in the United States from the beginning of the twentieth century. Progress was much slower in Britain. Apart from the largest industrial companies, the application of management accounting did not become common until about 1970. Even now, there is evidence that many smaller entities still depend on what is sometimes called 'back of the envelope' exercises for managerial planning and control purposes. It should also be noted that over the same period, manufacturing industry in many industrial nations has given way to service industries. This means that many of the traditional management accounting issues, such as stock control and pricing, standard costing and product costing are of much less significance than they once were. Nevertheless, they are still of some considerable relevance and we will be covering them in subsequent chapters.

Activity 12.2	Write down two reasons why, following the Industrial Revolution, it became apparent that accounting, as practised previously, was not geared to working out the cost of individual products.

Main functions

The overall role of a management accountant is to provide information for management purposes. Six specific functions can be readily identified: planning, control, cost accounting, decision making, financial management, and auditing.

The interrelationship of these functions is shown in Figure 12.3 and we outline them briefly in the rest of this section.

Planning

Planning can be classified into two broad groupings: long-term and short-term.

Long-term planning

Long-term planning is commonly called *strategic planning* or *corporate planning*. We will refer to it as 'strategic planning' because this appears to be the most widely used term. *Strategy* is a military term meaning the ability to plan and organize manoeuvres in such a way that the enemy is put at a disadvantage. Over the last 20 years, strategic planning has become an important managerial function in both profit-making and not-for-profit

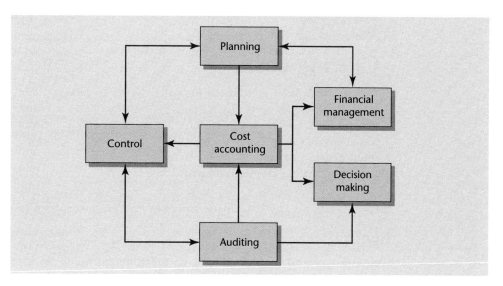

Figure 12.3 Management accounting: main functions

entities. In essence, it involves working out what the entity wants to achieve in the long term (i.e. beyond a calendar year) and how it intends to achieve it.

There are six basic steps involved in preparing a strategic plan. A summary is shown in Table 12.1.

Strategic planning is not specifically a management accounting function. The senior management of the entity will probably set up a multidisciplined strategic planning team that may include a management accountant. The management accountant's major role will be to collect data and to provide information (mainly of a financial nature) required by the team.

Short-term planning

Accountants normally refer to short-term planning as *budgeting*, the 'short term' being regarded as being a period of up to a calendar year. Budgeting is covered in Chapter 15.

Table 12.1 Steps in preparing a strategic plan

Step	Action	Question to be asked
1	Establish the entity's objective (e.g. to earn a minimum of 20% on capital employed)	*'Where do we want to be in x years' time?'*
2	Assess the entity's current position	*'Where are we now?'*
3	Evaluate the external factors (economic, financial, political and social) that will apply during the period of the plan	*'What is the outside world likely to be like?'*
4	Specify the differences between the current position and the required future one	*'What gaps are there between where we are now and where we want to be?'*
5	Conduct a SWOT analysis	*'What are our strengths, weaknesses, opportunities and threats?'*
6	Put the strategic plan together	*'What do we have to do to get towards where we want to go?'*

Cutting costs

The oil giant Shell is reported to have made plans to cuts costs. Rather unusually the axe is about to fall on the accounting function. The move has come about because of lower prices that the company is getting for its oil and gas.

This is certainly one way of cutting costs but this is not usually what management accountants mean when they talk about *controlling* them!

Source: Adapted from www.accountancyage.com/articles/print2242953, 27 May 2009.

Control

A clear plan of what an entity wants to do and how it intends to get there is clearly preferable to having no plan at all. Otherwise the entity will just drift. However, an additional benefit of planning is that it can also form part of the control mechanism of the entity. What management accountants do is to measure what has actually happened over a certain period of time and then compare it with what was planned to happen. Any apparent significant differences (or *variances* as they are called) are investigated, and if they are not acceptable then action is taken to ensure that future actual events will meet the agreed plan. It may be found, for example, that the actual price paid for some raw materials was £5 per kilo when the plan allowed for a payment of only £4.50 per kilo. Why was there a variance? Was it poor planning? Was it impossible to estimate the actual price more accurately? Was it inefficient purchasing? Were higher-quality materials purchased and if so, was there less wastage?

Not all variances are unwelcome. For instance, 1000 units might have been sold when the plan only allowed for sales of 950 units. The reasons for this variance should still be investigated, and if this *favourable* trend were deemed likely to continue then it would be necessary to ensure that additional resources (e.g. production, administration, distribution, and finance) were made available to meet higher expected levels of sales.

Note that it would be the responsibility of the management accountants to coordinate the investigation of any variances and report back to the entity's senior management. *It would not be the management accountant's responsibility to take any form of disciplinary action.* This is a point that is not always understood by those employees who come into contact with management accountants!

Further aspects of control are covered in Chapters 15 and 16.

Activity 12.3

Planning involves working out what you want to happen. Control involves (a) looking at what has happened, then (b) taking action if the actual events are different from the planned events. But the control element happens after the events. So how can they be controlled? Write down reasons why trying to control events after they have happened may be of some benefit.

Cost accounting

Historically, cost accounting has been the main function of management accounting. It is now much less significant, and other functions, such as the provision of information for decision making, have become much more important. The cost accounting function involves the collection of the entity's ongoing costs and revenues, the recording of them in a double-entry book-keeping system (a task that these days is normally done by computer), the balancing of the 'books' and the extraction of information as and when required by management. Cost accounting also involves the calculation of *actual costs* of products and services for stock valuation, control and decision-making purposes.

We deal with cost accounting in Chapter 13.

News clip

Accounting error

The owners of Magners cider, the C & C group, have admitted that revenues did not rise by 3% in the four months to the end of June 2009 as previously reported. They fell by 5%. Apparently an error occurred when data were transferred incorrectly from the internal accounting system to the spreadsheet used for producing the trading statement.

Source: Adapted from *The Financial Times*, 14 July 2009, p. 17.

Decision making

The provision of information for decision making is now one of the major functions of management accountants. Although actual costs collected in the cost accounting records may provide some guidance, decision-making information usually requires dealing with anticipated or expected future costs and revenues and it may include data that would not normally be incorporated in a traditional accounting ledger system.

Most decisions are of a special or 'one-off' nature and they may involve much ingenuity in obtaining information that is of assistance to managers in considering a particular decision. Note that it is the managers themselves who will (and should) take the decision, not the management accountants.

Various aspects of decision making are covered in Chapters 17, 18 and 19.

Financial management

The financial management function associated with management accounting generally is again one that has become much more significant in recent years. Indeed, financial management has almost become a discipline in its own right. Its main purpose is to seek out the funds necessary to meet the planning requirements of the entity economically, to make sure that they are available when required and that they are used efficiently and effectively.

Along with economy, effectiveness and efficiency are known as the three 'Es'. CIMA defines them as follows:

Economy: Acquisition of resources of appropriate quantity and quality at minimum cost.
Effectiveness: Utilization of resources such that the output of the activity achieves the desired result.
Efficiency: Achievement of either maximum useful output from the resources devoted to an activity or the required output from the minimum resource input.

(CIMA: Official Terminology, 2005)

Financial management is not covered in any depth in this book, although we do return briefly to some aspects of it in Chapter 19.

Auditing

Auditing involves the checking and verification of accounting information and accounting reports. There are two main types of audit: external and internal.

News clip

Underground gap

Auditors have discovered serious deficiencies in accounting procedures involving London Underground maintenance companies. Metronet's reported divisional costs could not be clearly linked to the company's management accounts. It was also found that Tube Lines spends proportionately more on its finance function operations than does Metronet.

Source: Adapted from *Accountancy Age*, 27 July 2007, p. 2.

External auditing may be regarded as part of the financial accounting function, while internal auditing is more of a management accounting responsibility. External auditors work for an outside entity, while internal auditors are employees of the entity itself and they are answerable to its management. In practice external and internal auditors work closely together. Internal auditors' remit may also be extended to assessing the economy, effectiveness and efficiency of management systems generally instead of concentrating almost exclusively on the cost and financial records.

The management accountant's involvement in auditing is not considered any further in this book.

Activity 12.4

Match each item in Column A with the most appropriate item in Column B.

A	B
Auditing	Financing activities
Controlling	Governing activities
Cost accounting	Recording activities
Decision making	Determining activities
Financial managing	Checking activities
Planning	Devising activities

Behavioural considerations

The collection of data and the supply of information are not neutral activities. They have an impact on those who are involved in supplying and receiving such material. The impact can be strongly negative and it can adversely affect the quality of the data or information. In turn, this may cause management to make some erroneous decisions because of unreliable data and biased information. This is a feature of the job that accountants are now trained to recognize, i.e. the *behavioural impact* that *they* may have on other employees. What relevance has this for non-accountants?

Much of the information collected and stored in a financial accounting system is backed by legislation and neither accountants nor non-accountants can ignore what is

Figure 12.4 The modern management accountant: a model diplomat

required regardless of their own personal views. The legal position puts financial accountants in a powerful position because, if necessary, they can *demand* what they want from other employees.

Management accountants cannot make such demands as there are no statutory requirements to produce management accounts or even any management accounting standards. Their power, as such, comes from the close working relationship that they have with the directors and other senior managers. There is no doubt that in practice this puts them in an extremely strong position.

However, irrespective of the source of the power that accountants may have in making demands on other employees, modern thinking suggests that it is unwise to exercise it too obviously. Accountants are now taught that they have a much better chance of obtaining what they want when they want it by working *with* other employees rather than by ordering them around.

This approach to dealing with other staff works best, of course, if it is reciprocated. So as a non-accountant you too should regard accountants more as friends rather than as enemies, i.e. try to work with them rather than against them. Some non-accountants may find this hard to do especially if they have had some unfortunate confrontations with accountants in the past. However, remember that it is usually better to talk than to fight (*jaw jaw, rather than war war*) and that accountants are basically employed to provide a service for other employees.

So in return for cooperating fully with your accountants and getting the service that you want and that they can provide, what approach can you expect them to adopt? We suggest that their behaviour towards you should be as follows:

- *Cooperative.* Treat you as an equal and make it clear that your work is just as important as what they do.
- *Non-autocratic.* Avoid being autocratic, condescending and superior.
- *Diplomatic.* Be courteous, patient, polite and tactful.
- *Informative.* Explain in some detail why, what and when some information is required and in what form.
- *Helpful.* Assist in digging out the information that they require.
- *Considerate.* Take into account your other responsibilities and give you a realistic amount of time to provide any information that they require.
- *Courteous.* Avoid threatening implicitly or explicitly any disciplinary action.
- *Instructive.* Guide you through the mechanics of the management accounting system that relate to your responsibilities.

In practice, the above requirements may be somewhat idealistic. Sometimes, for example, senior managers do not encourage a participative approach and they may not always be willing to provide appropriate training courses. The management accountants in the entity then have a responsibility to point out to the senior managers that the planning and control systems that operate in such an environment are not likely to be particularly successful.

It must also not be forgotten that the relationship between management accountants and non-accountants is not one-sided and that non-accountants have an equal responsibility to be cooperative. Clearly, management accountants will find it difficult to work with staff who adopt a resentful or surly manner and who try to make life difficult for them.

Activity 12.5	Suppose that as a departmental manager you received an e-mail from the chief management accountant containing the following statement:

> *I wish to inform you that you overran your budget by £10,000 for March 2011. Please inform me immediately what you intend to do about this overspend. Furthermore, I will need to know why you allowed this gross piece of mismanagement to occur.*

Jot down what your feelings would be if you had received such an e-mail. Then rewrite the above using a more tactful tone.

❗ Questions you should ask

Some entities impose a management accounting system on their managers and they are expected to do just as they are told. However, experience suggests that such an approach does not work. It is much better to involve staff in the detailed implementation and operation of information systems. What approach does *your* own organization take? We suggest that you ask the following questions (but remember to be tactful!).

- Who wants this information?
- What is it for?
- What's going to happen to it?
- Will I get some feedback?
- What will I be expected to do about it?
- May I suggest some changes?
- How can I help to improve what is done?

Conclusion

This chapter has provided a foundation for a more detailed study of management accounting. Management accounting is one of the six main branches of accounting. Its main purpose is to supply information to management for use in planning and controlling an entity and in decision making. It grew largely out of the simple financial accounting systems used in the late nineteenth century when it became apparent that such systems could not provide managers with the day-to-day information that such systems needed, e.g. for use in stock control and for product costing purposes. In the early part of the twentieth century management accounting came to be increasingly recognized as a useful planning and control mechanism. More recently it has become an integral part of overall managerial decision making. The discipline now has six main recognizable functions: planning, control, cost accounting, decision making, financial management and auditing.

There are no statutory or mandatory professional requirements that govern the practice of management accounting. Nevertheless, management accounting techniques are now regarded as being of considerable benefit in assisting an entity to achieve its longer-term objectives. As a result, management accountants tend to hold senior positions in most entities and they may wield considerable power and influence. However, their work can be largely ineffective and the quality of the information that they provide poor if they do not receive the wholehearted support of their fellow employees. Unless this is forthcoming, the eventual decisions taken by management, based on the information provided by the management accountants, may possibly lead to problems in the running of the entity.

Key points

1 Management accounting is one of the six main branches of accounting.

2 Its main purpose is to collect data and provide information for use in planning and control and for decision making.

3 Management accounting evolved in the late nineteenth century out of the simple financial accounting systems used at the time when more detailed information was needed for stock control and for production costing purposes.

4 It began to be used as a planning and control technique in the early part of the twentieth century.

5 In more recent years, management accounting techniques have become incorporated into managerial decision making.

6 Six main functions of modern management accounting can now be recognized: planning, control, cost accounting, decision making, financial management and auditing.

7 Management accounting practices can have a negative impact on both the providers and the users of information if management accountants adopt an autocratic and non-participative attitude.

8 A negative approach to management accounting requirements may result in poor-quality information and erroneous decision making.

Check your learning

The answers to these questions can be found within the text.

1 What is meant by 'management accounting'?

2 List six ways in which it is different from financial accounting.

3 Suggest two reasons why in pre-industrial times there was no need for entities to have a management accounting system.

4 For what purposes did nineteenth century managers need a more detailed costing system?

5 What is meant by 'strategic planning'?

6 How does it differ from budgeting?

7 What are the six steps involved in preparing a strategic plan?

8 What is meant by 'control'?

9 Describe briefly the nature of cost accounting.

10 What is meant by 'decision making'?

11 What is the main purpose of financial management?

12 To what extent are management accountants involved in auditing?

13 Why should management accountants be aware of the behavioural impact of information supply?

News story quiz

Remember the news story at the beginning of this chapter? Go back to that story and reread it before answering the following questions.

This news story is interesting because it shows what pressure companies are now under to disclose much more about their activities than perhaps has been the case in the past. Of course, the agencies providing financial help to companies are in a powerful position to demand what they want.

Questions

1 Why should management accounts be highly sensitive?

2 Why might a company's published accounts be inadequate for credit insurance purposes?

3 Would the internal *financial* accounts not be sufficient for this purpose?

4 What additional information would the management accounts provide?

Tutorial questions

The answers to questions marked with an asterisk can be found in Appendix 4.

12.1 Examine the usefulness of management accounting in a service-based economy.

12.2 The first step in preparing a strategic plan is to specify the entity's goals. Formulate three possible objectives for (a) a manufacturing entity and (b) a national charity involved in animal welfare.

12.3 Assess the importance of taking into account behavioural considerations when operating a management accounting system from the point of view of (a) the management accountant; and (b) a senior departmental manager.

12.4* Distinguish between financial accounting and management accounting.

12.5* Describe the role of a management accountant in a large manufacturing entity.

12.6 Outline the main steps involved in preparing a strategic plan.

12.7 What is the difference between 'planning' and 'control'?

12.8 'Management accountants hold an extremely powerful position in an entity, and this enables them to influence most of the decisions.' How far do you think that this assertion is likely to be true in practice?

Further practice questions, study material and links to relevant sites on the World Wide Web can be found on the website that accompanies this book. The site can be found at www.pearsoned.co.uk/dyson

A big purchasing initiative

Siemens set to lower profit forecast

Daniel Schäfer

Siemens is set to lower its profit forecast on Wednesday as a deeper-than-expected recession spoils the engineering group's ambitious profit growth plans.

Peter Löscher, Siemens' chief executive, is expected to ditch the projection that the operating profit in the three sectors will reach €8bn–€8.5bn ($10.6bn–$11.3bn) in the current financial year, which ends in September.

In the first quarter, the company cheered markets with a better-than-expected 20 per cent increase in operating profit to more than €2bn.

However, profits in the pivotal industry sector, which makes everything from train carriages to light bulbs, fell in the quarter, forcing Siemens to follow other industrial companies in drastically reducing working hours.

By June, 19,000 workers will be expected to be part of a government-sponsored scheme to reduce working hours.

The financial crisis has reached Siemens, but Siemens itself is not in crisis, Joe Kaeser, Siemens' chief financial officer, said recently.

Order income will keep falling in the second quarter. But thanks to the company's large order backlog in the healthcare and energy sectors, Siemens' revenues and profits are likely to grow further.

A base effect will help Siemens, as it had large one-off restructuring costs in the year before. But analysts said Siemens was better positioned to cope with the recession because it started cutting costs even before the crisis hit.

Mr Löscher, who in 2007 became the first outsider in 161 years to

head Siemens, has not only sold further non-core subsidiaries, but has also launched a programme to save €1.2bn in overheads by 2010.

The next effort to cut costs will be unveiled this week when Barbara Kux, a Siemens' management board member who came in late last year, announces details of a purchasing initiative.

Ms Kux recently said that she would reduce the number of the company's 370,000 suppliers by 20 per cent.

She is not expected to unveil a top-line figure but analysts expect savings of about €1bn this year – a sum that will be much welcomed by Mr Löscher to achieve Siemens' new forecast.

www.ft.com, 26 April 2009.

Source: Reproduced with permission from *The Financial Times*.

Questions relating to this news story can be found on page 297 ➡

About this chapter

In the previous chapter we explained something about the nature and purpose of management accounting, why and how it developed as a separate branch of accounting, and what its main functions are today. One such function is *cost accounting*.

Cost accounting involves collecting detailed financial data about products and services, and the recording of that data. The data may then be extracted from the books of account, summarized and presented to the management of an entity. The managers will use the information presented to them for planning and control purposes.

The information may take various forms depending on what it is to be used for. At the very least, managers are usually interested in knowing the profit or loss made by individual products or services. For convenience, we will call this process *product costing*.

Following the Industrial Revolution, the new type of managers in the nineteenth century attempted to base their selling prices on what products had cost to make. Unfortunately, the financial accounting systems at that time could not provide the information required so a separate branch of accounting called *cost accounting* slowly began to develop. In the twentieth century cost accounting has been subsumed into a much broader branch of accounting now generally referred to as *management accounting*.

Even so, accountants still cost products using a technique that has hardly changed in over 100 years. This technique is known as *absorption costing*. In broad terms, absorption costing involves the following procedure:

- isolate those costs that can be easily identified with a particular product;
- apportion the non-indentifiable costs.

Accountants describe the first stage as *allocating* the direct costs and the second stage as *absorbing* the indirect costs. In this chapter we cover the first stage and in the next chapter the second stage.

<table>
<tr>
<td>**Learning objectives**</td>
<td>

By the end of this chapter, you should be able to:

- **identify material, labour and other direct costs;**
- **describe three important methods of charging direct material costs to production;**
- **calculate prime costs.**

</td>
</tr>
</table>

! Why this chapter is important

This is the first of two chapters covering the subject of cost accounting. As a non-accountant you may be puzzled why you need to know *anything* about cost accounting. It might seem reasonable to assume that you can safely leave that subject to your accountants. We do not think so.

There are two broad reasons why we hold this view. In order to be a really successful manager we think that you need to know something about cost accounting for two reasons: (1) to achieve greater control over the resources for which you are responsible, and (2) to make better decisions. This chapter will help you do both of these things when dealing with materials. The treatment of what accountants call *direct material* costs requires a decision to be made about the price at which materials should be charged to production. If managers get the pricing decision wrong it can have some serious and often adverse consequences for the survival of the company. So it is far too important a decision for you to delegate it entirely to your accountants. They will usually supply you with all the cost and financial information that you need but you will be in a much better position to assess its reliability and usefulness if you are familiar with its source, the assumptions made in preparing it and the methods used to compile it.

Responsibility accounting

A cost accounting system will normally be based on what is called 'responsibility accounting'. *Responsibility accounting* has a number of identifiable features. They are as follows:

- *Segments.* The entity is broken down into separate identifiable segments. Such segments are known as 'responsibility centres'. There are three main types:
  - (i) *Cost centres.* A cost centre is a clearly defined area of responsibility under the overall control of a designated individual to which the costs directly associated with the specified area are charged. There are two main types of costs centres: *production* cost centres where products are manufactured or processed, e.g. a machining department or an assembly area; and *service* cost centres where a service is provided to other cost centres, e.g. the personnel department or the canteen. Cost centres can take a number of forms such as a department, a production line, a machine, a product or a sales area.
  - (ii) *Profit centres.* A profit centre is similar to a cost centre except that both costs and revenues associated with the centre are charged to it. It is then possible to calculate the profit or loss for each profit centre. The oil division of a large chemical company is an example of a profit centre.
  - (iii) *Investment centres.* An investment centre is similar to a profit centre except that it is also responsible for all the major investment decisions that relate to that centre. A division of a large multinational company is an example of an investment centre.
- *Boundaries.* The boundaries of each segment will be clearly established.
- *Control.* A manager will be put in charge of each separate segment.
- *Authorization.* Segmental managers will be given the independence to run their segments as autonomously as possible.

By identifying different segments within an entity it is then possible to isolate the various costs and revenues associated with each segment. This means that segmental managers can then be made solely responsible for planning, budgeting and controlling all their segment's activities and for making any decisions that affect it. They will also, of course, be held responsible for whatever does or does not happen within it.

| Activity 13.1 | What are your first thoughts about responsibility accounting? Do you think that it is possible to divide a complex organization into neat little segments? Is it realistic to say to someone 'you're in complete charge of that segment'?

How much autonomy do you think a cost centre manager can really be given? Base your answer on the following scale. |

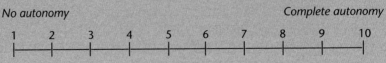

No autonomy   *Complete autonomy*

1   2   3   4   5   6   7   8   9   10

Classification of costs

While in theory a responsibility accounting system enables costs and revenues to be easily identified on a segmental basis (from now on we will refer to all responsibility centres simply as 'cost centres'), in practice it is not always easy to identify each cost with a particular cost centre because there are some costs that are so general and so basic that no one manager has control over them, e.g. fcatory rental and business rates. Such costs are levied on a property as a whole and they do not relate directly to any particular cost centre.

Activity 13.2	Specify which cost centre you think should be charged with the cost of a company's factory rent and business rates.

Costs that are easily and economically identifiable with a particular segment are known as *direct costs*. So if it is possible to identify all the costs of the entity with particular cost centres then there is no problem because by definition *all* costs must be direct costs. While this may be true at the cost centre level it is usually not true at the product or unit level. Some costs will certainly be easy to identify with particular units (classed as *direct unit costs*) but there will be other costs (classed *as indirect unit costs*) where it is much more difficult to relate them to units of production, e.g. canteen costs or the wages department expenses. In what way, therefore, is it possible to charge some of the indirect costs to individual units? In practice, it is not easy but we explain how it might be done in the next chapter.

Irrespective of whether costs are classified into the direct or indirect categories, we also need to have some idea of their nature, so they are usually broken down into their *elements*, i.e. whether they are material costs, labour costs or other types of costs. The *elements of cost* are shown in diagrammatic form in Figure 13.1. This breakdown is similar to the one we adopted for manufacturing accounts in Chapter 6.

There are two particular points to note about Figure 13.1. Firstly, in a competitive market, selling price can rarely be determined on a 'cost-plus' basis, i.e. total cost of sales plus a profit loading. If the entity's prices are higher than its competitors, then it is not likely to sell very many units. However, if its selling prices are lower than its competitors then it might sell many units but the profit on each unit may be low. Even so its competitors are likely to bring down their prices very quickly. So when the market largely determines selling prices, it is vital that the entity's total costs are strictly controlled and monitored so that the gap between its total sales revenue and its total cost of sales (i.e. its profit) is as wide as possible. Secondly, the classification shown will not necessarily be relevant for all entities. For example, an entity in the service sector (such as insurance broker) is not likely to have any direct or indirect production costs.

Figure 13.1 is based on what is called *total absorption costing*. This is a method whereby *all* costs of the entity are charged to (or absorbed into) particular products irrespective of their nature. If only production costs are absorbed into product costs, the system is referred to simply as absorption costing.

There is also another important costing method known as *marginal* costing. This method involves classifying costs into their fixed and variable elements. Fixed costs are those that do not change irrespective of how many units are produced (i.e. regardless of output). Variable costs are those costs that do change and change directly proportionally to the number of units produced. We shall be dealing with marginal costing in Chapter 17.

We can now begin our detailed study of direct costs. We start with direct materials.

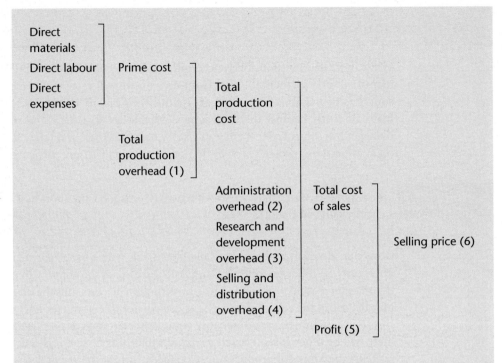

Figure 13.1 The elements of cost

Source: Based on Chartered Institute of Management Accountants (2005). CIMA Official Terminology. Oxford: CIMA Publishers.

Notes

1 Total production overhead includes those indirect production costs that cannot be easily identified with specific units or processes.
2 Administration overhead includes the non-production costs of operating the entity.
3 Research expenditure includes the cost of working on new products and processes. Development expenditure will include those costs associated with trying to improve existing products, processes and production techniques.
4 Selling and distribution overhead includes the cost of promoting the entity's products and services and the cost of delivering them to its customers or clients.
5 A profit loading may be added to the total cost of sales in order to arrive at the unit's selling price.
6 In this chapter we only go as far as the prime cost level.

Direct materials

News clip

Inventory error

Oil and gas services company Hamworthy has discovered an overstatement in its inventory values totalling £4.6 million. The company said that it had taken immediate action to improve processes and strengthen internal controls and management in order to prevent any recurrence.

Source: Adapted from www.accountancyage.com/articles/print/2225200, 3 September 2008.

Materials consist of raw materials and component parts. Raw materials are those basic ingredients that are incorporated into the production of a product, such as flour, sugar, and raisins used in making cakes. Component parts include miscellaneous ready-made goods or parts that are purchased (or manufactured specially) for insertion into a main product, e.g. a car radiator.

As we discussed earlier, a direct cost is one that can be easily and economically identified with a particular segment, such as a cost centre or a particular product. However, there is a problem when relating this definition to materials. It might be easy and economic to identify them *physically* with a particular segment but it does not necessarily follow that it is then easy to attach a cost to them. There are two main problems. Firstly, *size*. We might be able to identify a few screws used in assembling a chair, for example, but it would not be worthwhile costing them separately because their relative value is so small. Such costs would, therefore, be classified as *indirect* material costs. Secondly, *timing*. Materials may have been purchased at different times and at different prices, so it might not be possible to know whether 1000 kg of material held in stock had been purchased at £1, £2 or £3 per kilo. This problem applies particularly when materials that are purchased in separate batches are stored in the same containers, e.g. grains and liquids.

In such circumstances, it is necessary to determine an appropriate pricing method. Many such methods are available but as the price of materials charged to production also affects the value of closing stock, regard has to be had to the financial reporting requirements of the entity. In management accounting we are not bound by any statutory or mandatory professional requirements, and so we are perfectly free to adopt any stock valuation method we wish. Unfortunately, if the chosen method is not acceptable for financial reporting purposes, we would have to revalue the closing stock for the annual accounts. This may be a very expensive exercise. We would, therefore, normally adopt a pricing method that is suitable both for the annual accounts and for management accounting purposes. This means adopting the requirements contained in *SSAP 9* (Stocks and long-term contracts). There are three preferred methods (assuming that the specific unit cost cannot be identified). We summarize each of them below. They are also shown in diagrammatic format in Figure 13.2.

- *First-in, first-out (FIFO)*. This method adopts the first price at which materials have been purchased.
- *Average cost*. An average cost may be calculated by dividing the total value of materials in stock by the total quantity. There are a number of acceptable averaging methods but we will be using the *continuous weighted average* (CWA) cost method.
- *Standard cost*. This method involves estimating what materials are likely to cost in the future. Instead of the actual price, the *estimated* or *planned* cost is then used to charge out the cost of materials to production. The standard cost method is usually adopted as part of a standard costing system. We shall not be considering it any further in this chapter because we will be dealing with standard costing in Chapter 16.

Activity 13.3

Assuming that you do not know the specific unit price of some materials, which method would you use to price them? Tick the appropriate box below and insert the main reason for your choice.

FIFO ☐   Average cost ☐   Standard cost ☐

Main reason:

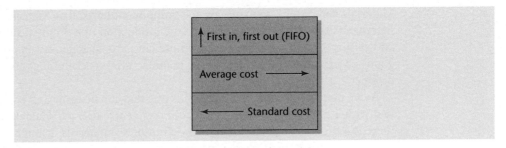

Figure 13.2 Direct material costing methods

First-in, first-out

Number errors

Wolverine Tube, the American copper producer, has found a number of errors in its inventory. The errors were discovered in previously issued financial statements. As a result the release of its second quarter figures had to be delayed.

Source: Adapted from www.accountancyage.com/articles/print/2224241, 22 August 2008.

We will now use a calculative example to explain how the FIFO and the continuous weighted average pricing methods work. It is sensible to issue the oldest stock to production first, followed by the next oldest and so on, and this should be done wherever possible. This method of storekeeping means that old stock is not kept in store for very long, thus avoiding the possibility of deterioration or obsolescence. However, as some materials may be stored in such a way that they become a mixture of old and new stock it is then not possible to identify each separate purchase. Nevertheless, in pricing the issue of stock to production there seems to be some logic in following the first-in, first-out procedure and charge production with the oldest price first, followed by the next oldest price and so on. The procedure is as follows:

1 Start with the price paid for the oldest material in stock and charge any issues to production at that price.
2 Once all of the goods originally purchased at that price have been issued, use the next-oldest price until all of that stock has been issued.
3 The third-oldest price will be used next, then the fourth oldest, and so on.

The use of the FIFO pricing method is illustrated in Example 13.1.

Although Example 13.1 is a simple one, it can be seen that if the amount of material issued to production includes a number of batches purchased at different prices, the FIFO method involves using a considerable number of different prices.

The advantages and disadvantages of the FIFO method may be summarized as follows.

Advantages

- The method is logical.
- It appears to match the physical issue of materials to production.
- The closing stock value is closer to the current economic value.

Example 13.1	**The FIFO pricing method of charging direct materials to production**

The following information relates to the receipts and issue of a certain material into stock during January 2012:

Date	Receipts into stores			Issue to production
	Quantity units	Price £	Value £	Quantity units
1.1.12	100	10	1 000	
10.1.12	150	11	1 650	
15.1.12				125
20.1.12	50	12	600	
31.1.12				150

Required:

Using the FIFO method of pricing the issue of goods to production, calculate:

(a) the issue prices at which goods will be charged to production;
(b) the closing stock value at 31 January 2012.

Answer to Example 13.1

(a) The issue price of goods to production:

Date of issue	Tutorial note	Units	Calculation	£
15.1.12	(1)	100	units × £10 =	1 000
	(2)	25	units × £11 =	275
		125		1 275
31.1.12	(3)	125	units × £11 =	1 375
	(4)	25	units × £12 =	300
		150		1 675

(b) Closing stock:

	£
25 units × £12 =	300
Check:	
Total receipts (£1000 + £1650 + £600)	3 250
Total issues (£1275 + £1675)	2 950
Closing stock	300

Tutorial notes

1 The goods received on 1 January 2012 are now assumed to have all been issued.

2 This leaves 125 units in stock out of the goods received on 10 January 2012.

3 All the goods purchased on 10 January 2012 are assumed to have been issued.

4 There are now 25 units left in stock out of the goods purchased on 20 January 2012.

● The stores ledger account is arithmetically self-balancing and there are no adjustments that have to be written off to the profit and loss account.
● It meets the requirements of *SSAP 9.*
● It is acceptable for UK tax purposes.

Disadvantages

● It is arithmetically cumbersome.
● The cost of production relates to out-of-date prices.

Continuous weighted average

Inventory write-down

The construction company Barratt has written off £495m of its inventories. This is some 27% of the total value. Other house builders are expected to follow suit. Barratt's Chief Executive believes such a practice helps morale because it lowers the effective input cost of land and that gives divisions the opportunity to make a profit in a 'grim market'. He argues that it is better to focus management on a profit margin rather than 'a margin of loss'.

Source: Adapted from www.ft.com/cms, 9 March 2009.

In order to avoid the detailed arithmetical calculations involved in using the FIFO method, it is possible to substitute an *average* pricing method. There are a number of different types but we are going to use the continuous weighted average (CWA) method. This method may require frequent changes to be made to the issue prices depending on the number of orders purchased. Although it appears very complicated, it is the easiest one to use *provided* that the receipts and issues of goods are recorded in a stores ledger account. An example of a manual stores ledger account is shown in Figure 13.3 opposite.

You will note from Figure 13.3 that the stores ledger account shows both the quantity and the value of the stock in store at any one time. The CWA price is obtained by dividing the total value of the stock by the total quantity. A new price will be struck each time new purchases are taken into stock.

The method is illustrated in Example 13.2 opposite. We use the same data as in Example 13.1 but we have taken the opportunity to present a little more information, so that we can explain more clearly how a CWA price is calculated.

The main advantages and disadvantages of the CWA method are as follows.

Advantages

- The CWA is easy to calculate, especially if a stores ledger account is used.
- Prices relating to previous periods are taken into account.
- The price of goods purchased is related to the quantities purchased.
- The method results in a price that is not distorted either by low or high prices, or by small or large quantity purchases.
- A new price is calculated as recent purchases are taken into stock, and so the price is updated regularly.

Disadvantages

- A CWA price tends to lag behind current economic prices.
- The CWA price may not relate to any actual price paid.
- It is sometimes necessary to write-off any arithmetical adjustments in the stock ledger account to the profit and loss account.

We now move on to have a look at the other main type of direct cost: labour.

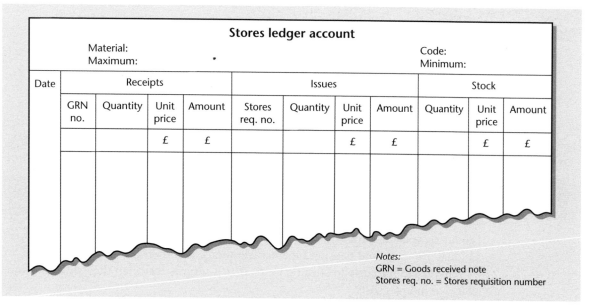

Material: Maximum:								Code: Minimum:		

Stores ledger account

Date	Receipts				Issues				Stock		
	GRN no.	Quantity	Unit price	Amount	Stores req. no.	Quantity	Unit price	Amount	Quantity	Unit price	Amount
			£	£			£	£		£	£

Notes:
GRN = Goods received note
Stores req. no. = Stores requisition number

Figure 13.3 **Example of a stores ledger account**

Example 13.2

The CWA pricing method of charging direct materials to production

You are presented with the following information relating to the receipt and issue of a certain material into stock during January 2012:

Date	Receipts into stores			Issues to production			Stock balance	
	Quantity units	Price £	Value £	Quantity units	Price £	Value £	Quantity units	Value £
1.1.12	100	10	1 000				100	1 000
10.1.12	150	11	1 650				250	2 650
15.1.12				125	10.60	1 325	125	1 325
20.1.12	50	12	600				175	1 925
31.1.12				150	11.00	1 650	25	275

Note:
The company uses the continuous weighted average method of pricing the issue of goods to production.

Required:
Check that the prices of goods issued to production during January 2012 have been calculated correctly.

Answer to Example 13.2

The issue prices of goods to production during January 2012 using the continuous weighted average method have been calculated as follows:

$$15.1.12 \quad \frac{\text{Total stock value at 10.1.12}}{\text{Total quantity in stock at 10.1.12}} = \frac{2\,650}{250} = \underline{\underline{£10.60}}$$

$$25.1.12 \quad \frac{\text{Total stock value at 20.1.12}}{\text{Total quantity in stock at 20.1.12}} = \frac{1\,925}{175} = \underline{\underline{£11.00}}$$

Activity 13.4	Taking into account the various advantages and disadvantages, which direct material pricing method do you regard as being the best? Use a scale of 1 to 4 (1 being your top choice).
	Unit cost [ ]
	First-in, first-out (FIFO) [ ]
	Continuous weighted average [ ]
	Standard cost [ ]

Direct labour

Labour costs include the cost of employees' salaries, wages, bonuses, and the employer's national insurance and pension fund contributions. Wherever it is practical to do so, we will charge labour costs to specific units. If it is impractical then they will have to be treated as indirect costs.

The identification and pricing of direct labour is much easier than with direct materials. Basically, the procedure is as follows.

1 Employees working on specific units are required to keep a record of how many hours they spend on each unit.
2 The total hours worked on each unit is multiplied by the appropriate hourly rate.
3 A percentage amount is added to the total to allow for the employer's other labour costs, e.g. national insurance, pension fund contributions and holiday pay.
4 The total amount is then charged directly to that unit.

The procedure is illustrated in Example 13.3.

Example 13.3	**The charging of direct labour cost to production**
	Alex and Will are the two employees working on Unit X. Alex is paid £10 an hour and Will £5. Both men are required to keep record of how much time they spend on each job they do. Alex spent 10 hours and Will 20 when working on Unit X. The employer has estimated that it costs him an extra 20 per cent on top of what he pays them to meet his contributions towards national insurance, pension contributions and holiday pay.
	Required: Calculate the direct labour cost of producing Unit X.

Answer to Example 13.3

Calculation of the direct labour cost:

	Hours		Rate per hour		Total
			£		£
Alex	10	×	10	=	100
Will	20	×	5	=	100
					200
Employer's costs (20%)					40
Total direct labour cost					240

It should be made clear that in practice it is by no means easy to obtain an accurate estimate of the direct labour cost of one unit. Indeed, if it is very difficult to do so, it will probably not be worthwhile. Even in those cases where there is no doubt that employees were working on a particular unit (as in Example 13.3) we depend on them keeping an accurate record. If you have ever had to do this in your own job you will know that this is difficult, especially if you are frequently being switched from one job to another, or you spend lots of time chatting in the corridor!

No matter what the difficulty, it is important that management should emphasize to employees just how important it is for them to keep an accurate record of their time. Labour costs may form a high proportion of total cost (e.g. in service industries) and so tight control is important. This is especially the case if tender prices are based on total unit cost. A high cost could mean that the company fails to get a contract, whereas too low a cost would reduce the amount of profit that the entity makes.

Other direct costs

Apart from material and labour costs, there may be other types of cost that can be relatively easily identified with specific units. These are, however, somewhat rare because unlike materials and labour it is usually difficult to trace a direct physical link to specific units unless, for example, some specialist plant is hired to work on one particular job. It would then be possible to charge the hire cost specifically to that job.

Irrespective of the difficulties of identifying other expenses with production, it is important to make every effort do so. Otherwise, the indirect charge just becomes bigger and bigger, and that then causes even greater distortions when it comes to pricing for new jobs.

 Questions you should ask

We suggest that you put the following questions to your management accountants.

- What is included in material costs?
- What criteria do you use for determining whether the costs are direct or indirect?
- What method do you use for charging them out to production?
- How do you determine whether labour costs are direct or indirect?
- What system is used to ensure that time spent on specific jobs is recorded accurately?
- Are there any other costs that could be classified as direct?
- What are they?
- What criteria can we use for charging them to specific units?

Conclusion

Responsibility accounting is a management control system that involves dividing an entity into segments and placing each segment under the control of a designated manager. Three main types of segments may be identified: cost centres (responsible for costs only), profit centres (responsible for costs and revenues) and investment centres (responsible for costs, revenues and investment decisions). Control is achieved by giving each manager complete responsibility for the costs incurred by his or her centre (and for any revenues received). Such costs (and revenues) can then be said to be *direct* to that centre. However, direct costs are normally defined as those that can be easily attributed to specific cost units. Those costs that cannot be easily attributed to specific cost units are known as *indirect* costs.

A direct cost is a cost that can be easily and economically identified with a specific cost centre. Some direct costs can then be identified with specific units or products. Those that cannot be so identified are known as *indirect* costs.

Costs are usually classified into elements of cost. By building the costs up in layers it is possible to determine a selling price, although market conditions have also to be taken into account when fixing selling prices.

Direct material costs include raw materials and component parts. If the cost of materials used in a particular product is known then there is no problem in charging them out to products. The unit cost will be used. Otherwise, a pricing method has to be selected. The recommended ones are first-in, first-out, an averaging method or the standard cost. Direct labour costs are those costs that can be easily attributed to specific units. They are charged out on the basis of hours worked and the hourly rate paid plus an allowance for employer's employment costs, such as national insurance, pension contributions and holiday pay. There may be other direct costs that can also be attributed to specific units but these are relatively rare.

Key points

1 Product costing has three main purposes: stock valuation, the planning and controlling of costs, and the determination of selling prices.

2 The procedure involves isolating those costs that are easy and economic to identify with specific units. Such costs are described as *direct costs*. Those costs that are not easy or economic to identify with specific costs are known as *indirect costs*. The total of indirect costs is known as *overhead* (or *overheads*).

3 Some material costs can be physically identified with specific units and their cost ascertained easily. In cases where it is difficult to isolate the cost of material used in production, e.g. where batches of materials are purchased at different prices and where they are stored collectively, an estimated price has to be determined. There are three acceptable methods for pricing materials (apart from being able to use the unit cost itself): first-in, first-out, average cost, and standard cost. The average cost method recommended in this book is known as the *continuous weighted average* (CWA) cost method.

4 Wherever possible, labour costs should be charged directly to specific units. Employees will need to keep time sheets that record the hours they have spent working on specific jobs. The amount charged to a particular unit will then be the time spent working on that unit multiplied by the respective hourly wage rate.

5 Some other services may also be identifiable with specific units, e.g. the hire of a machine for a particular contract. The cost of such services should be charged directly to production if it can be easily and economically determined.

Check your learning

The answers to these questions can be found within the text.

1 What is meant by 'responsibility accounting'?

2 What is (a) a cost centre, (b) a profit centre, (c) an investment centre?

3 What is (a) a direct cost, (b) an indirect cost?

4 What is meant by the 'elements of cost'?

5 What is meant by 'prime cost'?

6 What are direct materials?

7 What four methods may be used for charging direct materials out to production?

8 What is meant by 'direct labour'?

9 How is it collected and charged out to production?

10 Give an example of a direct cost other than materials or labour.

News story quiz

Remember the news story at the beginning of the chapter? Go back to that story and reread it before answering the following questions.

This article illustrates the complexity of dealing with purchases in a very large company. It would appear that Siemens has 370,000 suppliers. Imagine the number of staff and the paperwork involved in dealing with that number. Then, when the orders arrive they have to be checked, stored and issued to production. It is at that point that a decision has to be taken about what price they should be charged out to production.

Questions

1 What will be the impact of a fall in orders on Siemens's direct material pricing policy?

2 What impact will a fall in orders have on the company's inventory costs?

3 How will the new purchasing initiative enable costs to be cut by as much as €1 billion in one year?

Tutorial questions

The answers to questions marked with an asterisk can be found in Appendix 4.

13.1 Examine the argument that an arbitrary pricing system used to charge direct materials to production leads to erroneous product costing.

13.2* The following stocks were taken into stores as follows:

1.1.12   1000 units @ £20 per unit.
15.1.12   500   units @ £25 per unit.

There were no opening stocks.

On 31.1.12 1250 units were issued to production.

Required:
Calculate the amount that would be charged to production on 31 January 2012 for the issue of material on that date using each of the following methods of material pricing:

(a) FIFO (first-in, first-out)
(b) continuous weighted average.

13.3* The following information relates to material ST 2:

		Units	Unit price £	Value £
1.2.10	Opening stock	500	1.00	500
10.2.10	Receipts	200	1.10	220
12.2.10	Receipts	100	1.12	112
17.2.10	Issues	400	–	–
25.2.10	Receipts	300	1.15	345
27.2.10	Issues	250	–	–

Required:
Calculate the value of closing stock at 28 February 2010 assuming that the continuous weighted average method of pricing materials to production has been adopted.

13.4 You are presented with the following information for Trusty Limited:

2011	Purchases (units)	Unit cost £	Issues to production (units)
1 January	2 000	10	
31 January			1 600
1 February	2 400	11	
28 February			2 600
1 March	1 600	12	
31 March			1 000

Note: There was no opening stock.

Required:
Calculate the value of closing stock at 31 March 2011 using each of the following methods of pricing the issue of materials to production:

(a) FIFO (first-in, first-out)
(b) continuous weighted average.

13.5 The following information relates to Steed Limited for the year to 31 May 2012:

	£
Sales	500 000
Purchases	440 000
Opening stock	40 000

Closing stock value using the following pricing methods:

	£
FIFO (first-in, first-out)	90 000
Continuous weighted average	79 950

Required:
Calculate Steed Limited's gross profit for the year to 31 May 2012 using each of the above closing stock values.

13.6 Iron Limited is a small manufacturing company. During the year to 31 December 2012 it has taken into stock and issued to production the following items of raw material, known as XY1:

Date 2012	Receipts into stock			Issues to production
	Quantity (litres)	Price per unit £	Total value £	Quantity (litres)
January	200	2.00	400	
February				100
April	500	3.00	1 500	
May				300
June	800	4.00	3 200	
July				400
October	900	5.00	4 500	
December				1 400

Notes:
1 There were no opening stocks of raw material XY1.
2 The other costs involved in converting raw material XY1 into the finished product (marketed as Carcleen) amounted to £7000.
3 Sales of Carcleen for the year to 31 December 2012 amounted to £20,000.

Required:
(a) Illustrate the following methods of pricing the issue of materials to production:
   1 first-in, first-out (FIFO)
   2 continuous weighted average.
(b) Calculate the gross profit for the year using each of the above methods of pricing the issue of materials to production.

Well positioned

Boeing cuts jobs to shrink overheads

Michael Meeham

Boeing expects to shed 4,500 jobs in its Commercial Airplanes unit this year as it trims overhead 'to ensure competitiveness.'

The cuts were expected; Boeing Chairman and CEO Jim McNerney has previously indicated jobs would be shed. This will bring total BCA employment to about 63,500 workers – the level it had at the start of 2008.

The lost jobs are to be concentrated in administrative positions as BCA strives to reduce overhead costs and discretionary spending, rather than in airplane production. Boeing has been boosting production rates to keep up with demand for the past three years.

'We are taking prudent actions to make sure Boeing remains well posi-tioned in today's difficult economic environment,' BCA President and CEO Scott Carson said.

In a statement, Boeing said normal attrition and cuts in contract labour 'will account for some of the job reductions, layoffs of Boeing employees also are necessary.' Most of the jobs will be lost in Washington, Boeing's biggest jobs base and the state where it's seen the largest increase in recent employment.

After the mass layoffs sparked by the 9/11 airline downturn, Boeing began adding jobs in 2004 and has steadily increased employ-ment since then.

White orders declined to 662 last year from a high of 1,422 in 2007, the company has built up an order backlog of more than 3,700 aircraft over the past three years – so it doesn't lack production demand.

Total company employment stood at 160,738 on 31 January 2008, and climbed to 164,202 by 30 September, largely on the strength of hiring at BCA. Employment levels there were at 63,200 at the end of 2007. They rose as high as 68,010 by 31 October and then declined to 67,659 on 31 December. At their high point they were still about 30,000 below the pre 9/11 levels. Lean manufac-turing techniques are credited with allowing the company to boost production despite much lower employment levels.

Aviation Week, 9 January 2009.

Source: Reproduced with permission from McGraw-Hill Education.

Questions relating to this news story can be found on page 320 ➡

About this chapter

This is the second of two chapters in Part 4 that deal with *cost accounting*. We have split our study of cost accounting into two parts because the subject is too big to deal with in one. Chapter 13 dealt with direct costs while this one covers indirect costs. By the end of the chapter you will have been shown how accountants have traditionally gone about calculating product costs. In recent years the traditional method has been severely criticized, so we will also outline a relatively new technique for dealing with indirect costs (or overheads). This technique is called *activity-based costing* (ABC) and its proponents make great claims for it.

Learning objectives

By the end of this chapter, you should be able to:

- outline the nature of overheads, i.e. indirect production and non-production costs;
- calculate unit costs using absorption costing;
- assess its usefulness;
- explain what is meant by activity-based costing;
- summarize its advantages and disadvantages.

! Why this chapter is important

In the previous chapter we suggested that you needed to know something about cost accounting for three main reasons:

- to achieve greater control over what you manage;
- to make better decisions;
- to get involved in the material pricing decision.

The first two reasons hold good for this chapter but there is another reason that relates directly to the contents of this chapter.

The treatment of indirect costs in product costing is fairly questionable and there is much controversy in accounting circles about its usefulness and reliability. So you should not leave it entirely to the accountants to decide what to do. As a non-accountant and as a manager you have to get stuck right into the debate but you cannot do that if you don't know what the accountants are talking about.

This chapter will help you to talk to accountants at their level and enable *you* to decide what is best for *your* department when it comes to dealing with the 'overheads'.

Production overhead

News clip

Overhead control

According to the Japanese sales manager of Karmann, the German contract car manufacturer, Japanese car manufacturers have become more sophisticated in their cost accounting. As their supplier networks have grown they now look very carefully at the additional overheads that may be incurred such as training and translation costs. It may be 10% cheaper but in the sales manager's view 'localization' is not worth it if it costs 30% more to look after local suppliers.

Source: Adapted from www.ft.com/cms, 17 March 2009.

In the previous chapter we suggested that if management accounting is going to be used as part of a control system, it is necessary for all costs within an entity to become the direct responsibility of a designated cost centre manager. In this section we will examine how the *production* overhead gets charged to specific units. 'Production' relates to the output of any type of entity although it is more usually associated with those types of entities that manufacture a physical or a tangible product. 'Overheads' is a substitute term for indirect costs. An indirect cost is one that cannot easily be identified with a specific unit of output, a cost centre, a profit centre or an investment centre.

The charging of production overhead to specific units is rather a complicated procedure. It is known as *absorption costing*. In order to make it easier for you to follow we will take you through it slowly in three stages. As shown in Figure 14.1 the three stages are: (1) allocation; (2) apportionment; and (3) absorption. The figure shows the terms associated with the technique and also how costs are absorbed into one unit.

Activity 14.1	Insert the name of three factory departments whose running costs are likely to be treated as a production overhead.
	(1) (2) (3)

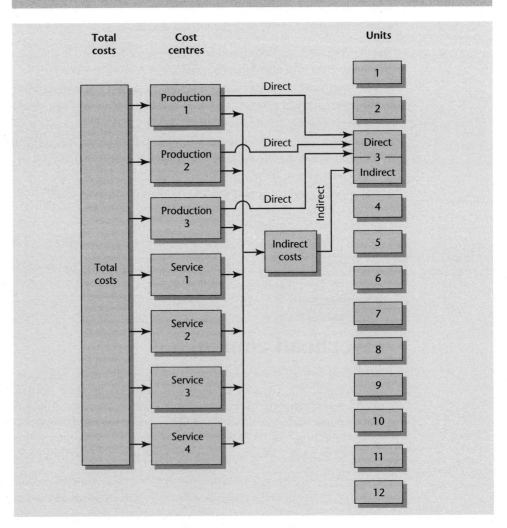

Figure 14.1 Absorption costing system: flow of costs

Stage 1: Allocate all costs to specific cost centres

Allocation is the process of charging the entire cost of an item to a cost centre (or a cost unit) without needing to apportion it or share it out in any way. It is essential that all costs are first allocated to a cost centre because they then become the responsibility of the manager of that centre. Some costs may be difficult to identify with a particular cost centre because they can be associated with a number of cost centres, e.g. factory rent or business rates. Nevertheless, such costs should be charged to a specific cost centre and not a 'general' or a 'sundry' one (even though the relationship may be largely nominal). This requirement is very important because if it is not strictly applied some costs will not be monitored and they will then just spiral out of control.

After the costs have been allocated to a cost centre, the next step is to divide them into two broad categories: *production* cost centres and *service* cost centres. Production cost centres are those departments or sections where the product is manufactured or partly manufactured. *Service* cost centres are those sections or departments that provide a service to other cost centres (including other service cost centres).

Once we have classified the cost centres into 'production' and 'service' we move on to Stage 2.

Stage 2: Share out the production service cost centre costs

There are two ways of sharing out the production service cost centre costs.

- Take *each* cost in each cost centre and charge the cost individually to all the other production and production service cost centres that have benefited from the service provided, e.g. the canteen and the personal department.
- Charge out the *total* of each production service cost centre's costs to all the other production and production service cost centres that have benefited from the service provided.

In practice a combination of both methods is usually adopted, i.e. some costs are charged out individually while the remainder are charged out in total.

Irrespective of which method is adopted the costs are usually shared out using some quantative factor. A few of the more common methods are described below.

- *Numbers of employees.* This method would be used for those service cost centres that provide a service to individual employees, e.g. the canteen, the works manager's office, and the wages office. Costs will then be apportioned on the basis of the number of employees working in a particular production department as a proportion of the total number of employees working in all production cost centres.
- *Floor area.* This method would be used for such cost centres as cleaning and building maintenance.
- *Activity.* Examples of where this method might be used include the drawings office (on the basis of drawings made), materials handling (based on the number of requisitions processed) and the transport department (on the basis of vehicle operating hours).

A problem arises in dealing with the apportionment of service cost-centre costs when service cost centres provide a service for each other. The wages office, for example, will probably provide a service for the canteen staff, and in turn the canteen staff may provide a service for the wages staff. Before the service cost-centre costs can be apportioned among the production cost centres, therefore, the service cost-centre costs have to be charged out to each other.

Unfortunately, the problem becomes circular because it is not possible to charge some of the canteen costs to the wages office until the canteen has been charged with some of the costs of the wages office. Similarly, it is not possible to charge out the wages office costs until part of the canteen costs have been charged to the wages office. The problem is shown in diagrammatic form in Figure 14.2. The treatment of *reciprocal service costs* (as they are called) can become an involved and time-consuming process unless a clear policy decision is taken about their treatment. There are three main ways of dealing with this problem.

1 *Ignore interdepartmental service costs.* If this method is adopted, the respective service cost-centre costs are only apportioned among the production cost centres. Any servicing that the service cost centres provide for each other is ignored.

2 *Specified order of closure.* This method requires the service cost-centre costs to be closed off in some specified order and apportioned among the production cost centres and the remaining service cost centres. As the service cost centres are gradually closed off, there will eventually be only one service cost centre left. Its costs will then be apportioned among the production cost centres. Some order of closure has to be specified, and this may be quite arbitrary. It may be based, for example, on those centres that provide a service for the largest number of other service cost centres, or it could be based on the cost centres with the highest or the lowest cost in them prior to any interdepartmental servicing. It could also be based on an estimate of the benefit received by the other centres.

3 *Mathematical apportionment.* Each service cost centre's total cost is apportioned among production cost centres and other service cost centres on the basis of the estimated benefit provided. The effect is that additional amounts keep being charged back to a particular service cost centre as further apportionment takes place. It can take a very long time before there is no more cost to charge out to any of the service cost centres. But when that point is reached, all the service cost-centre costs will then have been charged to the production cost centres. This method involves a great deal of exhaustive arithmetical apportionment. It is also very time-consuming, especially when there are a great many service cost centres. Although it is possible to carry out the calculations manually, it is only pratical if done by computer.

In choosing one of the above methods it should be remembered that they all depend on an *estimate* of how much benefit one department receives from another. Such an estimate amounts to no more than an informed guess. It appears pedantic therefore, to build an involved arithmetical exercise on the basis of some highly questionable assumptions. So we suggest that interdepartmental servicing charging should be ignored.

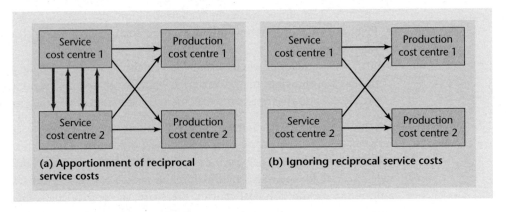

Figure 14.2 Service cost centre reciprocal costs

We have covered some fairly complicated procedures in dealing with Stages 1 and 2. So, before moving on to Stage 3, we use Example 14.1 to illustrate the procedure.

Example 14.1

Charging overhead to cost centres

You are provided with the following indirect cost information relating to the New Manufacturing Company Limited for the year to 31 March 2012:

Cost centre:	£
Production 1: indirect expenses (to units)	24 000
Production 2: indirect expenses (to units)	15 000
Service cost centre A: allocated expenses	20 000
Service cost centre B: allocated expenses	8 000
Service cost centre C: allocated expenses	3 000

Additional information:
The estimated benefit provided by the three service cost centres to the other cost centres is as follows:

Service cost centre A: Production 1 50%; Production 2 30%; Service cost centre B 10%; Service cost centre C 10%.
Service cost centre B: Production 1 70%; Production 2 20%; Service cost centre C 10%.
Service cost centre C: Production 1 50%; Production 2 50%.

Required:
Calculate the total amount of overhead to be charged to cost centre units for both Production cost centre 1 and Production cost centre 2 for the year to 31 March 2012.

Answer to Example 14.1

New Manufacturing Co. Ltd
Overhead distribution schedule for the year to 31 March 2012

Cost centre	Production		Service		
	1	*2*	*A*	*B*	*C*
	£	£	£	£	£
Allocated indirect expenses	24 000	15 000	20 000	8 000	3 000
Apportion service cost centre costs:					
A (50 : 30 : 10 : 10)	10 000	6 000	(20 000)	2 000	2 000
B (70 : 20 : 0 : 10)	7 000	2 000	–	(10 000)	1 000
C (50 : 50 : 0 : 0)	3 000	3 000	–	–	(6 000)
Total overhead to be absorbed by specific units	44 000	26 000	–	–	–

Tutorial notes

1 Units passing through Production cost centre 1 will have to share total overhead expenditure amounting to £44,000. Units passing through Production cost centre 2 will have to share total overhead expenditure amounting to £26,000. The number of units passing through both departments may be the same. They might be assembled, for example, in cost centre 1 and packed in cost centre 2.

2 The total amount of overhead to be shared amongst the units is £70,000 (44,000 + 26,000) or (£24,000 + 15,000 + 20,000 + 8000 + 3000). The total amount of overhead originally collected in each of the five cost centres does not change.

Tutorial notes continued

3 This exhibit involves some interdepartmental reapportionment of service cost centre costs. However, no problem arises because of the way in which the question requires the respective service cost centre costs to be apportioned.

4 The objective of apportioning service cost-centre costs is to share them out among the production cost centres so that they can be included in the cost of specific units.

Activity 14.2

What accounting term best fits each of the following one-word dictionary definitions?

Dictionary definition	Accounting term
(1) Assign	
(2) Spread	
(3) Engross	

We can now move on to examine stage 3 of the absorption process.

Stage 3: Absorb the production overhead

Once all the indirect costs have been collected in the production cost centres, the next step is to charge the total amount to specific units. This procedure is known as *absorption*.

The method of absorbing overhead into units is normally a simple one. Accountants recommend a single factor, preferably one related as closely as possible to the movement of overhead. In other words, an attempt is made to choose a factor that directly correlates with the amount of overhead expenditure incurred. Needless to say, like so much else in accounting, there is no obvious factor to choose!

There are six main methods that can be used for absorbing production overhead. They are all based on the same equation:

$$\text{Cost centre overhead absorption rate} = \frac{\text{total cost centre overhead}}{\text{total cost centre activity}}$$

The formulae for each of the six methods are as follows.

(1) Specific units

$$\text{Absorption rate} = \frac{\text{total cost centre overhead}}{\text{number of units processed in the cost centre}}$$

This method is the simplest to operate. The same rate is applied to each unit and so it is only suitable if the units are identical.

(2) Direct materials cost

$$\text{Absorption rate} = \frac{\text{total cost centre overhead}}{\text{cost centre total direct material costs}} \times 100$$

The direct material cost of each unit is then multiplied by the absorption rate.

It is unlikely that there will normally be a strong relationship between the direct material cost and the level of overheads. There might be some special cases, but they are probably quite unusual, e.g. where a company uses a high level of precious metals and its overheads strongly reflect the cost of safeguarding those materials.

(3) Direct labour cost

$$\text{Absorption rate} = \frac{\text{total cost centre overhead}}{\text{cost centre total direct labour costs}} \times 100$$

The direct labour cost of each unit is then multiplied by the absorption rate.

Overheads tend to relate to the amount of time that a unit spends in production and so this method may be particularly suitable since the direct labour cost is a combination of hours worked and rates paid. It may not be appropriate, however, where the total direct labour cost consists of a relatively low level of hours worked and of a high labour rate per hour because the cost will not then relate very closely to time spent in production.

(4) Prime cost

$$\text{Absorption rate} = \frac{\text{total cost centre overhead}}{\text{prime cost}} \times 100$$

The prime cost of each unit is then multiplied by the absorption rate. This method assumes that there is a close relationship between prime cost and overheads.

As there is probably no close relationship between either direct materials or direct labour and overheads, it is unlikely that there will be much of a correlation between prime cost and overheads. So the prime cost method tends to combine the disadvantages of both the direct materials cost and the direct labour cost methods without having any real advantages of its own.

(5) Direct labour hours

$$\text{Absorption rate} = \frac{\text{total cost centre overhead}}{\text{cost centre total direct labour hours}}$$

The direct labour hours of each unit are then multiplied by the absorption rate.

This method is highly acceptable, especially in those cost centres that are labour intensive because time spent in production is largely related to the cost of overhead incurred.

(6) Machine hours

$$\text{Absorption rate} = \frac{\text{total cost centre overhead}}{\text{cost centre total machine hours}}$$

The total machine hours used by each unit is then multiplied by the absorption rate.

This is a most appropriate method to use in those departments that are machine intensive. There is probably quite a strong correlation between the amount of machine time that a unit takes to produce and the amount of overhead incurred.

The various absorption methods are illustrated in Example 14.2.

Think of all the costs of running a factory. Apart from direct material and direct labour costs, what other costs are likely to be involved? List three of them and then attach to each one the main factor that is likely to cause them either to increase or to decrease.

Example 14.2

Calculation of overhead absorption rates

Old Limited is a manufacturing company. The following information relates to the assembling department for the year to 30 June 2012:

	Assembling department
	Total
	£000
Direct material cost incurred	400
Direct labour incurred	200
Total factory overhead incurred	100
Number of units produced	10 000
Direct labour hours worked	50 000
Machine hours used	80 000

Required:

Calculate the overhead absorption rates for the assembling department using each of the following methods:

(a) specific units
(b) direct material cost
(c) direct labour cost
(d) prime cost
(e) direct labour hours
(f) machine hours.

Answer to Example 14.2

(a) Specific units:

$$OAR = \frac{TCCO}{Number\ of\ units} = \frac{£100\,000}{10\,000} = \underline{£10.00\ per\ unit}$$

(b) Direct material cost:

$$OAR = \frac{TCCO}{Direct\ material\ cost} \times 100 = \frac{£100\,000}{400\,000} \times 100 = \underline{25\%}$$

(c) Direct labour cost:

$$OAR = \frac{TCCO}{Direct\ labour\ cost} \times 100 = \frac{£100\,000}{200\,000} \times 100 = \underline{50\%}$$

(d) Prime cost:

$$OAR = \frac{TCCO}{Prime\ cost} \times 100 = \frac{£100\,000}{400\,000 + 200\,000} \times 100 = \underline{16.67\%}$$

(e) Direct labour hours:

$$OAR = \frac{TCCO}{Direct\ labour\ hours} = \frac{£100\,000}{50\,000} = \underline{£2.00\ per\ direct\ labour\ hour}$$

(f) Machine hours:

$$OAR = \frac{TCCO}{Machine\ hours} = \frac{£100\,000}{80\,000} = \underline{£1.25\ per\ machine\ hour}$$

Example 14.2 illustrates the six absorption methods outlined in the text. In practice, only one absorption method would normally be chosen for each production cost centre, although different production cost centres may adopt different methods, e.g. one may choose a direct labour-hour rate and another may adopt a machine-hour rate.

The most appropriate absorption rate method will depend on individual circumstances. A careful study would have to be made of the correlation between (a) direct materials, direct labour, other direct expenses, direct labour hours and machine hours; and (b) total overhead expenditure. However, it is generally accepted that overhead tends to move with time, so the longer a unit spends in production the more overhead it will incur. So if this is the case, labour-intensive cost centres should use the direct labour hour method while machine-intensive departments should use the machine hour method.

A comprehensive example

At this stage it will be useful to illustrate overhead absorption in the form of a comprehensive example, although that does not mean that we are going to use hundreds of costs centres! The example chosen uses the minimum amount of information for us to bring together all the basic principles of overhead absorption.

Example 14.3

Overhead absorption

Oldham Limited is a small manufacturing company producing a variety of pumps for the oil industry. It operates from one factory that is geographically separated from its head office. The components for the pumps are assembled in the assembling department; they are then passed to the finishing department, where they are painted and packed. There are three service cost centres: administration, stores and work study.

The following information is relevant for the year to 30 June 2012:

Allocated cost-centre overhead costs:	£000
Administration	70
Assembling	25
Finishing	9
Stores	8
Work study	18

Additional information:

1 The allocated cost centre overhead costs are all considered to be indirect costs as far as specific units are concerned.
2 35,000 machine hours were worked in the assembling department, and 60,000 direct labour hours in the finishing department.
3 The average number of employees working in each department was as follows:

Administration	15
Assembling	25
Finishing	40
Stores	2
Work study	3
	85

➡

Example 14.3 continued

4 The stores received 15,000 requisitions from the assembling department, and 10,000 requisitions from the finishing department. The stores department did not provide a service for any other department.

5 The work study department carried out 2000 chargeable hours for the assembling department and 1000 chargeable hours for the finishing department.

6 One special pump (code named MEA 6) was produced. It took 10 machine hours of assembling time, and 15 direct labour hours were worked on it in the finishing department. Its total direct costs (materials and labour) amounted to £100.

Required:

(a) Calculate an appropriate absorption rate for:
    (i)   the assembling department,
    (ii) the finishing department.

(b) Calculate the total factory cost of the special MEA 6 pump.

Answer to Example 14.3(a)

Oldham Ltd
Overhead distribution schedule for the year to 30 June 2012

	Production			Service	
Cost centre	Assembling	Finishing	Adminis-tration	Stores	Work study
	£000	£000	£000	£000	£000
Allocated overhead costs (1)	25	9	70	8	18
Production					
Apportion administration:					
25 : 40 : 2 : 3 (2)	25	40	(70)	2	3
Apportion stores: 3 : 2 (3)	6	4	–	(10)	–
Apportion work study: 2 : 1 (4)	14	7	–	–	(21)
Total overhead to be absorbed	70	60	–	–	–

Tutorial notes

1 The allocated overhead costs were given in the question.

2 Administration costs have been apportioned on the basis of employees. Details were given in the question. There were 85 employees in the factory but 15 of them were employed in the administration department. Administration costs have, therefore, been apportioned on a total of 70 employees, or £1000 per employee. The administration department is the only service department to provide a service for the other service departments, so no problem of interdepartmental servicing arises.

3 The stores costs have been apportioned on the number of requisitions made by the two production cost centres, that is 15,000 + 10,000 = 25,000, or 3 to 2.

4 The work study costs have been apportioned on the basis of chargeable hours, i.e. 2000 + 1000 = 3000, or 2 to 1.

Calculation of chargeable rates:

1 Assembling department:

$$\frac{\text{TCCO}}{\text{Total machine hours}} = \frac{£70\,000}{35\,000} = £2.00 \text{ per machine hour}$$

2 Finishing department:

$$\frac{\text{TCCO}}{\text{Total direct labour hours}} = \frac{£60\,000}{60\,000} = £1.00 \text{ per direct labour hour}$$

It would seem appropriate to absorb the assembling department's overhead on the basis of machine hours because it appears to be a machine-intensive department. The finishing department appears more labour intensive and so its overhead has been absorbed on that basis.

Answer to Example 14.3(b)

MEA 6: Calculation of total factory cost

	£	£
Direct costs (as given in note 6)		100
Add: factory overhead:		
Assembling department (10 machine hours × £2.00 per MH)	20	
Finishing department (15 direct labour hours × £1.00 per DLH)	15	35
Total factory cost		135

Non-production overhead

News clip

Tailoring costs and cuts

Dress2Kill, a modern bespoke tailoring service in London, has had to cut its costs owing to a downturn in business following the banking crisis. Sales had been booming but the business had too much stock and high overheads. So two out of the three shops were closed and eight out of twenty staff were made redundant. Within six months overheads had been reduced from £70,000 to £30,000. Oh, and the book-keeper was fired for failing to warn the owner of the risks that had been taken.

Source: Adapted from www.ft.com/cms, 11 May 2009.

In the previous section we concentrated on the apportionment and absorption of *production* overheads. Most companies will, however, incur expenditure on activities that are not directly connected with production activities. For example, there could be selling and distribution costs, research and development costs, and head office administrative expenses. How should these types of cost be absorbed into unit cost?

Before this question can be answered, it is necessary to find out *why* we would want to apportion them. There are three possible reasons:

- *Control*. The more that an entity's costs are broken down, the easier it is to monitor them. It follows that just as there is an argument for having a detailed system of responsibility accounting at cost centre level, so there is an argument for having a similar system at unit cost level. However, in the case of non-production expenses this argument is not a very strong one. The relationship between units produced and non-production overhead is usually so remote that no meaningful estimate of the benefit received can be made. So the apportionment of non-production overhead is merely an arithmetical exercise, and no manager could be expected to take responsibility for costs charged to their cost centre in this way. From a control point of view, therefore, the exercise is not very helpful.

- *Selling price*. In some cases, it might be necessary to add to the production cost of a specific unit a proportion of non-production overhead in order to determine a selling price that covers all costs and allows a margin for profit. This system of fixing selling prices may apply in some industries, e.g. in tendering for long-term contracts or in estimating decorating costs. In most cases, however, selling prices are determined by the market and companies are not usually in a position to fix their selling prices based on cost with a percentage added on for profit (known as cost-plus pricing).

● *Stock valuation.* You might think that we need to include non-production overheads in valuing stocks but as *SSAP 9* does not permit them to be included they are usually ignored, even in management accounting. This is largely because much more work will be involved if the management accounts had to be altered to suit the requirements of the financial accounts.

It is obvious from the above summary that there are few benefits to be gained by charging a proportion of non-production overhead to specific cost units. In theory, the exercise is attractive because it would be both interesting and useful to know the *actual* cost of each unit produced. In practice, however, it is impossible to arrive at any such cost, and so it seems pointless becoming engaged in a purely spurious arithmetical exercise.

The only real case for apportioning non-production overhead applies where selling prices can be based on cost. What can be done in those situations? There is still no magic formula and an arbitrary estimate has still to be made. The easiest method is simply to add a percentage to the total production cost, perhaps based on this relationship between non-production overhead and total cost. This is bound to be a somewhat questionable method, since there can be no close relationship between production and non-production activities. It follows that the company's tendering or selling-price policy should not be too rigid if it is based on this type of cost-plus pricing.

Activity 14.4	You are a manager in a company that manufactures consumer products. Market prices are competitive and you need to keep down your costs. Do you think that charging non-production overhead to unit costs serves any purpose in this context? Tick the box below as appropriate and then give your reasons.

Yes ☐   No ☐

Why? _____

Predetermined absorption rates

An absorption rate can be calculated on a historical basis (i.e. after the event), or it can be predetermined (i.e. calculated in advance).

As we have argued, there is no close correlation between fixed overhead and any particular measure of activity: it can only be apportioned on what seems to be a reasonable basis. However, if we know the total actual overhead incurred, we can make sure that it is all charged to specific units, even if we are not sure of the relationship that it has with any particular unit.

In order to do so we need to know the *actual cost of overheads* and the *actual activity level* (whether measured in machine hours, direct labour hours or on some other basis). In other words, we can only make the calculation when we know *what* has happened.

The adoption of *historical* absorption rates is not usually very practicable. We have to wait until the actual period is over before an absorption rate can be calculated, the products costed and the customers invoiced. It is therefore, preferable to use what is known as a *predetermined absorption rate*. This involves estimating the overhead likely to be incurred and the direct labour hours (or machine hours) that are expected to be worked. If one or other of these estimates turns out to be inaccurate then we would have either undercharged our customers (if the rate was too low), or overcharged them (if the rate was too high).

This situation could be very serious for a company. Low selling prices caused by using a low absorption rate could have made the company's products very competitive, but there is not much point in selling a lot of units if they are being sold at a loss. Similarly, a high absorption rate may result in a high selling price. Each unit may then make a large profit but not enough units may be sold to enable the company to make an overall profit.

The difference between the actual overhead incurred and the total overhead charged to production (calculated on a predetermined basis) gives rise to what is known as a *variance*. If the actual overhead incurred is in excess of the amount charged out, the variance will be *adverse*, i.e. the profit will be less than expected. However, if the total overhead charged to production is less than was estimated then the variance will be *favourable*. The effect of this procedure is shown in diagrammatic form in Figure 14.3. Other things being equal, a favourable variance gives rise to a higher profit, and an adverse variance results in a lower profit.

It is a cardinal rule in costing that variances should be written off to the profit and loss account at the end of the costing period in which they were incurred. It is not considered fair to burden the next period's accounts with the previous period's mistakes. In other words, we should start off the new accounting period with a clean sheet.

Throughout the preceding sections we have clearly expressed many reservations about the way in which accountants have traditionally dealt with overheads. In recent years, dissatisfaction about overhead absorption has become widespread, and now a different technique called *activity-based costing* is being advocated. We review it briefly in the next section.

Activity 14.5	Fill in the missing words.

(a) _____ means to estimate beforehand an appropriate absorption rate.
(b) The difference between the actual overhead incurred and the total overhead charged is known as a _____ .

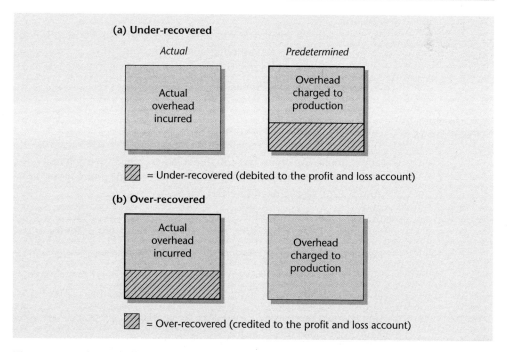

Figure 14.3 Predetermined rates under- and over-recovery of overhead

Activity-based costing

As we have seen, the calculation of product costs involves identifying the *direct costs* of a product and then adding (or absorbing) a proportion of the *indirect costs* (i.e. the overheads) to the total of the direct costs.

This was the method used for most of the twentieth century. It was only in the 1980s that it began to be apparent that the traditional method of absorbing overhead was inappropriate in an advanced manufacturing environment. As the traditional method involves calculating the total cost of overheads in a particular cost centre and charging them out to particular units on a time basis, the total cost is *averaged* among those units that flow through that particular cost centre. The assumption behind this procedure is that the more time that a unit spends in production, the more overhead it will incur. Such an assumption means, of course, that no distinction is made between fixed and variable overhead. It also means that irrespective of whether a particular unit causes a certain cost to arise in a cost centre, it is still charged with a proportion of that cost.

We will use an example to illustrate this point. The details are contained in Example 14.4.

Example 14.4

Overhead absorption: the unfairness of the traditional approach

In Jasmine Ltd's production cost centre 1, two units are produced: Unit A and Unit B, the total overhead cost being £1000. This is made up of two costs: (1) machine set-up costs of £800; and (2) inspection costs of £200. Overhead is absorbed on the basis of direct labour hours. The total direct labour hours (DLH) amount to 200. Unit A requires 150 DLH and Unit B 50 DLH.

The machinery for Unit A only needs to be set up once whereas Unit B requires nine set-ups. Unit A and Unit B both require two inspections each.

Required:
(a) Calculate the total overhead to be charged to Unit A and to Unit B using:
    (i)   the traditional method of absorbing overhead
    (ii) a fairer method based on set-up and inspection costs
(b) Prepare a table comparing the two methods.

Answer to Example 14.4

(a) (i) The traditional method
The absorption rate is £5 per direct labour hour (£1000 total overhead ÷ 200 direct labour hours). As Unit A has 150 direct labour hours spent on it, it will absorb £750 (150 DLH × £5) of overhead. Unit B has 50 direct labour hours spent on it; it will, therefore, absorb £250 of overhead (50 DLH × £5).

(a) (ii) A fairer method
Each set-up costs £80 [£800 ÷ 10 (1 set-up for A + 9 set-ups for B)].

Each inspection costs £50 [£200 ÷ 4 (2 inspections for A + 2 inspections for B)].

The total overhead charged to Unit A, therefore, would be £180: £80 for set-up costs (1 set-up × £80) plus £100 inspection costs (2 inspections × £50).

Unit B would be charged a total of £820: £720 of set-up costs (9 set-ups × £80) and £100 inspection costs (2 inspections × £50).

The fairer method illustrated here is known as *activity-based costing*.

(b) Comparing the two methods
The table below compares the two approaches to overhead absorption:

Jasmine Limited

Product	Overhead absorbed on a traditional basis	Overhead absorbed on an activity basis
	£	£
A	750	180
B	250	820
Total	1 000	1 000

Example 14.4 illustrates the potential unfairness of the traditional method of absorbing overhead. As the method *averages* the total cost among particular units, those units that do not benefit from a particular activity bear a disproportionate amount of the total cost. In the above example, Unit A should only be charged £180 of overhead (compared with £750 under the traditional method), whereas Unit B should be charged £820 (compared with £250 under the traditional method).

It follows that if the eventual selling price is based on cost, the traditional method would grossly inflate Unit A's selling price and deflate Unit B's selling price. Unit A's selling price would probably be highly uncompetitive and only a few units might be sold. Unit B's selling price would probably be highly competitive. So a great many units of Unit B might be sold but the total sales revenue may not be sufficient to recover all the overhead costs.

The fairer method that we have described is called activity-based costing (ABC). In order to illustrate the principles behind ABC, we have made reference to just one cost centre. However, in practice overheads for the whole of the entity (including both manufacturing and non-manufacturing overheads) would be dealt with collectively. They would then be allocated to *cost pools*, i.e. similar areas of activity. It is estimated that even in the largest entities a total of about 30 cost pools is the maximum number that it is practicable to handle. This means that some costs may be allocated to a cost pool where there is only a distant relationship between some of the costs. In other words, like the traditional method of absorbing overheads, ABC also involves some averaging of costs.

Once the overheads have all been allocated to an appropriate cost pool, a *cost driver* for each pool is selected. A cost driver is the main cause of the costs attached to that pool. Once again some approximation is necessary because some costs collected in that pool may only have a loose connection with the selected driver. By dividing the total cost in a particular cost pool by the cost driver, an overhead cost per driver can be calculated. For example, suppose the total overhead cost collected in a particular cost pool totalled £1000 and the costs in that pool were driven by the number of material requisitions (say 200), the cost driver rate would be £5 per material requisition (£1000 cost ÷ 200 material requisitions).

The final stage is to charge an appropriate amount of overhead to each unit benefiting from the service provided by the various cost pools. So if a particular unit required 10 material requisitions and the cost driver rate was £5 per material requisition, it would be charged £50 (£5 per material requisition × 10 requisitions). Of course, it may benefit from the services provided by a number of other cost pools, so it would collect a share of overhead from each of them as well.

The above procedures are illustrated in Example 14.5.

Example 14.5	**Activity-based costing (ABC)**

Shish Limited has recently introduced an ABC system. The following details relate to the month of March 2012.

1 Four cost pools have been identified: parts, maintenance, stores and administration.
2 The cost drivers that were identified with each cost pool are: total number of parts, maintenance hours, number of material requisitions and number of employees.
3 Costs and activities during the month were:

Cost pool	Total overhead £000	Activity	Quantity
Parts	10 000	Number of parts	500
Maintenance	18 000	Number of maintenance hours	600
Stores	10 000	Number of material requisitions	20
Administration	2 000	Number of employees	40

4 500 units of Product X3 were produced. This production run required 100 parts and 200 maintenance hours; 6 material requisitions were made and 10 employees worked on the units.

Required:
Using ABC, calculate the total amount of overhead absorbed by each unit of Product X3 in March 2012.

Answer to Example 14.5

Shish Ltd

Cost pool	Overhead	Cost driver	Cost driver rate	Usage by Product X3	Overhead cost charged to Product X3
(1)	(2) £000	(3)	(4) £	(5)	(6) £
Parts	10 000	500 parts	20	100 parts	2 000
Maintenance	18 000	600 hours	30	200 hours	6 000
Stores	10 000	20 requisitions	500	6 requisitions	3 000
Administration	2 000	40 employees	50	10 employees	500
Total overhead to be absorbed by Product X3					11 500

1 Column (4) has been obtained by dividing the data in column (2) by the data in column (3).
2 The data in column (6) has been obtained by multiplying the data in column (4) by the data in column (5).
3 The total amount of £11,500 shown in column (6) is the total amount of overhead to be absorbed by Product X3.

Solution
The total amount of overhead to be absorbed by each unit of Product X3 would be £23 (£11,500 ÷ 500 units).

ABC is an attempt to absorb overhead on the demands that a particular unit in production makes of the various resources that it uses before it is completed and becomes part of the 'finished stock'. In traditional overhead absorption costing, a unit is charged with the *average* charge for overheads irrespective of what proportion relates to that specific unit. This means that some units are charged with more than their fair share of overheads while others are perhaps charged with much less.

There is no difference in principle between ABC and traditional overhead absorption costing. ABC simply looks for a closer relationship between individual activities and the relationship that they have with specific units of production, while the traditional method adopts a more general approach. However, ABC does not require any distinction to be made between production overhead and non-production overhead – an issue that is largely ignored in traditional overhead absorption.

Activity 14.6	Tick the box in the relevant column.

	True	False
Activity-based costing (ABC) has been practised for over 100 years.		
ABC is simply a more complicated way of absorbing overheads.		
The main problem with ABC is in selecting appropriate cost drivers		

! Questions you should ask

The topic covered in this chapter is one that should encourage non-accountants to ask some very searching questions. We suggest that you use the following as a starting point.

- Have you had any problems in identifying some costs with particular cost centres?
- If so, which?
- How did you decide which cost centre to charge them to?
- What methods have you used to charge service cost centre costs to production cost centres?
- Have you ignored any interservice cost centre charging?
- If not, how have you dealt with the problem?
- What activity bases have you used to absorb overheads into product costs?
- Have you worked out absorption rates on a historical or a predetermined basis?
- What have you done about non-production overheads?
- Is there a case for switching to activity-based costing?

Conclusion

In this chapter we have continued our study of cost accounting that began in Chapter 13. In it we have explained how production overheads are absorbed into product costs. In summary, the procedure is as follows.

1 Allocate all costs to appropriate cost centres.

2 Distinguish between production and service cost centres.

3 Examine the individual costs in each production service cost centre and, where possible, apportion them on some equitable basis to other cost centres.

4 Apportion the total of any remaining service cost centre costs either (1) to production cost centres or (2) to production cost centres as well as other service cost centres. If (2), continue to reapportion the service cost centre costs until they have all been charged to production cost centres.

5 Select an absorption method based on either the number of units flowing through a particular cost centre or on the time a unit spends in the cost centre based on direct labour cost, direct labour hours or machine hours.

6 Divide the total overhead in each production cost centre by the selected absorption factor.

7 Charge each unit with its share of overhead (e.g. direct labour hours or machine hours $\times$ the absorption rate).

8 Add the amount calculated to the total direct cost of that unit.

It is also necessary to determine whether the above procedure should be done on a historical or a predetermined basis and whether non-production overheads should also be absorbed into product cost.

The above method has been in use for well over 100 years. Some academics and practitioners do not believe that it is suitable for modern manufacturing methods. In recent years a new method called *activity-based costing* has been adopted by some large companies. ABC is similar to traditional overhead absorption costing except that both production and non-production overheads are assigned to one of a number of identifiable cost pools. The main factor that causes those overheads to be incurred (known as a *cost driver*) is identified and a cost driver rate calculated (the pool overhead divided by the cost driver). Products are then charged with their share of each of the cost pool overheads.

Key points

1 In order to charge unit costs with a share of production overheads, *all* costs should first be identified with a specific cost centre.

2 Some cost centres provide a service to other cost centres. These are known as *service cost centres*. The various costs collected in the service costs centres should be shared out on an apportionment basis among the other cost centres. Some costs collected in the service cost centres may be apportioned separately; otherwise, the *total service cost centre cost* will be apportioned. An element of cross-charging arises when the service centres provide services for each other. This can be resolved either by ignoring any cross-charging, apportioning the total of the service centre costs in some specified order, or by mathematical apportionment.

3 Once the production cost centres have received their share of the service centre costs, an absorption rate for each production cost centre should be calculated. The traditional method is to take the total of each production cost centre's indirect cost (i.e. its overhead) and divide it either by the actual (or planned) direct labour hours, or by the machine hours actually worked (or planned to be worked) in that particular cost centre.

4 The absorption rate calculated for each production cost centre is used to charge each unit passing through that cost centre with a share of the production overhead.

5 The total production cost of a particular unit can then be calculated as follows:

direct materials cost + direct labour cost + direct expenses + share of production overhead = total production cost.

6 The absorption of non-production overhead (head office adminstration expenses, selling and distribution costs, and research development costs) is not recommended, except when it may be required for pricing purposes.

7 Absorption rates will normally be predetermined, i.e. they will be based on planned costs and anticipated activity levels.

8 The under-absorption or over-absorption of overhead should be written off to the profit and loss account in the period when it was spent.

9 In recent years a new way of dealing with the absorption of overheads called *activity-based costing* has been suggested. ABC involves charging overheads to common cost pools, identifying what main factor drives the costs in each of the respective pools, and then calculating a cost driver rate. Units are then charged with their share of each of the pool costs.

Check your learning

The answers to these questions can be found within the text.

1 What is (a) a production cost centre, (b) a service cost centre?

2 What do the terms 'allocate', 'apportion' and 'absorb' mean?

3 Suggest three ways that service cost centre costs may be charged to other cost centres.

4 What is meant by 'reciprocal service costs'?

5 Indicate three ways to deal with them.

6 What is the basic formula for absorbing production overheads into product costs?

7 List six methods of how this may be done.

8 What is non-production overhead?

9 How should it be absorbed into product costs?

10 What is a predetermined absorption rate?

11 What is meant by under- and over-recovery of overhead?

12 What do the initials 'ABC' mean?

13 What is a cost pool and a cost driver?

14 How does ABC differ from traditional absorption costing?

News story quiz

Remember the news story at the beginning of this chapter? Go back to that story and reread it before answering the following questions.

In 2009 Boeing was one of many companies throughout the world that announced a cut in overheads in an attempt to avoid making a loss. But what is really meant by 'overheads'?

Questions

1 To what extent do you think that making 4500 employees redundant is related to cutting overheads?

2 If most of the job losses are to come from administrative positions what impact is this likely to have on the main business of the company?

3 What do you think the President and CEO of Boeing means when he states that this action is being taken to make sure that the company is 'well positioned'?

Tutorial questions

The answers to questions marked with an asterisk may be found in Appendix 4.

14.1 'Arithmetical precision for precision's sake.' How far is this statement true of the traditional methods used in absorbing overheads into product costs?

14.2 Has total absorption costing any relevance in a service industry?

14.3 Some non-accountants believe that the technique of overhead absorption was devised simply to provide jobs for accountants. How far do you agree?

14.4 How should reciprocal service costs be dealt with when calculating product costs?

14.5 Assess the usefulness of activity-based costing in managerial decision making.

14.6* Scar Limited has two production departments and one service department. The following information relates to January 2012:

		£
Allocated expenses:		
Production department:	A	65 000
	B	35 000
Service department		50 000

The allocated expenses shown above are all indirect expenses as far as individual units are concerned.

The benefit provided by the service department is shared among the production departments A and B in the proportion 60 : 40.

Required:
Calculate the amount of overhead to be charged to specific units for both production department A and production department B.

14.7* Bank Limited has several production departments. In the assembly department it has been estimated that £250,000 of overhead should be charged to that particular department. It now wants to charge a customer for a specific order. The relevant data are:

	Assembly department	Specific unit
Number of units	50 000	–
Direct material cost (£)	500 000	8.00
Direct labour cost (£)	1 000 000	30.00
Prime cost (£)	1 530 000	40.00
Direct labour hours	100 000	3.5
Machine hours	25 000	0.75

The accountant is not sure which overhead absorption rate to adopt.

Required:
Calculate the overhead to be absorbed by a specific unit passing through the assembly department using each of the following overhead absorption rate methods:
(a) specific units
(b) percentage of direct material cost
(c) percentage of direct labour cost
(d) percentage of prime cost
(e) direct labour hours
(f) machine hours.

14.8 The following information relates to the activities of the production department of Clough Limited for the month of March 2012:

	Production department	Order number 123
Direct materials consumed (£)	120 000	20
Direct wages (£)	180 000	25
Overhead chargeable (£)	150 000	
Direct labour hours worked	30 000	5
Machine hours operated	10 000	2

The company adds a margin of 50 per cent to the total production cost of specific units in order to cover administration expenses and to provide a profit.

Required:
(a) Calculate the total selling price of order number 123 if overhead is absorbed using the following methods of overhead absorption:
direct labour hours;
machine hours.
(b) State which of the two methods you would recommend for the production department.

14.9 Burns Limited has three production departments (processing, assembly and finishing) and two service departments (administration and work study). The following information relates to April 2012:

	£
Direct material	
Processing	100 000
Assembling	30 000
Finishing	20 000

Direct labour

Processing (£4 × 100 000 hours)	400 000
Assembling (£5 × 30 000 hours)	150 000
Finishing (£7 × 10 000 hours) + (£5 × 10 000 hours)	120 000
Administration	65 000
Work study	33 000

Other allocated costs

Processing	15 000
Assembling	20 000
Finishing	10 000
Administration	35 000
Work study	12 000

Apportionment of costs:

	Process %	Assembling %	Finishing %	Work study %
Administration	50	30	15	5
Work study	70	20	10	–

Total machine hours: Processing 25 000

All units produced in the factory pass through the three production departments before they are put into stock. Overhead is absorbed in the processing department on the basis of machine hours, on the basis of direct labour hours in the assembling department, and on the basis of the direct labour cost in the finishing department.

The following details relate to unit XP6:

	£	£
Direct materials		
Processing	15	
Assembling	6	
Finishing	1	22
Direct labour		
Processing (2 hours)	8	
Assembling (1 hour)	5	
Finishing [(1 hour × £7) + (1 hour × £5)]	12	25
Prime cost		47

XP6: Number of machine hours in the processing department = 6

Required:
Calculate the total cost of producing unit XP6.

14.10 Outlane Limited's overhead budget for a certain period is as follows:

	£000
Administration	100
Depreciation of machinery	80
Employer's national insurance	10
Heating and lighting	15
Holiday pay	20
Indirect labour cost	10
Insurance: machinery	40
property	11
c/f	286

		£000
	b/f	286
Machine maintenance		42
Power		230
Rent and rates		55
Supervision		50
		663

The company has four production departments: L, M, N and O. The following infor-mation relates to each department.

Department	L	M	N	O
Total number of employees	400	300	200	100
Number of indirect workers	20	15	10	5
Floor space (square metres)	2 000	1 500	1 000	1 000
Kilowatt hours' power consumption	30 000	50 000	90 000	60 000
Machine maintenance hours	500	400	300	200
Machine running hours	92 000	38 000	165 000	27 000
Capital cost of machines (£)	110 000	40 000	50 000	200 000
Depreciation rate of machines (on cost)	20%	20%	20%	20%
Cubic capacity	60 000	30 000	10 000	50 000

Previously, the company has absorbed overhead on the basis of 100 per cent of the direct labour cost. It has now decided to change to a separate machine-hour rate for each department.

The company has been involved in two main contracts during the period, the details of which are as follows:

Department	Contract 1: Direct labour hours and machine hours	Contract 2: Direct labour hours and machine hours
L	60	20
M	30	10
N	10	10
O	–	60
	100	100

Direct labour cost per hour in both departments was £3.00.

Required:
(a) Calculate the overhead to be absorbed by both contract 1 and contract 2 using the direct labour cost method.
(b) Calculate the overhead to be absorbed using a machine-hour rate for each department.

Further practice questions, study material and links to relevant sites on the World Wide Web can be found on the website that accompanies this book. The site can be found at www.pearsoned.co.uk/dyson

When budgets go wrong

Was Dickens right?

Annual income twenty pounds, annual expenditure nineteen nineteen six, result happiness. Annual income twenty pounds, annual expenditure twenty pounds ought and six, result misery. (Mr Micawber in *David Copperfield* by Charles Dickens).

Kesa, Europe's third largest electrical retailer was presumably reasonably happy because its actual sales for the year to 30 April 2009 fell by 6.2 per cent – only slightly above the budgeted loss of between 5 and 6 per cent. By contrast WPP, the world's largest marketing and communications group was perhaps feeling miserable because its actual adjusted margins (a measure of profitability) were expected to be 12.5 per cent against a budget of 14.3 per cent. The shortfall arose largely because the company had failed to reduce its staff costs in line with the expected fall in sales.

But it's not only in the private sector that there can be differences between the actual and the budgeted results. For example, the National Audit Office qualified the 2008/2009 results of five government departments – including the Treasury! The Treasury had apparently incurred £24bn more expenditure than had been authorised by Parliament.

Budgets also go wrong in other countries in both the private and public sectors. A somewhat extreme case arose in the United States. It involved a company called KV Pharmaceutical Company. Its audit committee found problems not only with the company's budgetary control procedures but it also uncovered deficiencies in managerial conduct, human resource functions, and compliance with the Food and Drug Administration. Some very severe measures had to be taken including strengthening and enhancing the internal audit, budgeting and forecasting processes.

As a result of all these events there may have been some misery among the staff at KV Pharmaceutical. The Chairman would certainly have felt miserable because he was fired. In such circumstances even Dickens might have struggled hard to find a much more explicit way of describing it.

Sources: Based on www.ft.com, 24 June 2009; www.ft.com, 27 June 2009; *The Financial Times*, 27 August 2009; www.AccountancyAge.com, 21 July 2009; *St Louis Business Journal*, 23 June 2009.

Questions relating to this news story can be found on page 342 ➡

About this chapter

This chapter explores the nature and purpose of a budget. It outlines the various types of budgets, how they all fit together and how they may be used to keep a tight control of an entity's operations. It also explains that budgets and budgetary control are not neutral techniques. They have an impact on human behaviour and this has to be taken into account when using them.

Learning objectives

By the end of this chapter, you should be able to:

● describe the nature and purpose of budgeting and budgetary control;

● list the steps involved in operating a budgetary control system;

● describe the difference between fixed and flexible budgets;

● outline the behavioural consequences of a budgetary control system.

! Why this chapter is important

The more knowledge that you have as a manager, the more influence you will be able to exert. This applies particularly to budgeting. So this chapter is important for the following reasons.

● Your job will probably involve you in supplying information for budgetary purposes. It is easier to supply what is needed if you know what it is for and how it will be used.

● You are likely to have to prepare a budget for your department. Obviously, it is easier to do this if you have had some training in how to do it.

● You may be supplied with various reports that show your budgeted results against actual results. You may then be asked what you are going to do to correct any variance. The impact that this will have on you will depend on a number of factors, such as how familiar you are with the way that the information has been compiled, what inherent deficiencies it may have and what reliability you can place on it.

Budgeting is not a process that is of interest only to accountants. It should involve the whole entity. As a manager you will find that if you throw yourself wholeheartedly into the process it will help you to do your job more effectively.

Budgeting and budgetary control

News clip

Line by line

When asked how costs could be cut dramatically, Dave Barger, Chief Executive Officer of JetBlue said that his team regularly went through the company's budget 'line by line' in order to find whether cost savings could be made that had the least impact on customers and crew members.

Source: Adapted from *Fortune*, 8 December 2008, p. 16.

We start our analysis by explaining what we mean by a 'budget' and 'budgetary control'.

Budget

The term *budget* is probably well understood by the layman. Many people, for example, 'budget' for their own household expenses even if it is only by making a rough comparison between next month's salary and the next month's expenditure. Such a budget may not be very detailed but it contains all the main features of what accountants mean by a budget. There are as follows:

● *Policies*: a budget is based on the policies needed to fulfil the objectives of the entity.
● *Data*: it is usually expressed in monetary terms.
● *Documentation*: it is usually written down.
● *Period*: it relates to a future period of time.

Most entities will usually prepare a considerable number of what might be called sub-budgets. A manufacturing entity, for example, might prepare sales, production and administration budgets. These budgets would then be combined into an overall budget known as a *master budget*. A master budget is made up of a budgeted profit and loss account, a budgeted balance sheet and a budgeted cash flow statement.

Once a master budget has been prepared, it will be examined closely to see whether the overall plan can be accommodated. It might be the case, for example, that the sales budget indicates a large increase in sales. This will have required the production budgets to be prepared on the basis of this extra sales demand. The cash budget, however, might show that the entity could not finance the extra sales and production activity out of its budgeted cash resources, so additional financing arrangements will have to be made because obviously no entity would normally turn down the opportunity of increasing its sales.

Budgets are useful because they encourage managers to examine what they have done in relation to what they *could* do. However, the full benefits of a budgeting system only became apparent when it is used for *control* purposes. This involves making a constant comparison between the actual results and the budgeted results, and then taking any necessary corrective action. This procedure is called 'budgetary control'.

Activity 15.1	Write down three reasons why a manufacturing company might prepare budgets.

Budgetary control

When the actual results for a period are compared with the budgeted results and it is seen that there are material (or significant) differences (called variances) then corrective action must be taken to ensure that future results will conform to the budget. This is the essence of budgetary control, as can be seen in Figure 15.1. It has several important features.

● *Responsibilities*: managerial responsibilities are clearly defined.
● *Action plan*: individual budgets lay down a detailed plan of action for a particular sphere of responsibility.
● *Adherence*: managers have a responsibility to adhere to their budgets once the budgets have been approved.
● *Monitoring*: the actual performance is monitored constantly and compared with the budgeted results.
● *Correction*: corrective action is taken if the actual results differ significantly from the budget.

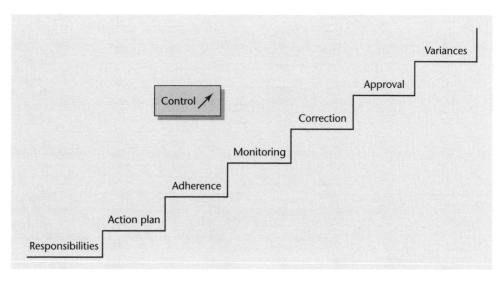

Figure 15.1 Budgetary control: features

- *Approval*: departures from the budget are only permitted if they have been approved by senior management.
- *Variances*: those that are unaccounted for are subject to individual investigation.

Any variance that occurs should be investigated carefully. The current actual performance will then be immediately brought back into line with the budget if this is considered necessary. Sometimes the budget itself will be changed, e.g. if there is an unexpected increase in sales. Such changes may, of course, have an effect on the other budgets and so cannot be done in isolation.

Now that we have outlined the nature and purpose of budgeting and budgetary control, we are in a position to investigate how the system works.

Procedure

> **News clip**
>
> # Sandwiches and sausage rolls
>
> The bakery chain Greggs is budgeting for 'marginally positive' 'like-for-like sales growth' this year. Apparently the recession has helped the company's results because more people are seeking value by purchasing its 99p sandwiches and 55p sausage rolls.

Source: Adapted from www.ft.com/cms, 11 March 2009.

In order to make it easier for you to follow the budget procedure we will break it down into four main stages: (1) who administers it; (2) what they aim to do; (3) the length of the budget period; and (4) how the master budget is made up. These four stages are shown in pictorial form in Figure 15.2. We start by first examining the administration of the budget process.

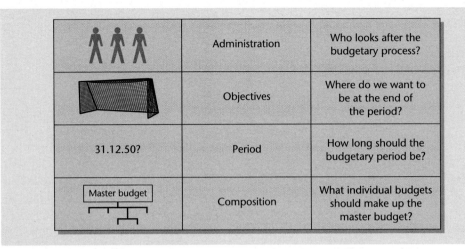

(figure)	Administration	Who looks after the budgetary process?
(figure)	Objectives	Where do we want to be at the end of the period?
31.12.50?	Period	How long should the budgetary period be?
Master budget	Composition	What individual budgets should make up the master budget?

Figure 15.2 Budget procedure

Administration

The budget procedure may be administered by a special budget committee or it may be supervised by the accounting function. It will be necessary for the budget committee to lay down general guidelines in accordance with the company's objectives and to ensure that individual departments do not operate completely independently. The production department, for example, will need to know what the company is budgeting to sell so that it can prepare its own budget on the basis of those sales. However, the detailed production budget must still remain the entire responsibility of the production manager.

This procedure is in line with the concept of responsibility accounting (see Chapter 13). If the control procedure is to work properly, managers must be given responsibility for clearly defined areas of activity, such as their particular cost centre. They are then fully answerable for all that goes on there. Unless managers are given complete authority to act within clearly defined guidelines, they cannot be expected to account for something for which they are not responsible. This means that if the budgeting control system is to work, managers must help prepare, amend and approve their own cost centre's budget.

Activity 15.2	A budget can act as a measure against which actual performance can be matched. However, some experts argue that when a measure becomes a target ('you must meet your budget') it becomes meaningless. To what extent do you think that budgeting is a waste of time? Mark your response on a scale like the one below.

Waste of time   *Valuable means of control*

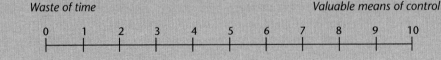

Objectives

The budget procedure starts with an examination of the entity's objectives. These may be very simple. They may include, for example, an overall wish to maximize profits, to foster better relations with customers, or to improve the working conditions of employees. Once an entity has decided on its overall objectives, it is in a position to formulate some detailed plans.

These will probably start with a *forecast*. There is a technical difference between a forecast and a budget. A forecast is a prediction of what is *likely* to happen, whereas a budget is a carefully prepared plan of what *should* happen.

Period

The main budget period is usually based on a calendar year. It could be shorter or longer depending on the nature of the product cycle. The fashion industry, for example, may adopt a short budget period of less than a year, while the construction industry may opt for a five-year period. Irrespective of the industry, however, a calendar year is usually a convenient period to choose as the base period because it fits in with financial accounting requirements.

Besides determining the main budget period, it is also necessary to prepare budgets for much shorter periods. These are required for budgetary control purposes in order to compare the actual results with the budgeted results on a frequent basis. The sub-budget periods for some activities may need to be very short if very tight control is to be exercised over them, e.g. the cash budget may need to be broken down into weeks, while the administration budget only into quarters.

Composition

In order to give you as wide a picture of the budgeting process as possible we will assume that we are dealing with a manufacturing company in the private sector. In practice the structure and content is likely to be extremely complex but we have stripped it down to its bare minimum. Even so, if you look at Figure 15.3 you will see that it still looks very involved. But don't worry. Later on in the chapter we will be using a quantitative example to illustrate the process and then it should all click into place.

In commercial organizations, the first budget to be prepared is usually the sales budget. Once the sales for the budget period (and for each sub-budget period) have been determined the next stage is to calculate the effect on production. This will then enable an agreed level of activity to be determined. The *level of activity* may be expressed in so many units or as a percentage of the theoretical productive capacity of the entity. Once the level of activity has been established then departmental managers can be instructed to prepare their budgets on that basis.

Let us assume, for example, that 1000 units can be sold for a particular budget period. The production department manager will need this information in order to prepare his budget. This does not necessarily mean that he will budget for a production level of 1000 units because he will also have to allow for the budgeted level of opening and closing stocks.

The budgeted production level will then be translated into how much material and labour will be required to meet that particular level. Similarly, it will be necessary to prepare overhead budgets. Much of the general overhead expenditure of the company (such as factory administrative costs, head office costs and research and development expenditure) will be fixed and it will not be affected by the activity level. One type of overhead, however, that may be affected by the activity level is the sales and distribution overhead budget because, for example, an increase in the number of units sold may involve additional delivery costs.

Not all entities start the budget process with sales. Local authorities are a good example. They usually prepare a budget on the basis of what they are likely to spend. The total budgeted expenditure is then compared with the total amount of council tax (after allowing for grants and other income) needed to cover it. If the political cost of an

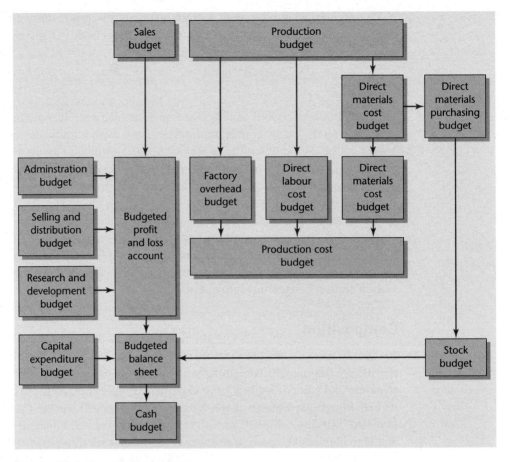

Figure 15.3 Functional budgets

Source: Adapted from Chartered Institute of Management Accountants (2005). CIMA Official Terminology, Oxford: CIMA Publishers.

increase in council tax appears to be too high then the council will require a reduction in the budgeted expenditure. Once the budget has been set, and the council tax has been levied on that basis, departments have to work within the budgets laid down. However, since the budget will have been prepared on an estimate of the actual expenditure for the last two or three months of the old financial year, account has to be taken of any a surplus or shortfall brought forward into the current year. If the estimate eventually proves excessive, the local authority will have overtaxed for that year. This means that it has got some additional funds available to cushion the current year's expenditure. Of course, if it has undertaxed for any balance brought forward, departments might have to start cutting back in the current year.

This process is quite different in the private sector because the budgeted sales effectively determine all the other budgets. In a local authority it is the expenditure budgets

Activity 15.3	(a) Assuming that a company has overestimated the budgeted level of activity, suggest ways in which it can bring its actual results back into line with the budget.
	(b) If a local authority has underestimated its expenditure for the last two months of the old financial year (February and March) what can it do to cover the deficit in the new financial year (April to the next March)?

that determine what the council tax should be and it is only the control exercised by central government and by the local authority itself that places a ceiling on what is spent.

A budget prepared for a particular department, cost centre or any other responsibility centre is known as a *functional budget*. Once all the functional budgets have been prepared, they are combined into the *master budget*. The master budget is, in effect, a consolidated budgeted profit and loss account, a budgeted balance sheet and a budgeted cash flow statement.

An initial draft of the master budget may not be acceptable to the senior management of the company. This may be because it cannot cope with that particular budgeted level of activity, e.g. as a result of production or cash constraints. Indeed, one of the most important budgets is the *cash budget*. The cash budget translates all the other functional budgets (including that for capital expenditure) into cash terms. It will show in detail the pattern of cash inputs and outputs for the main budget period, as well as for each sub-budget period. If it shows that the company will have difficulty in financing a particular budgeted level of activity (or if there is going to be a period when cash is exceptionally tight), the management will have an opportunity to seek out alternative sources of finance.

This latter point illustrates the importance of being aware of future commitments, so that something can be done in advance if there are likely to be constraints (irrespective of their nature). The master budget usually takes so long to prepare, however, that by the time it has been completed it will be almost impossible to make major alterations (although IT developments are now making this less of a difficulty). It is then tempting for senior management to make changes to the functional budgets without referring them back to individual cost-centre managers. It is most unwise to make changes in this way because it is then difficult to use such budgets for control purposes. If managers have not agreed to the changes, they will argue with considerable force that they can hardly take responsibility for budgets that have been imposed on them.

Activity 15.4	XYZ Limited is a manufacturing company. It prepares an annual master budget. Suggest the length of the sub-budget period for each of the following functions: (a) cash; (b) purchasing; and (c) research.

In the next section we use a comprehensive example to illustrate how all the functional budgets fit together.

A comprehensive example

Activity 15.5	List three benefits that you think the preparation of a master budget provides.

It would be very difficult to follow the basic procedures involved in the preparation of functional budgets if we used an extremely detailed example. The example that we are going to work through cuts out much of the detail and only illustrates the main procedures. Nevertheless, there are still 14 steps to take!

| Example 15.1 | ## Preparation of functional budgets |

Sefton Limited manufactures one product known as EC2. The following information relates to the preparation of the budget for the year to 31 March 2012:

1 Sales budget details for product EC2:
   Expected selling price per unit: £100.
   Expected sales in units: 10,000.
   All sales are on credit terms.

2 EC2 requires 5 units of raw material E and 10 units of raw material C. E is expected to cost £3 per unit, and C £4 per unit. All goods are purchased on credit terms.

3 Two departments are involved in producing EC2: machining and assembly. The following information is relevant:

	Direct labour per unit of product (hours)	Direct labour rate per hour £
Machining	1.00	6
Assembling	0.50	8

4 The finished production overhead costs are expected to amount to £100,000.

5 At 1 April 2011, 800 units of EC2 are expected to be in stock at a value of £52,000, 4500 units of raw material E at a value of £13,500, and 12,000 units of raw materials at a value of £48,000. Stocks of both finished goods and raw materials are planned to be 10 per cent above the expected opening stock levels as at 1 April 2011.

6 Administration, selling and distribution overhead is expected to amount to £150,000.

7 Other relevant information:
   (a) Opening trade debtors are expected to be £80,000. Closing trade debtors are expected to amount to 15 per cent of the total sales for the year.
   (b) Opening trade creditors are expected to be £28,000. Closing trade creditors are expected to amount to 10 per cent of the purchases for the year.
   (c) All other expenses will be paid in cash during the year.
   (d) Other balances at 1 April 2011 are expected to be as follows:

	£	£
Share capital: ordinary shares		225 000
Retained profits		17 500
Proposed dividend		75 000
Fixed assets at cost	250 000	
Less: Accumulated depreciation	100 000	
		150 000
Cash at bank and in hand		2 000

8 Capital expenditure will amount to £50,000, payable in cash on 1 April 2011.

9 Fixed assets are depreciated on a straight-line basis at a rate of 20 per cent per annum on cost.

Required:
As far as the information permits, prepare all the relevant budgets for Sefton Limited for the year to 31 March 2012.

Answer to Example 15.1

In order to make it easier for you to become familiar with the budgeting procedure we will take you through it step by step.

Step 1: Prepare the sales budget

Units of EC2		Selling price per unit		Total sales value
		£		£
10 000	×	100	=	1 000 000

Step 2: Prepare the production budget

	Units
Sales of EC2	10 000
Less: Opening stock	800
	9 200
Add: Desired closing stock (opening stock + 10%)	880
Production required =	10 080

Step 3: Prepare the direct materials usage budget

Direct materials:
E: 5 units × 10 080   =   50 400 units
C: 10 units × 10 080   =   100 800 units

Step 4: Prepare the direct materials purchases budget

Direct materials:	=	E (units)	C (units)
Usage (as per Step 3)		50 400	100 800
Less: Opening stock		4 500	12 000
		45 900	88 800
Add: Desired closing stock (opening stock + 10%)		4 950	13 200
		50 850	102 000
		× £3	× £4
Direct material purchases	=	£152 550	= £408 000

Step 5: Prepare the direct labour budget

	Machining	Assembling
Production units (as per Step 2)	10 080	10 080
× direct labour hours required	× 1 DLH	× 0.50 DLH
	10 080 DLH	5 040 DLH
× direct labour rate per hour	× £6	× £8
Direct labour cost =	£60 480	= £40 320

Step 6: Prepare the fixed production overhead budget

Given: £100 000

Answer to Example 15.1 *continued*

Step 7: Calculate the value of the closing raw material stock

Raw material	Closing stock* (units)		Cost per unit £		Total value £
E	4 950	×	3	=	14 850
C	13 200	×	4	=	52 800
					67 650

*Derived from Step 4.

Step 8: Calculate the value of the closing finished stock

	£	£
Unit cost:		
Direct material E: 5 units × £3 per unit	15	
Direct material C: 10 units × £4 per unit	40	55
Direct labour for machining: 1 hour × £6 per DLH	6	
Direct labour for assembling: 0.50 hours × £8 per DLH	4	10
Total direct cost	=	65
× units in stock		× 880
Closing stock value	=	57 200

Step 9: Prepare the administration, selling and distribution budget

Given: £150 000

Step 10: Prepare the capital expenditure budget

Given: £50 000

Step 11: Calculate the cost of goods sold

	£
Opening stock (given)	52 000
Manufacturing cost:	
Production units (Step 2) × total direct cost (Step 3) = 10 080 × £65	655 200
	707 200
Less: Closing stock (Step 8: 880 units × £65)	57 200
Cost of goods sold (10 000 units)	= 650 000

(or 10 000 units × total direct costs of £65 per unit)

Step 12: Prepare the cash budget

	£	£
Receipts		
Cash from debtors:		
Opening debtors	80 000	
Sales	1 000 000	
	1 080 000	
Less: Closing debtors (15% × £1 000 000)	150 000	
		c/f 930 000

	b/f	£	£
			930 000

Payments
Cash payments to creditors:

		£	£
Opening creditors		28 000	
Purchases [Step 4: (£152 550 + 408 000)]		560 550	
		588 550	
Less: Closing creditors (£560 550 × 10%)		56 055	532 495
Wages (Step 5: £60 480 + 40 320)			100 800
Fixed production overhead			100 000
Administration, selling and distribution overhead			150 000
Capital expenditure			50 000
Dividend paid for 2011			75 000
			1 008 295

	£
Net receipts	(78 295)
Add: Opening cash	2 000
Budgeted closing cash balance (overdrawn)	(76 295)

Step 13: Prepare the budgeted profit and loss account

	£	£
Sales (Step 1)		1 000 000
Less: Variable cost of sales (Step 8: 10 000 × £65)		650 000
Gross margin		350 000
Less: Fixed production overhead (Step 6)	100 000	
Depreciation [(£250 000 + 50 000) × 20%]	60 000	160 000
Production margin		190 000
Less: Administration, selling and distribution Overhead (Step 9)		150 000
Budgeted net profit		40 000

Step 14: Prepare the budgeted balance sheet

	£	£	£
Fixed assets (at cost)			300 000
Less: Accumulated depreciation			160 000
			140 000
Current assets			
Raw materials (Step 7)		67 650	
Finished stock (Step 8)		57 200	
Trade debtors (15% × £1 000 000)		150 000	
		274 850	
Less: Current liabilities			
Trade creditors			
[Step 4: 10% × (£152 550 + 408 000)]	56 055		
Bank overdraft (Step 12)	76 295	132 350	142 500
			282 500
Financed by:			
Share capital			
Ordinary shares			225 000
Retained profits (£17 500 + 40 000)			57 500
			282 500

Fixed and flexible budgets

News clip

Budgeting for typewriters

The New York Police Department are still using old-fashioned typewriters because vouchers and property forms are still recorded on carbon paper. The outdated equipment is so cumbersome that officers are less likely to make arrests for minor offences. During the last two years the NYPD has spent more than £612,000 on buying and upkeeping new typewriters. And that means that they still have to budget for them!

Source: Adapted from www.guardian.co.uk/world/2009, 17 July 2009.

The master budget becomes the detailed plan for future action that everyone is expected to work towards. However, some entities only use the budgeting process as a *planning* exercise. Once the master budget has been agreed, there may be no attempt to use it as a control technique. So the budget may be virtually ignored and it may not be compared with the actual results. If this is the case, then the company is not getting the best out of the budgeting system.

As was suggested earlier, budgets are particularly useful if they are also used as a means of control. The control is achieved if the actual performance is compared with the budgeted performance. Significant variances should then be investigated and any necessary corrective action taken.

The constant comparison of the actual results with the budgeted results may be done either on a *fixed* or a *flexible* budget basis. A fixed budget basis means that the actual results for a particular period are compared with the original budgets. This is as you would expect because the budget is a measure and a measure has to be rigid: you would get some very misleading results if you used an elastic ruler to measure distances! Similarly, an elastic-type budget might also give some highly unreliable results. In some cases, however, a variable measure is used in budgeting in order to allow for certain circumstances that might have taken place *since* the budgets were prepared. Accountants call this *flexing* the budget. A flexible budget is an original budget that has been amended to take account of the *actual* level of activity.

This procedure might appear somewhat contradictory. Surely changing a budget once it has been agreed is similar to using an elastic ruler to measure distances? This is not necessarily the case in budgeting.

As we explained earlier, in order to prepare their budgets, some managers (especially production managers) will need to be given the budgeted level of activity. This means that such budgets will be based on a given level of activity. If the *actual* level of activity is greater (or less) than the budgeted level, however, managers will have to allow for more (or less) expenditure on materials, labour and other expenses.

Suppose, for example, that a manager has prepared his budget on the basis of an anticipated level of activity of 70 per cent of the plant capacity. The company turns out to be much busier than expected and it achieves an actual level of activity of 80 per cent. The production manager is likely to have spent more on materials, labour and other

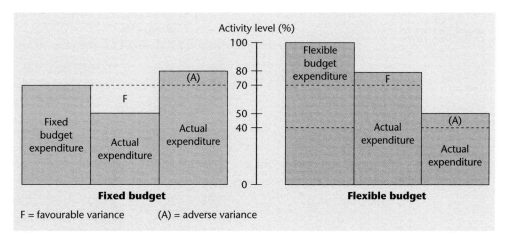

Figure 15.4 Flexing the budget

expenses than he originally thought. If the actual performance is then compared with the budget, i.e. on a fixed budget basis, it will look as though he had spent a great deal more than he had anticipated. And, of course, he has, although *some* of it, at least, must have been beyond his control because of the increased activity. It is considered only fair, therefore, to allow for those costs for which he is not responsible. So there is a need to flex the budget, i.e. revise it on the basis of what it would have been if the manager had budgeted for an activity of 80 per cent instead of 70 per cent. The other assumptions and calculations made at the time the budget was prepared (such as material prices and wage rates) would not be amended. Figure 15.4 portrays this argument in pictorial form, which perhaps makes it easier for you to understand.

If a company operates a flexible budget system, the budgets may be prepared on the basis of a wide range of possible activity levels. This is a time-consuming method, and managers would be very lucky if they prepared one that happened to be identical to the *actual* level of activity. The best method is to wait until the actual level of activity is known before the budget is flexed.

The operation of a flexible budgetary system is shown in Example 15.2.

Example 15.2

Flexible budget procedure

The following information had been prepared for Carp Limited for the year to 30 June 2012.

	Budget	Actual
Level of activity	*50%*	*60%*
	£	£
Costs:		
Direct materials	50 000	61 000
Direct labour	100 000	118 000
Variable overhead	10 000	14 000
Total variable cost	160 000	193 000
Fixed overhead	40 000	42 000
Total costs	200 000	235 000

Required:
Prepare a flexed budget operating statement for Carp Limited for the year to 30 June 2012.

Answer to Example 15.2

Carp Ltd
Flexed budget operating statement for the year 30 June 2012

Activity level	Fixed budget 50%	Flexed budget 60%	Actual costs 60%	Variance (col. 2 less col. 3) favourable/ (adverse)
	£	£	£	£
Direct materials	50 000	60 000	61 000	(1 000)
Direct labour	100 000	120 000	118 000	2 000
Variable overhead	10 000	12 000	14 000	(2 000)
Total variable costs	160 000	192 000	193 000	(1 000)
Fixed overhead	40 000	40 000	42 000	(2 000)
Total costs	200 000	232 000	235 000	(3 000)

Tutorial notes

1 All the budgeted *variable* costs have been flexed by 20% because the actual activity was 60% compared with a budgeted level of 50%, i.e. a 20% increase

$$\left(\frac{60\% - 50\%}{50\%} \times 100\right)$$

2 The budgeted fixed costs are not flexed because, by definition, they should not change with activity.

3 Instead of using the total fixed budget cost of £200,000, the total flexed budget costs of £232,000 can be compared more fairly with the total actual cost of £235,000.

4 Note that the terms 'favourable' and 'adverse' (as applied to variances) mean favourable or adverse to profit. In other words, profit will be either greater (if a variance is favourable) or less (if it is adverse) than the budgeted profit.

5 The reasons for the variances between the actual costs and the flexed budget will need to be investigated. The flexed budget shows that even allowing for the increased activity, the actual costs were in excess of the budget allowance.

6 Similarly, it will be necessary to investigate why the actual activity was higher than the budgeted activity. It could have been caused by inefficient budgeting or by quite an unexpected increase in sales activity. While this would normally be welcome, it might place a strain on the productive and financial resources of the company. If the increase is likely to be permanent, management will need to make immediate arrangements to accommodate the new level of activity.

Activity 15.6

On a scale of 0 to 5 how far do you think that a flexible budgeting system leads to a loss of managerial control (0 being total loss and 5 being no loss whatsoever)?

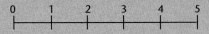

Behavioural consequences

Budgeting and budgetary control systems are not neutral. They have an impact on people causing them to react favourably, unfavourably or with indifference. If managers react favourably then their budgets are likely to be accurate and relevant. Similarly, any information provided for them will be welcomed and it will be taken seriously. As a result, any necessary corrective action required will be pursued with some vigour.

Working together

Finance and marketing professionals have sometimes had a disjointed working relationship. Now the Chartered Institute of Management Accountants has got together with the Chartered Institute of Marketing and the Direct Marketing Association. It is felt that there is a need for a closer working relationship at a time when businesses may be tempted to slash marketing budgets in order to cut costs.

Source: Adapted from *Financial Management*, June 2009, p. 7.

Managers who react unfavourably or with indifference may prepare budgets that are inaccurate or irrelevant and under considerable protest. Obviously such managers are not likely to take seriously any notice or any action based on suspect data.

It follows from the above that for a budgeting and budgetary control systems to work effectively, a number of important elements must be present, as seen in Figure 15.5 and summarized below.

- *Consultation*. Managers must be consulted about any proposal to install a budgeting or a budgetary control system.
- *Education and training*. Managers must undergo some education and training so that they are fully aware of the relevance and importance of budgeting and budgetary control systems and the part that they are expected to play.
- *Involvement*. Managers must be directly involved in the installation of the system and especially so in their own responsibility centre.
- *Independence*. Managers should prepare their own budgets (subject to some general guidelines) instead of having them imposed on them. Imposed budgets (as they are called) usually mean that managers do not take them seriously and they will then disclaim responsibility for any variances that may have occurred.
- *Non-disciplinary*. Managers should not be disciplined for any variances (especially if a budget has been imposed) unless they are obviously guilty of negligence. Budgetary control is a means of finding out *why* a variance occurred. It is not supposed to be a vehicle for disciplining managers.

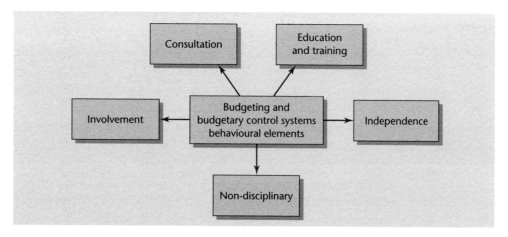

Figure 15.5 Budgeting: behavioural elements

With regards to the last point, if managers believe that the budgeting or budgetary control system operates against them rather than for them, they are likely to undermine it. This may take the form of *dysfunctional behaviour*, i.e. behaviour that may be in their own interest but not in the best interests of the company. They may, for example, act aggressively, become uncooperative, blame other managers, build a great deal of slack (i.e. tolerance) into their budgets, make decisions on a short-term basis or avoid making them altogether, and spend money unnecessarily up to the budget level that they have been given.

All of these points emphasize the importance of consulting managers and involving them fully in both the installation and operation of budgeting and budgetary control systems. If this is not the case, experience suggests that such systems will not work.

Activity 15.7	As a departmental manager you budgeted to spend £10,000 in 2013. You spent £9000. You budgeted to spend £12,000 in 2014 but you were told you could only spend £11,000 as you had 'over-budgeted in 2013'. What are you likely to do when you come to prepare your budget for 2015?

! Questions you should ask

This is a most important chapter for non-accountants because you are likely to be involved in the budgetary process no matter what junior or senior position you hold. If your employer uses an imposed budgetary control system you may not have as much freedom to ask questions but you might want to point out as diplomatically as you can that there are problems with such systems. You might also like to put the following questions to the accountants and senior managers.

- How far is the time spent on preparing budgets cost effective?
- Do you think that budgets prepared for a calendar year is too long a period?
- Should those costs (and revenues) that relate to a longer timescale be apportioned to sub-budget periods?
- Is it appropriate to compare actual events with fixed budgets or should we use flexible budgets?
- Why can't I be responsible for preparing my own department's budget?
- Why do you alter my budget after I have prepared it?
- Do you expect me to be responsible for any variances that are outside my control?
- Why punish me and my staff when we were not responsible either for the budget or for what went wrong with it?

Conclusion

The full benefits of budgeting can only be gained if it is combined with a budgetary control system. The preparation of budgets is a valuable exercise in itself because it forces management to look ahead to what *might* happen rather than to look back at what *did* happen. However, it is even more valuable if it is also used as a form of control.

Budgetary control enables actual results to be measured frequently against an agreed budget (or plan). Departures from that budget can then be quickly spotted and steps taken to correct any unwelcome trends. There is a strong case for arguing that the comparison of actual results with a fixed budget may not be particularly helpful if the actual level of activity is different from that budgeted. It is recommended, therefore, that actual results should be compared with a flexed budget.

As so many functional budgets are based on the budgeted level of activity, it is vital that it is determined as accurately as possible, since an error in estimating the level of activity could affect the whole of the company's operational and financial activities. So it is important that any difference between the actual and the budgeted level of activity is investigated carefully.

Budgeting and budgetary control systems may be resented by managers and they might then react to the systems in such a way to protect their own position. This may not be of benefit to the entity as a whole.

Key points

1 A budget is a short-term plan.

2 Budgetary control is a cost control method that enables actual results to be compared with the budget, thereby enabling any necessary corrective action to be taken.

3 The preparation of budgets will be undertaken by a budget team.

4 Managers must be responsible for producing their own functional budgets.

5 Functional budgets are combined to form a master budget.

6 A fixed budget system compares actual results with the original budgets.

7 In a flexed budget system the budget may be flexed (or amended) to bring it into line with the actual level of activity.

8 A budgeting and budgetary control system is not neutral. It may cause managers to act in a way that is not in the best interests of the entity.

Check your learning

1 What is a budget?

2 List its essential features.

3 What is meant by 'budgetary control'?

4 List its essential features.

5 What is a variance?

6 What is a forecast?

7 How long is a normal budgeting period?

8 What is a sub-budget period?

9 What administration procedures does a budgeting system require?

10   In a commercial organization, which budget is normally the first to be prepared?

11   What initial criterion is given to production managers before they begin to prepare their budgets?

12   What is meant by a functional budget?

13   List six common functional budgets.

14   What is meant by a fixed budget?

15   What is meant by a flexible budget?

16   Why is it desirable to prepare one?

17   List five desirable behavioural elements necessary to ensure a budgeting system is effective.

News story quiz

Remember the news story at the beginning of this chapter? Go back to that story and reread it before answering the following questions.

This news story relates to a number of examples of budgets being over-spent, i.e. the actual result being unfavourable to profit. But the actual results may sometimes be favourable to profit.

Questions

1   From a budgetary control point of view can a budget under-spend be regarded as 'happiness' and budget over-spend be described as 'misery'?

2   Is a small percentage difference between the actual and the budgeted results of an entity something to get worried about?

3   Why do you think that the UK government's budgetary control system appears to be so deficient?

Tutorial questions

The answers to questions marked with an asterisk can be found in Appendix 4.

15.1   The Head of Department of Business and Management at Birch College has been told by the Vice Principal (Resources) that his departmental budget for the next academic year is £150,000. What comment would you make about the system of budgeting used at Birch College?

15.2   Suppose that when all the individual budgets at Sparks plc are put together there is a shortfall of resources needed to support them. The Board suggests that all departmental budgets should be reduced by 15 per cent. As the company's Chief Accountant, how would you respond to the Board's suggestion?

15.3   Does a fixed budget serve any useful purpose?

15.4 'It is impossible to introduce a budgetary control system into a hospital because if someone's life needs saving it has to be saved irrespective of the cost.' How far do you agree with this statement?

15.5* The following information has been prepared for Tom Limited for the six months to 30 September 2011:

Budgeted production levels for product X

	Units
April	140
May	280
June	700
July	380
August	300
September	240

Product X uses two units of component A6 and three units of component B9. At 1 April 2011 there were expected to be 100 units of A6 in stock, and 200 units of B9. The desired closing stock levels of each component were as follows:

Month end 2011	A6 (units)	B9 (units)
30 April	110	250
31 May	220	630
30 June	560	340
31 July	300	300
31 August	240	200
30 September	200	180

During the six months to 30 September 2011, component A6 was expected to be purchased at a cost of £5 per unit, and component B9 at a cost of £10 per unit.

Required:
Prepare the following budgets for each of the six months to 30 September 2011:
(a) direct materials usage budget;
(b) direct materials purchase budget.

15.6* Don Limited has one major product that requires two types of direct labour to produce it. The following data refer to certain budget proposals for the three months to 31 August 2012:

Month	Production units
June	600
July	700
August	650

Direct labour hours required per unit:

	Hours	Budgeted rate per hour £
Production	3	4
Finishing	2	8

Required:
Prepare the direct labour cost budget for each of the three months to 31 August 2012.

15.7 Gorse Limited manufactures one product. The budgeted sales for period 6 are for 10,000 units at a selling price of £100 per unit. Other details are as follows:

1 Two components are used in the manufacture of each unit:

Component	Number	Unit cost of each component £
XY	5	1
WZ	3	0.50

2 Stocks at the beginning of the period are expected to be as follows:
4000 units of finished goods at a unit cost of £52.50.
Component XY: 16,000 units at a unit cost of £1.
Component WZ: 9,600 units at a unit cost of £0.50.

3 Two grades of employees are used in the manufacture of each unit:

Employee	Hours per unit	Labour rate per hour £
Production	4	5
Finishing	2	7

4 Factory overhead is absorbed into unit costs on the basis of direct labour hours. The budgeted factory overhead for the period is estimated to be £96 000.

5 The administration, selling and distribution overhead for the period has been budgeted at £275 000.

6 The company plans a reduction of 50 per cent in the quantity of finished stock at the end of period 6, and an increase of 25 per cent in the quantity of each component.

Required:
Prepare the following budgets for period 6:
(a) sales
(b) production quantity
(c) materials usage
(d) materials purchase
(e) direct labour
(f) the budgeted profit and loss account.

15.8 Avsar Limited has extracted the following budgeting details for the year to 30 September 2013:

1 Sales: 4000 units of V at £500 per unit
7000 units of R at £300 per unit

2 Materials usage (units):

	Raw material		
	O1	I2	L3
V	11	9	12
R	15	1	10

3 Raw material costs (per unit):

	£
O1	8
I2	6
L3	3

4 Raw material stocks:

	Units		
	O1	I2	L3
Opening stock	1300	1400	400
Closing stock	1400	1000	200

5 Finished stocks:

	Units	
	V	R
Opening stock	110	90
Closing stock	120	150

6 Direct labour:

	Product	
	V	R
Budgeted hours per unit	10	8
Budgeted hourly rate (£)	12	6

7 Variable overhead:

	Product	
	V	R
Budgeted hourly rate (£)	10	5

8 Fixed overhead: £193,160 (to be absorbed on the basis of direct labour hours).

Required:

(a) Prepare the following budgets:
   (i) sales;
   (ii) production units;
   (iii) materials usage;
   (iv) materials purchase; and
   (v) production cost.
(b) Calculate the total budgeted profit for the year to 30 September 2013.

15.9 The following budget information relates to Flossy Limited for the three months to 31 March 2013:

1 **Budgeted profit and loss accounts:**

Month	January	February	March
	£000	£000	£000
Sales (all on credit)	2000	3000	2500
Cost of sales	1200	1800	1500
Gross profit	800	1200	1000
Depreciation	(100)	(100)	(100)
Other expenses	(450)	(500)	(600)
	(550)	(600)	(700)
Net profit	250	600	300

2   **Budgeted balance sheets:**

Budgeted balances	December £000	January £000	February £000	March £000
Current assets:				
Stocks	100	120	150	150
Debtors	200	300	350	400
Short-term investments	60	–	40	30
Current liabilities:				
Trade creditors	110	180	160	150
Other creditors	50	50	50	50
Taxation	150	–	–	–
Dividends	200	–	–	–

3 Capital expenditure to be incurred on 20 February 2013 is expected to amount to £470,000.
4 Sales of plant and equipment on 15 March 2013 is expected to raise £30,000 in cash.
5 The cash at bank and in hand on 1 January 2013 is expected to be £15,000.

Required:
Prepare Flossy Limited's cash budget for each of the three months during the quarter ending 31 March 2013.

15.10 Chimes Limited has prepared a flexible budget for one of its factories for the year to 30 June 2012. The details are as follows:

% of production capacity	30% £000	40% £000	50% £000	60% £000
Direct materials	42	56	70	84
Direct labour	18	24	30	36
Factory overhead	22	26	30	34
Administration overhead	17	20	23	26
Selling and distribution overhead	12	14	16	18
	111	140	169	198

Additional information:
1 The company only expects to operate at a capacity of 45%. At that capacity, the sales revenue has been budgeted at a level of £135,500.
2 Variable costs per unit are not expected to change, irrespective of the level of activity.
3 Fixed costs are also not likely to change, irrespective of the level of activity.

Required:
Prepare a flexible budget for the year to 30 June 2012 based on an activity level of 45%.

Further practice questions, study material and links to relevant sites on the World Wide Web can be found on the website that accompanies this book. The site can be found at www.pearsoned.co.uk/dyson

Standard costing going ... going ... gone?

Lean accounting concepts

Lean accounting is a mystery to most business people and accountants. They have heard of lean manufacturing but not lean accounting. Lean accounting evolved in the manufacturing environment and hasn't made much progress into lean thinking applications. There are a number of ways lean accounting can be applied in a variety of situations. It is perfect for managing and measuring results in tough economic times.

Initially lean accounting got traction because it had the capability of overcoming the problems associated with standard costing. Standard costing is driven by labor efficiency, machine utilization, and absorption of overhead. These standard cost techniques were traditionally used by managers to build excessive inventories and generate positive variances to improve GAAP profitability leading to higher management incentive bonuses.

The economic recession has created a need for lean accounting. However, since most accountants haven't used lean tools, the application goes unused. Lean accounting deals with tracking throughput or revenue and the associated variable costs required to generate those sales. Understanding that lean contribution from sales directly improves the bottom line is critical. You don't spend funds unless it is associated with generating revenue. Since lean accounting provides better information for decision making it has the impact of increasing sales. In a slower economy, companies need tools like value stream costing and similar lean decision-making applications.

AccountingWEB.com, 2 April 2009.

Source: Reproduced with permission from AccountingWEB, Inc.

Questions relating to this news story can be found on page 366 ➡

About this chapter

This chapter examines *standard costing*, another planning and control technique used in management accounting. Like budgeting and budgetary control, standard costing involves estimating future sales revenue and product costs. But standard costing goes into much more detail: the total *budgeted* cost is broken down into the elements of cost (direct materials, direct labour, variable overhead and fixed overhead) and these costs are then compared with the *actual* cost of those elements. The difference between the standard cost and the *actual* cost is known as a variance. Variances are usually analysed into a volume variance and a price variance and sometimes these variances themselves are broken down into sub-variances. Significant variances are then investigated and immediate action is taken to correct any unexpected or unwelcome ones. The difference between budgeted sales and actual sales can also be analysed into volume and price variances.

Standard costing is of particular relevance in manufacturing industry where specific products or processes are produced repetitively.

! Why this chapter is important

Standard costing is an important management accounting planning and control technique and you need to know what it is and how it works if you are to become a really effective and self-aware manager. This chapter is important, therefore, for three reasons:

● you could be required to provide information for standard-costing purposes;
● you may be presented with standard-costing operating statements;
● you need to know what action to take in order to control unexpected trends.

Operation

The operation of a standard-costing system requires virtually everyone in an entity to be involved to some extent. The system depends on the supply of a vast amount of information from every cost centre throughout the entity and the personnel who are best placed to supply it are those who work in the various cost centres. It is not, however, a one-way process. Once the information has been processed it is fed back to those people who supplied it originally. They are then expected to use that information to deal with any significant variances.

If a standard-costing system is to work properly it is vital that it is fully supported by those people it is supposed to help. If they do not think that it is of any benefit to them they are then likely to provide inaccurate information and to discount subsequent reports based on it. If this is how they do behave then the system might as well be abandoned because it will result in ineffective planning and control.

Definitions

There are four important standard-costing terms you need to be familar with:

> 1 **Standard**: *the amount or level set for the performance of a particular activity.*
> 2 **Standard cost**: *the planned cost for a particular level of activity.*
> 3 **Variance**: *the difference between the standard (or planned) cost and the actual cost.*
> 4 **Variance analysis**: *an investigation into and an explanation of why variances occurred.*

Uses

Four main purposes of standard costing can be identified:

- *Stock valuation.* The standard-cost method of stock valuation is the expected or planned price that the entity expects to pay for its materials. Its advantages are that it is simple to use and it can remain stable for some time. The main difficulties are in establishing a standard cost and in coping with significant differences between the actual costs and the standard costs.
- *Control.* By comparing in detail actual costs against the standard costs on a frequent basis swift action can be taken to correct any departures from what was planned.
- *Performance measurement.* Standard costing provides information that enables an entity to determine if it is meeting its objectives.
- *Pricing.* The information provided by a standard-costing system helps entities to set their selling prices.

Application

Standard costing is an extremely useful planning and control technique that is particularly useful in those manufacturing companies where the production process is repetitive and identical units are constantly being turned out. This enables a general standard to be set that meets most situations. Non-repetitive operations do not enable a standard to be set very easily because by definition each operation tends to be different.

Standard costing is a development of the early twentieth century. By 1918 the basic equations that are still in use today had been devised. At the beginning of the twenty-first century manufacturing techniques are very different from those a hundred years ago, e.g. purchases are made to order and inventories are kept low. It might be thought, therefore, that standard costing would no longer be relevant. The research evidence available suggests that this is not so and that standard costing is still used quite widely.

Period

The standard-costing period will usually be the same as that for the main budget and sub-budget periods. Short periods are preferred so that the actual results can be compared frequently with the standard results. Corrective action can then be taken quickly before it is too late to do anything about any unexpected trends. Short standard-costing periods may also be necessary where market or production conditions are subject to frequent changes or where it is particularly difficult to prepare long-term plans.

Standards

The preparation of standard costs requires great care and attention. As each element of cost is subject to detailed arithmetical analysis, it is important that the initial information is accurate. Indeed, the information produced by a standard-costing system will be virtually worthless if subsequent analyses reveal that variances were caused by inefficient budgeting or standard setting.

In preparing standard costs, management will need to be informed of the level of activity to be used in preparing the standard costs, i.e. whether the entity will need to operate at, say, 80 per cent or 90 per cent of its theoretical capacity. An activity level should be chosen that is capable of being achieved. It would be possible to choose a standard that was *ideal*, i.e. one that represented a performance that could be achieved only under the most favourable of conditions. Such a standard would, however, be unrealistic, because it is rare for ideal conditions to prevail. An ideal standard is a standard that is attainable under the most favourable conditions and where no allowance is made for normal losses, waste and machine downtime.

A much more realistic standard is called an *attainable* standard. Such a standard is one that the entity can expect to achieve in reasonably efficient working conditions. In other words, it is accepted that some delays and inefficiencies, e.g. waste and machine downtime will occur, but it is also assumed that management will attempt to minimize them.

You may also come across the term *basic* standards. These are standards that are left unchanged over long periods of time. This enables some consistency to be achieved in comparing actual results with the same standards over a substantial period of time but they may become so out of date that meaningful comparisons are not possible.

Activity 16.1	Your company bases its standard costs on an ideal level of activity, i.e. no allowance is made for natural losses such as evaporation and the standard costs can only be achieved in entirely favourable conditions. As a cost centre manager, what would your reaction be when you received a report showing that your centre had a number of large unwelcome variances? What would you do about such variances?

Cost data

The cost data needed to operate a standard-costing system is considerable. The main requirements are as follows.

- *Direct materials*: types, quantities and price.
- *Direct labour*: grades, numbers and rates of pay.
- *Variable overhead*: the total variable overhead cost broken down into various categories, such as employee and general support costs.
- *Fixed overhead*: the total fixed overhead, likewise broken down into various categories such as employee costs, building costs and general administration expenses.

The above summary shows that the standard cost of a particular unit comprises four elements: direct materials, direct labour, variable overhead and fixed overhead. In turn, each element comprises two factors, namely quantity and price. In Example 16.1 we show you how the standard cost of a specific unit is built up.

| Example 16.1 | **Calculation of the total standard cost of a specific unit using absorption costing** |

	£
● Direct materials	
Quantity × price (2 units × £5)	10
● Direct labour	
Hours × hourly rate (5 hours × £10)	50
● Variable overhead	
Hours × variable overhead absorption rate per hour (5 hours × £6)	30
● Fixed overhead	
Hours × fixed overhead absorption rate per hour (5 hours × £3)	15
Total standard cost per unit	105

Note: The example is based on fictitous data. It assumes that the unit cost is calculated on the basis of standard absorption costing. This is the most common method of standard costing. It is also possible to adopt a system of standard *marginal* costing (see Chapter 17).

Standard hours and the absorption of overhead

Standard absorption costing requires overhead to be absorbed on the basis of *standard* hours. In a non-standard costing system it is absorbed on the basis of *actual* hours. A standard hour represents the amount of work that should be performed in an hour assuming that it is done in standard conditions, i.e. in *planned* conditions. Each unit is given a standard time of so many hours in which the work should be done.

So the total standard time will be calculated as follows:

Number of units × standard hours per unit

It is *not* calculated by multiplying the number of units by the *actual* hours per unit.

Sales

As well as calculating cost variances some companies do the same for sales, although this is thought to be much less common. A detailed analysis of the budgeted sales is needed to obtain the number of each product to be sold and its selling price. Such information will be needed not just for the overall budget period but also for each sub-budget period.

There are a number of ways in which sales variances may be calculated. We could just deal with actual and budgeted sales revenue but in this book we are going to adopt a method based on *sales profit* as this method is thought to be of much greater interest and relevance to managers. Basically it involves taking the actual sales revenue and then deducting the *standard* cost of those sales (not the actual cost). The balance is then compared with the budgeted profit. Any difference between the actual cost and the standard cost is taken care of when the cost variances are calculated. We will explain how it works in a little more detail later in the chapter.

Activity 16.2	Tick the appropriate column.		

		True	*False*
(a)	A standard costing system absorbs overhead on the basis of actual hours.		
(b)	A standard costing period has to be at least one year long.		
(c)	Sales variances cannot be broken down into both price and quantity variances.		
(d)	Normal losses are ignored in setting an attainable standard.		
(e)	Standard costing is an out-of-date technique.		

Performance measures

Management may find it useful if some performance measures are extracted from the standard costing data. Such measures pinpoint the level of efficiency of the entity, help managers to spot unfavourable trends and enable them to take immediate corrective action. There are three specific performance measures that we are going to cover in this chapter: the efficiency ratio, the capacity ratio and the production volume ratio (see Figure 16.1).

Referring to Figure 16.1, the actual hours are those direct labour hours actually worked. The budgeted direct labour hours are those that were expected or planned to be worked. Standard hours produced measure the actual output produced in standard direct labour hours. If each unit produced *should have* taken (say) five hours and 100 units were produced, the total hours produced would be 500 (5 DLH × 100). The budget might have been planned on the basis of 120 units, in which case the total standards labour hours would have been 600 (5 DLH × 120). In a machine-intensive cost centre, machine hours would be substituted for direct labour hours. The formula for each performance measure is outlined below.

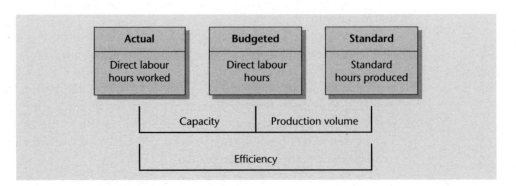

Figure 16.1 Three performance measures

The efficiency ratio

This ratio compares the total standard (or allowed) hours of units produced with the total actual hours taken to produce those units. The formula is:

$$\frac{\text{Standard hours produced}}{\text{Actual direct labour hours worked}} \times 100$$

Reminder:

The standard hours produced = the standard direct labour hours of production for the *actual* activity.

The efficiency ratio enables management to check whether the company has produced the units in more or less time than had been allowed.

The capacity ratio

This ratio compares the total actual hours worked with the total budgeted hours. It is calculated as follows:

$$\frac{\text{Actual direct labour hours worked}}{\text{Budgeted direct labour hours}} \times 100$$

The capacity ratio enables management to ascertain whether all of the budgeted hours (i.e. all the hours *planned* to be worked) were used to produce the actual units.

The production volume ratio

This compares the total allowed hours for the work actually produced with the total budgeted hours. It is calculated as follows:

$$\frac{\text{Standard hours produced}}{\text{Budgeted direct labour hours}} \times 100$$

The production volume ratio enables management to compare the work produced (measured in terms of standard hours) with the budgeted hours of work. This ratio gives management some information about how effective the company has been in using the budgeted hours.

In Example 16.2 we show you how to calculate these three ratios.

Example 16.2

Calculation of efficiency, capacity and production volume ratios

The following information relates to the Frost Production Company Limited for the year to 31 March 2011:

1 Budgeted direct labour hours: 1000
2 Budgeted units: 100
3 Actual direct labour hours worked: 800
4 Actual units produced: 90

➡

Example 16.2
continued

Required:
Calculate the following performance ratios:
(a) the efficiency ratio
(b) the capacity ratio
(c) the production volume ratio.

Answer to
Example 16.2

(a) The efficiency ratio:

$$\frac{\text{Standard hours produced}}{\text{Actual direct labour hours worked}} \times 100 = \frac{900^*}{800} \times 100 = \underline{112.5\%}$$

* Each unit is allowed 10 standard hours (1000 hours/100 units). Since 90 units were produced, the total standard hours of production must equal 900.

It would appear that the company has been more efficient in producing the goods than was expected. It was allowed 900 hours to do so but it produced them in only 800 hours.

(b) The capacity ratio:

$$\frac{\text{Actual direct labour hours worked}}{\text{Budgeted hours}} \times 100 = \frac{800}{1000} \times 100 = \underline{80\%}$$

All of the time planned to be available (the capacity) was not utilized, either because it was not possible to work 1000 direct labour hours or because the company did not undertake as much work as it could have done.

(c) The production volume ratio:

$$\frac{\text{Standard hours produced}}{\text{Budgeted hours}} \times 100 = \frac{900^*}{1000} \times 100 = \underline{90\%}$$

* As calculated for the efficiency ratio.

It appears that if 90 units had been produced in standard conditions, another 100 hours would have been available (10 units × 10 hours). Since the 90 units only took 800 hours to produce, at least another 20 units $\left(\frac{1000 - 800}{10}\right)$ could have been produced in standard conditions.

Comments

The budget allowed for 100 units to be produced and each unit was expected to take 10 direct labour hours to complete, a total budgeted activity of 1000 direct labour hours. However, only 90 units were actually produced. If these units had been produced in standard time, they should have taken 900 hours (90 units × 10 direct labour hours). These are the standard hours produced. The 90 units were completed in 800 actual hours. It appears, therefore, that the units were produced more efficiently than had been expected. The management will still need, of course, to investigate why only 90 units were produced and not the 100 units expected in the budget.

We can now move on to examine how standard cost variances may be calculated and whether they may be viewed as being either favourable or unfavourable. We do so in the next section.

Activity 16.3 Fill in the missing words.

(a) Capacity ratio = ———— ratio + ———— ratio.

(b) Standard hours produced = ———— direct labour hours for the ———— activity.

Cost variances

News clip

CIMA

Ian Herbert, a CIMA learning assessor, has argued in a magazine article that management accounting techniques such as standard costing, throughput accounting, and just-in-time management are still relevant even though the service sector has become more important. He argues that there are three reasons why this is so: (1) the world manufactures more goods than ever before; (2) many manufacturing processes are now outsourced to third parties; and (3) the *principles* of traditional techniques can be applied to the service sector.

Source: Adapted from *Financial Management*, April 2009, p. 53.

Structure

The difference between actual costs and standard costs may result in two main variances: price and quantity. These variances may either be favourable (F) to profit or adverse (A). This means that the actual prices paid or costs incurred can be more than anticipated (adverse to profit) or less than anticipated (favourable to profit). Similarly, the quantities used in production can result in more being used (adverse to profit) or less than expected (favourable to profit).

The standard production cost variances are shown in Figure 16.2. The formulae you need are shown below.

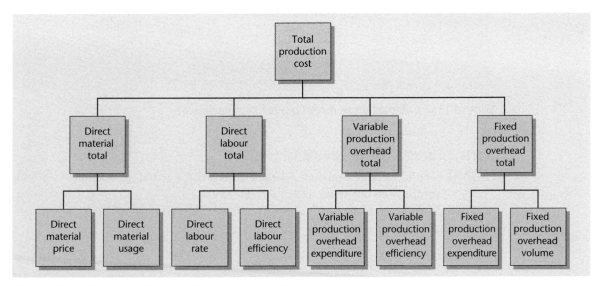

Figure 16.2 Main standard production cost variances

Direct materials

1 **Total** = (actual cost per unit × actual quantity used) – (standard cost per unit × standard quantity for actual production)
2 **Price** = (actual cost per unit – standard cost per unit) × total actual quantity used
3 **Usage** = (total actual quantity used – standard quantity for actual production) × standard cost

These relationships are shown in Figure 16.3.

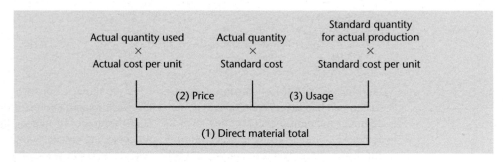

Figure 16.3 Calculation of direct material cost variances

Direct labour

1 **Total** = (actual hourly rate × actual hours) – (standard hourly rate × standard hours for actual production)
2 **Rate** = (actual hourly rate – standard hourly rate) × actual hours worked
3 **Efficiency** = (actual hours worked – standard hours for actual production) × standard hourly rate

These relationships are shown in Figure 16.4.

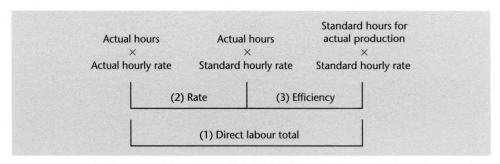

Figure 16.4 Calculation of direct labour cost variances

Variable production overhead

1 **Total** = actual variable overhead – [standard hours for actual production × variable production overhead absorption rate (VOAR)]
2 **Expenditure** = actual variable overhead – (actual hours worked × VOAR)
3 **Efficiency** = (standard hours for actual production – actual hours worked) × VOAR

These relationships are shown in Figure 16.5.

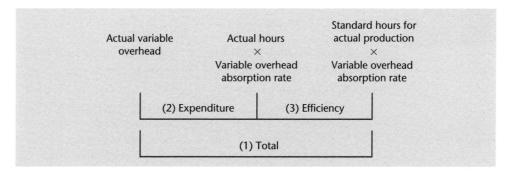

Figure 16.5 Calculation of variable production overhead variances

Fixed production overhead

1 **Total** = actual fixed overhead − [standard hours of production × fixed overhead absorption rate (FOAR)]

2 **Expenditure** = actual fixed overhead − budgeted fixed expenditure

3 **Volume** = budgeted fixed overhead expenditure − (standard hours for actual production × FOAR)

These variances are shown in Figure 16.6.

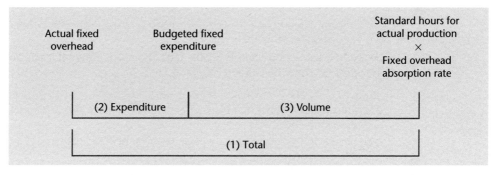

Figure 16.6 Calculation of fixed production overhead variances

Activity 16.4 List twelve main cost variances.

A comprehensive example

We will now use a comprehensive example to illustrate the main cost variances. The details are contained in Example 16.3.

Example 16.3	**Calculation of the main cost variances**

The following information has been extracted from the records of the Frost Production Company Limited for the year to 31 March 2011:

	£
Budgeted costs per unit:	
Direct materials (15 kilograms × £2 per kilogram)	30
Direct labour (10 hours × £4 per direct labour hour)	40
Variable overhead (10 hours × £1 per direct labour hour)	10
Fixed overhead (10 hours × £2 per direct labour hour)	20
Total budgeted cost per unit	100

The following budgeted data are also relevant:

1 The budgeted production level was 100 units.
2 The total standard direct labour hours amounted to 1000.
3 The total budgeted variable overhead was estimated to be £1000.
4 The total budgeted fixed overhead was £2000.
5 The company absorbs both fixed and variable overhead on the basis of direct labour hours.

Actual costs:	£
Direct materials	2 100
Direct labour	4 000
Variable overhead	1 000
Fixed overhead	1 600
Total actual costs	8 700

Note: 90 units were produced in 800 actual hours, and the total actual quantity of direct materials consumed was 1400 kilograms.

Required:
(a) Calculate the direct materials, direct labour, variable production overhead and fixed production overhead total cost variances.
(b) Calculate the detailed variances for each element of cost.

Answer to Example 16.3(a)	In answering part (a) of this question the first thing that we need to do is to summarize the total variance for each element of cost for the actual 90 units produced:

	Actual costs	Total standard cost for actual production	Variance
	£	£	£
Direct materials	2 100	2 700 (1)	600 (F)
Direct labour	4 000	3 600 (2)	400 (A)
Variable production overhead	1 000	900 (3)	100 (A)
Fixed production overhead	1 600	1 800 (4)	200 (F)
Total	8 700	9 000	300 (F)

Notes:
(a) F = favourable to profit; A = adverse to profit.
(b) The numbers in brackets refer to the tutorial notes below.

Tutorial notes

1 The standard cost of direct material for actual production = the actual units produced × the standard direct material cost per unit, i.e. 90 × £30 = £2700.

2 The standard cost of direct labour for actual production = the actual units produced × standard direct labour cost per unit, i.e. 90 × £40 = £3600.

3 The standard variable cost for actual performance = the actual units produced × variable overhead absorption rate per unit, i.e. 90 × £10 = £900.

4 The fixed overhead cost for the actual performance = the actual units produced × fixed overhead absorption rate, i.e. 90 × £20 = £1800.

Comments on the answers to Example 16.3(a)

Example 16.3(a) shows that the total actual cost of producing the 90 units was £300 less than the budget allowance. An investigation would need to be made in order to find out why only 90 units were produced when the company had budgeted for 100. Although the 90 units have cost £300 less than expected, a number of other variances have contributed to the total variance. So assuming that these variances are considered significant, they would need to be carefully investigated in order to find out what caused them.

As a result of calculating variances for each element of cost, it becomes much easier for management to investigate why the actual production cost was £300 less than expected. However, by analysing the variances into their major causes, the accountant can provide even greater guidance. This is illustrated in part (b) of the example.

Answer to Example 16.3(b)

In answering part (b) of Example 16.3, we will deal with each element of cost in turn. As we do so we will take the opportunity to comment on the results.

Direct materials

1 Price = (actual cost per unit − standard cost per unit)
× total actual quantity used

∴ the price variance = (£1.50 − 2.00) × 1400 (kg) = <u>£700 (F)</u>

The actual price per unit was £1.50 (£2100/1400) and the standard price was £2.00 per unit. There was, therefore, a total saving (as far as the price of the materials was concerned) of £700 (£0.50 × 1400). This was favourable (F) to profit.

2 Usage = (total actual quantity used − standard quantity for actual production)
× standard cost

∴ the usage variance = (1400 − 1350) × £2.00 = <u>£100 (A)</u>

In producing 90 units, Frost should have used 1350 kilograms (90 × 15 kg) instead of the 1400 kilograms actually used. If this extra usage is valued at the standard cost (the difference between the actual price and the standard cost has already been allowed for), there is an adverse usage variance of £100 (50 (kg) × £2.00).

3 Total = price + usage:

∴ the total direct materials variance = £700 (F) + £100 (A) = <u>£600 (F)</u>

The £600 favourable total variance was calculated earlier in answering part (a) of the question. This variance might have arisen because Frost purchased cheaper materials. If this were the case then it probably resulted in a greater wastage of materials, perhaps because the materials were of an inferior quality.

Direct labour

1 Rate = (actual hourly rate − standard hourly rate) × actual hours worked

∴ the rate variance = (£5.00 − £4.00) × 800 DLH = <u>£800 (A)</u>

The actual hourly rate is £5.00 per direct labour hour (£4000/800) compared with the standard rate per hour of £4. Every extra actual hour worked, therefore, resulted in an adverse variance of £1 or £800 in total (£1 × 800).

2 Efficiency = (actual hours worked – standard hours for actual production) × standard hourly rate.

$$\therefore \quad \text{the efficiency variance} = (800 - 900) \times £4.00 = \underline{£400 \text{ (F)}}$$

The actual hours worked were 800. However, 900 hours would be the allowance for the 90 units actually produced (90 × 10 DLH). If these hours were valued at the standard hourly rate (differences between the actual rate and the standard rate having already been allowed for when calculating the rate variance), a favourable variance of £400 arises. The favourable efficiency variance has arisen because the 90 units took less time to produce than the budget allowed for.

3 Total = rate + efficiency

$$\therefore \quad \text{the total direct labour variance} = £800 \text{ (A)} + £400 \text{ (F)} = \underline{£400 \text{ (A)}}$$

The £400 adverse total variance was calculated earlier in answering part (a) of the question. It arises because the company paid more per direct labour hour than had been budgeted, although this was offset to some extent by the units being produced in less time than the budgeted allowance. This variance could have been caused by using a higher grade of labour than had been intended. Unfortunately, the higher labour rate per hour was not completely offset by greater efficiency.

Variable production overhead

1 Expenditure = actual variable overhead – (actual hours worked × variable production overhead absorption rate)

$$\therefore \quad \text{the expenditure variance} = £1000 - (800 \times £1.00) = \underline{£200 \text{ (A)}}$$

2 Efficiency = (standard hours for actual production – actual hours worked) × variable production overhead absorption rate

$$\therefore \quad \text{the efficiency variance} = (900 - 800) \times £1.00 = \underline{£100 \text{ (F)}}$$

3 Total = expenditure + efficiency

$$\therefore \quad \text{the total variable production overhead variance}$$
$$= £200 \text{ (A)} + £100 \text{ (F)} = \underline{£100 \text{ (A)}}$$

The adverse variance of £100 (A) arises because the variable overhead absorption rate was calculated on the basis of a budgeted cost of £10 per unit. In fact the absorption rate ought to have been £11.11 per unit (£1000/90) because the total actual variable cost was £1000. There would, of course, be no variable production overhead cost for the ten units that were not produced. The £100 adverse total variance was calculated earlier in answering part (a) of the example.

Fixed production overhead

1 Expenditure = actual fixed overhead – budgeted fixed expenditure

$$\therefore \quad \text{the expenditure variance} = £1600 - £2000 = \underline{£400 \text{ (F)}}$$

The actual expenditure was £400 less than the budgeted expenditure. This means that the fixed production overhead absorption rate was £400 higher than it needed to have been if it had been the only fixed overhead variance.

2 Volume = budgeted fixed overhead – (standard hours of production × fixed production overhead absorption rate)

$$\therefore \quad \text{the volume variance} = £2000 - (900 \times £2.00) = \underline{£200\ (A)}$$

As a result of producing fewer units than expected, £200 less overhead has been absorbed into production.

3 The fixed production overhead total variance was calculated earlier in answering part (a) of the question. The simplified formula is as follows:

$$\text{Total} = \text{expenditure} + \text{volume}$$

$$= £400\ (F) + £200\ (A) = \underline{£200\ (F)}$$

As the actual activity was less than the budgeted activity, only £1800 of fixed overhead was absorbed into production instead of the £2000 expected in the budget. However, the actual expenditure was only £1600 so the overestimate of expenditure compensated for the overestimate of activity.

Activity 16.5	Think of a reason why a favourable direct materials price variance might be offset by an adverse direct materials usage variance. Similarly, why might an adverse direct labour rate variance be offset by a favourable direct labour efficiency variance?

Sales variances

In an *absorption* costing system, a total sales variance would be classified into a selling price variance and a sales volume profit variance (see Figure 16.7).

The formulae are outlined below and they are also shown in diagrammatic form in Figure 16.8.

1 Total sales variance = [actual sales revenue – (actual sales quantity × standard cost per unit)] – (budgeted quantity × standard profit per unit)

2 Selling price variance = [actual sales revenue – (actual sales quantity × standard cost per unit)] – (actual quantity × standard profit per unit)

An alternative formula for the calculation of the selling price variance is as follows: (actual selling price per unit – standard selling price per unit) × actual sales quantity.

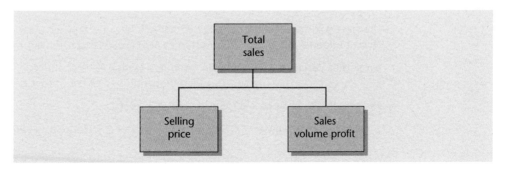

Figure 16.7 Main sales variances

3 **Sales volume profit variance** = (actual quantity – budgeted quantity) × standard profit per unit

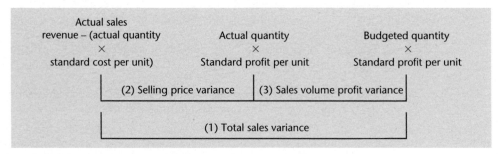

Figure 16.8 Calculation of sales profit variances

The use of sales variance formulae is illustrated in Example 16.4.

Calculating sales variances

The following data relate to Frozen Limited for the year to 31 July 2011:

	Budget/standard	Actual
Sales (units)	100	90
Selling price per unit	£10	£10.50
Standard cost per unit	£7	–
Standard profit per unit	£3	

Required:
Calculate the sales variances.

Answer to Example 16.4

Selling price variance = [actual sales revenue – (actual sales quantity × standard cost per unit)] – (actual quantity × standard profit per unit)

= [£945 – (90 units × £7)] – (90 units × £3) = (£945 – 630) – 270 = £45 (F)

The actual selling price per unit was £0.50 more than the standard selling price (£10.50–10.00) and so the variance is favourable. Other things being equal, the profit would be £45 higher than budgeted *for the actual number of units sold*.

Sales volume profit variance = (actual quantity – budgeted quantity) × standard profit per unit
The standard profit is £3 per unit.

(90 units – 100 units) = 10 × £3 = £30 (A)

The sales volume profit variance is £30 adverse because only 90 units were sold instead of the budgeted amount of 100 units. As a result, £30 less profit was made.

Total sales variance = [actual sales revenue – (actual sales quantity × standard cost per unit)] – (budgeted quantity × standard profit per unit)

The actual sales revenue = £945 (90 units × £10.50).

[£945 – (90 units × £7)] – (100 units × £3) = (£945 – 630) – 300 = £15 (F)

When the £45 favourable selling price is set off against the £30 adverse sales volume profit variance, there is a favourable total sales variance of £15 (£45 – 30).

Activity 16.6	Assuming that the demand for Product X is elastic, what effect might a reduction in its selling price have on its sales volume profit variance?	

Operating statements

Once all the variances have been calculated they may be summarized in the form of an operating statement. There is no standardized format for such a statement but the one used in Example 16.5 gives you a good idea of what one looks like.

The structure used in Example 16.5 is particularly helpful because it shows the link between the budgeted profit and the actual profit. This means that management can trace the main causes of sales and cost variances. In practice the statement would also show the details for each product.

Example 16.5

Preparation of a standard cost operating statement

Example 16.3 gave some information relating to the Frost Production Company Limited for the year to 31 March 2011. The cost data used in that example will now be used to illustrate the structure of a standard cost operating statement, along with some additional information.

Additional information:
1 Assume that the budgeted sales were 100 units at a selling price of £150 per unit.
2 90 units were sold at £160 per unit.

Required:
Prepare a standard cost operating statement for the year to 31 March 2011.

Answer to Example 16.5

Frost Production Company Limited. Standard cost operating statement for the year to 31 March 2011:

	(F) £	(A) £	£
Budgeted sales (100 × £150)			15 000
Budgeted cost of sales (100 × £100)			10 000
Budgeted profit			5 000
Sales volume profit variance (1)			(500)
Budgeted profit from actual sales			4 500
Variances: (2)			
Sales price (3)	900		
Direct materials usage		100	
Direct materials price	700		
Direct labour efficiency	400		
Direct labour rate		800	
Variable overhead efficiency	100		
Variable overhead expenditure		200	
Fixed overhead volume		200	
Fixed overhead expenditure	400		
	2 500	1 300	1 200
Actual profit			5 700

*Answer 16.5
continued*

1 **Sales volume profit variance** = (actual quantity – budgeted quantity) × standard profit per unit
= (90 – 100) × £50 = £500 (A)

2 Details of the cost variances were shown in the answer to Example 16.3.

3 **Selling price variance** = (actual selling price per unit – standard selling price per unit) × actual sales quantity
= (£160 – £150) × 90 = £900 (F)

The operating profit statement will help management to decide where to begin an investigation into the causes of the respective variances. It is unlikely that they will all be investigated. It may be company policy, for example, to investigate only those variances that are particularly significant, irrespective of whether they are favourable or adverse. In other words, only *exceptional* variances would be investigated. A policy decision would then have to be taken on what was meant by 'exceptional'.

Activity 16.7

Suppose that you were the managing director of a medium-sized manufacturing company. Which managers do you think should be supplied with a copy of the company's four-weekly standard cost operating statement?

 Questions you should ask

The calculation of standard cost variances is a complex arithmetical exercise. As a non-accountant it is unlikely that you will have to calculate variances but it is important for you to have some idea of how it is done so that you are in a stronger position to find out what happened. You can then take any necessary corrective action.

So what questions should you ask? We suggest that you can use the following as a basis for any subsequent investigation.

● Was the given level of activity accurate?

● Was the standard set realistic?

● Is there anything unusual about the actual events?

● Is the measure (i.e. the standard) reliable?

● Are there any particular variances that stand out?

● Are there any that are the main cause of any total variance?

● Is there a linkage between variances, e.g. between a favourable price variance and an unfavourable quantity/volume variance?

● Are there any factors that were not apparent at the time that the standards were set?

Conclusion

We have come to the end of a complex chapter. You may have found that it has been extremely difficult to understand just how standard cost variances are calculated.

Fortunately, it is unlikely that, as a non-accountant, you will ever have to calculate them for yourself. It is sufficient for your purposes to understand their meaning and to have some idea of the arithmetical foundation on which they are based.

Your job will usually be to investigate the *causes* of the variances and to take necessary action. A standard costing system is supposed to help managers plan and control the entity much more tightly than can be achieved in the absence of such a system. However, it can only be of real benefit if it is actually used by managers.

Key points

1 A standard cost is the planned cost of a particular unit or process.

2 Standard costs are usually based on what is reasonably attainable.

3 Actual costs are compared with standard costs.

4 Corrective action is taken if there are any unplanned trends.

5 Three performance measures used in standard costing are the efficiency ratio, the capacity ratio and the production volume ratio.

6 Variance analysis is an arithmetical exercise that enables differences between actual and standard costs to be broken down into the elements of cost.

7 The degree of analysis will vary, but usually a total cost variance will be analysed into direct material, direct labour, variable overhead and fixed overhead variances and sub-analysed into quantity and expenditure variances.

8 Sales variances may also be calculated, the total sales variance being analysed into a selling price variance and a sales volume profit variance.

9 The variances help in tracing the main causes of differences between actual and budgeted results but they do not *explain* what has actually happened – they are merely the starting point for a more detailed investigation.

Check your learning

1 Explain what is meant by the following terms: (a) a standard, (b) a standard cost, (c) a variance, (d) variance analysis.

2 List four uses of standard costing.

3 What type of entities might benefit from a standard costing system?

4 How long should a standard costing period be?

5 What is (a) a basic standard, (b) an attainable standard, (c) an ideal standard?

6 Name four types of information required for a standard costing system.

7 What is meant by 'a standard hour'?

8 Name three standard cost performance measures.

9 What are their respective formulae?

10 Complete the following equations:

(a) direct materials total = _____ + _____

(b) direct labour total = _____ + _____

(c) variable production overhead total = _____ + _____

(d) fixed production overhead total = _____ + _____

11 What is (a) an adverse variance, (b) a favourable variance?

12 Complete this equation: total sales variance = _____ + _____

13 Complete this statement: a standard cost operating statement links the budgeted profit to the _____ _____ for the period.

News story quiz

Remember the news story at the beginning of this chapter? Go back to that story and reread it before answering the following questions.

We do not deal with 'lean accounting' in this book. It's a very new area of accounting and it has not yet caught on. All you need to know for the purposes of this news story is that the proponents of lean accounting believe that traditional management accounting techniques are inappropriate for modern manufacturing practices. Try to answer the following questions based on your impression of standard costing that you have obtained from reading this chapter and any practical experience you have of working for an organization.

Questions

1 Do you think that standard costing is an outdated management control technique?

2 Is it a fair criticism to argue that standard costing is driven by 'labor (sic) efficiency, machine utilisation and absorption of overhead'?

3 Why should standard costing necessarily lead to 'excessive inventories that generate positive variances'?

Tutorial questions

The answers to questions marked with an asterix can be found in Appendix 4.

16.1 Is it likely that a standard-costing system is of any relevance in a service industry?

16.2 'Standard costing is all about number crunching, and for someone on the shop floor it has absolutely no relevance.' Do you agree with this statement?

16.3 'Sales variance calculations are just another example of accountants playing around with numbers.' Discuss.

16.4* You are presented with the following information for X Limited:

Standard price per unit: £10.
Standard quantity for actual production: 5 units.

Actual price per unit: £12.
Actual quantity: 6 units.

Required:
Calculate the following variances:

(a) direct material total variance
(b) direct material price variance
(c) direct material usage variance.

16.5 The following information relates to Malcolm Limited:

Budgeted production: 100 units.
Unit specification (direct materials): 50 kilograms × £5 per kilogram = £250.
Actual production: 120 units.
Direct materials used: 5400 kilograms at a total cost of £32,400.

Required:
Calculate the following variances:

(a) direct material total
(b) direct material price
(c) direct material usage.

16.6* The following information relates to Bruce Limited:

Actual hours: 1000.
Actual wage rate per hour: £6.50.
Standard hours for actual production: 900.
Standard wage rate per hour: £6.00.

Required:
Calculate the following variances:

(a) direct labour total
(b) direct labour rate
(c) direct labour efficiency.

16.7 You are presented with the following information for Duncan Limited:

Budgeted production: 1000 units.
Actual production: 1200 units.
Standard specification for one unit: 10 hours at £8 per direct labour hour.
Actual direct labour cost: £97,200 in 10,800 actual hours.

Required:
Calculate the following variances:

(a) direct labour total
(b) direct labour rate
(c) direct labour efficiency.

16.8* The following overhead budget has been prepared for Anthea Limited:

Actual fixed overhead: £150,000.
Budgeted fixed overhead: £135,000.
Fixed overhead absorption rate per hour: £15.
Actual hours worked: 10,000.
Standard hours of production: 8000.

Required:
Calculate the following fixed production overhead variances:

(a) total
(b) expenditure
(c) volume.

16.9* Using the data contained in the previous question, calculate the following perform-ance measures:

(a) efficiency ratio
(b) capacity ratio
(c) production volume ratio.

16.10 The following information relates to Osprey Limited:

Budgeted production: 500 units.
Standard hours per unit: 10.
Actual production: 600 units.
Budgeted fixed overhead: £125,000.
Actual fixed overhead: £120,000.
Actual hours worked: 4900.

Required:
Calculate the following fixed production overhead variances:

(a) total
(b) expenditure
(c) volume.

16.11 Using the data from the previous question, calculate the following performance measures:

(a) efficiency ratio
(b) capacity ratio
(c) production volume ratio.

16.12* Milton Limited has produced the following information:

Total actual sales: £99,000.
Actual quantity sold: 9000 units.
Budgeted selling price per unit: £10.
Standard cost per unit: £7.
Total budgeted units: 10,000 units.

Required:
Calculate:

(a) the selling price variance
(b) the sales volume profit variance
(c) the sales variance in total.

16.13 You are presented with the following budgeted information for Doe Limited:

Sales units	100
Per unit:	£
Selling price	30
Cost	(20)
Profit	10
Actual sales	120 units
Actual selling price per unit	£28

Required:
Calculate the sales variances.

16.14 The budgeted selling price and standard cost of a unit manufactured by Smillie Limited is as follows:

	£
Selling price	30
Direct materials (2.5 kilos)	5
Direct labour (2 hours)	12
Fixed production overhead	8
	25
Budgeted profit	5

Total budgeted sales: 400 units

During the period to 31 December 2012, the actual sales and production details for Smillie were as follows:

	£
Sales (420 units)	13 440
Direct materials (1260 kilos)	2 268
Direct labour (800 hours)	5 200
Fixed production overhead	3 300
	10 768
Profit	2 672

Required:
(a) Prepare a standard cost operating statement for the period to 31 December 2012 incorporating as many variances as the data permit.
(b) Explain what the statement tells the managers of Smillie Limited.

16.15 Mean Limited manufactures a single product, and the following information relates to the actual selling price and actual cost of the product for the four weeks to 31 March 2012:

	£000
Sales (50 000 units)	2 250
Direct materials (240 000 litres)	528
Direct labour (250 000 hours)	1 375
Variable production overhead	245
Fixed production overhead	650
	2 798
Loss	(548)

The budgeted selling price and standard cost of each unit was as follows:

	£
Selling price	55
Direct materials (5 litres)	10
Direct labour (4 hours)	20
Variable production overhead	5
Fixed production overhead	15
	50
Budgeted profit	5

Total budgeted production: 40 000 units.

Required:

(a) Prepare a standard cost operating statement for the four weeks to 31 March 2012 incorporating as many variances as the data permit.

(b) Explain how the statement may help the managers of Mean Limited to control the business more effectively.

Further practice questions, study material and links to relevant sites on the World Wide Web can be found on the website that accompanies this book. The site can be found at www.pearsoned.co.uk/dyson

Chapter 17 | Contribution analysis

Tough at the top

Alcatel-Lucent surges on break-even target

Andrew Parker

Alcatel-Lucent, the Franco-American telecoms equipment maker, on Thursday slipped to an operating loss in the second quarter, but said it still planned to break even for the full year.

Ben Verwaayen, Alcatel-Lucent's chief executive, said the company expected to hit its target of break-even at the level of adjusted operating income, partly through further cost cutting.

Mr Verwaayen is leading a turn-round of the telecoms equipment maker, which has yet to make a success of the 2006 merger between its French and American predecessor companies.

All the telecoms equipment manufacturers are getting hit in the economic downturn, as fixed line and mobile phone operators cut their capital spending.

The company reported revenue of €3.9bn ($5.5bn) for the three

months to June 30, down 4.8 per cent compared to the same period last year.

It recorded net income of €14m, compared to a €1.1bn loss in the second quarter last year. The improvement was because of some one-off items, including a €255m tax-free capital gain on the sale of Alcatel-Lucent's 21 per cent stake in Thales, the French defence electronics maker.

www.ft.com, 30 July 2009.

Source: Reproduced with permission from *The Financial Times*.

Questions relating to this news story can be found on page 393 ➡

About this chapter

In the previous two chapters we have been concerned with the planning and control functions of management accounting. We now turn our attention to another important function of management accounting, *decision making*. In this chapter we explore a basic technique of decision making known as *contribution analysis*.

Contribution analysis is based on the premise that in almost any decision-making situation some costs are irrelevant, that is they are not affected by the decision. They can, therefore, be ignored. In such circumstances management should concentrate on the *contribution* that a project may make. Contribution (C) is the difference between the sales revenue (S) of a project and the variable or extra costs (V) incurred by investing in that project. Other things being equal, as long as S – V results in C being positive then management should go ahead or continue with the project. If C is positive it means that something is left over to make a *contribution* to the fixed (or remaining) costs (F) of the entity. If the fixed costs have already been covered by other projects then the contribution increases the entity's profit.

Learning objectives

By the end of this chapter, you should be able to:

● explain why absorption costing may be inappropriate in decision making;

● describe the difference between a fixed cost and a variable cost;

● use contribution analysis in managerial decision making;

● assess the usefulness of contribution analysis in problem solving.

! Why this chapter is important

Of all the chapters in this book this is the most relevant and vital for non-accountants. Why? Whatever job you are doing and at whatever level, you will be required to make or to take decisions. Many of those decision will be straightforward day-to-day ones such as, '*Do we order a week's or a month's supply of paper towels?*' Other decisions will be more significant and long-term, for example '*Should we increase our selling prices?*' or '*Do we buy this other company?*'

While there is a cost implication in these sorts of decisions, it is unlikely that you would have to do the detailed calculations for yourself. Your accountants will do this for you and then present you with the results. However, in order to make sense of the information and to take an informed decision you need to know where the information has come from and how it has been compiled.

This is a valid point irrespective of the particular issue but it is especially valid for specific one-off decision making. If such decisions are based on absorbed costs you might make a spectacularly wrong decision because it would not be based on the project's *relevant* costs, i.e. those costs that are affected by that particular decision.

This chapter will help you to appreciate more clearly the nature of relevant costs and their importance in managerial decision making. As a result, you will be able take more soundly based decisions and be more confident about their eventual outcome.

Marginal costing

News clip

Outsourcing

According to a report by Create Research, asset managers are cutting their fixed costs by outsourcing instead of carrying out middle and back office jobs in-house. Stephen Wynne, chief executive of PNC Global Investment Services, admits that such a move causes some restructuring costs but 'the fixed expense becomes a variable one'.

Source: Adapted from www.ft.com/cms/s, 5 April 2009.

Chapters 13 and 14 dealt with cost accounting. The costing method described in some detail in those chapters is known as *absorption costing*. The ultimate aim of absorption costing is to charge out all the costs of an entity to individual units of production.

The method involves identifying the *direct costs* of specific units and then absorbing a share of the *indirect costs* into each unit. Indirect costs are normally absorbed on the basis of direct labour hours or machine hours. Assuming that an overhead absorption rate is predetermined, i.e. calculated in advance, this method involves estimating the total amount of overhead likely to be incurred and the total amount of direct labour hours or machine hours expected to be worked. So the absorption rate could be affected by the total cost of the overhead, the hours worked or by a combination of cost and hours.

The total of the indirect costs (the overhead) is likely to be made up of a combination of costs that will change depending on how many units a department produces and those costs that are not affected by the number of units produced. Costs that change with activity are known as *variable costs*. It is usually assumed that variable costs vary directly with activity, e.g. if 1 kg costs £1, then 2 kg will cost £2, 3 kg will cost £3 and so on. Those costs that do not change with activity are known as *fixed costs*.

As we argued in Chapters 13 and 14, if we are attempting to work out the total cost of manufacturing particular units, or if we want to value our stocks, it is appropriate to use absorption costing. Most cost book-keeping systems are based on this method of costing but absorption costing is not normally appropriate in decision making as the fixed element inherent in most costs may not be affected by a particular decision.

Suppose that a manager is costing a particular journey that a member of staff is proposing to make to visit a client. The staff member has a car that is already taxed and insured, so the main cost of the journey will be for petrol (the car may also depreciate slightly more quickly and it may require a service sooner). The tax and insurance costs will not be affected by one particular journey: they are *fixed costs*, no matter how many extra journeys are undertaken. The manager is, therefore, only interested in the *extra* cost of using the car to visit the client and he can then compare the cost of using the car with the cost of the bus, the train or going by air. Note that cost alone would not necessarily be the determining factor in practice; non-quantifiable factors such as comfort, convenience, fatigue and time would also be important considerations.

The extra cost of making the journey is sometimes described as the *marginal cost*. Hence the technique used in the above example is commonly referred to as *marginal costing*. Economists also use the term 'marginal cost' to describe the extra cost of making an additional unit (as with the extra cost of a particular journey). When dealing with production activities, however, units are more likely to be produced in batches. It would then be more appropriate to substitute the term *incremental costing* and refer to the *incremental cost*, meaning the extra cost of producing a batch of units. As the terms 'marginal costing' and 'marginal cost' are so widely used, however, we will do the same.

The application of marginal costing revolves round the concept of what is known as *contribution*. We explore this concept in the next section.

Activity 17.1	A business college has recently considered starting some extra evening classes on basic computing. The college runs other courses during the evening. The proposed course fee has been based on the lecturer's fee and the cost of heat, light, caretaking and other expenses incurred solely as a result of running the extra classes. However, the principal has insisted that a 25% loading be added to the fee to go towards the college's day-to-day running costs. This is in accordance with the college's normal costing procedures.

Give reasons why the principal's requirement may be inappropriate when costing the proposed evening class lectures.

Contribution

News clip

Variable cost restructuring

The media buying and market research company Aegis is proposing to cut 780 jobs across 40 countries. In talking to analysts and investors John Napier, the Chairman and interim chief executive, said that 2009 was likely to be a tougher year than 2008. As well as reducing staff by 5% by restructuring, Aegis is also proposing to bring variable costs such as incentives into line with 'a negative growth environment'.

Source: Adapted from www.ft.com/cms/s, 19 March 2009.

In order to illustrate what is meant by 'contribution' we will use a series of equations. The first is straightforward:

$$\text{sales revenue} - \text{total costs} = \text{profit (or loss)} \tag{1}$$

The second equation is based on the assumption that total costs can be analysed into variable costs and fixed costs:

$$\text{total costs} = \text{variable costs} + \text{fixed costs} \tag{2}$$

By substituting equation 2 into equation 1 we can derive equation 3:

$$\text{sales revenue} - (\text{variable costs} + \text{fixed costs}) = \text{profit (or loss)} \tag{3}$$

By rearranging equation 3 we can derive the following equation:

$$\text{sales revenue} - \text{variable costs} = \text{fixed costs} + \text{profit (or loss)} \tag{4}$$

Equation 4 is known as the *marginal cost equation*. We will simplify it by substituting symbols for words, namely sales revenue = S, variable costs = V, fixed costs = F, and profit = P (or loss = L). The equation now reads as follows:

$$S - V = F + P \tag{5}$$

But where does contribution fit into all of this? Contribution (C) *is the difference between the sales revenue and the variable costs of that sales revenue.* So, in equation form:

$$S - V = C \tag{6}$$

Contribution can also be looked at from another point of view. If we substitute C for $(S - V)$ in equation 5, the result will be:

$$C = F + P \qquad (7)$$

In other words, contribution can be regarded as being either the difference between the sales revenue and the variable costs of that sales revenue or the total of fixed cost plus profit.

What do these relationships mean in practice and what is their importance? The meaning is reasonably straightforward. If an entity makes a contribution, it means that it has generated a certain amount of sales revenue and the variable cost of making those sales is less than the total sales revenue $(S - V = C)$. So there is a balance left over that can go towards contributing towards the fixed costs $(C - F)$; any remaining balance must be the profit $(C - F = P)$. Alternatively, if the contribution is insufficient to cover the fixed costs, the entity will have made a loss: $C - F = L$.

The importance of the relationships described above in equation format is important for two main reasons. First, fixed costs can often be ignored when taking a particular decision because, by definition, fixed costs will not change irrespective of whatever decision is taken. This means that any cost and revenue analysis is made much simpler. Second, managers can concentrate on decisions that will maximize the contribution, since every additional £1 of contribution is an extra amount that goes toward covering the fixed costs. Once the fixed costs have been covered then every extra £1 of contribution is an extra £1 of profit.

Activity 17.2	Company M's annual sales were £100,000, its variable costs £40,000 and its fixed costs £50,000.
	Calculate the profit for the year using the marginal cost equation.

Assumptions

News clip

More losses reported

Uniq's overall losses got worse in the first six months of the year as restructuring and pension costs along with reduced sales took their toll. The UK business, however, was close to break-even with a loss of £1.3 million as the chilled food group gained extra business from Marks & Spencer and the Co-operative.

Source: Adapted from www.ft.com/cms/s, 30 July 2009.

The marginal cost technique used in contribution analysis is, of course, based on a number of assumptions. They may be summarized as follows:

- total costs can be split between fixed costs and variable costs;
- fixed costs remain constant irrespective of the level of activity;

- fixed costs do not bear any relationship to specific units;
- variable costs vary in direct proportion to activity.

The reliability of the technique depends very heavily on being able to distinguish between fixed and variable costs. Some costs may be semi-variable, i.e. they may consist of both a fixed and variable element. Electricity costs and telephone charges, for example, both contain a fixed rental element plus a variable charge. The variable charge depends on the units consumed or the number of telephone calls made. Such costs are relatively easy to analyse into their fixed and variable elements.

In practice, it may be difficult to split other costs into their fixed and variable components. The management accountants may need the help of engineers and work study specialists in determining whether a particular cost is fixed or variable. They may also have to draw on a number of graphical and statistical techniques. These techniques are somewhat advanced and beyond this book, so for our purposes we will assume that it is relatively easy to analyse costs into their fixed and variable components.

Activity 17.3	Reread the assumptions summarized above. Do you think that these assumptions are reasonable? Rank them in the order of how far you think that they are generally valid (1 = the most valid; 2 = the next most valid, and so on).

Format

In applying the marginal cost technique, the cost data are usually arranged in a vertical format on a line-by-line basis. The order of the data reflects the marginal cost equation $(S - V = F + P)$. This format enables the attention of managers to be directed towards the contribution that may arise from any particular decision. This is now called *contribution analysis*. The basic procedure is illustrated in Example 17.1.

Example 17.1	**A typical marginal cost statement**

	Symbol	Product A £000	Product B £000	Product C £000	Total £000
Sales revenue (1)	S	100	70	20	190
Less: variable costs of sales (2)	V	30	32	18	80
Contribution (3)	C	70	38	2	110
Less: fixed costs (4)	F				60
Profit (5)	P				50

Notes:
- The number in brackets after each item description refers to the tutorial notes below.
- The marginal cost equation is represented in the 'symbol' column, i.e. $S - V = C$; $C = F + P$; and thereby $S - V = F + P$.

Tutorial notes

1 The total sales revenue would normally be analysed into different product groupings. In this example there are three products: A, B and C.

2 The variable costs include direct materials, direct labour costs, other direct costs and variable overheads. Variable costs are assumed to vary *in direct proportion* to activity. Direct costs will normally be the same as variable costs, but in some cases this will not be so. A machine operator's salary, for example, may be fixed under a guaranteed annual wage agreement. It is a direct cost in respect of the machine but it is also a fixed cost because it will not vary with the number of units produced.

3 As explained above, the term *contribution* is used to describe the difference between the sales revenue and the variable cost of those sales. A positive contribution helps to pay for the fixed costs.

4 The fixed costs include all the other costs that do not vary in direct proportion to the sales revenue. Fixed costs are assumed to remain constant over a period of time. They do not bear any relationship to the units produced or the sales achieved. So it is not possible to apportion them to individual products. The *total* of the fixed costs can only be deducted from the *total contribution*.

5 The total contribution less the fixed costs gives the profit (if the balance is positive) or a loss (if the balance is negative).

Managers supplied with information similar to that contained in Example 17.1 may subject the information to a series of 'What if?' questions such as the following.

● What would the profit be if we increased the selling price of product A, B or C?
● What would be the effect if we reduced the selling price of product A, B or C?
● What would be the effect if we eliminated one or more of the products?
● What would happen if we changed the quality of any of the products so that the variable cost of each product either increased or decreased?
● Would any of the above decisions have an impact on fixed costs?

Activity 17.4	Rearrange the following data in a marginal cost format. Annual rent £3000; direct labour £20,000; direct material £10,000; sales £75,000; staff salaries £47,000.

Application

News clip

Rentokil on the rise

Rentokil beat expectations as its first-half results were better than expected. It was reported that the 'washrooms to pest control business' made progress in cutting costs and improving productivity. This helped to double operating cash flows in the six months to June 2009. The City Link had, however, continued to make a loss but chief executive Alan Brown expected it to break even by the end of the year.

Source: Adapted from www.ft.com/cms/s, 1 August 2009.

As we have seen, the basic assumptions used in marginal costing are somewhat simplistic. In practice, they would probably only be regarded as appropriate when a particular decision was first considered. Thereafter each of the various assumptions would be rigorously tested and they would be subject to a number of searching questions such as: 'If we change the selling price of this product, will it affect the sales of the other products?' 'Will variable costs always remain in direct proportion to activity?' or 'Will fixed costs remain fixed irrespective of the level of activity?'

We will now use a simple example to illustrate the application of the technique. The details are shown in Example 17.2. This illustrates the effect of a change in variable costs on contribution.

Example 17.2	Changes in the variable cost			
	One unit	Proportion	100 units	1000 units
	£	%	£	£
Sales revenue	10	100	1000	10 000
Less: variable costs	5	50	500	5 000
Contribution	5	50	500	5 000

Tutorial notes to Example 17.2

1   The selling price per unit is £10, and the variable cost per unit is £5 (50 per cent of the selling price). The contribution, therefore, is also £5 per unit (50 per cent of the selling price).

2   These relationships are assumed to hold good no matter how many units are sold. So if 100 units are sold the contribution will be £500; if 1000 units are sold there will be a contribution of £5000, i.e. the contribution is assumed to remain at 50 per cent of the sales revenue.

3   The fixed costs are ignored because it is assumed that they will *not* change as the level of activity changes.

Every extra unit sold will increase the profit by £5 per unit *once the fixed costs have been covered* – an important qualification. This point is illustrated in Example 17.3.

Example 17.3	Changes in profit at varying levels of activity				
Activity (units)	1000	2000	3000	4000	5000
	£	£	£	£	£
Sales	10 000	20 000	30 000	40 000	50 000
Less: variable costs	5 000	10 000	15 000	20 000	25 000
Contribution	5 000	10 000	15 000	20 000	25 000
Less: fixed costs	10 000	10 000	10 000	10 000	10 000
Profit/(Loss)	(5 000)	–	5 000	10 000	15 000

Tutorial notes to Example 17.3

1   The exhibit illustrates five levels of activity: 1000 units, 2000 units, 3000 units, 4000 units and 5000 units.

2   The variable costs remain directly proportional to activity at all levels, i.e. 50 per cent. The contribution is, therefore, 50 per cent (100% – 50%). The contribution per unit may be obtained by dividing the contribution at any level of activity level by the activity at that level, e.g. at an activity level of 1000 units the contribution per unit is £5 (£5000 ÷ 1000).

Tutorial notes to Example 17.3 continued

3 The fixed costs do not change, irrespective of the level of activity.

4 The contribution needed to cover the fixed costs is £10,000. As each unit makes a contribution of £5, the total number of units needed to be sold in order to break even, i.e. to reach a point where sales revenue equals the total of both the variable and the fixed costs, will be 2000 (£10,000 ÷ £5).

5 When *more* than 2000 are sold, the increased contribution results in an increase in profit. So, when 3000 units are sold instead of 2000, for example, the increased contribution is £5000 (£15,000 – 10,000); the increased profit is also £5000 (£5000 – 0). Similarly, when 4000 units are sold instead of 3000, the increased contribution is another £5000 (£20,000 – 15,000) and the increased profit is also £5000 (£10,000 – 5000). Finally, when 5000 units are sold instead of 4000 units, the increased contribution is once more £5000 (£25,000 – 20,000), as is the increased profit (£15,000 – 10,000).

6 The relationship between contribution and sales is known (rather confusingly) as the *profit/volume* (or P/V) ratio. Note that it does not mean *profit* in relationship to sales but the *contribution* in relationship to sales.

7 Assuming that the P/V ratio does not change, we can quickly calculate the profit at any level of sales. All we need to do is to multiply the P/V ratio by the sales revenue and then deduct the fixed costs. The balance will then equal the profit at that level of sales. It is also easy to accommodate any possible change in fixed costs if the activity level moves above or below a certain range.

Example 17.2 and Example 17.3 are simple examples but we hope that they demonstrate just how useful contribution analysis can be in managerial decision making. While the basic assumptions may be somewhat questionable, they can readily be adapted to suit more complex problems.

Activity 17.5

You are presented with the following data: number of units sold 5000, sales revenue £50,000, variable costs £25,000, fixed costs £10,000.

If the company wanted to make the same amount of profit, how many units would have to be sold if the fixed costs rose to £15,000?

Charts and graphs

Contribution analysis lends itself to the presentation of information in a pictorial format. Indeed, the $S - V = F + P$ relationship is often easier to appreciate when it is reported to managers graphically.

The most common format is in the form of what is called a *break-even chart*. A break-even chart is illustrated in Example 17.4. The chart is based on the data used in Example 17.3.

Example 17.4 shows quite clearly the relationships that are assumed to exist when the marginal costing technique is adopted. Sales revenue, total costs and fixed costs are all assumed to be linear, so they are all drawn as straight lines. Note also the following points.

● When no units are sold, the sales revenue line runs from the origin up to £50,000 when 5000 units are sold. It may then continue as a straight line beyond that point.
● The total cost line is made up of both the fixed costs and the variable costs. When there is no activity the total costs will be equal to the fixed costs, so the total cost line runs from the fixed cost point of £10,000 up to £35,000 when 5000 units are sold. It may then continue beyond that point.

● The fixed cost line is drawn from the £10,000 point as a straight line parallel to the *x* axis irrespective of the number of units sold.

In practice, the above relationships are not likely to hold good over the range of activity indicated in the example. They are usually assumed to remain valid over only a small range of activity. This is known as the *relevant range*. In this example the relevant range may be from (say) 1000 to 3000 units. Above or below these levels the selling prices, the variable costs and the fixed costs may all change.

While this point might appear to create some difficulty, it should be appreciated that wide fluctuations in activity are not normally experienced. It is usually quite reasonable to assume that the entity will be operating in a fairly narrow range of activity and that the various relationships will be linear. It must also be remembered that the information is meant to be only a *guide* to managerial decision making and that it is impossible to be absolutely precise.

Example 17.4	**A break-even chart**

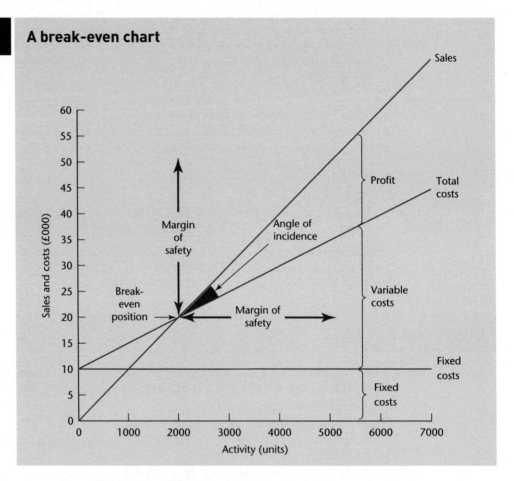

Tutorial notes to Example 17.4

1   The total costs line is a combination of the fixed costs and the variable costs. So it ranges from a total cost of £10,000 (fixed costs only) at a nil level of activity, to £35,000 when the activity level is 5000 units (fixed costs of £10,000 + variable costs of £25,000).

2   The angle of incidence is the angle formed between the sales line and the total cost line. The wider the angle, the greater the amount of profit. A wide angle of incidence and a wide margin of safety (see note 3) indicates a highly profitable position.

*Tutorial notes
to Example 17.4
continued*

3 The margin of safety is the distance between the sales achieved and the sales level needed to break even. It can be measured either in units (along the *x* axis of the graph) or in sales revenue terms (along the *y* axis).

4 Activity (measured along the *x* axis) may be measured either in units or as a percentage of the theoretical maximum level of activity, or in terms of sales revenue.

You will see that the break-even chart shown in Example 17.4 does not show a separate variable cost line. This may be somewhat confusing, and so sometimes the information is presented in the form of a *contribution graph*. A contribution graph based on the data used in Example 17.4 is illustrated in Example 17.5. Can you spot the differences between the two examples?

Example 17.5

A contribution graph

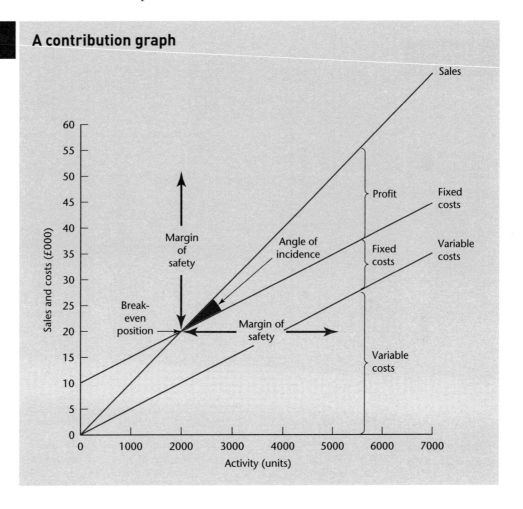

- The contribution graph shows the variable cost line ranging from the origin when there is no activity to £25,000 when 5000 units are sold. It then continues beyond that point in a straight line.
- The fixed cost line is drawn parallel to the variable cost line, i.e. higher up the *y* axis. As the fixed costs are assumed to remain fixed irrespective of the level of activity, the fixed cost line runs from £10,000 when there is no activity to £35,000 when 5000 units are sold. It is then continued as a straight line beyond that point.
- The fixed cost line also serves as the total cost line.

Apart from the above differences, the break-even chart and the contribution graph are identical. Which one should you adopt? There is no specific guidance that we can give since the decision is one largely of personal preference. The break-even chart is more common, but the contribution chart is probably more helpful since the fixed and the variable cost lines are shown separately.

One problem with both the break-even chart and the contribution graph is that neither shows the *actual amount of profit or loss* at varying levels of activity. So, if you wanted to know what the profit was when (say) 4000 units were sold, you would have to use a ruler to measure the distance between the sales line and the total cost line. This is not very satisfactory so in order to get over this problem we can use a *profit/volume chart* (or graph).

A profit/volume chart shows the effect of a change in activity on profit. An example of such a chart is shown in Example 17.6. It is based on the data used in Example 17.3.

Example 17.6	**A profit/volume chart**

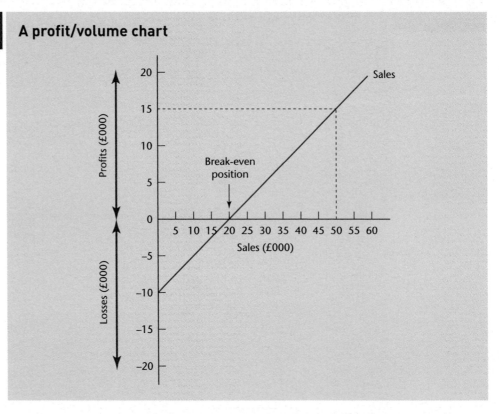

Tutorial notes to Example 17.6

1 The *x* axis can be represented either in terms of units, as a percentage of the activity level or in terms of sales revenue.

2 The *y* axis represents profits (positive amounts) or losses (negative amounts).

3 With sales at a level of £50,000, the profit is £15,000. The sales line cuts the *x* axis at the break-even position of £20,000 sales. If there are no sales, the loss equals the fixed costs of £10,000.

As you can see from Example 17.6 the profit/volume chart only shows the entity's *total* profit or loss. It does not show the profit or loss made on individual products. It is possible to do so although the result is somewhat simplistic (see Example 17.7).

<table>
<tr><td rowspan="2" style="background:#333;color:#fff">**Example 17.7**</td><td colspan="5">**Tilsy Limited**</td></tr>
</table>

Example 17.7

Tilsy Limited

You are presented with the following information.

Product	A	B	C	Total
	£	£	£	£
Sales	5 000	20 000	25 000	50 000
Less: variable costs	3 000	10 000	12 000	25 000
Contribution	2 000	10 000	13 000	25 000
Less: fixed costs				10 000
Profit				15 000

Additional information:
Assume that Tilsy first began manufacturing and selling Product A, then Product B, and finally Product C. Its fixed costs remained constant at £10,000 irrespective of whether it was dealing with one, two or all three of these products.

Required:
Prepare a profit/volume chart showing the impact on its profit/(loss) of the individual product ranges.

Answer to Example 17.7

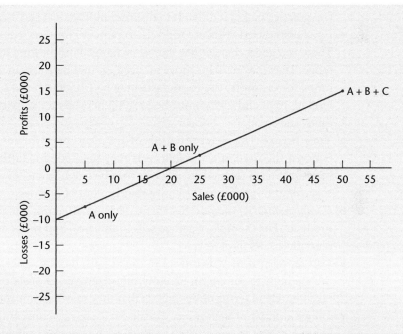

1 If Product A is the first product, the company makes a loss of £8000 (£2000 – 10,000). Once Product B is introduced a profit of £2000 is made [(£2000 + 10,000) – 10,000]. Then when Product C is added the profit becomes £15,000 [(£2000 + 10,000 + 13,000) – 10,000].

2 It would be possible to plot the three product ranges in a different order, e.g. Product B, then Product C, then Product A; or possibly Product C, then Product A, then Product B.

3 The disclosure of the impact of individual products on profit is useful because it can highlight the performance of a poorly performing product. Product A does make a small contribution of £2000 (£5000 – 3000) but this is not sufficient to offset the fixed costs of £10,000. It is only when Product B is introduced that the company begins to make a profit. The chart shows this fairly clearly.

Activity 17.6	On a scale of 1 to 5, how useful do you think that the following diagrams are to management (5 = very useful; 1 = not at all useful)?

(a) a break-even chart ☐

(b) a contribution graph ☐

(c) a profit/volume chart ☐

Reservations

The assumptions adopted in preparing marginal cost statements and their use in contribution analysis lead to a number of important reservations about the technique. The main ones are as follows.

- *Cost classification.* Costs cannot be easily divided into fixed and variable categories.
- *Variable costs.* Variable costs do not necessarily vary in direct proportion to sales revenue at all levels of activity. The cost of direct materials, for example, may change if supplies are limited or if they are bought in bulk. It is also questionable whether direct labour should be treated as a variable cost (as is often the case) since current legislative practice makes it difficult to dismiss employees at short notice.
- *Fixed costs.* Fixed costs are unlikely to remain constant over a wide range of activity. There is a good chance that they will change both beyond and below a fairly narrow range. They may perhaps move in 'steps', so that between an activity level of 0 and 999 units, for example, the fixed costs may be £10,000, be £12,000 between an activity level of 1000 and 2999 units, be £15,000 between an activity level of 3000 and 5000 units, and so on.
- *Time period.* The determination of the time period over which the relationship between the fixed and variable costs may hold good is difficult to determine. In the very short term (say a day), all costs may be fixed. In the long term (say five years), all costs may be variable as the entity could go out of business.
- *Complementary products.* A specific decision affecting one product may affect other products. For example, a garage sells both petrol and oil. A decision to stop selling oil may affect sales of petrol.
- *Cost recovery.* It may be unwise to exclude fixed costs altogether from the analysis. In the medium-to-long term an entity must recover all of its costs. Decisions cannot be taken purely in terms of the impact that they may have on contribution.
- *Diagrammatic presentations.* Break-even charts, contribution graphs and profit/volume charts are somewhat simplistic. The sales of individual products are considered in total and it is assumed that any change made to one product will have a proportionate effect on all the other products.
- *Non-cost factors.* Decisions cannot be taken purely on the basis of cost. Sometimes factors that cannot be easily quantified and costed are more important, e.g. comfort, convenience, loyalty, reliability or speed.
- *Behavioural factors.* In practice, behavioural factors also have to be considered. Individuals do not always act rationally and an actual behaviour pattern may be quite different from what was expected. A decrease in the selling price of a product, for

example, may reduce the quantity of good purchased because it is *perceived* to be of poor quality.

The factors listed above are all fairly severe reservations of the marginal costing technique and its use in contribution analysis. Nevertheless, experience suggests that it has still a useful part to play in managerial decision making, provided that the basis on which the information is built is understood, its apparent arithmetical precision is not regarded as a guarantee of absolute certainty, and non-cost factors are also taken into account.

With these reservations in mind, we can now move on to look at the technique in a little more detail. Before we do so, however, it would be useful to summarize the main formulae so that it will be easier for you to refer back to them when dealing with the various examples.

Activity 17.7	Reread the reservations outlined above. Judging them from a non-accountant's point of view, select the three most significant weaknesses of the marginal costing approach and summarize them.

Formulae

Earlier in the chapter we explained that marginal costing revolves around the assumption that total costs can be classified into fixed and variable costs. This then led us on to an explanation of what we called the *marginal cost equation*, i.e. $S - V = F + P$. This equation can be used as the basis for a number of other simple equations that are useful in contribution analysis. The main ones are summarized below.

Abbreviation:

- Sales – variable cost of sales = contribution $\qquad S - V = C$

- Contribution – fixed costs = profit/(loss) $\qquad C - F = P/(L)$

- Break-even (B/E) point = contribution – fixed costs $\qquad C - F$

- B/E in sales value terms = $\dfrac{\text{fixed costs} \times \text{sales}}{\text{contribution}} \qquad \dfrac{F \times S}{C}$

- B/E in units = $\dfrac{\text{fixed costs}}{\text{contribution per unit}} \qquad \dfrac{F}{C \text{ per unit}}$

- Margin of safety (M/S) in sales value terms = $\dfrac{\text{profit} \times \text{sales}}{\text{contribution}} \qquad \dfrac{P \times S}{C}$

- M/S in units = $\dfrac{\text{profit}}{\text{contribution per unit}} \qquad \dfrac{P}{C \text{ per unit}}$

Example 17.8 illustrates the use of some of these formulae.

Example 17.8

The use of the marginal cost formulae

The following information relates to Happy Limited for the year to 30 June 2012.

Number of units sold: 10,000

	Per unit	Total
	£	£000
Sales	30	300
Less: Variable costs	18	180
Contribution	12	120
Less: Fixed costs		24
Profit		96

Required:
In value and unit terms, calculate the following:
(a) the break-even position
(b) the margin of safety.

Answer to Example 17.8

(a) Break-even position in value terms:

$$\frac{F \times S}{C} = \frac{£24\,000 \times 300\,000}{120\,000} = £60\,000$$

Break-even in units:

$$\frac{F}{C\ \text{per unit}} = \frac{£24\,000}{12} = 2000\ \text{units}$$

(b) Margin of safety in value terms:

$$\frac{P \times S}{C} = \frac{£96\,000 \times 300\,000}{120\,000} = £240\,000$$

Margin of safety in units:

$$\frac{P}{C\ \text{per unit}} = \frac{£96\,000}{12} = 8000\ \text{units}$$

Tutorial note   Note the relationship between the sales revenue and the margin of safety. The sales revenue is £300,000 and £60,000 of sales revenue is required to break even. The margin of safety is, therefore, £240,000 (£300,000 – 60,000).

Activity 17.8

Using the data in Example 17.8 prepare (a) a break-even chart; and (b) a profit/volume chart.

It would now be helpful to incorporate the principles behind contribution analysis into a simple example. Example 17.9 outlines a typical problem that a board of directors might well face.

Example 17.9	**Marginal costing**

Looking ahead to the financial year ending 31 March 2012, the directors of Problems Limited are faced with a budgeted loss of £10,000. This is based on the following data.

Budgeted number of units: 10,000

	£000
Sales revenue	100
Less: Variable costs	80
Contribution	20
Less: Fixed costs	30
Budgeted loss	(10)

The directors would like to aim for a profit of £20,000 for the year to 31 March 2012. Various proposals have been put forward, none of which require a change in the budgeted level of fixed costs. These proposals are as follows:

1 Reduce the selling price of each unit by 10 per cent.
2 Increase the selling price of each unit by 10 per cent.
3 Stimulate sales by improving the quality of the product, which would increase the variable cost of the unit by £1.50 per unit.

Required:
(a) For each proposal calculate:
    (i)   the break-even position in units and in value terms;
    (ii) the number of units required to be sold in order to meet the profit target.
(b) State which proposal you think should be adopted.

Answer to Example 17.9

Problems Limited
(a) (i) and (ii)

Workings:	£
Profit target	20 000
Fixed costs	30 000
Total contribution required	50 000

The budgeted selling price per unit is £10 (£100 000/10 000). The budgeted variable cost per unit is £8 (£80 000/10 000).

The budgeted outlook compared with each proposal may be summarized as follows:

Per unit:	Budgeted position	Proposal 1	Proposal 2	Proposal 3
	£	£	£	£
Selling price	10	9	11	10.00
Less: Variable costs	8	8	8	9.50
(a) Unit contribution	2	1	3	0.50
(b) Total contribution required to break even (= fixed costs) (£)	30 000	30 000	30 000	30 000

Answer to Example 17.9 *continued*

(c) Total contribution required to meet the profit target (£)

Total contribution required to meet the profit target (£)	50 000	50 000	50 000	50 000
Number of units to break even [(b)/(a)]	15 000	30 000	10 000	60 000
Number of units to meet the profit target [(c)/(a)]	25 000	50 000	16 667	100 000

(b) Comments

1 By continuing with the present budget proposals, the company would need to sell 15,000 units to break even or 25,000 units to meet the profit target. So in order to break even the company needs to increase its unit sales by 50% $\left(\dfrac{£15\,000 - 10\,000}{10\,000} \times 100 \right)$ and by 150% $\left(\dfrac{£25\,000 - 10\,000}{10\,000} \times 100 \right)$ to meet the profit target.

2 A reduction in selling price of 10% per unit would require unit sales to increase by 200% $\left(\dfrac{£30\,000 - 10\,000}{10\,000} \times 100 \right)$ in order to break even and by 400% $\left(\dfrac{£50\,000 - 10\,000}{10\,000} \times 100 \right)$ to meet the profit target.

3 By increasing the selling price of each unit by 10%, the company would only have to sell at the budgeted level to break even, but its unit sales would have to increase by 66.7% $\left(\dfrac{£16\,667 - 10\,000}{10\,000} \times 100 \right)$ to meet the profit target.

4 By improving the product at an increased variable cost of £1.50 per unit, the company would require a 500% $\left(\dfrac{£60\,000 - 10\,000}{10\,000} \times 100 \right)$ increase in unit sales to break even, or a 900% $\left(\dfrac{£100\,000 - 10\,000}{10\,000} \times 100 \right)$ increase to meet the profit target.

Conclusion

It would appear that increasing the selling price by 10% would be a more practical solution for the company to adopt. In the short run, at least, it will break even and there is the possibility that sales could be sufficient to make a small profit. In the long run this proposal has a much better chance of meeting the profit target than do the other proposals. Some extra stimulus would be needed, however, to lift sales to this level over such a relatively short period of time. It is not clear why an increase in price would increase sales, unless the product is one that only sells at a comparatively high price, such as cosmetics and patent medicines. It must also be questioned whether the cost relationships will remain as indicated in the example over such a large increase in activity. In particular, it is unlikely that the fixed costs will remain entirely fixed if there were to be a 66.7% increase in sales.

Limiting factors

When optional decisions are being considered, the aim will always be to maximize contribution because the greater the contribution then the more chance there is of covering the fixed costs and of making a profit. When managers are faced with a choice, therefore, between (say) producing product A at a contribution of £10 per unit or of producing product B at a contribution of £20 per unit, they would normally choose product B. Sometimes, however, it may not be possible to produce unlimited quantities of product B because there could be limits on how many units could either be sold or produced. Such limits are known as *limiting factors* (or key factors).

Limiting factors may arise for a number of reasons. It may not be possible, for example, to sell more than a certain number of units, there may be production restraints (such as shortages of raw materials, skilled labour or factory space), or the company may not be able to finance the anticipated rate of expansion.

If there is a product that cannot be produced and sold in unlimited quantities, then it is necessary to follow a simple rule in order to decide which product to concentrate on producing. The rule can be summarized:

> **choose the work that provides the maximum contribution per unit of limiting factor employed.**

This sounds very complicated but it is easy to apply in practice. In outline, the procedure is as follows (we will assume that direct labour hours are in short supply).

1 Calculate the contribution made by each product.
2 Divide the contribution that each product makes by the number of direct labour hours used in making each product.
3 This gives the contribution per direct labour hour employed (i.e. the limiting factor).
4 Select the project that gives the highest contribution per unit of limiting factor.

So if we had to choose between two jobs, say A and B, we would convert A's contribution and B's contribution into the amount of contribution earned for every direct labour hour worked on A and on B respectively. We would then opt for the job that earned the most contribution per direct labour hour. The technique is illustrated in Example 17.10.

Example 17.10

Application of key factors

Quays Limited manufactures a product for which there is a shortage of the raw material known as PX. During the year to 31 March 2012, only 1000 kilograms of PX will be available. PX is used by Quays in manufacturing both product 8 and product 9. The following information is relevant:

Per unit:	Product 8	Product 9
	£	£
Selling price	300	150
Less: Variable costs	200	100
Contribution	100	50
P/V ratio $\left(\dfrac{£100}{300} \times 100\right)$ and $\left(\dfrac{£50}{150} \times 100\right)$	$33\frac{1}{3}$	$33\frac{1}{3}$
Kilograms of PX required	5	2

Required:
State which product Quays Limited should concentrate on producing.

Answer to Example 17.10

	Product 8	Product 9
	£	£
Contribution per unit	100	50
Limiting factor per unit (kg)	÷ 5	÷ 2
Contribution per kilogram	= 20	= 25

Decision:
Quays should concentrate on product 9 because it gives the highest contribution per unit of limiting factor.

Check:
Maximum contribution of product 8:

200 units (1000kg/5) × contribution per unit = 200 × £100 = £20 000

Maximum contribution of product 9:

500 units (1000kg/2) × contribution per unit = 500 × £50 = £25 000

In Example 17.10 it was assumed that there was only one limiting factor, but there could be many more. This situation is illustrated in Example 17.11. The basic data are the same as for Example 17.10.

Example 17.11

Marginal costing using two key factors

Information:
1 Assume now that it is not possible for Quays Limited to sell more than 400 units of product 9.
2 The company would aim to sell all of the 400 units because product 9's contribution per unit of limiting factor is greater than product 8's. The total contribution would then be £20,000 (400 × £50).
3 The 400 units would consume 800 units of raw materials (400 × 2 kilograms), leaving 200 (1000 – 800) kilograms for use in producing product 8.
4 Product 8 requires 5 kilograms per unit of raw materials, so 40 units (200kg ÷ 5kg) could be completed at a total contribution of £4000 (40 × £100).

Summary of the position:

	Product 8	Product 9	Total
Units sold	40	400	
Raw materials (kilograms used)	200	800	1 000
Contribution per unit (£)	100	50	
Total contribution (£)	4 000	20 000	24 000

Note: The £24,000 total contribution compares with the contribution of £25,000 that the company could have made if there were no limiting factors affecting the sales of product 9.

Activity 17.9

A few examples of limiting factors are given in the text. Make a list of them. Now think about the concept. An entity will choose to make and sell as many units as it can of those products that make the highest contribution per unit of limiting factor. What other specific factors might stop it from doing so? Add them to your list.

> ### ❗ Questions you should ask
>
> When you have a specific decision to take as a manager, it is almost certain that your accountants will do the detailed calculative work for you. They are likely to present you with a summary of their results and their recommendations.
>
> We will assume that you have asked them for some guidance on a specific decision that you have to take. What should you ask them when you receive the information? The following questions are suggested, although you will, of course, need to adapt them depending on the circumstances.
>
> - Where have you got the basic data from?
> - What estimates have you had to make in adapting the original data?
> - Has the information been compiled on a contribution basis?
> - If not, why not? What other method have you used? Why is the contribution approach not appropriate in this case?
> - If the contribution approach has been used, how have the variable costs been separated from the fixed costs?
> - Have you assumed that variable costs move in direct proportion to sales revenue?
> - Over what timescale are the fixed costs fixed?
> - Over what time period will the various cost relationships last?
> - What impact will your recommendations have on other aspects of the business?
> - What non-quantifiable factors have you been able to take into account?
> - What non-quantifiable factors have been ignored?
> - Generally, how reliable is the information that you have given me?
> - What confidence can I have in it?
> - Is there anything else that I should know?

Conclusion

Contribution analysis is particularly useful in short-term decision making but it is of less value when decisions have to be viewed over the long term. The system revolves around two main assumptions:

- some costs remain fixed irrespective of the level of activity;
- other costs vary in direct proportion to sales.

These assumptions are not valid over the long term but provided that they are used with caution then they can be adopted usefully in the short term.

It should also be remembered that the technique is only a *guide* to decision making and that non-cost factors have to be taken into account.

In the next chapter we use contribution analysis to deal with other managerial problems.

Key points

1 Total cost can be analysed into fixed costs and variable costs.

2 Fixed costs are assumed to be unrelated to activity. They may be ignored in making short-term managerial decisions.

3 A company will aim to maximize the *contribution* that each unit makes to profit.

4 The various relationships between costs can be expressed in the form of an equation: $S - V = F + P$, where S = sales, V = variable costs, F = fixed costs and P = profit.

5 It may not always be possible to maximize unit contribution because materials, labour, finance or other factors may be in short supply.

6 In the long run, fixed costs cannot be ignored.

Check your learning

The answers to these questions can be found within the text.

1 What system of costing is normally used for the costing of products and for stock valuation purposes?

2 Why is this system not suitable for specific decision making?

3 What is meant by 'decision making'?

4 What term is given to the extra cost of an event?

5 What is meant by 'incremental costing'?

6 What is (a) a fixed cost, (b) a variable cost?

7 What is meant by the term 'contribution'?

8 What is the marginal cost equation?

9 List four main assumptions that underpin marginal costing.

10 What is a break-even chart?

11 What is meant by the terms (a) 'break-even', (b) 'angle of incidence', (c) 'margin of safety'?

12 What is a contribution graph?

13 What is a profit/volume chart?

14 List six assumptions that are adopted when preparing a marginal cost statement.

15 What is the formula for calculating (a) the break-even position in sales value terms, (b) the break-even position in units, (c) the margin of safety in sales value terms, (d) the margin of safety in units?

16 What is meant by a 'limiting factor'?

17 Give three examples of limiting factors.

18 State the rule that is used when activity is restricted by the presence of a limiting factor.

News story quiz

Remember that news story at the beginning of this chapter? Go back to that story and reread it before answering the following questions.

This is yet another story of a company struggling to break even still less make a profit during a deep recession. The story is of particular interest to us because it illustrates the concept of break-even that we have outlined in this chapter. It makes the point for us that when trading conditions are difficult a company may strive merely to 'break even' by cutting costs. And in case we sometimes forget, cutting costs usually means that employees lose their jobs – often with tragic consequences.

Questions

1 What do you think Mr Verwaayen means by the phrase 'expected to hit its target of break-even at the level of adjusted operating income'?

2 Is it possible to break even by any other means?

3 How would a one-off tax-free gain on the sale of Thales affect Alcatel-Lucent's break-even position?

Tutorial questions

The answers to questions marked with an asterisk can be found in Appendix 4.

17.1 'It has been suggested that although contribution analysis is fine in theory, fixed costs cannot be ignored in practice.' Discuss this statement.

17.2 'Contribution analysis described in textbooks is too simplistic and is of little relevance to management.' How far do you agree with this statement?

17.3 Do break-even charts and profit graphs help management to make more meaningful decisions?

17.4* The following information relates to Pole Limited for the year to 31 January 2012.

	£000
Administration expenses:	
Fixed	30
Variable	7
Semi-variable (fixed 80%, variable 20%)	20
Materials:	
Direct	60
Indirect	5
Production overhead (all fixed)	40
Research and development expenditure:	
Fixed	60
Variable	15
Semi-variable (fixed 50%, variable 50%)	10
Sales	450

Selling and distribution expenditure:

Fixed	80
Variable	4
Semi-variable (fixed 70%, variable 30%)	30

Wages:

Direct	26
Indirect	13

Required:
Using the above information, compile a contribution analysis statement for Pole Limited for the year to 31 January 2012.

17.5* You are presented with the following information for Giles Limited for the year to 28 February 2012:

	£000
Fixed costs	150
Variable costs	300
Sales (50 000 units)	500

Required:
(a) Calculate the following:
  (i) the break-even point in value terms and in units
  (ii) the margin of safety in value terms and in units.
(b) Prepare a break-even chart.

17.6 The following information applies to Ayre Limited for the two years to 31 March 2011 and 2012 respectively:

Year	Sales	Profits
	£000	£000
31.3.2011	750	100
31.3.2012	1 000	250

Required:
Assuming that the cost relationships had remained as given in the question, calculate the company's profit if the sales for the year to 31 March 2012 had reached the budgeted level of £1,200,000.

17.7 The following information relates to Carter Limited for the year to 30 April 2012:

Units sold: 50,000

Selling price per unit	£40
Net profit per unit	£9
Profit/volume ratio	40%

During 2013 the company would like to increase its sales substantially, but to do so it would have to reduce the selling price per unit by 20 per cent. The variable cost per unit will not change, but because of the increased activity the company will have to invest in new machinery which will increase the fixed costs by £30,000 per annum.

Required:
Given the new conditions, calculate how many units the company will need to sell in 2013 in order to make the same amount of profit as it did in 2012.

17.8 Puzzled Limited would like to increase its sales during the year to 3l May 2012. To do so, it has several mutually exclusive options open to it:

- reduce the selling price per unit by 15 per cent;
- improve the product resulting in an increase in the variable cost per unit of £1.30;

- spend £15,000 on an advertising campaign;
- improve factory efficiency by purchasing more machinery at a fixed extra annual cost of £22,500.

During the year to 31 May 2011, the company sold 20,000 units. The cost details were as follows:

	£000
Sales	200
Variable costs	150
Contribution	50
Fixed costs	40
Profit	10

These cost relationships are expected to hold in 2012.

Required:
State which option you would recommend and why.

17.9 The following information relates to Mere's budget for the year to 31 December 2012:

	Product			
	K	L	M	Total
	£000	£000	£000	£000
Sales	700	400	250	1350
Direct materials	210	60	30	300
Direct labour	100	200	200	500
Variable overhead	90	60	50	200
Fixed overhead	20	40	40	100
	420	360	320	1100
Profit/(loss)	280	40	(70)	250
Budgeted sales (units)	140	20	25	

Note: Fixed overheads are apportioned on the basis of direct labour hours.

The directors are worried about the loss that product M is budgeted to make and various suggestions have been made to counteract the loss, viz.:

- stop selling product M;
- increase M's selling price by 20 per cent;
- reduce M's selling price by 10 per cent;
- reduce its costs by purchasing a new machine costing £350,000, thereby decreasing the direct labour cost by £100,000 (the machine would have a life of five years; its residual value would be nil).

Required:
Evaluate each of these proposals.

You're fired ... maybe

Job losses can sometimes be a false economy

Andrew Taylor

Life is about to get even tougher in the jobs market, with employers expected to announce a spate of redundancies over the next few months.

Businesses, if they can avoid it, do not fire people in the run-up to Christmas. Harsh decisions tend to be postponed until after the holidays.

Hence the foreboding that January and February will see even more job losses, as employers decide they can wait no longer to respond to plummeting order books.

However, cutting permanent jobs is expensive – particularly if employers are only going to have to replace axed staff when trading improves.

A study published this week by the Chartered Institute of Personnel and Development (CIPD) calculated the 'real' average cost of firing a worker at more then £16,000. And this did not take into account the psychological effect that redundancies have on surviving staff in terms of lower morale, productivity and output.

Instead of pursuing short-term savings, employers might be better off if they respond 'by retaining their people, rather then downsizing and risking long-term damage to their business', says the CIPD.

Recent moves to introduce short-term working and extended Christmas breaks, as an alternative to cutting permanent staff, suggest that some manufacturing employers, have heeded this lesson.

www.ft.com, 8 January 2009.

Source: Reproduced with permission from *The Financial Times*.

Questions relating to this news story can be found on pages 414–415 ➡

About this chapter

In the previous chapter we suggested that the use of absorption costing in most decision-making situations may lead to some unwise decisions. We suggested that a contribution approach using marginal costing would normally be more appropriate. Marginal costing involves classifying costs on a fixed/variable basis, instead of on a direct/indirect basis as in absorption costing. There are, however, other ways of classifying costs and we outline some of them in this chapter.

The chapter also uses your overall knowledge of management accounting to examine some specific decision-making situations. We cover four main types of decision:

● those that involve determining whether to close or shut down a plant or a factory;
● those that involve deciding whether we supply or make our own materials and components;
● those that involve determining what price to charge for goods and services;
● those that involve deciding what price to charge for one-off or special orders.

Learning objectives

By the end of this chapter, you should be able to:

- outline the nature of decision making;
- list six ways of classifying costs for decision-making purposes;
- incorporate cost and financial data into specific decision-making situations.

! Why this chapter is important

The previous chapter was one of the most important in the book and this one is also very important. It tells you a little more about decision making and the classification of costs. It then uses some numerical examples to illustrate the particular direction that various decisions should take.

The chapter is heavily biased towards helping you as a non-accountant to make and take effective decisions. This means that it is *essential* if you are to become an all-round first-class manager.

Nature and purpose

News clip

Decision-making challenge

Paul Boyle, the Chief Executive of the Financial Reporting Council, has argued in a recent speech that the corporate governance challenge is about making boards more effective. He believed that the main challenge was to improve both decision making and the behaviour of directors.

Source: Adapted from www.frc.org.uk/press/pub1878, 25 February 2009.

We start our examination of this important topic by examining the nature and purpose of decision making.

The term *decision* will be familiar to you in your everyday life. It means coming to a conclusion about a particular issue, e.g. when to get up in the morning, whether to have tea or coffee for breakfast, or choosing between a holiday and buying some new clothes. Similarly, in a managerial context, decisions have to be taken about whether or not to sell in particular markets, buy some new machinery or spend more money on research.

Management accountants will be involved in collecting data and supplying information for such decisions. While the information that they supply will be primarily of a financial nature, they will highlight other considerations that need to be taken into account before a decision is made. The eventual decision will rest with the responsibility centre manager concerned. It may well be that non-cost factors turn out to be more important than measurable financial considerations. For example, an entity may buy components from an external supplier because they are cheaper. But what happens if the supplier becomes unreliable? It might then be worth the extra cost of manufacturing the components internally in order to avoid the risk of any disruption to normal production.

The information required for decision-making purposes tends to be more wide-ranging and less constrained than that used in cost accounting. Its main characteristics are summarized below and they are also shown in Figure 18.1.

- *Forward looking.* While historical data may be used as a guide, information for decision making is much more concerned with what *will* happen rather than with what *did* happen. As so much of the information required is concerned with the future, considerable initiative and intuitive judgement is required in being able to obtain it.
- *One-off decisions.* Decision making often involves dealing with a problem that is unique. So a solution has to be geared towards dealing with that particular problem.
- *Data availability.* While some of the data required for decision making may be extracted from the cost accounting system, much of what is required may have to be specially obtained.
- *Net cash flow.* Managers will be concerned with the impact that a decision may have on the expected net cash flow of a particular project, i.e. future cash receipts less future cash expenditure. The calculation of periodic profit and loss based on accruals and prepayments will be largely irrelevant.
- *Relevant costs.* Costs and revenues that are not affected by a decision are excluded from the analysis. For example, fixed costs would normally be ignored because they are not likely to change.
- *Opportunity costs.* Those benefits that would be foregone or lost as a result of taking a particular decision are known as opportunity costs. They form an important part of any decision-making analysis. You may decide, for example, to look after your own garden yourself instead of doing some paid overtime. The opportunity cost would be the wages or salary you lose by not working overtime less the amount you save by not employing a gardener.
- *Probability testing.* Much of the information used in problem solving is speculative because it relates to the future and so it is advisable to carry out some probability testing. This is an extremely complex area and it goes beyond this book. In broad terms it involves calculating the *expected value* of a particular project or proposal. The basic idea is demonstrated in Example 18.1.

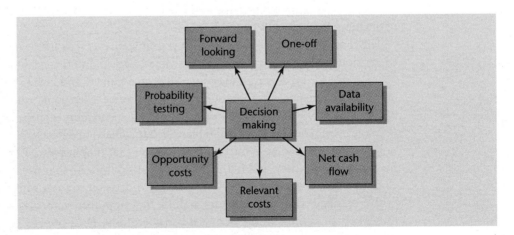

Figure 18.1 The nature of decision making

Example 18.1	**Probability testing**

Company X sells one product codenamed A1. The marketing department has estimated that the sales of A1 for a forthcoming budget period could be £1000, £1500 or £2000. On further investigation it would appear that there is a 70 per cent chance that the sales will be £1000, a 20 per cent chance that the sales will be £1500 and a 10 per cent chance that the sales will be £2000.

Required:
Calculate the expected value of sales for product A1 during the forthcoming budget period.

Answer to Example 18.1

The question requires us to calculate the expected value of the sales of A1 for the forthcoming period. It might be easier for you to think of the expected value as the *weighted average*, which perhaps provides a clue to what is required. In order to calculate the expected values the budgeted sales figures are multiplied by their respective chances or probabilities. So:

Budgeted sales (1)	Probability (2)	Expected value (3)
£	%	£
1 000	70	700
1 500	20	300
2 000	10	200
	100	1 200

Tutorial notes

1 The expected value (or weighted average) of the sales for the forthcoming budget period is £1200 as per column (3).

2 The answer has been obtained by multiplying the three estimated levels of sales by their respective probabilities (column (1) multiplied by column (2)).

3 In this exhibit, the probabilities are expressed in percentage terms. When combined they should always total 100%. Note that sometimes they are expressed in decimal terms; they should then total 1.0 (in our example 0.7 + 0.2 + 0.1 = 1.0).

4 The probabilities are estimates. They may be made partly on past experience, partly on an investigation of the market and partly on instinct. In other words they might be better described as 'guesstimates'.

5 Does the solution make sense? The expected value is £1200; this is £200 more than the lowest level of sales of £1000; the probability of this level being achieved is 70 per cent. So the chance of the sales being at least £1000 is quite high. By contrast, there is only a 20 per cent probability that the sales could be as high as £1500 and only a 10 per cent chance that they could reach £2000. It seems reasonable to assume, therefore, that the sales are likely to be nearer £1000 than £1500. So £1200 appears to be a reasonable compromise.

Activity 18.1	Tick the appropriate box.

In decision making:	True	False
(a) Profit is not usually taken into account when considering the launch of a new product.		
(b) Qualitative factors are ignored because they cannot be quantified.		
(c) Net cash flow will always be the deciding factor in going ahead with a proposed project.		

Cost classification

News clip

Bringing out the axe

The Japanese car-maker Toyota announced its quarterly results on Tuesday. They beat expectations. But, like its peers, Toyota has had to bring out the axe, managing to save $1.5 billion of fixed costs in the quarter. Unfortunately most of it was offset by exchange rate effects.

Source: Adapted from www.ft.com/com/cms, 4 August 2009.

As we have demonstrated in previous chapters, costs and revenues may be classified into various categories depending upon the purpose for which they are going to be used. In cost accounting, information is required mainly for product costing and stock valuation purposes, and so the most important category is the distinction between direct costs and indirect ones.

A direct/indirect cost classification is not normally appropriate in decision making. The preferred classification is that relating to fixed and variable costs but you will come across other cost classifications. We show the main ones used in decision making in Figure 18.2 along with a brief explanation of them below.

Fixed and variable costs

We covered such costs in the previous chapter. Fixed costs are those that are likely to remain unchanged irrespective of the level of activity. Variable costs are those that move directly proportional to activity – one unit results in £1 of variable cost, two units results in £2 of variable cost, three units in £3 of variable cost and so on.

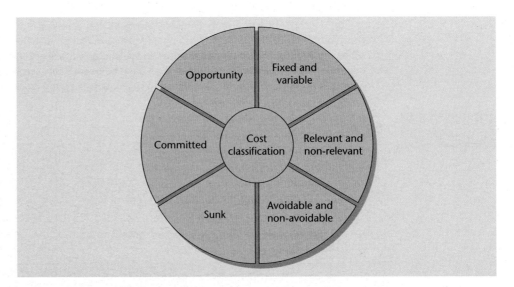

Figure 18.2 Cost classification

In theory, those costs classified as 'fixed' will remain the same irrespective of whether the entity is completely inactive or if it is operating at full capacity. In practice, fixed costs tend to remain fixed only over a relatively small range of activity range and only in the short term.

The assumption that fixed costs remain unchanged means that they do not normally need to be taken into account. In other words, they can be ignored because they will not be affected by the decision and they are not relevant in any consideration of the issues.

Relevant and non-relevant costs

Relevant costs are those future costs that are likely to be affected by a particular decision. It follows that non-relevant costs are those that are *not* likely to be affected by the decision. This means that non-relevant costs, such as fixed costs (although they are not always irrelevant), can be excluded from any cost analysis.

Avoidable and non-avoidable costs

Avoidable costs are those that may be saved by not taking a particular decision. Non-avoidable costs will still be incurred if the decision is taken. Avoidable and non-avoidable costs are very similar to relevant and non-relevant costs and sometimes the terms are used synonymously.

Sunk costs

Sunk costs are those that have already been incurred as a result of a previous decision. So they are not relevant as far as future decisions are concerned and they can be excluded from any decision-making analysis.

Committed costs

A committed cost arises out of a decision that has previously been taken, although the event has not yet taken place. For example, a proposal to increase the capacity of a factory from 1000 to 1500 units per annum will result in increased capital expenditure. A decision to accept the proposal means that certain costs are *committed* and it only becomes a matter of time before there is a cash outflow. Once the proposal has gone ahead and it has been paid for, the costs become *sunk* costs. Committed costs (like sunk costs) are not relevant as far as *future* decisions are concerned.

Opportunity costs

We referred to opportunity costs in the previous section of this chapter. Just to remind you, an opportunity cost is a measure of the net benefit that would be lost if one decision is taken instead of another decision. Opportunity costs are not normally recorded in the cost accounting system because they are difficult to quantify, so when making a decision they may need to be estimated.

Activity 18.2

Carla Friar is a mature student at university. Her university fees and maintenance cost her £7000 a year. Carla gave up her job in a travel centre to become a full-time student. Her take-home pay was then £20,000 a year but she also lost various travel concessions worth £1000 a year. As a student she has little free time, she socializes infrequently and so she does not spend much. This saves her about £2000 a year but, of course, she misses her friends and her nights out.

What factors do you think that Carla should take into account in trying to work out the opportunity cost of becoming a student?

Types of decision

We now turn to some specific decisions that managers may have to take. They are shown in diagrammatic format in Figure 18.3. The figure is followed by an explanation of each decision. The purchase of capital assets is another important decision that managers have to take but we leave this topic to the next chapter as we need more space to discuss it.

Closure and shutdown decision

News clip

Idling plants

The largest aluminium maker in the US, Alcoa, has announced a lower than expected loss. It achieved this by an aggressive cost-cutting exercise that has resulted in jobs being slashed and idling plants. The company reported that it had managed to achieve $280 million of over-head savings in 2009 – representing 134 per cent of its target for the year.

Source: Adapted from www.ft.com/cms, 8 July 2009.

A common problem that managers may face from time to time is whether to close some segment of the enterprise, such as a product, a service, a department or even an entire factory. This is a *closure* decision, the assumption being that the closure would be permanent. A similar decision may have to be taken in respect of a temporary closure. This is known as a *shutdown* decision.

A closure decision sometimes needs to be taken because a segment within the overall entity may have become unprofitable, out of date or unfashionable and therefore no future is seen for it. A decision to close a segment of an entity temporarily would be taken when the segment's problems are likely to be overcome in the near future. So a segment may be unprofitable at the moment but it is expected to recover in (say) a year's time.

Closure and shutdown decisions are often required because a segment is regarded as being 'unprofitable'. The definition of 'unprofitable' has to be looked at very closely.

Type	Question
Closure and shutdown	Will it be temporary or permanent?
Make or buy	Do we make our own or buy outside?
Pricing	Should it be market based or cost based?
Special orders	Will it be profitable?
Capital investment	How much will it cost?

Figure 18.3 Types of decision

A product, for example, may not be making a *profit* but it may be making a *contribution* towards the fixed costs of the company. Should it be abandoned? Great care would need to be taken before such a decision was taken. The abandonment of one product may have an impact on the sales of other products in such circumstances, it may even be beneficial to sell the product below its variable cost (at least in the short term).

Closure and shutdown decisions are not easy to make because they often require staff to be made redundant. They cannot be determined purely on narrow cost grounds, as other wide-ranging factors may need to be considered. We illustrate a relatively straightforward closure decision in Example 18.2 below.

Make or buy decisions

News clip

Outsourcing deals reviewed

In an attempt to cut costs many firms are now attempting to renegotiate their outsourcing contract deals or parcel off elements to different suppliers. But Graham Beck, the senior sourcing adviser at PA Consulting, believes that this may be unwise. It may cut costs, he argues, 'but you will be responsible for putting it all back together again and integrating all your suppliers'.

Source: *Financial Management*, June 2009, p. 7.

Example 18.2

A closure decision

Vera Limited has three main product lines: 1, 2 and 3. The company uses an absorption costing system, and the following information relates to the budget for the year 2012.

Product line	1	2	3	Total
Budgeted sales (units)	10 000	4 000	6 000	
	£000	*£000*	*£000*	*£000*
Sales revenue	300	200	150	650
Direct materials	100	40	60	200
Direct labour	50	70	80	200
Production overhead	75	30	35	140
Non-production overhead	15	10	5	30
	240	150	180	570
Profit (Loss)	60	50	(30)	80

Additional information:
1 Both direct materials and direct labour are considered to be variable costs.
2 The total production overhead of £140,000 consists of £40,000 variable costs and £100,000 fixed costs. Variable production overheads are absorbed on the basis of 20 per cent of the direct labour costs.
3 The non-production overhead of £30,000 is entirely fixed.
4 Assume that there will be no opening or closing stock.

Required:
Determine whether product line 3 should be closed.

Answer to Example 18.2

Points

1 The first step in determining whether to recommend a closure of product line 3 is to calculate the *contribution* that each product line makes.
2 In order to do so, it is necessary to rearrange the data given in the question in a marginal cost format, i.e. separate the fixed costs from the variable costs.
3 If product line 3 makes a contribution then other factors will have to be taken into account before an eventual decision can be made.

Calculations

Product line	1	2	3	Total
Budgeted sales (units)	10 000	4 000	6 000	
	£000	£000	£000	£000
Sales revenue	300	200	150	650
Less: Variable costs:				
Direct materials	100	40	60	200
Direct labour	50	70	80	200
Variable production overhead (question note 2: 20% of direct labour cost)	10	14	16	40
	160	124	156	440
Contribution	140	76	(6)	210

Less: Fixed costs:		
Production overheads (£140 – 40)		(100)
Non-production overheads (See question note 3)		(30)
Profit		80

Observations

It would appear that product line 3 neither makes a profit nor contributes towards the fixed costs. Should it be closed? Before such a decision is taken a number of other factors would have to be considered. These are as follows.

● Are the budgeted figures accurate? Have they been checked? How reliable are the budgeted data?
● What method has been used to identify the direct material costs that each product line uses? Is it appropriate for all three product lines?
● The question states that direct labour is a variable cost. Is direct labour really a variable cost? Is the assessment of its cost accurate and realistic?
● Variable production overheads are absorbed on a very broad basis related to direct labour costs. Does this method fairly reflect product line 3's use of variable overheads?
● Product line 3 appears to result in only a small negative contribution. Can this be made positive by perhaps a small increase in the unit selling price or by the more efficient use of direct materials and direct labour?
● Assuming that the cost data supplied are both fair and accurate, would the closure of product line 3 affect sales for the other two product lines or the overall variable costs?
● If closure of product line 3 is recommended, should it be closed permanently or temporarily? More information is needed of its prospects beyond 2012.

The decision

Clearly, without more information it is impossible to come to a firm conclusion. Assuming that the cost accounting procedures are both accurate and fair, it would appear that *on purely financial grounds*, product line 3 should be closed. However, until we have more information we cannot put this forward as a conclusive recommendation.

Make or buy decisions require management to determine whether to manufacture internally or purchase externally. Should a car company, for example, manufacture its own components or purchase them from specialist suppliers? Similarly, should a glass manufacturer concentrate on producing glass and purchase its packaging and safety equipment externally? In local government should a housing department employ its own joiners or contract outside firms to do the necessary work? In modern parlance these types of decisions are known as 'outsourcing'.

The theory beyond make or buy decisions revolves round the argument that entities should do what they are best at doing and employ others to undertake the peripheral activities. In other words, they should concentrate on their main objective and contract out or 'privatize' (in the case of governmental activities) all other essential activities.

A decision to contract out may often be taken simply because it appears to be cheaper (in monetary terms) to do so. This may be an unwise decision. There could be vital non-financial and non-quantifiable factors that are just as important as cost. For example, it may not be possible to obtain exactly what the company wants, or there could be delays in receiving some vital supplies. Both of these difficulties could cause a breakdown or hold-up to the company's own production. This might ultimately prove to be more expensive than manufacturing internally. So when deciding to make or buy, *all* factors should be built into the analysis, even though it may be difficult to quantify some of them.

A simple make or buy decision is illustrated in Example 18.3.

Example 18.3	**A make or buy decision**

Zam Limited uses an important component in one of its products. An estimate of the cost of making one unit of the component internally is as follows.

	£
Direct materials	5
Direct labour	4
Variable overhead	3
Total variable cost	12

Additional information:
1 Fixed costs specifically associated with manufacturing the components are estimated to be £8000 per month.
2 The number of components normally required is 1000 per month.

An outside manufacturer has offered to supply the components at a cost of £18 per component.

Required:
Determine whether Zam Limited should purchase the components from the outside supplier.

Answer to Example 18.3	**Points**

Assuming that the cost data given in the question are accurate, the first step in answering the question is to calculate the cost of manufacturing the components internally. Although the variable cost of each unit is given, there are some fixed costs directly associated with manufacturing internally and these have to be taken into account.

The fixed costs cause us a problem because the monthly activity levels may vary. However, we can only work on the data given in the question, i.e. 1000 units per month.

➡

Answer to Example 18.3 continued

Calculations

Total cost of manufacturing internally 1000 units per month of the component:

	£
Total variable cost (1000 units × £12)	12 000
Associated fixed costs	8 000
Total cost	20 000
Total unit cost (£20 000 ÷ 1000)	£20

Tutorial notes

1 Assuming that Zam Limited requires 1000 units per month, it would be cheaper to obtain them from the external supplier (£20 compared with £18 per component).

2 The above assumption is based on purchases of 1000 units. The more units required, the cheaper they would be to manufacture internally. In order to match the external price, the fixed costs can be no more than £6 per unit (the external purchase price of £18 less the internal variable cost of £12 per unit). If the fixed costs were to be limited to £6 per unit, the company would need to manufacture 1334 units (£8000 ÷ £6). The total cost would then be the same as the external cost (£24,000), but it would involve a one-third increase in the activity level.

3 The cost data should be checked carefully (especially the estimated associated fixed costs) and the monthly activity level reviewed. It might then be possible to put forward a tentative recommendation.

The decision

Given the data provided in the question, it would be cheaper to purchase the components externally. This would free some resources within Zam Limited enabling it to concentrate on manufacturing its main product.

However, there are a number of other considerations that need to be taken into account. In particular the following questions would need to be asked.

● How accurate are the cost data?
● How variable is the monthly activity level?
● Is the external supplier's component exactly suited to the company's purposes?
● How reliable is the proposed supplier?
● Are there other suppliers who could be used in an emergency and at what cost?
● What control could be exercised over the quality of the components received?
● How firm is the quoted price of £18 per component, and for what period will that price be maintained?
● How easy would it be to switch back to internal manufacturing if the supplier proved unreliable?

It follows that much more information (largely of a non-cost nature) would be required before a conclusive decision could be taken.

Activity 18.3

A company is considering outsourcing the manufacture of a vital component used in one of its most profitable products. It finds that it would be cheaper to buy the component externally than to make it internally. List all the non-cost factors that you think should be considered before it is decided to purchase the component externally. Then identify which you think is the most important one.

Pricing decisions

News clip

Munich Re

Munich Re, the world's largest reinsurer, has coped well in the financial crisis. The second quarter results were better than the first quarter and this July's insurance treaty renewals showed a price increase of 4.4%. Mr von Bomhard, the Chief Executive, said that he was not unhappy with the pricing level but he thought that the market should shift more quickly into a 'hardening mode'.

Source: Adapted from www.ft.com/cms, 5 August 2009.

A very important decision that managers have to make in both the profit-making sector and the not-for-profit sector is that relating to pricing. Supermarkets, for example, have to price their goods, while local authorities have to decide what to charge for adult education, leisure centres and meals on wheels.

Two types of pricing decisions can be distinguished. The first relates to the prices charged to customers or clients external to the entity. We will refer to this type as *external* pricing. The second type relates to prices charged by one part of an entity to another part, such as when components are supplied by one segment to another segment. This type of pricing is known as *transfer* pricing. We will deal with each type separately.

External pricing

External selling prices may be based either on market prices or on cost (see Figure 18.4). We will deal first with market-based prices.

Market-based pricing

Many goods and services are sold in highly competitive markets. This means that there may be many suppliers offering identical or near-identical products and they will be competing fiercely in respect of price, quality, reliability and service. If the demand for a product is *elastic*, then the lower the price the more units that will be sold. The opposite also applies and higher prices will result in fewer goods being sold. The demand for most everyday items of food, for example, is elastic.

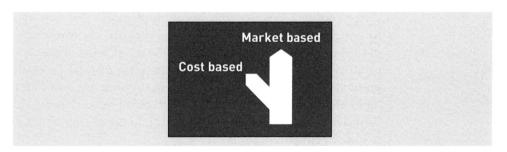

Figure 18.4 External pricing decisions

It follows that when demand is elastic it is unlikely that individual sellers can determine their own selling prices. So within narrow limits, they will have to base their selling prices on what is being charged in the market. Otherwise if they charge more than the market price their sales will be reduced. If they charge less than the market then their sales will increase but the market will quickly adjust to a lower level of selling prices.

Where market conditions largely determine a supplier's selling prices, it is particularly important to ensure that tight control is exercised over costs. Otherwise the gap between total sales revenue and total costs (i.e. the profit) will be insufficient to ensure an adequate return on capital employed.

In some cases the demand for goods is *inelastic* – i.e. price has little or no effect on the number of units sold. The demand for writing paper and stationery, for example, tends to be inelastic, probably because it is an infrequent purchase and it is not a significant element in most people's budgets. So when the demand for goods is inelastic, suppliers have much more freedom in determining their own selling prices and they may then base them on cost.

Cost-based pricing

There are a number of cost-based pricing methods. We summarize the main ones below and the circumstances in which they are most likely to be used.

- *Below variable cost.* This price would be used:
  - when an entity was trying to establish a new product on the market;
  - when an attempt was being made to drive out competitors;
  - as a loss leader, i.e. to encourage other goods to be bought.

  A price at this level could only be sustained for a very short period (unless it is used as a loss leader) since each unit sold would not be covering its variable cost.
- *At variable cost.* Variable cost prices may be used:
  - to launch a new product;
  - to drive out competition;
  - in difficult trading conditions;
  - as a loss leader; price could be held for some time but ultimately some contribution will be needed to cover the fixed costs.
- *At total production cost.* This will include the unit's direct costs and a share of the production overheads. Prices at this level could be held for some time (perhaps when demand is low) but eventually the entity would need to cover its non-production overheads and to make a profit.
- *At total cost.* This will include the direct cost and a share of both the production and non-production overheads. Again, such prices could be held for a very long period, perhaps during a long recession, but eventually some profit would need to be earned.
- *At cost plus.* The cost-plus method would either relate to total production cost or to total cost. The 'plus' element would be an addition to the cost to allow for non-production overhead and profit (in the case of total production cost) and for profit alone (in the case of total cost). In the long run, cost-plus prices are the only option for a profit-making entity. However, if prices are based entirely on cost then inefficiencies may be automatically built into the pricing system and this could lead to uncompetitiveness.

Activity 18.4   Make a list of all the factors that you think may determine the demand for a product.

Transfer pricing

Transfer pricing problems

Dixons (DGS International) has been informed that it is in breach of HM Revenue and Custom transfer pricing guidelines and it may have to pay back hundreds of millions of pounds. Transfer pricing relates to the value placed on assets or goods moved internally from one subsidiary to another – usually across international borders. HMRC pursues cases where it believes the price has been set artificially low for tax purposes.

Source: Adapted from www.accountancyage.com/articles/print/2240985, 23 April 2009.

In large entities it is quite common for one segment to trade with another segment. So what is 'revenue' to one segment will be 'expenditure' to the other. This means that when the results of all the various segments are consolidated, the revenue recorded in one segment's books of account will cancel out the expenditure in the other segment's books. Does it matter, therefore, what prices are charged for internal transfers?

The answer is 'Yes it does' because some segments (particularly if they are divisions of companies) are given a great deal of autonomy. They may have the authority, for example, to purchase goods and services from outside the entity. They almost certainly will do so if the price and service offered externally appears to be superior to any internal offer and this may cause them to suboptimize, i.e. to act in *their* own best interest although it may not be in the best interests of the entity as a whole.

Let us suppose that segment A fixes its transfer price on a cost-plus basis, say at £10 per unit. Segment B finds that it can purchase an identical unit externally at £8 per unit. Segment B is very likely to accept the external offer. But segment A's costs may be based on *absorbed costs*. The *extra cost* (i.e. the variable cost) of meeting segment B's order may be much less than the external price of £8 per unit. In these circumstances it may not be beneficial for the *entity as a whole* for segment B to purchase the units from an outside supplier.

It follows that a transfer price should to be set at a level that will encourage a supplying segment to trade internally and to discourage a receiving segment to buy its goods externally. There are various transfer-pricing methods that can be adopted (see Figure 18.5). We review the main ones below.

- *Market price.* If there are identical or similar goods and services offered externally, transfer prices based on market prices will neither encourage nor discourage supplying or receiving segments to trade externally.
- *Adjusted market price.* Market prices may be reduced in recognition of the lower costs attached to internal trading, e.g. advertising, administration and financing costs. This method encourages segments to trade with each other.
- *Total cost or total cost plus.* A transfer price based on total cost will include the direct costs plus a share of both production and non-production overhead. Total cost-plus methods allow for some profit. The main problems attached to the total-cost methods is that they build inefficiencies into the transfer price (as there is no incentive to control costs) and they therefore encourage suboptimization.

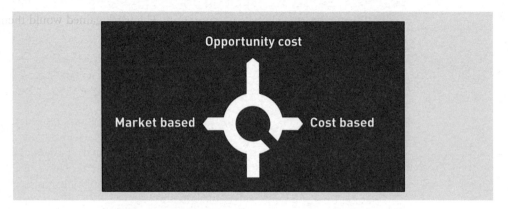

Figure 18.5 Transfer pricing decision

- *At variable cost or variable cost plus.* The variable cost method itself does not encourage a supplying segment to trade internally as no incentive is built into the transfer price, but a percentage addition may provide some incentive since it enables some contribution to be made towards fixed costs. However, transfer prices based on variable costs may be very attractive to *receiving* segments as the transfer price normally compares favourably with the external price. If the variable cost method is adopted it is recommended that it is based on the *standard* variable cost.
- *Negotiated price.* This method involves striking a bargain between the supplying and receiving segments based on a combination of market price and costs. As long as the discussions are mutually determined this method can be highly successful.
- *Opportunity cost.* This method may be somewhat impractical, but if the costs can be quantified it is the ideal one to adopt. A transfer price based on the opportunity cost comprises two elements: first, the standard variable cost in the supplying segment, and second the entity's opportunity cost resulting from the transaction. It is the second element that is the hardest to determine.

Activity 18.5

What is the best way out of the transfer price dilemma? Should it be based on market prices or on costs? Suppose as a manager you have the freedom to negotiate your own transfer prices with other divisional managers. Summarize the arguments that you would use in any ensuing discussions.

Special orders

On some occasions an entity may be asked to undertake an order beyond its normal trading arrangement and to quote a price for it. Such arrangements are known as *special orders*. The potential customer or client would normally expect to pay a lower price than the entity ordinarily charges, as well as possibly receiving some favourable treatment. What pricing policy should the entity adopt when asked to quote for a special order? Much will depend on whether it has some surplus capacity. If this is the case, it may be prepared to quote a price below variable cost if it wants to avoid a possible shutdown. However, the minimum price that it would *normally* be willing to accept would be equal to the incremental (or extra) cost of accepting the order.

The incremental cost involved may be the equivalent of the variable cost. Prices based at or below the variable cost would be extremely competitive, thereby helping to ensure that the customer accepted the quotation. The work gained would then absorb some of the entity's surplus capacity and help to keep its workforce occupied. There is also the possibility that the customer may place future orders at prices that would enable the entity to make a profit on them. But there is then the danger that in the meantime more profitable work has to be rejected because the entity cannot cope with both the special order and the additional work.

A price in excess of the variable cost would make a contribution towards fixed costs and this would clearly be the preferred option. The quoted price would have to be judged very finely because the higher the price the greater the risk that the customer would reject the quotation. So the decision would involve trying to determine what other suppliers are likely to charge and what terms they would offer.

An indication of the difficulties associated with determining whether a special order should be accepted is demonstrated in Example 18.4.

Example 18.4	**A special order**

Amber Limited has been asked by a customer to supply a specially designed product. The customer has indicated that he would be willing to pay a maximum price of £100 per unit. The cost details are as follows.

Unit cost	£	£
Contract price		100
Less: Variable costs		
Direct materials	40	
Direct labour (2 hours)	30	
Variable overhead	10	80
Contribution		20

At a contract price of £100 per unit, each unit would make a contribution of £20. The customer is prepared to take 400 units, and so the total contribution towards fixed costs would be £8000 (400 units × £20). However, Amber has a shortage of direct labour and some of the staff would have to be switched from other orders to work on the special order. This would mean an average loss in contribution of £8 for every direct labour hour worked on the special order.

Required:
Determine whether Amber Limited should accept the special order.

Answer to Example 18.4

In order to determine whether Amber Limited should accept the special order, the extra contribution should be compared with the loss of contribution by having to switch the workforce from other orders. The calculations are as follows.

	£
Total contribution from the special order (400 units × £20 per unit)	8 000
Less: the opportunity cost of the normal contribution foregone	
[800 direct labour hours (400 units × 2 DLH) × £8 per unit]	6 400
Extra contribution	1 600

Tutorial notes

Before coming to a decision, the following points should also be considered. You will see that they range well beyond simple cost factors.

1 The costings relating to the special order should be carefully checked.

2 The customer should be asked to confirm in writing that it would be willing to pay a selling price of £100 per unit.

3 Determine whether the customer is likely to place additional orders for the product or not.

4 Check that the *average* contribution of £8 per direct labour hour, obtained from other orders, applies to the workforce that would be switched to the special order, i.e. is the contribution from the other orders that would be lost more or less than £8 per direct labour hour?

5 Is it possible that new staff could be recruited to work on the special order?

6 Is more profitable work likely to come along in the meantime? Would it mean that it could not be accepted during the progress of the order?

Recommendation

Assuming that the points raised in the above notes are satisfied, then the recommendation would be to accept the special order at a price of £100 per unit. This would mean that Amber's total contribution would be increased by £1600.

The management accountant's main role in dealing with special orders would be to supply historical and projected cost data of the financial consequences of particular options. The eventual decision would be taken by senior management using a wide range of quantitative and qualitative information. The type of questions asked would be similar to some of the issues covered in the tutorial notes in the solution to Example 18.4.

Activity 18.6

The country is experiencing a deep recession. Trade is very bad. Then, rather unexpectedly, Company X is asked to supply one of its main products to a new customer, but unfortunately at a price well below the product's variable cost. In two adjacent columns list (a) all the reasons why it should accept the order; and (b) why it should be rejected. Overall, what would be your decision?

! Questions you should ask

The questions that you should put to your accountants about any specific decision-making problem will revolve round the robustness of the data that they have used and any non-quantitative factors they have incorporated into their recommendations. You could use the following questions as a guide.

- Where have you got the data from?
- How reliable are the basic facts?
- What assumptions have you adopted?
- Have you included only relevant costs?
- Have you tested the results on a probability basis?
- What non-quantitative factors have you been able to identify?
- Is it possible to put any monetary value on them?
- Do you think that we should go ahead with this proposal?

Conclusion

An important function of the management accountant in the twenty-first century is to assist in managerial decision making. In such a role the primary task of the accountant is to provide managers with financial and non-financial information in order to help them make more effective decisions. Although the information provided may include much historical data, decision making often means dealing with future events, so the information provided consists of a great deal of speculative material. This means that the management accountant needs to exercise considerable skill and judgement in collecting information that is both accurate and relevant for a particular purpose. Non-relevant information can be ignored as it only obscures the broader picture.

The significance of including only relevant data is seen when managers have to make special decisions, such as whether to close or shut down a segment of an entity, make or provide goods and services internally instead of obtaining them from an outside supplier, determine a selling price for the entity's goods and services, or whether to accept a special order and at what price. These are all-important and complex decisions and managers need reliable information before they can make them.

Key points

1 Decision making involves having to resolve an outcome for a specific problem.

2 The information required relates to the future, it is specific to the problem, it may have to be collected specially for the task and it is geared towards estimating the future net cash flows of particular outcomes.

3 The information provided to management should include only relevant costs and revenues, with an estimate of any opportunity costs.

4 The data used in a management accounting information report should be subject to some probability testing.

5 The terms 'fixed and variable costs', 'relevant and non-relevant costs', 'avoidable and non-avoidable costs', 'sunk costs', 'committed costs' and 'opportunity costs' are all of special significance in decision making.

6 Closure and shutdown decisions should be based on the contribution earned or likely to be earned on the segment under consideration and compared with the likely closure or shutdown costs.

7 Generally it is more profitable to make goods or to provide services internally than to obtain them externally if their variable cost is less than or equal to external prices.

8 The pricing of goods and services for selling externally will normally be determined by the market price for similar goods and services. In some cases, however, selling prices can be based on cost. Depending on market conditions, the cost could be at or below variable cost, the absorbed or the total absorbed cost, with or without an addition for profit.

9 The internal transfer of goods and services should be based on market price or adjusted market price. Where this is not possible, any price at or in excess of the variable cost should be acceptable.

➡

Key points
continued

10 The ideal transfer price is one that is based on the standard variable cost in the supplying segment plus the entity's opportunity cost resulting from the transaction.

11 Special orders should be priced so that they cover their variable cost. There may be some circumstances when it is acceptable to price them below variable cost but this can only be a short-term solution. Any price in excess of variable costs helps to cover the entity's fixed costs.

12 Cost and financial factors are only part of the decision-making process. There are other factors of a non-financial and non-quantifiable nature (such as behavioural factors) that must be taken into account.

Check your learning

1 Define what is meant by a 'decision'.

2 List seven main characteristics of decision-making data.

3 Identify six ways of classifying costs.

4 What is an opportunity cost?

5 What is meant by a closure or a shutdown decision?

6 What is meant by a make or buy decision?

7 What is meant by a pricing decision?

8 What are the two main types of pricing decisions?

9 What is meant by a market price?

10 List six cost-based pricing methods.

11 What is the basic problem in determining pricing between segments within the same entity?

12 How might it be resolved?

13 What is meant by a special order?

14 How does it differ from the general pricing problem?

News story quiz

Remember the news story at the beginning of this chapter? Go back to that story and reread it before answering the following questions.

At times of economic difficulty companies seek to cut their costs. This often means making staff redundant but, as this article points out, this may not always be the best decision.

Questions

1 If your company was facing economic difficulty where would you first look to cut costs?

2 Assuming that you had to cut employment costs what options would you consider before making staff redundant?

3 What longer-term factors would have to be taken into account before you opted for redundancies?

Tutorial questions

The answers to questions marked with an asterisk can be found in Appendix 4.

18.1 This chapter has emphasized that it is managers that make decisions and not management accountants. How far do you agree with this assertion?

18.2 Many of the solutions to the problems posed in this chapter depend on being able to isolate the variable cost associated with a particular decision. In practice, is it realistic to expect that such costs can be readily identified and measured?

18.3 Assume that you were an IT manager in a large entity and that the services that you provide are made available to both internal and external parties. Specify how you would go about negotiating an appropriate fee for services sought by other departments within the entity.

18.4* Micro Limited has some spare capacity. It is now considering whether it should accept a special contract to use some of the spare capacity. However, this contract will use some specialist direct labour that is in short supply. The following details relate to the proposed contract:

	£000
Contract price	50
Variable costs:	
Direct materials	10
Direct labour	30

In order to complete the contract, 4000 direct labour hours would be required. The company's budget for the year during which the contract would be undertaken is as follows:

	£000
Sales	750
Variable costs	(500)
Contribution	250
Fixed costs	(230)
Profit	20

There would be 50,000 direct labour hours available during the year.

Required:

Determine whether the special contract should be accepted.

18.5* Temple Limited has been offered two new contracts, the details of which are as follows:

Contract	(1)	(2)
	£000	£000
Contract price	1000	2100
Direct materials	300	600
Direct labour	300	750
Variable overhead	100	250
Fixed overhead	100	200
	800	1800
Profit	200	300
Direct materials required (kilos)	50000	100000
Direct labour hours required	10000	25000

Note:

The fixed overhead has been apportioned on the basis of direct labour cost. Temple is a one-product firm. Its budgeted cost per unit for its normal work for the year to 31 December 2012 is summarized below.

	£
Sales	6000
Direct materials (100 kilos)	700
Direct labour (200 hours)	3000
Variable overhead	300
Fixed overhead	1000
	5000
Profit	1000

The company would only have the capacity to accept one of the new contracts. Unfortunately, materials suitable for use in all of its work are in short supply and the company has estimated that only 200,000 kilos would be available during the year to December 2012. Even more worrying is the shortage of skilled labour, only 100,000 direct labour hours are expected to be available during the year. The good news is that there may be an upturn in the market for its normal contract work.

Required:

Calculate

(a) the contribution per unit of each limiting factor for
    (i)   the company's normal work
    (ii) Contract 1
    (iii) Contract 2.
(b) The company's maximum contribution for the year to 31 December 2012, assuming that it accepts either Contract 1 or Contract 2.

18.6 Agra Limited has been asked to quote a price for a special contract. The details are as follows:

1 The specification required a quotation for 100,000 units.
2 The direct costs per unit for the order would be: materials £3, labour £15, distribution £12.

3 Additional production and non-production overhead would amount to £500,000, although £100,000 could be saved if the order was for less than 100,000 units.
4 Agra's normal profit margin is 20 per cent of total cost.

Required:
Recommend a minimum selling price if the order was for:
(a) 100,000 units
(b) 80,000 units.

18.7 Foo Limited has been asked to quote for a special order. The details are as follows:

1 Prices are to be quoted at order levels of 50,000, 100,000 and 150,000 units respectively. Foo has some surplus capacity and it could deal with up to 160,000 units.
2 Each unit would cost £2 for direct materials, and £12 for direct labour.
3 Foo normally absorbs production and non-production overhead on the basis of 200 per cent and 100 per cent respectively of the direct labour cost.
4 Distribution costs are expected to be £10 per unit.
5 Foo's normal profit margin is 20 per cent of the total cost. However, it is prepared to reduce this margin to 15 per cent if the order is for 100,000 units, and to 10 per cent for an order of 150,000 units.
6 The additional non-production overhead associated with this contract would be £200,000, although this would be cut by £25,000 if the output dropped below 100,000 units.

Required:
Suggest
(a) a selling price per unit that Foo Limited might charge if the contract was for 50,000, 100,000 and 150,000 units respectively;
(b) the profit that it could expect to make at these levels.

18.8 Bamboo Limited is a highly specialist firm of central heating suppliers operating exclusively in the textiles industry. It has recently been asked to tender for a contract for a prospective customer. The following details relate to the proposed contract.

1 Materials:
   ● £20,000 of materials would need to be purchased.
   ● £10,000 of materials would need to be transferred from another contract (these materials would need to be replaced).
   ● Some obsolete stock would be used. The stock had originally cost £18,000. Its current disposable value is £4000.
2 The contract would involve labour costs of £60,000, of which £30,000 would be incurred regardless of whether the contract was undertaken.
3 The production manager will have to work several evenings a week during the progress of the contract. He is paid a salary of £30,000 per year, and on successful completion of the contract he would receive a bonus of £5000.
4 Additional administrative expenses incurred in undertaking the contract are estimated to be £1000.
5 The company absorbs its fixed overheads at a rate of £10 per machine hour. The contract will require 2000 machine hours.

Required:
Calculate the minimum contract price that would be acceptable to Bamboo Limited.

18.9 Dynasty Limited has been involved in a research project (code named DNY) for a number of months. There is some doubt as to whether the project should be completed. If it is, then it is expected that DNY will require another 12 months' work. The following information relates to the project.

1 Costs incurred to date are £500,000.

2 Sales proceeds if the project continues will be £600,000.

3 Direct material costs amount to £200,000. The type of material required for DNY had already been purchased for another project, and it would cost £20,000 to dispose of it.

4 Direct labour costs have come to £150,000. The direct labour used on DNY is highly skilled and it is not easy to recruit the type of staff required. In order to undertake DNY, some staff would have to be transferred from other projects. This would mean that there was a total loss in contribution from such projects of £350,000.

5 Research staff costs amount to £200,000. The staff would be made redundant at the end of project DNY at a cost of £115,000. If they were to be made redundant now, there would be a cost of £100,000.

6 The company can invest surplus cash at a rate of return of 10 per cent per annum.

7 Non-production overhead budgeted to be apportioned to DNY for the forthcoming 12 months amounts to £60,000.

Required:

Determine whether or not the DNY project should continue.

Further practice questions, study material and links to relevant sites on the World Wide Web can be found on the website that accompanies this book. The site can be found at **www.pearsoned.co.uk/dyson**

Fixing the roof

Does IT work: Shopkeepers need to show their agility

Stephen Pritchard

Consumer spending figures are flat in the UK and a report by consultancies PwC and Retail Forward published last month predicted that retail sales in the US would be flat, or even negative, this year.

The poor outlook has hit capital spending plans. Gartner, the IT industry research firm, estimates that half the world's top 10 retailers will cut their capital spending plans in half.

But at the same time, there are pockets of investment. Again according to Gartner, 'cash-rich' companies are poised to make significant investments. And retailers across the board are looking to technology as a way of cutting costs, winning new business or exploiting gaps in the market left by others.

'Many retailers have slashed their capital spending by between 30 and 70 per cent,' says John Davidson, joint author of the Gartner report. 'They are also scaling back on the number of projects.'

There are two challenges for retailers – and especially those with large physical estates.

The first is that consumer spending overall is down, and the prospect of deflation in a number of markets is making consumers cautious about parting with their cash

The second challenge is to compete with leaner online outlets with lower fixed overheads, lower staff costs and often, more attractive customer service. So-called 'multi-channel' strategies, for example, where retailers allow customers to order goods online but collect them from a store, have tended to add to the shopkeeper's costs.

www.ft.com, 13 May 2009.

Source: Reproduced with permission of *The Financial Times*.

Questions relating to this news story can be found on pages 440–441 ➡

About this chapter

This is the third chapter in Part 4 of the book dealing with management accounting decision making. It explains how various calculative techniques can help management select a particular investment. Accountants call this exercise *capital investment appraisal*. The chapter also explores the main sources of external short-, medium- and long-term finance available for the financing of a project once it has been selected.

By the end of this chapter, you should be able to:

- describe what is meant by capital investment appraisal;
- identify five capital investment appraisal techniques;
- incorporate such techniques into quantitative examples;
- recognize the significance of such techniques;
- list the main external sources of financing capital investment projects.

! Why this chapter is important

As a junior manager you may be involved in capital investment decisions. At this stage of your career not much money will be involved and all you might be doing is deciding which one of two filing cabinets your section should buy. As you become more senior, the projects will become bigger and perhaps cost millions of pounds. You will have to decide which to go for and how they should be financed.

Such decision making will involve a consideration of various projects on both a quantitative and a qualitative basis. Your accountants will process the data for you, and they may use one of the techniques discussed in this chapter. They will then present you with the results. It is extremely unlikely that you will be involved in the detailed number crunching but in order to make a decision about which project you should select you will need to question your accountants about their recommendations.

You will not be able to do so with any confidence unless you have some knowledge of their methods. This chapter provides you with the basic material. After studying it you will be in a much better position to make your own capital investment decisions and not just do what your accountants tell you to do.

Background

News clip

Capital expenditure cut

In order to improve its performance Punch Taverns is to undergo a cut-price makeover even though it is short of cash.

In order to help pay for it Punch has announced a 20% cut in its capital expenditure budget.

Source: Adapted from *The Observer Business and Media*, 26 April 2009, p. 2.

Accountants make a distinction between *capital* expenditure and *revenue* expenditure. Expenditure of a capital nature provides a benefit to an entity for more than a year. Revenue expenditure does so for only one year and it has to be renewed if the benefit is to be continued.

Besides its long-term nature some other features of capital expenditure may be distinguished. They include the following:

- its purpose is to help the entity achieve its long-term objectives;
- it will often involve huge sums of money being spent on major projects;
- it may have a considerable impact on how many staff the entity employs and how they react;
- the benefits may be spread over very many years;
- it is difficult to assess precisely what those benefits will be.

All entities would find it difficult to survive if they did not invest in some form of capital expenditure from time to time, and they certainly would not be able to grow and to develop. Plant and machinery will begin to wear out and become obsolete, for example, while in the longer term buildings will need to be replaced. In addition many entities have to set aside resources for projects that do not relate directly to their main business, such as the provision of leisure and social facilities for their employees.

All entities, whether public or private, usually have to select from a long list of possible capital investment projects because they certainly will not have either the time or the resources to do them all at once. So which should they choose? And how should they be financed? This chapter begins to answer these sort of questions.

Main methods

News clip

Off the balance sheet

A European accounting standard means that many of the government's capital expenditure projects will be able to be kept 'off the books'. This means that many hospitals, clinics, schools, waste and local authority projects can continue to be built under private finance initiatives (PFIs) without counting against the government's capital expenditure totals.

Source: Adapted from www.ft.com/cms/s, 13 May 2009.

In this section we are going to examine the main methods used in capital investment (CI) appraisal. We will assume that we are dealing mainly with profit-making entities. Such entities will expect all their projects to make a profit except for those undertaken on health, social and welfare grounds (these types of project are particularly difficult to assess). There are five main techniques that accountants can use in CI appraisal. They are shown in diagrammatic form in Figure 19.1 and we examine each of them in the following subsections.

Payback

The payback method is an attempt to estimate how long it would take before a project begins to pay for itself. For example, if a company was going to spend £300,000 on

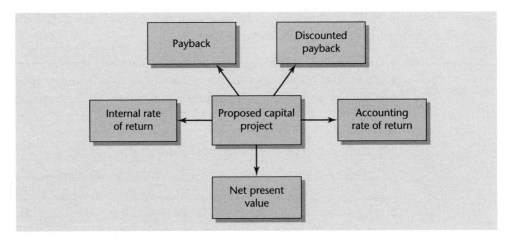

Figure 19.1 Capital investment appraisal methods

purchasing some new plant, the accountant would calculate how many years it would take before £300,000 had been paid back in cash. The recovery of an investment in a project is usually measured in terms of *net cash flow*. This is the difference between cash received and cash paid during a defined period of time. In order to adopt this method the following information is required:

- Total cost of the investment.
- Amount of cash instalment payable on the investment.
- Accounting periods in which the instalments will be paid.
- Cash receipts and any other cash payments connected with the project.
- Accounting periods in which they fall.

As the payback measures the rate of recovery of the original investment in terms of net cash flow, it follows that non-cash items (such as depreciation and profits and losses on sales of fixed assets) are not taken into account.

The payback method is illustrated in Example 19.1.

Example 19.1	**The payback method**

Miln Limited is considering investing in some new machinery. The following information has been prepared to support the project:

	£000	£000
Cost of machinery		20
Expected net cash flow:		
Year 1	1	
2	4	
3	5	
4	10	
5	10	30
Net profitability		10

Required:
Calculate the prospective investment's payback period.

Answer to Example 19.1

The payback period is as follows:

			£000
	Cumulative net cash flow:		
Year	1		1
	2	(£1 000 + £4 000)	5
	3	(£5 000 + £5 000)	10
	4	(£10 000 + £10 000)	20
	5	(£20 000 + £10 000)	30

The investment will, therefore, have paid for itself at the end of the fourth year. At that stage £20,000 will have been received back from the project in terms of net cash flow and that sum would be equal to the original cost of the project.

As can be seen from Example 19.1 the payback method is a fairly straightforward technique, but it does have several disadvantages. These are as follows:

- An estimate has to be made of the amount and the timing of cash instalments due to be paid on an original investment.
- It is difficult to calculate the net cash flows and the period in which they will be received.
- There is a danger that projects with the shortest payback periods may be chosen even if they are not as profitable as projects with a longer payback period. The payback method only measures cash flow; it does not measure profitability.
- The total amount of the overall investment is ignored and comparisons made between different projects may result in misleading conclusions. A project with an initial investment of £10,000 may have a shorter payback period than one with an initial investment of £100,000, although in the long run the larger investment may prove more profitable.
- The technique ignores any net cash flows received after the payback period.
- The timing of the cash flows is not taken into account: £1 received now is preferable to £1 received in five years' time. So a project with a short payback period may recover most of its investment towards the end of its payback period while another project with a longer payback period may recover most of the original investment in the first few years. There is clearly less risk in accepting a project that recovers most of its cost very quickly than in accepting one where the benefits are deferred.

Irrespective of these disadvantages, the payback method has something to be said for it. While it may appear to be rather simplistic, it does help managers to compare projects and to think in terms of how long it takes before a project has recovered its original cost.

Activity 19.1

What do you think about the simple payback method? Tick the appropriate column.

	True	False
(a) It is easy to understand.		
(b) It is too simple.		
(c) It is good enough for most capital investment decisions.		

Discounted payback

The simple payback method ignores the timing of net cash receipts but this problem can be overcome by *discounting* the net cash receipts. You will probably be familiar with discounting in your everyday life. You know, for example, that if you put £91 into the building society and the rate of interest is 10% per annum, your original investment will be worth about £100 [£91 + £9 (10% × £91)] at the end of the year. We could look at this example from another point of view. Assuming a rate of interest of 10% per annum, what amount of money do you have to invest in the building society in order to have £100 at the end of the year? The answer is, of course, £91 (ignoring the odd 10p). In other words, £91 received now is about the same as £100 received in a year's time. This is what is meant by *discounting*. The procedure is as follows:

1 Calculate the future net cash flows.
2 Select an appropriate rate of interest.
3 Multiply the net cash flows by a discount factor.

The discount factor will depend on the cost of borrowing money. In the case of the building society example above, the discount factor is based on a rate of interest of 10%. The factor itself is 0.9091, i.e. £100 × 0.9091 = £90.91. To check: take the £90.91 and add the year's interest, i.e. £90.91 × 10% = £9.091 + £90.91 = £100.00. You will not have to calculate discount factors as they are readily available in tables. We include one in Appendix 2 on page 478 of this book.

In order to confirm that you understand the point about discounting, turn to Appendix 2. Look along the top line for the appropriate rate of interest: in our case it is 10%. Work down the 10% column until you come to the line opposite the year (shown in the left-hand column) in which the cash would be received. In our example, the cash is going to be received in one year's time, so it is not necessary to go further than the first line. The present value of £1 receivable in a year's time is, therefore, 0.9091, or £90.91 if £100 is to be received in a year's time.

Activity 19.2	Assuming a rate of interest of 15% per annum, what is the present value of £200 receivable in two years' time?

We can now show you how the discounted payback method works. We do so in Example 19.2.

Example 19.2	**The discounted payback method**

Newland City Council has investigated the possibility of investing in a new project, and the following information has been obtained:

	£000	£000
Total cost of project		500
Expected net cash flows:		
Year 1	20	
2	50	
3	100	
4	200	
5	300	
6	30	700
Net return		200

Required:
Assuming a rate of interest of 8%, calculate the project's overall return using the following methods:
(a) payback
(b) discounted payback.

Answer to Example 19.2

(a) Payback method

Year	Net cash flow	Cumulative net cash flow
	£000	£000
0	(500)	(500)
1	20	(480)
2	50	(430)
3	100	(330)
4	200	(130)
5	300	170
6	30	200

Calculation:
After 4 years the total cash flows received = £370,000 (£20,000 + 50,000 + 100,000 + 200,000). The £30,000 still necessary to equal the original cost of the investment (£500,000 – 370,000) will be met part way through Year 5, i.e. (£130,000 ÷ 300,000) × 12 months = 5.2 months. So the payback period is about 4 years and 5 months (41 months), assuming that the net cash flows accrue evenly throughout the year.

(b) Discounted payback

Year	Net cash flow	Discount factors	Present value at 8% [Column (2) × Column (3)]	Cumulative present value
(1)	(2)	(3)	(4)	(5)
	£000		£000	£000
0	(500)	1.0000	(500)	(500)
1	20	0.9259	19	(481)
2	50	0.8573	43	(438)
3	100	0.7938	79	(359)
4	200	0.7350	147	(212)
5	300	0.6806	204	(8)
6	30	0.6302	19	11

Calculation:
Using the discounted payback method, the project would recover all of its original cost during Year 6. Assuming that the net cash flows accrue evenly, this would be about the end of the fifth month because (£8000 ÷ 19,000) × 12 months = 5.1 months. So the discounted payback period is about 5 years 5 months (65 months).

The discounted payback method has the following advantages.

● Relatively easy to understand.
● Not too difficult to compute.
● Focuses on the cash recovery of an investment.
● Allows for the fact that cash received now may be worth more than cash receivable in the future.

- Takes more of the net cash flows into account than is the case with the simple payback method because the discounted payback period is always longer than the simple payback method.
- Enables a clear-cut decision to be taken, since a project is acceptable if the discounted net cash flow throughout its life exceeds the cost of the original investment.

However, like the simple payback method, it has some disadvantages.

- Sometimes difficult to estimate the amount and timing of instalments due to be paid on the original investment.
- Difficult to estimate the amount and timing of future net cash receipts and other payments.
- Not easy to determine an appropriate rate of interest.
- Net cash flows received after the payback period are ignored.

Irrespective of these disadvantages, the discounted payback method can be usefully and readily adopted by those entities that do not employ staff specially trained in capital investment appraisal techniques.

Activity 19.3	On balance do you think that the discounted payback method (a) is more helpful than the payback method in capital investment appraisal; and (b) is relatively easy to understand?

(a) Yes [ ]   No [ ]   (b) Yes [ ]   No [ ]

Accounting rate of return

The *accounting rate of return* (ARR) method attempts to compare the *profit* of a project with the capital invested in it. It is usually expressed as a percentage. The formula is as follows:

$$ARR = \frac{profit}{capital\ employed} \times 100$$

Two important problems arise from this definition.

- *Definition of profit.* Normally, the average annual net profit earned by a project would be used. However, as explained in earlier chapters, accounting profit can be subject to a number of different assumptions and distortions (e.g. depreciation, taxation and inflation) and so it is relatively easy to arrive at different profit levels depending on the accounting policies adopted. The most common definition is to take profit before interest and taxation. The profit included in the equation would then be a simple average of the profit that the project earns over its entire life.
- *Definition of capital employed.* The capital employed could be either the initial capital employed in the project or the average capital employed over its life.

So, depending on the definitions adopted, the ARR may be calculated in one of two ways:

- Using the original capital employed:

$$ARR = \frac{average\ annual\ net\ profit\ before\ interest\ and\ taxation}{initial\ capital\ employed\ on\ the\ project} \times 100$$

● Using the average capital employed:

$$ARR = \frac{\text{average annual net profit before interest and taxation}}{\text{average annual capital employed on the project}^{*}} \times 100$$

$$^{*} \frac{\text{Initial capital employed + residual value}}{2}$$

The two methods are illustrated in Example 19.3.

| Example 19.3 | **The accounting rate of return method** |

Bridge Limited is considering investing in a new project, the details of which are as follows:

Project life		*5 years*
	£000	*£000*
Project cost		50
Estimated net profit:		
Year 1	12	
2	18	
3	30	
4	25	
5	5	
Total net profit	90	

The estimated residual value of the project at the end of Year 5 is £10,000.

Required:
Calculate the accounting rate of return of the proposed new project using:
(a) the original capital employed
(b) the average capital employed.

Answer to Example 19.3

The accounting rate of return would be calculated as follows:

(a) *Using the initial capital employed*:

$$\frac{\text{Average annual net profits}}{\text{Cost of the investment}} \times 100$$

Average annual net profits = £18 000 (£90 000/5)

$$\therefore \text{Accounting rate of return} = \frac{£18\,000}{50\,000} \times 100 = \underline{36\%}$$

(b) *Using the average capital employed*:

$$\frac{\text{Average annual net profits}}{\text{Average capital employed}} \times 100$$

$$= \frac{£18\,000}{\frac{1}{2}(£50\,000 + 10\,000)} \times 100 = \underline{60\%}$$

Like the payback and discounted payback methods, the accounting rate of return method has several advantages and disadvantages.

Advantages
- Compatible with a similar accounting ratio used in financial accounting.
- Relatively easy to understand.
- Not difficult to compute.
- Draws attention to the notion of overall profit.

Disadvantages
- Net profit can be subject to different definitions, e.g. it might or it might not include the depreciation on the project.
- Not always clear whether the original cost of the investment should be used, or whether it is more appropriate to substitute an average for the amount of capital invested in the project.
- Use of a residual value in calculating the average amount of capital employed means that the higher the residual value, the lower the ARR. For example, with no residual value, the ARR on a project costing £100,000 and an average net profit of £50,000 would be 100%, i.e.:

$$\frac{£50\,000}{\frac{1}{2} \times (100\,000 + 0)} \times 100 = \underline{100\%}$$

With a residual value of (say) £10,000, the ARR would be 90.9%, i.e.:

$$\frac{£50\,000}{\frac{1}{2} \times (100\,000 + 10\,000)} \times 100 = \underline{90.9\%}$$

The estimation of residual values is very difficult but it can make all the difference between one project and another.

- Gives no guidance on what is an acceptable rate of return.
- Benefit of earning a high proportion of the total profit in the early years of the project is not allowed for.
- Method does not take into account the time value of money.

Irrespective of these disadvantages, the ARR method may be suitable where very similar short-term projects are being considered.

Activity 19.4	What are your views on the accounting rate of return capital investment appraisal method? Tick the box that best reflects your own views.
	(a) Useless [ ] (b) Could be of some help [ ] (c) Extremely useful [ ]

Net present value

Unlike the payback and ARR capital investment appraisal methods, the net present value (NPV) method does take into account the time value of money. In summary the procedure is as follows.

1 Calculate the annual net cash flows expected to arise from the project.
2 Select an appropriate rate of interest, or required rate of return.
3 Obtain the discount factors appropriate to the chosen rate of interest or rate of return.
4 Multiply the annual net cash flow by the appropriate discount factors.
5 Add together the present values for each of the net cash flows.
6 Compare the total net present value with the initial outlay.
7 Accept the project if the total NPV is positive.

Example 19.4 illustrates this procedure.

Example 19.4

The net present value method

Rage Limited is considering two capital investment projects. The details are outlined as follows:

Project	1	2
Estimated life	3 years	5 years
Commencement date	1.1.01	1.1.01
	£000	£000
Project cost at year 1	100	100

Estimated net cash flows:

Year:	1	20	10
	2	80	40
	3	40	40
	4	–	40
	5	–	20
		140	150

The company expects a rate of return of 10% per annum on its capital employed.

Required:
Using the net present value method of project appraisal, assess which project would be more profitable.

Answer to Example 19.4

Rage Ltd

Project appraisal:

	Project 1			Project 2		
Year	Net cash flow	Discount factor	Present value	Net cash flow	Discount factor	Present value
(1)	(2)	(3)	(4)	(5)	(6)	(7)
	£	10%	£	£	10%	£
1	20 000	0.9091	18 182	10 000	0.9091	9 091
2	80 000	0.8264	66 112	40 000	0.8264	33 056
3	40 000	0.7513	30 052	40 000	0.7513	30 052
4	–	–	–	40 000	0.6830	27 320
5	–	–	–	20 000	0.6209	12 418
Total present value			114 346			111 937
Less: Initial cost			100 000			100 000
Net present value			14 346			11 937

Tutorial notes

1 The net cash flows and the discount factor of 10% (i.e. the rate of return) were given in the question.

2 The discount factors may be obtained from the discount table in Appendix 2.

3 Column (4) has been calculated by multiplying column (2) by column (3).

4 Column (7) has been calculated by multiplying column (5) by column 6.

Both projects have a positive NPV, but project 1 will probably be chosen in preference to project 2 because it has a higher NPV, even though its total net cash flow of £140,000 is less than the total net cash flow of £150,000 for project 2.

The advantages and disadvantages of the NPV method are as follows:

Advantages
- Use of net cash flows emphasizes the importance of liquidity.
- Different accounting policies are not relevant as they do not affect the calculation of the net cash flows.
- Time value of money is taken into account.
- Easy to compare the NPV of different projects and to reject projects that do not have an acceptable NPV.

Disadvantages
- Difficulties may be incurred in estimating the initial cost of the project and the time periods in which instalments must be paid back (although this is a common problem in CI appraisal).
- Difficult to estimate accurately the net cash flow for each year of the project's life. This is a problem that is again common to most other methods of project appraisal.
- Not easy to select an appropriate rate of interest. The rate of interest is sometimes referred to as the *cost of capital*, i.e. the cost of financing an investment. One rate that could be chosen is that rate which the company could earn if it decided to invest the funds outside the business (the external rate of interest). Alternatively an internal rate of interest could be chosen. This rate would be based on an estimate of what return the company expects to earn on its existing investments. In the long run, if the internal rate of return is lower than the external rate then it would appear more profitable to liquidate the company and invest the funds elsewhere. A local authority does not have the same difficulty because it would probably use a rate of interest set by central government.

NPV is considered to be a highly acceptable method of CI appraisal. It takes into account the timing of the net cash flows, the project's profitability and the return of the original investment. However, a project would not necessarily be accepted just because it had an acceptable NPV as non-financial factors have to be allowed for. In some cases less profitable projects (or even projects with a negative NPV) may go ahead, for example if they are concerned with employee safety or welfare.

Activity 19.5	How easy did you find the net present value method of capital investment appraisal to understand? Tick which applies.

(a) Very difficult [ ]   (b) Difficult [ ]   (c) Neither difficult nor easy [ ]   (d) Easy [ ]
(e) Very easy [ ]

Internal rate of return

The internal rate of return (IRR) method is also based on discounting. It is very similar to the NPV method, except that instead of discounting the expected net cash flows by a *predetermined* rate of return, it estimates what rate of return is required in order to ensure that the total NPV equals the total initial cost.

In theory, a rate of return that is lower than the entity's required rate of return would be rejected but in practice the IRR would only be one factor to be taken into account in deciding whether to go ahead with the project. The method is illustrated in Example 19.5.

<table>
<tr><td>**Example 19.5**</td><td>

The internal rate of return method

Bruce Limited is considering whether to invest £50,000 in a new project. The project's expected net cash flows would be as follows:

Year	£000
1	7
2	25
3	30
4	5

Required:
Calculate the internal rate of return for the proposed new project.
</td></tr>
</table>

Answer to Example 19.5

Bruce Ltd

Calculation of the internal rate of return:

Step 1: Select two discount factors
The first step is to select two discount factors, and then calculate the NPV of the project using both factors. The two factors usually have to be chosen quite arbitrarily but they should preferably cover a narrow range. One of the factors should produce a *positive* NPV, and the other factor a *negative* NPV. In this question factors of 10% and 15% have been chosen to illustrate the method. In practice, you may have to try various factors before you come across two that are suitable for giving a positive and a negative result.

Year	Net cash flow	Discount factors		Present value	
(1)	(2)	(3)	(4)	(5)	(6)
		10%	15%	10%	15%
	£			£	£
1	7 000	0.9091	0.8696	6 364	6 087
2	25 000	0.8264	0.7561	20 660	18 903
3	30 000	0.7513	0.6575	22 539	19 725
4	5 000	0.6830	0.5718	3 415	2 859
Total present values				52 978	47 574
Initial cost				50 000	50 000
Net present value				2 978	(2 426)

Notes:

1 Column (2) has been obtained from the question.

2 Columns (3) and (4) are based on the arbitary selection of two interest rates of 10% and 15% respectively. The discount factors may be found in Appendix 2.

3 Column (5) has been calculated by multiplying column (2) by column (3).

4 Column (6) has been calculated by multiplying column (2) by column (4).

The project is expected to cost £50,000. If the company expects a rate of return of 10%, the project will be accepted because the NPV is positive. However, if the required rate of return is 15% it will not be accepted because its NPV is negative. The maximum rate of return that will ensure a *positive* rate of return must, therefore, lie somewhere between 10% and 15%, so the next step is to calculate the rate of return at which the project would just pay for itself.

Step 2: Calculate the specific break-even rate of return

To do this, it is necessary to interpolate between the rates used in Step 1. This can be done by using the following formula:

$$IRR = \text{positive rate} + \left(\frac{\text{positive NPV}}{\text{positive NPV} + \text{negative NPV*}} \times \text{range of rates} \right)$$

*Ignore the negative sign and add the positive NPV to the negative NPV.

So in our example:

$$IRR = 10\% + \left(\frac{2978}{(2978 + 2426)} \times (15\% - 10\%) \right)$$
$$= 10\% + (0.5511 \times 5)$$
$$= 10\% + 2.76\%$$
$$= \underline{\underline{12.76\%}}$$

The project will be profitable provided that the company does not require a rate of return in excess of about 13%. Note that the method of calculation used above does not give the precise rate of return (because the formula is only an approximation), but it is adequate enough for decision-making purposes.

Example 19.5 shows that the IRR method is similar to the NPV method in two respects:

- the initial cost of the project has to be estimated as well as the future net cash flows of the project; and
- the net cash flows are then discounted to their net present value using discount tables.

The main difference between the two methods is that the IRR method requires a rate of return to be estimated in order to give an NPV equal to the initial cost of the investment. The main difficulty arises in deciding which two rates of return to use so that one will give a positive NPV and the other will give a negative NPV. You will find that you may have to have many attempts before you arrive at two suitable rates!

The advantages and disadvantages of the IRR method may be summarized as follows.

Advantages
- Emphasis is placed on liquidity.
- Attention is given to the timing of net cash flows.
- Appropriate rate of return does not have to be calculated.
- Method gives a clear percentage return on an investment.

Disadvantages
- Not easy to understand.
- Difficult to determine two rates within a narrow range.
- Method gives only an approximate rate of return.
- Gives some misleading results in complex CI situations, e.g. if there are negative net cash flows in subsequent years and where there are mutually exclusive projects.

As a non-accountant, you do not need to be too worried about the details of such technicalities. All you need to know is that in practice the IRR method has to be used with some caution.

Activity 19.6

With reference to the internal rate of return method of capital investment appraisal: (a) examine the advantages and disadvantages in the text; (b) score each one on a scale of 1 to 3 [1 = not very important; 2 = important; 3 = very important]; (c) add up your scores for each advantage and disadvantage; (d) take the total score for all the advantages away from the total score for all the disadvantages.

What is the net result? The advantages or the disadvantages? Does your result match your basic instincts about the IRR method?

Selecting a method

Of the five capital investment appraisal methods we have covered, which one is the most appropriate?

We consider it important that the time value of money is taken into account in a CI appraisal since the profitability of a future project may be grossly optimistic if such a concept is ignored. The discounted payback method, the net present value method and the internal rate of return method all meet this requirement.

The internal rate of return method involves some complex calculations, although the overall result is relatively easy to understand. Nonetheless, it may be a little too sophisticated for most entities. The discounted payback method is simple to understand and it is intuitively appealing. Its main disadvantage is that net cash flow received after the payback period may be ignored. Almost by default, therefore, the net present value method would appear to be the most favoured method. The main difficulty with the NPV method is the selection of a suitable rate of return for a particular project. So great care needs to be taken before accepting or rejecting a project based on the NPV method because it is highly dependent on the arbitrary determination of a specified rate of return.

Activity 19.7

The text has covered five methods of capital investment appraisal. Rank them in order of usefulness (1 being the most useful and 5 being the least useful).

Net cash flow

News clip

Cheaper prices

Retailers have been hammering away at suppliers' contracts in order to make savings or pass on cheaper prices to customers. Judith McKenna, Asda's finance director, says that retailers have an arsenal of weapons that they can use to cut prices. With suppliers, for example, they have three main levers: extend payment days, cut inventories to improve working capital, and drive down the amount they pay for goods.

Source: Adapted from www.ft.com/cms/s, 29 April 2009.

Four of the capital investment appraisal methods that we have covered in this chapter require the calculation of a project's net cash flow (payback, discounted payback, NPV and IRR). This is obviously not an easy task because it requires making a great many assumptions and estimates of what might happen in the future – possibly for very many years ahead. There are two issues in particular that can cause a problem: the impact of inflation on future net cash flows and the treatment of taxation. We discuss each of these problems below.

Inflation

In simple terms, inflation means that in (say) a year's time £1 received *then* will not buy the same amount of goods and services as £1 received *now* (see Figure 19.2). So if we calculate future net cash flow on the basis of the currency's value *now* we are, in effect, expecting to receive less cash in the future. Or to put it another way, we should estimate our future net cash flows on the basis of what it will take to purchase the equivalent of £1 of goods and services now. For example, if prices have risen by 10 per cent in a year, you will need to spend £1.10 in a year's time to buy exactly the same goods and services as you could today for £1.

There are two ways of allowing for inflation in capital investment appraisal: (1) indexing; and (2) adjustment of the rate of return. Brief explanations of both methods are given below.

- *Indexing*. Future net cash flows may be indexed using a recognized price index. For example, assume that the net cash flow arising from a particular project will be £100 in Year 1, £150 in Year 2 and £200 in Year 3. The relevant current price index at the beginning of Year 1 is 100 but the index is expected to rise to an average level of 120 for Year 1, 140 for Year 2 and 175 for Year 3. In order to compare the net cash flows over the next three years more fairly, they need to be put on the same price base. If they are indexed, Year 1's net cash flow becomes £83 [(£100 × 100) ÷ 120]; Year 2's net cash flow becomes £107 [(£150 × 100) ÷ 140]; and Year 3's net cash flow becomes £114 [(£200 × 100) ÷ 175]. The adjusted future net cash flows of £83, £107 and £114 for Years 1, 2 and 3 respectively will then be incorporated into a CI exercise and discounted at the entity's cost of capital.
- *Adjusting the rate of return*. Instead of indexing, we could select a higher rate of return. The easiest approach would be to add the expected rate of inflation to the entity's cost of capital. So with inflation at a rate of 5% per annum and a required rate of return of 10%, £100 receivable in 12 months would be discounted at a rate of return of 15%, i.e. £86.96 [(£100 × 100) ÷ 115, or using discount tables £100 × 0.8696].

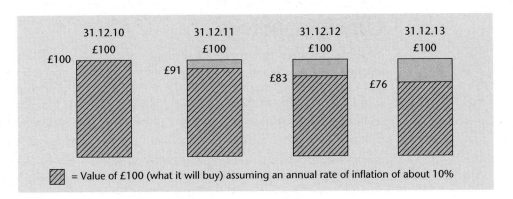

= Value of £100 (what it will buy) assuming an annual rate of inflation of about 10%

Figure 19.2 The impact of inflation

Taxation

Corporation tax is based on the *accounting profit* for the year. In order to calculate the amount of *tax payable* for the year, the accounting profit is adjusted for those items that are not allowable against tax, e.g. depreciation. There are also tax concessions that are not included in the calculation of accounting profit. Capital allowances, for example, are a tax allowance given when fixed assets are purchased. In essence, they are the equivalent of a depreciation allowance. Sometimes up to 100% capital allowances are given so that the entire cost of purchase can be deducted from the profit in the year that a fixed asset was purchased. This means that in the year in the year of purchase, other things being equal, the amount of corporation tax will be low, although in later years it will probably be higher.

So in estimating future net cash flows it is necessary to forecast what changes are likely to take place in the taxation system, what allowances will be available, what effect any changes will have on the amount of corporation tax payable and in what periods tax will have to be paid. Needless to say, the forecasting of such events is enormously difficult!

Activity 19.8	In calculating net cash flow for capital investment appraisal purposes, which method do you think is the most useful for dealing with the following problems? Tick the relevant box.

(1) *Inflation*: (a) indexing   [ ]
              (b) adjust the rate of return   [ ]

(2) *Taxation*: (a) current rate of corporation tax   [ ]
              (b) likely corporation tax rate for each year of the project's life   [ ]

Sources of finance

News clip

Homebuilder purchase

One of the largest homebuilders in the USA, Pulte, has announced that it was going to buy its rival Centex for $1.3 billion in stock. The deal will double the amount of cash on Pulte's balance sheet and allow it to cut $1 billion of debt off its balance sheet. It also expects to save $250 million in overheads and $100 million in debt expenses.

Source: Adapted from www.ft.com/cms/s, 9 April 2009.

Once a decision has been taken to invest in a particular project it is then necessary to search out a suitable method of financing it. There are a considerable number of available sources (both internal and external) although they vary depending on what type of entity is involved. Central and local government, for example, are heavily dependent on current tax receipts for financing capital investment projects, while charities rely on loans and grants. In this section we will concentrate on the sources of external finance available to companies. Such sources depend on the time period involved.

For convenience, we will break our discussion down into the short term, the medium term, and the long term. The various sources of finance are shown in diagrammatic format in Figure 19.3 and we discuss each of them below.

Short-term finance

There are five major sources of external short-term finance.

- *Trade credit*. This is a form of financing common in all companies (and for all other entities). An entity purchases goods and services from suppliers and agrees to pay for them some days or weeks after they have been delivered. This method is so common that sometimes discounts are given for prompt payment. By delaying the payment of creditors, the entity's immediate cash needs are less strained and it may be able to finance projects that otherwise could not be considered. However, it is clearly only a temporary method of financing projects (particularly long-term ones). The entity is also highly vulnerable to pressure from its creditors. This method often operates in tandem with a demand for debtors to settle their accounts promptly.
- *Bank overdraft*. This is a form of loan where the bank's customer is allowed to draw out more from the bank than has been deposited. An entity's overdraft may have to be secured by a *floating charge*. This means that the bank has a general claim on any of the entity's assets if the entity cannot repay the overdraft. There is usually an upper limit, the amount overdrawn can usually be called in at any time and the interest charge may be high. The main advantages of an overdraft are that it is flexible and that interest is normally only charged on the outstanding balance on a daily basis.
- *Factoring*. Factoring relates to an entity's debtors. There are two types of factoring:
  - recourse factoring, where an entity obtains a loan based on the amount of its debtor balances;

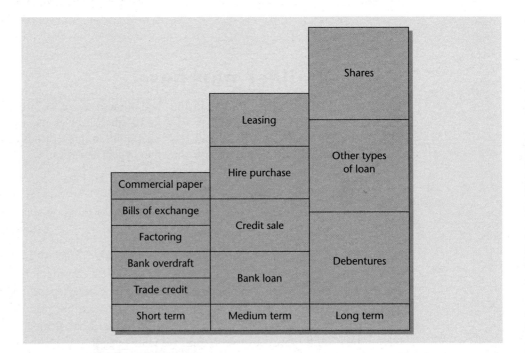

Figure 19.3 Sources of finance

- non-recourse factoring, where the debtor balances are sold to a factor and the factor then takes responsibility for dealing with them.

  Factoring is a convenient way of obtaining ready cash but either the interest rate on the loan or the discount on the invoices may be high.

- *Bill of exchange.* This is simply an invoice that has been endorsed (i.e. accepted) by a merchant bank. It can then be sold by the legal holder to obtain immediate finance. The interest charged depends on the creditworthiness of the parties involved, and if a company has a poor reputation then it will expect to pay more interest.

- *Commercial paper.* This is a form of short-term borrowing used by large listed companies. It is a bearer document, i.e. a person to whom the document is payable without naming that person.

Activity 19.9	Five main sources of external short-term finance are outlined in the text. Can you identify other sources of both internal and external short-term finance that may possibly be available to a company? List as many as you can.

Medium-term finance

There are four main types of external medium-term finance.

- *Bank loan.* Banks may be prepared to lend a fixed amount to a customer over a medium- to long-term period. The loan may be secured on the company's assets and the interest charge may be variable. Regular repayments of both the capital and the interest will be expected. Bank loans are a common form of financing but the restrictions often placed on the borrower may be particularly demanding.

- *Credit sale.* This is a form of borrowing in which the purchaser agrees to pay for goods (and services) on an instalment basis over an agreed period of time. Once the agreement has been signed, the legal ownership of the goods is passed to the purchaser and the seller cannot reclaim them. Sometimes very generous terms can be arranged, e.g. no payment may be necessary for at least 12 months, but the basic cost of the goods may be far higher than other suppliers are charging.

- *Hire purchase.* HP is similar to a credit sale except that the seller remains the legal owner of the goods until all payments due have been completed. An immediate deposit may be necessary, followed by a series of regular instalments. Once the goods have been paid for the ownership passes to the purchaser. HP is usually an expensive method of financing the purchase of fixed assets.

- *Leasing.* This is a form of renting. A fixed asset (such as a car or a printing press) remains legally in the ownership of the lessor. In the case of some leases the asset may never actually be returned. In effect, the lessee becomes the *de facto* owner. Leasing can be expensive although if the lessor passes on what can sometimes be very generous tax allowances it can be a reasonably economic method of financing projects.

Activity 19.10	The following are four forms of external medium-term finance. Rank your preferences in rank order (1 to 4). Bank loans [ ] Credit sales [ ] Hire purchase [ ] Leasing [ ]

Long-term finance

External long-term finance can generally be obtained from three main sources.

- *Debentures.* These are formal long-term loans made to a company; they may be for a certain period or open-ended. Debentures are usually secured on all or some of an entity's assets. Interest is payable but because it is allowable against corporation tax debentures can be an economic method of financing specific projects.
- *Other types of loan*:
  - *Loan capital* is a form of borrowing in which investors are paid a regular amount of interest and their capital is eventually repaid. The investors are creditors of the entity but they have no voting rights.
  - *Unsecured loan stock* is similar to debenture stock except that there is no security for the loan. The interest rate tends to be higher than that on debenture stock because of the greater risk.
  - *Convertible unsecured loan stock* gives stockholders the right to convert their stock into ordinary shares at specified dates.
  - *Eurobond loan capital* can be obtained by borrowing overseas in the 'Euro' market. The loans are usually unsecured and they are redeemed at their face value on a certain date. Interest is normally paid annually. The rate depends partly on the size of the loan and partly on the particular issuer.
- *Shares.* Expansion of the company could be financed by increasing the number of ordinary shares available, either on the open market or to existing shareholders in the form of a *rights issue*. An increase in an entity's ordinary share capital dilutes the holding of existing shareholders and all shareholders will expect to receive increasing amounts of dividend. Alternatively new or additional preference shares could be offered; preference shareholders would have an automatic right to a certain percentage level of dividend and so the issue of preference shares limits the amount of dividend available to ordinary shareholders.

Activity 19.11	You are in a small business as (a) a sole trader, (b) a partnership, and (c) a limited liability company. You wish to purchase some new machinery costing £50 000. In each case, which main form of financing the project would you prefer? (a) _____ (b) _____ (c) _____

❗ Questions you should ask

Capital investment appraisal is a most important decision-making function. The selection of a particular project and the most appropriate means of financing it are difficult decisions to make. As a senior manager you will receive some expert advice on what you can do. Ultimately, the final decision will be one for you. As far as the financial data are concerned, what questions should you put before your accountants? We suggest that the following may provide a framework for some detailed questioning.

- What capital appraisal method have you used?
- Why did you select that one?
- What problems have you encountered in calculating the net cash flow (or estimated net profit)?
- What allowances have you made for inflation and taxation?
- What rate of return have you used and why?
- What qualitative factors do you think should be taken into account?
- Are you able to put a monetary cost or value on them?

Conclusion

CI appraisal is a complex and time-consuming exercise. It is not possible to be totally accurate in determining the viability of individual projects but a valid comparison can usually be made between them.

Managers tend to be very enthusiastic about their own sphere of responsibility. As a result a marketing manager may be *sure* that additional sales will be possible, a production director may be *certain* that a new machine will pay for itself quickly and the data processing manager may be *convinced* that a new high-powered computer is essential.

In helping management to choose between such competing projects, the accountant's role is to try to assess their costs and to compare them with the possible benefits. Once a choice has been made he then has to ensure that the necessary finance will be available for them. CI appraisal should not be used as a means of blocking new projects. It is no different from all the other accounting techniques. It is meant to provide additional guidance to management and ultimately it is the responsibility of management to ensure that other factors are taken into account.

Key points

1 Capital investment appraisal forms part of the budgeting process.

2 There are five main methods of determining the viability of a project:
- payback
- discounted payback
- accounting rate of return
- net present value
- internal rate of return.

3 All the methods listed above have their advantages and disadvantages but the recommended methods are discounted payback and net present value.

4 Capital expenditure may be financed by a variety of external sources (as well as internal). Sources of short-term finance for entities include trade credit, bank overdrafts, factoring, bills of exchange and commercial paper. Medium-term sources include bank loans, credit sales, hire purchase and leasing. Long-term sources include debentures and other types of loans, and share issues.

Check your learning

The answers to these questions can be found within the text.

1 What is the distinction between capital and revenue expenditure?

2 List five characteristics associated with capital expenditure.

3 What is meant by 'net cash flow'?

4 What is the payback method of capital investment appraisal?

5 What information is needed to adopt it?

6 List four disadvantages of the payback method.

7 What is the discounted payback method of capital investment appraisal?

8 What is meant by 'discounting'?

9 What does a discount factor depend on?

10 List four advantages and four disadvantages of the discounted payback method.

11 What is the accounting rate of return method of capital investment appraisal?

12 What formula should be used in adopting it?

13 And how should (a) the numerator and (b) the denominator be determined?

14 List three advantages and three disadvantages of the accounting rate of return method.

15 What is the net present value method of capital investment appraisal?

16 Outline seven steps needed to adopt it.

17 List three advantages and three disadvantages of the method.

18 What is the internal rate of return method of capital investment appraisal?

19 What is its basic objective?

20 What formula is used to determine the required rate of return?

21 List three advantages and three disadvantages of the method.

22 How may (a) inflation and (b) taxation be allowed for in capital investment appraisal?

23 List three main external sources of (a) short-term finance, (b) medium-term finance and (c) long-term finance.

News story quiz

Remember the news story at the beginning of this chapter? Go back to that story and reread it before answering the following questions.

This is yet another news story of companies struggling to stay in business during a particularly deep recession. As the story indicates, one way of saving money is to cut capital expenditure. But that could mean that if a company survives the recession it will not be in a position to take full advantage of an upturn in the market. This story suggests that an investment in IT will help retailers survive the recession.

Questions

1 How can 'technology' help the retail industry to cut costs, win new business or exploit gaps in the market?

2 What sources of finance are open to retailers to finance such expenditure when spending is down and consumers are reluctant to part with their cash?

3 How far do you think the retailers' problems during the recession have been caused by not providing for the bad times during the good times?

Tutorial questions

The answers to questions marked with an asterisk can be found in Appendix 4.

19.1 'In capital expenditure appraisal, management cannot cope with any technique that is more advanced than payback.' How far do you think that this assertion is likely to be true?

19.2 'All capital expenditure techniques are irrelevant because:
(a) they cannot estimate accurately future cash flows;
(b) it is difficult to select an appropriate discount rate.'
Discuss.

19.3 Do any of the traditional capital investment appraisal techniques help in determining social and welfare capital expenditure proposals?

19.4 'We can all dream up new capital expenditure proposals', asserted the Managing Director, 'but where is the money coming from?' How might the proposals be financed?

19.5* Buchan Enterprises is considering investing in a new machine. The machine will be purchased on 1 January in Year 1 at a cost of £50,000. It is estimated that it will last for five years, and it will then be sold at the end of the year for £2000 in cash. The respective net cash flows estimated to be received by the company as a result of purchasing the machine during each year of its life are as follows:

Year	£	
1	8 000	(excluding the initial cost)
2	16 000	
3	40 000	
4	45 000	
5	35 000	(exclusive of the project's sale proceeds)

The company's cost of capital is 12%.

Required:
Calculate:
(a) the payback period for the project
(b) its discounted payback period.

19.6* Lender Limited is considering investing in a new project. It is estimated that it will cost £100,000 to implement, and that the expected net profit after tax will be as follows:

Year	£
1	18 000
2	47 000
3	65 000
4	65 000
5	30 000

No residual value is expected.

Required:
Calculate the accounting rate of return of the proposed project.

19.7* The following net cash flows relate to Lockhart Limited in connection with a certain project that has an initial cost of £2,500,000:

Year	Net cash flow £000	
1	800	(excluding the initial cost)
2	850	
3	830	
4	1 200	
5	700	

The company's required rate of return is 15%.

Required:
Calculate the net present value of the project.

19.8 Moffat District Council has calculated the following net cash flows for a proposed project costing £1,450,000:

Year	Net cash flow £000	
1	230	(excluding the initial cost)
2	370	
3	600	
4	420	
5	110	

Required:
Calculate the internal rate of return generated by the project.

19.9 Prospect Limited is considering investing in some new plant. The plant would cost £1,000,000 to implement. It would last five years and it would then be sold for £50,000. The relevant profit and loss accounts for each year during the life of the project are as follows:

Year to 31 March	1 £000	2 £000	3 £000	4 £000	5 £000
Sales	2 000	2 400	2 800	2 900	2 000
Less: Cost of goods sold					
Opening stock	–	200	300	550	350
Purchases	1 600	1 790	2 220	1 960	1 110
c/f	1 600	1 990	2 520	2 510	1 460

	b/f	1 600	1 990	2 520	2 510	1 460
Less: Closing stock		200	300	550	350	50
		1 400	1 690	1 970	2 160	1 410
Gross profit		600	710	830	740	590
Less: Expenses		210	220	240	250	300
Depreciation		190	190	190	190	190
		400	410	430	440	490
Net profit		200	300	400	300	100
Taxation		40	70	100	100	10
Retained profits		160	230	300	200	90

Additional information:

1 All sales are made and all purchases are obtained on credit terms.
2 Outstanding trade debtors and trade creditors at the end of each year are expected to be as follows:

Year	Trade debtors	Trade creditors
	£000	£000
1	200	250
2	240	270
3	300	330
4	320	300
5	400	150

3 Expenses would all be paid in cash during each year in question.
4 Taxation would be paid on 1 January following each year end.
5 Half the plant would be paid for in cash on 1 April Year 0, and the remaining half (also in cash) on 1 January Year 1. The resale value of £50,000 will be received in cash on 31 March Year 6.

Required:
Calculate the annual net cash flow arising from the purchase of this new plant.

19.10 Nicol Limited is considering investing in a new machine. The machine would cost £500,000. It would have a life of five years and a nil residual value. The company uses the straight-line method of depreciation.

It is expected that the machine will earn the following extra profits for the company during its expected life:

Year	Profits
	£000
1	200
2	120
3	120
4	100
5	60

The above profits also represent the extra net cash flows expected to be generated by the machine (i.e. they exclude the machine's initial cost and the annual depreciation charge). The company's cost of capital is 18%.

Required:
(a) Calculate:
  (i) the machine's payback period; and
  (ii) its net present value.
(b) Advise management as to whether the new machine should be purchased.

19.11 Hewie Limited has some capital available for investment and is considering two projects, only one of which can be financed. The details are as follows:

	Project (1)	Project (2)
Expected life (years)	4	3
	£000	£000
Initial cost	600	500
Expected net cash flows (excluding the initial cost) Year		
1	10	250
2	200	250
3	400	50
4	50	–
Residual value	Nil	Nil

Required:
Advise management on which project to accept.

19.12 Marsh Limited has investigated the possibility of investing in a new machine. The following data have been extracted from the report relating to the project:

Cost of machine on 1 January Year 6: £500,000.
Life: four years to 31 December Year 9.
Estimated scrap value: Nil.
Depreciation method: Straight-line.

Year	Accounting profit after tax £000	Net cash flows £000	
6	100	50	(excluding the initial cost)
7	250	200	
8	250	225	
9	200	225	
10	–	100	

The company's required rate of return is 15%.

Required:
Calculate the return the machine would make using the following investment appraisal methods:
(a) payback
(b) accounting rate of return
(c) net present value
(d) internal rate of return.

Further practice questions, study material and links to relevant sites on the World Wide Web can be found on the website that accompanies this book. The site can be found at www.pearsoned.co.uk/dyson

Emerging issues

Adapting to the environment

Accountants given green reporting guidance

Rachael Singh

Accountants are being encouraged to improve their knowledge about environmental reporting as companies and public bodies face growing pressure to reduce their carbon footprint.

The climate change bill, which requires the UK to reduce emissions by 80% from 1990 levels by 2050, brings green policies into the corporate mainstream.

To help accountants through the thicket of green regulations and targets the Association of Chartered Certified Accountants has released the second in its series of sustainability briefings.

The guide provides guidance to accountants on dealing with environmental reporting. It includes advice on understanding regulatory and voluntary requirements as well as new legislation, risk management, establishing a framework for

measurement of financial and non-financial reporting.

It also covers how to adapt environmental policies into the day-to-day operations of finance departments and how finance staff can provide clear information on the subject to a board of directors.

Steve Priddy, director of technical policy and research at ACCA, said: 'There is uncertainty and anxiety among our members about carbon, sustainability and green house gas emissions. Our members from around the world have said they want some clarification so they can do their job.'

Later this year, the UK will implement the Carbon Reduction Commitment which requires companies that spend £500,000 or more on its energy bills to pay for their carbon usage prior to using it.

The companies will be ranked in a league table based on how much they cut their carbon consumption. Their position in the table will determine the size of the rebate the companies will receive the following year.

The CRC is expected to have significant implications for company accounts and auditors.

Rachel Jackson, head of social and environmental issues at ACCA, said: 'Accountants have always needed to adapt to their evolving professional landscape. The next significant development is the emergence of sustainability issues within core business practice.'

The briefings have been published in association with KPMG and Accountability, a global not-for-profit network.

Accountancy Age, 12 February 2009.

Source: Reproduced with permission from Incisive Media Ltd.

Questions relating to this news story can be found on page 469 ➡

About this chapter

In this last chapter in the book we deal with some emerging issues in management accounting. Basic management accounting practice has hardly changed in over 100 years and although some new techniques were introduced as the twentieth century progressed there were few changes until about 1980. Since that time the discipline of management accounting has begun to be reviewed and reconsidered as a result of major developments in the commercial and industrial world.

This chapter explores some of the changes that have taken place in the business environment towards the end of the twentieth century and the impact that such changes are having on management accounting. We then review some of the developments that are gradually gaining wider acceptance as the twenty-first century progresses.

<table>
<tr>
<td>

Learning objectives

</td>
<td>

By the end of this chapter, you should be able to:

● summarize the changes in the business environment during the last 30 years;
● explain why changes in the commercial and industrial environment have affected traditional management accounting practice;
● outline the nature and purpose of a number of recent developments in management accounting practice.

</td>
</tr>
</table>

❗ Why this chapter is important

This chapter is important for non-accountants for the following reasons.

● You will be able to judge the value of any management accounting information presented to you if you have some knowledge of its historical development.
● You will be able to contribute to any debate that involves examining whether or not traditional management accounting practices have a place in the new business environment.
● You will be able to question your accountants on the proposals that they may have for introducing new management accounting developments into your own entity.
● You will be able to determine whether the management accounting function could be reorganized in order to provide managers with a better service.

The business environment

The Second World War had a profound effect on the financial, economic, political and social life of the United Kingdom. The country had to be rebuilt. A great deal of damage had been done to the infrastructure, there had been a lack of investment in its traditional industries, and the UK (like many other countries in Europe) found it difficult to compete with emerging countries in overseas markets. Many of these countries had a large labour force and the UK found that they could sell their goods much more cheaply than it could. Furthermore, as they were able to create entirely new businesses it was much easier to introduce new ways of doing things. By contrast the UK had an industrial base rooted in the nineteenth century with a backward rather than a forward looking approach to business.

The main country that heralded the new business era was Japan. Prior to the Second World War Japan had been a relatively unknown and somewhat primitive country. The impact of the war required it to be almost completely rebuilt and modernized without having the benefit of many indigenous raw materials. Japan's leaders realized that the country could only survive if it sold high-quality low-cost products to the rest of the world. It had to start from an almost zero industrial base but progress was helped by the close family traditions of Japanese culture and society. It took some time but eventually Japan was able to introduce the most modern practices into its industrial life.

These practices enabled the Japanese to be flexible in offering high-quality and reliable competitive products to its customers and deliver them on time. A detailed discussion of the managerial philosophy and various production techniques used by the Japanese is beyond this book but the following significant developments were pioneered in Japan.

- *Advanced manufacturing technology (AMT)*. AMT production incorporates highly automated and highly computerized methods of design and operation. It enables machines to be easily and cheaply adapted for short production runs, thereby enabling the specific requirements of individuals to be met.

- *Just-in-time (JIT) production*. Traditional plant and machinery were often time-consuming and expensive to convert if they needed to be switched from one product to another. Once the plant and machinery was set up, therefore, long production runs were the norm. This meant that goods were often manufactured for stock (resulting in heavy storage and finance costs). By contrast, AMT leads to an overall JIT philosophy in which an attempt is made to manufacture goods only when they have been specifically ordered by a customer. The JIT approach has implications for management accountants. As goods are only manufactured when ordered, raw materials and components are purchased only when they are required for a particular order. So no stock pricing problem arises and stock control becomes less of an issue since stock levels will, by definition, be kept to a minimum.

- *Total quality management (TQM)*. Another approach that the Japanese have incorporated into their production methods is TQM. The basic concept reflects two basic objectives:
  (1) *Getting it right the first time.* Whatever task is being undertaken it should be done correctly the first time that it is attempted. This means that there should then be savings on internal failure costs as there is no wastage, reworking, re-inspections, downgrading or discounted prices. There will also be savings on external costs such as repairs, handling, legal expenses, lost sales and warranties. There could, however, be additional preventive costs (e.g. planning, training and operating the system) as well as appraisal costs such as administration, audit and inspection.
  (2) *The quality of the output should reflect its specification.* In this context the concept of 'quality' should not be confused with the feeling of 'luxury'. A small mass-produced car, for example, may be regarded as a quality product (because its performance meets its specification) in exactly the same way that we equate a Rolls-Royce motor car with exceptional quality.

Activity 20.1 | Do you think that a just-in-time production system avoids the type of materials pricing problem discussed in Chapter 13? List the reasons why it may do and why it may not.

The industrial changes that had taken place in Japan were observed by other countries (especially the United States) and the new developments were subsequently adopted in many countries throughout the world albeit mainly in large international companies rather than in small domestic ones.

Other changes that took place after the end of the Second World War were more general. Among those that particularly affected the UK were the following:

- *Decline of manufacturing industry*. Traditional extractive and heavy manufacturing industries (such as coal mining, iron and steel, shipbuilding and car manufacturing) are now much less important and in some cases non-existent. Those manufacturing industries that do still exist are much less labour intensive than they used to be and labour costs themselves can no longer be regarded as a variable cost.

● *Growth of service industries.* There has been a growth of service industries such as finance services, entertainment, information supply and tourism. Service entities do not generally employ the thousands of employees that manufacturing industries used to employ. The service sector now forms a major part of the economy of the UK.

● *Organization change.* Another noticeable development that has taken place in recent years in both the profit-making and not-for-profit sectors is the move to *outsourcing* or *privatization*. This means that entities now concentrate on their core activities; everything else is bought in or supplied from outside the entity. For example, firms that build bathrooms and kitchens may subcontract electricians, joiners and plumbers to do the basic work on a job-by-job basis and an industrial company may employ an outside organization to look after its payroll.

● *Automation and computerization.* Production processes and administrative backup is now intensively automated and computerized. Indeed, the impact of computerization has been phenomenal. Most employees now have a personal computer on their desk giving them ready access to a vast internal and external data bank. This means that if they need (say) a report on a particular issue they can download it immediately without waiting for the accountants to do it for them. These developments are likely to become so significant that management accounting procedures in the near future will hardly be recognizable to today's practitioners.

Management accounting changes

The developments that have taken (and are still taking) place in business life in recent years have already had an effect on current management practices. However, as we mentioned in Chapter 12, during the period 1920 to 1980 management accounting changed very little and there were very few new developments. Since 1980 the pace has quickened and many entities have incorporated new ideas into their management accounting procedures. Such changes have tended to be mainly in medium- and large-scale industrial entities. The pace has been much less obvious in smaller service-based and not-for-profit entities.

We should not expect, therefore, a *revolution* to take place in management accounting practices over the next few years. We can expect more of a slow *evolutionary* process and it might take at least another 30 years before nineteenth-century management accounting practices are phased out gradually.

What changes can we expect? Although the pace will be slow, we suggest the following.

● The collection, recording, extraction and summary of data for information purposes will be performed entirely electronically. This management accounting function will no longer be serviced by a large army of management accountants.

● As JIT procedures become dominant, stock control, materials pricing and stock valuation will become relatively insignificant tasks.

● Product costing will still be important but overhead absorption techniques will become more sophisticated and all the basic data will be processed by computer.

● Budgeting and budgetary control procedures will also become much more computerized and they will be capable of being subject to a variety of different possible outcomes.

● Standard costing is likely to become less significant in a TQM environment but if it does survive it will be possible to produce different standard costs for a variety of different outcomes.

● Management accountants will become more like business analysts specializing in the financial implications of decision making and they will use a wide variety of both internal and *external* data.

● Management accountants will constantly be having to develop and incorporate new techniques in order to cope with a commercial and industrial world that will be subject to rapid change.

It follows that if the above changes do take place, future non-accountants are likely to meet a very different type of management accountant from the one that they are familiar with today. Tomorrow's management accountant will be much more of a team player, less bound to arithmetical recording of past events and more involved in taking highly informed decisions about future events.

Taking into account the changing business environment and the need for management accounting to adapt to such changes, which of the newer *techniques* can we see management accountants developing over the next few years? We review some of the possibilities in the following sections, but remember that progress is likely to be evolutionary rather than revolutionary. In the next section we explain how we have come to select the topics that we have chosen for discussion.

Activity 20.2	By this stage of the book you should have a good knowledge of the purpose of management accounting and the techniques used. List three changes that you would like to see incorporated into management accounting practice.

Selected techniques

As we have indicated earlier in the chapter, there were few new management accounting developments during much of the twentieth century. There are now signs that the pace of change is beginning to quicken, possibly because of rapid and enormous changes in information and production technology. An increase in the number of universities teaching and researching accounting has also possibly helped to awaken an interest in financial reporting and, perhaps to a lesser extent, in management accounting.

We have chosen ten fairly new management accounting techniques to discuss in this chapter. Our selection is somewhat arbitrary although it is based on current discussions in management accounting circles and on the techniques that professional and university accounting students are now required to study for their examinations. So there is a chance that by the time you become a manager the young accountants of the future may have put them into practice.

In order to simplify our discussion we will deal with the topics in alphabetical order so that it will be easier for you refer to them quickly if you need to check on a particular technique. They are: (1) activity-based management; (2) backflush costing; (3) better and beyond budgeting; (4) environmental accounting; (5) performance measurement; (6) product life cycle costing; (7) strategic management accounting; (8) target costing; (9) throughput accounting; and (10) value chain analysis. These topics are also shown in that order in Figure 20.1.

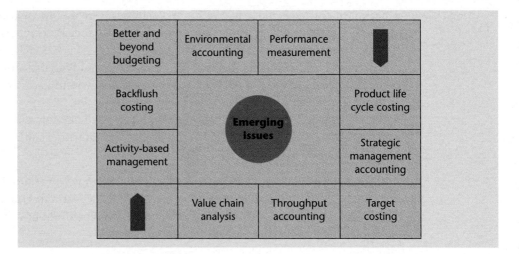

Figure 20.1 Emerging issues

Activity-based management

Activity-based management (ABM) is a management control technique involving the identification of activities, establishing the cost of those activities and the actual management of them.

In Chapter 14 we discussed a fairly new development in costing called activity-based costing. ABC is a management accounting technique used to determine how much of an entity's overhead should be charged to individual products. ABM is a refinement of ABC. There are two main differences: (i) ABM can be used in all types of entity and not just those that manufacture products; and (ii) it encompasses *all* costs and not just overheads. So ABM may be regarded as a means of assessing an entity's performance.

The basic procedure is as follows.

1 Determine the key activities undertaken by the entity.
2 Collect all the costs attached to each activity.
3 Charge them to appropriate cost pools.
4 Select a cost driver, i.e. identify the main factor that largely determines each activity.
5 Calculate the cost driver rate for each cost pool.

Sometimes the total cost in each cost pool is classified into core, support and diversionary activities or into value added or non-value added activities. If the diversionary or non-value added costs appear to be unacceptable, immediate steps would, of course, be taken either to reduce or eliminate them altogether.

It is also possible to calculate the ABM contribution. The concept is very similar to the one we met in marginal costing in Chapter 17. The ABM contribution formulae are as follows:

> *Sales revenue – activity pool costs = ABM contribution*
> *ABM contribution – remaining costs = profit/(loss)*
> *∴ Sales revenue – activity pool cost = remaining costs*

The activity pool costs include all the costs of making the products, providing the necessary services and delivering the products to the customer. The remaining costs must, by definition, relate to the provision of future activities (such as research and development) otherwise they would have been included in the pool costs. ABM proponents argue that it would be incorrect to regard such costs as part of current activities because they relate to a future time period. In financial accounting, research expenditure would normally be written off in the period in which it was incurred although in certain circumstances development expenditure may be deferred to a future period.

ABM provides a number of benefits. Among them are the following.

- Budgets become more reliable because a closer link is established between demand and the resources required to satisfy that demand.
- Diversionary activities can be more easily recognized and costs reduced accordingly.
- Profitability is improved because more accurate product costs are established.
- Unit output costs can be calculated (activity output costs/output volume) and these can assist in performance measurement.

However, as with most management accounting techniques there are some problems involved in operating an ABM system:

- It is difficult to reduce the number of activities to a practical level.
- The precise boundary between activities is often difficult to determine.
- The method causes resentment and jealousy as it cuts across traditional departmental structures.
- It is not always clear to the workforce who is in charge of a particular activity (as opposed to a department).

Not surprisingly, then, although ABM has been a widely discussed topic for the last 20 years it has not been widely adopted. That may be about to change as there are some signs that at least the more forward-thinking companies are now in the process of implementing it.

Activity 20.3 What do you think your reaction would be if a company you worked for switched from being organized on departmental lines to one being based on activities so that you all worked in multidisciplinary teams? List your likely reactions.

Backflush costing

Backflush costing is a product costing technique whereby costs are traced back to a product *after* its production process has been completed, i.e. flushed back. The conventional costing method is to attach costs to products at each stage of the production process. This involves a considerable amount of cost book-keeping but backflush costing cuts out a great deal of it.

The introduction of just-in-time production methods has encouraged the development of this new costing method. As we commented earlier, JIT purchasing involves ordering materials from a supplier only when a customer has placed an order. So when the materials are received they go straight into production; they are not taken into stock, they do not need to be stored, and it is easy to get them out of stock when they are required. By keeping stock at a minimum (most companies keep *some* stock) less space is required, waste is reduced, and there is less documentation checking and controlling. So overall store-keeping costs tend to be lower than in a traditional system.

At some point backflush costing requires a product to have a cost attached to it. So when and at what point does this happen? There are three possible stages (known as trigger points) when the costing could take place. They are as follows.

1 *On completion.* This is the purest and possibly the simplest form of backflush costing. No entries would be made in the books of account until the units are transferred to the finished goods store. The accounts used would primarily be the stores ledger account (for direct materials), the conversion cost account (for direct labour and overheads), and the cost of goods sold account,

2 *On purchase and completion.* This method uses two trigger points: (1) an entry would be made in the purchases account when the raw materials are first purchased. In a JIT system this would almost always be in response to a specific order. And then (2) on completion of the order entries would be made in the conversion cost account and the cost of goods sold account.

3 *On purchase and sale.* This method also uses two trigger points. (1) on purchase of the materials for a specific order; and (2) when the sale has actually taken place. This method means that if for some reason or other the goods are not immediately sold there could be a considerable delay before the details could be entered in the books of account.

Irrespective of which trigger point is selected the cost charged to the completed units would normally be either the budgeted cost or the standard cost.

Backflush costing has a number of apparent benefits. Among them are:

● There is much less book-keeping and what remains is simpler.
● It is cheaper to run than the conventional method of costing.
● The store-keeping function is much reduced.

However, there are some problems:

● There are fewer control signal points such as material mix and yield variances.
● The audit trail is made more difficult because there is no sequencing of costs.
● For financial reporting purposes it is in conflict with generally accepted accounting principles (GAAP) mainly because there is no work-in-progress account.

Notwithstanding these problems it is argued that backflush is ideally suited when JIT procedures are employed, the production cycle time is short and inventory levels are kept low.

Activity 20.4	Under a backflush costing system which trigger point would you recommend?
	On completion [ ] On purchase and completion [ ] On purchase and sale [ ]

Better and beyond budgeting

In Chapter 15 we examined the nature and purpose of budgeting and budgetary control. However, our discussion was strictly limited to the traditional approach to the subject – one that has been widely adopted over very many years. This approach is known as *incremental* budgeting. In brief, incremental budgets are prepared by (a) taking last year's budget (it is usually for a year); (b) adjusting it for any expected changes during the forthcoming year; and then (c) increasing the costs and revenues by the expected rate of inflation during the budget period.

This method of budgeting has been increasingly subject to a whole barrage of criticism in recent years. Among the many problems that can arise are the following.

- It is not related to the strategic aims of the entity.
- Budgets are prepared annually and they soon get out of date.
- The system is organized on a departmental basis.
- The budgets are based largely on last year's budget.
- Inefficiencies and inherent weaknesses are automatically built into the system.
- The focus is on financial outcomes and not on operational ones.
- Broad sweeping top-down changes are often made at the last minute, e.g. instruction from the managing director: '*Knock 10% off everyone's budget*'.
- Budgeting is a costly exercise in terms of time, energy and resources.

The above defects are just some of the criticisms that can be levelled against incremental budgeting but they should be sufficient for you to appreciate why there is now a demand for something better. Indeed, some accountants call it just that: 'better budgeting'. But other accountants are keen to go 'beyond budgeting'. It is not always clear what the difference is between these two approaches but perhaps the better budgeting movement is more evolutionary while the beyond budgeting movement is more much revolutionary.

Better budgeting

The demand for better ways of budgeting is not new but it has intensified in recent years owing to the enormous technological changes that have swept the westernized world. Some of the proposed changes that have been advocated over the last 30 years or so are summarized below.

- *Rolling budgets.* Budgets are still prepared on an incremental basis but as the year progresses the first month's budget is knocked off and the first month of the next year is added. This procedure continues month by month as the year goes on. This method means that the budget is less out of date than is the case with a pure incremental budgeting system but otherwise it is still subject to all its other defects.
- *Zero-based budgeting (ZBB).* This method ignores last year's budget. Budgets are prepared on the basis of a complete new set of assumptions and outcomes that relate to the forthcoming year. So changed circumstances are taken into account but ZBB still suffers from most of the problems associated with incremental budgeting.
- *Activity-based budgeting (ABB).* This is a much more recent development following the recent interest in activity-based costing. Assuming that the activities of the entity have been grouped into cost pools and appropriate cost drivers selected, the budgets will be prepared on a cost pool and cost driver basis. ABC has not, as yet, been widely adopted in industry so it follows that ABB is at a very early stage of development. It is clearly an improvement on incremental budgeting but its major weaknesses are that it is still being based largely on a non-strategic approach, it tends to be done only annually, it soon gets out of date, and it is firmly based on last year's budget.

Beyond budgeting

The beyond budgeting approach is a recognition that the world is very different from what it was in the nineteenth century. In recent years there has been an information technology revolution, plant and machinery have become more sophisticated, and companies are managed in a much more participative style than ever they were in Victorian times. Employees too are no longer as submissive as they used to be and their feelings need to be recognized and their recommendations should be taken seriously. All of these factors have encouraged the growth of the radical 'beyond budget' movement.

You might think that the term is rather a strange one. This is because its main proponents do not think that it is sufficient to merely have a radical overhaul of budgeting itself. They want a completely new management model albeit with budgeting at the heart of it. As they put it, they want to go *beyond* budgeting. We do not have the space here to explore this new management model in any depth so we will limit our discussion to some of the basic proposals.

It would be misleading to suggest that the movement is at the stage of being able to recommend a workable substitute for incremental budgeting but we can begin to identify some of the changes that are needed. They are as follows.

- Budgets should be related to the entity's strategy.
- They should cover a shorter period of time (perhaps as short as three months).
- Rolling forecasts based on various *outcomes* should be adopted instead of the traditional cost centre budgets.
- There should be a concentration on activities and processes rather than on departmental cost centres.
- Discretionary costs, such as advertising, marketing, research and training costs from the short-term forecasts, should be excluded.
- Non-financial as well as financial data should be included.
- Data relating to the company's competitors should also be included.
- Managers should be allowed greater autonomy when preparing their forecasts.
- Staff should be given bonuses for meeting the targets set for them.

The above requirements are far-reaching although some of them are beginning to be incorporated into many advanced manufacturing companies. What needs to happen now is for them to be welded together so that they form a workable comprehensive model that can replace incremental budgeting. We wait with interest to see how long it will take.

Activity 20.5	Identify the one crucial factor that in your view makes incremental budgeting ineffective in controlling the revenues and costs of a large industrial company. Give reasons for your choice.

Factor _____

Reasons _____

Environmental accounting

News clip

Global warming information

The world's big corporations are failing to provide a full account to investors of the risks and potential costs of climate change. A report from the Ceres network of green organizations and investors and the Environmental Defence Fund has found that shareholders are given only minimal information about global warming and the effect that it might have on their 'bottom line'.

Source: Adapted from *The Guardian*, 4 June 2009, p. 25.

Environmental accounting is a form of accounting that captures, records, extracts, summarizes and reports information of both a financial and non-financial nature that specifically relates to the environment. If the information is used mainly for internal purposes it is known as *environmental management accounting* and simply as *environment accounting* when it is provided for parties external to an entity. For convenience we will refer to both types as environmental accounting or EA.

EA's primary aim is simple: to provide information for management so that corrective action can be taken in order to reduce the impact of the entity's activities on the environment. A secondary aim is to report on the entity's performance in achieving that aim.

EA is a very new branch of accounting. We can trace its origins back to an influential report published in 1975 called *The Corporate Report*. This report broke new ground when it argued that companies had a wider responsibility to the community than simply reporting to shareholders. It identified six main user groups that have an interest in a company's performance (see Chapter 2). It argued that such groups are not just interested in having some financial information: they also want to know how the company fits in to the social, economic and political environment in which it operates. This suggestion was valid in 1975 but it is even more so today.

Over the last 20 years there has been a growing interest in and concern about the *physical* environment as the vast majority of scientists have given starker and starker warnings about its future, largely because of the apparent threat to the world caused by global warming. Some observers do not agree with this view but two almost indisputable facts are clear:

1 The world's population has got bigger and bigger.
2 There is a general clamour for living standards to rise.

As a result of these two phenomena a number of consequences arise:

● Natural resources become scarcer because some cannot be replaced as quickly as they are being consumed.
● The switch from a largely agrarian world to an advanced technological one has resulted in considerable air, land and water pollution.
● The climate does appear to be changing as more and more carbon is released into the atmosphere.
● It becomes more difficult to find the means of disposing of huge amounts of human waste without spoiling huge tracts of land and polluting water supplies.

No doubt as you worked your way through school you became very well aware of these problems. You probably feel very concerned about them and you might possibly be campaigning to get something done to stop them happening. By contrast to the attitude of young people, it has taken accountants, at least in their professional role, some time to accept that there is a problem. Credit is due in part to a number of academic accountants who have produced a great deal of research on this subject. The various professional accountancy bodies eventually began to support them and now EA often features in their respective syllabi.

In the meantime many companies had also begun to collect data about environmental matters. One sign indicating that they are now being taken much more seriously is that almost any large manufacturing company's annual report and accounts contains some sort of environmental report. Indeed, Cairn Energy, for example, an oil company, publishes a separate 'Corporate Responsibility Report'. The one for 2008 is 44 pages long. It has a separate section called 'Behaving responsibly towards the environment' which is six pages long. Its main headings include: (a) environmental impacts; air quality, energy consumption, water consumption, waste and prevention of spills; (b) environmental compliance; and (c) climate change. The contents of this report give you some idea of what is involved in EA.

As the public become more concerned about environmental matters, many companies have set up an environment management team. Until recently accountants were not generally members of such a team. That is now changing. What part do they play in the work of such a team? We can identify four specific responsibilities:

1 Converting the environmental implications of proposed projects into financial terms.
2 Providing financial data identifying environmental benefits and costs of ongoing projects.
3 Preparing both financial and non-financial environmental performance measures.
4 Ensuring that all environment reports comply with statutory and professional accounting requirements.

A traditional accounting system would not and cannot identify those costs and revenues that we might now describe as being 'environmental'. So when an EA system is introduced into an entity the existing accounting system needs to be adapted so that it provides the required information about environmental costs and possible benefits. But what are they? We will deal first with the costs.

Some environmental costs will be tangible such as direct materials and direct labour costs. Other costs will be intangible such as the costs of dealing with the opposition to a proposed addition to a factory. Once it has been agreed what is 'environmental', the accountants should not have undue difficulty in identifying the tangible costs, although it almost certainly will be more difficult to quantify the intangible costs. Once all the costs have been isolated they may then be classified under appropriate headings. The US Environment Protection Agency has suggested the following classification. We have also included some examples of what might be included in each category.

- *Conventional company costs*: capital equipment, materials, salvage value.
- *Upfront*: site preparation, R&D, installation.
- *Regulatory*: monitoring, training, pollution control.
- *Voluntary*: community outreach, annual reports, landscaping.
- *Back-end:* closure, disposal of inventory, site survey.
- *Contingent*: penalties and fines, personal injury damage, natural resource damage.
- *Image and relationship costs*: corporate image, relationship with workers, relationship with host communities.

We now turn to examine some environmental benefits. Among them are the following:

- *Capital cost savings*: these may arise from better project design resulting in increased production, less pollution and less wastage.
- *Revenue savings*: such savings could come through more efficient use of resources, e.g. materials, energy, water and the sale of waste products.
- *Intangible savings*: these may be very difficult to identify and to put a monetary value on them but environmental considerations may result in better labour relations, improved corporate image and enhanced acceptance of the brand image.

As far as accountants are concerned the collection, recording and reporting of the possible recognizable costs and revenues are what accountants are skilled at doing but, as we have indicated, many (if not most) of the environmental costs and revenues are difficult to quantify and so to cost in financial terms. A move towards environmental accounting takes accountants into almost unknown territory but it is a journey that should be as exciting as it is important.

Activity 20.6	Answer the following questions. Tick as appropriate.

Answer the following questions. Tick as appropriate.

1 Do you think that global warming is a major worry?   Yes/no

2 How bad is it (on a scale of 1 to 10)?

   Very bad   Not at all

   1 _____ 10

3 Do you think that there is a need for some form of environmental accounting?   Yes/no

4 If yes, what should it include? If no, why not?

Performance measurement

Performance measurement is a collective term embracing a whole range of techniques which incorporate both financial and non-financial data as a means of assessing an entity's performance in achieving its objectives.

The concept and practice of measuring the performance of an entity is not new. Indeed, traditional profit and loss accounts and balance sheets that include the previous year's results is one form of performance measurement. If data are extracted from such a source and converted into 'ratios' (as we demonstrated in Chapter 10) then we have incorporated both financial and to some extent non-financial information into our analysis. Such an exercise meets our definition of performance measurement. But the methods that have been practised for decades are increasingly seen to be inadequate and unsatisfactory? Why?

A number of reasons can be identified. They are as follows.

- The traditional methods of performance measurement rely almost exclusively on accounting information.
- Accounting information is based on (a) questionable assumptions, assertions and arguments; (b) it is historical; and (c) non-financial data are largely ignored.
- External data are not included.

Advocates of change argue that what is needed is:

- Non-financial data should be included.
- Comparison should be made with the entity's competitors.
- Greater use should be made of statistical information.

As a result of the deficiencies of the traditional method of measuring performance and the changes that need to be made, a number of possible replacements have been suggested. We will review briefly just two of the leading contenders: benchmarking and the balanced scorecard.

Benchmarking

Benchmarking simply means the incorporation of comparative data into performance measurement. According to CIMA (2005), benchmarking can take four different forms:

1 *Internal:* comparisons are made between different units or functions within the same industry.

2 *Functional*: comparisons are made with the best external practitioners regardless of the industry.

3 *Competitive*: comparisons are made with the entity's direct competitors.

4 *Strategic*: a form of competitive benchmarking but its purpose is to take strategic action and to make organizational changes.

There is a danger of *information overload* in extending performance measurement beyond financial data and by including comparisons with other entities. Information overload is not a problem with another idea: the balanced scorecard.

The balance scorecard

The balanced scorecard is a performance measurement device that aims to link an entity's objectives with its performance. The idea was put forward by two American academics, Kaplan and Norton, in a series of articles and books (see, for example Kaplan, R.S. and Norton, D.P. (1992) 'The Balanced Scorecard – Measures That Drive Performance', *Harvard Business Review*, January/February).

An adapted version of Kaplan and Norton's balanced scorecard is illustrated in Figure 20.2. It has four *perspectives*. These relate to the organizational activity of the entity. Each perspective has a basic question linked to it:

1 *Financial*: how do we look to shareholders?

2 *Internal business process*: what must we excel at?

3 *Innovation and learning*: can we continue to improve value?

4 *Customer*: how do customers see us?

Each perspective then has a number of *objectives*. In turn each objective has a *measure* (such as the staff turnover ratio) and a *target* set for it (say 3 per cent per annum). In addition, managers are expected to come up with an initiative, i.e. what measures they would take to achieve each objective.

	Objectives	Measures	Targets	Initiatives
Financial perspective 1 2 3				
Internal business process perspective 1 2 3				
Innovation and learning perspective 1 2 3				
Customer perspective 1 2 3				

Figure 20.2 A balanced scorecard

Source: Adapted from Kaplan, R.S. and Norton, D.P. (1996) 'Using the balanced scorecard as a strategic management system', *Harvard Business Review*, January/February. With permission from Harvard Business School Publishing.

The model is flexible and can be adapted to individual circumstances so there could be any number of objectives attached to each perspective. But this would, of course, increase the number of measures, targets and initiatives and this could lead to information overload.

Some academic observers suggest that the balanced scorecard idea has now become part of mainstream management practice. If that is so then you are highly likely to come across it when you become a manager in almost any type of entity. However, we would be cautious about just how widely it has been adopted. The idea might now be more than 20 years old but the evidence so far suggests that it is still appropriate to treat it is as an emerging issue.

Activity 20.7	Bearing in mind all the problems that there are in obtaining reliable data, for performance measurement purposes, which of the following options would you prefer (tick as appropriate)?

(a) Financial performance measures only   [ ]
(b) Non-financial performance measures only   [ ]
(c) A combination of both financial and non-financial performance measures   [ ]

Reasons: _____

Product life cycle costing

Product life cycle costing is a costing technique that captures, records and reports on the cost of making a product from the moment that someone has an idea until the time that there is no sign that it ever existed. The essence of this form of costing is captured in its description as 'cradle to grave' costing (see Figure 20.3). In those entities that do not manufacture a physical product it is known simply as 'life cycle costing'. It should be noted that although it might be thought of as a costing *method* its primary purpose is cost *management*. We start with a description of a product's 'life cycle'.

Just as humans go through various stages during their life (childhood, adolescence, adulthood, youth, middle age, old age) so do products. We can distinguish three main phases that most products go through. They are as follows.

1 *Development.* An initial idea is worked up into a design, a prototype is built and then tested. If successful the prototype goes into production. This phase can account for up to 80 per cent of the overall cost in many advanced technological industries.
2 *Manufacturing.* The product is manufactured and goes on to the market. Some products have a short life, perhaps only a few days, whereas others may last for decades. Irrespective of the length of their life it is possible to recognize four distinct stages, as shown in Figure 20.3: (a) an introductory period when it takes some time before the product begins to take off; (b) a growth period as sales begin to climb; (c) a period of maturity when sales are at their height; (d) finally a period of decline as sales begin to fall off (sometimes quite rapidly).
3 *Disposal.* The product is eventually taken off the market and it is no longer manufactured. The product line has to be dismantled, the plant and possibly the building demolished, and any left-over materials and waste products buried or dumped (one hopes safely although, alas, that is not always the case).

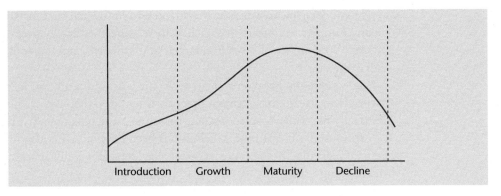

Figure 20.3 The product life cycle

Source: Fox, H. (1973) 'A framework for functional coordination', *Atlanta Economic Review*, 23(6): 8–11. With permission from the Federal Reserve Bank of Atlanta.

All three of these phases, of course, incur costs. In a traditional costing system the research and development costs would be written off (or charged) in the period in which they were incurred. Disposal costs would be treated similarly. There would normally be no attempt to charge either the initial costs or the disposal costs directly to the product during the manufacturing stage. This means, of course, that the units being manufactured are in effect being undercharged and the profit that they generate is being overstated.

The American defence industry in the early 1960s is credited with being one of the first organizations to recognize this deficiency and to do something about it. And so product life cycle costing was born. The justification for it is that it gives a more accurate assessment of product profitability if both the development costs of a product and its eventual disposal costs are included in the production costs.

Among the perceived benefits of product life cycle costing are the following:

● The technique minimizes the possibility that the research team will be carried away with 'a great idea' regardless of whether it is likely to be profitable.
● Emphasis is placed on the impact of cost at every stage of development.
● A more realistic assessment is provided of product profitability.
● Greater consideration is given to the eventual treatment of waste and its disposal cost.

But equally there are some obvious problems:

● Good ideas might be stifled at an early stage because of their apparent high cost.
● It is not easy to estimate the length of a product's life.
● The three phases of the life cycle are difficult to cost especially the disposal costs.

Perhaps these problems are such that even 50 years after its introduction product life cycle costing has still not been widely adopted. Nonetheless, it has several factors going for it and perhaps this is why it is included in accounting examination syllabi.

| Activity 20.8 | Suppose you were asked to work out the costs of disposing of nuclear waste. List all the possible factors that you would have to take into account.

How realistic would such an exercise be in practice?

Not at all   Quite possible
1 ————————————————————————————— 10 |

Strategic management accounting

News clip

Bean counters no longer

As the British public sector heads for recession, Charles Tilley, Chief Executive of the Chartered Institute of Management Accountants (CIMA), stresses the importance of putting strategy and management into accounting, not just bean counting.

Source: Adapted from *Accountancy Age*, 24 October 2008.

SMA is an advanced form of management accounting that includes internally generated financial and non-financial data along with comparable data relating to an entity's competitors.

The term has been generally adopted since 1981 when Simmonds introduced it to a wider audience in a magazine article (*Management Accounting*, 59, pp. 26–29). SMA is not strictly a 'technique' but a development of the conventional form of management accounting. SMA has the potential to change the existing practice quite radically while at the same time turning management accountants into sophisticated business managers instead of remaining as number-crunching back-room technicians.

It is possible to distinguish three distinct differences between traditional management accounting and SMA. They are as follows:

1 SMA places a greater emphasis on relating management accounting information to the *strategies* of the entity.
2 It includes much more *non-financial* data about an entity's operating activities.
3 It incorporates data about the entity's direct *competitors*.

We will now comment briefly about each of these differences.

Recent accounting literature is full of references to 'strategy'. Strategy is usually described in terms of its military usage. A workable dictionary definition is as follows:

> *The science and art of conducting a military campaign by the combination and employment of means on a broad scale for gaining advantage in war.*
> Source: Funk, C.E., Editor (1946) *New Standard Dictionary of the English Language*. New York: Funk and Wagnall's Company.

Or perhaps more relevant for our purposes:

> *The use of stratagem or artifice in business or politics.*
> Source: Funk, 1946.

If we apply these definitions to education you will probably find that your module has probably got an aim (*what are we trying to do in this module?*) and a number of objectives (*how are we going to achieve that aim?*). Similarly the aim of a profit-making business might be (say) to make a minimum return of 20 per cent on capital employed per annum. The management would then have to work out how to achieve that aim. It might, for example, plan to do so by working towards achieving a gross profit of 50 per cent per annum and attempt reducing overheads by 5 per cent per annum.

So in simple terms, if an entity has adopted an SMA approach, the management accountants would have provided information that compares the actual results with the set objectives. For example, '*We aimed for a reduction in overheads of 5 per cent over the year as a whole but we are operating at a level of only 3 per cent*. Under a conventional management accounting system the accountants would compare the 3 per cent reduction this year with last year's 2 per cent (say). The company is clearly doing better this year than it did last year but it is not meeting its objective, i.e. that of making 5 per cent for the year as a whole. This point might be further emphasized, or course, if the external competitors were reducing their overheads by 7 per cent.

Just as in education, where lecturers set module aims and objectives which force them into thinking deeply about what they are trying to do and how they are going to go about it, it is so in business. That is a useful exercise in itself, but it is even more useful if you then compare how the business is doing with what you wanted it to do. In that sense the past is irrelevant: what has gone has gone. It is the future that matters.

Unfortunately SMA is not easy to put into practice. Setting aims and objectives should be fairly easy, as is the collection of internal data. The difficult bit is in obtaining comparable information about the entity's competitors. But even if this is a problem there is no reason why an SMA approach should not be tried. Comparing actual data with data based on objectives is still a highly valuable way to control costs and to take better decisions. Nonetheless, management accounting is slow to change and as yet there is little evidence to suggest that SMA has been widely adopted.

Activity 20.9	What future do you think there is for strategic management accounting? Is it perhaps just a passing fancy of university accounting lecturers? Mark your response on the scale below: 0 = no future at all; 10 = a great future for it.

0 _____ 10

Target costing

Target costing is a costing technique that establishes the cost of a product by first determining the selling price and then deducting a desired profit margin from that selling price. The balance is the total maximum cost allowable for developing, manufacturing and selling the product. Or, if we put it in equation terms:

> *Target selling price – desired profit = target cost*

Traditional absorption costing works the other way round: the selling price is determined by first working out how much a product may take to make and sell and then adding on a desired profit level, i.e.:

> *(Direct material costs + direct labour costs + overheads) + desired profit = selling price.*

In reality, of course, the selling price cannot always be determined this way because competitors' prices have to be taken into account. That may mean going back to see whether any cost reductions can be made or possibly cutting back on the desired profit level.

A target costing approach is similar to the conventional costing approach except it is much more intensive and inclusive, involving employees, suppliers and customers. Suppose, for example, that a company is proposing to launch a new product on to the market. After some sophisticated market research it is believed that it could be sold at

£10 per unit. The company wishes to achieve a profit of £1 per unit. So no more than £9 per unit can be incurred in making and selling it. However, the initial estimates suggest that it would cost £11 per unit. That means that a rigorous cost cutting exercise would have to be undertaken, examining every stage of the product's life cycle starting from the original design to the eventual scrapping of the product. Its specification, the manufacturing process, and the selling and distribution procedure would all have to be thoroughly investigated and re-costed to see if they could be eliminated, minimized or improved and the cost of them reduced.

This process often needs to be so rigorous in order to get the cost down that target costing goes way beyond traditional cost accounting practices. Indeed, some accountants argue that target costing should be renamed *target cost management*. We will, however, stick to the term by which it is best known.

Target costing originated in the automobile industry in Japan. Its main objectives were to reduce costs, improve product quality, provide what customers wanted, and bring new products on to the market when the time was right. The technique is believed to have a great deal going for it although as yet it does not appear to have caught on in the Western world. The following are some of its perceived benefits.

● An emphasis is placed on *customers* being a key factor in an entity's survival.
● Cooperation among staff is enhanced.
● A culture of and a search for continuous improvement is created.
● New ideas are brought forward for the development of new products and processes.

But naturally there are some problems in operating a target costing system.

● Problems arise in forecasting changes in market and technological developments.
● It is difficult to determine a whole range of factors: customers' needs, predict competitors' activities and responses, derive an accurate target price (even with the use of sophisticated market research techniques), and estimate a share of development costs and non-production overheads.

Activity 20.10	How realistic (on a scale of 1 to 10) do you think it is to expect managers to achieve a target set for them when it is based on an estimated selling price and an expected profit margin?

Completely realistic   *Quite unrealistic*
1 _____ 10

How would managers behave if given such a target?

Try to meet it: Yes [ ]   Ignore it [ ]   Try to work to it [ ]

Throughput accounting

Throughput accounting/costing is a costing technique that enables the throughput of a process to be calculated, *throughput* being defined as the difference between sales revenue and direct material cost.

In principle, therefore, it is very similar to marginal costing except that in marginal costing *all* variable costs are deducted from sales revenue and the balance is referred to as *contribution*. Indeed, an alternative name for throughput accounting (or costing) is *super variable costing*. Throughput accounting also recognizes that in the modern world it is unrealistic to assume that labour costs can be regarded as a direct expense. The two techniques are contrasted in Figure 20.4 below.

Throughput costing is a technique developed by Goldratt and Cox in their book *The Goal* (1986, North River Press). It revolves around the concept that all activities at some time or other are restricted by *constraints*, thereby leading to the development of a theory known as the *theory of constraints* (TOC). For example, a company might be able to sell all it can produce but it is limited or constrained by a shortage of skilled labour. It may also be limited by a *bottleneck* in the production process.

A bottleneck is a resource that cannot supply all that is demanded of it. Suppose, for example, that Machine A produces units that are then transferred to Machine B. A manufactures 100 units per hour but B can only cope with 50 units an hour. If A continues to produce 100 units per hour, large stocks of the unfinished units will be built up until such time that B can deal with them. They will then have to be stored somewhere and storage is expensive. Management must seek to remove the bottleneck occurring at B as quickly as possible. In the meantime A must limit its output to 50 units per hour. This would be quite a radical approach and one that is contrary to traditional practice. It means that staff working on A will become 'idle' (the term is not meant to be pejorative) and no manager likes to see his staff hanging around doing nothing. If the problem is not resolved quickly then eventually the staff might have to be laid off albeit, one hopes, temporarily.

The elimination of bottlenecks means that more and more materials can be processed without being held up. The more that are processed, the more that can be sold and the more profitable an entity becomes. So the main aim of management should be to concentrate on increasing the *throughput* of materials and that means that managers need to be constantly making sure that there are no bottlenecks.

Throughput accounting is at an early stage of development and it is perhaps too soon to know whether it is likely to be widely adopted. Some of its claimed advantages are as follows:

Marginal cost statement		Throughput accounting statement	
	£		£
Sales revenue	<u>20 000</u>	Sales revenue	20 000
Direct materials	6 000	Direct materials	<u>6 000</u>
Direct labour	3 000		
Other direct expense	<u>1 000</u>		
	<u>10 000</u>		
Contribution	10 000	*Throughput contribution*	14 000
Fixed costs	<u>5 000</u>	Operating expenses	<u>9 000</u>
Profit	<u>5 000</u>	*Profit*	<u>5 000</u>

Figure 20.4 Simplified marginal cost and throughput accounting systems

- It is easy to understand and to implement.
- Direct material costs can be easily identified.
- Labour costs are not treated as a variable cost.
- Variable costs do not have to be identified and costed.
- An emphasis is placed on value added coming from selling and not by continuing to increase output.
- Attention is focused on eliminating constraints and bottlenecks.
- Products can be easily ranked on the basis of their profitability.

The basic concept of throughput accounting is so simple and so intuitively appealing that there would appear to be few problems in putting it into practice. But there are some; among them are the following:

- It is difficult to accept that sometimes it is appropriate to stop production.
- Coping with staff lay-offs (even on a temporary basis) is a major labour relations problem.
- Less attention may be given to the control of 'other operating expenses'.
- Concentrating on throughput contribution may draw attention away from overall profitability.

Activity 20.11	On a scale of 1 to 10, how appealing is the concept behind throughput accounting?

(a) As an idea:
Not at all   Very highly
1 _____ 10

(b) As a practical proposition:
Not at all   Very highly
1 _____ 10

Value chain analysis

Value chain analysis (VCA) is an investigatory technique used to assess the value added to a product as it goes through a sequence of activities right from the development stage through to the point when it is delivered to the customer. The sequence of activities is known as the *value chain* (see Figure 20.5).

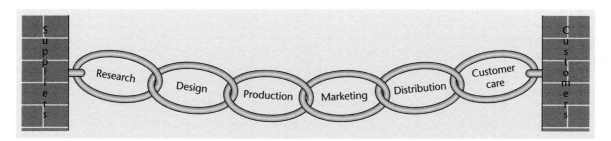

Figure 20.5 A production company's value chain

Source: Based on Porter, M.E. (1985) *Competitive Advantage: Creating and Sustaining Superior Performance.* New York, NY: Free Press.

VCA was developed by M.E. Porter in a book called *Competitor Advantage: Creating and Sustaining Superior Performance* published in 1985. The title of the book gives a clue about the technique's objective. It is argued that by determining the value added to the product at every stage of the manufacturing process a company can gain an advantage over its competitors. Porter distinguished between *primary* activities (such as operations, marketing and sales) and *support* activities, e.g. procurement and human resource management.

A value chain analysis involves six basic steps. In summary they are as follows.

1 *Divide the entity into strategic business units (SBUs).* An SBU is a part of an entity responsible for a defined activity such as planning, development, production and marketing. Note that VCA may be used in service entities but the value chain will not then be as long or as complicated as it is for a manufacturing entity.
2 *Identify those activities within each SBU that add value.* These activities will be similar to the ones illustrated in Figure 20.5.
3 *Allocate revenue, costs and assets to each value-creating activity.* The procedures required here are basically the same as those accountants use to set up an investment cost centre.
4 *Identify a cost driver for each value activity.* The cost driver cost is obtained by dividing the value added by the cost driver.
5 *Compare the result for each value added activity.* You should now be able to spot fairly quickly those activities that appear to add little value. You can then consider whether the activity can be made more efficient, whether it could be bought-in ('outsourced') or even eliminated altogether.
6 *Compare the overall results with other similar entities.* This will not be easy because the information required may be difficult to get and even then it may not be strictly comparable.

You may have spotted that the above procedure is very similar to activity-based costing. Perhaps the major difference is basically between the way that the costs and revenues are classified: ABC classifies them into activity cost pools while VCA puts them into stages or sequences.

VCA is a complicated exercise. It involves identifying and distinguishing between different 'sequences' and then costing them. The next step after that involves selecting just one factor that drives the activity in each sequence. However, while there may be some difficulties in putting VCA into practice it is probably a worthwhile exercise since non-value adding activities can be quickly spotted. But then something has to be done about them and that certainly will not be easy.

| Activity 20.12 | List the similarities that you can spot between activity-based costing/management and value chain analysis. |

Questions you should ask

This chapter has outlined some of the changes that have begun to take place in management accounting since about 1980. Progress has, however, been slow. You might like to check what changes your own company (or any other entity) has experienced or is proposing to make. We suggest that you ask the following questions.

● Are our management accountants now expected to become business managers rather than number crunchers?

● If so, are they going to be decentralized and located in separate operating units?

● Are we going to be able to access accounting reports and statements direct from our PCs instead of waiting for the accountants to contact us?

● Are we moving towards a more strategic management approach?

● Can we expect to receive as much non-financial as well as financial information and will it include details about our competitors?

● Are we proposing to replace our costing system with one that is more up to date and, if so, what will take its place?

● Are we going to put as much emphasis on environmental reporting as we do on financial reporting?

Conclusion

Part 4 of this book has dealt with management accounting. We have concentrated on traditional management accounting techniques and their usefulness for managers. Most of those techniques originated in the late nineteenth and early twentieth centuries and they have hardly changed at all during the last 100 years.

In the meantime great changes have taken place in economic activity, especially since the Second World War ended in 1945. The main developments first took place in the Far East in countries that were not bound by past practices. They were able to build up their industries using different organizational structures and new production methods. Labour was cheap and increasing automation and development in information technology hastened the changes that were taking place.

All of this resulted in the decline of old industries in countries like the UK. Indeed, the UK found it impossible to compete with these emerging nations. The result was that by the end of the twentieth century the UK had very little manufacturing industry and its economy was largely serviced based.

These changes in the business environment have begun to have a significant impact on management accounting practices. Until 1980 there had been little movement but change became necessary as the 'old world' began to realize that it too had to accept some fundamental changes to business life. Orders were hard to get, customers were more demanding, prices were competitive, costs had to be controlled more rigorously, goods and services had to be of the highest quality and an efficient aftercare service was vital.

Traditional management techniques could not cope with these requirements so they also had to change. Perhaps the most significant change has been a move towards *activity-based costing* (see Chapter 14) subsequently extended to *activity-based management*. Even so, only large industrial companies have taken much interest in either ABC or ABM and much work still needs to be done in encouraging medium and small industrial entities and many service entities of their usefulness.

There are also some other issues that are not necessarily new, such as better budgeting and performance measurement, but which are now receiving greater attention. Perhaps one emerging issue above all else is the attention currently being given to environmental matters. Many companies appear to be taking it very seriously and some of them are even publishing their own reports. It cannot be long now before the accountancy profession issues an environmental accounting standard.

We should not expect major changes to take place in management accounting practice very quickly, or indeed on any extensive scale. Such developments take a long time to become known and to become accepted. Progress will be slow and it will certainly be evolutionary rather than revolutionary.

Key points

1 Management accounting developed as a main branch of accounting towards the end of the nineteenth century.

2 By 1925 most management accounting techniques used today were in place and there was little further development until about 1980.

3 The decline of old industries in the Western world and the emergence of new economies in the Far East (particularly Japan), the introduction of new management philosophies (such as total quality management and just-in-time procedures), and new technologically based industries have together necessitated the development of more relevant management accounting techniques.

4 We can expect a slow movement towards incorporating relatively new management accounting techniques into practice over the next few years. A more strategic management accounting approach is likely, involving comparing actual results with their set objectives, more non-financial data and comparative studies of competitors' results.

5 Activity-based management will probably become more widespread, and better (if not beyond) budgeting procedures will be devised.

6 One almost certain development will be a move towards environmental costing, accounting and reporting.

7 Throughput accounting, backflush costing, target costing, value chain analysis, and product life cycle costing will all probably be increasingly adopted by large technology-based companies.

Check your learning

The answers to these questions can be found within the text.

1 What were the main causes of industrial change after the Second World War?

2 What do the following initials mean: AMT, JIT, TQM?

3 List four major causes of the change in the UK economic environment over the last 30 years.

4 Identify four implications for management accounting of such changes.

5 What do the initials ABM and ABCM stand for?

6 What is the difference between ABC and ABM?

7 List the four stages in an ABM exercise.

8 What is the difference between better budgeting and beyond budgeting?

9 List five ways by which traditional budgeting could be improved.

10 What is environmental accounting?

11 What is performance measurement?

12 What is benchmarking?

13 What is a balanced scorecard?

14 What is meant by strategic management accounting?

15 What is the main feature that distinguishes it from traditional management accounting?

16 What are the four perspectives into which it may be classified?

17 What is a target cost?

18 List six links that make up a production company's value chain.

News story quiz

Remember the news story at the beginning of this chapter? Go back to that story and reread it before answering the following questions.

Environmentalists are almost in despair at the apparent widespread lack of interest and concern there appears to be about the impact that climate change could be having on the environment. This article suggests that accountants are now beginning to get much more involved in what is commonly referred to as the green agenda. Maybe the environmentalists will be much encouraged when such a traditionally and highly conservative profession has joined the cause!

Questions

1 What role do you think management accountants should play in environmental reporting?

2 What type of information should be included in an environmental reporting system?

3 How far should the environmental monitoring and reporting process be tied in to the existing financial and management accounting system?

Tutorial questions

20.1 'Ugh!' snorted the chairman when confronting the chief accountant. 'Strategic management accounting is another of those techniques dreamed up by you and your mates to keep you in a job.' Could the chairman have a point?

20.2 'Activity-based management is fine in theory but impossible in practice.'

Discuss.

20.3 How far do you think that short budget forecasts would be more useful than budgets tied in with the traditional annual financial reporting system?

20.4 Do you think that environmental management accounting is of any benefit to a company?

20.5 Do you think that target costing serves any useful purpose in a service entity?

20.6 'Value chain analysis is just another version of activity-based management.'

Discuss.

20.7 Compare and contrast each of the following management accounting techniques and then, giving your reasons, select the one that in your opinion is most likely to be useful to a non-accounting manager: backflush costing; product life cycle costing; and throughput accounting.

Further practice questions, study material and links to relevant sites on the World Wide Web can be found on the website that accompanies this book. The site can be found at www.pearsoned.co.uk/dyson

Fixed and flexible budgets

After preparing this case study you should be able to:

• distinguish between fixed and flexible budgets;

• evaluate a budgetary control variance report;

• indicate what action should be taken to deal with any reported variances.

Background

Location:	Larkhill, Central Scotland
Company:	Larkhill Products Limited
Personnel:	Robert Jordan, Product Manager
	Dave Ellis, Management Accountant

Synopsis

Robert Jordan recently joined Larkhill Products Limited as a product manager. The company manufactures, distributes and sells a range of popular card games. At the end of his first month in post, Robert received the following statement from the management accountant.

Larkhill Products Limited
Monthly variance report: January 2012

	Per unit	Original budget	Flexed budget	Actual	Quantity variance	Price variance	Total variance
		Units	Units	Units			
Sales volume		20 000	18 000	18 000			2 000 (A)
Production volume		20 000	18 000	18 500			1 500 (A)
	£	£000	£000	£000	£000	£000	£000
Sales	40	800	720	648	–	72(A)	72(A)
Direct material	18	360	324	360	45(F)	81(A)	36(A)
Direct labour	12*	240	216	270	90(F)	144(A)	54(A)
	30	600	540	630	135(F)	225(A)	90(A)
Contribution	10	200	180	18			162(A)
Fixed costs		150	150	140		10(F)	(10)(F)
Profit/(loss)		50	30	(122)	135(F)	287(A)	152(A)

*3 DLH × £4.

Robert left school at the age of 18 with a couple of GCE Advanced Level passes. He had started his career promoting double glazing for a local company before moving into selling central heating systems. He was good at persuading people to buy and for the first ten years of his career he rarely stayed in one job for longer than two years. His ability and experience enabled him to gain promotion to more senior positions in sales and marketing.

He was never interested in going to college or university and he was far too busy to think of studying part-time for some sort of qualification. So when he joined Larkhill he knew a great deal about selling but little about the other functional activities of the company, e.g. accounting, distribution, human relations and production. His interview had not been handled particularly well, but Robert was good at dealing with people so he had been able to give the impression that he had a wide knowledge of business.

Robert panicked when he received the management accountant's statement. What was it? What did it mean? What was he supposed to do with it? Dare he ask anybody to help him?

After thinking about the problem overnight he decided to tackle it head on. The next morning he telephoned Dave Ellis, the management accountant. Robert was very authoritative and at the same time apologetic. 'Sorry about this, Dave,' he wheedled, 'as you know, I'm new here and my other companies had different ways of doing things. I'd appreciate it if you would do me a position paper about the monthly variance report.' He then indicated in more detail what he wanted. Dave agreed to supply him with some more information.

Robert was pretty sure that he had not convinced Dave about the reason why he wanted a 'position paper'. Nevertheless, he was confident that charm and warm words would see him through an embarrassing problem – as it always had.

Required:

Prepare an explanation for Robert Jordan, explaining what the monthly variance report means and what action is needed.

Standard cost operating statements

Learning objectives

After preparing this case study you should be able to:

- describe the nature and purpose of a standard cost operating statement;
- evaluate the information presented in such a statement;
- suggest ways in which that information may be enhanced.

Background

Location:	Burnley, Lancashire
Company:	Amber Textiles Limited
Personnel:	Ted Finch, Managing Director

Synopsis

Amber Textiles Limited is a small textile processing company based in Burnley in Lancashire. It is one of the few remaining such companies in the United Kingdom but it too is struggling to survive as a result of intense competition from the Far East.

The board of directors has been well aware for some time that if the company is to continue in business, it must retain its customer base by being extremely competitive. There is little scope to increase selling prices and so costs have to be controlled extremely tightly.

The Board has done everything possible to control the company's costs. For example, it recently introduced an 'information for management' (IFM) system. The system involves using budgets for control purposes but it also produces standard costs for each of the company's main product lines. A firm of management consultants installed the system with the assistance of the company's small accounting staff.

The new IFM system seemed to involve an awful lot of paperwork and the managing director, Ted Finch, was struggling to cope with the sheer volume of reports that mysteriously appeared on his desk almost every day. By profession, Ted was a textile engineer. He had little training in numerical analysis and none related to accounting.

One morning, shortly after the new system was up and running, he found the following statement on his desk.

Amber Textiles Limited
Standard Cost Operating Statement

Period: Four weeks to 31 March 2012

	£	£	£
Budgeted sales			700 000
Budgeted cost of sales			(490 000)
			210 000
Sales volume profit variance			17 600
Budgeted profit from actual sales			227 600
Variances	Favourable	Adverse	
Sales price		20 000	
Direct material price	6 700		
Direct material usage	15 400		
Direct labour rate		17 600	
Direct labour efficiency	20 800		
Variable production overhead expenditure		3 140	
Variable production overhead efficiency	2 600		
Fixed production overhead expenditure		30 000	
Fixed production overhead volume	12 000		
	57 500	70 740	(13 240)
Actual profit			214 360

Ted studied the statement carefully. What was it? How had it been produced? What did it mean? What was he supposed to do with it?

He was still somewhat puzzled after studying it for some time so he decided to telephone the management consultants responsible for installing the IFM system. They referred him to a manual that they had prepared, a copy of which lay untouched on top of Ted's bookshelf. Sure enough, the manual contained an explanation and an example of a 'standard costing operating statement'.

After studying the relevant section, Ted felt a little more confident about what he was supposed to do with the standard cost operating statement. Nevertheless, he thought that it might be useful to take some advice. So he contacted his chief accountant and asked him to prepare a written report reviewing the statement. He stressed that he wanted to know precisely what action he should take (if any) to deal with its contents.

Required:

(a) Prepare the section of an *Information for Management* manual dealing with standard cost operating statements. The section should include an outline of the nature and purpose of such a statement, an explanation of its contents and the action management should take on receiving it.

(b) With regard to the specific standard cost operating statement for the four weeks to 31 March 2012, prepare a report explaining what the data mean, what interrelationship there may be among the variances, and what specific action Ted Finch might expect his line managers to take in dealing with it.

(c) Outline what additional information might be useful to include in a standard cost operating statement.

Pricing

After preparing this case study you should be able to:

- distinguish between an absorption costing approach and a marginal costing approach;
- prepare a quotation for a customer using a number of different costing approaches;
- identify a number of other factors that must be considered when preparing a quotation.

Background

Location:	Dewsbury, West Yorkshire
Company:	Pennine Heating Systems Limited
Personnel:	Ali Shah, Managing Director
	Hugh Rodgers, Production Manager

Synopsis

Pennine Heating Systems Limited is a small heating and ventilation system company located in the West Yorkshire town of Dewsbury. It provides customer-designed systems for small businesses. The systems are designed, manufactured and installed specially for each customer. This means that each individual contract has to be priced separately.

The company had expanded rapidly in recent years but as it had done so its overhead costs had continued to increase. The managing director, Ali Shah, had always insisted that contracts should be priced on an absorption cost basis. This was not a problem in the early days of the company. There was then a considerable demand for what Pennine Systems was able to offer and customers almost always accepted whatever was quoted.

More recently, however, the demand for heating and ventilation systems had become less strong, competitors had come into the market, the national economy was in recession and customers were much more conscious about their costs than they used to be when the economy was expanding.

So while Pennine's reputation was good it had to be particularly sensitive about the price that it charged for its orders. Indeed, Ali sensed that the company was beginning to lose some business because its quotations were too high. He wondered whether he should review the pricing system in order to make sure that the company attracted sufficient business.

Ali was reminded of what he had intended to do late one Friday night when a request for a quotation landed on his desk. On the Monday, he asked Hugh Rodgers, his production manager to cost and price it. He had the results on the Wednesday morning. Hugh's calculations were as follows.

	£
Direct materials	14 000
Direct labour	41 500
Prime cost	55 500
Factory overhead	11 100
Factory cost of production	66 600
Administration overhead	6 660
Selling and distribution overhead	9 990
Total operating cost	83 250
Profit	16 650
Suggested contract price	99 900*

*say £100 000.

Note:

Factory overhead, administration overhead, and selling and distribution overhead are added to the factory cost of production at rates of 20%, 10% and 15% respectively. A profit loading of 20% is then added to the total operating cost.

Ali suspected that a contract price of £100,000 may be too high to gain the contract but he wondered whether the company could afford to accept a much lower price. He asked Hugh to conduct an intensive investigation of the cost build-up and other matters relating to the contract. Hugh did so and he discovered, *inter alia*, the following information.

1 All the overheads include a share of the fixed costs of the company. 75% of the factory overhead, 80% of the administration overhead, and 60% of the selling and distribution overhead are fixed costs.
2 Hugh has been informed privately that a number of other companies have been asked to quote for the contract and that three other companies are being considered at contract prices of £70,000, £75,000 and £95,000 respectively.

Required:

(a) Advise Ali Shah what price Pennine Heating Systems Limited should quote for the contract.
(b) Outline what factors other than price Ali should take into account before offering a firm quotation.

Appendix 1 — Further reading

This book contains sufficient material for most first-year modules in accounting for non-accounting students. Some students may require additional information, however, and it may be necessary for them to consult other books when attempting exercises set by their tutors.

There are many very good accounting books available for *accounting* students, but they usually go into considerable technical detail. *Non-accounting* students must use them with caution otherwise they will find themselves completely lost. In any case, non-accounting students do not need to process vast amounts of highly technical data. It is sufficient for their purpose if they have an understanding of where accounting information comes from, why it is prepared in that way, what it means and what reliance can be placed on it.

Bearing these points in mind, the following books are worth considering.

Financial accounting

Elliott, B. and Elliott, J. (2008) *Financial Accounting and Reporting*, 11th edn, Financial Times/Prentice Hall, Harlow. This is an excellent textbook that is now into its eleventh edition. It should be a very useful reference book for non-accounting students.

Holmes, G. and Sugden, A. (2008) *Interpreting Company Reports and Accounts*, 10th edn, Financial Times/Prentice Hall, Harlow. A well-established text that deals with company financial reporting in some detail.

Wood, F. and Sangster, A. (2008) *Business Accounting*, Volumes 1 and 2, 11th edn, Financial Times/Prentice Hall, Harlow. Wood is the master accounting-textbook writer. His books can be recommended with absolute confidence.

Management accounting

Arnold, J. and Turley, S (1996) *Accounting for Management Decisions*, 3rd edn, Financial Times Prentice Hall, Harlow. This book is aimed at first- and second-year undergraduate and professional courses. Non-accounting students should be able to follow it without too much difficulty.

Drury, C. (2008) *Management and Cost Accounting*, 7th edn, Cengage Learning, London. This book has become the established British text on management accounting. It is a big book in every sense of the word. Non-accounting students should only use it for reference.

Hopper, T., Scapen, R.W. and Northcott, D. (eds) (2007) *Issues in Management Accounting*, 3rd edn, Prentice-Hall Europe, Harlow. This book will be useful for those students who are interested in current developments in management accounting. However, be warned! It is written in an academic style and some of the chapters are very hard going. It is also now somewhat dated.

Horngren, C.T., Foster, G., Datar, S. and Rajan, M. (2008) *Cost Accounting: International Version: A Managerial Emphasis*. 13th edn, Prentice Hall, Harlow. Horngren is a long-established American text. It will be of benefit to non-accounting students mainly for reference purposes.

Smith, J.A. (ed.) (2007) *Handbook of Management Accounting*, 4th edn, CIMA Publishing/Elsevier, Oxford. This handbook contains 54 chapters on an extremely wide range of management accounting topics. It should be useful for non-accounting students when preparing essays or reports on emerging issues in management accounting.

Appendix 2 — Discount table

Present value of £1 received after *n* years discounted at *i* %

i / *n*	1	2	3	4	5	6	7	8	9	10
1	0.9901	0.9804	0.9709	0.9615	0.9524	0.9434	0.9346	0.9259	0.9174	0.9091
2	0.9803	0.9612	0.9426	0.9246	0.9070	0.8900	0.8734	0.8573	0.8417	0.8264
3	0.9706	0.9423	0.9151	0.8890	0.8638	0.8396	0.8163	0.7938	0.7722	0.7513
4	0.9610	0.9238	0.8885	0.8548	0.8227	0.7921	0.7629	0.7350	0.7084	0.6830
5	0.9515	0.9057	0.8626	0.8219	0.7835	0.7473	0.7130	0.6806	0.6499	0.6209
6	0.9420	0.8880	0.8375	0.7903	0.7462	0.7050	0.6663	0.6302	0.5963	0.5645

i / *n*	11	12	13	14	15	16	17	18	19	20
1	0.9009	0.8929	0.8850	0.8772	0.8696	0.8621	0.8547	0.8475	0.8403	0.8333
2	0.8116	0.7929	0.7831	0.7695	0.7561	0.7432	0.7305	0.7182	0.7062	0.6944
3	0.7312	0.7118	0.6931	0.6750	0.6575	0.6407	0.6244	0.6086	0.5934	0.5787
4	0.6587	0.6355	0.6133	0.5921	0.5718	0.5523	0.5337	0.5158	0.4987	0.4823
5	0.5935	0.5674	0.5428	0.5194	0.4972	0.4761	0.4561	0.4371	0.4190	0.4019
6	0.5346	0.5066	0.4803	0.4556	0.4323	0.4104	0.3898	0.3704	0.3521	0.3349

Chapter 1   **1.2**   (a) account (b) double-entry book-keeping (c) profit (d) entity (e) Industrial Revolution.

1.3   (a) false (b) false (c) true (d) true (e) false.

1.4   The AAT. It is not a chartered body and it is not considered to be one of the six major professional accountancy bodies.

1.5

Type of entity	Advantage	Disadvantage
Sole trader	The owner has total control of the business	It may be difficult to obtain sufficient finance
Partnership	The management of the business is shared	If the business is unsuccessful the partners may go bankrupt
Limited liability company	The liability of the owners is restricted	Certain financial information about the company has to be disclosed publicly

1.6   Broadcasting: quasi-governmental.
Famine relief: social organization.
Postal deliveries: quasi-governmental.
Social services: local government.
Work and pensions: central government.

Chapter 2   **2.2**   *Advantages*

Easy to compare this year's events with those that happened a year ago.
Annual comparisons are commonly made in other spheres and therefore acceptable.
A year reflects the normal climatic seasonal pattern.

Disadvantages
It is an artificial period of time.
It is either too short or too long for certain types of businesses.
Some of the information included in the annual accounts could be well over 12 months old by the time it is reported and it may by then be out of date.

2.3   Revenue should only be recognized when there is a high possibility that it will exceed the costs to date plus costs to be incurred. Even then only a proportion of the anticipated profit should be taken before the contract has been completed. Subject to these provisos, there may be a case for taking some profit towards the end of 2012.

Chapter 3	**3.1**	(a) Assets = capital + liabilities. (b) Twice.

3.2 (a) A record or a history of a certain event.
(b) A book in which a number of accounts are kept (a book of account).
(c) To receive something or the value received.
(d) To give something or the value given.

3.3 (a) Cash account; sales account.
(b) Rent paid account; bank account.
(c) Wages account; cash account.
(d) Purchases account; bank account.
(e) Ford's account; sales account.

3.4 The entries are on the wrong side.

3.5

Debit	*Credit*
(a) Suppliers	Cash
(b) Office rent	Bank
(c) Cash	Sales
(d) Bank	Dividends received

3.6 A debit balance on an account means that the total on the debit side is greater than the total on the credit side. A credit balance is the opposite.

3.7 (a) no (b) yes (c) no.

Chapter 4	**4.1**	(a) false (b) false (c) false.

4.2 (a) Land; property; plant and machinery; furniture and fittings.
(b) Stocks; trade debtors; other debtors; insurance paid in advance; bank; cash.
(c) Bank overdraft; trade creditors; other creditors; electricity owing.

4.3 (a) £3 500 [£10 000 less (2 000 + 6 000 − 1 500)]
(b) £4 000 [£10 000 less (2 000 + 6 000 − 2 000)]
(c) £4 500 [£10 000 less (2 000 + 6 000 − 2 500)]

4.4 £2 250 (£50 000 − 5 000 = 45 000 ÷ 20)

4.6 £4 500 [£4 000 + 1 000 − 500]

4.7 £11 000 [£3 000 + 10 000 − 2 000]

4.8 Probably yes. Debit the profit and loss account and credit Gibson's account. £70 000 (£75 000 − 5 000).

4.9 £1 500 [£9 000 − (250 000 × 3%)]. It will increase his profit by £1 500.

4.10 (a) Issued share capital, debenture receipts, capital expenditure.
(b) Provisions, depreciation, bad debts.

Chapter 5	**5.2**	*Advantages*

Free from personal bankrupcy
The business carries on in perpetuity
Gives some status in the community.

Disadvantages
Formal accounting records to be kept
The Companies Act 2006 accounting requirements apply
Disclosure of information to the public.

5.3 (a) net profit for the year before taxation (b) dividends.

5.4 (a) current liabilities (b) loans (c) fixed assets (d) capital (e) current assets.

Chapter 7 **7.1** Payment of trade creditors.

7.2 Issue of debenture stock, fixed assets purchased.

7.4 (a) false (b) false (c) true (d) false (e) true (f) false.

Chapter 10 **10.2** (a) true (b) true (c) true.

10.3 (a) £40 938 (b) stocks.

10.8

Company	Effect
A	Not much
B	Considerable
C	Highly significant

Chapter 11 **11.4** The expected profit on the contract is now £100 000 [£500 000 − (300 000 + 100 000)]. Depending upon a review of the expected outcome, it might be appropriate to claim some profit on account. One way would be to apportion the expected profit on the basis of costs incurred to date as a proportion of the total cost. This would give a profit of £75 000 for Year 3 (£100 000 × 300 000/400 000). However, as the contract is only 60% through it life, some accountants might reduce this by an arbitrary factor of 2/3. The profit taken would then be £50 000 (£75 000 × 2/3). This is a normal accounting approach to the problem of revenue/profit recognition on contract work. But notice how judgemental the whole exercise appears to be.

Chapter 12 **12.4** Checking, governing, recording, determining, financing, devising.

Chapter 14 **14.5** (a) predetermined (b) variance.

Chapter 17 **17.2** S − V = F + P so £100 000 − 40 000 = 50 000 + 10 000, i.e. P = £10 000

17.4

	£000	£000
Sales		75
Less: variable costs		
Direct material	10	
Direct labour	20	30
		45
Less: fixed costs		
Staff salaries	47	
Rent	3	50
Loss		(5)

17.5   The contribution per unit is £5 (£50 000 – 25 000/5 000) so another 1 000 units would have to be sold.

17.8   (a) Break-even chart

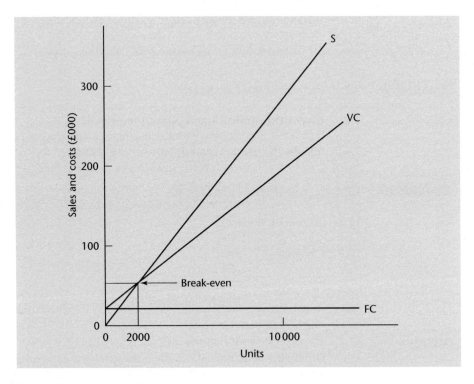

(b) Profit/volume graph

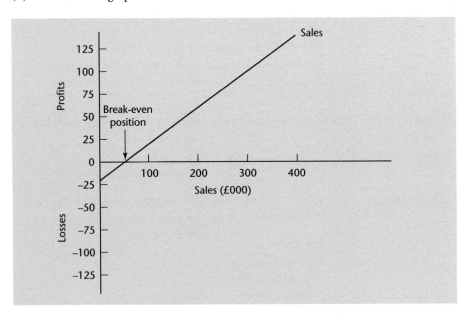

Chapter 19   **19.2**   £151.22 (£200 × 0.7561)

Chapter 1   **1.4**   Accountants collect a great deal of information about an entity's activities and then translate it into monetary terms – a language that everyone understands. The information that is collected can help non-accountants to do their job more effectively because it provides them with better guidance on which to make decisions. Any eventual decision is still theirs. Futhermore, all managers must be aware of the statutory accounting obligations to which their organization has to adhere if they are to avoid taking part in unlawful acts.

1.5   To collect and store detailed information about an entity's activities.
To abstract and summarize information in the most effective way for the requirements of a specified user or group of users.

1.6   None. The preparation of management accounts is for the entity to decide whether they serve a useful purpose.

1.8   Statutory obligations are contained in the Companies Act 2006. In addition, listed companies have to abide by certain mandatory professional requirements.

Chapter 2   **2.4**   (a) Matching
(b) Historic cost
(c) Quantitative
(d) Periodicity
(e) Reliability
(f) Going concern

2.5   (a) Relevance
(b) Entity
(c) Comparability
(d) Materiality
(e) Historic cost
(f) Realization

2.6   (a) Entity
(b) Reliability
(c) Periodicity
(d) Reliability
(e) Dual aspect
(f) Realization

Chapter 3 **3.4** Adam's books of account:

Account

Debit	Credit
(a) Cash	Capital
(b) Purchases	Cash
(c) Van	Cash
(d) Rent	Cash
(e) Cash	Sales
(f) Office machinery	Cash

3.5 Brown's books of account:

Account

Debit	Credit
(a) Bank	Cash
(b) Cash	Sales
(c) Purchases	Bank
(d) Office expenses	Cash
(e) Bank	Sales
(f) Motor car	Bank

3.10 Ivan's ledger accounts:

Cash Account

		£			£
1.9.10	Capital	10 000	2.9.10	Bank	8 000
12.9.10	Cash	3 000	3.9.10	Purchases	1 000

Capital Account

		£			£
			1.9.10	Cash	10 000

Bank Account

		£			£
2.9.10	Cash	8 000	20.9.10	Roy	6 000
30.9.10	Norman	2 000			

Purchases Account

		£			£
3.9.10	Cash	1 000			
10.9.10	Roy	6 000			

Roy's Account

		£			£
20.9.10	Bank	6 000	10.9.10	Purchases	6 000

Sales Account

		£			£
			12.9.10	Cash	3 000
			15.9.10	Norman	4 000

Norman

		£			£
15.9.10	Sales	4 000	30.9.10	Bank	2 000

3.11 Jones's ledger accounts:

Bank Account

		£				£
1.10.11	Capital	20 000	10.10.11	Petty cash		1 000
			25.10.11	Lang		5 000
			29.10.11	Green		10 000

Capital Account

		£			£
			1.10.11	Bank	20 000

Van Account

		£	£
2.10.11	Lang	5 000	

Lang's Account

		£			£
25.10.11	Bank	5 000	2.10.11	Van	5 000

Purchases Account

		£	£
6.10.11	Green	15 000	
20.10.11	Cash	3 000	

Green's Account

		£			£
28.10.11	Discounts received	500	6.10.11	Purchases	15 000
29.10.11	Bank	10 000			

Petty Cash Account

		£			£
10.10.11	Bank	1 000	22.10.11	Miscellaneous expenses	500

Sales

		£			£
			14.10.11	Haddock	6 000
			18.10.11	Cash	5 000

Haddock

		£			£
14.10.11	Sales	6 000	30.10.11	Discounts allowed	600
			31.10.11	Cash	5 400

Cash Account

		£			£
18.10.11	Sales	5 000	20.10.11	Purchases	3 000
31.10.11	Haddock	5 400			

Miscellaneous Expenses

		£	£
22.10.11	Petty cash	500	

Discounts Received Account

		£			£
			28.10.11	Green	500

Discounts Allowed Account

		£	£
30.10.11	Haddock	600	

3.13 (a), (b) and (c) Pat's ledger accounts:

Cash Account

		£			£
1.12.10	Capital	10000	24.12.10	Office expenses	5000
29.12.10	Fog	4000	31.12.10	Grass	6000
29.12.10	Mist	6000	31.12.10	Seed	8000
			31.12.10	Balance c/d	1000
		20000			20000
1.1.11	Balance b/d	1000			

Capital Account

		£			£
			1.12.10	Cash	10000

Purchases Account

		£			£
2.12.10	Grass	6000			
2.12.10	Seed	7000			
15.12.10	Grass	3000			
15.12.10	Seed	4000	31.12.10	Balance c/d	20000
		20000			20000
1.1.11	Balance b/d	20000			

Grass's Account

		£			£
12.12.10	Purchases returned	1000	2.12.10	Purchases	6000
31.12.10	Cash	6000	15.12.10	Purchases	3000
31.12.10	Balance c/d	2000			
		9000			9000
			1.1.11	Balance b/d	2000

Seed's Account

		£			£
12.12.10	Purchases returned	2000	2.12.10	Purchases	7000
31.12.10	Cash	8000	15.12.10	Purchases	4000
31.12.10	Balance c/d	1000			
		11000			11000
			1.1.11	Balance b/d	1000

Sales Account

		£			£
			10.12.10	Fog	3000
			10.12.10	Mist	4000
			20.12.10	Fog	2000
31.12.10	Balance c/d	12000	20.12.10	Mist	3000
		12000			12000
			1.1.11	Balance b/d	12000

Fog's Account

		£			£
10.12.10	Sales	3 000	29.12.10	Cash	4 000
20.12.10	Sales	2 000	31.12.10	Balance c/d	1 000
		5 000			5 000
1.1.11	Balance b/d	1 000			

Mist's Account

		£			£
10.12.10	Sales	4 000	29.12.10	Cash	6 000
20.12.10	Sales	3 000	31.12.10	Balance c/d	1 000
		7 000			7 000
1.1.11	Balance b/d	1 000			

Purchases Returned Account

		£			£
			12.12.10	Grass	1 000
31.12.10	Balance c/d	3 000	12.12.10	Seed	2 000
		3 000			3 000
			1.1.11	Balance b/d	3 000

Office Expenses Account

		£			£
24.12.10	Cash	5 000			

Tutorial note

It is unnecessary to balance off an account and bring down the balance if there is only a single entry in it.

(d) Pat's trial balance:

Pat
Trial balance at 31 December 2010

	£ *Dr*	£ *Cr*
Cash	1 000	
Capital		10 000
Purchases	20 000	
Grass		2 000
Seed		1 000
Sales		12 000
Fog	1 000	
Mist	1 000	
Purchases returned		3 000
Office expenses	5 000	
	28 000	28 000

3.14 (a) Vale's books of account:

Bank Account

		£			£
1.1.11	Balance b/d	5 000	31.12.11	Dodd	29 000
31.12.11	Fish	45 000	31.12.11	Delivery van	12 000
31.12.11	Cash	3 000	31.12.11	Balance c/d	12 000
		53 000			53 000
1.1.12	Balance b/d	12 000			

Capital Account

		£			£
			1.1.11	Balance b/d	20 000

Cash Account

		£			£
1.1.11	Balance b/d	1 000	31.12.11	Purchases	15 000
31.12.11	Sales	20 000	31.12.11	Office expenses	9 000
31.12.11	Fish	7 000	31.12.11	Bank	3 000
			31.12.11	Balance c/d	1 000
		28 000			28 000
1.1.12	Balance b/d	1 000			

Dodd's Account

		£			£
31.12.11	Bank	29 000	1.1.11	Balance b/d	2 000
31.12.11	Balance c/d	3 000	31.12.11	Purchases	30 000
		32 000			32 000
			1.1.12	Balance b/d	3 000

Fish's Account

		£			£
1.1.11	Balance b/d	6 000	31.12.11	Bank	45 000
31.12.11	Sales	50 000	31.12.11	Cash	7 000
			31.12.11	Balance c/d	4 000
		56 000			56 000
1.1.12	Balance b/d	4 000			

Furniture Account

		£			£
1.1.11	Balance b/d	10 000			

Purchases Account

		£			£
31.12.11	Dodd	30 000			
31.12.11	Cash	15 000	31.12.11	Balance c/d	45 000
		45 000			45 000
1.1.12	Balance b/d	45 000			

Sales Account

		£				£
			31.12.11	Cash		20 000
31.12.11	Balance c/d	70 000	31.12.11	Fish		50 000
		70 000				70 000
			1.1.12	Balance b/d		70 000

Office Expenses Account

		£		£
31.12.11	Cash	9 000		

Delivery Van Account

		£		£
31.12.11	Bank	12 000		

(b) Vale's trial balance:

Vale
Trial balance at 31 December 2011

	Dr	Cr
	£	£
Bank	12 000	
Capital		20 000
Cash	1 000	
Dodd		3 000
Fish	4 000	
Furniture	10 000	
Purchases	45 000	
Sales		70 000
Office expenses	9 000	
Delivery van	12 000	
	93 000	93 000

Chapter 4 **4.7** Ethel's accounts:

Ethel
Trading, profit and loss account for the year to
31 January 2010

	£
Sales	35 000
Less: Purchases	20 000
Gross profit	15 000
Less: Expenses:	
Office expenses	11 000
Net profit	4 000

Ethel
Balance sheet at 31 January 2010

Fixed assets	£	£
Premises		8000
Current assets		
Debtors	6000	
Cash	3000	
	9000	
Less: Current liabilities		
Creditors	3000	6000
		14000
Financed by:		
Capital		
Balance at 1 February 2009		10000
Net profit for the year		4000
		14000

4.8 Marion's accounts:

Marion
Trading, profit and loss account for the year to 28 February 2011

	£000	£000
Sales		400
Less: Purchases		200
Gross profit		200
Less: Expenses:		
Heat and light	10	
Miscellaneous expenses	25	
Wages and salaries	98	133
Net profit		67

Marion
Balance sheet at 28 February 2011

Fixed assets	£000	£000
Buildings		50
Current assets		
Debtors	30	
Bank	4	
Cash	2	
	36	
Less: Current liabilities		
Creditors	24	12
		62

	£000	£000
Financed by:		
Capital		
Balance at 1 March 2010		50
Net profit for the year	67	
Less: Drawings	55	12
		62

4.12 (a) Lathom's trading account:

Lathom
Trading account for the year to 30 April 2010

	£	£
Sales		60 000
Less: Cost of goods sold:		
Opening stock	3 000	
Purchases	45 000	
	48 000	
Less: Closing stock	4 000	44 000
Gross profit		16 000

(b) The stock would be shown under current assets, normally as the first item.

4.14 Standish's accounts:

Standish
Trading, profit and loss account for the year
to 31 May 2012

	£	£
Sales		79 000
Less: Cost of goods sold:		
Opening stock	7 000	
Purchases	52 000	
	59 000	
Less: Closing stock	12 000	47 000
Gross profit		32 000
Less: Expenses:		
Heating and lighting	1 500	
Miscellaneous	6 700	
Wages and salaries	17 800	26 000
Net profit		6 000

Standish
Balance sheet at 31 May 2012

	£	£
Fixed assets		
Furniture and fittings		8 000
Current assets		
Stock	12 000	
Debtors	6 000	
Cash	1 200	
	19 200	
Less: *Current liabilities*		
Creditors	4 300	14 900
		22 900
Financed by:		
Capital		
Balance at 1 June 2011		22 400
Net profit for the year	6 000	
Less: Drawings	5 500	500
		22 900

4.17 Pine's accounts:

Pine
Trading, profit and loss account for the year to
30 September 2012

	£	£
Sales		40 000
Less: Cost of goods sold:		
Purchases	21 000	
Less: Closing stock	3 000	18 000
Gross profit		22 000
Less: Expenses:		
Depreciation: furniture		
(15% × £8 000)	1 200	
General expenses	14 000	
Insurance (£2 000 − 200)	1 800	
Telephone (£1 500 + 500)	2 000	19 000
Net profit		3 000

Pine
Balance sheet at 30 September 2012

	£	£	£
Fixed assets			
Furniture			8 000
Less: Depreciation			1 200
		c/f	6 800

	£	£	£
			b/f 6 800
Current assets			
Stock		3 000	
Debtors		5 000	
Prepayments		200	
Cash		400	
		8 600	
Less: Current liabilities			
Creditors	5 900		
Accrual	500	6 400	2 200
			9 000
Financed by:			
Capital			
At 1 October 2011			6 000
Net profit for the year			3 000
			9 000

Chapter 5   **5.4**   Margo Ltd's accounts:

Margo Limited
Profit and loss account for the year to 31 January 2010

	£000
Profit for the financial year	10
Tax on profit	3
Profit after tax	7
Proposed dividend (10p × £50)	5
Retained profit for the year	2

Margo Limited
Balance sheet at 31 January 2010

	£000	£000	£000
Fixed assets			
Plant and equipment at cost			70
Less: Accumulated depreciation			25
			45
Current assets			
Stocks		17	
Trade debtors		20	
Cash at bank and in hand		5	
	c/f	42	45

	£000	£000	£000
		b/f 42	45
Less: Current liabilities			
Trade creditors	12		
Taxation	3		
Proposed dividend	5	20	22
			67

Capital and reserves	Authorized	Issued and fully paid
	£000	£000
Share capital (ordinary shares of £1 each)	75	50
Profit and loss account (£15 + 2)		17
		67

5.5 Harry Ltd's accounts:

Harry Limited
Profit and loss account for the year to 28 February 2011

	£000	£000
Gross profit for the year		150
Administration expenses		
[£65 + (10% × £60)]	71	
Distribution costs	15	86
Profit for the year		64
Taxation		24
Profit after tax		40
Dividends: Ordinary proposed	20	
Preference paid	6	26
Retained profit for the year		14

Harry Limited
Balance sheet at 28 February 2011

	£000	£000	£000
Fixed assets			
Furniture and equipment at cost			60
Less: Accumulated depreciation			42
			18
Current assets			
Stocks		130	
Trade debtors		135	
Cash at bank and in hand		10	
	c/f	275	18

	£000	£000	£000
		b/f 275	18
Less: Current liabilities			
Trade creditors	25		
Taxation	24		
Proposed dividend	20	69	206
			224

Capital and reserves	*Authorized, issued and fully paid*
	£000
Ordinary shares of £1 each	100
Cumulative 15% preference shares of £1 each	40
Share premium account	20
Profit and loss account (£50 + 14)	64
	224

5.6 Jim Ltd's accounts:

(a)

Jim Limited
Trading and profit and loss account for the year to 31 March 2011

	£000	£000	£000
Sales			270
Less: Cost of goods sold:			
Opening stock		16	
Purchases		124	
		140	
Less: Closing stock		14	126
Gross profit			144
Less: Expenses:			
Advertising		3	
Depreciation: furniture			
and fittings (15% × £20)	3		
vehicles (25% × £40)	10	13	
Directors' fees		6	
Rent and rates		10	
Telephone and stationery		5	
Travelling		2	
Wages and salaries		24	63
Net profit			81
Corporation tax			25
Net profit after tax			56
Proposed dividend			28
Retained profit for the year			28

Jim Limited
Balance sheet at 31 March 2011

	Cost	Depreciation	Net book value
	£000	£000	£000
Fixed assets			
Vehicles	40	20	20
Furniture and fittings	20	12	8
	60	32	28
Current assets			
Stocks		14	
Debtors		118	
Bank		11	
		143	
Less: Current liabilities			
Creditors	12		
Taxation	25		
Proposed dividend	28	65	78
			106

	Authorized	Issued and fully paid
	£000	£000
Capital and reserves		
Ordinary shares of £1 each	100	70
Profit and loss account (£8 + 28)		36
		106

(b) According to Jim Limited's balance sheet as at 31 March 2011 the value of the business was £106,000. This is misleading. Under the historic cost convention the balance sheet is merely a statement listing all the balances left in the double-entry book-keeping system after the preparation of the profit and loss account.

It would be relatively easy, for example, to amend the balance of £106,000 by adjusting the method used for calculating depreciation and for valuing stocks. Furthermore, when a business is liquidated it does not necessarily mean that the balances shown in the balance sheet for other items (e.g. fixed assets, debtors and creditors) will be realized at their balance sheet amounts. There will also be costs associated with the liquidation of the business.

Chapter 6   **6.4**   Megg's accounts:

Megg
Manufacturing account for the year to 31 January 2010

	£000	£000
Direct materials:		
Stock at 1 February 2009	10	
Purchases	34	
	44	
Less: Stock at 31 January 2010	12	
Materials consumed		32
Direct wages		65
Prime cost		97
Factory overhead expenses:		
Administration	27	
Heat and light	9	
Indirect wages	13	49
		146
Work-in-progress at 1 February 2009	17	
Less: Work-in-progress at 31 January 2010	14	3
Manufacturing cost of goods produced		149

6.5   Moor's accounts:

Moor
Manufacturing account for the year to 28 February 2011

	£	£
Direct materials:		
Stock at 1 March 2010	13 000	
Purchases	127 500	
	140 500	
Less: Stock at 28 February 2011	15 500	125 000
Direct wages		50 000
Prime cost		175 000
Factory overheads		27 700
		202 700
Work-in-progress at 1 March 2010	8 400	
Less: Work-in-progress at 28 February 2011	6 300	2 100
Manufacturing cost of goods produced		204 800

Chapter 7 **7.4** (a) Dennis Ltd's accounts using FRS 1 format:

Dennis Limited
Cash flow statement for the year ended 31 January 2010

	£000
Net cash inflow from operating activities	4
Capital expenditure	
Payments to acquire tangible fixed assets	(100)
	(96)
Management of liquid resource and financing	
Issue of ordinary share capital	100
Increase in cash	4

Reconciliation of operating profit to net cash inflow from operating activities

	£000
Operating profit (£60 – 26)	34
Increase in stocks	(20)
Increase in debtors	(50)
Increase in creditors	40
Net cash inflow from operating activities	4

(a) Dennis Ltd's accounts using IAS 7 format:

Dennis Limited
Cash flow statement for the year ended 31 January 2010

	£000	£000
Cash flows from operating activities		
Profit before taxation (£60 – 26)	34	
Adjustments for:		
Increase in trade and other receivables (£250 – 200)	(50)	
Increase in inventories (£120 – 100)	(20)	
Increase in trade payables (£220 – 180)	40	
Cash generated from operations	4	
Net cash from operating activities		4
Cash flows from investing activities		
Purchase of property, plant and equipment (£700 – 600)	(100)	
Net cash used in investing activities		(100)
Cash flows from financing activities		
Proceeds from issue of share capital (£800 – 700)	100	
Net cash used in financing activities		100
Net increase in cash and cash equivalents		4
Cash and cash equivalents at 1 February 2009		6
Cash and cash equivalents at 31 January 2010		10

(b) Dennis Limited generated £4000 cash from its operating activities during the year to 31 January 2010. It also increased its cash position by that amount during the year. However, it did invest £100,000 in purchasing some tangible fixed assets during the year, but this appeared to be paid for out of issuing another £100,000 of ordinary shares.

The cash from operating activities seems low. Its probably needs to examine its stock policy and its debtor collection arrangements because both stocks and debtors increased during the year. Its creditors also increased. Taken together, these changes might indicate that it is beginning to run into cash flow problems.

7.5   Frank Ltd's accounts using FRS1 format:

Frank Limited
Cash flow statement for the year ended 28 February 2012

	£000
Net cash inflow from operating activities	70
Management of liquid resources and financing	
Issue of debenture loan	60
Purchase of investments	(100)
Increase in cash	30

Reconciliation of operating profit to net cash inflow from operating activities

	£000
Operating profit (£40 – 30)	10
Depreciation charges	20
Increase in stocks	(30)
Decrease in debtors	110
Decrease in creditors	(40)
Net cash inflow from operating activities	70

No details of debenture interest were given in the question.

Reconciliation of net cash flow to movement in net debt:

	£000	£000
Increase in cash in the period	30	
Cash inflow from increase in debt	(60)	(30)
Net debt at 1.3.11		(20)
Net debt at 28.2.12		(50)

Analysis of changes in net debt:

	At 1.3.11	Cash flows	At 28.2.12
	£000	*£000*	*£000*
Cash at bank	(20)	30	10
Debt due after 1 year	–	(60)	(60)
Total	(20)	(30)	(50)

(a) Frank Ltd's accounts using IAS 7 format

Frank Limited
Cash flow statement for the year ended 28 February 2012

	£000	£000
Cash flows from operating activities		
Profit before taxation (£40 – 30)	10	
Adjustments for:		
Depreciation (£100 – 80)	20	
	30	
Decrease in trade and other receivables		
(£110 – 220)	110	
Increase in inventories (£190 – 160)	(30)	
Decrease in trade payables (£160 – 200)	(40)	
Cash generated from operations	70	
Net cash from operating activities		70
Cash flows from investing activities		
Purchase of shares	(100)	
Net cash used in investing activities		(100)
Cash flows from financing activities		
Proceeds from long-term borrowings (£60 – 0)	60	
Net cash used in financing activities		60
Net increase in cash and cash equivalents		30
Cash and cash equivalents at 1 March 2011		(20)
Cash and cash equivalents at 28 February 2012		10

(b) The cash flow statement for the year ended 28 February 2012 tells the managers of Frank Limited that the company increased its cash position by £30,000 during the year. Its operating activities generated £70,000 in cash. This was supplemented by issuing £60,000 of debenture stock making the total increase in cash £130,000. However, £100,000 of cash was used to purchase some investments.

More tests would need to be done but on the limited evidence available, the company's cash position as at the end of the year looked healthy.

Chapter 10 **10.4** **Betty**
Accounting ratios year to 31 January 2011:

(a) Gross profit ratio:

$$\frac{\text{Gross profit}}{\text{Sales}} \times 100 = \frac{30}{100} \times 100 = \underline{\underline{30\%}}$$

(b) Net profit ratio:

$$\frac{\text{Net profit}}{\text{Sales}} \times 100 = \frac{14}{100} \times 100 = \underline{\underline{14\%}}$$

(c) Return on capital employed:

$$\frac{\text{Net profit}}{\text{Capital}} \times 100 = \frac{14}{48} \times 100 = \underline{\underline{29.2\%}}$$

(d) Current ratio:

$$\frac{\text{Current assets}}{\text{Current liabilities}} = \frac{25}{6} = \underline{\underline{4.2 \text{ to } 1}}$$

(e) Acid test:

$$\frac{\text{Current assets} - \text{stock}}{\text{Current liabilities}} = \frac{25 - 10}{6} = \underline{\underline{2.5 \text{ to } 1}}$$

(f) Stock turnover:

$$\frac{\text{Cost of goods sold}}{\text{Stock}} = \frac{70}{10} = \underline{\underline{7 \text{ times}}}$$

(g) Debtor collection period:

$$\frac{\text{Trade debtors}}{\text{Credit sales}} \times 365 = \frac{12}{100} \times 365 = \underline{\underline{44 \text{ days}}} \text{ (rounded up)}$$

10.5 **James Limited**
Accounting ratios year to 28 February 2012:

(a) Return on capital employed:

$$\frac{\text{Net profit before taxation and dividends}}{\text{Shareholders' funds}} \times 100 = \frac{90}{620} \times 100 = \underline{\underline{14.5\%}}$$

(b) Gross profit:

$$\frac{\text{Gross profit}}{\text{Sales}} \times 100 = \frac{600}{1200} \times 100 = \underline{\underline{50\%}}$$

(c) Mark-up:

$$\frac{\text{Gross profit}}{\text{Cost of goods sold}} \times 100 = \frac{600}{600} \times 100 = \underline{\underline{100\%}}$$

(d) Net profit:

$$\frac{\text{Net profit before taxation and dividends}}{\text{Sales}} \times 100 = \frac{90}{1200} \times 100 = \underline{\underline{7.5\%}}$$

(e) Acid test:

$$\frac{\text{Current assets} - \text{stock}}{\text{Current liabilities}} = \frac{275 - 75}{240} \times 100 = \underline{\underline{0.83 \text{ to } 1}}$$

(f) Fixed assets turnover:

$$\frac{\text{Sales}}{\text{Fixed assets (NBV)}} = \frac{1200}{685} = \underline{\underline{1.75 \text{ times}}}$$

(g) Debtor collection period:

$$\frac{\text{Trade debtors}}{\text{Credit sales}} \times 365 = \frac{200}{1200} \times 365 = \underline{\underline{61 \text{ days}}} \text{ (rounded up)}$$

(h) Capital gearing:

$$\frac{\text{Long-term loans}}{\text{Shareholders' funds} + \text{long-term loans}} \times 100 = \frac{100}{720} \times 100 = \underline{\underline{13.9\%}}$$

Chapter 12 **12.4** The main function of *accounting* is to collect quantifiable data, translate it into monetary terms, store the information and extract and summarize it in a format convenient for those parties who require such information.

Financial accounting and management accounting are two important branches of accounting. The main difference between them is that financial accounting specializes in supplying information to parties *external* to an entity, such as shareholders or governmental departments. Management accounting information is mainly directed at the supply of information to parties *internal* to an entity, such as the entity's directors and managers.

12.5 A management accountant employed by a large manufacturing entity will be involved in the collecting and storing of data (largely, although not exclusively, of a financial nature) and the supply of information to management for planning, control and decision-making purposes. Increasingly, a management accountant is seen to be an integral member of an entity's management team responsible for advice on all financial matters.

Depending on seniority, the management accountant may be involved in some routine and basic duties such as the processing of data and the calculation of product costs and the valuation of stocks. At a more senior level, the role may be much more concerned with advising on the financial impact of a wide variety of managerial decisions, such as whether to close down a product line or determining the selling price of a new product.

Chapter 13 **13.2** Charge to production:
(a) FIFO:

		£
1000 units	@ £20 =	20 000
250 units	@ £25 =	6 250
Charge to production		26 250

(b) Continuous weighted average:

Date	Units		Value £
1.1.12	1 000	@ £20	20 000
15.1.12	500	@ £25	12 500
	1 500		32 500

$$\text{Average} = \frac{£32\,500}{1\,500} = \underline{\underline{£21.67}}$$

Charge to production on $31.1.12 = 1\,250 \times £21.67 = \underline{\underline{£27\,088}}$

13.3 Value of closing stock

Material ST 2

	Stock	Units	Total stock value £	Average unit price £
1.2.10	Opening	500	500	1.00
10.2.10	Receipts	200	220	
		700	720	1.03
12.2.10	Receipts	100	112	
		800	832	1.04
17.2.10	Issues	(400)	(416)	
25.2.10	Receipts	300	345	
		700	761	1.09
27.2.10	Issues	(250)	(273)	
28.0.10	Closing stock	450	488	

Chapter 14 **14.6** Scar Ltd's overhead:

Scar Limited
Overhead apportionment January 2012:

	Production Department		Service Department
	A £000	B £000	£000
Allocated expenses	65	35	50
Apportionment of service department's expenses in the ratio 60 : 40	30	20	(50)
Overhead to be charged	95	55	–

14.7 Bank Ltd's overhead:

Bank Limited
Assembly department – overhead absorption methods:

(a) Specific units:

$$\frac{\text{Total cost centre overhead}}{\text{Number of units}} = \frac{£250\,000}{50\,000} = \underline{\underline{£5 \text{ per unit}}}$$

(b) Direct materials:

$$\frac{\text{Total cost centre overhead}}{\text{Direct materials}} \times 100 = \frac{£250\,000}{500\,000} \times 100 = 50\%$$

Therefore 50% of £8 = $\underline{\underline{£4 \text{ per unit}}}$

(c) Direct labour:

$$\frac{\text{Total cost centre overhead}}{\text{Direct labour}} \times 100 = \frac{£250\,000}{1\,000\,000} \times 100 = 25\%$$

Therefore 25% of £30 = £7.50 per unit

(d) Prime cost:

$$\frac{\text{Total cost centre overhead}}{\text{Prime cost}} \times 100 = \frac{£250\,000}{1\,530\,000} \times 100 = 16.34\%$$

Therefore 16.34% of £40 = £6.54 per unit

(e) Direct labour hours:

$$\frac{\text{Total cost centre overhead}}{\text{Direct labour hours}} = \frac{£250\,000}{100\,000} = £2.50 \text{ per direct labour hour}$$

Therefore £2.50 of 3.5 DLH = £8.75 per unit

(f) Machine hours:

$$\frac{\text{Total cost centre overhead}}{\text{Machine hours}} = \frac{£250\,000}{25\,000} = £10 \text{ per machine hour}$$

Therefore £10 of 0.75 = £7.50 per unit

Chapter 15

15.5 Direct materials budget for Tom Ltd:

TOM LIMITED

(a) Direct materials usage budget:

	Number of units						
Month	*30.4.11*	*31.5.11*	*30.6.11*	*31.7.11*	*31.8.11*	*30.9.11*	*Six months to 30.9.11*
Component:							
A6 (2 units for X)	280	560	1 400	760	600	480	4 080
B9 (3 units for X)	420	840	2 100	1 140	900	720	6 120

(b) Direct materials purchase budget:

Component A6							
Material usage (as above)	280	560	1 400	760	600	480	4 080
Add: Desired closing stock	110	220	560	300	240	200	200
	390	780	1 960	1 060	840	680	4 280
Less: Opening stock	100	110	220	560	300	240	100
Purchases (units) ×	290	670	1 740	500	540	440	4 180
Price per unit =	£5	£5	£5	£5	£5	£5	£5
Total purchases	£1 450	£3 350	£8 700	£2 500	£2 700	£2 200	£20 900

Month	*30.4.11*	*31.5.11*	*30.6.11*	*31.7.11*	*31.8.11*	*30.9.11*	*Six months to 30.9.11*

Number of units

Component B9							
Material usage (as above)	420	840	2 100	1 140	900	720	6 120
Add: Desired closing stock	250	630	340	300	200	180	180
	670	1 470	2 440	1 440	1 100	900	6 300
Less: Opening stock	200	250	630	340	300	200	200
Purchases (units)	470	1 220	1 810	1 100	800	700	6 100
Price per unit	£10	£10	£10	£10	£10	£10	£10
Total purchases	£4 700	£12 200	£18 100	£11 000	£8 000	£7 000	£61 000

15.6 Direct labour budget for Don Ltd:
Don Limited
Direct labour cost budget:

	Quarter 30.6.12	31.7.12	31.8.12	*Three months to 31.8.12*
Grade:				
Production (units) ×	600	700	650	1 950
Direct labour hours per unit =	3	3	3	3
Total direct labour hours	1 800	2 100	1 950	5 850
Budgeted rate per hour (£) ×	4	4	4	4
Production cost (£) = *c/f*	7 200	8 400	7 800	23 400

	Quarter 30.6.12	31.7.12	31.8.12	*Three months to 31.8.12*
Production cost (£) = *b/f*	7 200	8 400	7 800	23 400
Finishing (units)	600	700	650	1 950
Direct labour hours per unit ×	2	2	2	2
Total direct labour hours =	1 200	1 400	1 300	3 900
Budgeted rate per hour (£) ×	8	8	8	8
Finishing cost (£) =	9 600	11 200	10 400	31 200
Total budgeted direct labour cost (£)	16 800	19 600	18 200	54 600

Chapter 16   **16.4** Variances for X Ltd:

(a) Direct materials total variance: £

Actual price per unit × actual quantity = £12 × 6 units   72
Less: Standard price per unit × standard quantity for
    actual production = £10 × 5 units   50
    22   (A)

(b) Direct materials price variance:
(Actual price – standard price) × actual quantity
= (£12 – 10) × 6 units
£12   (A)

(c) Direct materials usage variance:
(Actual quantity – standard quantity) × standard
price = (6 – 5 units) × £10
£10   (A)

16.6 **Variances for Bruce Ltd:**

(a) Direct labour total variance: £

Actual hours × actual hourly rate = 1000 hrs × £6.50 — 6 500

Less: Standard hours for actual production ×

standard hourly rate = 900 hrs × £6.00 — 5 400

£1 100 (A)

(b) Direct labour rate variance:

(Actual hourly – standard hourly rate)

× actual hours = (£6.50 – 6.00) × 1000 hrs — £500 (A)

(c) Direct labour efficiency variance:

(Actual hours – standard hours for actual production)

× standard hourly rate = (1000 hrs – 900) × £6.00 — £600 (A)

16.8 **Overhead variances for Anthea Ltd:**

(a) Fixed production overhead total variance: £

Actual fixed overhead — 150 000

Less: Standard hours of production × fixed

production overhead absorption rate = (8000 hrs × £15) — 120 000

£30 000 (A)

(b) Fixed production overhead expenditure variance:

Actual fixed overhead – budgeted fixed overhead =

(£150 000 – 135 000) — £15 000 (A)

(c) Fixed production overhead volume variance:

Budgeted fixed overhead – (standard hours of

production × fixed production overhead

absorption rate) = [£135 000 – (8000 × £15)] — £15 000 (A)

16.9 **Performance measures for Anthea Ltd:**

Performance measures:

(a) Efficiency ratio:

$$\frac{SHP}{Actual\ hours} \times 100 = \frac{8000}{10\,000} \times 100 = \underline{\underline{80\%}}$$

(b) Capacity ratio:

$$\frac{Actual\ hours}{Budgeted\ hours^*} \times 100 = \frac{10\,000}{9000} \times 100 = \underline{\underline{111.1\%}}$$

(c) Production volume ratio:

$$\frac{SHP}{Budgeted\ hours^*} \times 100 = \frac{8000}{9000} \times 100 = \underline{\underline{88.9\%}}$$

$$^*\frac{135\,000}{15}$$

16.12 Selling price variance for Milton Ltd:

(a) Selling price variance:

[Actual sales revenue – (actual quantity × standard cost per unit)] £9000 (F)
– (actual quantity × standard profit per unit) = [£99 000 –
(9000 × £7)] – (9000 × £3*) =

* £10 – 3

(b) Sales volume profit variance:

(Actual quantity – budgeted quantity) × standard
profit = (9000 units – 10 000) × £3 £3000 (A)

(c) Sales variances = £9000 (F) + 3000 (A) = £6000 (F)

Chapter 17 **17.4** Contribution analysis for Pole Ltd:

Pole Limited
Marginal cost statement for the year to 31 January 2012

	£000	£000
Sales		450
Less: Variable costs:		
Direct materials	60	
Direct wages	26	
Administration expenses: variable (£7 + 4)	11	
Research and development expenditure: variable (£15 + 5)	20	
Selling and distribution expenditure: variable (£4 + 9)	13	130
		320
Contribution		
Less: Fixed costs:		
Administration expenses (£30 + 16)	46	
Materials: indirect	5	
Production overhead	40	
Research and development expenditure (£60 + 5)	65	
Selling and distribution expenditure (£80 + 21)	101	
Wages: indirect	13	270
Profit		50

17.5 Break-even chart for Giles Ltd:

Giles Limited

(a) (i) *Break-even point*:

In value terms:

$$\frac{\text{Fixed costs} \times \text{sales}}{\text{Contribution}} = \frac{£150\,000 \times 500}{(500 - 300)} = \underline{\underline{£375\,000}}$$

In units:

	£
Selling price per unit (£500 ÷ 50)	10
Less: Variable cost per unit (£300 ÷ 50)	6
Contribution per unit	4

$$\frac{\text{Fixed costs}}{\text{Contribution per unit}} = \frac{£150\,000}{4} = \underline{\underline{37\,500 \text{ units}}}$$

(ii) *Margin of safety*:

In value terms:

$$\frac{\text{Profit} \times \text{sales}}{\text{Contribution}} = \frac{£50\,000 \times 500}{200} = \underline{\underline{£125\,000}}$$

In units:

$$\frac{\text{Profit}}{\text{Contribution per unit}} = \frac{£50\,000}{4} = \underline{\underline{12\,500 \text{ units}}}$$

(b) *Break-even chart*:

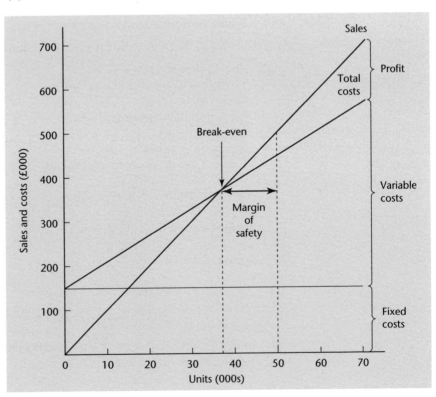

Chapter 18   **18.4**   **A special contract for Micro Ltd:**

Budgeted contribution per unit of limiting factor for the year:

$$\frac{£250\,000}{50\,000} = \underline{\underline{£5 \text{ per direct labour hour}}}$$

Contribution per unit of limiting factor for the special contract:

	£	£
Contract price		50 000
Less: Variable costs:		
Direct materials	10 000	
Direct labour	30 000	40 000
Contribution		10 000

Therefore contribution per unit of limiting factor:

$$\frac{£10\,000}{4\,000 \text{ DLH}} = \underline{\underline{£2.50 \text{ per direct labour hour}}}$$

Conclusion:

The special contract earns less contribution per unit of limiting factor than does the *average* of ordinary budgeted work. It may be profitable to accept the contract if either it displaces less profitable work or surplus direct labour hours are available. A careful assessment should be undertaken to ascertain whether much more profitable work would be found than is the case with the contract if it will displace other more profitable contracts that could arise in the near future.

18.5   Contributions for Temple Ltd:

(a) **Calculation of the contribution per unit of limiting factor**

(i)   Normal work:

	£
Sales	6 000
Direct materials (100 kilos)	700
Direct labour (200 hours)	3 000
Variable overhead	300
	4 000
Contribution	2 000

Contribution per unit of key factor:

$$\text{Direct materials: } \frac{£2000}{100 \text{ kilos}} = \underline{\underline{£20 \text{ per kilo}}}$$

$$\text{Direct labour: } \frac{£2000}{200 \text{ direct labour hours}} = \underline{\underline{£10 \text{ per direct labour hour}}}$$

(ii) and (iii) Calculation of the contribution per unit of limiting factor for each of the proposed two new contracts:

	Contract 1	Contract 2
	£000	£000
Contract price	1 000	2 100
Less: Variable costs		
Direct materials	300	600
Direct labour	300	750
Variable overhead	100	250
	700	1 600
Contribution	300	500

Contribution per unit of key factor:

	Contract 1	Contract 2
Direct materials	£300	£500
	50 kilos	100 kilos
=	£6 per kilo	£5 per kilo
Direct labour	£300	£500
	10 DLH	25 DLH
=	£30 per DLH	£20 per DLH

Summary of contribution per unit of limiting factor:

	Direct materials	Direct labour
	£	£
Normal work	20	10
Contract 1	6	5
Contract 2	30	20

(b) **Calculation of the total maximum contribution**

Contract 1
If Contract 1 is accepted, it will earn a total contribution of £300,000. This will leave 150,000 kilos of direct material available for its normal work (200,000 kilos maximum available, less the 50,000 used on Contract 1). This means that 1,500 units of ordinary work could be undertaken (150,000 kilos divided by 100 kilos per unit).

However, Contract 1 will absorb 10,000 direct labour hours, leaving 90,000 DLH available (100,000 DLH less 10,000 DLH). As each unit of ordinary work uses 200 DLH, the maximum number of units that could be undertaken is 450 (90,000 DLH divided by 200 DLH). Thus the maximum number of units of ordinary work that could be undertaken if Contract 1 is accepted is 450 and NOT 1500 units if direct materials were the only limiting factor. As each unit makes a contribution of £2000, the total contribution would be £900,000 (450 units × £2000).

The total maximum contribution, if Contract 1 is accepted, is therefore, £1,200,000 (£300,000 + 900,000).

Contract 2
If Contract 2 is accepted, only 100,000 kilos of direct materials will be available for ordinary work (200,000 kilos maximum available less 100,000 required for Contract 2). This means that only 1000 normal jobs could be undertaken (100 000 kilos divided by 100 kilos required per unit).

Contract 2 would absorb 25,000 direct labour hours, leaving 75,000 available for normal work (100,000 maximum DLH less the 25,000 DLH used by Contract 2). As each unit of normal work takes 200 hours, only 375 units could be made (75,000 DLH divided by 200 DLH per unit). Thus if this contract is accepted, 375 is the maximum number of normal jobs that could be undertaken.

This would give a total contribution of £750,000 (375 units multiplied by £2000 of contribution per unit).

If Contract 2 is accepted, the total maximum contribution would be £1,250,000, i.e. Contract 2's contribution of £500,000 plus the contribution of £750,000 from the normal work.

The decision
Accept Contract 2 because the maximum total contribution would be £1,250,000 compared with the £1,200,000 if Contract 1 was accepted.

Tutorial notes
1 The various cost relationships are assumed to remain unchanged at all levels of activity.
2 Fixed costs will not be affected irrespective of which contract is accepted.
3 The market for Temple's normal sales is assumed to be flexible.
4 Contract 2 will absorb one-half of the available direct materials and one-quarter of the available direct labour hours. Would the company want to commit such resources to work that may be uncertain and unreliable and that could have an adverse impact on its normal customers?

Chapter 19 **19.5** **Payback for Buchan Enterprises:**
(a) Payback period:

Year	Investment outlay	Cash inflow	Net cash flow	Cumulative cash flow
	£	£	£	£
1	(50 000)	8 000	(42 000)	(42 000)
2	–	16 000	16 000	(26 000)
3	–	40 000	40 000	14 000
4	–	45 000	45 000	59 000
5	–	37 000	37 000	96 000

Net cash flow becomes positive in Year 3. Assuming the net cash flow accrues evenly, it becomes positive during August: $(26/40 \times 12) = 7.8$ months. The payback period, therefore, is about 2 years 8 months.

(b) Discounted payback period:

Year	Net cash flow	Discount factor @ 12%	Discounted net cash flow	Cumulative net cash flow
	£		£	£
0	(50 000)	1.0000	(50 000)	(50 000)
1	8 000	0.8929	7 143	(42 857)
2	16 000	0.7929	12 686	(30 171)
3	40 000	0.7118	28 472	(1 699)
4	45 000	0.6355	28 598	26 899
5	37 000	0.5674	20 994	47 893

Discounted net cash flow becomes positive in Year 4. Assuming the net cash flow accrues evenly throughout the year, it becomes positive in January of Year 4 (1699/ 28,598 × 12 = 0.7). Discounted payback period therefore equals 3 years 1 month. This value is in contrast with the payback method, where the net cash flow becomes positive in August of Year 3 (i.e. 2 years 8 months).

19.6 Lender Ltd's accounting rate of return:

$$\text{Accounting rate of return (APR)} = \frac{\text{average annual net profit after tax}}{\text{cost of the investment}} \times 100\%$$

$$= \frac{\frac{1}{5}(\pounds18\,000 + 47\,000 + 65\,000 + 65\,000 + 30\,000)}{100\,000} \times 100\%$$

$$= \frac{45\,000}{100\,000} \times 100\%$$

$$= \underline{\underline{45\%}}$$

Note: Based on the average investment, the ARR

$$= \frac{\pounds45\,000}{\frac{1}{2}(100\,000 + 0)} \times 100\%$$

$$= \underline{\underline{90\%}}$$

19.7 Net present value for a Lockhart project:

Net present value:

Year	Net cash flow £000	Discount factor @15%	Present value £000
1	800	0.8696	696
2	850	0.7561	643
3	830	0.6575	546
4	1 200	0.5718	686
5	700	0.4972	348
Total present value			2 919
Initial cost			2 500
Net present value			419

Index